Latin American International Law in the Twenty-First Century

Latin American International Law in the Twenty-First Century

Edited by

ALEJANDRO CHEHTMAN

Dean and Professor of Law, Escuela de Derecho, Universidad Torcuato Di Tella, Argentina

ALEXANDRA HUNEEUS

Evjue Bascom Professor of Law, University of Wisconsin, USA

SERGIO PUIG

Joint Chair in International Economic Law, EUI, Italy
Evo DeConcini Professor of Law, UArizona, USA

OXFORD
UNIVERSITY PRESS

OXFORD
UNIVERSITY PRESS

Oxford University Press is a department of the University of Oxford.
It furthers the University's objective of excellence in research, scholarship,
and education by publishing worldwide. Oxford is a registered trade mark of
Oxford University Press in the UK and in certain other countries.

Published in the United States of America by Oxford University Press
198 Madison Avenue, New York, NY 10016, United States of America.

Library of Congress Cataloging-in-Publication Data
Names: Chehtman, Alejandro, editor. | Huneeus, Alexandra, 1967– editor. |
Puig, Sergio (Law teacher), editor.
Title: Latin American international law in the twenty-first century /
[edited by] Alejandro Chehtman, Alexandra Huneeus, Sergio Puig.
Description: New York : Oxford University Press, 2025. |
Includes bibliographical references and index. |
Identifiers: LCCN 2024056766 | ISBN 9780197753989 (hardback) |
ISBN 9780197753996 (epub) | ISBN 9780197754009 (updf) |
ISBN 9780197754016 (online)
Subjects: LCSH: International law—Latin America.
Classification: LCC KZ4116 .L39 2025 | DDC 341.098—dc23/eng/20241125
LC record available at https://lccn.loc.gov/2024056766

DOI: 10.1093/9780197754016.001.0001

Printed by Marquis Book Printing, Canada

Note to Readers

This publication is designed to provide accurate and authoritative information in regard to the subject matter covered. It is based upon sources believed to be accurate and reliable and is intended to be current as of the time it was written. It is sold with the understanding that the publisher is not engaged in rendering legal, accounting, or other professional services. If legal advice or other expert assistance is required, the services of a competent professional person should be sought. Also, to confirm that the information has not been affected or changed by recent developments, traditional legal research techniques should be used, including checking primary sources where appropriate.

(Based on the Declaration of Principles jointly adopted by a Committee of the American Bar Association and a Committee of Publishers and Associations.)

To Eduardo and Graciela, for their love, support, and example
A.C.

To Ion, Lucas, and Amaia, with love and gratitude
A.H.

To Daria, Diego, and Negar, for their love, resilience, and kindness
S.P.

Contents

Acknowledgments

This project was conceived in the quiet of the first COVID-19 quarantine, when Zoom was still a novelty. It has accompanied us through vital challenges and cross-continental moves. The toddlers are now in school, a teenager in college, and our mutual work relationships have become friendships. Throughout we have counted on the support of many others. At Oxford University Press we thank Merel Alstein, for believing in the project and pushing us to persist; and Robert Cavooris and Lisa Butts, for their patience and support on all matters relevant to the project. We also want to thank Doris Salcedo for kindly authorizing us to use an image of Shibboleth for the cover.

The work for this project has been presented at several venues. We are grateful to the Di Tella Law School, the Center for Global Legal Studies of University of Wisconsin Law School, and the Arizona Law School, for hosting Latin American International Law (LAIL) workshops, virtual and hybrid; to the American Society for Comparative Law, the American Society for International Law, and the Latin American Society for International Law, for the opportunity to present the project or its chapters at early stages; and to *AJIL Unbound*, for publishing a symposium of essays on LAIL themes by our volume authors.

Committing to write a chapter to an edited volume is an act of faith. We are grateful to our authors for trusting us with their work. We are also grateful to those who have provided comments and suggestions that have helped steer the project in new directions, including Arnulf Becker Lorca, Jorge Contesse, Fabia Fernandez Carvalho, Xisca Pou, and Steven Ratner.

We thank our families for bearing with the long Zoom calls at odd hours and with debates about whether LAIL exists and what is its nature. We hope this volume provides an inspired answer to those questions.

Contributors

Ana Micaela Alterio, PhD is Full Professor, ITAM (Instituto Tecnológico Autónomo de México), Ciudad de México, MX, CONAHCYT (Consejo Nacional de Humanidades, Ciencias y Tecnologías), Ciudad de México, MX, MX. https://orcid.org/0000-0001-8729-9647

Amaya Álvez Marín, PhD is Full Professor, Faculty of Law, Universidad de Concepción, Concepción, CL. https://orcid.org/0000-0002-1510-7770

Helena Alviar García, SJD is Full Professor of Law, Sciences Po, Paris, FR. https://orcid.org/0000-0002-3707-2724

Maryluz Barragan Gonzalez is Deputy Director/Researcher, Center of Studies on Law, Justice and Society, Bogota, CO. https://orcid.org/0009-0009-2419-3787

Arnulf Becker Lorca is Chair in Public International Law, European University Institute, Florence, IT. https://orcid.org/0000-0002-0767-7634

Laura Betancur-Restrepo is Associate Professor, Faculty of Law, Universidad de los Andes, Bogota, CO. https://orcid.org/0000-0002-5124-8431

Lina M. Céspedes-Báez, SJD is Full Professor, Universidad del Rosario, Bogotá, CO. https://orcid.org/0000-0002-5602-0559

Alejandro Chehtman, is Dean and Professor of Law, Escuela de Derecho, Universidad Torcuato Di Tella, Argentina. https://orcid.org/0000-0002-6765-2957

Jorge Contesse is Professor of Law, Rutgers Law School, Newark, US

Louise Fawcett, MPhil, DPhil is Professor of International Relations, Department of Politics and International Relations, University of Oxford, Oxford, UK. https://orcid.org/0000-0003-4282-0982

Fabia Fernandes Carvalho, PhD is Lecturer in international law at FGV Sao Paulo Law School, Getulio Vargas Foundation (FGV), Sao Paulo, BR. https://orcid.org/0000-0003-1394-154X

Ximena Fuentes, DPhil is Professor of International Law, Faculty of Law, University of Chile, Santiago, CL. https://orcid.org/0009-0004-8260-1228

George Rodrigo Bandeira Galindo is Associate Professor, University of Brasilia, BR. https://orcid.org/0000-0002-0071-5861

Beatriz Garcia, PhD is Associate Professor, Sorbonne University Abu Dhabi, Abu Dhabi, United Arab Emirates

Roberto Gargarella is Senior Researcher, CONICET/University Pompeu Fabra, Buenos Aires, AR

Manuel A. Gómez is Professor of Law, College of Law, Florida International University, Miami, FL. https://orcid.org/0000-0003-3780-5876

Ezequiel Gonzalez-Ocantos is Professor of Comparative and Judicial Politics, Department of Politics and International Relations, University of Oxford, Oxford, UK

Claudio Grossman Guiloff is Professor of Law and Dean Emeritus, R. Geraldson Scholar International and Humanitarian Law, American University Washington College of Law, Washington DC, USA

Alexandra Huneeus is Evjue Bascom Professor of Law, University of Wisconsin, USA. https://orcid.org/0000-0003-0296-3209

María Teresa Infante Caffi is Professor of International Law, University of Chile, Santiago, CL. https://orcid.org/0009-0007-0838-3332

Steven L. B. Jensen, PhD is Senior Researcher, Research Department, The Danish Institute for Human Rights, Copenhagen, DK. https://orcid.org/0000-0003-0640-0008

David Landau is Mason Ladd Professor and Associate Dean for International Programs, Florida State University College of Law, Tallahassee, FL. https://orcid.org/0000-0002-4990-0400

Fernando Lusa Bordin is College Associate Professor in Law, Sidney Sussex College, University of Cambridge, UK

Mónica Mazariegos-Rodas, PhD is Coordinator, Department of Law and Political Sciences Research, Institute of Studies in Socio-Humanistic Sciences, Vice Provost's Office of Research and Projection, Rafael Landivar University, Guatemala City, GT

Pablo Mijangos y González, PhD in History is Edmund J. and Louise W. Kahn Chair in History, Southern Methodist University, Dallas, TX

Mariana Mota Prado, LLM, JSD is Professor of Law and William C. Graham Chair in International Law and Development, University of Toronto, Toronto, CA. https://orcid.org/0000-0002-5555-8859

Federica Paddeu is Associate Professor and Derek Bowett Fellow in Law, Queens' College, University of Cambridge, Cambridge, UK. https://orcid.org/0000-0002-7040-8453

Mónica Pinto is Professor of Law & Dean Emerita, Facultad de Derecho, Universidad de Buenos Aires, Buenos Aires, AR

Rodrigo Polanco is Senior Lecturer and Researcher, World Trade Institute-University of Bern, Bern, CH, Swiss Institute of Comparative Law, Lausanne, CH. https://orcid.org/0000-0003-1974-5523

Enrique Prieto-Rios, LLBB, MA, PhD is Associate Professor, Faculty of Law, Universidad del Rosario, Bogotá, CO. https://orcid.org/0000-0002-1798-7855

Sergio Puig is Joint Chair in International Economic Law, EUI, Italy and Evo DeConcini Professor of Law, UArizona, USA. https://orcid.org/0000-0001-9007-4406

Elizabeth Salmón, PhD is Professor of Law, Pontifical Catholic University of Peru, Lima, PE. https://orcid.org/0000-0003-4034-8418

Wayne Sandholtz, PhD is Professor, Department of Political Science and International Relations and Gould School of Law, University of Southern California, Los Angeles, CA. https://orcid.org/0000-0002-8314-0038

Juan Pablo Scarfi, PhD is Professor of International Relations, Institute of Political Science, Pontificia Universidad Catolica de Chile, Santiago, CL. https://orcid.org/0000-0002-7096-568X

Kathryn Sikkink, PhD is Professor of Public Policy, Harvard Kennedy School, Harvard University, Cambridge, MA. https://orcid.org/0000-0003-0335-742X

René Urueña is Associate Professor, Faculty of Law, Universidad de los Andes (Colombia), Universidad de los Andes (Colombia), CO. https://orcid.org/0000-0002-4551-3198

Eduardo Valencia-Ospina, PhD (Javeriana University, Bogotá); LLM (Harvard) is Member and Chair, United Nations (International Law Commission), Geneva, CH, International Court of Justice, The Hague, NL

Giovanny Vega-Barbosa, LLM is Legal Expert and Chief of Investment Arbitration Group, Agencia Nacional de Defensa Jurídica del Estado de Colombia, Bogotá, CO. https://orcid.org/0000-0001-6126-0760

Pedro A. Villarreal, PhD is Senior Research Fellow, Max Planck Institute for Comparative Public Law and International Law, Heidelberg, DE. https://orcid.org/0000-0003-4216-1542

Abbreviations

AAAQ	availability, accessibility, affordability, and quality
ABC	Argentina, Brazil, Chile
AIIL	American Institute of International Law
ALBA	Bolivarian Alternative for the Americas
APDH	*Asamblea Permanente por los Derechos Humanos*
ARAPNET	Advanced Research Projects Agency Network
ARS	Articles on the Responsibility of States
AUC	*Autodefensas Unidas de Colombia*
BNDG	National Bank of Genetic Data
BOAI	Budapest Open Access Initiative
BRICS	intergovernmental organization comprising Brazil, Russia, India, China, South Africa, Iran, Egypt, Ethiopia, and the United Arab Emirates
CASTALA	Conferences on the Application of Science and Technology to the Development of Latin America
CCTs	conditional cash transfers
CELAC	Community of Latin American and Caribbean States
CEPAL	Comisión Económica para América Latina y el Caribe
CERD	Convention on the Elimination of All Forms of Racial Discrimination
CICIG	Commission against Impunity in Guatemala
CILAC	Open Forum of Sciences of Latin America and the Caribbean
CLCS	Commission on the Limits of the Continental Shelf
CONADEP	*Comisión Nacional sobre la Desaparición de Personas*
DNS	domain names system
ECLAC	UN Economic Commission for Latin America and the Caribbean
ECOSOC	Economic and Social Council
ECtHR	European Court of Human Rights
EEAF	*Equipo Argentino de Antropología Forense*
EEZ	exclusive economic zone
ERP	*Ejército Revolucionario del Pueblo*
ESCR	economic, social and cultural rights
EUTR	EU Timber Regulation
FARC	Revolutionary Armed Forces of Colombia
FCPA	Foreign Corrupt Practices Act
FLEGT	Forest Law Enforcement Governance and Trade
FONAFIFO	National Forestry Fund
FTAs	free trade agreements
GATT	General Agreement on Trade and Tariffs

GHG	greenhouse gases
GRULAC	Group of Latin American and Caribbean Countries
IACtHR	Inter-American Court of Human Rights
IACW/CIM	Inter-American Commission on Women
IADB	Inter-American Development Bank
IAHRS	Inter-American Human Rights System
ICCC	International Computer Communication Conference
ICCPR	International Covenant on Civil and Political Rights
ICESCR	International Covenant on Economic, Social and Cultural Rights
ICJ	International Court of Justice
ICPPED	International Convention for the Protection for All People from Enforced Disappearances
ICSID	International Centre for Settlement of Investment Disputes
ICTR	International Criminal Tribunal for Rwanda
ICTY	International Criminal Tribunal for the former Yugoslavia
IDPs	internally displaced persons
IEL	international economic law
IHL	international humanitarian law
ILO	International Labour Organization
IMF	International Monetary Fund
INTAL	Institute for the Integration of Latin America and the Caribbean
IP	Internet Protocol
IPR	intellectual property rights
ISB	International Sanitary Bureau
ISI	import substitution industrialization
ISP	internet service provider
ITLOS	International Tribunal for the Law of the Sea
JDA	joint development agreement
JPL	Justice and Peace Law
LAIL	Latin American international law
LDCs	less developed countries
LIO	Liberal International Order
NAFTA	North American Free Trade Agreement
NAIL	new approaches to international law
NGOs	nongovernmental organizations
NIAC	non-international armed conflict
OA	open access
OAS	Organisation of American States
OECD	Organisation for Economic Co-operation and Development
PES	payments for ecosystem services
PLACTS	*Pensamiento Latinoamericano en Ciencia Tecnología y Sociedad*
PTAs	preferential trade agreements
REDD+	Reducing Emissions from Deforestation and Forest Degradation
SIDs	small island developing states

SLADI	Sociedad Latinoamericana de Derecho Internacional/Latin American Society of International Law
SMEs	small and medium enterprises
SRE	Secretariat of Foreign Affairs, or Secretaría de Relaciones Exteriores
STA	Science and Technology Studies
STF	Supreme Federal Tribunal
TCP	Transmission Control Protocol
TRIPS	Trade-Related Aspects of Intellectual Property Rights
TWAIL	Third World approaches to international law
UNICO	UN Conference on International Organization
UDHR	Universal Declaration on Human Rights
UNASUR	Union of South American Nations
UNCAT	UN Convention against Torture and Other Cruel, Inhuman or Degrading Treatment or Punishment
UNCITRAL	UN Commission on International Trade Law
UNCTAD	UN Conference on Trade and Development
UNDP	United Nations Development Programme
UNESCO	United Nations Educational, Scientific and Cultural Organization
UNFCCC	United Nations Framework Convention on Climate Change
URL	Uniform Resource Locator
US	United States
USAID	United States Agency for International Development
USIA	United States Information Agency
USMCA	United States–Mexico–Canada Agreement
VCLT	Vienna Convention on the Law of Treaties
WHO	World Health Organization
WTO	World Trade Organization

Introduction to Latin American International Law

Alejandro Chehtman, Alexandra Huneeus, and Sergio Puig

I. Introduction

In 1909, Chilean jurist Alejandro Álvarez laid out his argument for the existence of a regional law of the Americas in the *American Journal of International Law*.[1] His objective was to carve out a more prominent place for Latin America in the then emerging US-led geopolitical order.[2] The article, subsequently turned into a book, became a manifesto not for a Latin American international law but for a Pan-American international law—a regional legal order encompassing the Americas in their entirety, with the United States at the helm. Pan-Americanism has since consolidated into an influential and pervasive regional legal and political project, spawning key institutions and instruments, such as the 1933 Montevideo Convention, the Inter-American Development Bank, and the Organisation of American States (OAS), among others.

Of course, Alvarez's Pan-American vision was not the only contender; ideas around regionalism and international law have long been contested among Latin Americans. Álvarez's brand of regional law was more US-centric than that of other publicists and construed itself both as a continuation and a recalibration of earlier proposals such as the Drago and the Calvo Doctrines, both of which sought to claim greater sovereign rights against foreign meddling. While these jurists disagreed on how Latin American states should position themselves in the face of foreign powers—and the United States in particular—they were united by a vision of a shared community of practice of international law at the regional level. They all believed, in the late nineteenth and early twentieth centuries, that there was something distinctive and important about the practices, doctrines, and aims of international law in the Western Hemisphere

[1] Alejandro Álvarez, "Latin America and International Law," 3 *American Journal of International Law* 3 (1909): 269.

[2] Liliana Obregón, "Noted for Dissent: The International Life of Alejandro Alvarez," *Leiden Journal of International Law* 19 (2006): 983.

Alejandro Chehtman, Alexandra Huneeus, and Sergio Puig, *Introduction to Latin American International Law*
In: *Latin American International Law in the Twenty-First Century.* Edited by: Alejandro Chehtman, Alexandra Huneeus, and Sergio Puig, Oxford University Press. © Oxford University Press 2025.
DOI: 10.1093/9780197754016.001.0001

and that Latin American countries and publicists had an important role to play therein.

Over a century later, the dynamics of regionalism have changed dramatically and, indeed, are quickly changing anew even as we write this introduction. These transformations make it important to explore the regional projects and practices of our current geopolitical era, while also studying the projects of the past anew, guided by a contemporary set of questions, problems, and priorities. That is the work of this volume. Like the work of the turn-of-the-twentieth-century regionalist writers, it is animated by the observation that Latin America continues to be a source of new doctrines, theory, and legal institutions that hardly receive enough attention, and by a normative commitment to the idea of regional projects in international law. But in contrast to those thinkers, we did not set out to advance a particular project or vision. Rather, we sought to explore the competing visions of regional law that coexist today, their respective sensibilities, normative commitments, and institutional innovations, with an eye to scholarly trends and legal practice.

Our first goal, in other words, is to showcase Latin American international law (LAIL), by which we refer to the doctrine, institutions, practice, and scholarship of international law in Latin America and the Caribbean. Latin Americans are currently fostering an understanding of international law that is more plural and inclusive than the Creole elite (*Criollos*) and US-led projects of the past. The volume draws our attention to emerging strains of legal thought and practice. It explores a current era of decentered regional legal projects, introducing and critically engaging with some of Latin America's original ideas and practices concerning international law and diplomacy that do not necessarily revolve around traditional centers of power—or do so in more complex ways than the diplomat-led projects of the past. As Anne Orford argues, "bringing the concept of regional orders to the foreground can open up a new and timely set of questions about politics, representation, and the future of international law."[3] It can allow us to understand law as enabling both power and resistance to it and examine different ways in which ideas can be articulated and institutionalized, as well as the possibility of alternative views about what international law is and what it should be. Thus, we also present Latin American ideas and doctrines as forms of resistance that can both contribute to and challenge "mainstream," "global" approaches.

We also aim to showcase leading and emerging scholars in the region who are rewriting the canons of international law scholarship. What was once a stodgy and exceedingly formalist field has been transformed in recent decades, not least

[3] Anne Orford, "Regional Orders, Geopolitics, and the Future of International Law," *Current Legal Problems* 74 (2021): 149.

by the incursion of constitutional law into its midst. Latin American international law is no longer the exclusive domain of male and creole diplomats, government lawyers, and international law scholars but now belongs to a broader group of actors—including Indigenous activists, historians, economists, and sociologists of different genders—who are bringing new perspectives into the field of practice and scholarship alike. Like their predecessors, many of these actors have been trained in the traditional centers of power and knowledge creation, and they continue to teach and work in academic institutions of the so-called Global North, writing mostly in English. But others play fundamental roles in advising civil society, defending marginalized groups, and protecting public goods such as the environment and the oceans. In sum, Latin American international law scholarship has ceased to be a discipline animated exclusively by a relatively uniform group of local elites, even if it maintains its connections with local and global centers of power.

Finally, our purpose is to advance scholarship on Latin American law and scholarship on regionalism in international law. The book is not conceived as a collection of country studies, but rather it follows five different entry points into the study of LAIL: history, theory and method, institutions and practice, new doctrines, and current challenges. We chose this structure because it throws into relief themes that cut across the region, allowing us to study trends across borders. Indeed, an important insight emerges from this exercise: there is a new canon of Latin American international law in the twenty-first century. It has several distinctive features: (1) scholarship continues to revisit the old doctrines and arguments of the past, including the efforts of Latin America to insert itself into the European and American-led orders, but now with the critical twist that this was a particular class of Latin Americans, who were vested in suppressing other voices within their own states; (2) increasingly, international law is constructed not only by diplomats and foreign ministries but also by judges, civil society, Indigenous peoples, interdisciplinary scholars, women, and others whose voices were previously absent; (3) the law of human rights, constructed through the inter-American system in dialogue with domestic courts and other actors, is the area of greatest cohesion, development, and originality in contemporary LAIL; (4) the United States and Europe have been displaced as the region's main interlocutors. We develop the argument for a twenty-first-century LAIL not in the introduction but in the epilogue to this volume, as it is the payoff (or one of them) for engagement with the chapters in between.

In this introduction, we next turn to show how the contemporary geopolitical landscape demands reengagement with, but also rethinking of, regional law (section II). Section III provides a brief preview of the sections and chapters of the volume. Section IV closes with a reflection on shibboleths, fissures, and the book's cover art.

II. Why Revisit These Questions Now?

Throughout the time that Álvarez and others sought to construct a regional identity through law, the United States loomed as the most powerful center of influence; the "other" with and against which the region asserted itself in its relationship to Europe. However, current political, economic, and scholarly trends are offsetting this fundamental dualism, introducing a greater variety of important players and projects. In this section we highlight five sources of change that we believe are affecting legal and political landscapes throughout the region, and ultimately reshaping both the practice and study of regional and international law.

Top among these is the decentering of the United States in Latin America's trade and economic balance. There is a dramatic shift in geopolitical power unmatched since the close of World War II. A rising China—and a higher risk of conflict as states and non-state actors exploit new sources of power—continues to erode long-standing norms and institutions created after the War. China has displaced the United States as the top trading partner of South America and has become the second largest trading partner for Latin America overall. The change has been abrupt. When China joined the World Trade Organization (WTO) in the early 2000s, it represented only 2 percent of Latin American trade volumes.[4] The effects of China's rise in trade (and investment) and corresponding shifts in geopolitical power are already manifest and will transform globalization as economic and production networks shift and diversify. For example, twenty Latin American countries are part of the Belt and Road Initiative, three have signed free trade agreements (FTAs) with China and seven have signed comprehensive strategic partnerships with China, including Brazil and Mexico. Moreover, states have withdrawn recognition of Taiwanese sovereignty in recent years; today "only seven countries in the region still recognize it."[5] These changes already reflect a change in global norms, rules, and institutions. Conversely, Latin American governments feel less pressure to hew to US soft power, resulting, some argue, in the rise of authoritarianism, as aspiring authoritarians can find a friendly counterpart in China human rights abuses notwithstanding.[6] In this context, the United States has vastly neglected Latin America. It has emphasized anti-narcotics and anti-immigration policies, while overlooking opportunities

[4] Diana Roy, "China's Growing Influence in Latin America," Council on Foreign Relations, June 15, 2023, accessed June 26, 2024, https://www.cfr.org/backgrounder/china-influence-latin-america-argentina-brazil-venezuela-security-energy-bri.

[5] Ibid.

[6] Charles Eder and David O. Shullman, "How China Exports Authoritarianism," *Foreign Affairs*, September 16, 2021, accessed June 26, 2024, https://www.foreignaffairs.com/articles/china/2021-09-16/how-china-exports-authoritarianism. This role was occupied by the United States in the context of Cold War politics during the 1960s and 1970s.

for a more productive engagement around the social, political, and economic development of the region.

A second, related transformation results from the democratic stagnation or backsliding in the region (and elsewhere).[7] Among other reasons, weak state capacity, tenuous rule of law, fragile traditions of tolerance for opposition, high inequality, corruption, and militaries with a strong role in politics have affected the region, especially in recent times. Populist presidents with authoritarian tendencies—including Presidents Andrés Manuel Lopez Obrador (Mexico), Jair Bolsonaro (Brazil), Javier Milei (Argentina), Nayib Bukele (El Salvador), Hugo Chávez and Nicolás Maduro (Venezuela), and the reprise of Daniel Ortega (Nicaragua)—have appeared, further challenging a rule-based international order with the United States at the center. These governments sometimes work together to reshape the agendas of international organizations such as the OAS, and to reconfigure the underpinnings of international politics more generally. One might object that everything old is new again: Latin America has cycled between periods of authoritarianism and democracy since independence. Each time, however, it is different. Salient differences with the past include the emergence of a new, multipolar world and the general decline of support for democratic government, including in the United States. Key to this transformation are the challenges imposed by the technologies in a digital age, and how they facilitate the spread of misinformation. China, Russia, and other actors, in varying ways, are supporting illiberal regimes by sharing technology and expertise for digital repression. Among the effects of misinformation is the decline of support for multilateral cooperation, especially when US interests conflict with the interest of such actors. One obvious effect of international law on this transformation is the challenge of its effectiveness when large segments of societies mistrust and target international institutions and "globalist" politicians.[8]

The third transformation affecting regional international projects stands in tension with the first two. Decades of steady gains in prosperity and other aspects of human development have improved lives in the region and raised peoples' expectations. In many countries, these trends have stagnated during rapid social and technological changes. Hence, societies across the region are demanding states to address domestic problems. A growing mismatch between what publics expect and what governments can deliver might generate more social movements, political volatility, erosion of democracy, and expanding roles for alternative providers of governance that implicate international law, including

[7] Tom Ginsburg, "Authoritarian International Law?" *American Journal of International Law* 114 (2020): 221–260.

[8] James Bell et al., "International Cooperation Welcomed across 14 Advanced Economies," Pew Research Center, September 21, 2020, accessed June 26, 2024, https://www.pewresearch.org/global/2020/09/21/international-cooperation-welcomed-across-14-advanced-economies/.

human rights law. This was not the case when Álvarez and his interlocutors wrote in the early twentieth century—then, international law was conceived of as the law of nations, no more and no less. This was the height of the Westphalian understanding of the world order. International law belonged to the executive branch and foreign ministries, was practiced in the region exclusively by the *criollo* diplomats of the Americas, and represented *criollo* elite interests on the international plane. Today, a more diverse group of actors and interests at national and subnational levels have begun leveraging international law for their own political projects, transcending state-led foreign policy in a way unthinkable in the Álvarez era. Some argue, for example, that judges, constitutional lawyers, and human rights lawyers are constructing a new regional constitutional practice, *a ius constitucional commune* in Latin America.[9] This practice has not emerged in the top-down manner of the state-orchestrated regional projects of the twentieth century. Instead, it is the result of rights litigation involving a transnational ecosystem of actors such as nongovernmental organizations (NGOs), victim advocacy groups, and national courts, and using the language of jurisprudence rather than diplomacy. Similarly, autochthonous social movements have harnessed the language of rights to create a new regional practice around legal pluralism. This is especially evident in the role of Indigenous rights advocates and the use of the International Labor Organization Convention 169 to ground the right of Indigenous peoples to free, prior, and informed consultation, among others.

The fourth transformation that impacts regional law and politics is environmental degradation. Climate change creates greater food and water insecurity in the region, increasing migration from poor or especially affected countries, precipitating new health challenges, and contributing to unprecedented biodiversity losses. These trends will severely impact Latin America. It is home to the "lungs of the planet," as the Amazon Forest is called, as well as some of the world's most biodiverse ecosystems. It also encompasses regions, for example, in Mexico, Central America, Bolivia, and Chile, that are suffering climate change-induced drought and water shortages, and regions, such as the Caribbean, that are battered by ever more violent storms and rising seas. These weather events are contributing to massive "irregular" migration and will continue to do so, impacting the United States (and its domestic politics) and the way the country interacts with the region. Moreover, national security arguments will be deployed by many nations for combating climate change and adapting to the resulting shared global challenges, with likely consequences for international cooperation. It is also the case that a crisis creates opportunity. Latin American

[9] Armin *von Bogdandy et al., "Ius Constitutionale Commune in Latin America: A Regional Approach to Transformative Constitutionalism," in Transformative Constitutionalism in Latin America: The Emergence of a New Ius Commune, ed. Armin von Bogdandy et al. (Oxford: Oxford University Press, 2017).*

and Caribbean countries are forging innovative responses to this threat through international law. All countries are parties to the Paris Agreement, and many have signed other relevant treaties, including the Escazú Agreement, a regional treaty that protects information and activism around environmental causes. Latin American states also belong to the Inter-American Human Rights System (IAHRS), which has declared a right to a healthy environment and has begun creating human rights standards for states' responses to climate change.

Finally, the pace and reach of technological developments is transforming human experiences and capabilities while creating new tensions and disruptions in the region. Not only has global competition for elements of technological supremacy, such as lithium, increased, but new technologies and applications are reshaping the human experience. The pace of technological change could increase societal tensions between those with the access, ability, and power to adapt and those who are unable or unwilling to change. Some communities and countries could make rapid advancements while others may be left behind with little hope of catching up, exacerbating inequalities within and between states. In this process, public-private partnerships for investment, research, and development will be critical for attaining many technological breakthroughs and advantages. In this process, core corporate, group, and national interests do not easily align, increasing tensions between governments and corporations. National interests in certain technologies can be at odds with corporate interests in increasing profits. Notably, concerns about privacy and control of data streams and trade in industrial goods and other technologies are likely to lead to greater interventions in trade and investment policies. This dynamic can also lead to reliance on national security arguments, which are notoriously hard to evaluate, to regulate business actors.

Taken together, these trends amount to a dramatic shift that challenges the centrality of traditional pan-Americanism debates. This volume is largely an exploration of the scholarship on international law emerging in light of this new geopolitical landscape.

III. Twenty-First-Century Latin American International Law: Myriad Perspectives and Projects

The volume is divided into five parts: history, theory and methods, institutions and practice, new doctrines, and contemporary challenges. While there is inevitably something arbitrary about assigning these rich essays into the five categories—each essay could claim to belong to more than one part—it is also the case that each part throws into relief a different aspect of Latin American international law.

Part I: History

The first part, focused on historical approaches, portrays Latin America as an equal partner in the construction of international law. Many of the chapters return to the theorists and doctrines of the past—what we might refer to as the nineteenth- and twentieth-century LAIL canon—but each adds formerly underexplored perspectives, including new voices, methods, and arguments. Part I also demonstrates different disciplinary approaches to historical arguments, including writers who identify as historians, political scientists, legal scholars, and theorists, and some who claim more than one disciplinary identity.

In his chapter on the Spanish American Concordats, Pablo Mijangos performs the work of the historian, building arguments from primary documents and other archival material and engaging with debates about the role of a little-studied instrument in nineteenth-century governance. Even as his chapter engages with the historiography of the time, it also demonstrates that delving into early postcolonial history can enrich our understanding of international law and its relationship to the nation-state. Mijangos argues that the concordats, or diplomatic agreements between governments and The Holy See over the handling of ecclesiastical affairs in the new nation-states, played an important role in this new era. However, they are also important because they presage the relationship of international law and nation-state governments that would evolve in the twentieth century and hold important lessons about soft power and international agreements.

Next, Louise Fawcett performs the work of the international relations scholar. Her account shows Latin American individuals and states as equal partners that played a unique role in creating modern international law. She provides a sweeping view of the work of three public intellectuals, Andres Bello, Carlos Calvo, and Alejandro Álvarez. She also includes a discussion of the often-ignored women who helped shape the region's approach to international law in this period.

In a similar vein, Fabia Fernandes Carvalho argues for the significance of two Mexican diplomats from the interwar period: Isidro Fabela and his work advancing the legal principle of nonintervention, and Genaro Estrada, who promoted the doctrine of nonrecognition. These two figures, she argues, helped crystallize "a legalistic Mexican engagement with the vocabulary of international law" in the interwar period. Theirs was a distinctly Latin American political project that sought to stand on equal terms with the European community of nations and to eliminate foreign control of natural resources and economic dependency.

Juan Pablo Scarfi, a historian, turns to the interwar period. The Montevideo Convention (1933) was famously a continental platform for codifying the principles of sovereign equality, state independence, and (absolute) non-intervention. It also endorsed a declaratory approach to statehood. In his contribution, Scarfi excavates the ideas, sensibilities, and political movements that led to this influential treaty. He contrasts the competing positions between the Pan-American movement, the Mexican Constitution (1917), and the anti-interventionist and anti-imperialist movements. Scarfi suggests that the Montevideo Convention inadvertently made the international legal order less liberal through its absolutist defense of sovereign equality and non-intervention.

From the field of political science, Stephen Jensen and Kathryn Sikkink echo the theme of regional contributions to the construction of international law. They show that human rights law as a liberatory (or emancipatory) project of social change has its roots in Latin American and Caribbean states. Latin American diplomats and jurists played a central role in including human rights language in the UN Charter. They later were responsible for the first intergovernmental declaration of human rights, the American Declaration on Rights and Duties of Man of April 1948, which became a benchmark for the Universal Declaration of Human Rights (UDHR). In the 1960s, a newly decolonized Caribbean state, Jamaica, made fundamental contributions by reshaping the field of human rights. In these human rights initiatives, Latin America and Caribbean countries worked cooperatively with the United States, but more often without US leadership or in opposition to US policy. Further, they advanced a more capacious understanding of human rights that included social and economic rights.

Where the other chapters in this part celebrate Latin American contributions to international law, legal scholars Arnulf Becker Lorca and Amaya Alvez turn the narrative in a more critical and inward direction. The authors highlight how these interventions were also part and parcel of a project that aimed to complete the colonization or elimination of the Indigenous peoples of the Americas. International law doctrines such as *uti posseditis*, celebrated by Alejandro Álvarez as a Latin American innovation, allowed the early republics to claim sovereignty over Indigenous land that they did not yet possess or govern in any real sense, but over which they aimed to gain dominion. Thus, they excluded Indigenous peoples from participation in the international legal order. Becker Lorca and Alvez spotlight key moments in which international law was used to strip Indigenous peoples of land and autonomy, highlighting key moments that have been previously overlooked.

Part II: Theories and Methods

Scholarship in Latin American international law has finally begun to overcome disciplinary boundaries and engage with diverse disciplines and theoretical approaches, greatly enriching the field of study. In Part I, scholars from different disciplines—spanning history, political theory, political science, and law—joined in the inquiry over the history of Latin American international law. Part II shows that this disciplinary and theoretical ecumenism is more generally a feature of international law in the region. Written by a mix of law professors, diplomats, and political theorists, it includes chapters on sociolegal approaches, critical approaches, feminist approaches, law and development, and democratic theory.

The section begins with a tour of international law's engagement with social science through the prism of international economic law (IEL). Sergio Puig shows the fruits of IEL studies that employ theory and methods from disciplines that range from law and economics to anthropology. Puig closes by arguing that interdisciplinary IEL scholarship is a promising site through which to imagine alternatives to the current global economic order. Mariana Mota Prado then focuses on one strand of economic theory that has played an important role in Latin American legal reform movements: law and development. She offers three examples from three different decades—dependency theory, Hernando Soto's writing on property rights and bureaucratic reforms, and conditional cash transfers—to explore a different phase of the intellectual history of international development. Each reveals a distinct way in which "local" ideas interact with "international" paradigms and thus offers a different answer to the perennial question of whether different societies want to develop similarly.

René Urueña's chapter offers a new angle on discussions of economic development. He demands that we analyze together concepts that we usually hold apart: theories about economic and technological development in Latin America, on the one hand, and international law, on the other. After tracing the relationship of these concepts over the twentieth century, he calls for a contemporary reengagement with how technology is deeply connected to a particular place—with important distributive implications. Further, he exhorts greater engagement with international law as providing for transnational regulatory regimes; for example, by creating legal structures such as the UNCTAD's (UN Conference on Trade and Development) Technology Transfer Code or the TRIPS (Trade-Related Aspects of Intellectual Property Rights) regime, while at the same time creating a vocabulary for domestic or regional initiatives.

Part II then presents two critical perspectives on law that have gained footing in the academy, Third World approaches to international law (TWAIL) and critical feminism. Latin America was one of the earliest regions of the world to achieve independence from European colonization, but it was a latecomer to TWAIL. George Rodrigo Bandeira Galindo explores the region's recent engagement, tracing how a growing group of scholars have raised friendly challenges to TWAIL, such as pushing TWAIL to engage further with the Indigenous peoples of the Americas. He closes with a review of theorists such as Arnulf Becker Lorca and Liliana Obregon who view the project of Latin American international law itself as an exclusionary *criollo* construct. Ana Micaela Alterio uses the judgment of *Vicky Hernadez v. Honduras* by the Inter-American Court of Human Rights to explore disputes between Latin American feminisms. The judgment pushes against the limits of binary approaches in human rights law, using an evolutionary interpretative approach to extend human rights protection to trans people. Alterio applauds the decision as having the potential to shatter "the stability" of essentialist legal systems. But she notes with concern the dissents based on a more exclusionary view of feminism, reflecting on the divergence of views within feminism that continue to play out in the region.

Also adopting a more critical lens, Roberto Gargarella reprises his argument against international court adjudication of rights. Using the example of the Inter-American Court of Human Rights, he argues that dominant models concerning the relationship between international tribunals and local authorities are deeply flawed because they fail to give due deference to decisions made through a dialogue among equals in a democratic polity.

The section closes with an examination of the legal theory often described as Latin American law's defining feature, positivism. In contrast to natural law theory, positivism considers that legal norms are the result of decisions made by those who have the power and authority to create law. Ambassador Ximena Fuentes shows how, as international law itself moved toward a positivist self-definition in the nineteenth century, Latin Americans seized the new theory to shield themselves from European claims rooted in natural law. Against the doctrine of discovery, which might have allowed Europeans and North Americans to claim unoccupied lands, they posited the principle of *uti posseditis*; against claims of the sovereign right to protect nationals in foreign jurisdictions, they posited the principle of non-intervention. Thus, positivism became the pole star of international law theory and practice in the region.

Part III: Institutions and Practice

Part III further develops the theme that the study of international law is no longer the study of formal legal doctrine. Not only does contemporary scholarship include different disciplines and theoretical approaches (as demonstrated in Parts I and II); it also includes study of a rich set of institutions and practices. This part includes a discussion of the role of courts in the region, including the unique role played by both the International Court of Justice (ICJ) and the Inter-American Court. But it also takes us beyond the realm of law and courts, with chapters on legal education, the legal profession, and truth commissions.

Eduardo Valencia-Ospina and Giovanny Vega-Barbosa analyze the dense relationship that Latin American states have with the ICJ: No other region so frequently calls on the ICJ to resolve their disputes. After adding nuance to the picture by assessing the varied practices of Latin American states before the ICJ through three relevant periods, they identify confidence as the defining contemporary feature to describe Latin American states' frequent invocation of the Court.

Elizabeth Salmon's chapter on truth commissions turns to another uniquely Latin American practice. She goes further than just noting that Latin America was home to the first truth commissions, zoning in on a particular function that these commissions have played. Latin American states have been loath to recognize the existence of an armed conflict in their territory. Reviewing the cases of Argentina, Chile, El Salvador, Guatemala, Peru, and Colombia, Salmon shows how truth commissions have stepped in to fill the void, formally labeling situations of violence as non-international armed conflict, with important consequences for the application of international humanitarian, criminal, and human rights law.

Manuel A. Gómez argues that the growing role of international law in the region is reshaping the legal profession, including legal education. It has incentivized a new cadre of legal professionals focused on international dispute resolution, acting on behalf of multinational corporations, states, and similar actors in the case of international arbitration. However, at the law school level, it has also resulted in the growth of legal clinics that increase access to justice for victims of human rights violations, refugees, and other marginalized communities. Monica Pinto also points to legal education. She queries the changing concept of Latin American international law by tracing the evolution of legal education in the region. In a compact but sweeping history, she shows how doctrinal developments and education reflected the political challenges of five historical periods, starting with the colonization of the Americas. She concludes with the critical observation that significant barriers exist for the region's international law practitioners.

Part III closes with two chapters that explore the entanglement of international and national courts through rights law. David Landau shows the growing role of comparative international law in Latin America. Focusing on three rights areas—same-sex marriage, social rights, and Indigenous free, prior, and informed consultation—he argues that a set of leading domestic courts are the main protagonists in constructing human rights norms. These norms then spread throughout the region and are adopted and disseminated by the Inter-American Court of Human Rights. However, he also notes that limits of norm diffusion: consensus over norms occurs only where domestic political factors allow. In some rights matters, the region's judiciaries "wildly" diverge. Jorge

Contesse provides a historical review of the work of the two most prominent human rights institutions, the Inter-American Commission and Court. He celebrates the vitality of these bodies, particularly in the struggle against military dictatorships. But he also cautions that the Court's overzealous interpretations of its mandate in recent years could eventually weaken the human rights system by undermining its legal legitimacy.

Part IV: Doctrinal Innovation

Even as international law scholarship has spread its wings and engaged with different methods, theories, and approaches, the law itself remains a central site of analysis and action. Part IV returns to old-school doctrine. Here, however, the focus is not the usual LAIL canon of nineteenth-century doctrines such as *uti posseditis,* asylum, and the principle of non-intervention. Rather, we turn to a new era of doctrinal innovation. Part IV showcases the contemporary vibrancy of international law construction in the region. It is written by a mix of legal scholars and leading practitioners, and those who wear both hats.

The part begins with three areas of international law that have grown through deep and creative engagement with some of the region's most difficult problems, including mass state-sponsored atrocity. Claudio Grossman, one of the group of lawyers who helped shape litigation before the IAHRS into what it is today, provides an in-depth analysis of one of reparations in the region, from the Calvo Doctrine in the late 1800s to the advancement of the concept of integral reparations by the IAHRS. He also extends the analysis to other institutions in dialogue with the IAHRS, showing its impact outside the region, and closes with concern for how the rise in populist politics may impact this doctrine.

Alejandro Chehtman provides a detailed mapping of legal and institutional innovation in the field of transitional justice in Latin America. He explores the forces and actors that led to establishing the first truth commission and the seminal junta's trials in Argentina. He further dissects the key innovations in truth, justice, and peace that allow Latin American interventions against mass atrocity to be construed as a laboratory of experimentation, innovation, failures, and influential outcomes. Ultimately, the chapter advances three central claims. First, it shows the key dynamics between victims' organizations, legal scholars, and judicial operators that underpin these vibrant, productive, and influential experiments. Second, it reflects the regional scope of the dialogue and cross-fertilization between initiatives (experiments). Finally, it articulates how relevant actors reinterpreted and used human rights discourse to pursue their grievances, transforming it into a mainstream, arguably dominant framework to address not only state repression and violence but all forms of injustice.

Maryluz Barragan González traces how racism has been inscribed into the legal systems of Latin America and then points to two significant developments in the struggle toward greater equality. First, she highlights the jurisprudence of ILO Convention 169 on the rights of Indigenous and Tribal peoples. Latin American courts have been decisive in defining the content of the right to prior consultation of Indigenous peoples and Afro-descendant communities. Second, she points to the historical reparations movement carried out by the Caribbean Community or CARICOM (officially formed in 1973 by the Chaguaramas Treaty). This platform has led the conversation regarding reparations to compensate for the legacy of the treatment of enslaved people and colonization. It proposes the return of public debts that Caribbean countries paid to their colonizers so they could be independent nations, problematizing current international law and the relationship between European countries and their former colonies.

A key area of doctrinal development has been human rights, whether they sit at the international or constitutional level, or, increasingly, the two at once. In recent years, a group of scholars has argued that the practice of human rights and constitutional rights in the region has given rise to an *ius contitucionale in Latin America* (ICCAL), or "a transformative constitutional project" that "seeks to achieve and promote human rights, democracy, and the rule of law and analyze how the region has embraced and implemented these constitutional normative values." In their chapter, Lina M. Céspedes-Báez, Enrique Prieto-Rios, and Mónica Mazariegos-Rodas take on the many critics of the ICCAL theory showing how the "communities of practice" in Latin America have strategically appropriated and mobilized transformative constitutionalism's narratives and ways of interpreting the law to grant agency and guarantee the human rights of subalterns in the region.

Maria Teresa Infante, ambassador and judge, reviews maritime delimitation in the region. Judge Infante walks the reader through the different fora and diverse sources of law that states have turned to for maritime delimitation and explores the different factors, including geographical and geostrategic elements (or legal geography), that shape decision-making. Infante argues against the idea of a regional practice in maritime delimitation, showing that the contingencies of each case drive the practice.

Part IV closes by returning to more traditional LAIL subjects with a chapter by Fernando Lusa Bordin and Federica Paddeu. In recent years, Latin American states have drawn on their historical experience to advocate for an orderly and restrictive regime of countermeasures, to curb unilateral action and interventionism. They have also remained committed to asserting their juridical equality and actively shaping international law through codification and favor the adoption of a convention on state responsibility. Both projects invoke two key postulates of traditional "American international law": juridical equality of states and non-intervention. Through this effort, they hope, the international community will come together in an earnest multilateral endeavor to create greater legal certainty.

Part V: Contemporary Challenges

The volume closes with contemporary challenges. Part V points to areas of concern where Latin America is not necessarily known as an innovator—yet—but where there is a need for innovation considering the regional context and where interesting doctrinal and institutional developments are beginning to unfold.

Ezequiel González-Ocantos and Wayne Sandholtz analyze how Latin American countries have grappled with the "eruption" of transnational corruption norms, laws, and regimes, both translating and creating internationally sanctioned anticorruption standards. They trace an important shift in the framing of the issue of corruption since the late 1980s. Initially, corruption gained salience during the region's transition to more open market economies. The response to corruption was to create a series of international treaties and concomitant changes to domestic legal frameworks and key law enforcement institutions to bolster horizontal accountability. Today, corruption is increasingly framed as a human rights issue in the region, as a way to curb corruption and the excesses of anticorruption crusades.

Helena Alviar and Laura Betancur explore tensions between the aims of achieving peace and the demands imposed by international institutions and treaties, by discussing the negotiations and 2016 peace agreement between the Colombian government and the FARC guerrillas. The case offers an interesting example of the tense, complex, and far-reaching interaction between international law and domestic goals of ending civil conflict. The text analyzes how different actors made strategic use of international law according to their political preferences or economic goals. The Colombian peace treaty is relevant to other jurisdictions as it is the first peace agreement achieved since the International Criminal Court entered into force, and challenges key assumptions about what the Rome Statute demands.

Beatriz Garcia explores the current forms of environmental cooperation in Latin America. She examines whether new pathways could be open, especially regarding forest conservation, given new regulatory trends focused on global supply chains targeting commodities associated with forest destruction. Agricultural and forestry products represent a large share of Latin American domestic markets, while commodity exports, particularly to China and the United States, are likely to grow. This leads to the question of whether international norms targeting global supply chains could be instrumental in reshaping Latin American forest conservation efforts. The argument is that these regulations open an opportunity to refocus Latin American cooperation into more tangible actions toward forest and biodiversity conservation.

Alexandra Huneeus argues that the Inter-American Court is poised to play a distinct role in the complex new realm of global climate emergency litigation. Four international courts are being called on to issue judgments on questions of state responsibilities in the face of climate change, including the International Court of Justice, the European Court of Human Rights, and the International Tribunal for the Law of the Sea. But the Inter-American Court is uniquely suited to the task given its rich jurisprudence on socioeconomic rights and differential harm doctrines which can inform questions about climate justice for front-line communities and other vulnerable groups.

Pedro Villareal discusses overarching regional challenges in the field of international health law, with an emphasis on communicable disease pandemics. While COVID-19 represents the most acute disease-related problem in an entire century, the chapter shows how the regional dimension not only plays a role but may actually be a determining factor in the pandemic's longer-term impact. The chapter looks at the legal landscape, including the role of the IAHRS, and identifies the structural ailments that distinguish the region. It concludes by underscoring how the legal challenges posed by the COVID-19 pandemic in the region should be understood in light of rampant economic inequality and the resulting social exclusion of marginalized groups.

Rodrigo Polanco pushes against the lack of acknowledgement of Latin American contributions to the internet, including the creation of Cybersyn in Chile in the early 1970s. Polanco presents the participation of countries of the region in regulating the Web, with particular emphasis on one of its more essential uses—digital trade. Latin American countries have made a distinct contribution to advancing principles such as open access and net neutrality. In addition, they have pioneered the inclusion of e-commerce and data flow provisions in preferential trade agreements.

The volume closes with an epilogue in which, based on the insights of the chapters, we try to answer the question, "What characterizes Latin American international law in our time, in the practice and in the scholarship of international law?" The volume reveals a new canon of Latin American international law in the twenty-first century, with its own strengths and its own blind spots.

IV. On the Cover

The book's cover shows a picture of Shibboleth, an intervention by Colombian artist Doris Salcedo, prepared for and originally exhibited in the Turbine Hall at Tate Modern Gallery, London, from 2007 to 2008.

Shibboleth confronts us with a 167-meter-long crack, a fracture that operates as an allegory of division, segregation, and exclusion. The title comes from an Old Testament passage about a people who recognized who belonged to it—and who did not—from how they pronounced this word. Salcedo herself indicated that the work "represents borders, the experience of immigrants, . . . and of racial hatred. It is the experience of a Third World person coming into the heart of Europe."

Shibboleth works as a powerful allegory of Latin American international law, its journey to the Global North, and the internal, indeed deep divisions that persist in this region. Although the chapters in this volume often highlight new voices, Latin America is a region still struggling with violence, a colonial past, and structural racism that has marginalized so many, including Indigenous and Afro-descendant people. Shibboleth also points to how lawyers and legal scholars use the language and structure of formal law to distinguish the law from politics, and to distinguish themselves as a profession. Admittedly, the borders between international law scholarship and other disciplines have grown more porous through growing interdisciplinary dialogue, leading to a rich new era of international law scholarship. But we must remain conscious of the limits of this new era, as well as of drawing conclusions from this particular set of essays, rich as they are. Although the crack in Turbine Hall was filled in after the closure of the exhibit in the Tate Modern in London, it is still visible as a powerful reminder of divisions in the past and emerging in the present in complex ways.

PART I
HISTORY

1

The Spanish American Concordats (1821–1875)

Pablo Mijangos y González

I. Introduction

Since the twelfth century, the Holy See has frequently used concordats to settle jurisdictional disputes with secular sovereigns and reframe the relations between civil and ecclesiastical authorities in different parts of the world. Although this kind of diplomatic agreement has had a tremendous impact on the history of polities with a sizable Catholic community, the historiography of international law rarely mention it. Leaving aside the biases of historiography centered in the Anglosphere, the concordats' absence in this field may be due to their legal peculiarities: the church has no independent means to ensure their observance (it can only exercise the remedies provided by secular legislations) and they are signed by the Holy See, an ancient religious entity whose international status has suffered significant challenges since the Protestant Reformation and whose current legal nature was defined until the Lateran Accords of 1929.[1] Despite these characteristics, though, concordats deserve to be fully addressed by the historiography of international law because, in essence, they are agreements between two sovereign entities—one secular and one religious—and because they belong to the complex legal order of a global community of believers. In the case of Spanish America, where Catholicism has been the predominant religion since colonial times, concordats' relevance has been difficult to overlook.

Since there are no comparable legal instruments in the other major religions, it is necessary to understand why the Catholic tradition had to develop this one in the first place. Although religion deals in principle with the spiritual realm, it usually has a visible public presence and can exercise profound influence in every corner of social life. This can be said about every religious faith but is especially true of Catholicism. Notwithstanding the church's traditional interest in regulating its own affairs, many aspects of religious life strongly overlap with

[1] It is important to distinguish the Holy See, as global head of the Catholic Church, from the extinct Pontifical States and the contemporary Vatican City State, two territorial entities that were created to protect the papacy's independence.

Pablo Mijangos y González, *The Spanish American Concordats (1821–1875)* In: *Latin American International Law in the Twenty-First Century.* Edited by: Alejandro Chehtman, Alexandra Huneeus, and Sergio Puig, Oxford University Press. DOI: 10.1093/9780197754016.003.0001

secular law and earthly political concerns: it suffices to think about the management of ecclesiastical property, church taxation, family law, religious education, and clerical appointments. This is the reason why the Church has always had to negotiate with civil authorities on how to deal with the so-called matters of "mixed jurisdiction." The local churches themselves conduct most negotiations of this sort, but concordats have had a special place in history because they usually arise from highly explosive conflicts and require an *ad hoc* reformulation of general principles of church governance. In those cases of special relevance, the Holy See—as the supreme echelon of the ecclesiastical hierarchy, fully independent from secular rule—has historically assumed the exclusive power to negotiate and authorize the legal status of the Catholic Church in any polity. As Roland Minnerath observes, it is no coincidence that the first concordat (that of Worms, in 1122) came about after the Gregorian Reform that dramatically strengthened the powers of the papacy.[2]

The history of concordats in Spanish America began relatively late, after the collapse of the Spanish Empire in the 1820s. Before Independence, Church-state relations in the Americas had been managed through the system of Royal Patronage, which gave the Spanish Crown broad powers over the government and administration of ecclesiastical affairs in the New World. Although Spanish legal doctrine understood Patronage as an intrinsic element of state sovereignty, the system's original foundations were a series of sixteenth-century papal bulls addressed to the Spanish kings. Unsurprisingly, once the Spanish Empire vanished from the scene, the whole system entered into crisis, and the new republican governments—the inheritors of Royal sovereignty—began to clash with the clergy over the scope of their respective jurisdictions, leading in some cases to large-scale political conflicts. In this context, the Holy See gradually began to consider the signature of concordats with the Spanish American republics. As with the Napoleonic concordat of 1801, a broad agreement with each of these young republics was expected to solve the existing tensions and facilitate the local churches' reorganization after years of ongoing revolutions. Legally speaking, the first Spanish American concordats were the most ambitious attempt at solving the crisis of religious governance that was then affecting the region.

This chapter focuses on the concordats signed by Pope Pius IX with the Spanish American nations during the 1850s and 1860s. They constitute an important chapter in the history of international law, not just because they were high-level agreements between sovereign powers but mainly because these concordats were one of the earliest and most evident examples of international

[2] Roland Minnerath, "The Position of the Catholic Church Regarding Concordats from a Doctrinal and Pragmatic Perspective," *Catholic University Law Review* 47, no. 2 (Winter 1998): 468.

norms clashing with constitutional law. As the chapter will show, during the first decades of independent life, most Spanish American nations attempted to preserve the old Patronage system by codifying its basic principles in their respective constitutions. This was a pragmatic response to pressing state needs and a clear assertion of national sovereignty (which seemed necessary considering the early republics' fragility). Since this unilateral solution to the crisis of church governance was never accepted by the Holy See, almost every Spanish American republic eventually tried to negotiate a concordat in the hope of getting the pope's blessing for their existing laws. The problems began when Roman officials attempted to impose a uniform model of church governance for the entire region, leading to concordat proposals that often conflicted with national laws. What would happen when an international accord contradicted or modified a series of rules established by constitutional clauses? Which legal order would prevail? This crucial question of international law—seen today in the frequent reluctance of many governments to enforce international human rights—first appeared in the region when the church's search for uniformity clashed with the constitutions' unbending assertion of national rule.

II. Problems of Religious Governance in the Early Republics

To understand the need for concordats in Spanish America, it is first necessary to understand the crisis of governance that both the Catholic Church and the new republican governments faced after Independence. As mentioned before, for over three centuries, Church-state relations in the Spanish Empire had been managed through the system of Royal Patronage, which gave the Spanish Crown broad powers over the government and administration of ecclesiastical affairs.[3] This system became ever more encompassing and led to countless conflicts of jurisdiction during colonial times, but at least was deemed legitimate by the clergy and the general population. A new set of religious problems in the region began in the 1820s when the severance of bonds between Spain and its former colonies led to questioning the continuity and legitimacy of state control of the Church: Did the new sovereigns need the pope's authorization to rule over the local Catholic clergy and manage its considerable wealth? Were priests and parishioners bound to obey bishops appointed by weak governments? Assuming that the new republics were uniformly Catholic (as asserted by all the constitutions of this period), what were the concrete duties of the state toward the Catholic faith?

[3] For a general overview, see Alberto de la Hera, *Iglesia y Corona en la América española* (Madrid: Editorial MAPFRE, 1992).

The fierce debates over National Patronage have been thoroughly studied and cannot be adequately addressed here.[4] It is enough to say that, despite the irregular continuity of traditional practices, by the mid-nineteenth century no country in the region had been capable of finding a mutually acceptable solution to their many problems of religious governance. The Holy See clearly acknowledged the damage created by this situation. In its confidential dossier about the concordat proposal submitted by Bolivia in 1851, the Congregation of Extraordinary Ecclesiastical Affairs recognized that the absence of appropriate rules on Church-state relations had been extremely detrimental to the different churches of the region. In the first place, some national governments had abolished the tithe or relaxed its enforcement, thus depriving the clergy of their main source of sustenance. Second, the same governments had exercised a broad power of appointing clerical authorities, which in some countries had provoked bitter internal conflicts within the Church over the legitimacy of the local hierarchy. In some other cases, the lack or delay of episcopal appointments had also created a crisis of clerical authority, which affected the performance of diocesan seminaries and eroded the internal discipline of the local clergy. In the same vein, the absence of regular communications between religious communities and their superiors in Europe had aggravated the existing crisis of the regular clergy, some of whose members led "publicly scandalous" lives. And to make things worse, the combination of politicized clerical appointments and a robust freedom of the press had favored the dissemination of "evil books" and "pernicious opinions," especially in public education.[5]

If the Catholic Church had good reasons for sitting at the negotiation table, the region's republican governments were almost desperate for an agreement with the Holy See. As Mexican statesman Lucas Alamán argued in 1853, Catholicism remained the strongest—and perhaps the only—cultural bond that tied together the inhabitants of the new republics.[6] Despite its many fractures and internal tensions, the Catholic Church provided a shared moral vocabulary and a powerful heritage of symbols, rituals, and feasts to societies marked by enormous ethnic, linguistic, social, economic, regional, and political differences. Since religious conflict was usually understood as a dangerous threat to national unity, and most republics seemed to be on the verge of political collapse, governments really wanted to secure the Catholic Church's support by finally ending the acrimonious patronage debate. At the same time, though, these weak Catholic

[4] See Michael P. Costeloe, *Church and State in Independent Mexico: A Study of the Patronage Debate, 1821-1857* (London: Royal Historical Society, 1978).

[5] Archivio Storico della Segreteria di Stato—Sezione per i Rapporti con gli Stati e le Organizzazioni Internazionali (ASRS), AA.EE.SS., Pio IX, Rapporti delle sessioni, Anno 1851, Sess. 303, Vol. XXI, Fasc. 3, ff. 49–52, 59–60.

[6] Lucas Alamán, "Carta a Antonio López de Santa Anna" (March 23, 1853), in *Lucas Alamán*, ed. Andrés Lira (Mexico City: Cal y Arena, 1997), 351.

republics also needed to assert their sovereignty vis-à-vis foreign powers and domestic power factors, such as regional *cacicazgos*, unruly armies, Indigenous communities, and the Catholic Church itself. For liberals and conservatives, obtaining the papal recognition of National Patronage was practically synonymous with preserving national sovereignty: the new republican governments had to enjoy the same ecclesiastical privileges the papacy had granted to the Spanish monarchy in the sixteenth century.

Beyond these questions of principle, the lack of new rules of religious governance also affected the state-building process in concrete ways.[7] To begin with, the new republics desperately needed to create a functional system of public finance, which was supposed to require the sale and circulation of church lands (*desamortización*), as well as the elimination of tithes and their substitution with secular taxes on private wealth. As a powerful landholder managing an immense network of parishes, schools, funds, and charities, the Church would only accept this measure in exchange for permanent state funding. In addition, these republics needed to modernize their legal systems and establish strong judiciaries capable of processing social conflicts in a uniform and timely fashion: this objective could not be realized if the ecclesiastical courts preserved their traditional jurisdiction and procedures and if members of the clergy kept enjoying a privileged legal status (*fuero*). Whereas the colonial order had allowed a complex coexistence of separate jurisdictions and legal regimes, the prevailing model of the national state required a more rational and uniform legal structure based upon the supremacy of civil law and the equality of all citizens. In this respect, a concordat could be a valuable instrument for reducing the jurisdictional boundaries of clerical tribunals and, thus, for enhancing the power of secular courts.

Finally, republican governments also wanted the clergy to become state officials in charge of taming and moralizing the popular classes. In a time when the central administration's reach beyond capital cities was minimal, parish priests and frontier missionaries were often seen as the only authorities capable of reforming an extremely disordered society. Lay politicians had not forgotten the leading role of many clerics during the Wars of Independence. They realized that bishops, cathedral canons, and ecclesiastical judges often enjoyed a greater influence over important local affairs than governors or lawmakers. From this perspective, the government's traditional right to present candidates for bishoprics and canonries and its parallel right to choose and supervise parish priests could never be renounced, for these powers were crucial instruments for

[7] See, among others, Pablo Mijangos, *Entre Dios y la república. La separación Iglesia-Estado en México, siglo XIX* (México: Tirant Lo Blanch/CIDE, 2018); Daniel Víctor Santilli, "El papel de la tributación en la formación del Estado. La contribución directa en el siglo XIX en Buenos Aires," *América Latina en la historia económica* 33 (enero-junio 2010): 33–63; Juan Pro, *La construcción del Estado en España. Una historia del siglo XIX* (Madrid: Alianza, 2019).

securing social order and political stability. There is no better example of this concern than the religious project of Gabriel García Moreno, who conquered the presidency of Ecuador in the 1860s. As Derek Williams explains, García Moreno aimed to transform Ecuador into a modern nation with improved transportation, a strong economy, a professional army, and a powerful government capable of asserting its presence in the most remote villages. To achieve this goal, however, he needed the church's help in civilizing the Ecuadorian people: who but the clergy would teach peasants the evils of drinking and immorality and the value of hard work, authority, and discipline?[8]

Although the need for new rules for conducting Church-state relations had been well-known since the early years of republican life, several factors delayed the beginning of concordat negotiations. On the church's side, perhaps the greatest obstacle was Pope Gregory XVI's reluctance to sign agreements of this kind. During his long reign between 1831 and 1846, the Holy See's foreign policy remained in the hands of the *zelanti*, a party of ultra-conservative clerics suspicious of the political regimes born out of the revolutions in Europe and the Americas.[9] For example, when, in 1837 and 1843, the Mexican government's envoys submitted concordat proposals centered on recognizing church patronage as a state right and reducing the tithe to half (to tax only 5 percent of the income instead of the traditional 10 percent), papal officers courteously replied that the pontiff's main concern was to preserve the canonical rights of the Church and that he preferred to negotiate each item of the proposal separately.[10] In the same vein, when the Nicaraguan plenipotentiary minister in Paris proposed the papal nuncio in France to negotiate a concordat in 1844, the Congregation decided to reject this proposal on the ground that there were too many "divisions, unions, and other political variations" in the new republics. A negotiation with such counterparts was too risky because new presidents did not honor the obligations assumed by their predecessors.[11] Not surprisingly, Gregory XVI only agreed to sign four treaties on specific topics with neighboring Naples (1834), Modena and Sardinia (both in 1841), and the Swiss canton of St. Gallen (1845).[12] The pope recognized the new nations' independence from Spain but never trusted the authorities of such remote and unstable republics.

It is difficult to summarize what happened on the other side of the Atlantic since the first three decades after Independence were characterized by chronic

[8] Derek Williams, "Assembling the 'Empire of Morality': State Building Strategies in Catholic Ecuador, 1861-1875," *Journal of Historical Sociology* 14, no. 2 (June 2001): 149–174.

[9] Nicholas Atkin and Frank Tallett, *Priests, Prelates, and People: A History of European Catholicism since 1750* (New York: Oxford University Press, 2003), 89–92.

[10] ASRS, AA.EE.SS., Gregorio XVI, Messico, Anno 1845, Pos. 113, Fasc. 595, ff. 70–85.

[11] ASRS, AA.EE.SS., Gregorio XVI, Nicaragua, Anno 1844, Pos. 8, Fasc. 543, f. 31.

[12] Angelo Mercati, *Raccolta di concordati su materia ecclesiastiche tra la Santa Sede e le autorità civili*, vol. 1 (Rome: Tipografia Poliglotta Vaticana, 1954), xix.

political instability in the entire region. Governments rose and fell due to factional strife, never-ending *pronunciamientos*, and fiscal penury: this general context made it very difficult to negotiate anything. In most cases, however, the crucial obstacle resided in the patronage clauses in the different national constitutions. With slight differences, republican constitutions declared Catholicism the official religion but simultaneously regulated the exercise of patronage powers, especially regarding clerical appointments.[13] For diplomatic purposes, these constitutional restrictions meant that patronage had to be recognized by the Holy See as an authority inherent in state sovereignty, and could never be understood as a privilege conceded by the popes. Furthermore, constitutional patronage clauses also implied that any agreement negotiated in Rome had to be coherent with the national legislation and approved by the respective national legislature, which opened the possibility for a total or partial rejection of the accords. The Holy See expected concordats to enjoy the same legal hierarchy of the constitution and to be quickly approved by the national executive power, with no need for additional sanction. Such an expectation could only materialize under strong, pro-clerical regimes that only prevailed in some countries during the middle decades of the century.

III. The Concordat Wave under Pope Pius IX

The death of Pope Gregory and the subsequent election of Cardinal Giovanni Mastai-Ferretti as Pope Pius IX in the summer of 1846 provided an opportunity to break the impasse in the negotiations between the Holy See and the Spanish American republics. Despite his later reputation as an arch-reactionary, when Pius IX rose to the papal throne, he was widely regarded as the liberals' hope: everyone expected him to remove the *zelanti* from power and to introduce moderate reforms in the government of the Papal States. And so he did, for during the first two years of his pontificate, Pius IX granted amnesty to political prisoners, issued a law establishing freedom of the press, arranged the introduction of railways and telegraph lines, and sanctioned a new constitution for his dominions.[14] His initial foreign policy also announced change, as he approved a concordat with czarist Russia (1847), started relations with the Ottoman Empire, and (unsuccessfully) invited the Orthodox churches to reunite with Rome.[15] Unlike his predecessor, Pius IX wanted to provide a lasting

[13] See Agustín Sánchez Andrés, "El marco constitucional de las relaciones entre Iglesia y Estado en América del Sur (1811-1900)," *Hispania Sacra* 50, no. 102 (1998): 589–610.

[14] Frank J. Coppa, *The Modern Papacy since 1789* (New York: Longman, 1998), 84–89.

[15] Giacomo Martina, "Pio IX," in *The Papacy: An Encyclopedia*, vol. 2, ed. Philippe Levillain (New York: Routledge, 2002), 1192–1194.

legal framework to the Spanish American churches and considered concordats the best means to fulfill that end. Negotiations would not be easy, but at least the door was finally open.

The pope accepted to open formal negotiations with the Republic of Chile in 1848. However, this initial attempt failed due to the Chilean ambassador's insistence on the papal recognition of National Patronage and the outbreak of the Roman revolution in the same year, which led the pope to reject his fragile liberalism and embrace a clearly conservative path. Having in mind the dangers of giving too much power to unfriendly regimes, the Congregation of Extraordinary Ecclesiastical Affairs argued against the Chilean concordat proposal because it was "contrary to the liberties and prerogatives of the Church" and because it "sanctioned many abuses already present in other places of the Americas."[16] But instead of rejecting concordats as such, what the congregation's members said was that the pope would only approve agreements that met two conditions: first, any concordat would have to be beneficial to the Church, and second, it would have to correct abusive but generally accepted practices, to serve as a model for future negotiations in the region. The Holy See did not have to wait long to receive a new and more attractive proposal, for the Bolivian government, moved by the explosive increase of tensions with the Church, entrusted General Andrés Santa Cruz with the task of settling pending affairs. One of Bolivia's most renowned statesmen, Santa Cruz was an excellent choice for this job because he had opposed the Roman revolution and had been warmly recommended as a loyal ultramontane by monsignor Gaetano Baluffi, the first internuncio to the Republic of New Granada (Colombia).[17]

Although it was partially rejected by Bolivia's National Convention and never entered into force, the Bolivian concordat of 1851 remains an important milestone in this story because it was the first Spanish American negotiation successfully concluded and because it became the standard model for the region. Broadly summarized, it could be said that this concordat involved several major accords, each more relevant for the Church or the state. The first five attended to the main interests of the Holy See: Catholicism would remain the state religion (art. 1); consequently, both private and public education, at all levels, would be imparted following Catholic principles and under the bishops' supervision, who would also enjoy the power to censor books on religion and morals (arts. 2 and 3); and, finally, the Bolivian government committed itself to sustain the clergy with

[16] ASRS, AA.EE.SS., Pio IX, Rapporti delle sessioni, Anno 1851, Sess. 303, Vol. XXI, Fasc. 3, ff. 56–57.

[17] Humberto Vázquez-Machicado, "La Diplomacia de Bolivia ante la Santa Sede. El mariscal Santa Cruz, diplomático en Europa," in *Obras Completas de Humberto Vázquez-Machicado y José Vázquez-Machicado*, ed. Guillermo Ovando-Sanz and Alberto M. Vázquez (La Paz, Bolivia: Editorial Don Bosco, 1988), 23–26, 34.

state funds, in compensation for the diminution of tithe income (art. 5). Even if the Church was to be financed by the state, it preserved full property rights over its corporate wealth, which remained protected by the same guarantees granted by national law to ordinary citizens (art. 18). Church real estate, therefore, would not be mandatorily auctioned. However, if church properties had already been privatized, the clergy would not molest the new owners (art. 20). Church wealth not destined for public worship could be subject to taxation (art. 19).[18]

If the first five agreements guaranteed the Catholic Church's financial viability in the country and its monopoly over the conscience of Bolivians, the following five answered the government's main political concerns. In the first place, the President of the Republic was to enjoy patronage powers, namely, the right to submit candidates for vacant bishoprics to the pope, appoint six canons for each cathedral chapter, and choose parish priests from lists of candidates elaborated by the bishops (arts. 7, 8, and 9). These powers ensured the Executive a considerable degree of control over the entire church hierarchy, on the condition that seminary education remained in the hands of the bishops and all candidates and appointees satisfied the traditional requirements of canon law (art. 12). In the second place, the pope and the bishops would preserve their power to create new dioceses and parishes, but always proceeding in accord with the government (arts. 10 and 11). Third, bishops and clergymen would swear an oath of allegiance to the Constitution and the Republic, committing themselves to never getting involved in political schemes contrary to "national independence or public tranquility" (art. 23). Fourth, all the nation's clerics would pray for the salvation of the President and the Republic after each religious celebration (art. 24). And fifth, the clergy's civil disputes and their judicial cases related to nonreligious crimes would thereafter be resolved by secular courts, provided that priests were treated respectfully and that criminal appeal courts included at least two clergymen (arts. 15 and 16).[19]

The Bolivian concordat eliminated the tithe, restricted clerical immunities, and transformed the clergy into a major political instrument of the government, all this without risking the republic's confessional character and the church's economic power. As a sign of goodwill toward Rome, Articles 4, 21, and 22 also allowed for free communication between the Holy See and the Bolivian church (thus eliminating the traditional *pase regio*), preserved the existing monasteries, authorized the free establishment of new religious orders, and pledged the government to support missions for the "conversion of the unfaithful" within the national territory (i.e., in the Indigenous lands that had not been reached by

[18] Concordat between the Holy See and Bolivia (1851), in *Datos y antecedentes para la celebración de un concordato* (La Paz, Bolivia: Imp. "La Libertad," 1883), 3–13.

[19] Ibid., 7–13, 15–17.

Western culture yet).[20] The most controversial provision, especially from the perspective of constitutional and international law, was Article 27, which defined the concordat as a "Law of the State" and abrogated all preceding "laws, ordinances, and decrees" on these matters. Article 28 disposed that the agreement had to be ratified within eighteen months, but it did not say by whom or what the consequence of a partial rejection would be.[21] As mentioned, the Holy See expected ratification to be a mere bureaucratic procedure, for it understood concordats as agreements between sovereigns endowed with a constitutional status. This is why, even if the concordat solved important problems, it was bound to clash with Bolivia's National Convention, which assumed itself to be the representative of the Sovereign People and regarded the constitution as the superior standard on ecclesiastical law.

The failure of Bolivia's concordat did not deter the pope from starting new negotiations in 1852, this time with the Republic of Guatemala. Like in the previous case, Guatemala entrusted this task to an experienced diplomat, Fernando de Lorenzana, Marquis of Belmonte, who was well-known at the papal court (and who would also be hired by other Central American countries for the same purpose[22]). Unlike Bolivia, however, the current president of Guatemala, conservative General Rafael Carrera, had tighter control of the political system and could guarantee an easy ratification process. The negotiations advanced quickly because the pope instructed the Congregation to use the Bolivian concordat as a model.[23] Signed on October 7, 1852, the Guatemalan concordat practically repeated the same language and became the official referent for future agreements. Besides the introduction of a conciliation phase in the ordinary disputes between clerics (art. 15), the only relevant difference was the preservation of the tithe along with an annual allocation of state funds for the Church (art. 4).[24] That same day, and also with Lorenzana's signature, Costa Rica formalized its concordat with the Holy See, in which the tithe was explicitly eliminated in exchange of state funding.[25] There were no more concordats in Spanish America until July 1861, when the Holy See signed one with Honduras, then followed by those with

[20] Ibid., 5, 15.

[21] Ibid., 17.

[22] On Lorenzana and the Central American concordats, see Carmela Velazquez Bonilla, *Entre la Santa Sede y Centroamérica. La Iglesia católica, la independencia y la producción del poder moderno, 1821-1870* (San José: Universidad de Costa Rica, 2021).

[23] ASRS, AA.EE.SS., Pio IX, Rapporti delle sessioni, Anno 1852, Sess. 309 II, Vol. XXI, Fasc. 7, f. 481.

[24] "Concordato fra Pio IX e la Repubblica di Guatemala," in *Raccolta di concordati su materie ecclesiastiche tra la Santa Sede e le autorità civili*, vol. 1 (Rome: Tipografia Poliglotta Vaticana, 1919), 810–821.

[25] "Concordato fra Pio IX e la Repubblica di Costarica," in *Raccolta di concordati su materie ecclesiastiche tra la Santa Sede e le autorità civili*, vol. 1, 801–802.

Nicaragua (October 1861), San Salvador (April 1862), Venezuela (July 1862), and Ecuador (October 1862).

Besides their content, what did these concordats have in common? First, they reveal the pope's desire for uniform Church-state law on a continental scale.[26] Pius IX clearly understood that the Spanish American republics came from the same legal and political tradition, that the "sister republics" would be watching and copying each other (as always), and that Church-state relations could not radically differ from the colonial past. Despite his openly reactionary discourse, the pope tried to find common ground between the liberals who demanded patronage powers and the conservatives who wanted to preserve the republics' Catholic identity at all costs. In the second place, these concordats showed that the Holy See's uniformizing policy in the Americas could only work under certain conditions. The government had an explicit conservative agenda in the seven nations that reached an agreement with Rome. Republican institutions were relatively weak, which facilitated the ratification process and created incentives to instrumentalize the Church as an effective tool for imposing moral discipline and ruling over a diverse and dispersed rural population (Ecuador was the clearest example of this). As we will see, this was not the case in the larger countries of the region, where liberals considered the Church to be a rival—and not an ally of—the state and where some in the clergy were desperate to get rid of secular patronage.

IV. Failed Negotiations

Since the Catholic Church was present in almost every corner of social life, concordat negotiations could deeply affect the political arrangements contained in national constitutions. To illustrate this point, it suffices to list the constitutional subjects touched by Bolivia's concordat: state religion, public and private education, freedom of expression, taxes, national budget, property rights, presidential powers, secular courts' jurisdiction, civic oaths, and the hierarchy of international norms. From the perspective of mid-nineteenth-century liberals, these subjects had to be discussed and defined within national assemblies, considering public opinion and having the national interest in mind. The nondemocratic nature of concordats, along with the liberals' fixation on national sovereignty, made it almost impossible for the Holy See to reach an agreement with the larger countries that also undertook this kind of negotiation. The Argentine Confederation, Perú, and Mexico should be added to the list initiated by Chile and Bolivia. What

[26] ASRS, AA.EE.SS., Pio IX, Rapporti delle sessioni, Anno 1852, Sess. 309 III, Vol. XXI, Fasc. 7, f. 493.

did the first three countries have in common? They inherited the institutional infrastructure of the old Spanish viceroyalties, had developed a stronger constitutional tradition (fiercely defended by a large class of liberal lawyers), and coexisted with powerful clerical structures that were not easy to tame. It is not surprising, then, that concordat negotiations were very different in these nations.

The case of Argentina resembles that of Chile. After the fall of dictator Juan Manuel de Rosas in 1852, the triumphant provincial governments adopted a new constitution in 1853, which declared Catholicism as the state religion but simultaneously introduced freedom of worship, considering the religious needs of British merchants in the country. This charter also granted patronage rights to Congress and the Executive, excluded the regular clergy from legislative assemblies, and eliminated the clerical *fuero*.[27] The pope did not want to break relations with the country, so he sent an apostolic delegate to Argentina and then, in 1858, received an ambassador who had instructions to negotiate a concordat. Alas, the negotiations ended quickly. The Argentinian envoy, Juan del Campillo, presented a proposal that repeated the patronage clauses of the 1853 constitution, while the Congregation of Extraordinary Ecclesiastical Affairs insisted on adopting an agreement like the Guatemalan concordat of 1852. Faced with the Congregation's refusal, Campillo argued that the accords had to be compatible with the national constitution or they would not be sanctioned by the "supreme powers of the State." The Holy See Replied that the proposal did not satisfy the Church but did not close the door for future negotiations.[28] As the distinguished jurist Dalmacio Vélez Sarsfield had also recognized in his 1854 treatise *Relaciones del estado con la iglesia*, it was better to preserve the status quo, for the Church met "an overall worthy and high need." The propagation of its doctrine, the "conservation of its institutions," and the "support for its authorities" were essential for maintaining public order.[29]

Perú approached the Holy See in 1852, right after Bolivia's concordat negotiations concluded. The Peruvian president commissioned Monsignor Bartolomeo de Herrera, a canon of Lima's cathedral chapter, to negotiate an agreement different from that of Bolivia but consistent with the project of a Catholic republic endowed with patronage powers. The Congregation did not immediately reject the project because it knew Perú's regional relevance: the country was undergoing an economic takeoff due to railway construction and

[27] Agustín Sánchez Andrés, "El marco constitucional de las relaciones entre Iglesia y Estado en América del Sur (1811-1900)," *Hispania Sacra* 50, no. 102 (1998): 592.

[28] ASRS, AA.EE.SS., Pio IX, Rapporti delle sessioni, Anno 1859, Sess. 357, Vol. XXV, Fasc. 5, ff. 367–371.

[29] Dalmacio Vélez Sarsfield, *Relaciones del estado con la iglesia* (1854), quoted and translated by Abelardo Levaggi, "Dalmacio Vélez Sarsfield (Argentina, 1800-74)," in *Law and Christianity in Latin America: The Work of Great Jurists*, ed. M. C. Mirow and Rafael Domingo (New York: Routledge, 2021), p. 107.

mining policy and becoming increasingly attractive to European immigrants.[30] Nonetheless, the negotiations quickly derailed because Canon Herrera did not have sufficient powers to undertake the negotiation, and a liberal revolution broke out in January 1854: the whole enterprise seemed too risky for the Holy See.[31] Besides, liberal opinion abhorred the idea of following the same steps of Bolivian General Santa Cruz and furiously opposed any measure that could be interpreted as a renunciation of Perú's sovereign rights. The jurist who best developed this argument was Francisco Javier Mariátegui, a distinguished magistrate, diplomat, and lawmaker who had taken part in the country's most important political moments since Independence. According to Mariátegui, concordats were "harmful," "unnecessary," and contrary to the church's ancient discipline, in which the election of bishops did not belong to the Roman pontiff but to the faithful themselves. Therefore, as a political body created by the same people of believers, the nation was the rightful holder of patronage powers and did not have to negotiate them with the devious Roman curia. Besides, the nation's progress required a policy of religious tolerance like that of the United States. In a century of remarkable intellectual advances, the Peruvian government should protect individual liberties and never restore the church's monopoly over education.[32]

The lack of adequate political conditions forced the Peruvian government to suspend concordat negotiations. This does not mean, however, that Perú moved toward a regime of Church-state separation. On the contrary, in parallel with Ecuador, the government's modernizing projects required the clergy's support on the ground: in a Catholic country, the Church remained an essential instrument for maintaining peace, order, and social discipline. The development of the Amazonic areas of the country, for instance, could not be accomplished without Catholic missionaries trained in the art of "civilizing" the Indigenous peoples.[33] Thus, despite Mariátegui's passionate opinion, the government kept pushing for a partial agreement with the Holy See, which was finally obtained in 1875. In the bull *Praeclara inter beneficia*, Pope Pius IX granted patronage powers to the Peruvian president on the condition that clerical wealth would be respected and Catholicism would remain the state religion.[34] It was not a comprehensive

[30] ASRS, AA.EE.SS., Pio IX, Rapporti delle sessioni, Anno 1853, Sess. 312, Vol. XXII, Fasc. 1, ff. 60–61.

[31] ASRS, AA.EE.SS., Pio IX, Perú, Anno 1854, Pos. 92, Fasc. 254, ff. 3–8. See also Giovanni Iannettone, "La misión de Herrera de 1852: el Perú y la Santa Sede en el siglo XIX," *Revista peruana de derecho internacional* LIII, no. 121 (enero–abril 2003): 51–82.

[32] Francisco Javier Mariátegui, *Reseña histórica de los principales concordatos celebrados con Roma, y breves reflexiones sobre el último habido entre Pío IX y el Gobierno de Bolivia* (Lima, Peru: Impreso por José Mira, 1856), prologue and 284–286.

[33] Pilar García Jordan, *Iglesia y poder en el Perú contemporáneo, 1821-1919* (Cusco: Centro de Estudios Regionales Andinos "Bartolomé de las Casas," 1991), 137–139, 169–171.

[34] Juan José Ruda Santolaria, "Las relaciones entre la Iglesia y el Estado a la luz de las constituciones peruanas del siglo XIX," *Revista de Estudios Histórico-Jurídicos* 24 (2002): 76–77.

accord, but it allowed both Church and state to avoid major religious conflicts like those that had taken place in neighboring New Granada in the 1850s.[35]

Mexico was, by far, the most conflicting scenario for the Catholic Church in the Americas during the nineteenth century. On the one hand, Mexican liberalism insisted on placing the Church under the state's sovereign jurisdiction, to facilitate a significant transformation of Mexican society.[36] Congress had approved instructions for negotiating a concordat since 1826. Still, all diplomatic missions in Rome failed because Mexican envoys were legally instructed to ask the pope to recognize Patronage as a sovereign right of the state. After the failed missions of 1837 and 1843, President Antonio López de Santa Anna made one last attempt to reach an agreement with the Holy See in 1854, but to no avail. The state would not benefit from giving the clergy total control over education and exhausting the treasury to support the Church, even if the government was in conservative hands.[37] Soon after, under liberal presidents Juan Álvarez and Ignacio Comonfort (1855–1857), the state suppressed the clerical *fuero*, imposed the forced sale of corporate lands, forbade priests from charging fees to poor parishioners, and broke down the barriers to non-Catholic education. Two years later, amidst a bloody civil war that soon would be followed by French military intervention, President Benito Juárez declared the separation of Church and state, nationalized clerical property, introduced freedom of worship, established civil marriage, abolished regulars' novitiates and religious confraternities, and banned public displays of religious fervor. Legally speaking, Mexico stopped being a Catholic nation in 1859.

The obsession with creating a powerful state after the military defeat against the United States in 1847–1848 and the presence of a strong and radical liberal movement certainly became two major obstacles in the negotiations with the Holy See. However, the Mexican case is also interesting because a considerable sector of the local clergy vehemently opposed secular patronage. From the perspective of such Mexican bishops as Clemente de Jesús Munguía, secular governments were dangerously incompetent to rule over the Church, which, in the end, remained the only stable institution in a country engulfed by permanent political turmoil. Besides, and more important from a legal perspective, they saw the Church as a "perfect juridical society," that is, as a "complete" and sovereign community in its own sphere, which was entitled to the same prerogatives

[35] On the Church-state conflict in New Granada (Colombia), see José David Cortés Guerrero, *La batalla de los siglos. Estado, Iglesia y religión en Colombia en el siglo XIX. De la Independencia a la Regeneración* (Bogotá: Universidad Nacional de Colombia, 2016).

[36] See Charles Hale, *Mexican Liberalism in the Age of Mora, 1821–1853* (New Haven CT: Yale University Press, 1968).

[37] ASRS, AA.EE.SS., Pio IX, Messico, Anno 1851-1861, Pos. 165, Fasc. 643, ff. 43–83.

enjoyed by all independent societies under international law.[38] According to this ecclesiological vision, the Catholic Church had a natural right to self-government and should only negotiate agreements with friendly and reliable régimes. This is one of the reasons Munguía, along with some other bishops, boycotted the concordat negotiations fostered by President Santa Anna and the first apostolic delegate in Mexico, Luigi Clementi, who believed that the Mexican church needed an accord of this kind.

Ecclesiastical records leave no doubt about the Mexican clergy's opposition to the concordat. In 1854, while the Mexican government was pushing forward the negotiations in Rome, the bishops of Guadalajara, Michoacán, Puebla, Chiapas, Sonora, Durango, and Nuevo León—that is, seven of the republic's ten prelates—began to write to each other to draft a joint plan of action, manifesting their skepticism about any agreement and their awareness of the interests at stake. At some point, some bishops even suggested that they had to "multiply the obstacles" in the path to a settlement with which they disagreed. Munguía, for instance, wrote to the bishop of Guadalajara that requesting the restoration of the civil enforcement of tithes would be sufficient to "frustrate" the concordat.[39] A year later, on May 1, 1855, after examining the official proposal submitted by the Mexican government, Munguía wrote a confidential letter to the pope recommending that he not celebrate a concordat with Santa Anna. According to the bishop, the Catholic Church had survived Mexico's "incessant revolutions" only because of its autonomy from temporal governments and "its exclusive dependence on Rome."[40] It was a matter of "life or death" that the "anarchical governments" of Mexico never regain patronal powers. If experience taught anything, it was that Mexican regimes "usually take much more than what is granted to them."[41]

A decade later, when Emperor Maximilian tried again to negotiate a concordat with Rome, domestic clerical opposition remained strong. Munguía, yet again, told the pope that an agreement with the new Mexican monarch would be "harmful" and "truly ruinous."[42] The French-backed Empire did not even have an army of its own; it was delegitimized by its "antinational character," overwhelmed by debt and economic crisis, beset by a "tenacious and uncompromising party," and threatened by the resurgence of the United States after the Civil War's end.[43] Besides, the prelate stressed, the Church was a "perfect and

[38] See Pablo Mijangos, *The Lawyer of the Church: Bishop Clemente de Jesús Munguía and the Clerical Response to the Mexican Liberal Reforma* (Lincoln: University of Nebraska Press, 2015), 114–136.

[39] Archivo Histórico del Arzobispado de Guadalajara, Sección: gobierno, Serie: obispos, Pedro Espinosa y Dávalos. 1826-1862. Caja 1. Año 1854.

[40] ASRS, AA.EE.SS., Pio IX, Messico, 1851-1861, Pos. 165, Fasc. 644, ff. 98–102.

[41] ASRS, AA.EE.SS., Pio IX, Messico, 1851-1861, Pos. 165, Fasc. 644, ff. 101–102.

[42] Archivio Apostolico Vaticano (AAV), Segreteria di Stato, Rubrica 251, Anno 1866, Fasc. 11, f. 112.

[43] AAV, Segreteria di Stato, Rubrica 251, Anno 1866, Fasc. 11, ff. 109–110.

visible society, independent and sovereign," which possessed the right to regulate its own affairs.[44] The Church stood to benefit more from Juarez's separation than from Maximilian's concordat. Interestingly, by 1865, Munguía's thoughts coincided perfectly with those of the Holy See. On the one hand, traditional concordat policy had not given the expected results in many countries: patronage powers rarely functioned as a deterrent to secularization and "impiety." On the other, the pope started to believe that, in a world of sovereign national states, it was better for the local churches to privilege unity with Rome and assert their spiritual autonomy. The First Vatican Council (1869–1870), indeed, not only affirmed the pope's infallibility and primacy but set the stage for a secular tendency of reduced state intervention in church affairs.[45]

V. Conclusion

The first concordat cycle in Spanish America ended in the 1870s, coinciding with the last years of Pius IX's pontificate. The First Vatican Council, the extinction of the Papal States, and the strong wave of anticlericalism unleashed by Germany's *Kulturkampf* convinced the pope that the times were not ripe for encouraging Church-state cooperation. As the Vatican Secretary of State, Cardinal Giacomo Antonelli, admitted to the British representative before the Holy See in 1869, Pius IX believed that "there was not one so-called Catholic Government that possessed moral courage enough to stem the revolutionary torrent of infidelity and immorality that threatened society."[46] In the countries where concordat policy had seemingly been successful, such as Guatemala or Ecuador, the fall of conservative regimes led to the suspension or the open breach of the existing agreements. In some others, liberal governments asked the Holy See to modify the concordat to incorporate reforms that were unacceptable to the pope. In 1873, for instance, El Salvador's ambassador requested the reduction of the bishops' powers in public schools, the banning of religious processions, and that the concordat declare Catholicism the "dominant religion in the state" (instead of "state religion"), to assure Protestants that they were equal before the law.[47] After the proposal's rejection, the government disputed the concordat.

The failure of the first concordat system in the 1870s reveals that it depended on political conditions that were far from permanent. As mentioned, the Holy See

[44] AAV, Segreteria di Stato, Rubrica 251, Anno 1866, Fasc. 11, f. 58--60.

[45] See John W. O'Malley, *Vatican I: The Council and the Making of the Ultramontane Church* (Cambridge, MA: Harvard University Press, 2018).

[46] Odo Russell to Earl of Clarendon, June 8, 1869, in *The Roman Question: Extracts from the despatches of Odo Russell from Rome, 1858-1870*, ed. Noel Blakiston (London: Chapman and Hall, 1962), 367.

[47] ASRS, AA.EE.SS., Pio IX, Rapporti delle sessioni, Anno 1873, Sess. 402, Vol. XXIX, Fasc. 1.

agreed to grant Patronage Powers in exchange for state funding for the Church and complete clerical control of public education. This bargain only seemed attractive to the weakest Spanish American republics (the Central American nations, Ecuador, and Venezuela), which in the 1850s and 1860s did not have the power to subdue the Church or replace the clergy's local authority with secular institutions. In the moment that an ongoing economic globalization began to stir the Latin American export economies—and thus to enrich the national budgets necessary for state building—the governments' traditional need of church support also began to diminish. It is not that societies suddenly became secularized, as many modernization theorists assumed: Catholicism remained the "dominant religion" in Spanish America well into the end of the twentieth century. What did take place, though, was a successful process of state consolidation that quickly rendered anachronistic the Holy See's foreign policy. As recognized by Antonelli, traditional agreements with Catholic sovereigns were a relic of the past: Church-state relations would now have to adjust to the constitutional logic of modern nations.

From the perspective of the history of international law, the end of the first concordat cycle also reveals the intrinsic weakness of this legal instrument in the developing world of nation-states. In the absence of supranational authorities with coercive powers, the observance of bilateral accords depended on the goodwill of the contracting parties; when this goodwill ceased to exist, the only way to honor international agreements consisted of enforcing them through such punishments as economic sanctions or a plain military invasion (as it happened to Mexico when President Juárez suspended the payment of external debt in 1861). If the Papal States had historically functioned as little more than a buffer for protecting Rome, their disappearance in 1870 rendered the Holy See a "soft power" merely endowed with spiritual authority: it did not have armies or economic leverage, only religious prestige among Catholics. Faced with the institutional might of liberal states, which became ever more authoritarian as the century ended, the Holy See first decided to strengthen the church's presence in society and then to wait for better political times. The new agreements with Guatemala and Ecuador (1881 and 1890, respectively), the Colombian concordat of 1887, and those that Pius XII signed with Ecuador (1937), Colombia (1942), and the Dominican Republic (1954) were the last attempts to protect the Spanish American churches through this kind of agreements. Once the Second Vatican Council reconciled Catholicism with modernity, the history of concordats entered into a new phase that deserves a separate explanation.

2

Early Internationalists

Bello, Calvo, and Álvarez and Beyond

Louise Fawcett

I. Introduction

This chapter examines the richness and diversity of early Latin American contributions to the development of international law across the nineteenth and first half of the twentieth century.[1] It shows the centrality of these interventions to the processes surrounding Latin America's insertion and terms of acceptance into the international community of states, processes that, with some exceptions, have been hitherto neglected by scholars. It is worth underlining at the outset that these are very early contributions to "international" law from a "developing country" or "Third World" perspective (though neither terms were then used) since Latin American states were among the first to win independence from European imperial powers and then to be recognized as independent states, mainly in the first three decades of the nineteenth century. This was a highly consequential moment. Marcela Ternavasio has highlighted the drama surrounding the process of "la aparición de la inédita doctrina de reconocimiento de los nuevos Estados nacidos de las crisis imperiales en el concierto internacional."[2] Their experience was, therefore, unique in both time and place. The next major waves of decolonization occurred in the mid-twentieth century, after two world wars and under different conditions. In that sense, Latin Americans, using

[1] The term "Latin America" appeared in the second half of the nineteenth century to refer to the newly independent Spanish-speaking republics. For one of its earliest uses, see José María Samper, "Reflexiones sobre la federación colombiana" November 22, 1855 (Samper refers to "la federación colombiana," as a union of Spanish American republics), https://repository.eafit.edu.co/bitstream/handle/10784/930/0084_1855.pdf?sequence=2&isAllowed=y (last visited June 26, 2024). See also Sebastián Mantilla Blanco, "José María Torres Caicedo and the Politics of International Law in the Nineteenth Century Latin America," *American Journal of Legal History* 61, no. 2 (2021): 180, 183; Carlos Marichal, "The Birth of International Studies of Latin America," *Foro Internacional* 55, no. 3 (2015). On Brazil's early exclusion, see Leslie Bethell, "Brazil and 'Latin América,'" *Journal of Latin American Studies*, 42, no. 3 (2010): 457–485.

[2] Marcela Ternavasio, *Los juegos de la política. Las independencias hispanoamericanas frente a la contrarrevolución* (Buenos Aires: Siglo Veintiuno Editores, 2021); Daniel Gutiérrez Ardila, *El reconocimiento de Colombia. Diplomacia y propaganda en la coyuntura de las restauraciones 1819-1831* (Bogota, Colombia: Universidad Externado, 2012).

Louise Fawcett, *Early Internationalists* In: *Latin American International Law in the Twenty-First Century*. Edited by: Alejandro Chehtman, Alexandra Huneeus, and Sergio Puig, Oxford University Press.
 DOI: 10.1093/9780197754016.003.0002

international law and institutions as a vehicle, played a pathbreaking and still underrecognized role in the expansion of international society.[3] This process, its significance, and legacies for the Americas and beyond, is the focus of this chapter.

The chapter centers principally on the work and influence of three prominent early publicists whose lives collectively spanned nearly two hundred critical years for the Americas: the Venezuelan-Chilean Andrés Bello, 1781–1865; Uruguayan-Argentinian Carlos Calvo, 1824–1906; and Chilean Alejandro Álvarez 1868–1960. Their extensive works are considered "classics" in the history of international law in Latin America,[4] but they also played interdependent and highly formative roles in shaping the politics, foreign policy, and international relations environment in the Americas and beyond, contributing to a regional culture of "legalismo."[5] This regional *legalismo*, in turn, informed broader developments in international law. Though each spent several years in Europe and was heavily influenced by European legal traditions and thought, all three were Latin American "internationalists" who dedicated their long careers to the cause of the newly independent Americas, the promotion of their place in the international system, and, by extension, the leveling and recrafting of the parameters of that system. Their collective, sometimes overlapping, sometimes diverging influences extended across the early American congresses[6] to the development of early Pan-American and later inter-American and an array of regional institutions from World War II to the present. They were also evident at multiple international fora, including the Hague Conferences, particularly the second in 1907, where Latin American states had a significant presence,[7] and in the debates surrounding the crafting of the League of Nations Covenant, the United Nations Charter, the International Court of Justice, and Bretton Woods institutions—all of which bear the hallmarks of Latin America's influence and legacies in matters related to the exercise of sovereignty, the equality of states, the principle of nonintervention and individual rights. Latin Americans were tenacious in pursuing these aims, but their efforts were not always welcomed by

[3] For the "orthodox," now outdated, account, see Hedley Bull and Adam Watson, *The Expansion of International Society* (Oxford: Oxford University Press, 1984); for a sensitive critique, see Carsten Schulz, "Civilisation, Barbarism and the Making of Latin America's Place in 19th Century International Society," *Millenium* 42, no. 3 (2014): 837–885.

[4] Hugo Caminos, "The Latin American Contribution to International Law," *American Society of International Law Proceedings* 80 (1986): 157.

[5] Nicole Jenne, "The Origin of Regional Ideas: International Law, External Legitimization and Latin America's 'legalismo," *Journal of the History of International Law* 24 (June 2022): 500–532.

[6] See Andrés Bello's 1844 essay, "Congreso Americano, *El Araucano*," in *Obras Completas* (hereafter OC) 2nd edition, 26 vols, (Caracas: Fundacion la casa de Bello 1981) Vol. X: 639-656; also Juan Bautista Alberdi, "Sobre la conveniencia de un congreso general americano; in *Alberdi: Obras Completas* (Buenos Aires: La Tribuna Nacional 1886) Vol II: 389–4012.

[7] Carsten Schulz, "Accidental Activists: Latin American Status-Seeking at The Hague," *International Studies Quarterly* 61, no. 3: 612–622.

established powers that sought to preserve an international hierarchy based on a particular understanding of "civilization." Indeed, their efforts were frequently resisted.[8] Before and between the two world wars, there was regular pushback on their demands to secure diplomatic recognition, equality of treatment, and freedom from intervention, as demanded in the Calvo Doctrine, discussed in the section below, but their insistence ultimately bore fruit in the new, more inclusive set of multilateral norms and practices that emerged after 1945.

If these institutional legacies reflect the influences of all three men, they were far from being the only significant legal scholars or publicists of this period, as other chapters in this volume reveal. They collaborated, debated, and conflicted with, or drew upon and refined, the work and ideas of others, both within and beyond the Americas. Other prominent jurists, many also from the so-called ABC (Argentina, Brazil, Chile) group of countries, include Juan Bautista Alberdi (1810–1884), José María Torres Caicedo (1830–1899), Luis María Drago (1859–1921), and Carlos Saavedra Lamos (1878–1959) from Argentina and Rui Barbosa (1849–1923) and Manoel Alvaro de Souza Sá Vianna (1860–1924) from Brazil. Mexican jurists and politicians, like Isidro Fabela (1882–1964) and Genaro Estrada (1887–1937), associated with the Carranza and Estrada doctrines, respectively, were active in the post-revolutionary period in defending Mexico's independence and new institutions against external encroachments.

The chapter addresses other neglected histories in Latin American international law (LAIL), notably the roles of Latin American women. Unsurprisingly, given the context of the time, the above list is male only and reflects the limited visibility of Latin American women, or any women, in international relations during this period.[9] Yet, Latin American women are important in the story of LAIL. By the early twentieth century, they had begun to have a significant impact on different arenas of regional and international politics. Many lacked the formal training and public profile of scholars like Bello, Calvo, and Álvarez, but Latin American women were highly active in and around the early Pan-American conferences (and what became the Inter-American Commission on Women) and the League of Nations and later the United Nations (UN), notably in the area of women's rights and emancipation.[10] Three contrasting examples from the period include the Uruguayan doctor Paulina Luisi (1875–1950), known as the "mother" of Latin American feminism; Minerva Bernardino (1907–1988),

[8] See Andrew Linklater, *The Idea of Civilisation and the Making of the Global Order* (Bristol, UK: Bristol University Press, 2021), esp. ch. 6.

[9] On the absence of women in international relations, see Patricia Owens at al., *Women's International Thought. Towards a New Canon* (Cambridge: Cambridge University Press, 2022).

[10] Katherine Marino, *Feminism for the Americas: The Making of an International Human Rights Movement* (Chapel Hill: University of North Carolina Press, 2019); Immi Tallgren, ed., *Portraits of Women in International Law: New Names and Forgotten Faces* (Oxford: Oxford University Press, 2023).

a lawyer from the Dominican Republic; and the Brazilian-born politician and diplomat Berta Lutz (1894–1976), the latter two being among the four women signatories to the UN Charter—the first international agreement to recognize equal rights for women.[11] Bringing women into the conversation offers a fresh dimension to a rather conservative interpretation of early LAIL—one which connects to later feminist studies and the advance of an international human rights regime in which Latin American men and women played a significant role.[12] There are further silences, and the chapter does not directly address the question of other excluded groups in the history of LAIL, notably the Indigenous peoples of the Americas who were swept up into the processes of "whitening" and "civilizing" in an attempt to bring the region into the mainstream of late nineteenth- and early twentieth-century international society.[13]

It is impossible to do justice to the combined *oeuvre* of the three individuals in question, let alone the collective contributions of Latin American scholars, activists, and publicists to international law in this period. Therefore, the aim is to offer a synthesis of Bello, Calvo, and Álvarez's regional and international contributions, to complement and integrate existing literature from international history, international law, and international relations. In this regard, the chapter embraces the so-called historical turn in international law and international relations as well as their "global" turns by paying attention to the different sites of international thought and action.[14] It also shares Jeremy Adelman's concern with uncovering the 'special relationship between Latin America and world history'.[15] Indeed, in making the work of these scholars more visible, this chapter challenges the prevalent assumption that global norms and practices derive only from the "Global North"[16] or that "Southern" actors, when acknowledged, are regarded as "subordinate" or "peripheral" players in international relations, implying secondary status as norm takers rather than norm makers. In unseating this narrative, it engages selectively with references to the relevant works and

[11] Rebecca Adami and Dan Plesch, *Women and the UN. A New History of Women's Rights*, (London: Routledge 2022).

[12] Margaret Keck and Kathryn Sikkink, *Activists beyond Borders* (Ithaca, NY: Cornell University Press, 1998).

[13] See Liliana Obregón, "Between Civilisation and Barbarism: Creole interventions in International Law," *Third World Quarterly*, 27, no. 5 (2006): 823; Arnulf Becker Lorca, *Mestizo International Law. A Global Intellectual History* (Cambridge: Cambridge University Press, 2015).

[14] For example, Marti Koskenniemi, *The Gentle Civiliser of Nations. The Rise and Fall of International Law* 1870-1960 (Cambridge: Cambridge University Press, 2002); George Lawson, "The Eternal Divide? History and International Relations," *European Journal of International Relations*, 18, no. 2 (2012): 203–226; Duncan Bell, *Empire, Race and Global Justice* (Cambridge: Cambridge University Press 2019).

[15] Jeremy Adelman, "Latin American and World Histories: Old and New Approaches to the Pluribus and the Unum," *Hispanic American Historical Review* 84, no. 3 (2004): 400.

[16] Eric Helleiner, "Principles from the Periphery: The Neglected Southern Sources of Global Norms," *Global Governance* 20, no. 3 (2014): 359–418.

activities of these three scholars and secondary sources from the interface of international law and international relations to provide an updated inventory of their most important contributions.[17]

The chapter proceeds as follows. First, it offers an overview of the principal international contributions of these three scholars and their immediate contemporaries: what distinguished, united, and divided them, for example, with regard to their international positioning on the relative merits of a broader "pan" or hemispheric vision versus a "Spanish/Latin American" or more *regionally* focused approach, which emerged early post-independence and then reemerged at different times and in different ways. The second section asks why the individual and collective contributions of these scholars remain relatively neglected, a question that cannot be answered simply by pointing to the predominance of Western-centered approaches and the relatively static literatures in international relations and international law, which continues to limit understanding by prioritizing selective Western sites of knowledge production. Answering the question also demands a discussion of the backgrounds, ideologies, and *representativeness* of these individuals—whether or not as largely "creole" (and male) ABC elites, they could legitimately represent the many voices, in José Martí's words, of *Nuestra América*.[18] The third and final section offers a longer, and more dynamic view of the legacies of Latin American legal scholarship for contemporary international institutions and order in the Americas and beyond. It exposes the contentious and often fractured nature of liberal internationalist narratives as reflected in ongoing debates about desired regional orders.

II. Bello, Calvo, and Álvarez and beyond: Context and Contribution

That the lives and work of Bello, Calvo, and Álvarez and their contemporaries had a profound impact on the sphere of Latin American politics and international

[17] Frank G. Dawson, "Lesser Developed Nations and International Law: The Latin American Experience," *Case Western Reserve Journal of International Law*, 13, no. 1 (1981): 37–81; see also Caminos, "The Latin American Contribution to International Law" More recent scholarship includes, Arnulf Becker Lorca, "International Law in Latin America or Latin American International Law? Rise, Fall, and Retrieval of a Tradition of Legal Thinking and Political Imagination," *Harvard International Law* Journal 47, no. 1 (2006); Jorge Esquirol, "Latin America," in *Oxford Handbook of the History of International Law*, ed. B. Fassbender and Ann Peters, (Oxford: Oxford University Press, 2012) 553–557; Liliana Obregón, "Colluding Worlds of the Lawyer, the Scholar and the Policy Maker: A View of International Law from Latin America," *Wisconsin Journal of International Law* 23, no. 1: (2005). For a feminist perspective, see Andrei Mamolea, "The Role of International Law in Paulina Luisi's Activism," in Tallgren, *Portraits of Women*, 444–454.

[18] José Martí, *Our America, Writings on Latin America and the Struggle for Cuban Independence*, ed. Eric Foner (New York: Praeger, 1977).

relations is evident. Though their objectives were similar—to promote and defend the existence and interests of the new American republics—their impact differed, reflecting time, place and conviction. These differences in approach were consequential for the development of international law and institutions. For Bello, Calvo, and fellow publicists like Drago and Fabela, the Spanish or *Latin* American domain was their primary concern in advancing the region's independent credentials and status in international law. For Álvarez, Barbosa, and the Pan-Americanists, the US-led *American* domain was seen as the most effective, indeed the only, vehicle to promote the interests of Latin America in the world. For Álvarez, the United States was a "natural" leader in this process and in shaping a distinctive "American" contribution to international law.[19] Unsurprisingly, as shown at the end of this section, some of these same issues—hemispheric versus Latin American perspectives—were reflected among the women's movements for gender equality, with some women, like Paulina Luisi, departing from the Pan-American script.[20] These dividing lines were not always rigid or clear-cut, but they were important in distinguishing their respective domains of action and influence and setting out future pathways.

While, as the introduction points out, it was this larger domain that has received the most attention, with the inter-American system dominating over Latin American regional arrangements, the relationship was often tense and competitive, with overlapping and contradictory processes and trends, which continue to be relevant to this day, as witnessed by the twenty-first-century emergence of "post-hegemonic" Latin American regionalisms as a direct response to US-dominated projects.[21] Such "pro-sovereignty" regionalisms invoke earlier debates, dating back to the independence period and recurring between the two wars or during the Cold War period when fears of Western hegemony spurred alternative projects for regional order, both economic and political.[22] As the shadow of the United States looms a little less large in the world, and alternative models and partners present themselves from among the "rising" powers, many inside the Global South (the expansion of the BRICS, an intergovernmental organization originally comprising Brazil, Russia, India, China and South Africa, to include Iran, Egypt, Ethiopia, and the United Arab Emirates, is one example), these alternative visions acquire more importance, and their histories retain all

[19] Juan Pablo Scarfi, "The Latin American Politics of International Law," *Cambridge Review of International Affairs* 35, no. 5 (2022): 671

[20] See Marino, *Feminism for the Americas*, 172–172, 227–228.

[21] Louise Fawcett, "The Evolution of Competitive Latin American Regionalism," in *Regionalism and Multilateralism*, ed. Thomas Meyer, José Luís de Sales Marques, and Mario Telò (New York: Springer, 2020): 108–126; Pia Riggirozzi and Diana Tussie, *The Rise of Post-Hegemonic Regionalism in the Americas* (New York: Springer, 2012).

[22] Louise Fawcett, "The Origins and Development of Regional Ideas in the Americas," in *Regionalism in the Americas*, ed. Louise Fawcett and Monica Serrano (London: Palgrave, 2005): 25–51.

their relevance. The Latin American story thus demands attention as part of the larger story of global international relations.

Andrés Bello, unlike his better-known successors, Calvo (and Drago) or Álvarez, was not associated with an "original" interpretation of international law. However, Bello is credited with the early origins of the Law of the Sea and delimitation of maritime spaces.[23] Even if there was no headline "Bello Doctrine," his significance deserves fresh attention since a close reading of Bello shows how he was, in many ways, the forefather of later traditions. His extensive coverage of multiple topics, adjusted to meet the evolving conditions of the time, anticipated Calvo, Drago, and Fabela in particular.[24] If Calvo is referred to as "el internacionalista más destacado," his debt to Bello is clear, as acknowledged in his treatise on international law when he wrote that "les auteurs les plus distingués sont unanimes à parler de l'œuvre de Bello avec éloge."[25]

Bello carved out an early and distinctive space for thinking about the role and rights of the independent Americas in the international system. The principal object of Bello's *Principios de Derecho Internacional* first published in 1832, was, as Iván Jaksić writes, "el fundar la legitimidad internacional de las naciones que surgían del proceso de independencia."[26] This widely consulted text provided the first systematic and complete treatment of the subject published in the Americas or in Spanish.[27] Not an "original" contribution in one sense, his work was one of "synthesis" and drew on multiple scholars—Suarez, Grotius, Hobbes, Pufendorf, Wolff, Vattel, Bynkershoek, Martens, Wheaton, Phillimore, and Kent[28]—it was novel in its application to the Americas and in its ambition to educate future generations of legal scholars and policymakers. It is fitting, therefore, to call his contribution "foundational."[29] Bello's treatise in international law was nested in a much larger body of work, which ranged from the use of the Spanish language in the Americas[30] to the question of how to maintain order in the new republics, a task to which his civil code was directed;[31] he was,

[23] Bello, *Obras Completas* (OC) (Caracas, Venezuela: Casa de Bello, 1981), X: 68. My thanks to Iván Jaksić for this point. See also Jeannette Irigoin Barrenne, "The Contribution of Andrés Bello to the Law of the Sea in the Chilean Civil Code," in *Law of the Sea from Grotius to the International Tribunal for the Law of the Sea*(Leiden, The Netherlands: Brill, 2015), 7–17.

[24] Obregón, "Colluding Worlds," 147–148.

[25] See Cepulveda, "Tres ensayos mexicanos"; Carlos Calvo, *Le Droit International. Théorique et Pratique* (5th ed., Paris, 1896), I: 109–110.

[26] Iván Jaksić, *Andrés Bello: La pasión por el orden* (Caracas: bid&co, 2007): 197.

[27] See Eduardo Plaza, "Prlogo: Introducción al Derecho Internacional de Andrés Bello," in Bello, *Obras Completas* (OC) (1st ed., Caracas, 1954), X: clxv; Fernando Murillo, *Andrés Bello. Historia de una vida y una obra* (Caracas: Casa de Bello, 1986), 385.

[28] Bello, OC X: xxvii

[29] Obregón, "Colluding Worlds," 147–148.

[30] Andrés Bello, *Gramática de la lengua castellana destinada al uso de los americanos*, in OC IV: 31.

[31] See Jaksić, *Andrés Bello*, 23.

therefore, a "complete scholar."[32] Order, broadly conceived, at home and abroad, was Bello's central concern—without it, the very survival of the new republics was at risk. Hence, the value he and other jurists, notably Alberdi, who wrote a treatise on the "crime" of war, placed on conflict avoidance and resolution made regional peace a highly valued prize and contributed to Latin America's reputation as a peaceful zone.[33]

Both Calvo and Drago were the architects of related legal doctrines that achieved notoriety in late nineteenth- and early twentieth-century debates on the region's burgeoning relations and interactions with external powers—relations that were central to economic and political development yet raised continuing questions about unequal treatment and the threat of renewed European interventions in the case of debt default, for example. In the context of the time, these doctrines proved foundational since they sought to shift the existing parameters of international law onto an equal footing by clearly establishing and narrowing the legitimate conditions for intervention.[34] They were closely related to Bello's position on the equality of states and the rights of foreign nationals: "Even the weakest republic enjoys the same rights and is subject to the same obligations as the most powerful empire," or (quoting de Martens) "the foreign creditor can only be asked to be placed on the same level as the state's other creditors."[35] However, they now addressed specific questions regarding diplomatic immunity and the threat of intervention in the case of nonpayment of debts. The Calvo Doctrine, articulated in 1868 following the French intervention in Mexico, sought to establish that in settling disputes between foreign nations and local governments, complaints and grievances should be subject to domestic courts. In other words, an alien should "resort to local remedies, thereby waiving diplomatic protection from his own government."[36] The Drago Doctrine, set out in a note of 1902 following joint European action against Venezuela, sought to outlaw the use of force for debt collection or losses suffered by overseas companies and individuals.[37] In both doctrines, the prior question of nonintervention was closely entangled with that of individual rights.

The regular articulation of these core principles by Latin American representatives at international fora, notably the Second Hague Conference and the different Pan-American conferences, hastened their eventual adoption in

[32] Rafael Caldera, *Andrés Bello* (London: Routledge 1977), 48.

[33] Bello, OC X: 195; Juan Bautista Alberdi, *El crimen de la guerra* (Buenos Aires: Cultura Argentina, 1915); Arie Kacowicz, *Zones of Peace in the Third World* (Albany: State University of New York Press, 1998).

[34] Calvo, *Droit International*, I: 351–352.

[35] Bello, OC X: 31, 48; also Bello, *Selected Writings*, 241, 253.

[36] Dawson, "Lesser Developed Nations and International Law," 49; Francesco Tamburini, "Historia y destino de la doctrina Calvo," *Revista de estudios histórico-jurídicos*, 24 (2002): 81–101.

[37] Luis M. Drago, "State Loans in their Relation to International Policy," *American Journal of International Law* 1, no. 3 (1907): 692–726.

international law. Latin American states themselves regularly adopted a "Calvo Clause" in their contractual arrangements,[38] but the doctrine itself (as first articulated) only secured US approval at the Pan-American Conference in Montevideo in 1933, coming to final fruition in the Charter of the Organization of American States (OAS) in 1948.[39] The Drago Doctrine, for its part, though embraced by Latin American countries, and partially recognized by the United States in the Porter Convention (1907), did not end an era of interventions. Extending the earlier Monroe Doctrine (1823), the Platt Amendment (1901), which set the conditions for Cuba's independence following the Spanish-American War, and the Roosevelt Corollary (1904), continued to reserve that right for the United States, at least in Central America and the Caribbean.

The pioneering efforts of Calvo and Drago, which sought to upend the discriminatory, hierarchical practices of the European-centered legal and diplomatic order, with its characteristic "gun-boat diplomacy," were appropriated by others. Post-revolutionary Mexico provided the context for two related doctrines. The Carranza Doctrine (1918), named after President Venustiano Carranza (1917–1920), of which Isidro Fabela was an architect, sought to tighten the conditions of nonintervention and sovereign equality in defense of Mexico's new institutions. The Estrada Doctrine (1930), named after Mexico's Foreign Secretary Genaro Estrada, called for de facto recognition of changes in government, rejecting the principle that allowed foreign governments to pass judgments on the legitimacy of a given regime. These doctrines also harked back to Bello's work regarding the recognition of new states: "Every nation which governs itself in any form whatsoever and has the ability to communicate directly with other nations, is in their eyes, a sovereign and independent state"; and "no state may dictate the type of government, religion, or administration of another."[40]

An important dimension of these debates was the growing power and influence of the United States and the parallel rise of the Pan-American movement, which, by the turn of the century, dominated hemispheric relations.[41] Inspired by the efforts of US Secretary of State James Blaine during his second term (1889–1892), pan-Americanism encompassed a growing range of activities, including a regular series of conferences, and involved multiple transnational

[38] M. Garcia-Mora, "The Calvo Clause in Latin American Constitutions and in International Law," *Marquette Law Review* 33, no. 4 (1950): 205.

[39] Tamburini, "Historia y destino de la doctrina Calvo"; César Cepúlveda, "La presencia viviente de Carlos Calvo," in César Cepúlveda et al., *Carlos Calvo: Tres ensayos mexicanos* (Mexico City: Secretaría de relaciones exteriores, 1974).

[40] Bello, OC X: 35, 39.

[41] David Sheinin (ed.), *Beyond the Ideal. Pan-Americanism in Inter-American Affairs* (New York: Praeger, 2001), 19–32.

networks from both North and South America.[42] Relevant to this discussion is the American Institute for International Law (AIIL), in whose foundation, in 1912, Álejandro Álvarez, and the US lawyer James Brown Scott, played a pioneering role. The AIIL and its work were important not just for designing and codifying a body of new laws applicable to the Americas but also because Latin American jurists played such a central, if undervalued, role.[43]

Álvarez reflected his contemporaries' beliefs about the role of international law and its codification to safeguard the interests of the new American republics in the international system.[44] Few would have disagreed with his claim that the entry of Latin American states had "widened the field of international law and modified its character."[45] Álvarez, however, further argued that the shared principles of "independence, liberty and equality" among *all* American states formed the basis for a distinctive "American" international law.[46] On this point, other publicists disagreed, including Calvo, with only the Argentinian Amancio Alcorta, in the words of Álvarez, "grasping the idea."[47] Another Argentinian, Alberdi, had earlier spoken of an "American" international law and an "American congress," but in reference only to what became Latin America. Andrés Bello, in contrast, had scarcely referred to an international law of the Americas as distinct from a generalized international law.[48] Two years after the publication of Álvarez's *Le droit international américain*, the Brazilian jurist Sá Vianna offered a firm rebuttal, declaring its "nonexistence."[49] These debates regarding an exclusive "regional" perspective on international law have lost some of their relevance today. However, they serve to underline the intense activity and the competing approaches among Latin American lawyers in their attempts to reframe international law to serve the interests of newly independent states.[50] While the set of "new" states was an admittedly limited one, and there were different status grades,[51] even in Latin America, where certain states (like Argentina, Brazil, and Chile) believed themselves superior, this nonetheless represented a significant

[42] See Mark J. Petersen, *The Southern Cone and the Origins of Pan America, 1888-1933* (Notre Dame: IN: University of Notre Dame Press), 3–8.

[43] See Juan Pablo Scarfi, *Hidden History of International Law in the Americas. Empire and Legal Networks* (Oxford: Oxford University Press, 2017).

[44] Obregón, "Colluding Worlds," 158.

[45] Alejandro Álvarez, "Latin America and International Law," *American Journal of International Law* 3, no. 2 (1909): 269.

[46] Ibid., 343; also *Le droit international américain* (Paris: Pedone, 1910).

[47] Álvarez, "Latin America and International Law," 352.

[48] Fernando Murillo, *Andrés Bello y el derecho Latinoamericano* (Caracas: Casa de Bello, 1987), 50–51.

[49] Manoel Alvaro de Souza Sá Vianna, "De la non existence de un droit international américain" (Rio de Janeiro: L Figueredo1912).

[50] See Becker Lorca, "International Law in Latin America."

[51] Edward Keene, "The Standard of Civilisation and the Expansion thesis," *Millenium* 43, no. 2 (2014).

opening up and leveling of international society, heralding the larger expansion which took place following decolonization after 1945.

Another distinguishing feature of Álvarez and his pan-Americanism was his belief in US hemispheric leadership, a position that led him to defend the Monroe Doctrine: first, and less controversially, because it provided the necessary safeguards against any return of European imperialism, and second, and more problematic, because it should be understood not as a unilateral but as an American doctrine, and "a part of what may be called American International Law."[52] He insisted that the doctrine was not a policy of imperialism or US hegemony and that it had the support of "all" American states.[53] In this respect, he shared the view of US President Woodrow Wilson of "pan-Americanism as a hemispheric model for a global order."[54] He defended the recent interventions of the United States in both the external and internal affairs of "certain Latin American States" including Venezuela, Cuba, and Panama, in the interest of preserving regional peace and order.[55] Here, like Wilson, Álvarez and his southern cone contemporaries drew a distinction between orderly and disorderly republics or between, in the hierarchical and often racist language of the period, "civilized" and "uncivilized" states. Central American and Caribbean states still belonged to the latter category, making them appropriate subjects for intervention, just as for Wilson, "self-determination" was an ideal principally for White Europeans.[56]

Indeed, many Latin American jurists and diplomats saw the Monroe Doctrine as a bulwark against European imperialism and pan-Americanism as a vehicle for containing the United States. Drago's 1902 note appealed to the Monroe Doctrine against European interference, but Drago and others worried about its extended use in an age of growing US power.[57] Alberdi critiqued the Monroe Doctrine as "colonialism," justifying "intervention against intervention."[58] Such concerns were captured in the writings of the day by, for example, Jose Martí and the poet Ruben Darío, who alternately warned of the malign effects of spreading US influence and the dangers of viewing the US as an "exemplary civilization."[59] Ada Ferrer powerfully describes how, in Cuba, the effects of the Monroe

[52] "Alejandro Álvarez, The Monroe Doctrine from the Latin American Point of View," *St. Louis Law Review* 2, no. 3 (1917): 137.

[53] Ibid., 144; also Álvarez, *Le droit international américain*, 173–179.

[54] Klaas Dykmann, "Pan-Americanism as a Hemispheric Model for a Global Order?," *Journal of the History of International Law* 24 (2022): 259–292.

[55] Álvarez, *Le droit international américain*, 165–72.

[56] See Lloyd E. Ambrosius, "Wilson, Alliances, and the League of Nations," in *Woodrow Wilson and American Internationalism* (Cambridge: Cambridge University Press, 2017), 133–157.

[57] Petersen, *Origins of Pan America*, 67–71.

[58] William Wheatley Pearson, "Alberdi's Views on the Monroe Doctrine," *HAHR* 3, no. 3 (1920): 370.

[59] Marti, *Our America*; José Enrique Rodó, *Ariel* (Austin: University of Texas Press, 1988).

Doctrine's exclusion of Europe protected and enabled the slavery and sugar plantation system in which the United States was heavily invested.[60]

Meanwhile, the League of Nations, in which the numerically significant Latin American states had invested great hopes, proved a disappointing institution.[61] This was not only because of US nonmembership and the persistence of a European power condominium—one designed to keep Latin Americans out of major decision-making.[62] It was also because of its ultimately feeble or tardy responses to interventions, occupations (the Circum-Caribbean), and wars, (the Chaco War 1932–1935), or the defense of 'small' states like Manchuria and Ethiopia, swallowed up by Japan and Italy, respectively.[63] Indeed, Álvarez suggested that the Monroe Doctrine better defended Latin American states than the vague wording of the League's Article 10, which undertook "to respect and preserve . . . the territorial integrity and existing political independence of all Members." In short, neither "American" nor "international" law provided an adequate defense to weak or new states, but Latin America increasingly made its presence felt.

Even as pan-Americanism gathered its share of critics and generated alternative prescriptions for regional order, including Latin American projects and the revivalist movement known as "Hispanismo," its influence prevailed. Álvarez remained committed to the Pan-American project and belief in the "spirit of American fraternity."[64] By the 1930s, following the Montevideo Conference, its contours had softened significantly as US President Roosevelt embraced the "Good Neighbour" policy, introducing a redesign of what later became the inter-American system." Further, notwithstanding its hegemonic properties, pan-Americanism offered numerous benefits to Latin American states including access to resources and markets and a forum where men (and women) had a voice and could exercise significant roles. Still, the undercurrents of Latin American reform and resistance would endure and resurface through the following seventy-five years in different projects to promote alternative regionalisms in the Americas and to reform inter-American institutions.

If Álvarez's interpretation of specific Latin American situations giving rise to an *American* law afforded him a central place in the history and development of American institutions, he is also recognized for his contribution to promoting

[60] Ada Ferrer, *Cuba. An American History* (New York: Scribner, 2021).

[61] Alan. McPherson and Yannick. Wehrli, 'Introduction' in Alan McPherson and Yannick Wehrli, eds., *Beyond Geopolitics. New Histories of Latin America at the League of Nations* (Albuquerque: University of New Mexico 2013): 1–6.

[62] See Carsten Schulz, ISA Working Paper 2023.

[63] See, Ronald Stuart Kain, "The Chaco Dispute and the Peace System," *Political Science Quarterly* 50, no. 3 (September 1935): 321–342, https://www.latinamericanstudies.org/paraguay/chaco-peace.pdf (last visited June 26, 2024).

[64] Scarfi, *Hidden History*, 171; Álvarez, "Latin America and International Law," 294.

and drafting an early international human rights regime and service at the International Court of Justice (ICJ) from 1946 to 1955.[65] At the ICJ, Álvarez was noted for his defense of the rights of small states, drawing on a longer tradition of Latin American involvement at the Permanent International Court of Justice (the ICJ's predecessor under the League of Nations) where a Brazilian jurist, Raul Fernandes, had successfully made the case for an "optional clause" to the Court's compulsory jurisdiction (to which forty-five Latin American states subscribed), to circumvent opposition by the great powers.[66] In regard to human rights, for Álvarez, like earlier publicists, the doctrine of nonintervention required careful harmonization with principles concerning individual rights, "regardless of nationality, gender, race, language or religion,"[67] particularly where equal treatment of foreigners and nationals were concerned. Though nonintervention and domestic sovereignty took precedence in the early years of state- and nation-building, Latin American jurists not only supported the human rights language of the UN Charter but were also party to drafting, in 1948, the American Declaration of Human Rights even before the UN adopted the Universal Declaration of Human Rights.[68]

Latin American women were also important in these processes in still under-acknowledged ways. Álvarez's work provides an entrée to the roles of Latin American women in advancing gender equality and *universal* human rights in international law. Though Álvarez, like earlier Latin American publicists, incorporated gender into his general claim for individual and state rights,[69] these became the centerpiece of a burgeoning women's movement in the Americas and the wider world, drawing on the rapidly changing social and economic conditions of the time.[70] If Álvarez spoke of an international law to reflect the "new tendencies of international life,"[71] for Latin American feminists, these

[65] Katharina Zobel, "Judge Alejandro Álvarez at the International Court of Justice (1946-1955)," *Leiden Journal of International Law* 19 (2006): 1017–1040; Keck and Sikkink, *Activists beyond Borders*, 81, 84–85.

[66] On Álvarez at the ICJ, see Liliana Obregón, "Noted for Dissent. The International Life of Alejandro Álvarez," *Leiden Journal of International Law* 19, no. 4 (2006): 989; on Fernandes, see Antonio Cançado Trinidade, *The Construction of a Humanised International Law* (Leiden, The Netherlands: Brill, 2015). Cançade also notes the precedent of the Central American Court (founded 1907) which operated continuously from 1908 to 1918 as heralding the "advance of the rule of law at the international level". See Antonio Augusto Cançado Trindade, "Towards Compulsory Jurisdiction," 238, accessed, June 26, 2024, https://www.oas.org/es/sla/ddi/docs/publicaciones_digital_XXXVII_curso_derecho_internacional_2010_Antonio_Augusto_Cancado_Trindade.pdf.

[67] Zobel, "Judge Alejandro Álvarez," 1022

[68] Keck and Sikkink, *Activists*, 85

[69] See also Bello's earlier defense of domestic laws taking precedence in marriages between nationals and foreigners. Andrés Bello, *Obras Completas* (OC), ed. Iván Jaksić, 16 (Santiago: Ediciones Biblioteca Nacional de Chile, 2022).

[70] Asuncion Lavrin, *Women, Feminism and Social Change in Argentina, Chile and Uruguay 1890-1940* (Lincoln: University of Nebraska Press, 1995).

[71] Álvarez, "The New International Law," *Transactions* (1929): 46.

"tendencies" squarely included the recognition of equal rights for women, making them major protagonists in the campaign for an equal rights treaty. Hence the critical link between equality for states and equality for women was established.

Lacking the public profile or production of individuals like Bello, Calvo, and Álvarez, Latin American women were nonetheless highly active in the late nineteenth and early twentieth centuries, in demanding both representation and equal rights for women within their own countries and in promoting the regional and international networks and institutions that called for their formal recognition. Apart from Luisi, Bernardino, and Lutz, other prominent activists committed to the principle of "women's sovereignty"[72] included two lawyers: Panamanian Clara González (1898–1990) and Ofelia Domínguez Navarro (1894–1976) from Cuba. Their early efforts focused on the Pan-American conferences (and what became the Inter-American Commission on Women (IACW/CIM), founded in 1928[73]), the League of Nations, and the UN Conference on International Organization (UNICO), prior to the signing of the UN Charter. A leading US feminist, Doris Stevens (1888–1963) first chaired the IACW, but the Latin American women were frequently more advanced and progressive than their North American peers, and major advances in this period may be attributed to them, as recent literature records.[74] Having finally secured the participation of female delegates, they pursued their demand for an equal rights treaty at Montevideo. This failed, but a nationality convention was passed, allowing independent nationality rights to married women, though these already existed in some Latin American countries.[75] Frustration at the slow pace of change and subordination to US leadership, however, led to defections from the IACW, notably Paulina Luisi, who came to view pan-Americanism as a cover for US hegemony, even a facilitator for authoritarian regimes.[76] She continued her work defending the rights of women and children in alternative fora, including the League of Nations.[77] It is true that Bernardino, for all her feminist activism, was closely associated with the Trujillo regime in the Dominican Republic.[78] Others, Bertha Lutz in particular, while sharing some of Luisi's concerns, remained within the movement, believing, like Álvarez, that pan-Americanism was the best vehicle to secure the necessary changes and codification of international law

[72] Marino, *Feminism for the Americas*, 9.

[73] See Inter-American Commission of Women, "Brief History of the Commission," available at https://www.oas.org/en/cim/history.asp (last accessed, June 26, 2024).

[74] Elise Dietrichson and Fatima Sator, "The Latin American Women," in Adami and Plesch, *Women and the UN*, 17–38.

[75] Marino, *Feminism for the Americas*, 73–74.

[76] Mamolea, "Paulina Luisi's Activism," 451.

[77] Marino, *Feminism for the Americas*, 76.

[78] Ellen DuBois and Lauren Derby, "The Strange Case of Minerva Bernardino," *Women's Studies International Forum* 32, no. 1 (2009): 43–50.

to progress their respective demands. In this way, just as an earlier generation of male jurists carved out space for Latin American interventions in international law in demanding equality between states, so did a generation of Latin American women, make their own mark placing them at the "vanguard" of the movement for women's rights and securing their inclusion in the United Nations Charter.[79]

In short, the combined efforts of Latin American men *and* women in this formative one hundred-year period shine a new light on their contribution to international law, affording them new agency. Recognising these efforts destabilizes long-held assumptions about the sources and development of international law. As discussed below, this story cannot be merely subsumed into a Eurocentric narrative or the US-dominated Pan-American movement. It is not marginal, but should be considered integral to debates about the expansion of international society. To categorize this story as a "regional" contribution is, in one sense, correct. The "region" of Latin America, as defined since the mid-1850s, given the uniqueness of its situation, had opened up singular possibilities for intervention in shaping global norms. In different ways, other regions would later enjoy similar opportunities in their interactions with international order and institutions, but not at such a formative moment in international law's development. Section III addresses why such relative ignorance has prevailed and seeks to correct the imbalance not only to gain a better grasp of the Latin American dimension of law and history but also to open up a wider window on how regional efforts promoted the development of international society.

III. Correcting Neglect

Though the above contributions, principally from Latin American men, have received some attention over the years, the relative *international* neglect of these scholars and publicists remains surprising, particularly in an era when scholars are calling for more attention to the roles of the Global South in a more "Global international relations" (IR), or to "Third World international law." In these discussions, until recently, references to Latin America have often been minimal, footnoted, or marginalized.[80] This knowledge gap can be explained in different ways: by timing, by the limited access to their work, by European or Western-centered approaches and disciplinary biases.

Timing is important: these were very early interventions in international law when its ownership was limited to the "great" powers. International attention

[79] Ibid.; Marino, *Feminism in the Americas*, 225–236.

[80] For example, Antony Anghie, *Imperialism, Sovereignty and the Making of International Law* (Cambridge: Cambridge University Press, 2005), 209; Amitav Acharya and Barry Buzan eds., *Non-Western IR Theory* (London: Routledge, 2010).

to works by these scholars has been limited by accessibility—only a selection of their original work is available in English. Andrés Bello's voluminous scholarship, including his work on international law,[81] has not been translated, though important extracts have been by leading Bello scholar and biographer Iván Jaksić.[82] The work of Carlos Calvo was published in Spanish and French.[83] Of the three, unsurprisingly, given his association with the United States, and his strong advocacy of pan-Americanism, a much more comprehensive selection of the works of Alejandro Álvarez, including his much-cited piece in the *American Journal of International Law*, have been published in English.[84] So, an appreciation of the work of these scholars and their contemporaries for the non-Spanish reader means reliance on secondary sources. Also unsurprising is that the contributions of Latin American women, indeed all women, have been similarly neglected until very recently.[85]

Related to the problem of visibility and access, another familiar explanation for this neglect is Eurocentrism, or "Western-centrism": the pervasive hegemony of Western thinking and scholarship when it comes to approaches to international relations in general, and to international law in particular, meaning that scant attention has been paid to scholars, publicists, and policymakers beyond a core group of Western states.[86] In Latin America, Eurocentrism is entangled with the European origins of early Latin American elites. Even as scholars began to challenge Eurocentrism, Latin America often fell between the cracks, for seemingly belonging to the West or being insufficiently "non-Western" due to the primarily European background and training of post-independence, "creole" elites, and their failure to provide a more radical response to the facts of Western hegemony. This meant that their essential contributions to the debates—for example, those surrounding establishing a "liberal" international order, were

[81] Bello, *Derecho Internacional*, 2 vols. OC X.

[82] Ívan Jaksić, ed., *Andrés Bello. Selected Writings of Andrés Bello* (Oxford: Oxford University Press 1997); Andrés Bello, *Scholarship and Nation Building in Nineteenth Century Latin America* (Cambridge: Cambridge University Press 2001).

[83] Carlos Calvo, *Derecho Internacional Teórico y práctico en Europa y América Latina* (Paris, 1868); Carlos Calvo, *Le droit international theorique et practique* (5th ed., Paris 1896).

[84] Alejandro Álvarez, "Latin America and International Law"; also Alejandro Álvarez, "The Monroe Doctrine from a Latin America Point of View," *Washington University Law Review* 2, no. 3 (1917): 135–146.

[85] Owens et al., *Women's International Thought*; Marino, *Feminism for the Americas.* One striking omission is Concepción Arenal from Spain, the first woman to write a history of international law: *El derecho de gentes* (Madrid: Imprenta de la revista de legislación 1879).

[86] On the general IR claim, see Amitav Acharya and Barry Buzan, *The Making of Global International Relations* (Cambridge: Cambridge University Press, 2019), with specific reference to Latin America, see Amitav Acharya, Melisa Deciancio, and Diana Tussie, eds., *Latin America in Global International Relations* (London: Routledge: 2021). In respect to international law, see B. S. Chimni, "Third World Approaches to International Law: A Manifesto," *International Community Law Review* 8 (2006): 3–27; on Eurocentrism, see Arnulf Becker Lorca, "Eurocentrism in the History of International Law," in Fassbender and Peters, *Oxford Handbook of the History of International Law*, 1034–1057.

ignored or misperceived.[87] Subsequent alignment with the United States and asymmetry in power relations further compounded the problem, contributing to "the silencing within the historical record" and the possibility of a more nuanced understanding of Latin America's relationship with the West and the wider world.[88]

While these arguments have been well rehearsed and partially rebuffed by scholars, they still need to be challenged to make Latin American "voices" better heard.[89] In addition, the repeated use of terms like "periphery" or "semi-periphery" in referring to "non-Western" countries and borrowing from work on structural theories of imperialism and underdevelopment[90] amplifies the problem by highlighting Latin America as a subordinate "other," worthy of only secondary attention as a norm taker.[91] This notion of periphery extends beyond the domain of international relations and law into the histories of democracy and international political economy. Regarding the former, resistance to imagining the possibility of Latin America contributing to debates on the origins of democracy is striking. Alexis De Tocqueville set the tone in his study, *Democracy in the Americas*, wondering if the South American revolutions and subsequent regional disorder merely reflected a "natural state' of the South American Spaniards."[92] In contrast, recent research on the origins of democracy and the expansion of suffrage has shown how its histories also need to start beyond the West.[93] On the latter, scholars demonstrate how Latin America's contribution has been regularly undervalued or "misperceived,"[94] and call attention to the "victories of Latin American economists to formulate a policy agenda, that gained them influence in the region and the world by situating the discussion of development in the world system of trade."[95] As with international law, there is a meaningful Latin

[87] See Fawcett, "Between West and Non-West"; On Calvo's "liberal" critique of imperialism, see Teresa Davis, "The Ricardian State. Carlos Calvo and Latin America's Ambiguous Origins Story," *Journal of the History of Int Law* 23, no. 1 (2020), 45; on Álvarez, see Arnulf Becker Lorca, "A Álvarez Situated: Subaltern Modernities and Modernisms that Subvert," *Leiden Journal of International Law* 19, no. 4 (2006): 883.

[88] Tom Long, *Latin America Confronts the United States. Asymmetry and Influence* (Cambridge, Cambridge University Press, 2015), 8–9; Robert Holden and Eric Zolov, *Latin America Confronts the United States: A Documentary History* (Oxford: Oxford University Press, 2010), xv.

[89] Arlene Tickner, "Hearing Latin American Voices in International Relations Studies," *International Studies Perspectives* 4 (2003).

[90] Johan Galtung, "A Structural Theory of Imperialism," *Journal of Peace Research* 8, no. 2 (1971): 81–117.

[91] See, for example, the "Periphery Series" of *Leiden Journal of International Law* (2006) "focusing attention on the role played by centre-periphery dynamics in international law."

[92] Alexis de Tocqueville, *Democracy in America* (New York Vintage 1945), 240.

[93] See Eduardo Posada-Carbo, Joanna Innes, and Mark Philp, eds., *Reimagining Democracy in Latin America and the Caribbean* (Oxford: Oxford University Press 2023).

[94] Diana Tussie and Fabrício Chagas Bastos, "Misrecognised, Misfit and Misperceived. Why Not a Latin American School of IPE?" *Review of International Political Economy* 30, no. 3 (2022): 891–913.

[95] Margarita Fajardo, *The World that Latin America Created* (Cambridge, MA: Harvard University Press, 2022), 12.

American-centered conversation on economic development and democracy's roots that demands more attention. And here, again, the roles and influences of women have suffered from double neglect, only reversed with contributions to the literature in more recent decades. The work of "cepalina" Brazilian Maria Conceiçião Tavares, an important figure in ECLA, has received far less attention than that of Enzo Faletto and Fernando Henrique Cardoso.[96] And only very recently has research revealed the critical place of women in debates about the expansion of suffrage in Latin America.[97]

If the politics, backgrounds, and representativeness of Latin American jurists have hitherto denied them a "Third World" label, this is a misrepresentation that needs correcting. First, the Third World is not a monolithic category. It did not exist as a concept in the mid-nineteenth century, nor did states then emerging from colonialism have the opportunity to issue a more radical "manifesto," one that would almost certainly have resulted in further interventions and the loss of sovereignty.[98] Context is everything here: Latin American elites, therefore, were cognizant of the need to work within and conform to the broad expectations of the emerging "liberal international order, but that order was also fluid and permitted room for negotiation and maneuver. Their "republican internationalism" tendencies support this position.[99] More assertive and radical responses came later, entangled in defense of Mexico's Revolution, against the increasingly hegemonic tendencies of pan-Americanism, of which the Platt Amendment was an example, or still later in the contributions of dependency theorists or the demands for a "new international economic order," and most recently in the wave of post-hegemonic regionalism.[100]

Each individual's contribution differed and necessarily reflected some specifics of time, place, and conviction. There are obvious risks in dealing with all three under one heading. Obregón, for example, distinguishes the "classical" contributions of Bello and Calvo from the "modernizing" stance of Álvarez.[101] Despite this diversity, however, there is a common thread running through their work regarding their ambitions for the independent Americas and their rightful place in the evolving international system, one that broke with established

[96] Ibid., 208–210.

[97] Eduardo Posada-Carbó, "The Long and Unfinished Road to Universal Suffrage: A Latin American Perspective, 1810-1985," in *Comparative Election Law* (Edward Elgar 2022), 250–272.

[98] Makau Mutua and Antony Anghie, "What Is TWAIL?" *Proceedings of the Annual Meeting* (American Society of International Law) 94 (April 2000): 31–40.

[99] Tom Long and Carsten Andreas Schulz, "Republican Internationalism: The Nineteenth Century Roots of Latin American Contributions to International Order," *Cambridge Review of International Affairs* (2021); J. Luis Rodriguez and Christy Thornton, "The Liberal International Order and the Global South: A View from Latin America, *Cambridge Review of International Affairs* 35, no. 5 (2022): 626–638.

[100] Riggirozzi and Tussie, *Post-Hegemonic Regionalism.*

[101] Obregón, "Noted for Dissent," 989.

norms and disrupted any "civilizational" calculus. Given that the system was, at that time, dominated by the norms and practices of major Western powers, it is unsurprising that much of their effort was directed toward securing absolute independence, full sovereignty, territorial integrity, and equality for Latin America in the family of states into which they were emerging. And, given the still prevailing hierarchies, it is also unsurprising that their successful efforts were often attributed to others.

Yet radical or reformist, Latin American jurists spoke with one voice, demanding better hearing, more rights, and representation in international fora. Law, the "gentle civilizer," was their chosen vehicle.[102] Latin American states, through their emergence and recognition as independent states and their iterated demands for equal treatment and peaceful dispute resolution, did offer a robust response to the facts of Western hegemony as it moved from Europe to the United States. Furthermore, with its creole (and mestizo) elites and mestizo societies, Latin America cannot correctly be located within any simple "West-non-West" binary but deserves attention on its own terms and in relation to the time and place of its emergence.[103] It should be considered part of the early and complex processes accompanying the "decolonization" or the *internationalization* of international law and society.[104]

IV. Conclusions and Legacies

This chapter has sought to extract and distill core elements of the thinking and scholarship of three key publicists and their contemporaries, men and women, to offer a more integrated and compelling account of Latin America's contribution to the development of international law during a critical period in its evolution in what was still a highly stratified and unequal international system.[105] This is a timely moment for such an exercise—with greater receptiveness to the TWAIL project within the larger Global IR story, as well as to how women's interventions have helped to define and transform the substance and practice of IR.[106]

In different ways and at times, since their lives crossed over three turbulent centuries, Bello, Calvo, and Álvarez exerted an extraordinary influence on the construction of a more "international" international law, one relevant not only to the Americas, with which they were most immediately concerned, but to

[102] Koskenniemi, *The Gentle Civiliser.*

[103] Fawcett, "Between West and Non-West," 679; Obregón, "Between Civilisation and Barbarism," 815–832; Becker Lorca, *Mestizo International Law.*

[104] Rajagopal, "International Law and Its Discontents," 176; Anghie, *Imperialism, Sovereignty and the Making of International Law*, 109, 209.

[105] Keene, "Standard of Civilization," 652–653.

[106] Owens et al., *Women's International Thought*, 1–22.

the wider world of international law as it emerged in the early decades of the twentieth century, and was gradually adapted by the appearance of new states and international institutions. In this regard, they were on the cusp of, and indeed integral to, a period of major change in the development and content of international law, what has been called "the end" of classical international law.[107] Whether or not they contributed to a specifically "American" international law, as suggested by Álvarez, or sought instead to revise, "enrich," and expand international law to the new states of the Americas is less immediate today.[108] Still, the region, as a unit of analysis, remains significant in these debates. Regions, historically and at present, have developed their own distinctive norms and institutional practices—increasingly so today as the legitimacy of global institutions is being challenged. What is important here is the use of the Americas, or Latin America, as a regional platform to internationalize law. In this process, their respective positions were important—all had views, not always aligned, on the uses of "regionalism" in the Americas; all left important legacies informing future practice.[109]

However, whether or not we conceive of any *regional* international law as distinct from the body of *universal* international law hardly changes the impact of their respective and collective contributions and the need to revisit them with twenty-first-century eyes, particularly at a time when scholars are rethinking the roles of the Global South in the construction of international law, order, and institutions.[110] Their long lives—all three publicists lived to be over eighty (as did Lutz and Bernardino) —experience, and interventions in the workings of law and international relations in different countries meant they had an enormous impact within Latin American states and beyond. Notwithstanding the legacies of Eurocentrism and powerful narratives of US economic and territorial expansion of this period, there was a "slow yet steady revision of the fundamentals of international law," one in which Latin American jurists played a central role.[111] Or, to borrow a phrase from Gargarella, just as Latin America was part of the "sala de máquinas" of constitutionalism,[112] it was also part of the "engine room"

[107] Arnulf Becker Lorca, "Sovereignty beyond the West: The End of Classical International Law," *Journal of the History of International Law*, 13, no. 1 (2011): 7–73.

[108] Becker Lorca, "International Law in Latin America or Latin American International Law?"; Apollin Kougne Zouapet, *Regional Approaches to International Law (RAIL): Rise or Decline of International Law?* (KFG Working Paper Series No. 46: Berlin 2021).

[109] Fawcett, "Origins and Development"; Pia Riggirozzi and Diana Tussie, *The Rise of Post-Hegemonic Regionalism in the Americas* (New York: Springer, 2012).

[110] See, for example, B. Rajagopal, "International Law and Its Discontents. Rethinking the Role of the Global South," *Proceedings of the Annual Meeting* (American Society of International Law) 106 (2012): 176–181.

[111] Greg Grandin, "Liberal Traditions in the Americas: Rights, Sovereignty and the Origins of Liberal Internationalism," *American Historical Review* 117, no. 1 (2012), 84.

[112] Roberto Gargarella, *La sala de máquinas de la Constitución: Dos siglos de constitucionalismo en América Latina 1810-2010* (Buenos Aires: Katz Editores,2014).

of international law, revealing the close interdependencies between the domestic and international contexts. Other chapters in this volume illustrate how, in matters concerning political, social, and economic rights, their legacies resonate through the evolution of international law and institutions in the Americas and beyond. As Brazil's UNICO delegate, Bertha Lutz told a colleague "the mantle is falling off the shoulders of the Anglo-Saxons" in advocating women's rights.[113] Beyond her bold claim, it is not too far-fetched to suggest that the design and evolution of inter-American institutions, and international institutions and regimes more generally, draw upon the influence of these individuals.[114]

In shedding further light on the formative role of Latin American states and peoples in the contemporary international relations of the period, this chapter has adopted a decentered lens that unsettles simple "Western-non-Western" binaries and accords greater agency to actors from outside the Western world.[115] Latin American men and women were present and active in significant debates about revisions to multiple arenas of international law, with profound consequences for the development of a more inclusive and indeed more "humane" international society.[116] Their actions invite fresh challenges to prevailing myths around that society's evolution, to expose its inequalities and open up the possibility of imagining a more plural and participatory international space.

113 Cited in Dietrichson and Sator, "Latin American Women," 17.

114 McPherson and Wehrli, *Beyond Geopolitics*. Eric Helleiner, *The Forgotten Origins of Bretton Woods*, (Ithaca, NY: Cornell University Press, 2014); Kathryn Sikkink, "Latin American Countries as Norm Protagonists and the Idea of International Human Rights," *Global Governance* 20, no. 3 (2014): 389–404.

115 See the interpretation of Deepesh Chakrabarty, *Provincializing Europe. Postcolonial Thought and Historical Difference* (Princeton, NJ: Princeton University Press, 2008). For the most recent work on Latin America's contributions to "Global International Relations," see Acharya et al., *Latin America in Global International*.

116 Judge Antonio Cançade Trindade, *The Construction of a Humanised International Law* (Brill 2017).

3

Nonintervention, Nonrecognition, and the Articulation of a Mexican Doctrine of International Law

Assessing the Contribution of Isidro Fabela and Genaro Estrada

*Fabia Fernandes Carvalho**

I. Introduction

This chapter will assess the international legal theses that two prominent Mexican diplomats put forward in the interwar period: Genaro Estrada (1887–1937) and Isidro Fabela (1882–1964). In the context of the post-revolutionary Mexican society, the engagement with international law proved to be a strategic move to showcase an autonomous Mexican position in the international sphere. In place of the negative image of a chaotic revolutionary country, the international arena was a convenient space for conveying the idea of a stable Mexico in full economic development. In this setting, international law and international institutions of the interwar period proved to be a productive vocabulary and space for Mexican post-revolutionary endeavors.

Genaro Estrada, the Mexican Secretary of Foreign Affairs (1930–1932), and Isidro Fabela, the Mexican delegate at the League of Nations and the International Labor Organization (1937–1940), were key figures in this context. They played an essential role in articulating and disseminating international legal theses that would eventually crystallize a legalistic Mexican engagement with the vocabulary of international law. Genaro Estrada addressed the issue of recognition in international law, and Isidro Fabela the principle of nonintervention.

The so-called Estrada Doctrine was a declaration by Genaro Estrada and published in the *Boletín Oficial de la Secretaría de Relaciones Exteriores* on

* My gratitude to Alexandra Huneeus, Alejandro Chehtman, Sergio Puig, and all participants of the two LAIL Handbook project workshops held in 2021 and 2022 for the productive discussion of the ideas explored in this contribution. I also want to thank Juan Pablo Scarfi for instigating comments about Isidro Fabela and Alejandro Rodiles Breton for the exchanges about Genaro Estrada. All English translations are the author's except where otherwise noted.

Fabia Fernandes Carvalho, *Nonintervention, Nonrecognition, and the Articulation of a Mexican Doctrine of International Law* In: *Latin American International Law in the Twenty-First Century.* Edited by: Alejandro Chehtman, Alexandra Huneeus, and Sergio Puig, Oxford University Press. © Oxford University Press 2025. DOI: 10.1093/9780197754016.003.0003

September 27, 1930, about the recognition of governments.[1] Revolutionary Mexico suffered from the consequences of the doctrine of recognition, "which allows foreign governments to pass upon the legitimacy of the regime existing in another country."[2] In a one-page declaration, Estrada clarified that granting recognition to a foreign regime would be "an insulting practice" that "offends the sovereignty of other nations."[3] Accordingly, no foreign nation would have the right to judge the replacement of governments. Importantly, Estrada asserted that the doctrine of recognition was mainly applied to Latin American republics. In cases of regime change in Europe, other nations did not make declarations about the recognition of governments. Therefore, Mexico would confine itself "to the maintenance or withdrawal, as it may deem advisable, of its diplomatic agents, and to the continued acceptance, also when it may deem advisable, of such similar accredited diplomatic agents as the respective nations may have in Mexico."[4]

Isidro Fabela's assertion of the principle of nonintervention was connected to the legal principles of the Mexican foreign policy employed at the League of Nations. These principles were informed by the Estrada and Carranza Doctrines; the latter also related to nonintervention and was enunciated earlier in the context of the US intervention in Veracruz in 1914.[5] Fabela articulated a strong position at the League, opposing acts of aggression by powerful states primarily in the context of the Spanish Civil War.[6] According to Fabela's legal interpretation, the League should not follow the French and British positions advocating nonintervention. To the Mexican diplomat and international lawyer, refusing assistance to the Spanish Republic, the *de jure* government of Spain, would constitute a form of intervention in the Spanish Civil War. In this setting, the Mexican material and political support to the Spanish Republic should be seen as a legal obligation under the League Covenant and, more broadly, international law.

The strategic engagement with the vocabulary of international law by Mexican diplomacy in the interwar period helped to crystallize a Mexican doctrine of international law, a legalistic and faithful take on international law based on the ideas of nonintervention and nonrecognition. At stake in this context was

[1] The English version is published as "Estrada Doctrine of Recognition," *The American Journal of International Law* (Supplement: Official Documents) 25, no. 4 (Oct. 1931): 203, https://doi.org/10.2307/2213173.

[2] Ibid.

[3] Ibid.

[4] Ibid.

[5] Juan Pablo Scarfi, "Mexican Revolutionary Constituencies and the Latin American Critique of US Interventionism," in *Revolutions in International Law. The Legacies of 1917*, ed. Anne Orford et al (Cambridge: Cambridge University Press, 2021), 222–241.

[6] Fabia Fernandes Carvalho Veçoso, "Mexican Post-Revolutionary Foreign Policy and the Spanish Civil War. Legal Struggles over Intervention at the League of Nations," in Anne Orford et al., *Revolutions in International Law*, 242–267.

the extrapolation of the revolutionary ideals to the international realm, together with a solid commitment to the notion of sovereignty and the State, to bring into action the objectives of the 1917 Mexican Constitution—especially article 27 on the country's sovereignty over subsoil mineral resources.[7]

This chapter will shed light on the particularities of the post-revolutionary Mexican engagement with international law and its innovative character compared to the experience of other countries in the Americas, particularly the articulation of international law in the context of Pan-Americanism. Exploring the emergence of the Mexican doctrine of international law in the interwar period can help us understand the ways in which a distinctly Latin American political project was coupled with the international legal vocabulary aiming not just to be part of the European community of nations but more ambitiously, put forward a form of internationalism that sought to eliminate foreign control of natural resources and economic dependency.[8] This feature of Mexican engagement with international law will become more apparent when assessing its connections to the project of oil nationalization during the presidency of Lázaro Cárdenas (1934–1940) later in this contribution.

However, Mexico's stance on international law has faced limits and challenges in achieving change and transformation in the global, regional, and domestic orders. Notably, the transmission and circulation of the Estrada Doctrine and Fabela's articulation of nonintervention after the interwar period show how Mexican international legalism was used to prevent more recent domestic debates about democracy and human rights.

The argument unfolds as follows. The next section explores Fabela's legal views on nonintervention. It starts with the principle of nonintervention, which has a long tradition in international law and Mexican internationalism. Moreover, the Estrada Doctrine is somehow a rearticulation of this principle, which justifies its assessment after Fabela's approach to nonintervention. Section II contextualizes their international legal thought in light of the circulation of ideas of anti-imperialism in Latin America, exploring the limits and possibilities of the Mexican stance toward international law.

[7] It is worth noting that nonintervention and nonrecognition were key principles in Latin American thinking about international law before the Mexican Revolution. Accordingly, see the Introduction to this volume, especially its first section, "Regionalist Projects in Latin American International Law," for early Latin American views on these principles.

[8] As put by the editors of this volume, *Latin American International Law* seeks "to explore the competing visions of regional law that coexist today, their respective sensibilities, normative commitments, and institutional innovations." Alejandro Chehtman, Alexandra Huneeus, and Sergio Puig, "Introduction," in this volume.

II. The Mexican Stance on Nonintervention in the Interwar Period

International law occupied a privileged place in the context of the Mexican Revolution and post-revolutionary Mexico.[9] In those two moments, Isidro Fabela's internationalism was vital in articulating Mexican foreign policies.[10] Generally, he had an active role in the country's political life and is also recognized as one of the most important Mexican jurists of the twentieth century. More specifically, as put by Juan Pablo Scarfi, Fabela's international legal thought played a crucial role in the progressive institutionalization of the revolutionary process in Mexico, both at the later stage of the revolution and during the 1930s reform efforts. Despite the limitations of the vocabularies of constitutional law and international law in fully incorporating the revolutionary constituencies shaped by the Mexican Revolution, new legal approaches were generated. The 1917 revolutionary Constitution and Mexican internationalism, which included a new stance on the relationship with the United States, illustrate these innovations.[11]

Fabela was awarded his law degree in 1908 by the *Escola Nacional de Jurisprudencia* in Mexico before the revolution started. Significantly, he actively participated in the *Ateneo de la Juventud* in his youth. The *Ateneo* was an organization that gathered Mexican intellectuals to rethink the ideas of positivism that had been circulating in the region since the last century, discussing the personalist and autocratic regime of Porfirio Díaz (1877–1880, 1884–1911) and imagining new possibilities for Mexico in the context of modernity in Latin America.[12]

Fabela had an active role in the Mexican Revolution as a member of the constitutionalist movement led by Venustiano Carranza, president of Mexico, at the later stage of the revolutionary process (1917–1920). In the context of the constitutionalists' struggle to emerge as the victorious faction of the revolution and build a new revolutionary state in Mexico, Fabela was commissioned to design and establish Mexico's diplomatic relations.[13] He worked to disseminate the ideals of the new revolutionary state and, as the Mexican diplomatic representative in many countries in Europe and Latin America from 1915 to 1917

[9] This section draws ideas from Fabia Fernandes Carvalho Veçoso, *Mexican Post-Revolutionary Foreign Policy*.

[10] Luis Ochoa Bilbao, Juan Pablo Padro Lallande, and Jesica Ayala Brito, "Isidro Fabela: Contexto Mundial y Derecho Internacional en la Política Exterior de la Revolución," *IUS Revista del Instituto de Ciencias Jurídicas de Puebla* 13, no. 43 (2019): 207–229, https://doi.org/10.35487/rius.v13i43.2019.429.

[11] Scarfi, "Mexican Revolutionary Constituencies," 219.

[12] Bilbao et al., "Isidro Fabela," 212. See also Scarfi, "Mexican Revolutionary Constituencies," 227–228.

[13] Bilbao et al., "Isidro Fabela," 213.

he sought to have Mexico recognized internationally. As a diplomatic representative, Fabela worked for the legitimacy of the constitutionalist government, establishing links with the spaces of intellectuality and culture.[14]

In the context of post-revolutionary Mexico in the 1930s, with an institutionalized and consolidated state, Fabela's work framed the role of international law in the country's foreign policy. This was concretely achieved through his appointments as the permanent Mexican delegate at the League of Nations and the International Labour Organization (1937–1940).[15]

Furthermore, Fabela's scholarly work was deeply embedded in the role of promoting and explaining Mexico's processes of institutional transformation after the revolution. He published on the revolution's history,[16] diplomatic history,[17] and quite extensively on international law topics such as intervention, neutrality law, and the Monroe and Drago Doctrines, among other publications.[18]

The legal principle of nonintervention employed by Mexico in the post-revolutionary context had already been articulated in the experience of the new revolutionary state under Carranza's presidency as the so-called Carranza Doctrine.[19] Importantly, Fabela's views on nonintervention evolved hand in hand with his changing views on US imperialism. His earlier continental sensibility based on the Monroe Doctrine was transformed in light of the 1914 US intervention in Veracruz. Fabela and Carranza reinterpreted "the Monroe Doctrine as an interventionist doctrine, rather than a continental principle," and the United States was seen in a new light "as an aggressive and imperialist neighbor intervening in the internal affairs and acting against Mexican sovereign autonomy."[20]

Fabela's radical stance on nonintervention would reappear in the interwar period under the presidency of Lázaro Cárdenas (1934–1940). It is worth noting that US imperialism was the clear focus of the early articulation of the principle of nonintervention. In the context of the League, even though the United States

[14] Ibid., 215.

[15] "Síntesis Biográfica del Doctor Don Isidro Fabela," in *Homenaje a Isidro Fabela*, ed. Comite de Amigos de Isidro Fabela (Mexico City: Universidad Nacional Autónoma de México, 1959), 703–706.

[16] Isidro Fabela, *Documentos Históricos de la Revolución Mexicana*, 5 vols. (Mexico City: Fondo de Cultura Económica, 1960–1964); Isidro Fabela, *História diplomática de la Revolución Mexicana (1912-1917)*, 2 vols. (México City: Fondo de Cultura Económica, 1958–1959). These publications reflect Fabela's views on the revolution from the perspective of a constitutionalist.

[17] Isidro Fabela, *Los Estados Unidos Contra La Libertad: Estudios de Historia Diplomatica Americana (Cuba, Filipinas, Panama, Nicaragua, Republica Dominicana)* (Barcelona: Talleres Graficos "Lux," 1920); Isidro Fabela, *Los precursores de la diplomacia mexicana* (Mexico City: Secretaría de Relaciones Exteriores, 1929).

[18] For a complete list of his publications, see www.isidrofabela.org.mx.

[19] For a detailed analysis of the international legal thought of Isidro Fabela in the context of the Mexican Revolution and the rise of the Carranza Doctrine, see Scarfi, "Mexican Revolutionary Constituencies."

[20] Ibid., 228.

was not involved in interwar cases of aggression,[21] Fabela's views on nonintervention would eventually be directed at US imperialism and the regional context in a renewed version of Mexican revolutionary nationalism. This form of nationalism focused on the state as the nation's builder and the economy's vector. In contrast, in the international realm, it would encompass the defense of multilateral principles and peace in consonance with the reality of a weaker country.[22] In such a modernist effort to strengthen Mexican national identity, the imperialism and interventionism of the United States would be depicted as the opposite stance.[23]

In the 1930s, Mexico enjoyed material conditions to defend in Geneva the peaceful settlement of international disputes, the principle of nonintervention, and the right to self-determination, adding to this "Mexican doctrine of international law" the collective security scheme of the League Covenant. In this setting, Mexican foreign policy opposed acts of aggression by powerful states in interwar conflicts. Accordingly, the role of Mexico in the League of Nations helped to bolster an autonomous Mexican position in the international sphere, transforming the negative image of a chaotic revolutionary country in international isolation.

For example, Fabela's legal thesis on regulating acts of aggression under the legal framework of the interwar period was fully attached to the Covenant rules on collective security and a vision of the world as interdependent. Under Fabela's legalistic stance, the provisions of the Covenant would substantively modify

[21] On American isolationism in the 1930s, the US Department of State asserts that "during the 1930s, the combination of the Great Depression and the memory of tragic losses in World War I contributed to pushing American public opinion and policy toward isolationism. Isolationists advocated non-involvement in European and Asian conflicts and non-entanglement in international politics. Although the United States took measures to avoid political and military conflicts across the oceans, it continued to expand economically and protect its interests in Latin America." "American Isolationism in the 1930s," Bureau of Public Affairs Department of State, The Office of Electronic Information, March 12, 2008, https://2001-2009.state.gov/r/pa/ho/time/wwii/102129.htm. Recent research shows a different role of the United States in the League. During the 1930s and 1940s, US government representatives and private actors had a prominent role in the technical organs of the League of Nations, such as the Health Organization and the Economic and Financial Organization. Putting together efforts of multilateralism and Pan-Americanism, the liberal elites of the United States aimed at a reformist stance toward capitalism. The technical organs of the League worked to regulate interdependence under a renovated view of economic governance in the international sphere. US actors had an important role in this context, supporting the establishment of missions in Latin America by both the Health Organization and the Economic and Financial Organization. For José Antonio Sánchez Román, the US engagement with the League via technical organs was a form of interventionism in Latin America aimed at stimulating free trade and the activities of US multinationals in the region. See José Antonio Sánchez Román, "El multilateralismo como intervencionismo. Estados Unidos y la Sociedade de Naciones in América Latina (1930-1946)," *Revista Complutense de Historia de América* 41 (2015): 47–69, https://hdl.handle.net/20.500.14352/24328.

[22] Luis Ochoa Bilbao, "Radiografía del Imperio: Los Estados Unidos Contra la Libertad, de Isidro Fabela," in *Pensar El Antiimperialismo. Ensayos de Historia Intelectual Latinoamericana, 1900-1930* (Mexico City: Colegio de Mexico, Universidad de Colima, 2012), 106–107.

[23] Ibid., 107.

the concept of neutrality.[24] When an armed conflict breaks out between one or more members of the League and another member state (or a nonmember state), all League members must break their commercial relations with the aggressor. Notably, the League Covenant did not establish a war declaration as mandatory.[25] League members should also apply the punishments decreed against the aggressor. Following the Covenant's provisions, a member state could be either nonbelligerent or pre-belligerent but not neutral.[26]

A critical legal issue in this context is how Fabela connected nonintervention to the new perspective on neutrality under the legal framework of the League Covenant. Accordingly, Fabela saw nonintervention as one of the legal consequences of neutrality and not vice versa.[27] Nonintervention could not be used as a legal proxy to assure a neutral status precisely because total neutrality was unavailable to the League members under the Covenant. As he put it when referring to the Spanish Civil War, "the alleged nonintervention that it is said to apply in Spain would be admissible only if neutrality could be decreed previously, but it is the case that the members of the League should not be neutral to the aggression that Spain is a victim."[28]

However, at the same time, the Cárdenas' regime did not aim to present Mexico as the protector of weaker countries in the international domain. Accordingly, Mexico kept a prudent and legalistic position at the League, which allowed its main objective to gain global respect through its role in the international organization. In other words, the Mexican position on nonintervention was ultimately more a defense of the Covenant than of a country suffering an act of aggression.[29]

In an international press declaration in April 1937, Fabela clarified that neutrality rules and nonintervention could be invoked as the legal foundation for denying help to the Spanish government by those few states that did not belong to the League. However, the League members could not rely on it, as Spain had the legal right to receive support through its government, the only representative of the Spanish state legally recognized by the League.[30]

[24] Isidro Fabela, *Neutralidad: estudio histórico, jurídico y político; la Sociedad de las Naciones y el continente americano ante la guerra de 1939-1940* (Mexico City: Biblioteca de Estudios Internacionales, 1940), 250.

[25] Ibid., 248.

[26] Ibid., 253.

[27] Jorge Castañeda, "La aportación de Isidro Fabela a la seguridad colectiva internacional," in *Homenaje a Isidro Fabela*, ed. Comite de Amigos de Isidro Fabela (Mexico City: Universidad Nacional Autónoma de México, 1959), 146–147.

[28] Fabela, *Neutralidad*, 263–264.

[29] Fabián Herrera León, *México en la Sociedad de Naciones, 1931-1940* (Mexico City: Secretaría de Relaciones Exteriores, Dirección General del Acervo Histórico Diplomático, 2014), 229–230.

[30] Fabela, *Neutralidad*, 264.

The connections between Mexico and Spain opened space for a more vigorous defense of nonintervention, which was directed to benefit Mexican domestic politics in light of the oil nationalization issue. In March 1938, Cárdenas nationalized Mexican oil based on Article 27 of the 1917 Constitution. This provision established that all subsoil mineral resources are the nation's property. Their private exploitation may only be carried out through concessions to Mexicans by birth or naturalization or to Mexican companies.

It is beyond the scope of this chapter to delve into the details of the Mexican process of nationalizing oil[31] and, more specifically, the emergence of a right to nationalize in international law. However, the pioneering character of the Mexican post-revolutionary context is noteworthy, especially if one considers that these debates reached the field of international law at a later stage.[32]

Fabela's stance on nonintervention at the League of Nations can be seen as a clear message to the international community. Nonintervention should be understood under the rules of international law and the League Covenant. This legalistic commitment would pave the way for Mexico's active role in confronting possible domestic attempts at intervention, especially considering US imperialism. In other words, the Mexican stance at the League would open space for this understanding of nonintervention for Mexico's benefit.[33]

The following section further interrogates the Mexican legalistic stance in the interwar period in light of the Estrada doctrine on recognition.

III. The Recognition of Governments: The Estrada Doctrine and the Core of Mexican Foreign Policy

> *Wilkie: ¿Cuál es la posición de México respecto a la Doctrina Estrada? La Doctrina Estrada parece ser muy contradictoria. ¿Cómo puede mantenerse esta doctrina en el concepto de que, si le conviene a México, retira a sus representantes diplomáticos? ¿Qué eso no constituye un*

[31] To illustrate, see José Ovalle Favela, "La nacionalización de las industrias petrolera y eléctrica," *Boletín Mexicano de Derecho Comparado* 40 (2007): 178–184, https://revistas.juridicas.unam.mx/index.php/derecho-comparado/article/view/3910/4927; Linda B. Hall, *Oil, Banks, and Politics, the United States and Postrevolutionary Mexico, 1917-1924* (New York: University of Texas Press, 1995); Jonathan C. Brown, *Oil and Revolution in Mexico* (Berkeley: University of California Press, 1993); Lorenzo Meyer, *Mexico and the United States in the Oil Controversy, 1917-1942* (New York: University of Texas Press, 1977).

[32] For example, Konstantin Katzarov, "The Validity of the Act of Nationalization in International Law," *Modern Law Review* 22 (1959): 639–648, https://www.jstor.org/stable/1091549. To be sure, Resolution 1803 (XVII) from the General Assembly of the United Nations, adopted on December 14, 1962, on permanent sovereignty over natural resources, is a milestone in these debates in international law. United Nations, "General Assembly resolution 1803 (XVII)," Audiovisual Library of International Law, https://legal.un.org/avl/ha/ga_1803/ga_1803.html.

[33] León and Andrés, *Contra tudo y contra todos*, 302–303.

rompimiento? ¿Qué cosa es la Doctrina Estrada? Si usted le dice a un enemigo: "Yo no estoy rompiendo relaciones con usted, pero yo no vengo más a su casa; yo no vuelvo a su casa, sino hasta que usted haga lo que yo quiero". ¿No es esto un rompimiento?

Cosío Villegas: Yo en este punto sí tengo opiniones muy definidas. Tengo la idea de que esta Doctrina Estrada se justificó cuando fue expuesta en 1930, por Genaro Estrada la primera vez, y tenía un sentido muy claro: era una posible defensa contra la inclinación intervencionista de Estados Unidos. Pero como un criterio para regir las relaciones de México con otros países, no como ha ocurrido con Brasil, con Honduras, con República Dominicana, o antes con Perú, es una doctrina que no tiene aplicación posible. Desde ese punto de vista yo estoy en absoluto desacuerdo con la Secretaría de Relaciones Exteriores. Es una doctrina insostenible, y que, además, México no ha sostenido ni siquiera con congruencia. . . . Por más que México insista en decir que si mantiene sus agentes diplomáticos, no representa la aprobación del gobierno, y que si los retira, no representa una reprobación. Por supuesto que eso representa en un caso la aprobación y en otro la reprobación.[34]

The conversation above between US historian James W. Wilkie and Mexican historian and writer Daniel Cosío Villegas in January 1965 illustrates the controversies around the Mexican thesis of recognition of governments as formulated by Genaro Estrada in 1930. How to keep a noninterventionist stance

[34] James W. Wilkie and Edna Monzón Wilkie, *Daniel Cosío Villegas. Un Protagonista de la Etapa Constructiva de la Revolución Mexicana. Entrevistas* (Mexico City: El Colegio de Mexico, 2011), 187–188.

Wilkie: What is Mexico's position regarding the Estrada Doctrine? The Estrada Doctrine seems to be very contradictory. How can this doctrine be maintained in the concept that, if it suits Mexico, it withdraws its diplomatic representatives? That doesn't constitute a breakup? What is the Estrada Doctrine? If you say to an enemy: "I am not breaking off relations with you, but I am not coming to your house anymore"; "I'm not going back to your house until you do what I want." Isn't this a breakup?

Cosío Villegas: At this point I do have very defined opinions. I have the idea that this Estrada Doctrine was justified when it was exposed in 1930, by Genaro Estrada the first time, and it had a very clear meaning: it was a possible defense against the interventionist inclination of the United States. But as a criterion to govern Mexico's relations with other countries, not as has happened with Brazil, with Honduras, with the Dominican Republic, or before with Peru, it is a doctrine that has no possible application. From that point of view I am in absolute disagreement with the Ministry of Foreign Affairs. It is an unsustainable doctrine, and one that, furthermore, Mexico has not supported even with consistency. . . . No matter how much Mexico insists on saying that if it maintains its diplomatic agents, it does not represent the government's approval, and that if it withdraws them, it does not represent a disapproval. Of course that represents approval in one case and disapproval in another. (Translation into English by the author)

while maintaining or withdrawing Mexican diplomatic agents in light of regime change in another country? Is it possible to detach how Mexico advances diplomatic relations from any substantive analysis of the new regime via recognition? Moreover, can such a "neutral" stance be kept over time in any case of regime change? In a nutshell, these were the questions posed by Wilkie to Cosío Villegas. These exchanges were used to contextualize research by Carlos David Aguirre Cortés to understand the motives behind adopting the Estrada Doctrine.[35]

The one-page Estrada Doctrine was directed to public servants of the Mexican state working abroad as diplomats from the Mexican Secretary of Foreign Affairs. In this setting, the formulation of the Estrada Doctrine was objective and straightforward.[36] Differently from Fabela's doctrinal legal articulation on nonintervention, the Estrada Doctrine offered clear direction to the Mexican diplomatic staff about recognizing governments. However, as a "memorándum de cuatro párrafos y poco más de una cuartilla de extension,"[37] the 1930 document offered a way to proceed that was based on international legal principles, especially nonintervention and the formal equality among states.

Although it was an official document with clear international legal consequences, a lawyer did not articulate the Estrada Doctrine. Estrada started his professional trajectory working as a journalist. His proximity to the world of letters evolved into writing essays (a classic form of Latin American literature) and poetry. He also worked as a literature teacher and bibliographer. In 1923, he started to work for the *Secretaría de Relaciones Exteriores* (SRE), where he developed a brilliant and rising career. Estrada worked to professionalize the diplomatic and consular service and created the Mexican diplomatic historical archives at the SRE. In sum, he was a respected intellectual and writer and, like a lineage of Mexican diplomats (and even other Latin American diplomats), had a robust knowledge of literature.[38]

[35] Carlos David Aguirre Cortés, "Los Motivos de Don Genaro: la Formulación de la Doctrina Estrada en 1930" (Master's thesis, Centro de Investigación y Docencia Económicas, A. C., División de Historia, 2014).

[36] "The declaration is, in effect, an announcement of instructions sent to the diplomatic representatives of Mexico to acquaint them with a new policy of their government." Philip C. Jessup, "The Estrada Doctrine," *The American Journal of International Law* 25, no. 4 (1931): 719–720, https://doi.org/10.2307/2189922.

[37] Aguirre Cortés, *Los Motivos de Don Genaro*, 25. "memorandum of four paragraphs and a little more than a page in length" (translation into English by the author).

[38] Cesar Sepúlveda, "Proyecciones internacionales, políticas y jurídicas de la Doctrina Estrada," *Revista Mexicana De Política Exterior* 12 (1986): 335, https://revistadigital.sre.gob.mx/index.php/rmpe/article/view/2284. For a more detailed (and celebratory) biography of Genaro Estrada, see Jorge Alfonso Calderón Salazar, "El Legado de Genaro Estrada," Cámara di Diputados, https://www.diputados.gob.mx/LeyesBiblio/muro/pdf/estrada_perfil.pdf.

As mentioned by Alejandro Rodiles Breton,[39] when the doctrine was enunciated in 1930, nonintervention was not yet a principle universally recognized—something that eventually crystallized in the 1945 Charter of the United Nations. European and US interventions in the region were part of the Latin American reality, and alien protection based on the use of force was a current practice of hegemonic states.[40] In this setting, the enunciation of the Estrada Doctrine followed the same path as previous Latin American doctrines on forcible debt collection and nonintervention, such as the Calvo and Drago doctrines. The former condemned "diplomatic or armed intervention as a lawful measure to enforce any pecuniary claim in international law." Therefore, domestic means of dispute settlement should be exhausted before the employment of any international scheme of alien protection. The latter asserted that international law does not allow for the coercive collection of public debt.

As an international lawyer interested in past articulations of international law in the region, my main interest lies in understanding how the Estrada Doctrine achieved legal authority in the field. Understanding the historical conditions for its emergence is essential, and it is an issue open to discussion about how we can interpret the past. Be as it may, it is beyond doubt that the Estrada Doctrine is traditionally recognized as one of the most important Mexican contributions to international law. Notably, the Mexican SRE had a crucial role in attaching legal prominence to the Estrada Doctrine, compiling legal opinions by Mexican and other Latin American jurists on the practice of recognition of governments as formulated by Estrada.[41] In 1996, the names of Isidro Fabela and Genaro Estrada were engraved in gold on the wall in the *Colección Muro de Honor* in the Mexican Chamber of Deputies. Their names were included as the precursors of the Mexican foreign policy, an initiative approved by all parliamentary groups.[42]

The issue of recognition of governments had been the subject of discussion in international law when the Estrada Doctrine was enunciated in 1930. Amos S. Hershey offered a good overview in a piece published in 1920, considering the practices of recognizing de facto governments by mostly European states and

[39] Alejandro Rodiles Bretón, "Il ruolo del Messico nell'ordine mondiale (e accanto agli USA)," *Rivista Italiana di Geopolitica* 8 (2017): 142, https://www.limesonline.com/rivista/il-ruolo-del-messico-nell-ordine-mondiale-e-accanto-agli-usa-14629649/.

[40] On the collection of debt through the use of force, see Fabia Fernandes Carvalho Veçoso, "Intervención, deuda externa y la conformación del orden espacial: el bloqueo de Venezuela revisitado (1902-1903)," *Revista Estudios Sociales* 59, no. 2 (2020): 41–62, https://doi.org/10.14409/es.v59i2.8853; Fabia Fernandes Carvalho Veçoso, "Resisting Intervention through Sovereign Debt: A Redescription of the Drago Doctrine," *Third World Approaches to International Law Review* 1 (2020): 74–92, https://twailr.com/twail-review/issue-1-2020/fabia-fernandes-carvalho-vecoso-resisting-intervention-through-sovereign-debt-a-redescription-of-the-drago-doctrine/.

[41] Aguirre Cortés, *Los Motivos de Don Genaro*, 20.

[42] Cámara de Diputados, "Muro de Honor. Salón de Plenos de la H. Cámara de Diputados. Letras de Oro. Isidro Fabela. Genaro Estrada," 2006, https://www.diputados.gob.mx/LeyesBiblio/muro/pdf/fabela.pdf.

the United States.[43] The author opened his text by asserting that recognizing de facto governments would be a "topic that seems to have almost wholly escaped the attention of so-called authorities or publicists on international law."[44] After citing doctrinal excerpts and assessing European and US state practice from the nineteenth century onward, Hershey concluded:

> The record shows that in every instance except Poland down to 1850 where any people has claimed independence by right of revolt the right of intervention has been exercised against the will of one or the other party to the dispute. In every instance the only question that has disturbed the intervening Powers has regarded neither the right nor the policy so much as the "time and mode" of action. The only difference between the European and American practice was that the United States aimed at moderating or restricting the extreme license of European intervention . . . The Practice of the United States, on the other hand, appears to have been governed by mixed motives of expediency, sympathy with democratic movements, and supposed legality.[45]

This excerpt illustrates the connections between the recognition of governments and the principle of nonintervention in international law. Estrada was right to make it clear that assessing substantive issues of the legitimacy of a new regime as a condition for granting recognition was a form of intervening in the internal affairs of the state in question. Accordingly, the Estrada Doctrine was formalized under the theory of declaratory recognition. That is, the new government (and most importantly, statehood) would not be dependent upon the legal scrutiny of other states by granting recognition.

The European practice shown by Hershey was related to contexts of civil wars, insurrections, provisory governments, state secession, and the related interventions by third states to support either the offended established government or the new political faction aiming to become the new government. On the other hand, the US state practice of recognizing de facto governments would be more connected to a substantive assessment of the legality and legitimacy of the new government, the so-called constitutive theory of recognition.[46]

[43] Amos S. Hershey, "Notes on the Recognition of De Facto Governments by European States," *American Journal of International Law* 14, no. 4 (1920): 400–518, https://www.jstor.org/stable/2187871.

[44] Ibid., 499.

[45] Ibid., 516–517.

[46] Arnulf Becker Lorca explored these two theoretical approaches to recognition in more detail. See Arnulf Becker Lorca, *Mestizo International Law* (Cambridge: Cambridge University Press, 2014), 933–940 (electronic version).

Indeed, the decade before the adoption of the Estrada Doctrine was marked by external pressure against Mexico. In such troubled years, the regime of the elected President Alvaro Obregón in 1920 was not immediately recognized by the United Kingdom and the United States despite being the de jure government of Mexico. Issues of alien protection in the context of internal rebellions in Mexico and the control over Mexican oil, among other questions, were related to this scenario.[47] Genaro Estrada was already a public servant at the SRE and could follow the legal struggles for Mexican recognition.

To Rodiles Bretón, the Estrada Doctrine put together recognition and nonintervention in an ambitious attempt to rebuild international law "post-*jus public europaeum*."[48] Here resides the importance of the doctrine and its authority in international law. Rodiles Bretón is correct in saying that the Estrada Doctrine aimed to oppose the European system of subjective evaluation by one state to another in the limited context of the family of civilized nations. Against such a form of constitutive recognition and contrary to the rules and practices of *jus public europaeum*, the Estrada Doctrine adopted a declaratory form of recognition.[49]

In this specific sense, the 1930 Estrada Doctrine and Fabela's approach to nonintervention can be seen as something more than a "creole attempt"[50] to be included in European international law. The Mexican Doctrine of international law aimed at more than inclusion and participation in a global order already established by Europe. The Mexican stance aimed at a substantive change in the rules of the international game, proposing the elimination of foreign control of natural resources and the end of economic dependency. In this setting, asserting an anti-imperial sensibility of the Mexican doctrine of international law is possible. Nevertheless, the circulation of this Mexican stance in different contexts over time showed the limits of such a sensibility in international law. The following sections address these issues.

[47] Sepúlveda, *Proyecciones internacionales*, 335–339.

[48] Rodiles Bretón, *Il ruolo del Messico nell'ordine mondiale*, 142. To Schmitt, "Por el contrario, surge en suelo americano una construcción radicalmente opuesta que se apoyaba en el princípio de la independencia de cada Estado, y por la que el reconocimiento según el Derecho de Gentes era calificado de medio inadmisible de intervención y por tanto era rechazado. **Este punto de vista posee el valor dialético de una antítesis lógica y conserva este valor aun cuando se aya convertido, en el aspecto de la política del poder, en un gesto débil.** Es el critério que ha quedado expresado en la llamada *Doctrina Estrada* mejicana, y que llega, de modo consecuente, hasta el extremo de considerar todo reconocimiento semejante como contrario al Derecho de Gentes e incluso como ofensa al Estado o al Gobierno presuntamente reconocido, y de rechazarlo en base a este razonamiento." Carl Schmitt, *El Nomos de La Tierra en el Derecho de Gentes del* "Ius publicum europaeum" (Granada: Comares, 2002), 334. (emphasis added).

[49] Rodiles Bretón, *Il ruolo del Messico nell'ordine mondiale*, 142.

[50] Liliana Obregón, "Completing Civilization: Creole Consciousness and International Law in Nineteenth-Century Latin America," in *International Law and Its Others*, ed. Anne Orford (Cambridge: Cambridge University, 2006), 247–264.

IV. The Mexican Doctrine in International Law and Anti-Imperialism

Various anti-imperial sensibilities have circulated in the region since the end of the nineteenth century. As put by Alexandra Pita González and Carlos Marichal Salinas, it is a recurrent idea in Latin American social thinking and in public debates to describe the region as a space open for domination by foreign countries. The region's political, economic, and military asymmetries would make Latin America easy prey to the hegemonic interests of the powerful states of the day. Others have sought to justify Latin American backwardness using imperial undertakings as a vital cause of such a state of affairs.[51]

Between the mid-nineteenth century and the 1930s, philosophical ideas related to progress and backwardness in the region were transformed. From a positivistic view of a barbaric past to be transformed into a civilized future by imitating foreign models, a more vigorous critique of US imperialism emerged. An understanding of the negative influence of external factors on Latin America accompanied it.[52]

To be sure, Latin American countries suffered numerous interventions and experienced political instability throughout their history. From the fears of the *Libertadores* for the recolonization of Latin American republics to the domestic challenges of a highly militarized society in the post-independence context,[53] as well as the many European interventions in the nineteenth century related to imperial rivalries mainly among Great Britain, France, and Spain, the region had become a space with constant challenges of political ordering. Nineteenth-century US expansionism also contributed to this context of political instability. Still, anti-imperial sensibilities would emerge in the late nineteenth century, which included the Latin American reactions to the 1898 US war with Spain and the occupation of Cuba.[54]

[51] Alexandra Pita González and Carlos Marichal Salinas, "Introducción: Pensar El Antiimperialismo," in *Pensar El Antiimperialismo. Ensayos de Historia Intelectual Latinoamericana, 1900-1930*, ed. Alexandra Pita González and Carlos Marichal Salinas (Colegio de Mexico: Universidad de Colima, 2012), 9.

[52] Ibid., 10.

[53] Tulio Halperín Donghi, *The Contemporary History of Latin America* (Durham, NC: Duke University Press, 1993), 74–76. The author explains that these issues had parallels in Brazil, although the independence of the former Portuguese colony did not happen through war. Importantly, the author explains that "increasing militarization added to the economic burdens of the new states, and it contained the seeds of future political instability. The leaders of irregular armed forces could easily become independent of the governments that organized them. The armies of the young Spanish American republics arrived at independence with far too many commissioned officers for peace-time purposes, and in most cases, dismissing them was risky. In order to retain the loyalty of their overgrown armies, the new governments had to invest a major portion of their resources in military payrolls, but for that they needed more state revenues. Extracting those revenues required, in turn, the further use of force in what became a self-perpetuating cycle." Halperín Donghi, *Contemporary History*, 75.

[54] Oscar Terán, "El primer antimperialismo latinoamericano," in *En busca de la ideología argentina* (Buenos Aires: Catálogos Editora, 1986), 85–97.

Latin American anti-imperialism lacked homogeneity in ideological, conceptual, and instrumental terms. Some authors focused on the nation-state as the preferential site to resist imperialism. In contrast, others articulated expanded forms of spatial order, including some sort of continental nationalism. Notably, imperialism occupied a vital space in the explorations of Latin American identity that can be seen in the typical modern literary text in the region, the "ensaio" (essay). The images of the other as the "Gringo" or "Yankee" were part of the processes of self-understanding of the "Latino" or "Iberamericano" in texts that created metaphors to articulate the problematic issues concerning the meaning of the nation in the region.[55] Moreover, the innovations in the relations between the United States and Latin America in the early twentieth century brought by the Roosevelt Corollary to the Monroe Doctrine paved the way for robust US interventionism in Latin American countries.[56]

In this setting, the early forms of Latin American anti-imperialism denounced the US territorial, commercial, and cultural expansionism. They presented a defensive countermove, a union between Latin American republics. The idea of Latin American unity was articulated around various essentialist features, being pre-Hispanic, colonial, or the particularities of the context of post-independence. In any case, Latin American unity constituted a monolithic entity, and the full realization of its potentialities had been stagnant, considering the constant presence of the other in the form of either colonialism or imperialism. To Oscar Terán, discourses articulating these forms of anti-imperialism circulated in the region from the end of the nineteenth century to the beginning of World War I.[57]

Broader intellectual discussions about the issues and prospects of applying the concept of modernity to Latin America help us to understand this context.[58] Generally speaking, modernity is seen in Latin America as something pertaining to different settings across time and space. Modernity will be found outside the region, in Western Europe or the United States. If Latin America is to be considered, modernity belongs to the region's future. As a contested notion,

[55] Gonzáles and Marichal Salinas, "Introducción," 10.

[56] The Roosevelt Corollary, established by President Theodore Roosevelt in 1904, stated that the United States would not accept European interventions to collect debt in the Americas. Roosevelt transformed the Monroe Doctrine "from a defensive, verbal opposition to new European colonisation in the Americas into an aggressive, military right of the United States to intervene in the affairs of any nation that appeared too instable to withstand a European attack." Alan McPherson, *A Short History of U.S. Interventions in Latin America and the Caribbean* (London: Wiley-Blackwell: 2016), 47. In the same vein, see the Introduction, in this volume.

[57] Terán, *El primer antimperialismo*, 85–86.

[58] Sergio Costa, "The Research on Modernity in Latin America: Lineages and Dilemmas," *Current Sociology* 67, no. 6 (2019): 838, https://doi.org/10.1177/0011392118807523.

modernity is "equated with a specific (distant) social formation and simultaneously represents a vision of the future whereby different forms of domination, also including dictatorships, are legitimized in the name of modernization." Moreover, having Europe or the United States as the idealized form of modernity justified the dominance of enlightened Latin American elites over the non-Europeanized Latin American masses.[59]

From the end of the nineteenth century to the beginning of the twentieth century, modernity was understood by intellectuals in the region as a transplant. European civilization (and later the United States) was seen as more developed and advanced and should be transferred into Latin America, not just by the import of institutions. Europeans should also migrate to Latin America to transform the local population's features, ensuring the desired progress. European scientific racism was imported into Latin America and had different articulations in different countries—from replacing the indigenous people with European immigrants in Argentina to a mixture of races in the case of Brazil.[60] As mentioned, nineteenth-century positivism and the views of modernization as a transplant would be transformed by a robust stance against US imperialism in Latin America. In other words, foreign influence would be seen as hindering modernization, preventing the region from flourishing appropriately.

Without US interventionism and the US-supported dictatorships in the Caribbean and Central America, the region would eventually experience more sustained progress. Not the nineteenth-century progress through the importation of foreign models but a changed notion of progress based on the affirmation of various forms of Latin American identity.[61] Notably, other activist perspectives animated by social movements, unions, anarchism, socialism, and communism also articulated variations of anti-imperialism in the region. The diversity of anti-imperial sensibilities makes it impossible to assert a homogeneous character to this way of thinking about interventionism in Latin America.

Between 1914 and 1930, efforts to modernize the region were connected to affirming different forms of Latin American identity by critiquing its opposite stance, US imperialism.[62] The Mexican doctrine of international law reflects this context. As discussed earlier in this chapter, resisting US interventions was at the core of Mexico's stance toward international law.

These previous considerations help us understand the Mexican legalistic stance on nonintervention and recognition. Fabela and Estrada were modernizers, but not in the sense of transplant and imitation. Their strong anti-imperial sensibility was related to a more optimistic take on Mexican (and Latin

[59] Ibid., 839.
[60] Ibid., 842–843.
[61] Gonzáles and Marichal Salinas, "Introducción," 12.
[62] Ibid., 12.

American) identity, marked by revolutionary proposals and social critique.[63] Still, the differences between Latin American countries as weaker actors and Europe and the United States as the Great Powers make clear their modernist approach and the search to diminish the distance between Mexico, Europe, and the United States. Mexican endeavors would be achieved not through the acritical imitation of foreign models but as a modernization process focused on the revolutionary self-transformation of Mexico. Notably, the transformative character of the Mexican stance must be pondered in light of its affirmation of a national form of capitalism based on the state and cultural autonomy.[64]

In this setting, international law was used to help consolidate Mexico's modern position in the international realm. The country's legalistic stance must be considered in light of this form of modernist anti-imperialism. If all Mexico was doing was following international law strictly during the interwar period, how could one argue that oil nationalization, for example, would be something that the international community would resist? Retrospectively, it is possible that Mexico's faith in international law was exaggerated, as the affirmation of an international legal principle had little impact on the outcomes of international events, including US interventionism.

Nevertheless, the Mexican doctrine of international law was distinct from other articulations of international law in the continent that were not animated by a robust anti-imperial sensibility. The crucial role of international law in the activities of the American Institute of International Law in the broader context of pan-Americanism, as explored by Juan Pablo Scarfi,[65] was related to a US civilizing mission in the region by promoting the international rule of law. In this setting, Fabela and Estrada's stances contrast with the more accommodating views of Alejandro Álvarez toward the United States, for example.[66]

V. Final Remarks: The Limits and Challenges of the Mexican Doctrine of International Law

This chapter has assessed the legal views of the Mexican diplomats Isidro Fabela and Genaro Estrada on the principle of nonintervention and the recognition of governments by the occasion of their emergence in the interwar period. Animated by a modernist anti-imperial sensibility, the Mexican doctrine of international law aimed to change certain aspects of international law, focusing

[63] Ibid., 23.
[64] Ibid., 24–25.
[65] Juan Pablo Scarfi, *The Hidden History of International Law in the Americas. Empire and Legal Networks* (Oxford: Oxford University Press, 2017).
[66] Ibid., 61–62.

on ending economic dependency and eliminating foreign control of natural resources.

However, later articulations of the Mexican doctrine of international law, in different contexts over time, show certain limits of this Mexican stance. Focusing on the Estrada Doctrine and its attempt to keep a form of "neutrality" in international affairs, in light of the political dominance of the *Partido Revolucionário Institucional* (PRI) for seven decades in the country, the doctrine started to be seen as a passive Mexican attitude toward the international.[67] In other words, the Estrada Doctrine could be used as a shield to prevent judgment over the PRI regime in Mexico. The discussion about promoting human rights and democracy domestically could not find an ally in international law.

The same can be said about the principle of nonintervention. At the end of the twentieth century, nonintervention could be used as a flexible formula to manage Mexico's ambivalence in opening its economy to international trade, at the same time preventing assessments of its political system.[68]

In this setting, this chapter recognizes the transmission processes of legal theses and interpretations over time. Assessing the Mexican stance on international law in the post-revolutionary context tells us a story of the role of international law in modernization projects in Mexico, moved by an anti-imperial sensibility against the United States. Moving across time, the legalistic Mexican position can be seen in a different light, with limitations and challenges related to the particularities of the political context in the country. However, retrieving Fabela and Estrada's legal theses might help us to better map regional political projects in international law in Latin America, adding political imagination to how we can think about transforming the region's challenges of today.

[67] Rodiles Bretón, *Il ruolo del Messico nell'ordine mondiale*, 142–143.

[68] Ibid., 143. On later articulation of the Mexican foreign policy, see illustratively Ana Covarrubias, "La Política Exterior 'Activa' . . . una vez más," *Foro Internacional* 191–192 (2008): 13–34 and Leonel Pereznieto Castro, "La Doctrina Estrada, una nota para su relectura," *Revista de Relaciones Internacionales de la UNAM* 89 (2002): 121–126.

4
The Montevideo Convention and Its Predecessors

Juan Pablo Scarfi

I. Introduction

The Montevideo Convention (1933) has been often seen as a turning point moment in the evolution of a regional Latin American approach to international law in the context of the formation of the inter-American system and the parallel institutionalization of the discipline across the region. At the same time, the Convention consolidated essentially the principles of nonintervention, state independence and autonomy (statehood), and sovereign equality and had broader effects and implications beyond the region and the inter-American system, shaping the international legal order and international organizations, especially the United Nations Charter. On the one hand, the principles of state independence and autonomy and the recognition of state personality (statehood) under international law were consolidated essentially in articles 5 and 6, for they asserted that "the fundamental rights of states are not susceptible of being affected in any manner whatsoever" and that "the recognition of a state merely signifies that the state which recognizes it accepts the personality of the other with all the rights and duties determined by international law. Recognition is unconditional and irrevocable."[1] On the other hand, the principles of sovereign equality among states and nonintervention were consecrated in articles 4 and 8, since they affirmed, respectively, that "states are juridically equal, enjoy the same rights, and have equal capacity in their exercise. The rights of each one do not depend upon the power it possesses to assure its exercise, but upon the simple fact of its existence as a person under international law" and that "no state has the right to intervene in the internal or external affairs of another."[2] These mentioned principles and the implications of these four articles of the Montevideo Convention were interconnected. This chapter revises standard interpretations of the Montevideo Convention, which have tended to regard it

[1] Séptima Conferencia Internacional Americana, *Actas y antecedentes con el índice general* (Montevideo: Imprenta Nacional, 1933).
[2] Ibid.

Juan Pablo Scarfi, *The Montevideo Convention and Its Predecessors* In: *Latin American International Law in the Twenty-First Century*. Edited by: Alejandro Chehtman, Alexandra Huneeus, and Sergio Puig, Oxford University Press. DOI: 10.1093/9780197754016.003.0004

as either a turning point and watershed moment for both international law and Latin America's contribution to it or the culmination of a series of continental projects for the codification of international law.[3]

Although this chapter concedes that the Montevideo Convention was a transformative moment, it argues that it was shaped by a wide range of precedents and predecessors, previous international and Pan-American conferences, as well as different regional legal and political traditions and experiences, including notably the Pan-American movement and its legal implications, the Mexican Constitution of 1917, and the rise of anti-interventionist and anti-imperialist aspirations. In other words, the road to Montevideo was the culmination of a long process of disciplinary consolidation and codification of international law across the continent, as well as progressive politicization of international law around a debate over the question of interventions.

Since the inception of the US-led Pan-American movement in 1890, a continental tradition of American international law was consolidated and institutionalized through the creation of the American Institute of International Law (AIIL), an organization created in Washington, DC by the United States and Chilean jurists James Brown Scott and Alejandro Álvarez and funded by the Carnegie Endowment for International Peace. It joined together all the national societies of international law of the continent and sought to advance a US-led approach to American international law. As leaders of the AIIL, Scott and Álvarez each advocated a humanitarian and solidarist approach to continental American international law. The AIIL put forward a series of projects to codify American international law and advocated a moderate approach to the principle of nonintervention. These projects set the grounds for the principles debated at the Montevideo Convention.

At the same time, outside the microcosms of the Pan-American movement and the AIIL, the rise of a legal anti-imperialist critique of US interventionism in Latin America contributed to a more robust approach to absolute nonintervention. Following the Mexican Revolution and Mexico's constitution of 1917, a small group of jurists in Mexico and Cuba adopted an anti-imperialist posture based on a legal critique of US unilateral interventionism in the region and the rebuke of the US Monroe Doctrine.[4] Unlike the AIIL, this tradition adopted a regionalist Latin American approach to international law, one

[3] Arnulf Becker Lorca, *Mestizo International Law: A Global Intellectual History, 1842-1933* (Cambridge: Cambridge University Press, 2014), 305–352; Juan Pablo Scarfi, *The Hidden History of International Law in the Americas: Empire and Legal Networks* (Oxford: Oxford University Press, 2017), 147–174. It is worth mentioning that in this chapter, I offer a slightly different exploration of the Montevideo Convention and the politics of international law in Latin America from that of my previous work.

[4] Juan Pablo Scarfi, "Mexican Revolutionary Constituencies and the Latin American Critique of US Intervention," in *Revolutions in International Law: The Legacies of 1917*, ed. Anne Orford et al. (Oxford: Oxford University Press, 2021), 218–241; Juan Pablo Scarfi, "Denaturalizing the Monroe Doctrine: The Rise of Latin American Legal Anti-imperialism in the Face of the Modern

founded on a pluralist and political awareness of the limitations of international law for moderating great power politics. These two opposing American and Latin American approaches to international law clashed with one another in the context of the Rio de Janeiro Commission of Jurists of 1927 and the Sixth Pan-American Conference held in Havana in 1928. These clashes stimulated a Latin American politicization of international law at Rio de Janeiro, Havana, and the Montevideo Convention.

Finally, the chapter also argues that the Montevideo Convention led to a rather paradoxical contribution of Latin America to the Liberal International Order (LIO) of 1945. It created the grounds for the formation of the LIO by advancing essentially nonliberal and anti-interventionist principles. It incepted globally in the United Nations Charter, particularly Articles 2(7) and 2(4), the principles of absolute nonintervention, statehood, and sovereign equality, moderating US liberal imperialism and interventionism. It made the LIO and the Bretton Woods System less liberal and consolidated the principle of the rights and duties of states, according to which great powers, in particular the United States, committed themselves to limit their liberal interventionist practices across the region.[5] The idea that great powers have duties to small states was a direct product, so this chapter argues, of the Latin American politicization of international law around a debate over interventions, especially US interventionism in the region.[6]

II. Early Latin American Initiatives for Consolidating the Principles of Nonintervention and Sovereign Equality

Latin American advocacy for the principle of nonintervention can be traced back to the work of foundational figures in the field of international law in the region since the early nineteenth century. For instance, Andrés Bello, the author of the first important treatise on international law published in Latin America (1832), proved to be a firm advocate of nonintervention. He sharply denounced the recourse to interventions in international affairs.[7] Similarly, Carlos Calvo, and the

US and Hemispheric Redefinition of the Monroe Doctrine," *Leiden Journal of International Law* 33 (2020): 541–555.

[5] Christy Thornton, "A Mexican International Economic Order? Tracing the Hidden Roots of the Charter of Economic Rights and Duties of States," *Humanity: An International Journal of Human Rights, Humanitarianism, and Development* 9, no. 3 (2018): 389–421.

[6] Juan Pablo Scarfi, "The Latin American Politics *of* International Law: Latin American Countries' Engagements *with* International Law *and* Their Contradictory Impact *on the* Liberal International Order," *Cambridge Review of International Affairs* 35, no. 5 (2022): 662–679.

[7] Andrés Bello, *Principios de Derecho Internacional* (Santiago: Imprenta de la Opinión, 1832). On Bello's advocacy of nonintervention, see Louise Fawcett, "Between West and non-West: Latin American Contributions to International Thought," *The International History Review* 34,

so-called Calvo Doctrine in particular, contributed to consolidating the principle of nonintervention as a basic standard for the region by the mid-nineteenth century. As originally formulated by Calvo, the Calvo Doctrine postulated that foreign citizens had to submit their claims to local courts since aliens should not be allowed to have more protection than domestic creditors.[8] In its standard formulation, the doctrine stated that states have rights to independence, sovereignty, and territorial integrity and thus they should not be exposed to any form of interference or intervention by other states.[9]

Yet by the early twentieth century, Latin American diplomats and jurists began to adopt a more concrete critical posture regarding European and US military interventions in the region, as well as to take a more active role in international and continental conferences, especially following the formation of the Pan-American movement and conferences. They generated, in turn, a major shift in standard beliefs about norms and eventually the progressive "legalization of diplomacy" and the adoption of a "legalist approach to international relations" in favor of the principle of nonintervention.[10] In this sense, the Drago Doctrine, formulated as a direct response to the 1902 blockade of Venezuela by Great Britain, Germany, and Italy for collecting public debts, was an important turning point regarding the rise of a Latin American legal anti-interventionist approach. Drawing on the precedent of the Calvo Doctrine and in a clear attempt to constrain European interventions in Latin America, the Argentine Minister of Foreign Affairs, Luis María Drago, sent a note to the Argentine minister in Washington, DC, Martín García Mérou, affirming categorically the basic principles of what later become known as the Drago Doctrine. He asserted: "In a word, the principle which [the Argentine Republic] would like to see recognized is: that the public debt cannot occasion armed intervention nor even the actual occupation of the territory of American nations by a European power."[11] The Drago Doctrine was originally articulated as a corollary of the Monroe Doctrine to the extent that Martín García Mérou regarded Drago's statement as "the first acknowledgment and acceptance of the Monroe Doctrine 'as a

no. 4 (2012): 679–704; and Isidro Fabela, *Intervención* (Mexico: Universidad Nacional Autónoma de México, 1959), 136.

[8] Carlos Calvo, *Derecho internactonal teórico y práctico de Europa y América* (Paris: D'Amyot, 1868).

[9] Francis Anthony Boyle, *Foundations of World Order: The Legalist Approach to International Relations, 1898-1922* (Durham, NC: Duke University Press, 1999), 109. See also Manuel R. Garcia-Mora, "The Calvo Clause in Latin American Constitutions and International Law," *Marquette Law Review* 33, no. 4 (1950): 205–219.

[10] Martha Finnemore, *The Purpose of Intervention: Changing Beliefs about the Use of Force* (Ithaca, NY: Cornell University Press, 2003), 24–51; Boyle, *Foundations*.

[11] Luis M. Drago, "Argentine Republic: Ministry of Foreign Relations and Worship," *American Journal of International Law* 1, no.1 (Supplement: Official Documents, 1907): 1–6.

principle of American public law by a nation of South America.'"[12] While the Monroe Doctrine (1823) epitomizes in its original formulation a synthesis between anticolonialism and US paternalism over Latin America, Drago sought to stress its former condition, drawing on the Monroe Doctrine as an anticolonial principle of absolute nonintervention in the Americas. However, he reframed it as a multilateral principle to be invoked by any country of the Americas, especially to protect weak countries of the region from powerful European nations when public debts were involved. Since it was formulated as a "Pan-American principle of inter-continental diplomacy" condemning interventions, the Pan-American conferences were, according to Drago, the ideal setting for debating the basic tenets of his doctrine.[13]

Eventually, the Drago Doctrine became a subject of debate at the Third Pan-American Conference of 1906 held in Rio de Janeiro, but it was debated more fervently in the context of the Second Hague Peace Conference of 1907. The Pan-American movement emerged in the United States in the 1880s and 1890s under the impulse of Secretary of State James Blaine as a US-led policy of economic, political, legal, and intellectual cooperation toward Latin America.[14] It has been regarded as a US-led movement of both hegemony and cooperation and "the friendly face of US dominance in the hemisphere,"[15] but pan-Americanism, above all, "played a central and lasting role in structuring inter-American relations."[16] Secretary of State Elihu Root contributed to giving a new impulse to the Pan-American movement along the lines of the promotion of peace and legal diplomacy. In this context, he visited South America, interacted with many jurists and diplomats from the region, including Drago and the Brazilian jurist and politician Ruy Barbosa, and thus became the main protagonist of the Third Pan-American Conference held in Rio de Janeiro in 1906.

[12] United States, *Papers Relating to the Foreign Relations of the United States* (Washington, DC: Government Printing Office, 1903), 1–6, quoted in David Sheinin, *Argentina and the United States: An Alliance Contained* (Atlanta: University of Georgia Press, 2006), 31; Arthur P. Whitaker, *The Western Hemisphere Idea: Its Rise and Decline* (London: Sothis Press, 1954), 88.

[13] Ernesto Quesada, "La doctrina Drago: su esencia y concepto amplio," *Revista de la Universidad de Buenos Aires* 43 (1919): 355.

[14] See David Healy, *James G. Blaine and Latin America* (Columbia: University of Missouri Press, 2001).

[15] David Sheinin, "Rethinking Pan Americanism: An Introduction," in *Beyond the Ideal: Pan Americanism in Inter-American Affairs*, ed. David Sheinin (New York: Praeger, 2000), 1; Juan Pablo Scarfi and Andrew Tillman, "Cooperation and Hegemony in US-Latin American Relations: An Introduction," in *Cooperation and Hegemony in US– Latin American Relations: Revisiting the Western Hemisphere Idea*, ed. Juan Pablo Scarfi and Andrew Tillman (New York: Palgrave Macmillan US, 2016,1–20).

[16] Juan Pablo Scarfi and David Sheinin, "Introduction: The Pan-American Shift from Apology for Empire to Imperial Critique to Latin American Agency," in *The New Pan-Americanism and the Structuring of Inter-American Relations*, ed. Juan Pablo Scarfi and David Sheinin (New York: Routledge, 2022), 2.

Root made a strategic move for renovating the Pan-American movement, especially securing seats for the Latin American delegations at the Second Hague Peace Conference (1907), since most of the states of the region had not been represented at the First Hague Peace Conference (1899). In the context of the Third Pan-American Conference and Root's reception in Argentina and Brazil, Barbosa and Drago regarded the United States as a "perfect model" and its republican constitution and the federal union as "our examples" for South American nations.[17]

In Root´s Banquet at the Opera House in Argentina, Drago reasserted the defense of his doctrine as a continental "principle of American diplomacy."[18] Root responded by supporting the Drago Doctrine and acknowledging explicitly that "the United States of America has never deemed it to be suitable that she use her army and navy for collection of ordinary contract debts of foreign governments to her citizens."[19] Yet the Drago Doctrine was only discussed formally in its full length in the context of the Second Hague Peace Conference where Drago represented the Argentine delegation and sought to maintain the basic tenets of his doctrine as a principle of absolute nonintervention. Yet the US delegation, under the instructions of Root and represented by Scott as a technical delegate, redefined the basic tenets of the Drago Doctrine through the Porter Convention. According to this latter convention, when recourse to arbitration is unsuccessful, the creditor maintains the right to take military action against the debtor country and may thus intervene. This resort to arbitration contradicted the principle of absolute nonintervention originally outlined by Drago. In his formal instructions to the US delegates, prepared in collaboration with Scott, Root stressed that the use of force for the collection of public debts "is not permissible until after" the claim has been arbitrated.[20] Root thus did not support the principle of absolute nonintervention and contributed in turn to denaturalizing the Drago Doctrine.[21] As is well-known, it was finally reframed under the lines of the Porter Convention.

The principle of sovereign equality was also discussed ardently at the Second Hague Peace Conference, and Barbosa was its most firm advocate in

[17] Juan Pablo Scarfi, *El imperio de la ley: James Brown Scott y la construcción de un orden jurídico interamericano* (Buenos Aires: Fondo de Cultura Económica, 2014), 64–66.

[18] "Speech of Dr. Luis M. Drago, President of the Reception Committee (Buenos Aires, August 17, 1906)," in *Latin America and the United States. Addresses by Elihu Root*, ed. Robert Bacon and James Brown Scott (Sydney, Australia: Wentworth Press, 1917), 96.

[19] "Reply of Mr. Root, (Buenos Aires, August 17, 1906)," in Bacon and Scott, *Latin America and the United States*, 98.

[20] Elihu Root, "Instructions to the American delegates to the Hague Peace Conferences," Department of State, Washington, DC, May 31, 1907, in *Instructions to the American Delegates to the Hague Peace Conferences and Their Official Reports*, ed. James Brown Scott, 76–77 (1916).

[21] For an analysis of the denaturalization of the Drago Doctrine, see Scarfi, *Hidden History*, 73–74.

Latin America. Indeed, he became known later as "the Eagle of the Hague."[22] Barbosa's advocacy for sovereign equality emerged as a direct reaction to the US delegation's proposal to create a permanent world court to solve international conflicts through legal means. Root and Scott envisioned the creation of a permanent judicial court composed of judges as an ideal replacement for the Permanent Court of Arbitration. The US delegation, led by Scott, prepared a project, in alliance with the British and German delegations, for an international judicial court comprising judges appointed in proportion to the population and wealth of each nation. They conceived the project as "the result of the conscientious work of three great Powers."[23]

Scott drafted the US proposal for a proportional rotation in the court's composition based on each nation's wealth and population. At The Hague, Scott sought to combine a rather formal attachment to the principle of sovereign equality with a hegemonic posture in favor of tracing distinctions regarding material interests between great powers and small states. He was convinced that the population and wealth of each nation were a direct manifestation of the size and importance of the businesses involved, and that when more businesses were at stake, the chance of affecting the material interests of states increased. According to Scott, great powers had more material interests involved and thus should have more representation and a much greater number of judges within the proposed court than small states. By contrast, Barbosa contended that each country, regardless of its power and the material interests involved, should have equal representation in the projected international judicial court, rejecting any distinctions between great powers and small states. Interestingly, when condemning the US proposal for a world court, drafted by Root and Scott as a nonegalitarian project, Barbosa drew on the formal defense of sovereign equality, originally delivered by Root at the Rio de Janeiro Pan-American Conference in 1906. Root famously asserted: "We deem the independence and equal rights of the smallest and weakest member of the family of nations entitled to as much respect as those of the greatest empire; and we deem the observance of that respect the chief guaranty of the weak against the oppression of the strong."[24] As Gerry Simpson has observed, the approach of Scott and Root associated with "pragmatic institution building" proved to be more appealing than the "doctrinaire

[22] Becker Lorca, *Mestizo*, 160; Gerry Simpson, *Great Powers and Outlaw States: Unequal Sovereigns in the International Legal Order* (Cambridge: Cambridge University Press, 2004), 132–164.

[23] This was the expression used by Edward Fry, member of the British delegation. See James Brown Scott, ed., *The Proceedings of the Hague Peace Conferences*, Vol. 2 (New York: Oxford University Press, 1920), 597.

[24] Elihu Root, "Speech of the Secretary of State, Honorary President of the Conference at the Third Conference of the American States" (Rio de Janeiro, July 31, 1906), in Bacon and Scott, *Latin America and the United States*, 10.

legalism" of Barbosa, for most jurists in the following three decades after the Second Hague Peace Conference tended to regard the construction of international legal institutions for the progressive development of international law as far more relevant than defending the principle of sovereign equality in the strict sense, as Barbosa did. In the end, the US delegation failed to get its project to create an international judicial court approved. Overall, the Second Hague Peace Conference offered a unique platform for the progressive consolidation of Latin American nations in international society, thus increasing their global status, as well as the discussion of regional aspirations, such as sovereign equality and nonintervention as epitomized in the Drago Doctrine.[25]

An important institutional and disciplinary impulse in favor of the consolidation of the principles of nonintervention and sovereign equality was introduced through the creation of Pan-American legal institutions, including the American Institute of International Law (AIIL), created in 1912, which prompted Latin American jurists to promote the codification of these principles and other regional legal aspirations as proper continental legal doctrines. The expansion of the Pan-American movement across the Americas motivated Scott and Alejandro Álvarez to envision and project the creation of a hemispheric legal organization to foster the adoption and codification of continental legal principles of "American international law." Álvarez became the most prominent advocate of American international law in the twentieth century. He drew an important distinction between the European legal tradition, centered on the notions of the balance of power, imperial competition, monarchism, and intervention, and an "American international law" based instead on the premises of continental solidarity, state independence, republicanism, and nonintervention.[26]

In 1911, Álvarez and Scott sent a letter to Root to draw on his support for this project, and they were explicit about the need to create a code of American international law for the Americas. They stated that "the American Institute should hold at Washington the first of its periodic meetings to discuss scientific questions of international law, especially those related to peace, so that little by little a code of international law might be drafted which should represent the enlightened thought of American publicists and be the result of their sympathetic collaboration."[27] In the context of the first institutional meeting of the AIIL held in 1915 in Washington, Scott prepared a Declaration of the Rights and Duties of

[25] Carsten Schultz, "Accidental Activists: Latin American Status-Seeking at the Hague," *International Studies Quarterly* 61, no. 3 (2017): 612–622.

[26] Alejandro Álvarez, *Le droit international américain: son fondement, sa nature* (1910).

[27] James Brown Scott and Alejandro Álvarez to Elihu Root, Washington, DC, June 3, 1911, quoted in James Brown Scott, "The Gradual and Progressive Codification of International Law," *American Journal of International Law* 21, no. 3 (1927): 417–450.

Nations.[28] In the second formal meeting of the AIIL, Álvarez drafted some preliminary projects for the codification of American international law.[29] The final version of these initial projects was completed by Álvarez in 1923 and later revised by the AIIL. They included important references to the principles of nonintervention and sovereign equality.

Yet Álvarez adopted a relatively moderate version of the principle of nonintervention based on a solidarist legal perspective, generating some scope for interference in exceptional circumstances when the rights of individuals or the collective interests of the international community were at stake.[30] He sought to grant the protection of the rights of individuals, advocating pioneering notions of human rights.[31] Álvarez proposed a moderate twist and thus departed from the approaches of Calvo and Drago to absolute nonintervention. Regarding the principle of nonintervention, the project prepared by Álvarez stated: "No State may intervene in the external or internal affairs of another American State, against its own will. The only interference that these could exert is amicable and conciliatory, without any character of imposition."[32] In regard to the principle of sovereign equality, it read:

> The states of the American continent, equal before the law, possess acquired rights to their complete independence, liberty, and sovereignty. These rights, as much as those they have over their territories, cannot be limited by any form in benefit of an extra-continental state, even if they count with the will and support of any American state.[33]

Álvarez saw sovereign equality and nonintervention, even in a moderate version, as two mutually interconnected principles. This project was revised by the AIIL and presented before the Pan-American Union to be discussed in the Rio de Janeiro Commission of Jurists of 1927 and the Sixth Pan-American Conference held in Havana in 1928. All in all, the principles of nonintervention and sovereign equality proved to be at the heart of the concerns of the leaders of the AIIL.

[28] James Brown Scott, *The American Institute of International Law: Its Declaration of Rights and Duties of Nations* (1916), 88.

[29] See Alejandro Álvarez, "Derechos fundamentales de los Estados," in *Actas, memorias y proyectos de las sesiones de la Habana (Segunda reunión del Instituto) 22 a 27 de enero de 1917,* ed. Instituto Americano de Derecho Internacional (New York: Oxford University Press, 1918), 378–390.

[30] See Stephen Neff, *Justice Among Nations: A History of International Law* (Cambridge, MA: Harvard University Press, 2014), 285–297.

[31] See Juan Pablo Scarfi, "Pan-American Human Rights: The Legacy of Pan-Americanism and the Intellectual Origins of the Inter-American Human Rights System," in Scarfi and Sheinin, *The New Pan-Americanism*, 138–162

[32] Alejandro Álvarez, *La codificación del derecho internacional en América: trabajos de la tercera Comisión de la Asamblea de Jurisconsultos reunida en Santiago de Chile* (1923), 98.

[33] Ibid., 98.

III. The Mexican Constitution of 1917 and the Consolidation of a Latin American Legal Anti-Interventionist Approach

The Mexican Revolution and the creation later of the Mexican Constitution of 1917 contributed to the consolidation of an anti-interventionist and defensive legal approach in Mexico, which drew on an existing regional Latin American legal tradition, in particular the Drago and Calvo doctrines. At the same time, they shaped a much broader Latin American legal critique of US interventionism in the 1910s and 1920s. The US intervention in Veracruz in 1914 was an important turning point in the germination of a robust absolute understanding of the principle of nonintervention. As a reaction to US intervention in Mexico, then President of Mexico, Venustiano Carranza, and his Minister of Foreign Affairs, Isidro Fabela, formulated the Carranza Doctrine, which entailed a rejection of the US Monroe Doctrine and the construction of an alternative anti-interventionist principle inspired by Latin American precedents.

The so-called Carranza Doctrine and the legal ideas of Fabela proved to be a source of inspiration for the Mexican Constitution of 1917 and, more importantly, for the reconstruction of the Latin American doctrine of absolute nonintervention. Fabela and Carranza, along with a small group of revisionist jurists, including the Cuban jurist Emilio Roig de Leuchsenring, moved away from the dominant Pan-American understanding of international law advocated by Álvarez, Scott, and the AIIL and adopted instead an anti-imperialist legal sensibility, especially concerned with safeguarding the sovereignty and international status of "weak nations" from power politics and the interventionist attitude of great powers, especially the United States.[34] More importantly, these legal doctrinal reconstructions promoted by Carranza, Fabela and Roig de Leuchsenring anticipated the institutional consolidation in the Montevideo Convention of 1933 of absolute non-intervention as an inter-American multilateral principle.

US intervention in Veracruz in the critical context of the Mexican Revolution in 1914 sought to depose Victoriano Huerta, who Carranza and Fabela considered a rival and traitor to the spirit of the revolution. US President Woodrow Wilson intervened in Mexico to safeguard Mexican sovereignty, but Carranza and Fabela strongly resented the intervention as an intrusion in the internal affairs and territorial and sovereign rights of Mexico. In fact, the Carranza Doctrine emerged largely as a legal and diplomatic defensive response to this US intervention. In this critical juncture, the ABC countries sought to

[34] Scarfi, "Denaturalizing the Monroe Doctrine"; Scarfi, "Mexican Revolutionary Constituencies," 220.

offer a peaceful mediation between the United States and Mexico.[35] Fabela and Carranza regarded even this proposed multilateral solution as an intromission in the internal affairs of Mexico.

Carranza and Fabela originally articulated the Carranza Doctrine between 1915 and 1918, consolidating it as a standard principle of Mexican approach to diplomacy and international law, as well as a new domestic constitutional principle in the years to come. Therefore, it is not a coincidence that the central tenets of the Carranza Doctrine were consolidated in this temporal interregnum and were also incorporated into Article 27 of the new Mexican Constitution. As Fabela himself observed, this famous article of the new constitution consolidated the principles of nonintervention and noninterference of foreign capital and commercial investment, setting sharp limitations for the exploitation of land and properties included in the national jurisdiction of the Mexican state and establishing equal status of foreigners and nationals for the acquisition of lands and properties in Mexico.[36]

In its standard formulation, the Carranza Doctrine was based on five central premises. First, it entailed explicitly rejecting the US Monroe Doctrine, conceived as an arbitrary interventionist principle with no legal value imposed by the United States over Latin American states without their consultation or need, violating their territorial integrity. Second, it established a connection between the principle of absolute nonintervention and sovereign equality, stating that all nations should be equal before the law and respect reciprocally their sovereignty, laws and institutions, "attaching themselves strictly and with no exceptions to the universal principle of non-intervention."[37] Unlike Álvarez who was in favor of collective interventions, Fabela believed that such concessions contributed to creating grounds to legitimize interventions.[38] Third, drawing on the Calvo and Drago doctrines, it stipulated that there should be no distinction between nationals and foreigners, and thus, they "should be equal against the state in which they reside."[39] In this sense, the Carranza Doctrine established, like the Calvo and Drago doctrines, that disputes over the collection of public debts between nationals and foreigners should be settled in national courts.

[35] See Mark T. Gilderhus, *Pan American Visions: Woodrow Wilson in the Western Hemisphere, 1913–1921* (Tuscon: University of Arizona Press, 1986), 37–45; Robert E. Quirk, *An Affair of Honor: Woodrow Wilson and the Occupation of Veracruz* (New York: W. W. Norton, 1964).

[36] *See* Texto original de la Constitución de 1917 y de las reformas publicadas en el Diario Oficial de la Federación del 5 de febrero de 1917 al 1o. de junio de 2009, Biblioteca Jurídica Virtual del Instituto de Investigaciones Jurídicas de la UNAM, 138–139; and Scarfi, "Mexican Revolutionary Constituencies," at 229.

[37] "La Doctrina Carranza," in *Isidro Fabela y la diplomacia mexicana*, ed. Fernando Serrano Migallón (México: Fondo de Cultura Económica, 1981), 192.

[38] Fabela, *Intervención*, 161.

[39] "La Doctrina Carranza," in *Isidro Fabela y la diplomacia mexicana*, ed. Fernando Serrano Migallón (México: Fondo de Cultura Económica, 1981), 192–193.

Fourth, it stressed that state legislation has to be uniform "without establishing distinctions based on nationality."[40] Finally, the fifth premise affirmed that "diplomacy should be based on the general interests of civilization and the establishment of universal confraternity" and thus, "it should not serve to exert pressure over the governments of weak nations, with the aim of obtaining modifications of the laws that are not convenient for the subjects of powerful nations."[41]

Fabela and Cuban jurist and historian Roig de Leuchsenring became fervent critics of US interventionism in Central America and the Caribbean in the late 1910s and 1920s and of the US uses and abuses of the Monroe Doctrine. They believed that the Monroe Doctrine did not have any legal status as a principle of international law, and thus, the US usage of the Monroe Doctrine as an elastic and flexible principle alternatively to promote Pan-American cooperation and legitimize interventions posed a threat to Latin American territorial integrity and sovereignty. Unlike the leaders of the AIIL, who advocated pan-Americanism and American international law, they favored a Latin American anti-interventionist approach to international law.

Roig de Leuchsenring gained prominence in Cuban legal and intellectual circles as a critic of US interventionism in the region and of the most articulated Cuban adversaries of the Platt Amendment, which legitimized, through a bilateral constitutional arrangement, US interventions in Cuba on a regular basis from 1903 to 1934. He was convinced that US interventions and the application of the Monroe Doctrine had been "terrible for the life of the Latin American republics."[42] In 1916, during the US occupation of the Dominican Republic, Roig de Leuchsenring drafted a declaration recommending that the AIIL condemn any interventions in the Americas categorically. It read: "None of the American states has the right nor could exert acts of domination, sovereignty or intervention over another state of the American continent."[43]

Although the AIIL did not adopt the declaration, it offers a testimony of the pioneering political pressure exerted by this group of pluralist Latin American jurists by the 1910s and 1920s for the consolidation of the principle of absolute nonintervention institutionalized later in the Montevideo Convention of 1933. In a similar vein, Fabela devoted an important book to examine empirically and critically US interventions in Central America and the Caribbean, also revisiting the case of US intervention in Veracruz in 1914.[44] It was a pioneering contribution to the incipient discipline of international relations written from the

[40] Ibid., 193.

[41] Ibid., 193.

[42] Emilio Roig de Leuchsenring, *La ocupación de la República Dominicana por los Estados Unidos y el derecho de las pequeñas nacionalidades de América* (La Habana: El Siglo XX, 1919), 63.

[43] Ibid., 64.

[44] Isidro Fabela, *Los Estados Unidos contra la libertad: Estudios de historia diplomática americana* (Barcelona: Talleres Gráficos Lux, 1920).

viewpoint of international law. In the preface, Fabela stated quite explicitly that he was against pan-Americanism and in favor of a Latin American regional approach to international law. He affirmed: "my purpose is to contribute to the formation of the history of North-American imperialism," and these "notes can be useful for the political and diplomatic history of America and the understanding of applied Pan-Americanism."[45]

IV. The Montevideo Convention and Its Impact on the Liberal International Order

As shown in the two previous sections, the Montevideo Convention was the culmination of a long process oriented toward the codification of continental principles of American international law, as promoted by the AIIL, and the consolidation of a radical anti-imperialist legal posture based on robust regional notions of absolute nonintervention, which emerged as a defensive reaction to European and especially US interventions in the region. The codification projects set the grounds for the germination of a continental political and legal debate over the principle of nonintervention. These contrasting legal attitudes and postures clashed at the Rio de Janeiro Commission of Jurists of 1927 and the Sixth Pan-American Conference held in Havana. The Montevideo Convention was the result of the tensions and politicization of international law between the legal projects of Álvarez, Scott, and the leaders of the AIIL and the radical anti-interventionist postures of Fabela and Roig de Leuchsenring who supported fervently instead the principle of absolute nonintervention. At the same time, "The South-American Anti-War Treaty of Non-aggression and Conciliation," proposed by Saavedra Lamas and known as the Saavedra Lamas Anti-War Treaty, provided an anti-interventionist framework, orienting the debates at the Montevideo Convention of 1933.

The debate over intervention at the Rio de Janeiro Commission became controversial among the community of jurists. The Costa Rican jurist Luis Anderson, who was also the Treasurer of the AIIL, took an active role in revising the codification projects and modifying its declaration on nonintervention drafted by Álvarez and promoting the elimination of the first two articles of the AIIL Declaration of the Rights and Duties of Nations drafted by Scott. These declarations were introduced in the original projects prepared by Álvarez, the AIIL, and the Pan-American Union. They were consistent with the spirit of the codification projects, which essentially combined the contradictory principles of nonintervention and the commitment to respect the rights of other nations.

[45] Ibid., 10

Like the moderate approach of Álvarez to nonintervention, the two articles of the AIIL Declaration stipulated a duty of not violating the rights of other nations, generating thus limitations to the sovereignty and independence of states and the principle of nonintervention.

Anderson's new proposal reframed nonintervention as an absolute principle since it stated: "No State could intervene in the internal affairs of another."[46] It was approved in turn with a "burst of applause."[47] The Argentine jurist Carlos Saavedra Lamas, who played a vital role at the Montevideo Convention, was a devoted and absolute supporter of Anderson's proposal.[48] However, Scott expressed his own reservations at Rio de Janeiro concerning the article on nonintervention, affirming that two exceptions had to be made on the grounds of humanitarian concerns and "reasons of humanity," as well as "self-defence."[49] He was in favor of maintaining a certain scope for US humanitarian interventions in Latin America to protect US citizens and properties in the region. The leaders of the AIIL, Scott and Alvarez, oscillated between a solidarist and humanitarian posture to generate a balance between the principle of nonintervention and the respect of the rights of other nations. Scott sought to create grounds for certain forms of humanitarian interventions.

At the Havana Conference, the tensions between advocates of absolute nonintervention and the solidarist and humanitarian posture of the leaders of the AIIL became even more pronounced. They led to the politicization of international law and the question of intervention. In the context of the preparations for the Havana Conference, Fabela sent a letter from Paris to the Latin American delegates, prompting them to condemn US interventions in the region, as well as the basic foundations of the Monroe Doctrine and the Pan-American movement. He addressed the following questions:

> 1) Is it Pan-Americanism compatible with the interventions carried out by the United States in some of the nations of the continent?; 2) What is the meaning and scope of the Monroe Doctrine?; 3) Does the Monroe Doctrine suit and bind the Latin Americans?; 4) Should Pan-Americanism persist or should be replaced by Latin-Americanism?[50]

[46] "International Commission of Jurists (Sessions held at Rio de Janeiro, Brazil, April 18th to May 20th, 1927), Public International Law: Projects to be Submitted for Consideration of the Sixth International Conference of Americas States," *American Journal of International Law* 22, special number (1927): 234–329.

[47] Camilo Barcia Trelles, *Doctrina de Monroe y cooperación internacional* (1931), 698.

[48] *Comisión Internacional de Jurisconsultos Americanos, Reunión de 1927*, Vol. 2 (1927), 98.

[49] Víctor M. Maúrtua, *Páginas diplomáticas: La codificación americana del derecho internacional (Ensayos, proyectos, discursos)* (Lima: Librería e Imprenta Gil, 1940), 364.

[50] Isidro Fabela, "A los señores Delegados Latinoamericanos," in Isidro Fabela, *Los Estados Unidos y la América Latina* (1921-1929)," *Cuadernos Americanos 16* (1955): 7–80.

By contrast, Víctor Maúrtua, who replaced Álvarez as Secretary General of the AIIL, prepared a polemical project, which was sharply resisted by the Latin American delegations for its condescension regarding legitimizing humanitarian interventions to protect US citizens and properties located in the region. Maúrtua sought to reintroduce the references to the articles of the AIIL Declaration of Rights and Duties of Nations into the codification projects, defending certain forms of humanitarian interventions in the name of the principles of solidarity, interdependence, and the interests of international community in a similar spirit to that of Álvarez, Scott, and the leaders of the AIIL. Maúrtua traced a sharp contrast between a "battle formula," associated with a "political gesture" and the principle of nonintervention, and "a juridical formula, frank, serene, expressive of what we estimate it should be the basis of universal international law," as represented by the AIIL Declaration of the Rights and Duties of Nations.[51] At the same time, Maúrtua's approach was in line with that of Scott and the US delegate Charles Evans Hughes, who defended the right to US humanitarian interventions as "a principle of international law."[52] Hughes famously affirmed:

> Now it is a principle of international law that in such case a government is fully justified in taking action—I would call it interposition of a temporary character—for the purpose of protecting the lives and property of its nationals. I could say that is not intervention. One can read in textbooks that that is not intervention. No country should forego its right to protect its citizens.[53]

Maúrtua's project contributed to framing the politicization over the question of intervention as a tension between a political and pluralist posture and a juridical and scientific one since the delegates from Argentina and El Salvador, Honorio Pueyrredón and Gustavo Guerrero, defensively rejected the project, speaking explicitly in the name of a necessary political posture, which proved consistent with that of Fabela, Roig de Leuchsenring, and Saavedra Lamas. In the end, the Havana Conference was a failure since there was no common agreement on the codification projects, and they could not be implemented. More importantly, it was certainly one of the most critical moments in international law and pan-Americanism in the Americas.[54] Yet, although the projects were revised at

[51] Maúrtua, *Páginas diplomáticas*, 119.

[52] Charles Evans Hughes, "Speech at the Last Plenary Session of the Sixth International Conference of American States, Havana, Cuba, 18th February, 1928," in *Report of the Delegates of the United States to the Sixth International Conference of American States* (held at Habana, Cuba, January 16 to February 20, 1928) (Washington, DC: Government Printing Office, 1928), 13–16, 14–15.

[53] Hughes, "Speech," 14–15.

[54] See Scarfi, *Hidden History*, 119–145.

the Montevideo Convention of 1933 in a similar controversial spirit, the debates were not as bellicose and polemical as those of Havana and Rio de Janeiro.

The debates over intervention did not threaten the whole Pan-American machinery and the inter-American system in 1933, in part because Argentine jurist and Minister of Foreign Affairs Carlos Saavedra Lamas was able to set the agenda of the Montevideo Convention beforehand, presenting his South American Anti-War Treaty there as a "fait accompli," and thus framing the discussion along the basic tenets outlined in the treaty.[55] Indeed, Saavedra Lamas presented the Anti-War Treaty before the League of Nations, taking a step back from the Pan American movement and the codification projects advanced by the AIIL in the 1920s. He had criticized US hegemonic leadership in these Pan-American initiatives for the codification of American international law and defended assertively the principle of absolute nonintervention in support of Anderson's proposal at the Rio de Janeiro Commission of Jurists.[56]

Saavedra Lamas played a leading role in the consolidation of the principle of absolute nonintervention and sovereign equality and state autonomy. These aspirations were not only addressed in the Anti-War Treaty, but they were also well-established before 1933, as has been shown, among a set of pluralist and politicized jurists, grouped in the margins from the legal canon and outside the confines of the AIIL and the Pan-American Union. The treaty was originally implemented as a South American Anti-War Treaty in the face of the Chaco War (1932–1935), involving the territorial dispute between Bolivia and Paraguay. It was signed by Argentina, Brazil, Chile, Paraguay, and Uruguay and was open to all the countries of the world. Indeed, the treaty adhered to the principle of absolute nonintervention as a South American doctrine, referencing the Drago Doctrine. In Article 3, it stated: "Contracting States undertake to use their best efforts to maintain peace [and] will bring the influence of public opinion, but in no case resort to intervention, either diplomatic or military."[57]

At the same time, the Anti-War Treaty adopted a pluralist and inclusive South American approach to international law, distinct from of US-led pan-Americanism, for it sought to include the different legal and political traditions of the region and presented itself as both a regional South American and universalist world initiative before the League of Nations. Saavedra Lamas was distrustful of pan-Americanism. He affirmed: "Pan-Americanism certainly represents a vast community regarding the moral unity of the continent, but it

[55] Greg Grandin, "Your Americanism and Mine: Americanism and anti-Americanism in the Americas," *The American Historical Review* 111, no. 4 (2006): 1042–1066.

[56] *See* Carlos Saavedra Lamas, *La crise de la codification et la doctrine argentine du droit international* (Paris: Editions Internationales, 1931).

[57] Carlos Saavedra Lamas, *Tratado Antibélico de no-agresión y de conciliación* (Buenos Aires: Ministerio de Relaciones Exteriores y Culto, República Argentina, 1933), 4.

should also be recognised that it involves something of a bilateral expression of the inevitable differences between the Latin and Anglo-Saxon worlds."[58]

The Montevideo Conference consolidated most of the principles contained in the Anti-War Treaty as inter-American principles, including absolute nonintervention, state autonomy, and independence and sovereign equality, moving away from US-led pan-Americanism.[59] Most Latin American delegations, notably those of Argentina, Cuba, and Mexico, condemned US interventions and supported the principle of absolute nonintervention. More importantly, Latin American jurists were able to press and bind the United States to the principles of nonintervention and sovereign equality and autonomy at the Montevideo Convention, adopting a multilateral and institutional approach based on the reciprocal treatment among states in the Americas.

The multilateral implications of these arrangements and formal recognition of the personality of the state under international law were institutionalized in Articles 4 and 6 of the Convention on the Rights and Duties of States, according to which "the rights of each state do not depend on the power that they have to guarantee its exercise, but upon the simple fact of its existence as a person under international law" and "the recognition of a state merely signifies that the state which recognizes it accepts the personality of the other with all the rights and duties determined by international law."[60] No doubt, Saavedra Lamas himself was the most devoted supporter of absolute nonintervention at Montevideo, since he amplified the scope of Anderson's original proposal presented at Rio de Janeiro, which had condemned interventions in the internal affairs of another state. Saavedra Lamas extended it successfully so that it also included the external affairs of other states. He went as far as to consider nonintervention an authentic right that could not be limited or moderated by any other right. He thus affirmed: "nonintervention is an elemental principle in juridical matters. It does not exist rights against rights. Sovereignty is a right; therefore, how could exist a right against sovereignty?"[61]

The debates over intervention that culminated in the Montevideo Convention contributed to consolidating the principles of absolute nonintervention and sovereign equality and the inter-American multilateral system and defining in turn the institutional feature of the modern multilateral international order associated with the LIO of 1945. By questioning the recourse to interventions, Latin American jurists consolidated not only the principles of nonintervention, inter-American multilateralism, and global modern multilateralism but also the importance of recognition for the constitution of the personality of

[58] Ibid., 14.
[59] Scarfi, *Hidden History*, 137–168; Becker Lorca, *Mestizo*, 337–352.
[60] Séptima Conferencia Internacional Americana, 139.
[61] Ibid., 122–123.

states (statehood) under international law, since their contributions and the Montevideo Convention also shaped the formulation of the UN Charter (1945), especially Articles 2(7) and 2(4).[62] In short, the principles of nonintervention and statehood were extended globally to international institutions beyond the inter-American system.

V. Conclusion: The Montevideo Convention and the Latin American Politics of International Law

The Montevideo Convention was more than a continental platform for the codification and institutionalization of the doctrines of absolute nonintervention, sovereign equality, and state independence and autonomy (statehood) as inter-American multilateral principles. It was above all, as this chapter has shown, the culmination of a long process in the construction of a political understanding of international law and thus Latin American politics of international law, which generated a politicization of these mentioned principles. Moreover, the Montevideo Convention also shaped globally the basic tenets of the so-called LIO and the UN Charter, introducing certain principles, notably absolute nonintervention, to moderate paradoxically US liberal imperialism and the practice of interventionism. It institutionalized the Convention of the Rights and Duties of States according to which great powers, notably the United States, have duties and commitments to small states, limiting their liberal interventionist practices with regard to small Latin American states.

The Montevideo Convention became in turn a platform for discussing the Latin American politics of international law and politicizing international law in the Americas. As such, it was influenced by the quest for institutionalizing the discipline of international law across the continent and creating a continental code of American international law, as well as the quest for consolidating the principle of absolute nonintervention to safeguard weak Latin American countries from great power politics. The idea that the region had a distinct legal and political feature, expressed in the form of American or Latin American international law, gained special prominence following the Montevideo Convention and especially in the 1940s and 1950s, but it adopted progressively the language of inter-American multilateralism.

Finally, the Montevideo Convention, as shown throughout this chapter, had ambivalent roots and complex outcomes, since it was the culmination of a progressive politicization of international law between two opposing legal

[62] See Ian Hurd, *International Organizations: Politics, Law, Practice* (Cambridge: Cambridge University Press, 2018), 48, 73.

approaches, a solidarist and humanitarian posture in favor of American international law, as advocated by the leaders of the AIIL, and a political and pluralist one in defense of Latin American international law, as promoted by Fabela, Roig de Leuhcsenring, and Saavedra Lamas. The convention thus generated a transition from US-led pan-Americanism to inter-American multilateralism. Following the Montevideo Convention, pan-Americanism and American international law could survive only with a new multilateral twist thanks to the tensions generated between these two approaches and the politicization of international law. The new inter-American languages and institutions of the inter-American system that emerged from this process in the 1940s, 1950s, and 1960s were not based on Pan-American or American international law or on Latin American international law, but they adopted instead the form of a new inter-American multilateral legal machinery.

5

Turning International Law against Indigenous Peoples

Arnulf Becker Lorca and Amaya Álvez Marín

I. Introduction

This chapter studies how international law shaped the fortunes of the Indigenous peoples of Latin America. Have international law rules, doctrines, and institutions protected their interests? What role did international law play in the dispossession of their lands? There are good reasons to answer the first question affirmatively. Since the times of the Spanish-Amerindian encounter, thanks to the teachings of Salamanca theologians like Francisco Vitoria and the advocacy of friars like Bartolome de Las Casas, Indigenous peoples were recognized as right-holders under the law of nations.[1] Although the actual impact of legal inclusion on the protection of Indigenous peoples' interests remains under dispute, Salamancan arguments about legal inclusion have been enlisted to identify an international legal tradition that, from colonial to more recent times, has not only recognized Indigenous peoples' rights but also enabled Indigenous activism.[2]

The adoption of Convention No. 169 on Indigenous and Tribal Peoples by the International Laboour Organization (ILO) in 1989 and the passing of the Declaration on the Rights of Indigenous Peoples by the General Assembly of the United Nations in 2007 culminated decades of Indigenous activism, which in the words of James Anaya, a renowned scholar and UN Rapporteur, marked a new era where "indigenous peoples have ceased to be mere objects of the discussion of their rights . . . and have become real participants in an extensive multilateral dialogue."[3] This trend, which has seen Indigenous peoples become

[1] The literature is enormous. For one example of twentieth-century Spanish scholarship reproducing the idea that Salamanca stood up for the rights of Indigenous people, see Luciano Pereña, *1920-2007. La idea de justicia en la conquista de América* (Madrid: Editorial MAPFRE, 1992).

[2] José Bengoa, *La emergencia indígena en América Latina* (Santiago, Chile: Fondo de Cultura Económica, 2000).

[3] S. James Anaya, *International Human Rights and Indigenous Peoples* (Boston: Aspen, 2009), 45

Arnulf Becker Lorca and Amaya Álvez Marín, *Turning International Law against Indigenous Peoples*
In: *Latin American International Law in the Twenty-First Century*. Edited by: Alejandro Chehtman, Alexandra Huneeus, and Sergio Puig, Oxford University Press.
DOI: 10.1093/9780197754016.003.0005

influential political actors on the national and international planes, has been powerful in Latin America.

Historian José Bengoa characterized this trend as the Indigenous irruption in Latin America.[4] One of the peculiarities of the irruption is that an ethnic discourse demanding new spaces of cultural and political autonomy has been pursued through the means of law. Bengoa sees the Indigenous cause as having merged with the struggle over the recognition of rights in a sort of "legal reconquest." "The question is clear," Bengoa affirms, "indigenous peoples exist in Latin America and have rights. Rather, they are acquiring or conquering them little by little. We are witnessing today a sort of conquest in reverse."[5] With the passing of the American Declaration of Indigenous Rights in 2016, this regional trend has only strengthened.

What about the question regarding Indigenous dispossession? If international law has been on the side of Indigenous peoples, did dispossession result from the law's frailty? When justice faces the hard realities of political and economic interest, it is tempting to vindicate the law that granted inclusion to Indigenous peoples and recognized their rights. This chapter challenges conventional wisdom, reassessing traditional answers to both questions and showing that the dispossession of Indigenous peoples happened within the law rather than as an abuse or violation of the law.

Indigenous rights advocates understand the late twentieth-century recognition of Indigenous rights to have brought international law back to its natural law origins, to the Spanish-Amerindian encounter, when the law of peoples defended Indigenous from the abuses by *conquistadores*. That is, even advocates seem to recognize that between the early nineteenth-century independence and the "Indigenous irruption" in the 1990s, international law was implicated in the dispossession of Indigenous peoples. During the nineteenth century, when a natural law-based law of peoples was replaced by a positivist international law that recognized legal subjectivity according to a standard of civilization, Indigenous peoples were excluded from the international community governed by law. This may indicate that exclusion was articulated not locally but internationally as a matter of legal doctrine. Or, more specifically, exclusion was articulated in Europe, where nineteenth-century international legal thought—and the standard of civilization—originated.

This chapter shows something different. It shows Latin American lawyers and publicists themselves "turning international against indigenous peoples." Latin American elites not only appropriated and reinterpreted international law doctrines to effect Indigenous dispossession, invoking, for example,

[4] Bengoa, *La emergencia indígena*.
[5] Ibid., 11

civilizational differences between Indigenous and local elites to render the former's land vacant and thus open to occupation by the new republics. They also invented legal doctrine to dispossess Indigenous peoples by way of inclusion in the law of the newly independent states. *Uti possidetis* is usually remembered as the international legal doctrine that emerged in the region to prevent conflicts between the new republics by recognizing colonial administrative boundaries as the boundaries between the new states. However, *uti possidetis* also introduced a legal fiction central to Indigenous dispossession. The fiction implied that the new republics of Spanish America occupied the whole extension of the territories inherited from colonial Spain, transforming Indigenous lands into state territory and Indigenous peoples into individuals entitled to citizenship, subjects of the laws of the Republic, and subject to its enforcement.[6]

We argue that this nineteenth-century pattern of dispossession by way of inclusion of the Indigenous within the law has continued structuring relations between Latin American states and Indigenous peoples until today. If including Indigenous peoples within domestic law, thus excluding them as international legal subjects, defines the nineteenth-century legal structure, in the twentieth century (until before the 1990s), Latin American international lawyers prevented potential change emerging from new international legal doctrines and institutions that could bestow Indigenous rights. We show that during the interwar period, the possible definition of Indigenous peoples as minorities subject to minority-treaty protections was considered by the League of Nations and strongly rejected by Latin American delegates. Then, we briefly show that in the post-1945 international order, as the right to self-determination crystalized, the potential inclusion of Indigenous peoples as peoples entitled to external self-determination was considered and ruled out by Latin Americans.

This chapter shows how international law has structured and justified the dispossession of Indigenous peoples in Latin America. But this is not the international law in the treatises written by the region's main authors. Neither the treatise by Andres Bello nor the one by Carlos Calvo explicitly justified the dispossession of Indigenous peoples as savages (see section VI.). Instead, the nineteenth-century international law we uncover is one where Bello and Calvo, as well as Europeans like the renowned Swiss diplomat Emer Vattel, are invoked by local politicians and publicists during debates about the treatment of Indigenous peoples.

This chapter examines *La cuestión de Arauco* (the Araucanian Question) as one concrete example—in Chile and in relation to one Indigenous people, the

[6] Marta Lorente Sariñena, "Uti possidetis, ita domini eritis. International Law and the Historiography of the Territory," in *Spatial and Temporal Dimensions for Legal History: Research Experiences and Itineraries*, vol. 6, ed. Massimo Meccarelli and María Julia Solla Sastre (Frankfurt am Main, Germany: Max Planck Institute for Legal History and Legal Theory, 2016), 131–172.

Mapuche—of the debates that in the nineteenth century justified Indigenous dispossession. Then, we will see twentieth-century Latin American international lawyers and diplomats defending the nineteenth-century interpretations of international law against Indigenous peoples' interests, arguing away the potential recognition of Indigenous peoples' rights as minority rights or as a right to self-determination. Did the "indigenous irruption in Latin America" during the 1990s break the historical continuities suggested in this chapter, the continuities of local publicists turning against Indigenous peoples?

We do not know. However, we know that Indigenous dispossession and subordination have been, in part, a (by)-product of the Latin American international law tradition. Therefore, confronting our regional legal tradition is the only way to understand how our predecessors turned international law against Indigenous peoples.[7] This chapter only begins this larger task.

II. *La cuestión de Arauco*

What is *la cuestión de Arauco*?—asked liberal congressman Benjamín Vicuña Mackenna in the 1868 parliamentary debates in Chile. It is a "great ghost, a bloody ghost" that has deceived us for generations—Vicuña Mackenna answered.[8] Araucanians—the congressman continued—are not the "imaginary race of mythological heroes" depicted in *La Araucana*, Alonso de Ercilla's sixteenth-century epic poem, where *Araucanos* resisted and never surrendered to the Spaniards.[9] Rather, "the Indians for whom the law and laws—*el derecho* y *la ley*—are so much invoked here are nothing . . . but bandits and highwaymen—*bandidos y salteadores de caminos*."[10] If they were never defeated it is because of Spaniards' "shameful mistake" not to continue the military offensive against them, when, influenced by a "delusional Jesuit's" idea to establish missions, Spain decided to pursue only a defensive war. It is time to change this three-centuries-long mistake, waging war against the barbarians—Vicuña Mackenna argued famously, crying out: "*delenda Arauco.*"[11]

[7] Another way to confront these darker legacies of our tradition is examining Indigenous resistance through international legal discourse throughout the periods explored here. We have engaged in that type of work elsewhere.

[8] Congreso Nacional de Chile, *Cámara de Diputados, Décimoquinto período legislativo, 1868*, 560.

[9] Alonso de Ercilla, *La Araucana* (Santiago, Chile: Pehuén Editores, 2001).

[10] Congreso Nacional de Chile, *Cámara de*, 563. The use of this expression was not innocent, as *saltadearoes de caminos* became a synonym for political enemies, when the laws criminalizing highwaymen were used to tackle constitutional emergencies in the absence of constitutional exceptions in the nineteenth-century liberal constitutions of Spain and Mexico. See José Antonio Aguilar, *En pos de la quimera: reflexiones sobre el experimento constitucional atlántico* (1st ed., México City: Fondo De Cultura Económica, 2000), 40.

[11] Congreso Nacional de Chile, *Cámara de Diputados*, 584.

Erecting himself as the Chilean Cato the Elder, Vicuña Mackenna evoked the Roman soldier and senator who repeatedly, after the end of each session of the Roman Senate, exhorted not just to invade but to conquer and annihilate the Carthaginian enemy, shouting: "*Carthago delenda est*"—Carthage must be destroyed.[12] The borrowing of this expression reflects Vicuña Mackenna's effort to elevate the *Arauco* question beyond local particularities, combining cultural stereotypes and anti-indigenous attitudes of the second half of the nineteenth century with legal arguments belonging to the law of peoples.

Taking sides with Rome, Vicuña Mackenna could cling to the Western tradition and inscribe the military campaign against the *Mapuche* in what was perceived as the larger conflict between civilization and barbarism.[13] Perceiving the Araucanian question as not a uniquely Chilean problem partly explains the relevance that the law of peoples acquired during parliamentary debates. "The problem of how to occupy territories inhabited by savages exists in all the countries of the Americas" Marcial Martínez, another liberal congressman, remarked.[14] Defining the *Arauco* question in these broader terms, Martínez advises not to follow the solution adopted in North America, where "invading on fire and blood . . . the indigenous race disappears."[15] For Vicuña Mackenna, in contrast, a war waged against the Indigenous peoples in the United States offered a paradigmatic example: "[T]he conquest of the Indian is essentially, as it has been in the United States, the conquest of civilization."[16] For Vicuña Mackenna, fighting for civilization is not only a moral but also a legal imperative: "[A] ccording to the law of nations, the conquest of barbarous, idle and vagabond peoples is perfectly legitimate."[17]

Invoking the law of nations may have seemed to Vicuña Mackenna and others across the region a safe bet to justify the conquest of Indigenous land. Throughout the nineteenth century, not just in Spanish America but globally, international law was reinterpreted to become the law of an international community of civilized nations. Under this emerging positive international legal order, some peoples and nations were understood as incapable of forming a state because they failed to meet a purported standard of civilization. Peoples falling short of

[12] On the appropriation of Cato's phrase by Vicuña Mackenna, see Alejandra Bottinelli Wolleter, "El oro y la sangre que vamos a prodigar. Benjamin Vicuna Mackenna, la ocupación de la Araucaníaa y la inscripcion del imperativo civilizador en el discurso público chileno," in *Historias de Racismo y discriminación en Chile*, ed. Rafael Gaune and Martin Lara (Santiago, Chile: Uqbar Editores, 2009), 105–122.

[13] Carsten-Andreas Schulz, "Civilisation, Barbarism and the Making of Latin America's place in Nineteenth-Century International Society," *Millennium* 42, no. 3 (August 2014): 837–859.

[14] Congreso Nacional de Chile, *Cámara de Diputados*, 557.

[15] Ibid., 557.

[16] Ibid., 565.

[17] Ibid., 610.

the standard were progressively excluded from international law.[18] International lawyers used different markers—religious, cultural, and racial—to sustain the distinction between civilized and non-civilized nations. They developed several legal doctrines to translate the distinction into legal regimes. According to the *terra nullius* doctrine, lands inhabited by Indigenous peoples were understood to be vacant and, therefore, open to legal acquisition by an occupying state.[19] At the same time, according to the *uti possidetis* doctrine, the new republics could lay claim to the whole of the territories inherited from Spain, regardless of actual occupation.[20] *Terra nullius, uti possidetis,* and the standard of civilization enabled Spanish American countries like Chile to dispossess indigenous peoples, like the *Mapuche*, by the force of law.

However, if the standard of civilization reflected nineteenth-century prejudices and preconceptions as well as valid international law, why was it necessary to defend, in long parliamentary sessions, a bill that merely sought to increase military forces in *Arauco*?

The historiography of international law, for a couple of decades now, has offered various accounts of international law's implication in Western colonialism, accounts in which positivism, the standard of civilization, *terra nullius,* and *uti possidetis* marshalled dispossession by excluding Indigenous peoples from international law.[21] There is much about this in Vicuña Mackenna's statement, his anti-Indigenous prejudices not being exceptional but a commonly held view among liberal elites. But in the Chilean parliamentary debates, a different account of the relationship between international law and Indigenous peoples emerges. Elites were divided on the *Arauco* question, some advocating for conquest, most supporting gradual occupation, but all enlisting the law of nations to back their positions. The law of nations that Spanish American lawyers enlisted reflected their ambiguity regarding the place of Indigenous peoples in the new republics. They had to tread carefully with doctrines excluding "savages" that could undermine the claim to sovereignty of their republics.

[18] See regarding Chile Gabriel Cid, "De la Araucanía a Lima: los usos del concepto civilización en la expansión territorial del Estado chileno 1855-1884," *Estudios Ibero-Americanos* 38, no. 2 (2012): 265–283. And see in general Robert A. Williams Jr., *The American Indian in Western Legal Thought: The Discourses of Conquest* (Oxford: Oxford University Press, 1992).

[19] As we will see, *terra nullius* was rarely invoked, and if it was it was mostly asked to establish Indigenous occupation. See Andrew Fitzmaurice, *Sovereignty, Property and Empire, 1500-2000* (Cambridge: Cambridge University Press, 2014).

[20] See Marcelo G. Kohen, *Possession contestée et souveraineté territorial* (Geneva, Switzerland: Graduate Institute Publications, 1997).

[21] In the Latin American context, Liliana Obregón's pioneering work has shown the project of civilization by Creole elites as part of the project of becoming members of the international community. See Liliana Obregón, "Creole Consciousness and International Law in Nineteenth-Century Latin America," in *International Law and Its Others*, ed. Anne Orford (Cambridge: Cambridge University Press, 2006), pp. 247–264; Liliana Obregón, "Carlos Calvo y la profesionalización del Derecho Internacional," *Revista Latinoamericana de Derecho Internacional* 3 (2015): 1–23.

III. Extending Law's Empire into Savage Territory

> "The indigenous territory is undoubtedly under the eminent dominion of the nation, but truth be told, this fact is more a legal fiction than a reality. The authorities of the Republic do not rule in that territory and they serve only as intermediaries between the savages and the civilized nation."[22]

With these words, Marcial Martínez rephrases the *Arauco* question as a question of bringing a legal fiction closer to reality. The legal fiction—*uti possidetis*—is the one affirming that the new republics inherited the administrative boundaries of colonial Spain. What type of power was exercised by the Republic within inherited territories? Here, disagreement begins. Some, such as Martínez, argued that the state had direct or eminent dominion, *dominium directum*, over inherited territories while recognizing that Indigenous peoples had indirect dominion, *dominium utile*, or merely possession over inhabited lands. Others, such as Vicuña Mackenna, assumed inherited territory to be just one seamless territory, regardless of the presence of Indigenous people who, neither having property nor occupying land, inhabited something like a *terra nullius*.

How to breach the gap between reality and fiction was another source of contention. For some, conquest by force was the only way to subdue the "barbarians." For most, however, the question was about the best way to occupy Indigenous territories, not just legally, but respecting "humanity and civilization."[23] That is, civilization both enabled and limited Indigenous dispossession. Gradual occupation, through commerce, missionary education, and land registration, was understood to be a peaceful and humane way to bring about civilization. It did not implicate waging war, but it did not exclude state violence to enforce the law, protect settlers, and punish crimes committed by Indigenous inhabitants, as well as legalized force in the process of land registration, as in the case of expropriation of vacant land. Controversy over Indigenous lands was wide-ranging. Here, we trace only the international legal dimension, identifying three positions adopted in the parliamentary debates: conquest, status quo, and occupation. We explored above the justifications for the conquest of the Mapuche by Mackenna and others; let us now turn to the arguments about the occupation.

[22] Congreso Nacional de Chile, *Cámara de Diputados*, 557.
[23] Ibid., 557.

IV. Status Quo, a Gradual and Civilized Occupation

What is the purpose of the bill—*reducir*—to submit the Indigenous to peace as the preamble states, or—*despojarlos*—despoil them by waging an offensive war, as the text of the bill announces? Manuel Antonio Matta posed this question during the parliamentary debate, pointing at the bill's contradiction to condemn what he saw as conquest. The problem we face is not simply a military problem but a question of "justice and civilization," Matta affirmed.[24] Defending what Vicuña Mackenna condemned as the status quo, Matta argued that keeping the boundary between areas controlled by the Republic and the *Mapuche* would gradually advance civilization while respecting Indigenous rights and the dignity of Chile.[25]

Matta did not dispute that civilization was a criterion justifying the Republic's authority over Indigenous land, nor did he dispute that Chile had direct or eminent dominion over its territory. However, civilization and direct dominion not only enabled but also structured—and to some extent limited—the gradual advance over *Mapuche* territory. Thus, Matta questions whether Chileans were the civilized party in interactions with Araucanians:

> [N]o matter how much it is said that we are civilized, and that they are barbarians, I do not believe we have reason to do what is intended with the Araucanians. And I base this not only on abstract theories of law that set the standard of conduct to which individuals and peoples should be subjected, and that prevent expropriation from being a fair means of acquisition, but also on facts.[26]

Matta disputed that *Mapuches* could be conquered, their property simply expropriated, citing looting, arson, pillaging, and violence by the Chilean army as the relevant facts.[27] Matta then concluded: "[T]here have been times in which Chileans living on the boundary have shown to be more barbarous than the Araucanians, and the army exceeding them."[28] Neither international law nor Andres Bello's treatise authorizes punishment with arson and pillage, Matta responded to the congressmen who had argued so. According to Matta, when discussing reprisals, Bello alludes to these as means to achieve a legitimate war

[24] Ibid., 548.
[25] "Honour and dignity require justice in the imposition of our law to the Araucanians, punishing them if they commit crimes, but not treating them a enemies, destroying their lands and houses." Ibid., 554.
[26] Ibid., 548.
[27] Ibid., 554–555.
[28] Ibid., 555.

objective and promptly obtain peace. Thus, reprisals are not legitimate if the objective is not to secure peace but to punish savage tribes.[29]

Matta shared with Vicuña Mackenna the use of the language of civilization to articulate ideas in line with the classical international law emerging during the second half of the nineteenth century. However, if we consider the standard of civilization as a doctrine with concrete meaning, Matta and Vicuña Mackenna disagreed. On the one hand, Matta constructed civilization as a standard that both enabled and regulated the occupation of Indigenous territory. Preserving the distinction between civilization and barbarism as the difference between Chileans and Indigenous required placing the latter under the protection of Chilean laws and justice. Thus, if Indigenous revolts resulted from provocations by Chilean settlers,[30] the Republic could enforce the law, punishing crime but not waging war against them as enemies.[31] At the same time, we see in Matta continuities with the pre-independence colonial law and pre-classical law of nations. If the colonial boundaries were inherited with the transfer of sovereignty from the Crown to the new republics, under (pre-classical) law of nations, the old distinction between *dominium directum* and *dominium utile* was inherited.

Martínez and Matta invoked this distinction, reassuring that the occupation of Indigenous land was only an exercise of *dominium directum*, bringing the legal fiction of *uti possidetis* closer to reality, but so that Indigenous peoples' property, that is, indirect dominium or *dominium utile*, was not affected. Respecting the requirements of "humanity and civilization," Indigenous property, and life, radical (as opposed to liberal) representatives advocated for a gradual and civilized occupation of *Arauco*.

V. Occupation, with the Force of the Law

Errázuriz, the war minister, defended the bill similarly in relation to *Mapuche* property. The talk about occupation—Errázuriz clarified—extends only to the state's "eminent domain," not to property occupied by Araucanians. Expanding the boundary southward, from the BíoBío to the Malleco rivers, according to a law passed in 1864, the state took control over Indigenous territory. Errázuriz explained that in the new territories, valuable land not occupied by the

[29] Ibid., 555.

[30] "[T]he resistance of the Indians has been nothing more than a legitimate act against the abuse of force." Ibid., 555.

[31] "[N]ot because the assailants wear epaulets [a military uniform's ornamental shoulder piece], do they stop herding Indians, cows, horses and rams without finding ourselves in the case of international law to which the Minister was referring [as justified]." Ibid., 555.

Indigenous, vacant land—*terrenos baldios*—had been acquired.[32] As Indigenous property owners mingled with new owners, with civilized Chileans, civilization was brought to these new territories, Errázuriz concluded.[33]

Progress is under threat by Indigenous resistance—Errázuriz warned, citing Bello: against Indigenous harassment, pillage, and assassination, the war against the savage is legal.[34] If, according to Bello, reprisals are legitimate measures between civilized states—Errázuriz asked—why can't they also justify punishment against savages, who rob and kill our citizens and take captive our spouses and children?[35]

These views of the Executive were further supported by Congressman Saavedra, who, as a military officer, had overseen the occupation plan. The Republic had the duty to protect Chilean inhabitants. But there was also another duty, to secure the territory of the state, for Indigenous uprisings could be used by foreign powers as opportunities to attack the country.[36] This happened during the war against Spain—Saavedra informed his colleagues. At that time, we did not have problems convincing the Araucanians that we intended only to occupy the territory peacefully, as we had helped them before during dire times, as the state would do with any other Chilean family—Saavedra noted, though warning that "we must never forget that the indigenous is always our enemy, that we will not defeat him easily, but through force."[37]

The bill passed. However, neither this nor other laws sanctioned conquest. Instead, submission, the so-called pacification—*pacificación de la araucanía*—came about after a series of punitive campaigns based on the power to enforce the law within Chilean territory—which, one should not forget, as the Chilean authorities admitted, included arson and destruction of *Mapuche* land, pillage, killing of those resisting, and the rape and assassination of children.[38] Indigenous dispossession resulted from these punitive campaigns to subdue rebellious Indigenous and from the transfer of land defined as vacant to settlers as well as the transfer of property owned by Indigenous to settlers-buyers. The point here is not to look at Indigenous dispossession resulting from enforcing the law, to bring civilization gradually and respecting property roghts of Indigenous individuals, as morally better than dispossession defined as the conquest of savages.

[32] Errázuriz was referring to a law passed in 1845 granting vacant land to foreigner settlers. See Myléne Valenzuela and Sergio Oliva, *Recopilación de legislación indígena 1813-2017*, Vol. I (Santiago, Chile: Editorial Librotecnia, 2018), 37.

[33] Congreso Nacional de Chile, *Cámara de Diputados*, 552.

[34] Ibid., 553.

[35] Ibid., 553.

[36] Ibid., 540–550.

[37] Ibid., 540–550.

[38] Joanna Crow, "Histories of Conquest: The Occupation of Araucanía and Its Consequences, 1862–1910," in *The Mapuche in Modern Chile* (Gainsville: University Press of Florida, 2013), 19–50.

The point, instead, is excavating the legal framework that enabled the process of Indigenous peoples' domination. Rather than a European international law imposing indigenous dispossession by means of the standard of civilization, we see local elites, politicians, and lawyers constructing a national legal discourse, a framework of nation-building, which also resulted in a framework of Indigenous domination. International law was only one of the pillars of this legal discourse, the others being constitutional law and private law. For example, *uti possidetis*, domestically, recognized in the constitutions of the new republics, created the fiction of a people exercising sovereignty over a delimited territory; internationally, as a doctrine recognized in Latin American international law, it extended a fiction of colonial law into post-independence law, the fiction that from the Crown to the republics, the sovereign exercised eminent or direct dominium over its entire territory, regardless of the indirect dominium of individuals possessing or owning land, including Indigenous peoples' lands. International law arguments, in conjunction with newly enacted post-independence private law, transformed Indigenous lands held under indirect dominium into individual private property through another fiction that lands not under possession or ownership (under indirect dominium) were "vacant land"; in consequence, lands not only under direct dominium of the state but also under indirect dominium could be transferred by the state to settlers as individual property plots.

This was a potent legal fiction underpinned by a potent nation-building ideology. It took more than a century to slowly realize the fiction and lots of violence to enforce it—if it has ever been fully realized, as Indigenous peoples, like the *Mapuche*, continue to resist the fiction today. The parliamentary debates of the 1860s illustrate one aspect of the dispossession of Indigenous peoples, namely the prevalence of the law-enforcement framework, which resulted from their inclusion as subjects within the territory of the Republic. The opposite trend, the exclusion of the Indigenous as savage, which we also saw in the debates, was carefully handled, for it could undermine the Republic's sovereignty. Let us consider this second aspect by looking at how local international legal thinking placed the Indigenous within international law and the larger nation-building project.

VI. Treading Carefully with Indigenous Peoples

The first international law thinking of the post-independence period was fully immersed in the nation-building project, laying down the doctrinal foundations for the new republics' claim to sovereignty and diplomatic recognition and for the drawing of their territorial boundaries and respect of their autonomy within those boundaries. A long road had to be traveled before these doctrines became rules of international law—culminating in the 1933 Montevideo Convention's inclusion of a formal definition of statehood, declaratory recognition, and non-intervention.[39] The foundations of this project were put down in the nineteenth century by men of letters like Andrés Bello in the mid-century and by Latin-Americans like Carlos Calvo, who, toward the end of the century, participated—as one of the men of 1873—in the formation of the modern discipline of international law.[40]

In laying down the nation's international-legal-building blocks, Bello first, and Calvo later, tread carefully when considering Indigenous people's place in the international legal order —if they were excluded, it could question the sovereignty of the new republics in the areas the Indigenous inhabited. Undoubtedly, the empire of law had to extend to the whole of the new republics' territory. Thus, as an essayist, Bello advocates "contain[ing] the barbarians and extend[ing] the benefits of civilization" to the southern provinces, for incursions and war by *Araucanos* are the natural causes of these provinces' misery.[41] As long as this threat is not removed—Bello argued—capitalists and entrepreneurs will not come to cultivate the land and establish industry. The relative tranquility obtained by force to prevent incursions from our "terrible neighbors, the indigenous," is not enough—Bello maintained, demanding: "more efficient and radical means" to provide safety to capitalist investments.[42]

In contrast, Bello, the international lawyer, was careful not to undermine the sovereignty claims of the new republics on grounds of the presence of "barbarians" within their territory. Explicit articulations of the standard of civilization to define American territories as *terra nullius* were rare in post-independence Spanish America. At the height of the civilizational rhetoric at the end of the nineteenth century, someone like Carlos Calvo does not simply deduce dispossession from the "uncivilized" life of Indigenous peoples.[43] It was

[39] Arnulf Becker Lorca, *Mestizo International Law* (Cambridge: Cambridge University Press, 2014).

[40] Martti Koskenniemi, *The Gentle Civilizer of Nations: The Rise and Fall of International Law 1870–1960* (Cambridge: Cambridge University Press, 2001).

[41] Andrés Bello, "Las Provincias del Sur," in *Obras completas,* Vol. XV (Santiago, Chile: Imprenta Cervantes, 1893), 249.

[42] Ibid., 249, 257. "[A]nother of the country's primary needs . . . consists in the security of the southern provinces, or the acquisition for the Republic of the vast possessions of the Indians which intercept the territory . . .; rendering almost impossible the establishment of frequent communication and of the other means which might be employed to propagate the benefits of a comparatively advanced civilization." Ibid., 248.

[43] Carlos Calvo, *Le droit international théorique et pratique précédé d'un exposé historique des progrès de la science du droit des gens,* Vol. 1 (1896), 207, 209, 408–409. First Calvo recognizes Indigenous possession:

> Where a country that does not belong to any State and is possessed by savage or barbarous peoples, one could recognize the necessary duty to extend the domain of civilization as justifying occupation by a civilized State; however, this cannot be admitted, . . . these barbarians possess their country; they use it as they wish; they make use of it in a way that suits their way of life, and they are not subject to anyone's law. (Ibid., 408)

Bello—decades before at the mid-century—who opened an argumentative path relying less on civilization than on direct dominium to justify the new republics' lawful occupation of Indigenous land. And Bello did so, appropriating Vattel.

Paraphrasing Vattel's famous passages on effective occupation, Bello explained that when a nation finds an uninhabited country without an owner, it can legitimately take possession, but only effective possession and the establishment of settlements sustain a claim to sovereignty and property.[44] Nations whose explorers find monuments erected by other nations as signs of possession pay no attention to these "empty ceremonies," like the Pope's bull conferring dominium over the New World.[45] Accompanying these paragraphs and probably noting the potential danger of Vattel's doctrine to the new republics, Bello adds in a lengthy footnote: "it must be confessed" that in the American continent, some powers have gone beyond Vattel, claiming exclusive rights to acquire land from natives, buying or conquering it from them.[46]

Conversant with universal international law via Vattel, Bello departs from it, by qualifying the view that only effective occupation is a legitimate title. Bello opts for the continuity of colonial law, arguing that the power that discovers or is first to occupy land exercises supremacy or direct dominium recognized by other nations. Invoking direct dominium, Bello can square Indigenous occupation with the rights of a discovering–occupying power that lacks effective occupation. Direct dominium, even under continuous Indigenous occupation, includes an exclusive right opposable to other powers over the claimed territory; it would, therefore, be a hostile aggression —Bello clarified—if a power disturbs the direct dominium of another nation. Moreover, direct dominium gives not only rights to settle disputes with indigenous over land use but also the right to acquire indirect property from the natives, buying it or conquering it.[47]

Then, however, Calvo argues that the state has complete dominion over its whole territory, regardless of actual possession by Indigenous peoples. States of the Americas, for Calvo, claim sovereignty to gradually administer and civilize their territory, allowing European settlers in: When a State is in possession of a country, all that the country contains becomes its property, even if its occupation is only effective over a portion of the country. If it leaves uncultivated or deserted areas, no one has the right to take possession of these areas without its consent. It is in the interest of the possessor state to preserve them for future use, and it is not accountable to anyone for the way in which it uses its property. . . . Such is the particular situation of the United States of North America, Mexico and the States of South America, which possess vast territories still unpopulated or inhabited by Savage tribes. It is understandable that colonization can only be established slowly and gradually in these vast regions, which is why most of the states of the undisputed national domain of which they are a part are making incessant efforts to attract European emigration. (Ibid., 409)

[44] Emer de Vattel, *The Law of Nations,* Book I, Chap. XVIII, §208; Andrés Bello, *Principios de derecho internacional,* chap. 2 (2nd ed., Paris: Librería de Garnier Hermanos, 1864), 32, 40, https://libros.uchile.cl/1103

[45] Bello, *Principios de derecho internacional,* 40–41.

[46] Ibid., 40–41.

[47] Ibid., 40–41.

Are all Indigenous groups and tribes capable of occupying lands? Bello answered again following and then departing from Vattel. "Pastoral tribes," which live wandering within a specific territory, without having divided the property between their members, possess the lands they occupy and, therefore, cannot be dispossessed without injustice.[48] "Wandering tribes," in contrast, are too small to inhabit land effectively. Their "elusive inhabitation"—*vaga habitación*—can pass neither as genuine and legitimate possession nor as a just and rational use of land. Leaving what is necessary for Indigenous subsistence, other men who can effectively use land and settle may occupy it without injustice. After paraphrasing Vattel, Bello once again added a qualification, arguing that the distinction between the two types of tribes, between what is actual possession and just and rational use of land from what is not, is difficult to establish. And here again, Bello turns to a footnote when departing from Vattel by way of quoting the German jurist Theodor Schmalz: "Ownership of land is acquired only by cultivation, because it must be the reward of work . . . Wherever the savage hunter or the nomadic herdsman leads a wandering life, land has no owner, and nothing forbids its cultivation by the industrious settler. By what title would native hordes arrogate to themselves the dominion of a soil they have not wanted to mark with labour?"[49]

Bello's international law textbook offered a legal framework not just to conduct the parliamentary debates of the 1860s in Chile but to respond the Indigenous question in Spanish America: the Republic has direct dominium, Indigenous peoples in principle, have indirect dominium; so when the Republic extends its authority into Indigenous land, their indirect dominium should be respected if considered a pastoral tribe, if they make "just and rational use" of their land, but if they do not, if their "elusive inhabitation" does not count as rational use of land and thus as valid possession, the Republic can solve the Indigenous question by transferring land to settlers and removing those who become an obstacle to bringing civilization as cultivation of land and establishment of industry.

While the Bello of the international law textbook offered a legal framework without mentioning the *Araucanos*, Bello the essayist argued for the latter alternative, calling for more radical and efficient ways to deal with the Indigenous, as Errázuriz quoted Bello in the parliamentary debate, waging war against them as reprisal for their belligerency; or as Saavedra later argued, placing *Araucanos* in reservations, so that they would be assimilated into "*la raza civilizada*" (the civilized race).[50]

[48] Ibid., 40–41.

[49] Ibid., 42, citing Theodor Schmalz, *Droits de Gens Européen*, Book IV, Chap. I (Paris: Chez N. Maze Libraire, 1823).

[50] Cornelio Saavedra, *Documentos relativos a la ocupación de Arauco que contienen los trabajos practicados desde 1861 hasta la fecha* (Santiago, Chile: Imprenta La Libertad, 1870), 15.

This nation-building legal framework, sustaining the domination of Indigenous peoples by advancing the empire of law, which coalesced around the middle of the nineteenth century, arguably has, in its fundamental elements, remained unchanged up to the present. It is worth repeating that we have argued about the rise of this framework as a regional phenomenon but that the process of Indigenous domination and dispossession should be understood in concrete terms in relation to a specific people in relation to a specific Republic. Here, we have only focused on the example of the Chilean state and the *Mapuche*. The story is very different in states where many Indigenous groups have historically coexisted, like Mexico, or Bolivia and Ecuador, which have recently recognized plurinationality in their constitutions. Thus, the argument that the nation-building legal framework continues to structure relations between Latin American states and Indigenous peoples requires a more nuanced and detailed explanation. In what follows, we will only look at two moments in the history of international law where fundamental elements of the nation-building legal framework could have been challenged by the rise of minorities as an international legal regime and in the rise of the right to self-determination. Latin American international lawyers and diplomats excluded Indigenous peoples from the application of the international regime for the protection of minorities during the first half of the twentieth century and from the decolonization regime, namely, the right to self-determination, during the second half of the twentieth century, arguing that Indigenous peoples were not a minority but assimilated citizens and that they were not a people of the type that has a right to self-determination.

VII. Not Minorities, but Assimilated Citizens

The discourse of assimilation of the Indigenous into the nation emerged in Latin America partly as product of the nineteenth-century nation-building framework we have examined. When in the twentieth century, specifically during the interwar period, a system of international protection for minorities emerged in Europe, Latin Americans, invoking assimilation, argued that it did not apply to Indigenous peoples, as they understood them as individual citizens enjoying formal equal rights. While the politics of assimilation could be understood as reflecting a commitment to abstract legal equality between Indigenous and non-Indigenous citizens, though only if the former assimilated to "civilized life," in relation to international lawyers' attitudes, assimilation reflected not only paternalism but also the unremitting prejudices we saw in nineteenth-century internationalists.

At the beginning of the twentieth century, the renowned Chilean jurist Alejandro Álvarez shared the same anti-Indigenous prejudices of most of his predecessors.[51] Highlighting the "amalgamation of races (the aborigines, the whites, and the negroes, together with the creole element)" in colonial Latin America, Álvarez clarifies that it was the "whites . . . although in the minority . . . [who] exercised control and guided a multitude which was in great part illiterate and ignorant."[52] This is why the creole element claimed for itself sovereignty over the entire territory of the independent republics, including unexplored territories and lands that "from time immemorial have been in possession of native tribes," Álvarez argued.[53] We have mentioned in this chapter that *uti possidetis* has been mostly understood as a doctrine that emerged to define the boundaries between the new republics. Álvarez, however, was fully aware of the second dimension we have mentioned regarding indigenous dispossession. Álvarez explains that the "*uti possidetis juris* of 1810" not only meant that the new republics claimed the territory they possessed at the moment of independence but also, adding the expression *juris*, meant that the republics had the right to possess that land, even if occupied by indigenous.[54] That there are no *nullius* territories in the Americas meant that Indigenous possession had no "international value," becoming a matter of internal public law instead of international law.[55]

These views on Indigenous peoples were engrained in the Latin American international law project as it achieved greater formalization during the interwar period, especially in the Montevideo Convention of 1933. Montevideo instituted a formal standard of statehood. A state comes into existence by the conjunction of a polity's formal attributes: territory, population, and government. Montevideo was, in consequence, an essential step toward the weakening of civilization as a standard to recognize international legal personality and, thus, sovereignty. This change arguably made the international community more plural but did not translate into Indigenous autonomy. On the contrary, it increased state pressure to consolidate sovereignty through effective control of territory inhabited by Indigenous peoples, increasing also the incentives for a policy of assimilation.

Latin American international law, as Álvarez explicitly mentioned, rendered the Indigenous question a matter of domestic public law rather than international

[51] See contributions by Arnulf Becker Lorca, Jorge Esquirol, Carl Landauer, Lialiana Obregon, and Katharina Zobel, special issue on life and work of Alejandro Álvarez, *Leiden Journal of International Law* 19, no. 4 (December 2006).

[52] Alejandro Álvarez, "Latin America and International Law," *American Journal of International Law* 3, no. 2 (1909): 271–272. Then, Álvarez describes independence as sparked from the "creole element, the only thinking part of the population." Ibid., 272.

[53] Ibid., 342–343

[54] Alejandro Álvarez, *Rasgos generales de la historia diplomática de Chile (1810-1910). Primera época, la emancipación* (Santiago, Chile: Imprenta Barcelona, 1911), 218–219, 222–223.

[55] Ibid., 342–343. Thus, Latin American states are responsible for the acts of tribes within their territory, even if they do not recognize the sovereignty of the state.

law. Latin American international lawyers and diplomats vigorously defended this arrangement against challenges originating from the emergence of bodies piercing sovereignty in the name of the protection of minorities after the creation of the League of Nations and the International Labor Organization (ILO), mechanisms that could potentially have been relevant for Indigenous peoples.

In the 1930s, the ILO became interested in the social conditions, poverty, and rurality of tribal and Indigenous peoples, including their protection. During the same period, Latin American states, steeped in what they conceived as the modernization of their societies, adopted a policy of assimilation of Indigenous peoples. In this context, the ILO concluded the first conventions for the protection of Indigenous peoples, focused on the regulation of abusive methods of recruiting workers and criminal sanctions for the breach of contract, for example.[56] From this interest in particular problems affecting Indigenous workers, the ILO moved toward a more global perspective on Indigenous issues, a vision of their participation in the national development project. ILO Convention 107, negotiated and signed in the 1950s, embodies a new assimilationist paradigm. Rather than achieving Indigenous autonomy, guaranteeing participation in development under equal rights and protecting Indigenous peoples in the modernization process were the convention's objectives.

The assimilationist paradigm framed the growing interest in Indigenous peoples within domestic law. Even when the international system was strengthened by the creation of intergovernmental organizations, such as the ILO and the League of Nations, and in the Americas, by the consolidation of the system of inter-American conferences and the process of codification of American international law, the Indigenous question was not internationalized, remaining within sovereignty's reserved domain. Latin American international lawyers and diplomats opposed the universal application of the system for the protection of minorities, arguing that the minority protection system should apply only to certain European States by virtue of the Treaty of Versailles, or as a condition of admission to the League of Nations.

In 1925, during the Seventh Assembly of the League of Nations, the Lithuanian delegation raised the issue of the universal application of minority protections. After World War I, during the Paris Conference, endorsement of the nationality principle in creating new states came with the imposition of treaty obligations to protect minority populations. Minority treaties were imposed only on Poland and then, among others, on new Eastern European states applying for League membership. The lack of universality (Germany and Italy, for example, were excluded) meant that the imposition of minority treaties was resented as a sign

[56] See ILO Conventions 50, 64, and 65, only recently abrogated by Report VII (2) 107 OIT meeting, 2018.

of humiliation.[57] This is why the Lithuanian representative argued that only a universally applicable treaty would resolve the violation of the principle of sovereign equality.

Opposition to the Lithuanian proposal came from Europe and Latin America.[58] The Brazilian delegate to the Assembly, Afranio de Mello-Franco, in charge of analyzing the Lithuanian proposal, explained that a general treaty for the protection of minorities would be impossible to apply in the Americas since there were no minorities in the region. The States of the region "had produced in them national organizations in which collective unity is complete."[59]

De Mello-Franco also commented on the Lithuanian proposal's effort to define the concept of minority more precisely. Arguing that minorities included not only racial, linguistic, and religious characteristics but also psychological, social, and historical ones, the Brazilian delegate, referring to the American reality, concluded that "mere coexistence of groups of persons forming racially different collective entities in the territory and under the jurisdiction of a State is not sufficient . . . to recognize . . . a minority requiring protection by the League of Nations."[60]

De Mello-Franco did not explicitly invoke Indigenous peoples, but for an ethnic or racial group to be recognized as a minority, he explicitly demanded the existence of a dispute between nationalities or the transfer of territory from one sovereign to another. The Brazilian delegate explicitly clarified that these circumstances did not exist in the Americas.[61]

This view on the inapplicability of universal protection of minorities was not unique to the Brazilian delegate but common among Latin Americans of the interwar period. For example, the prominent Colombian jurist Jesús María Yepes, writing for the Hague Academy, emphasized the absence in the region of "irreducible rivalries . . . antagonisms of race, language or religion."[62] For Yepes, the political, historical, and social particularities of the region had produced an American international law that not only was concerned with the problem of intervention and state responsibility but also reflected continental solidarity—unlike Europe, interested in the politics of the balance of power and in colonial and minority issues.[63]

[57] Mark Mazower, "Minorities and the League of Nations in Interwar Europe," *Daedalus*, 126, no. 2 (Spring 1997): 52.
[58] League of Nations, 7th General Assembly (1925), Sixth Meeting, *League of Nations Office Journal*, 141.
[59] Ibid., 141.
[60] Ibid., 141.
[61] Ibid., 141.
[62] Jesús María Yepes, "Les problèmes fondamentaux du droit des gens en Amérique," in *Collected Courses of the Hague Academy of International Law*, Vol. 47 (The Hague, The Netherlands: Hague Academy of International Law, 1934), 14.
[63] Ibid., 10–11.

Latin American attitudes regarding minorities responded to a careful analysis of the League of Nations' Mandates regime established by the infamous Article 22 of the Covenant. Article 22 represented a potential danger of intervention for Latin American states. This article established the League of Nations' guardianship over colonies and territories of the losers of the Great War that were "inhabited by peoples not yet able to stand by themselves under the strenuous conditions of the modern world." Mandates, by virtue of their resources and experience, were conferred on "advanced nations" to aid in the "welfare and development" of less developed peoples. Their tutelage—Article 22 clarified—formed a "sacred trust of civilization."

Supervision of Mandates was given to the League's Mandates Commission. Although the Commission operated for colonies and territories that ceased to be under the sovereignty of a state after the war, the reference in Article 22 to guarantees to provide for the welfare and development of the "Indigenous population" could bring potential supervision to Indigenous peoples of the Americas. It was no longer a hypothesis when a delegation sent by a native people, the Iroquois Confederacy represented by Deskaheh, arrived in Geneva with requests for mediation in its dispute with Canada.[64]

These examples of attitudes toward Indigenous peoples by Latin American states and their international lawyers show the shift from the discourse of civilization to modernization. In relation to Indigenous peoples, modernization was articulated as *indigenismo*.[65] From the point of view of *indigenismo*, native peoples were understood less as groups whose ethnic, social, and cultural characteristics separated them from the society that made up the state but as part of society, as vulnerable groups that should be carefully integrated through modernization.

Indigenist ideology entered the Latin American international regime in the 1930s. During the Seventh International American Conference of 1933, held in Montevideo, it was decided to organize the first inter-American Indigenist Congress.[66] The Eighth Conference of 1938, meeting in Lima, reiterated the organization of an Indigenist Congress, adopting a resolution on the protection of indigenous populations.[67] This resolution, contained in the conference's final

[64] See J. Rostowski, "The Redman's Appeal for Justice: Deskaheh and the League of Nations," in *Indians and Europe: An Interdisciplinary Collection of Essays*, ed. Christian F. Feest (Aachen, Germany: Edition Herodot, 1987), 435–453.

[65] Bengoa, *La emergencia indígena en América Latina*, 204–253.

[66] The International Conferences of American States 1933-1940, Seventh Conference, Resolution XCIII, First Supplement (Washington, DC: Carnegie Endowment for International Peace, 1940), 104.

[67] The International Conferences of American States 1933-1940, Eighth Conference, Resolution XIII, American Indigenous Experts Conference (Washington, DC: Carnegie Endowment for International Peace, 1940), 242; and The International Conferences of American States 1933-1940, Eighth Conference, Resolution XI, on the Indigenous population protection (Washington, DC: Carnegie Endowment for International Peace, 1940), 241.

act, defined Indigenous peoples as original peoples: "descendants of the first settlers of the American lands." But also as precarious subjects in need of guardianship, and as populations that have a preferential right to the protection of public authorities to compensate for the "deficiency" of their "physical and intellectual" development.[68] On the other hand, native peoples must be protected so that certain "positive indigenous values" can be preserved in the assimilation process. A policy of "complete integration" will ensure that Indigenous people participate effectively and on an equal footing in the life of the nation.[69]

The Indigenist Congress, which finally took place in April 1940, in Pátzcuaro, Michoacán, Mexico, further elaborated indigenist policies, approving a series of agreements and declarations on Indigenous political and social welfare, land distribution, irrigation, and education policies, among others, and the creation of the Inter-American Indian Institute based in Mexico.[70] The institute advanced indigenist ideology in the region for at least half a century until the breakdown of this paradigm in the 1990s.[71]

Indigenism aligned well with the Latin American diplomatic strategy of neutralizing the international regime for the protection of minorities. The minority regimes devised for Europe post-World War I protected groups not only from physical extermination but also from cultural, religious, or linguistic assimilation. Thus, recognized minorities enjoyed special rights, such as the right to private and public use of their native language and its teaching and to the exercise of religion and other cultural practices. However, it was not only the safeguarding of difference, characteristic of the minority regime, that was incompatible with indigenist assimilationism. The minority regime operated also as a substitute for self-determination.[72]

Minorities were entitled to protection when self-determination, as a principle used to redefine European borders after the World War I, could not apply for political reasons. The principles of self-determination (that each national group should enjoy self-government) and the minority regime (that a non-self-governing national group is protected in its particularities from the dominant national group in which it is embedded) were conceived to solve European problems. Yet, the mere possibility of extending these institutions to

[68] The International Conferences of American States 1933-1940, Eighth Conference, Resolution XI, 241.

[69] Ibid., 241.

[70] Congreso Indigenista Interamericano, *Acta final del Primer Congreso Indigenista Interamericano: celebrado en Patzcuaro, Michoacan, Mexico del 14 al 24 abril de 1940* (Wáshington, DC: Unión Panamericana, 1940).

[71] See Bengoa, *La emergencia indígena en América Latina*, 86–125.

[72] For an example of this idea, see, e.g., Josep L. Kunz, "The Present Status of the International Law for the Protection of Minorities," *American Journal of International Law* 48, no. 2 (1954): 282–287; and in general, see Patrick Macklem, *The Sovereignty of Human Rights* (New York: Oxford University Press, 2015), Chap. 5.

the Americas was understood to represent a great challenge to the autonomy of the states of the region. Thus, the post-1945 foreign policy of Latin American states remained firmly entrenched around preventing self-determination from even being contemplated. That the continuity of this foreign policy was possible, while human rights assumed a central role in the postwar international legal order, responded to the fact that human rights, as universal rights, cohered better with assimilationist indigenism than with a system of minority protection. Neither the United Nations Charter nor the Universal Declaration of Human Rights incorporated minorities as subjects of international protection.[73]

While new mechanisms for limiting and acquiring sovereignty (human rights and the right to self-determination) were emerging in the post-1945 order, Latin Americans reaffirmed the traditional position with respect to Indigenous peoples. As groups made up of individuals under state authority, Indigenous peoples would only be considered subjects of internationally recognized rights insofar as they were considered citizens. For example, during drafting negotiations of the International Covenant on Civil and Political Rights, delegates discussed the minority provision in the Universal Declaration of Human Rights. Latin American diplomats successfully proposed a restrictive definition of minority. The Chilean delegation headed by Humberto Díaz-Casanueva proposed the final wording of Article 27 of the Covenant, which, at the cost of logical inconsistency, left no doubt that the protection of minorities would only apply where minorities exist.[74] This repetitive language in the Chilean proposal was intended to make absolutely clear that Indigenous peoples could not be considered a minority.[75]

In contrast, the Soviet and Yugoslavian delegates proposed recognizing minority rights for individuals and groups belonging to ethnic, religious, or linguistic minorities that went beyond nondiscrimination and included cultural, linguistic, and religious rights and the right to political and economic life.[76] Díaz-Casanueva, the Chilean diplomat, declared sympathy for countries facing minority problems. However, he strongly opposed recognizing minorities without first defining the concept of minority. He equally objected to the inclusion

[73] Francesco Capotorti, *Study on the Rights of Persons Belonging to Ethnic, Religious and Linguistic Minorities* (New York: United Nations, 1991).

[74] Art. 27: "In those States in which ethnic, religious or linguistic minorities exist, persons belonging to such minorities shall not be denied the right, in community with the other members of their group, to enjoy their own culture, to profess and practice their own religion, or to use their own language." On the logically inconsistent wording of the definition of minority, see Timo Makkonen, *Identity, Difference and Otherness: The Concepts of "People," "Indigenous People" and "Minority" in International Law* (Helsinki, Finland: Erik Castrén Institute of International Law and Human Rights, 2000), 84.

[75] Chile, Amendment to the Draft Protection of Minorities. Doc. E/2256, Annex II, Section A III.

[76] United Nations, Economic and Social Council, Commission on Human Rights, Ninth Session, *Summary record of the 368th meeting held at the Palais des Nations* (Geneva, April 30, 1953). Doc. E/CN.4/SR.368, 4–8; Soviet proposal Document E/CN.4/L.222; Yugoslav proposal, Doc. E/CN.4/L.225.

of rights beyond nondiscrimination, since Latin American nations, with a "common language, origin and culture," have not had a minority problem.[77] It was in this context that Diaz-Casanueva thought it could be dangerous to have a general formula that could trigger minority protections in states that have no minorities, thus proposing the mentioned wording in Article 27 that limits protections to "well-established historical minorities," including the redundant expression "in States where minorities exist."[78]

Adopting the assimilationist paradigm during negotiations, Díaz-Casanueva was conscious of excluding indigenous peoples from minority protections in the human rights covenant, for the "young Latin-American countries seek the integration of their national communities."[79] Recognizing minority protections would be against the interest of Latin American states, not only because immigrants could claim special rights, but also because Indigenous peoples could claim minority rights. The Chilean delegate, using Mexico as an example, argued that when preserving their own ways of thinking and their own language, Indigenous groups have remained outside the benefits of modern civilization. It would be pure romanticism to transform Indigenous into minorities.[80] Seconding Díaz-Casanueva, the delegate of the United Kingdom, affirmed that "with the march of the civilizing process, underdeveloped groups will in the course of time be assimilated . . . it would be undesirable for States to be obliged to postpone an inevitable historical process."[81]

The outcome of these debates foreclosed minority protections of Indigenous peoples in Latin America. Opposition to minority rights reflected Latin Americans' fear of weakening national sovereignty. The opposition also reflected their conviction that Indigenous peoples were part of the nation and that, as part of the nation, it reflected the conviction that Indigenous do not form a people in the international law sense of a people with the right to self-determination. To the Latin American international lawyer, a danger had been averted. As Díaz-Casanueva explained, if states would have to guarantee special rights and privileges to minorities, this process would culminate in minorities claiming autonomy within the state.[82]

[77] United Nations, Economic and Social Council, Commission on Human Rights, Ninth Session, *Summary record of the 370th meeting held at the Palais des Nations* (Geneva, May 4, 1953). Doc. E/CN.4/SR.370, 5.

[78] U.N. Doc. E/CN.4/SR.370, 5. Díaz-Casanueva also proposed postponing the discussion of the article until the concept of minority was defined at a later date. This proposal was rejected. See U.N. Doc. E/CN.4/L.261 and Document E/CN.4/SR.371, 4.

[79] U.N. Doc. E/CN.4/SR.368, 10.

[80] Ibid., 10.

[81] U.N. Doc. E/CN.4/SR.369, 5.

[82] U.N. Doc. E/CN.4/SR.368p. 9.

Although international lawyers may have thought they had averted the danger of recognizing Indigenous autonomy while drafting minority rights, the threat resurfaced during deliberations on the right to self-determination. Latin Americans played an important role in the emergence of an international norm recognizing self-determination. However, reproducing the argumentative patterns used to deny minority rights, Latin American international lawyers argued strongly against extending self-determination to Indigenous peoples.[83]

VIII. Conclusion

Latin American men of letters, politicians, international lawyers, and diplomats laid down the legal foundations for Indigenous dispossession. While some argued that the matter was as simple as waging war against "the savage," we have shown that the position that predominated was one considering the expansion of the empire of the law as the justification for using force against Indigenous peoples.

The legal fiction of *uti possidetis* enclosed Indigenous peoples' lands and transformed Indigenous individuals into citizens.[84] The new republics, as we saw in the case of Chile, claimed direct dominium while leaving Indigenous peoples like the *Mapuches* with indirect dominium. When Indigenous peoples resisted, it was through law-enforcing violence that the legal fiction of *uti possidetis* became a reality. Otherwise, direct dominium did not infringe upon Indigenous property. However, if Indigenous lands were not under "just and rational use"—to use Andres Bello's term—lands were considered vacant. Dispossession, in this case, happened again within the law, as lands considered vacant were auctioned or given away to Chilean or foreign settlers bringing "civilization" to *Arauco*.

Has this continuity—between the nation-building framework and the exclusion of minority rights and self-determination—been broken by the "indigenous irruption in Latin America" after the 1990s? One may say so if one considers Indigenous peoples' activism invoking human rights, the ILO Convention, or even the right to self-determination. There is a long history of Indigenous resistance through international law in Spanish America and then Latin America, from Titu Cusi Yupanqui, the Inca who appropriated the law of nations in the

[83] A description of the diplomatic negotiations and the writings of Latin American international lawyers that contributed to the definition of the peoples enjoying a right to self-determination as those subject to colonial rule, excluding Indigenous peoples, goes beyond the limits of this chapter.

[84] In the case of Chile, as early as 1823, the protector of natives, a colonial authority was eliminated as Indigenous were to enjoy the legal rights and protection of citizenship. See Lei N° 10.084 de 10 de junio de 1823. Myléne Valenzuela and Sergio Oliva, *Recopilación de legislación indígena 1813-2017*, Book I, 34 (Santiago, Chile: Editorial Librotecnica, 2018).

sixteenth century, to the Coordinating Council of the Waorani Nationality of Ecuador Pastaza, who recently obtained judicial redress against an oil project for violation of the right to prior consultation.[85]

However, the struggle for Indigenous peoples' rights in general and the *Mapuche,* in particular, continues, as the problem of dispossession is not one of the past. The conflict between Indigenous communities and Latin American states remains, in many cases, unresolved. We have mentioned that demanding greater cultural and political autonomy characterized the Indigenous movement that emerged in the 1990s, and that international law became central to the demand for Indigenous rights. As the conflict remains unresolved and parties become entrenched in their positions and radicalized, the question of Indigenous rights under international law, including greater autonomy and a right to self-determination, looms large. At the same time, the nation-building framework is left potentially challenged. As this chapter focused on how Latin American politicians, diplomats, and international lawyers have turned international law against Indigenous peoples—expanding the law's empire as the project that produced indigenous dispossession—we hope to have offered insight to Indigenous intellectuals, lawyers, and activists who will be writing the next chapters in the history of legal appropriation and interpretation to turn international law toward Indigenous resistance.

[85] On Titu Cusi Yupanqui, see Arnulf Becker Lorca, "The Legal Mechanics of Spanish Conquest: War and Peace in Early Colonial Peru," in *The Justification of War and International Order. Past and Present,* ed. Lothar Brock and Simon Hendrik (Oxford: Oxford University Press, 2021). On the Waorani people, see "Boletín de Prensa por Resistencia Waorani y CONCONAWEP," *Amazon Frontlines,* April 26, 2019, https://amazonfrontlines.org/es/chronicles/victoria-waorani/ ; Also in general on Indigenous consultation, Meghan Morris et al., *Justicia Global 2. La consulta previa a pueblos indígenas. los estándares del derecho internacional* (Bogotá, Colombia: Universidad de los Andes, Programa de Justicia Global y Derechos Humanos), 1–52.

6

Latin American and Caribbean Contributions to Human Rights Law

Steven L. B. Jensen and Kathryn Sikkink

I. Introduction

Latin America and the Caribbean offer an illuminating lens through which to tell the story of international human rights law after 1945. The manifold contributions—including foundational ones—that emanated from the countries in the region and their changing roles in the historic evolution bring together domestic, regional, and international developments in ways that offer an excellent vantage point to capture the dynamics of the history of international human rights law.

Some scholars, pundits, and practitioners continue to assume and argue that the idea of human rights comes from the Global North and is imposed on the South, despite a body of scholarly work that has long provided evidence of a far more nuanced account.[1] Other scholars may inadvertently support this position

[1] Jan Herman Burgers, "Road to San Francisco: The Revival of the Human Rights Idea in the Twentieth Century, *Human Rights Quarterly* 14, no. 4 (1992): 447–477. Kathryn Sikkink, "Reconceptualizing Sovereignty in the Americas: Historical Precursors and Current practices," *Houston Journal of International Law* 19, no. 3 (1997): 705–729; Mary Ann Glendon, "Forgotten Crucible: The Latin American Influence on the Universal Human Rights Idea," *Harvard Human Rights Journal* 16 (2003): 27; Greg Grandin, "The Liberal Traditions in the Americas: Rights, Sovereignty, and the Origins of Liberal Multilateralism," *The American Historical Review* 117, no. 1 (2012): 68–91; Susan Waltz, "Universalizing Human Rights: The Role of Small States in the Construction of the Universal Declaration of Human Rights," *Human Rights Quarterly* 23, no. 1 (February 1, 2001): 44–72; Liliana Obregón, "The Colluding Worlds of the Lawyer, the Scholar and the Policymaker: A View of International Law from Latin America (Speaking Law to Power: International Law and Foreign Policy)," *Wisconsin International Law Journal* 23, no. 1 (2005): 145–172; Paolo Carozza, "From Conquest to Constitutions: Retrieving a Latin American Tradition of the Idea of Human Rights," *Human Rights Quarterly* 25, no. 2 (2003): 281–313; Kathryn Sikkink, *Evidence for Hope: Making Human Rights Work in the 21st Century* (Princeton, NJ: Princeton University Press, 2017), translated into Spanish as *Razones para la esperanza: La legitimidad y efectividad de los derechos humanos de cara al futuro* (Buenos Aires: Siglo XXI editores, 2018); Rainer Huhle, "América Latina y la Fundamentación del Sistema Internacional de Protección de los Derechos Humanos Después de la Segunda Guerra Mundial," in *Memoria: Revista sobre Cultura, Democracia y Derechos Humanos,* no. 4 (2008): 33–43.

Steven L. B. Jensen and Kathryn Sikkink, *Latin American and Caribbean Contributions to Human Rights Law* In: *Latin American International Law in the Twenty-First Century*. Edited by: Alejandro Chehtman, Alexandra Huneeus, and Sergio Puig, Oxford University Press.
DOI: 10.1093/9780197754016.003.0006

by failing to mention any Latin American sources as among the origins of human rights.[2]

This chapter explores the role of states from Latin America and the Caribbean as early protagonists of the international protection of human rights, focusing on their contributions in two "defining" periods for international human rights law, namely, the 1940s and the 1960s.[3] It demonstrates their contributions as a constitutive part of a global history of human rights because their influence was so far-reaching. We argue that international human rights law is both a product of and an integral part of Latin American international law. In the decades that followed the periods receiving attention in this chapter, both Latin American and Caribbean countries would have complicated and conflictual engagements with the international and regional human rights system. This should be kept in mind while analyzing regional engagements with human rights, but they are not the focus here. Instead, the two decades discussed show the region's formative influences on international human rights and provide a valid precursor to a larger story about Latin America and the Caribbean.

II. The 1940s: Latin America and the Early Years of Human Rights at the United Nations

Near the end of World War II (WWII), a global understanding emerged that human rights and democracy must be essential to the postwar order. No single individual or country led this process, but the many ideas circulating in the interwar and WWII period converged worldwide.[4] Support for the importance of human rights was particularly strong in Latin America, in part due to the unprecedented wave of democratization that swept through the region in the mid-1940s, bringing to power various governments of the center-left with strong backing from labor unions.[5] While the great powers stressed human rights in their war aims, they were much more hesitant to endorse the international

[2] For example, Pamela Slotte and Miia Halme-Tuomisaari eds., *Revisiting the Origins of Human Rights* (Cambridge: Cambridge University Press, 2015). An article on the case of Chile in the 1970s is featured at the end of the following volume, but Latin America is not featured in the earlier parts on the "Emergence of human rights regimes" and "Postwar universalism." See Stefan-Ludwig Hoffman, ed., *Human Rights in the Twentieth Century* (Cambridge: Cambridge University Press, 2011).

[3] Alejandra Huneeus, in this volume, and Jorge Contesse, in this volume, address different aspects of Latin American contributions to human rights.

[4] See, for example, Manu Bhagavan, *The Peacemakers: India and the Quest for One World* (New York: Palgrave Macmillan, 2013), 3.

[5] Leslie Bethell and Ian Roxborough, "Introduction: The Postwar Conjuncture in Latin America: Democracy, Labor, and the Left," in *Latin America Between the Second World War and the Cold War, 1944–1948*, ed. Leslie Bethell and Ian Roxborough (Cambridge: Cambridge University Press, 1992), 1–32; Hernan Santa Cruz, *Cooperar o perecer: El dilema de la comunidad mundial* (Buenos Aires: Grupo Editor Latinoamericano, 1984), 57.

protection of human rights through international law and institutions. There were deep divisions within the US and UK governments about including human rights in the postwar order.[6] As a result, the initial US drafts of the UN Charter contained no references to human rights, and the proposals that emerged from the Big Four meeting at Dumbarton Oaks in 1944 in preparation for the San Francisco conference contained only one reference to human rights.[7]

Latin American countries were disappointed because they were not consulted about the Dumbarton Oaks plans for a postwar organization, and also because the draft for the UN Charter did not incorporate various ideals they supported, including human rights.[8] To voice their concerns and formulate a collective policy, Latin American countries called an extraordinary meeting at the Chapultepec Castle in Mexico City in February 1945, the Inter-American Conference on Problems of War and Peace, which ended just weeks before the San Francisco conference began.

Before the meeting in Mexico, the Inter-American Juridical Committee prepared a detailed report of comments and recommendations on the Dumbarton Oaks proposal for the UN Charter. The committee said that it would be desirable to include in the charter of the new organization an international bill of rights, and some "machinery of international organization which could represent the will of the entire community and its collective interests."[9]

Delegates at the Mexico City meeting raised important issues: great-power dominance, the importance of international law, regional agreements for security, and economic and social problems. Human rights issues figured prominently in the speeches and resolutions.[10] Many Latin American states argued that WWII had created a worldwide demand that rights should be recognized and protected at the international level.[11] Resolutions also emphasized the

[6] Paul Gordon Lauren, *The Evolution of International Human Rights: Visions Seen* (Philadelphia, University of Pennsylvania Press, 1998), 162, 164–165, 167.

[7] Jacob Robinson, *Human Rights and Fundamental Freedoms in the Charter of the United Nations: A Commentary* (New York: Institute of Jewish Affairs, 1946), 17.

[8] Lauren, *The Evolution of International Human Rights,* 174–179; Sumner Welles, *Where Are We Heading?* (New York: Harper & Brothers, 1946), 34. See also Juan Pablo Scarfi, "Pan-American Human Rights. The Legacy of Pan-Americanism and the Intellectual Origins of the Inter-American Human Rights System," in *The New Pan-Americanism and the Structuring of Inter-American Relations,* ed. Juan Pablo Scarfi and David M. K. Sheinin (London: Routledge, 2022), 138–162.

[9] Inter-American Juridical Committee, *The Dumbarton Oaks Proposals: Preliminary Comments and Recommendations of the Inter-American Juridical Committee* (Washington, DC: Pan American Union, 1944), 2, 5–7.

[10] "Inter-American Conference on Problems of War and Peace, Mexico 1945 Final Act, 1945," in *Report of the Delegation of the United States of America to the Inter-American Conference on Problems of War and Peace, Mexico City, Mexico, February 21–March 8, 1945* (Washington, DC: U.S. Government Printing Office, 1946).

[11] *Report of the Delegation of the United States of America*; Johannes Morsink, *The Universal Declaration of Human Rights. Origins, Drafting, and Intent* (Philadelphia: University of Pennsylvania Press, 1999), 130–131.

"necessity" of a declaration of rights of man and the importance of international machinery and procedures to put the principles in the declaration into action; Cuba and Uruguay even submitted draft declarations of human rights. Acting on these concerns, the delegates instructed the Inter-American Juridical Committee to prepare a draft declaration of the rights and duties of man.[12] States also debated proposals from Ecuador and Guatemala about whether member states should take a firmer stand against military coups by agreeing collectively not to provide diplomatic recognition for governments that come to power through nondemocratic means. Samuel Moyn has argued that in this period, human rights were primarily a project of the Christian right rather than the secular left.[13] This is not supported by the evidence from Latin America, where substantial support came from the secular left as well as from some countries with more conservative Catholic traditions. Regime type was more important than religion. Authoritarian regimes in the region, including those stressing their Christian orientation, opposed human rights while democracies supported them.[14]

Of the fifty states at the San Francisco conference, eighteen were from the Global North, while thirty-one (or 62 percent) were from what we now call the Global South. This included nineteen countries from Latin America, the largest single regional group at the meeting, one from the Caribbean (Haiti), and eleven countries from other parts of the developing world.[15]

Latin American countries clarified that they supported sovereignty and nonintervention but also that these had to be subordinated to international law. For example, when discussing sovereignty, the Chileans clarified that "the State is lord of its territory, can grant itself whatever *democratic* form of government it may desire *within standards which respect the inalienable rights of man*."[16]

In their demands for the inclusion of human rights and democracy in the Charter, Latin Americans were supported by several US-based nongovernmental organizations (NGOs) present at the conference.[17] The British government gave the Latin American bloc credit for changing the US government's

[12] Inter-American Juridical Committee, "Draft Declaration of the International Rights and Duties of Man and Accompanying Report" (Washington, DC: Pan-American Union, March 1946), 57–58.

[13] Samuel Moyn, *Christian Human Rights* (Philadelphia: University of Pennsylvania Press, 2015), 8.

[14] Sikkink, *Evidence for Hope*, 69, 101, 231.

[15] South Africa (under white minority rule) is not included in either group. India was there in an observer capacity since it had not yet achieved full independence. See *Documents of the United Nations Conference on International Organization, San Francisco, 1945: Volume 3*, April 23 (New York: UN Information Organizations, 1945).

[16] *Documents of the United Nations Conference on International Organization, San Francisco, 1945*, 293 (emphasis added).

[17] See, for example, Sikkink, "Reconceptualizing Sovereignty in the Americas"; Morsink, *The Universal Declaration of Human Rights*; Glendon, "The Forgotten Crucible."

position on human rights at the San Francisco conference.[18] Without Latin American protagonism, it is unlikely that the Charter would have contained references to human rights.

The final UN Charter contains seven references to human rights, including critical amendments whereby the promotion of human rights is listed as one of the purposes of the organization. The Economic and Social Council (ECOSOC) is called on to set up a human rights commission, the only explicitly mandated commission in the Charter. In particular, the initiatives of the Latin American countries helped extend the Charter's economic, social, and human rights objectives, particularly Articles 55 and 56, on which later human rights work of the organization rested.[19]

In addition, Latin American delegates contributed to women's rights in the UN charter. Of the six official woman delegates at the San Francisco conference in 1945, half came from Latin America (the Dominican Republic, Brazil, and Uruguay). Two Latin American women—Bertha Lutz, the delegate from Brazil, and Minerva Bernardino, from the Dominican Republic—took the lead in promoting women's rights and received support from many of their colleagues in Latin America. They advocated language about the equal rights of men and women, including what later became Article 8 of the Charter, which said, "The United Nations shall place no restrictions on the eligibility of men and women to participate in any capacity and under conditions of equality in its principal and subsidiary organs." In doing so, they were opposed by woman delegates from the United States and Canada and by the woman advisers to the UK delegation.[20]

Including human rights language in the Charter of the United Nations was a critical juncture that channeled the history of postwar global governance in the direction of setting international norms and laws about promoting human rights.[21] This language was not the language of the great powers, and it was only adopted by the great powers in response to pressures from small states and civil society. In the case of the United States, President Roosevelt feared that the Senate would fail to ratify the UN Charter, as it had with the Versailles Treaty,

[18] Lauren, *The Evolution of International Human Rights*, 337, n.86.

[19] Santa Cruz, *Cooperar o perecer*, 69.

[20] See Katherine Marino, *Feminism for the Americas: The Making of an International Human Rights Movement* (Chapel Hill: University of North Carolina Press, 2019); Torild Skard, "Getting Our History Right: How Were the Equal Rights of Women and Men Included in Charter of the United Nations?," *Forum for Development Studies*, no. 1 (June 2008): 37–60; Bertha Lutz, "Mulheres na Conferência em São Francisco, relatório por Bertha Lutz. Nome: BR MN. BL. O. FEM 6/25, from Museu Nacional of Brazil." Translated into English, and posted as, Report by Bertha Lutz, Delegate from Brazil, at the website, Bertha Lutz, Museu Virtual http://lhs.unb.br/bertha/ (last accessed November 23, 2023).

[21] See, for example, Giovanni Capoccia and R. Daniel Kelemen, "The Study of Critical Junctures: Theory, Narrative, and Counterfactuals in Historical Institutionalism," *World Politics* 59, no. 3 (2007): 341–369.

and invited NGOs and representatives of labor unions to San Francisco with the specific purpose of mobilizing civil society in support of the Charter. After Roosevelt's death, only weeks before the San Francisco Conference, the new Truman administration worked to carry out Roosevelt's plans. The NGOs and labor unions convinced the US delegates that the human rights language was crucial for supporting the Charter. Once the United States agreed to support the human rights language, the other Great Powers followed suit.[22]

Some Latin American states and NGOs demanded an international organization with more far-reaching power to enforce international human rights norms. The Uruguayan delegation, for example, proposed that the UN Charter itself contain a "Declaration of Rights" and "a system of effective juridical guardianship of those rights."[23] Uruguay proposed to make it possible to suspend from the organization countries that persistently violated human rights.[24] The final language of the Charter on human rights is less firm than many states and NGOs desired since it calls on the UN to promote and encourage respect for human rights rather than actually to protect rights.[25]

III. From the American Declaration of the Rights and Duties of Man to the Universal Declaration of Human Rights

The UN Charter called on the new international organization to promote respect for human rights, but no intergovernmental enumeration of rights yet existed. Two different processes got underway for drafting a declaration of rights: an international process to draft the Universal Declaration of Human Rights (UDHR) and a regional process to draft the American Declaration. These two processes overlapped and were complementary, but drafting the American Declaration of the Rights and Duties of Man was always a step ahead of drafting the UDHR.[26] The reason was that, as mentioned in section II, the American

[22] Dorothy Robins, *Experiment in Democracy: The Story of U.S. Citizen Organizations in Forging the Charter of the United Nations* (New York: Parkside, 1971); Kathryn Sikkink, *Mixed Signals: U.S. Human Rights Policy and Latin America* (Ithaca, NY: Cornell University Press, 2004), 32–36.

[23] "New Uruguayan Proposals on the Dumbarton Oaks Proposals," *Documents of the United Nations Conference on International Organization, San Francisco, 1945:* Vol. 3 (New York: UN Information Organizations, 1945), 34.

[24] "Statement of Uruguayan Delegation of Its Position with Reference to Chapters I and II of the Charter as Considered by Committee I/1," *Documents of the United Nations Conference on International Organization, San Francisco, 1945:* Vol. 6 (New York: UN Information Organizations, 1945), 628–633.

[25] "Report of Rapporteur, Subcommittee I/1/A (Farid Zeineddine, Syria), to Committee I/1," *Documents of the United Nations Conference on International Organization, San Francisco, 1945* (New York: UN Information Organizations, 1945), 705.

[26] Huhle, "Latinoamérica: Continente de la Paz y los Derechos Humanos," 1–17. A third document could have been part of this story. In December 1948—based on a preliminary discussion from 1946 and parallel to the final UN meeting sessions focused on completing the UDHR—the Caribbean

states had requested a draft declaration of rights from the Inter-American Juridical Committee at the Mexico City conference in 1945. The UDHR drafting process had to wait until the states had ratified the UN Charter after the San Francisco meeting. The timing increased Latin America's influence on the UN process—even if it was the substance of the issues that mattered most.

The Inter-American Judicial Committee produced a complete draft declaration, including twenty-one articles and another fifty pages of full commentary, by December 31, 1945, only six months after the San Francisco conference had concluded. This document was published and circulated to member countries for comments in March 1946, before the UN Preparatory Committee tasked with drafting the UDHR had even held its first meeting.[27] The American states later expanded the American Declaration beyond this draft declaration. Still, all the core civil, political, economic, social, and cultural rights of the American Declaration were present in the draft. The American Declaration was completed before the second round of drafting of the UDHR, and it was influential in the text of the UDHR, particularly in the articles on social and economic rights.[28]

In April 1948, the American states met in Bogotá, Colombia to address several regional concerns, foremost among them creating a new regional organization, the Organization of American States (OAS). A vocal minority of states wanted a human rights declaration as part of the OAS Charter. In contrast, other states argued for less legally binding options, such as the self-standing American Declaration that eventually emerged.

The delegates considered the draft declaration prepared by the Inter-American Juridical Committee and added eight articles on rights and ten on duties. Of the thirty-eight articles in the American Declaration, twenty-eight are devoted to an enumeration of rights and ten to duties. Most discussions of duties in human rights law refer to the corresponding state duties that each right imposes. But the duties in the American Declaration are the complementary or supplementary duties that individuals have in addition to those of the state. This attention to duties sets the American Declaration apart from the UDHR, which does not list specific responsibilities, although it mentions them in Article 29.

Commission debated the development of a Caribbean Bill of Rights at its session in Guadeloupe. There was some interest in this, but the idea was effectively smothered by the United States, United Kingdom, France, and the Netherlands. See Steven L. B. Jensen, *The Making of International Human Rights: The 1960s, Decolonization, and the Reconstruction of Global Values*, (Cambridge: Cambridge University Press, 2016), 18–20.

[27] The UN Nuclear Preparatory Committee held its first meetings in April and May 1946. Inter-American Juridical Committee, *Draft Declaration of the International Rights and Duties of Man and Accompanying Report* (Washington, DC: Pan American Union, 1946); Morsink, *The Universal Declaration of Human Rights*, 4.

[28] John P. Humphrey, *Human Rights and the United Nations: A Great Adventure* (New York: Dobbs Ferry Transnational Publishers, 1984); Morsink, *The Universal Declaration of Human Rights*, 130.

The American Declaration of the Rights and Duties of Man was built upon the existing traditions and constitutions in Latin American countries.[29] Some authors argue that the Inter-American System of Human Rights emerged from the American Institute of International Law, founded by James Brown Scott and Alejandro Álvarez.[30] We argue that the inter-American human rights system had far more diverse origins, building on civic republicanism, Catholic social doctrine, and socialist thought in the region, including the 1917 Mexican Constitution.[31] This relates to what one scholar has called "inter-American constitutionalism," or the interaction between human rights developments and progressive constitutional developments in the region.[32] The idea of human rights was not a recent "legal transplant" in the region but a long-nourished and -cultivated local aspiration.[33]

The argument favoring a declaration won out over making human rights part of the binding OAS treaty. Some countries, like Mexico, motivated by its fear that human rights could be used to justify intervention, supported only a declaration of human rights, not a legally binding treaty, and worked to change the title from the "Declaration of the *International* Rights and Duties of Man," by removing the "international" and thus leaving more ambiguity about its purpose.[34] As a result of these disagreements and changes, some of the delegations to Bogotá were disappointed with the human rights results from the conference. The head of the Uruguayan delegation, Dardo Regules, said states' position on human rights was "the most timid and least obligatory."[35] The American Declaration nevertheless represents the first intergovernmental effort to flesh out the meaning of human rights for future international legal work.

All the rights in the UDHR appear first in the American Declaration, although the UDHR sometimes elaborates on these rights in greater detail. This heavy

[29] Fernando Berdion del Valle and Kathryn Sikkink, "(Re)discovering Duties: Individual Responsibilities in the Age of Rights," *Minnesota Journal of International Law* 26, no. 1 (2017): 189–245. Carozza, "From Conquest to Constitutions," 12.

[30] See M. Petersen and C-A Schulz, "Setting the Regional Agenda: A Critique of Posthegemonic Regionalism," *Latin American Politics and Society* 60, no. 1 (2018): 115–116; and Scarfi, "Pan-American Human Rights. The Legacy of Pan-Americanism and the Intellectual Origins of the Inter-American Human Rights System," 139.

[31] Berdion del Valle and Sikkink, "(Re)discovering Duties: Individual Responsibilities in the Age of Rights"; Carozza, "From Conquest to Constitutions," 12.

[32] Jorge Contesse, "Inter-American Constitutionalism: The Interaction between Human Rights and Progressive Constitutional Law in Latin America," in *Law and Society in Latin America: A New Map* ed. Cesar Rodriguez Garavito (London: Routledge, 2014), 220–234.

[33] Alan Watson, *Legal Transplants: An Approach to Comparative Law*, Virginia Legal Studies (Charlottesville: University Press of Virginia, 1974).

[34] Berdion del Valle and Sikkink, "(Re)discovering Duties: Individual Responsibilities in the Age of Rights."

[35] Dardo Regules, *La lucha por la justicia y por el derecho; apuntes sobre la IX Conferencia Panamericana reunida en Bogotá durante el mes de abril de 1948* (Montevideo, Uruguay: Barreiro y Ramos, 1949), 97.

influence of the American Declaration on the UDHR is not surprising because they share similar sources. When John Humphrey, the Canadian who served as the head of the UN Secretariat's Human Rights Division, wrote the Secretariat Outline (a draft bill of rights) for the Human Rights Commission to use in producing the eventual UDHR, he used as models drafts collected from law professors and NGOs as well as from other intergovernmental organizations, including the Pan-American Union.[36] Cuba, Panama, and Chile were the first countries to submit complete drafts of bills of rights to the commission. Each contained references to rights to education, food, health care, and other social security provisions.[37] Humphrey, a social democrat, was very sympathetic to the idea that the UDHR should include economic and social rights and used these drafts extensively in preparing the Secretariat's draft for the commission to consider. By way of these draft bills of rights submitted by Latin American delegations, "Humphrey took much of the wording and almost all of the ideas for the social, economic, and cultural rights from his first draft from the tradition of Latin American socialism."[38] The involvement of Latin American countries in including economic and social rights in the UDHR corrects a long-held belief that the economic and social rights in the UDHR were primarily the result of Soviet pressure.[39]

Latin American delegations, especially Mexico, Cuba, and Chile, were the first to insist that the American Declaration include the right to justice and almost single-handedly inserted language about it into the UDHR in what would become Article 8 of that Declaration. What they meant by the right to justice were judicial procedures that could protect individuals from abuse of authority by governments that violated their rights.

The probable source for Latin American proposals on the need for accountability in the American Declaration and the UDHR is the *Amparo* laws that existed in some, but not all, Latin American countries. This is a clear example of normative innovation where Latin American delegations took legal procedures from their own constitutional tradition, which were not present in the constitutions of the large common-law countries, and used them to craft an essential article of the new human rights declarations.

The Latin American delegates were not successful on all accounts. They faced hesitation or resistance to some of their proposals. For example, they failed to get one of the rights in the American Declaration included in the UDHR: the

[36] Humphrey, *Human Rights*, 31–32.

[37] Morsink, *The Universal Declaration of Human Rights*, 131.

[38] Ibid.

[39] Mary Ann Glendon, *A World Made New. Eleanor Roosevelt and the Universal Declaration of Human Rights* (New York: Random House, 2001); Morsink, *The Universal Declaration of Human Rights*; Humphrey, *Human Rights*.

right to petition. This generated a debate in the UN General Assembly's Third Committee in November 1948. Ecuador made a strong plea for its inclusion as part of the UDHR calling it "an essential corollary of human rights," because it would offer "a tool in the hands of the man in the street."[40]

Cuba and Uruguay backed Ecuador in this debate. The opposition mainly came from European countries—East and West—with issues of national sovereignty (Soviet Union) and the need for further study (United Kingdom) raised against the proposal. They were unwilling to accept such a proposal, and their opposition prevailed.

However, even these examples of failure reveal the stature that the Latin American region held in these international negotiations.[41] In their intervention in the debate, Belgium argued that including the right to petition in the American Declaration was "yet another proof that Pan-Americanism was ahead of other countries in international development."[42] It was a telling assessment of the state of international human rights diplomacy in the late 1940s.

The delegates who gathered in Bogotá and Paris in 1948 to complete drafting the American Declaration of Rights and Duties of Man and the UDHR did not believe that merely making a Declaration of Rights would be sufficient to provide international protection for rights, but they saw it as a crucial first step. "The human rights project of the 1940s was not stillborn but it arrived on the international scene without any privileged birthright. It would have to make its own way through the world."[43] That process of making its own way through the world was fraught with barriers and backtracking.

It took Latin American governments thirty years to move from the early and innovative American Declaration of the Rights and Duties of Man of 1948 to the entry into force of the leading regional human rights treaty, the American Convention of Human Rights in 1978. Progress on a human rights treaty ended as more countries suffered military coups. In the twenty years after the American Declaration of Rights and Duties of Man, every one of the twenty Latin American and Caribbean states present in the UN meetings of the 1940s (except for Costa Rica) suffered through at least one authoritarian regime that resisted the idea of

[40] Mr. Carrera Andrade (Ecuador), UN General Assembly, Third Committee, 158th Meeting, 25 November 1948, 699. A/C.3/SR.158.

[41] It is worth noting that in addition to the Latin American contributions to the UDHR debates, actors from the region also pushed other rights declarations at the UN General Assembly in parallel, thereby broadening the rights debate at this crucial moment. In November 1948, Argentina presented a Declaration of Old Age Rights to the UN General Assembly's Third Committee. See A/C.3/213/Rev. 1: Declaration of Old Age Rights. Argentina: Draft Resolution, November 26, 1948. The UDHR was still being negotiated at this point, and lack of time did not permit an in-depth discussion of the Argentine proposal.

[42] Mr. Dehousse (Belgium), UN General Assembly, 3rd Session, 3rd Committee, 159th Meeting, November 26, 1948, 706. A/C.3/SR.159.

[43] Jensen, *The Making of International Human Rights*, 46.

international protection of human rights. But, as momentum on international human rights law stalled in Latin America, the baton was picked up by a newly decolonized country in the Caribbean. They would lead the international community toward a whole new stage in the global protection of human rights.

IV. The 1960s: Jamaica and the Quest for an International Human Rights Protection System

Jamaica joined the United Nations in 1962 and wasted no time attempting to elevate human rights on the international agenda. In its maiden speech to the UN General Assembly, the Jamaican government linked peace and human rights and proposed an international year for human rights that would "seek cooperative methods of curing the denial of human rights whenever and wherever such a condition exists."[44] These were the initial steps in a political process that lasted from 1962 to 1968, which would transform the standing of human rights in international politics.

The pace of work for human rights promotion and protection at the United Nations slowed in the 1950s. In 1951, Uruguay submitted a detailed proposal for establishing a High Commissioner for Human Rights, a proposal discussed in subsequent years but not implemented until 1993.[45] In 1951 and 1952, Mexico and Haiti emerged as among the most outspoken critics of an attempt by the United Kingdom and the United States to close down the UN human rights structures. This was done under the seemingly obscure label of a UN "organizational efficiency review." In reality, it was an early attempt to smother human rights inside the new international organization. The proposal had the potential to change the normative-political trajectory of the United Nations but was—after moving through various UN structures under ECOSOC—eventually voted down in the UN General Assembly in February 1952.[46] This unsuccessful maneuvering by the United States inside the UN preceded the 1953 decision by the Eisenhower Administration—linked to the so-called Bricker Amendment Process—whereby the United States announced that it distanced itself from the drafting of the UN human rights covenants and declared that it was unlikely

[44] Hugh Shearer (Jamaica), UN General Assembly, 17th Session, 1145th Plenary Meeting, October 8, 1962, 378.

[45] See "Proposal for the Establishment of an Office of the United Nations High Commissioner (Attorney-General) for Human Rights," E/1992, annex VII (submitted to the Seventh session of the Commission on Human Rights in 1951).

[46] See Steven L. B. Jensen, "Inequality and Post-War International Organisation: Discrimination, the World Social Situation and the United Nations, 1948-1957," in *Histories of Global Inequality. New Perspectives*, ed. Christian Olaf Christiansen and Steven L. B. Jensen (London: Palgrave Macmillan, 2019), 137–139.

that the country would ever ratify them. The disappointment over the United States was clear and outspoken from several of their allies at the UN. In 1959, the question of creating "National Advisory Committees on Human Rights" came on the agenda of the Commission on Human Rights. Debate ensued, but no actions were taken. The 1950s appear as a decade where progress was continuously stalled at the UN regarding human rights, primarily by the opposition of the great powers.[47] This is a crucial reason 1962 stands out as a turning point.[48]

At the 1963 General Assembly, Jamaica followed up on its initial proposal by securing formal backing to designate 1968 as the "International Human Rights Year."[49] At this point, it was unclear what this would entail and whether it would have any effect. Jamaica, however, used this platform over the following years to challenge the great powers to accept that the international human rights law project would evolve despite their apparent skepticism or direct opposition. Jamaica effectively nurtured diplomatic alliances with a select group of states from the Global South and shaped the negotiation climate during the formative phase for international human rights law in the build-up to 1968. Costa Rica proved to be a particularly important ally in these endeavors. This was evident from 1964 when Costa Rica successfully advocated for Jamaica to be fast-tracked into the Commission on Human Rights as a new member due to its essential role in the field.[50] It proved to be a significant contribution.

By 1964, Jamaica had established itself as a leader in UN human rights diplomacy.[51] It provided momentum, structure, and a mobilizing timeline for this work. Also, it became increasingly clear that Jamaica promoted a holistic vision for advancing international human rights protection. It can best be described as an attempt to create a global human rights system with designated mechanisms at the national, regional, and international levels. This included evolving the necessary legal foundations, institutional infrastructure, and stronger and more

[47] Jan Eckel, *The Ambivalence of Good: Human Rights in International Politics Since the 1940s*, (Oxford: Oxford University Press, 2019), 51–75.

[48] Another factor was that the international human rights project in 1962 was redefined around the issues of race and religion which helped energize legal negotiations that had otherwise lingered for fourteen years since the adoption of UDHR. Jensen, *The Making of International Human Rights*, 102–173.

[49] See Document A/5493 and ADD.1: "Jamaica: request for the inclusion of an additional item in the agenda of the 18th session" (September 1963); UN General Assembly Resolution 1961 (XVIII), "Designation of 1968 as International Year for Human Rights," December 12, 1963.

[50] This included Costa Rica advocating with the US Mission to the UN in New York to make the United States support Jamaican membership of the Commission over potential Latin American candidates. US National Archives (College Park, MD), SOC-14 ECOSOC, Confidential Telegram from US UN Mission NY to Department of State, May 19, 1964.

[51] There is a domestic pre-history to Jamaica emerging as an international leader in human rights. See Steven L. B. Jensen, "'From this Era of Passionate Self-Discovery': Norman Manley, Human Rights and the End of Colonial Rule in Jamaica," in *Decolonization, Self-Determination and the Rise of Global Human Rights Politics*, ed. A. Dirk Moses, Marco Duranti, and Roland Burke (Cambridge: Cambridge University Press, 2020), 236–261.

transparent diplomatic processes for international deliberation on human rights violations.

Jamaica's efforts were based on a strategic reading of international affairs that gave prominence to the role of law. After 1964, the efforts were backed by the country's first foreign policy strategy for the multilateral domain, which emphasized three areas—human rights, international peacekeeping, and reform of international aid and trade—priorities that were to be pursued in an integrated manner. It was the first foreign policy of any nation that integrated human rights as a major priority area.

Jamaica's vision was an international legal order where human rights were to occupy a central role.[52] For example, Jamaica sent a letter to the members of the International Law Commission in September 1964 calling on them to consider a human rights provision in the Law of Treaties that was under development (today known as the 1969 Vienna Convention). They knew this law was primarily concerned with the relationship between states but felt their request to recognize that the individual in international law was still timely and relevant.[53]

At this point, Jamaica had already played a key role in initiating another relevant legal track, namely, "methods of fact-finding in international relations." Together with Mexico, Canada, Cyprus, Liberia, Netherlands, Pakistan, and Sweden, Jamaica had drafted a joint resolution on this question which the 1963 UN General Assembly adopted. It called for the UN Secretary-General to prepare a relevant study on the topic that included considering the feasibility of "a special international body for fact-finding."[54] The report was presented in May 1964. It provided the member states with a historical overview of international inquiries since the Hague Conventions in 1899 and 1907, through the League of Nations era before covering the post-1945 period with the United Nations. The initiative behind the report reads as a stepping-stone toward initiatives later in the decade related to fact-finding in the human rights field, most notably the creation of the UN Special Procedures in 1967.

Why did Jamaica embark on this diplomatic path? The fact is that human rights had been a live issue both in domestic Jamaican politics and in their foreign engagements in the years before Jamaican independence. This includes the noticeable decision by the Jamaican cabinet in June 1959 announcing the introduction of trade sanctions against South Africa. Jamaica deliberately used or further developed international legal techniques to address conflicts and human rights violations worldwide. It charted a diplomatic course—upon becoming an

[52] Hugh Shearer (Jamaica), UN General Assembly, 19th Session, 1293rd Plenary Meeting, December 7, 1964, 12. See also Jensen, *The Making of International Human Rights*, 88–89.

[53] The letter from Jamaica is included here: Reports of the International Law Commission, 17th and 18th Session (January & July 1966). A/6309/Rev.1, 127.

[54] A 5694: Report of the Secretary-General on methods of fact-finding, 1 May 1964.

independent nation—with a strong vision for internationalism that it pursued during the 1960s. Human rights and international peacekeeping were central elements herein. There may also be another factor to address this question. Jamaica's group affiliation was not settled upon their membership in the United Nations. This would normally imply membership of the Latin American and Caribbean regional group. However, one or two countries were hesitant to allow Jamaican membership because of the unsettled issue of British Honduras (today Belize). The states in question were concerned that Jamaica was too closely aligned with the United Kingdom—despite this being the colonial power from which they had achieved independence—and that this would influence their positions on British Honduras. Jamaica was thus without a regional grouping until this issue was resolved at the end of the 1960s. This situation may have inspired Jamaica to prioritize human rights on its own initiative, building alliances along the way (e.g., with Costa Rica).

The concrete steps that Jamaican diplomats took to realize their vision were manifold. Jamaica was simultaneously pushing forward with the plans for the International Year for Human Rights, which now, upon Jamaica's initiative, included the organization of the First World Conference on Human Rights that would take place over three weeks in the spring of 1968 (the precursor to the 1993 Vienna World Conference on Human Rights). The World Conference idea, when it was proposed in 1964, was met with resistance from both Western and communist states. The Jamaican UN Ambassador Egerton Richardson spent considerable effort grinding away at the resistance against broadening international human rights work. Costa Rica provided vocal support to the UN planning committee, arguing that the proposal came from a "feeling of urgency" aimed at promoting the cause of human rights more effectively.[55] Gradually, Richardson swayed Western European states and the United States to accept the idea, and he weakened communist opposition. The International Year in 1968 was established as a target date to ensure progress with international human rights during the intervening years and an opportunity to reassess the future. UN human rights diplomacy had never seen such a structured approach to its work.

The momentum was beneficial to the drafting and potential adoption of international human rights conventions. This dimension was still missing by the mid-1960s, meaning human rights had not yet become international law. The Jamaicans used the planning for the International Year to create "international machinery . . . aimed at ensuring implementation" of the human rights conventions, which was its second major priority in the build-up to 1968.[56]

[55] ST/SG/AC.5/SR.5: Mr Volio (Costa Rica), Committee on the International Year for Human Rights, July 10, 1964, 5.
[56] Ibid., p. 7.

Finalizing the ongoing legal drafting processes and securing adoption was now a primary goal for the International Human Rights Year process. This would soon bear fruit with the adoption of the 1965 Convention on Elimination of All Forms of Racial Discrimination and the two human rights covenants in 1966.

Adopting the 1965 Convention on Racial Discrimination was the first major result of the new Global South-led human rights diplomacy of the 1960s. It represented a breakthrough for international human rights law to the extent that it is reasonable to claim that this body of international law is built on a foundation of race.[57] The UN human rights debates that led to the convention—supported by the global politics of race in an international system shifting from a colonial world to a postcolonial one as an essential backdrop—transcended the sacred notions of sovereignty that were so closely guarded by a large number of UN member states. The ground shifted under firmly held positions, and the convention on racial discrimination established the precedent that paved the way for the two human rights covenants to be finally adopted in 1966.

These human rights conventions contained measures of implementation—including the so-called treaty bodies, which were part of the convention on racial discrimination and the Covenant on Civil and Political Rights. Two of Jamaica's allies led the UN negotiations that secured an agreement on this vital matter: Ghana and the Philippines. It allowed Jamaica to focus on other aspects of the human rights agenda. During the 1966 negotiations in the UN General Assembly on the International Covenant on Civil and Political Rights, Jamaica presented a proposal for inclusion in the Covenant of an article that would commit state parties to establish a "National Commission on Human Rights" with a mandate to monitor, advise, and report on "the status of the legislation, judicial decisions and administrative arrangements for the protection of the rights recognized in this Covenant."[58] It was deliberately worded to entail a protection mandate. Many states were not ready to consider such a proposal at this juncture, and it was neutralized by referring it to further study in the Commission on Human Rights and, therefore, not included in the Covenant.[59] In a parallel development, Jamaica also advocated for creating a UN Human Rights Council to replace the Commission on Human Rights.[60] These examples show how

[57] Jensen, *The Making of International Human Rights*, 102.

[58] UN General Assembly, Third Committee, "Jamaica: Amendment to the draft Covenant on Civil and Political Rights," A/C.3/L.1407, November 23, 1966.

[59] UN General Assembly, Third Committee, A/C.3/L.1408/Rev.1, December 8, 1966. This delayed the international agreement on establishing national human rights commissions for more than twenty-five years until 1993.

[60] US National Archives, RG 59/250/7/20, Soc 14, Box 3205: "1968 Human Rights Conference," Telegram 4908 from US UN Mission New York to Secretary of State, May 16, 1966. This was also unsuccessful and would only be realized in 2006 as part of UN Secretary-General Kofi Annan's UN reform agenda.

Jamaica's vision for institutionalizing human rights promotion and protection moved seamlessly between different levels.

With the adoption of three prominent human rights conventions within a year, the continued efforts moved into 1967 on a hopeful note. This was despite escalating violent crises across Southern Africa and elsewhere. The situation inspired renewed action in the human rights field. The need was to go beyond codification and instead find means to address serious human rights violations. The Commission on Human Rights had, in the 1940s, adopted a "No power to act" doctrine because states wanted to protect national sovereignty and hinder international action.[61] The doctrine had rendered the United Nations almost impotent when faced with violations. It was time to break new ground. Several proposals were under discussion at the February–March 1967 session of the Commission on Human Rights. Costa Rica had taken the lead on reviving the idea of a UN High Commissioner on Human Rights and was trying to plan for its establishment.[62] Argentina, Chile, Costa Rica, Guatemala, and Peru added to a Nigerian draft resolution focused on establishing regional commissions on human rights that would receive "information concerning gross violations of human rights and fundamental freedoms."[63] These proposals could serve as important steps to anchor human rights institutionally. However, a paradigm shift was still needed to counter the old "no power to act" doctrine. Jamaica tackled this head-on by working with Italy, Morocco, and Austria to call upon the Economic and Social Council to extend the terms of reference of the Commission on Human Rights so that it would have "the power to recommend and adopt general and specific measures to deal with violations of human rights."[64]

The UN Special Procedures emerged from these UN debates and decisions in early 1967, starting with an Ad Hoc Working Group of Experts on the Situation of Human Rights in Southern Africa and a Special Rapporteur on the Politics of Apartheid.[65] Fact-finding missions were now part of the UN human rights efforts. A whole group of states were involved in these decision-making

[61] M. E. Tardu, "United Nations Response to Gross Violations of Human Rights: The 1503 Procedure," *Santa Clara Law Review*, vol. 20, no. 3 (1980): 559.

[62] E/CN.4/L.831/Add.1:" Costa Rica: draft resolution on the creation of the post of United Nations High Commissioner for Human Rights," Commission on Human Rights, March 25, 1966; E/CN.4/AC.21/L.1: "Analytical and Technical Study Prepared by the Secretary-General" for the Working Group to Study Proposal to Create the Institution of a United Nations High Commissioner for Human Rights, December 30, 1966.

[63] E/4322: Commission on Human Rights, Report on the 23rd Session, February 20–March 23 1967, 87, 89.

[64] Ibid., 115.

[65] Elvira Dominguez-Redondo," The History of the Special Procedures: A 'Learning-by-Doing' Approach to Human Rights Implementation," in *The United Nations Special Procedures System*, ed. Aoife Nolan, Rosa Freedman, and Thérèse Murphy (Leiden, The Netherlands: Brill Nijhoff, 2017), 22–23.

processes, but it was no coincidence that the breakthrough came in the build-up to the International Year for Human Rights.

During these same months in early 1967, the Jamaican government hosted a UN human rights seminar on the "Effective Realization of Civil and Political Rights at the National Level" in Kingston. It revived attention on the Ombudsman institution and the role it could play in human rights protection around the world.[66] Jamaica also continued to advocate for the involvement of regional entities such as the Council of Europe and the Inter-American Commission in the UN's preparations for the 1968 Conference, as well as for the participation of NGOs in the conference. They met strong resistance from communist states but would prevail on the issue of civil society participation at the conference, which was now scheduled to take place in Tehran in April–May 1968. The Jamaican UN Ambassador Egerton Richardson was pushing for this NGO involvement to help bring more awareness to and make the human rights debates at the United Nations more transparent. At the same time, he was pushing for NGOs to take up the cause of human rights. At a UN conference for NGOs in September 1967, he challenged international civil society to intensify their efforts to prepare for the 1968 Conference after getting off to a "very late start."[67]

The preparations for the 1968 International Year for Human Rights faced considerable challenges. The Six-Day War in the Middle East in June 1967 brought a global political crisis to the United Nations that would have a detrimental impact on international human rights diplomacy. The communist world, Arab States, and several countries from the Global South wanted to narrow the agenda of the 1968 World Conference on Human Rights to focus solely on the occupied territories, apartheid, and colonialism. This was a dramatic narrowing of the agenda that Jamaica and its partners had been advocating. It placed the whole endeavor at considerable risk and certainly stifled the debate on establishing a UN Human Rights High Commissioner, which had been carried forward by a working group in the build-up to the Human Rights Year.

Egerton Richardson saw the consequences of this even before the Human Rights Year had unfolded. In his September 1967 speech, he gave this sobering assessment:

> I believe that the coercive powers we are attempting to give to international institutions will be of little effectiveness for a very long time to come.... National sovereignty, the big bad wolf of common international action, will continue

[66] ST/TAO/HR/29: Memorandum on UN Human Rights Seminar on the Effective Realization of Civil and Political Rights at the National Level, Kingston, Jamaica, April 25–May 8, 1967.

[67] Egerton Richardson speech at OPI Annual Conference for the Non-Governmental Organisations, September 13, 1967. Box 43: International Year for Human Rights (1968), Archive of the International League for the Rights of Man, New York Public Library.

> I fear, to frighten and to frustrate us—or frustrate you, the International Activists for a long time in the future.[68]

Richardson was both right and wrong in this assessment. Right, because 1968 would be a year of frustrations. The three-week 1968 Conference would see the whole first week obsess over whether to debate the occupied territories, to the detriment of other agenda items. The overall assessment of the 1968 Conference was that little was achieved. In August, the Warsaw Pact countries invaded Czechoslovakia, ending the "Prague Spring." In September 1968, Richardson gave a new assessment based on the events of the year, calling it "our moment of truth, when we came face to face with the nature of our beast—when we saw what it meant to be promoting the cause of Human Rights by working mainly through governments."[69] He now called on NGOs to carry the torch forward and bring the focus to the national level.

But Richardson's assessment was also wrong because he could not fully evaluate the significance of what had changed and what had been achieved through the Jamaica-led process of the International Human Rights Year from 1962 to 1968. It is reasonable to elaborate on these achievements to provide a fuller assessment of this Caribbean contribution to international human rights.

By the end of the 1968 International Human Rights Year, human rights became international law as the International Covenant on Elimination of All Forms of Racial Discrimination entered into force after achieving the required ratifications in early December 1968. The first international human rights mechanism—the UN Special Procedures—had been established in 1967. The First World Conference on Human Rights was held, and among its major results was an agreement to develop linkages between international human rights law and international humanitarian law. This was achieved through a Jamaica-sponsored resolution prepared in collaboration with the International Commission of Jurists. The whole process energized the regional European human rights system, which became apparent in the aftermath of the Human Rights Year and started yielding results in the early 1970s. It also impacted the Inter-American human rights system, which, from the mid-1960s, mobilized to finalize a regional human rights convention (formally adopted in San Jose, Costa Rica, in 1969). It is also possible to document an unprecedented national level mobilization and awareness raising around human rights in many countries worldwide. The first international NGO strategy on human rights was adopted in September 1968 with three focus areas: pushing for state ratification of human

[68] Ibid., 7.

[69] Egerton Richardson," The Perspective of the Tehran Conference," *Toward an NGO Strategy for the Advancement of Human Rights* (Conference Report), The International NGO Conference on Human Rights, Paris, September 1968, 25.

rights conventions, fact-finding missions and advocacy, and human rights education. Amnesty International's adoption of fighting torture in its mandate took place in 1968, with the Swedish NGO Committee for the Human Rights Year playing an influential role in this decision at the organization's 1968 international conference in Stockholm. Furthermore, Soviet dissidents behind the Iron Curtain used the International Human Rights Year as a platform for mobilizing against the Soviet state in their *samizdat* literature.[70]

Jamaica did not achieve its aim of creating an actual international human rights protection system where legal techniques were applied to address violations worldwide. They did, however, achieve a lot.[71] The examples cited in this chapter are by themselves all noteworthy achievements. Together, they provide a more comprehensive assessment of the International Human Rights Year as a process that brought forward new initiatives and positive change. Between the failures of intended aims and the successes of actual outcomes, we can understand Jamaica's—and by extension—the Caribbean's vital contribution to international human rights law during the 1960s.

V. Conclusions

This chapter documents processes that call into question some of the tropes of some recent human rights pundits and scholars. Based on substantial archival research, it details how much critical human rights work was done in the 1940s and the 1960s and the protagonist role played by Latin American and the Caribbean countries in those efforts. Human rights were embodied in international law as countries completed the drafting of the first three major human rights treaties: the Convention on the Elimination of All Forms of Racial Discrimination (CERD), the International Covenant on Civil and Political Rights (ICCPR), and the International Covenant on Economic, Social and Cultural Rights (ICESCR). Many of the important later developments and reforms of human rights work in the UN were first proposed in this period, often by actors from Latin America and the Caribbean, such as the creation of a High Commissioner for Human Rights, the empowerment of the UN Human Rights Commission to become an institution capable of doing human rights work, the creation of the myriad Special Procedures through which the Human Rights Commission carries out some of its work, especially fact-finding, and the conversion of the Commission into the Human Rights Council.

[70] This whole section draws on Jensen, *The Making of International Human Rights*, 174–208.

[71] Jamaica's domestic human rights story took a very different and more problematic direction after independence in the 1960s. See ibid., 201–204.

Latin American and Caribbean countries delivered—supported by key partners from the Global South, some partners in Europe, and a handful of NGOs—the international human rights project on the doorstep of the 1970s. This became a decade where Western states would embrace the project in their foreign policies, where Chile and Argentina would emerge as significant sites for contestations over human rights, Amnesty International and Helsinki Watch groups would show the potential of human rights NGOs, and Eastern European dissidents would capture the wider imagination of people around the world. The 1970s progress would depend on the foundations laid in the 1940s and the 1960s. Thus, we must recognize that the Latin American and Caribbean contributions to international human rights have been profound, substantive, and decisive.

PART II
THEORIES AND METHODS

7

Interdisciplinarity and LAIL

The Case of International Economic Law

Sergio Puig

I. Introduction

The field of international economic law developed and institutionalized significantly during the 1990s and 2000s. As global economic law's implications for politics, economics, and governance within states grew, so did its salience for interdisciplinary study. This is also true in Latin America, where interdisciplinary work proliferated, especially after the 2000s. Like in other regions, scholars from Latin America turned to disciplinary methods beyond the traditional study of legal doctrine, constituting part of a "new legal realist" approach in scholarship in the region often associated with the United States. This is a significant change in a region traditionally associated with legal positivism and a strong connection with European legal scholarship.

In this chapter, I discuss this turn by referencing the interdisciplinary encounters of international economic law in Latin America. After discussing different methodologies and substantive areas in general, I give examples of questions of interest (and the implications of the analysis) in the region. I highlight different methods within disciplines, including quantitative and qualitative approaches, and discuss how this relates to the slow but essential transformation of the scholarly tradition in the region. Ultimately, such transformation casts important light on how international economic law has influenced Latin American international law (LAIL), and the study of law more generally.

II. Methods and International Economic Law

This section summarizes the use of different methods in international economic law, including quantitative and qualitative approaches—such as surveys and large-N studies, experiments and quasi-experiments, comparative case studies, descriptive ethnographic and interview-based work, and rhetorical analytics—as well as critical and historical work. Such work sheds light on how international

Sergio Puig, *Interdisciplinarity and LAIL* In: *Latin American International Law in the Twenty-First Century.* Edited by: Alejandro Chehtman, Alexandra Huneeus, and Sergio Puig, Oxford University Press.
 DOI: 10.1093/9780197754016.003.0007

economic law is made, why it is made, and the conditions under which it has effects. I explain these methods by referencing five different types of interdisciplinary encounters that, along with Shaffer, I have dissected in a separate contribution.[1] In the following subsections, I relate this analysis to my discussion on LAIL.

Law and Economics

The dominant interdisciplinary form for the study of international economic law has long been economics, focusing on efficiency, optimization, and markets.[2] This work's importance reflected the growth of the trade law field in the 1990s and the market-oriented, neoliberal ideology of the time. All international trade law casebooks started with economic explanations for liberalizing trade and reasons to diverge from it considering market power, recapitulating the theories of Adam Smith, David Ricardo, Paul Samuelson, and Paul Krugman, among others. Building from these, Alan Sykes wrote a series of articles on the General Agreement on Trade and Tariffs (GATT), assessing economic and rational and public choice explanations of GATT rules and practices.[3]

The institutionalization of the World Trade Organization (WTO) dispute settlement—and, to a lesser extent, the North American Free Trade Association (NAFTA) and other regional trade agreements—soon attracted the attention of economists who worked with economically oriented legal scholars. A common theme was the need for more economic expertise in understanding and interpreting WTO law in WTO dispute settlement.[4] Economists were slower to examine international investment law. Recently, some economists have developed a law-and-economics approach to investment law under which developing countries in need of capital grant concessions to lower the cost of capital

[1] Sergio Puig and Gregory Shaffer, "Interdisciplinarity and International Economic Law," in *Encyclopedia on International Economic Law*, ed. Thomas Cottier and Krista N. Schefer (London: Edward Elgar, 2022), https://www.e-elgar.com/shop/usd/elgar-encyclopedia-of-international-economic-law-9781784713539.html.

[2] Classic treatises include John H. Jackson, *World Trade and the Law of GATT* (Indianapolis, IN: Bobbs Merrill, 1969), and Kenneth Dam, *The Gatt: Law and International Economic Organization* (Chicago: University of Chicago Press, 1977).

[3] Alan O. Sykes, "Protectionism as a 'Safeguard': A Positive Economic Analysis of the GATT 'Escape Clause' with Normative Speculations," *University of Chicago Law Review* 58 (1991): 255, 274–275 (characterizing GATT Article XIX as an escape clause for democracies, allowing them to respond to shocks in the political landscape). See also Alan O. Sykes, "Regulatory Protectionism and the Law of International Trade," *University of Chicago Law Review* 66 (1999): 1 (describing disputes that arise over the use of regulatory measures as protectionist devices).

[4] See, e.g., John H. Barton et al., *The Evolution of the Trade Regime: Politics, Law, and Economics of the GATT and the WTO* (Princeton, NJ: Princeton University Press, 2006), 213; K. Rose, "Do We Really Know that the WTO Increases Trade?" *American Economics Review* 94, no. 1 (2004): 112.

efficiently. These scholars likewise apply economic insights to assess the scope of investment agreements, standing, interpretive choices, and the structure of remedies and compensation.[5]

Recently, a "behavioralist" turn, questioning the sufficiency of rational choice assumptions, has impacted law and economics. For example, Anne van Aaken and Jurgen Kurtz developed a behavioral political economy approach to trade protectionism.[6] They explained protectionist policies in terms of "loss aversion," such that voters consider losses of jobs from trade rather than employment gains. In investment law, scholars have questioned rational actor models by examining the biases of arbitrators,[7] deploying behavioral approaches to understand the role of expertise in the interpretation of bilateral investment treaties,[8] and challenges to the social legitimacy of the investment law system.[9]

Political Science and the Political Economy of Law

In its multitudinous forms, power is a central variable in political science research. International relations realists explain much of international trade law regarding the market power that countries with large markets wield, be it the United States, China, or the European Union.[10] International relations "realists" theorize that the rules reflect the interests of dominant powers, which simply ignore them when they no longer serve their interest.[11]

As trade law was institutionalized, institutionalist-oriented political scientists studied international trade and investment law empirically to assess the

[5] Alan O. Sykes, "Public Versus Private Enforcement of International Economic Law: Standing and Remedy," *Journal of Legal Studies* 34 (2005): 631, 662 (concluding that private rights of action are valuable in the context of investment treaties). Emma Aisbett and Jonathan Bonnitcha, "A Pareto-Improving Compensation Rule for. Investment Treaties," *Journal of International and Economic Law* 24 (2021): 181.

[6] Anne van Aaken and Jürgen Kurtz, "Beyond Rational Choice: International Trade Law and the Behavioral Political Economy of Protectionism," *Journal of International Economic Law* 22 (2019): 601.

[7] Sergio Puig and Anton Strezhnev, "Affiliation Bias in Arbitration: An Experimental Approach," *Journal of Legal Studies* 46 (2017): 371.

[8] Yahli Shereshevsky and Tom Noah, "Does Exposure to Preparatory Work Affect Treaty Interpretation? An Experimental Study on International Law Students and Experts," *European Journal of International Law* 28 (2017): 1287, 1310 (finding that "preparatory work can play a significant role in decision making").

[9] Maria Laura Marceddu and Pietro Ortolani, "What Is Wrong with Investment Arbitration? Evidence from a Set of Behavioural Experiments," *European Journal of International Law* 31 (2020): 405, 410.

[10] R. Gilpin, *The Political Economy of International Relations* (Princeton, NJ: Princeton University Press, 1987).

[11] Jack L. Goldsmith and Eric A. Posner, *The Limits of International Law* (Oxford: Oxford University Press, 2005) (Goldsmith and Posner argued that nations will tend to pursue a self-interest as assessed by governing officials).

prospects for cooperative outcomes and different variables that explain the successful use of dispute settlement. Marc Busch and Eric Reinhardt assessed the relatively high success rate of resolving disputes under the more legalized WTO system.[12] Andrew Guzman and Beth Simmons studied whether power or legal capacity matters more for legal claims, using a research design focused on the identity of the respondent targeted by a developing state complainant.[13] They found that all but one of their proxies supported the legal capacity hypothesis, in contrast to a market power explanation.

Regarding investment law, Guzman explained that developing states are caught in a collective action problem.[14] They would be better off collectively if they could negotiate a multilateral treaty, but each developing state has an incentive to defect from the collective group to capture a greater share of the overall pool of investment. A vast body of work followed regarding the impact of bilateral investment treaties on investment patterns, deriving different conclusions in light of different specifications.[15] For example, Poulsen, Bonnitcha, and Yackee posit that the costs of bilateral investment treaties (BITs) significantly outweigh any possible benefits in general.[16] Their work builds on Yackee's work questioning whether international investment dispute settlement promotes significant new investment flows.[17]

Scholars have also assessed the effects of import competition on political support for particular policies.[18] This type of work has reinvigorated the assessment of the economic benefits of deep integration promoted by trade and investment agreements.[19] It helps drive more qualitative analyses by sociolegal scholars that contextualize the role of international economic law in modern societies.[20]

[12] Marc L. Busch and Eric Reinhardt, "Bargaining in the Shadow of the Law: Early Settlement in GATT/WTO Disputes," *Fordham International Law Journal* 24 (2000): 158.

[13] Andrew Guzman and Beth A. Simmons, "To Settle or Empanel? An Empirical Analysis of Litigation and Settlement at the World Trade Organization," *Journal of Legal Studies* 31 (2002): 205, 213 (demonstrating that states find it more difficult to settle trade disputes when the issue in dispute is not in a continuum, suggesting that states find it difficult to find compensatory transfers.)

[14] Andrew Guzman, "Why LDCs Sign Treaties That Hurt Them: Explaining the Popularity of Bilateral Investment Treaties," *Virginia Journal of International Law* 38 (1998): 639.

[15] J. Bonnitcha, L. Poulsen, and M. Waibel, *The Political Economy of the Investment Treaty Regime* (Oxford: Oxford University Press, 2017).

[16] L. Poulsen J. Bonnitcha, and Jason Yackee, Transatlantic Investment Treaty Protection, Paper No. 3 in the CEPS-CTR Project "TTIP in the Balance" (March 2015) available https://cdn.ceps.eu/wp-content/uploads/2015/03/SR102_ISDS.pdf.

[17] Jason Yackee, "Do Bilateral Investment Treaties Promote Foreign Direct Investment? Some Hints from Alternative Evidence," *Virginia Journal of International Law* 51 (2010): 397.

[18] J. B. Jensen, D. Quinn, and S. Weymouth, "Winners and Losers in International Trade: The Effects on US Presidential Voting," *International Organization* 71 (2017): 423.

[19] D. Rodrik, "What Do Trade Agreements Really Do?" *Journal of Economic Perspectives* 32 (2018): 73.

[20] Tim Dorlach and Paul Mertenskötter, "Interpreters of International Economic Law: Corporations and Bureaucrats in Contest over Chile's Nutrition Label," *Law and Society Review* 5 (2020): 571 (discussing the challenges to implement nutrition labeling regulation in Chile and the use of international trade and investment agreements in the process).

Sociology of Law

A core part of the discipline of sociology focuses on the institutionalization of norms. There are many exemplars of sociological approaches—from qualitative approaches that build on the work of Max Weber to quantitative work assessing the role of institutions and everyday legal practice. Two prominent approaches in international economic law, respectively, apply Pierre Bourdieu's field theory and the theory of transnational legal orders, the latter assessing the recursive relationship between international norm development and national and local law and practice. In both cases, scholars have engaged in fieldwork and sustained interviewing at multiple sites.

Applying frameworks influenced by Bourdieu regarding the role of professional and social capital in constructing law, Bryant Garth and Yves Dezalay analyzed international commercial arbitration.[21] They showed intense competition between arbitration sites and between American and European arbitrators—which helped shape and legitimize arbitration law. I used their work subsequently and applied network analysis to explore how factors such as social class, education, career, and expertise shape investment arbitration. Joseph Conti worked similarly regarding international trade law, assessing how "good cases" are constructed by a network of lawyers involved in WTO dispute settlement.[22]

Terence Halliday, Gregory Shaffer, and others have engaged in empirical projects assessing how norms develop, settle, and unsettle across state boundaries as part of what they conceptualize as "transnational legal orders."[23] This impressive work brings together old ("institutionalization") and new ("recursivity") social science concepts to develop testable hypotheses. They specify mechanisms that drive cycles of legal change beyond the state until a moving equilibrium (or relative "settlement") is reached in what they characterize as a transnational legal order. John Braithwaite and Peter Drahos conducted extensive earlier empirical work in this vein across areas of business law, including international trade and intellectual property law, focusing on the roles of state and non-state actors.[24] Shaffer applied this framework to assess the building of international trade law

[21] Y. Dezalay and B. Garth, *Dealing in Virtue* (Chicago: University of Chicago Press 1996).

[22] J. Conti, *Between Law and Diplomacy: The Social Contexts of Disputing at the World Trade Organization* (Stanford, CA: Stanford University Press, 2010).

[23] T. Halliday and G. Shaffer, *Transnational Legal Orders* (Cambridge: Cambridge University Press, 2015) (the edited volume contains examples in different contexts of international economic law of applying the theory).

[24] John Braithwaite and Peter Drahos, *Global Business Regulation* (Cambridge: Cambridge University Press, 2000).

capacity in China, Brazil, and India and its implications for the global trading system.[25] Block-Lieb and Halliday similarly applied it to the study of lawmaking by the United Nations Commission on International Trade Law (UNCITRAL), including how it regards investment law, bankruptcy law, and the carriage of goods by sea.[26]

Anthropology of Law

The core methodology in anthropology is ethnography, and this method has been used to study international economic law organizations, such as the World Bank and WTO. Galit Sarfaty analyzed the organizational culture of the World Bank to explore why it had not adopted a human rights policy or agenda at the time.[27] Annelise Riles studied international organizations of financial regulators to explain the loss of faith in both free-market regulation and state-led planning, as well as the use of expert tools.[28] These and other ethnographic approaches have provided alternative research paths to understand some of the failures of modern institutions in creating more equal societies.

In another line of research, Douglas Holmes and George Marcus theorized ethnographic work involving elites in which they treat elites not only as key informants but also as "epistemic partners" interested in understanding the processes being studied.[29] The interviews, in part, can be viewed as "collaborations" in the sense of forays into "making sense" of developments in the international economic law world. Shaffer (2021) applied this method in the study of the WTO, as have Anthea Roberts and Taylor Saint John (2021) in the study of investment law negotiations within UNCITRAL.[30]

[25] G. Shaffer, *Emerging Powers and the World Trading System: The Past and Future of International Economic Law* (Cambridge: Cambridge University Press, 2021).

[26] S. Block-Lieb and T. Halliday, *Global Lawmakers: International Organization in the Crafting of World Markets* (Cambridge: Cambridge University Press, 2017).

[27] Galit A. Sarfaty, *Values in Translation: Human Rights and the Culture of the World Bank* (Stanford, CA: Stanford University Press, 2012),

[28] A. Riles, *Collateral Knowledge: Legal Reasoning in the Global Financial Markets* (Chicago: University of Chicago Press, 2011).

[29] D. Holmes and G. Marcus, "Fast Capitalism: Para-Ethnography and the Rise of the Symbolic Analyst," in *Frontiers of Capital*, ed. Melissa S. Fisher and Greg Downey (Durham, NC: Duke University Press, 2006).

[30] G. Shaffer, *Emerging Powers and the World Trading System: The Past and Future of International Economic Law* (Cambridge: Cambridge University Press, 2021). Anthea Roberts and Taylor St. John, "Complex Designers and Emergent Design: Reforming the Investment Treaty System," *American Journal of International Law* 116 (2022): 96.

History and Critical Theory

The understanding and framing of international economic law problems have a contested history. Much of the conventional knowledge of international trade, investment, and monetary law begins with the challenges of the interwar period, where economic historians contend that tit-for-tat reprisals of currency devaluations and tariffs exacerbated international conflicts, as well as economic immiseration at home.[31] Other histories focus on the role of ideas, such as the Austrian school of ordo-liberals, in shaping the international trade regime.[32] Yet others assess the unintended consequences of early regime decisions, leading to investor-state dispute settlement.[33]

Critical theory, in contrast, often turns to history to delegitimate international economic law structures rather than to support them.[34] This is particularly apparent in international investment law, given its imperial legacies involving "gunboat diplomacy" to protect private companies' claims. It similarly extends to international trade law considering trade patterns between the "core" (industrial powers) and the "periphery" (developing country exporters of raw materials). For critical theorists, international economic law reflects asymmetric public and private power and constitutes capitalism.[35] Jothie Rajah, for example, uses rhetorical analysis to assess the World Bank's construction of rule-of-law rhetoric to further its economic development prescriptions.[36]

Some theorists critique "interdisciplinary" work because of the risk that functionalist-oriented social science work naturalizes understanding problems in ways that serve hegemonic interests.[37] Critical work aims to destabilize understandings of international economic law to open new imaginaries for what it could be, particularly in light of colonial legacies, as stressed by scholars of Third World approaches to international law (TWAIL).[38] Some of this analysis

[31] Douglas A. Irwin, *Clashing over Commerce: A History of US Trade Policy* (Chicago: University of Chicago Press, 2017).

[32] Quinn Slobodian, *Globalists: The End of Empire and the Birth of Neoliberalism* (Cambridge, MA: Harvard University Press, 2018)

[33] Taylor St. John, *The Rise of Investor-State Arbitration* (Oxford: Oxford University Press, 2017).

[34] Anne Orford, *International Law and the Politics of History* (Cambridge: Cambridge University Press, 2021).

[35] Katherina Pistor, *The Code of Capital: How the Law Creates Wealth and Inequality* (Princeton, NJ: Princeton University Press, 2019).

[36] J. Rajah, "Rule of Law as Transnational Legal Order," in *Transnational Legal Orders*, ed. T. Halliday and G. Shaffer (Cambridge: Cambridge University Press, 2015).

[37] Martti Koskenniemi, "Law, Teleology and International Relations: An Essay in Counterdisciplinarity," 26 *International Relations* 26 (2011): 3, 19–21 (emphasizing law's dependence upon style and the method of framing an argument over reliance upon empirical data); see also Martti Koskenniemi, "Miserable Comforters: International Relations as a New Natural Law," *European Journal of International Relations* 15 (2009): 395, 416 (discussing the effects of the indeterminacy of international law).

[38] Anthony Anghie, *Imperialism, Sovereignty and the Making of International Law* (Cambridge: Cambridge University Press, 2005); James Gathii, *War, Commerce, and International*

deploys Marxism to critique the capitalist bias of international economic law, which shapes the distribution of rights and duties and material outcomes among different communities and other constituencies of international law.[39]

III. Interdisciplinarity and International Economic Law

In section II, I discussed the methods and approaches in interdisciplinary international economic law (IEL) encounters and the types of questions scholars in the field are concerned with. In this section, I dissect some of the most essential interdisciplinary works about the field that centered on Latin America as an object of study. This analysis confirms what other scholars like Perrone have asserted: interdisciplinary IEL scholarship has been a mechanism for "imagining alternatives" to the current global economic order—an order developed with limited input from actors in this region.[40]

Investment

IEL scholars with an emphasis on Latin America have taken a particular interest in international investment law.[41] Partly, this results from the large number of investment cases brought against states in the region and partly from the growing popularity of international investment agreements and arbitration as cites for interdisciplinary explorations. Since many of the disputes involving states in the region as respondents concern oil and gas, mining, and energy sectors, the scholarship reflects a deep concern with the fairness of this legal regime. Such a regime seems to support an *extractivist* business logic—this is, it is designed to protect and insulate large investments for export markets, the "privatization" of

Law (Oxford: Oxford University Press, 2009); S. Pahuja, *Decolonising International Law* (Cambridge: Cambridge University Press, 2011).

[39] Ntina Tzouvala, *Capitalism as Civilisation: A History of International Law* (Cambridge: Cambridge University Press, 2020).

[40] Nicolás M. Perrone, "¿Un espacio para pensar alternativas? La academia latinoamericana de derecho internacional económico frente al orden económico global," *Revista Derecho del Estado* no. 36 (June 2016): 199, 199–226, https://doi.org/10.18601/01229893.n36.07.

[41] See, e.g., Felix Becker, *Los Tratados de Amistad, Comercio y Navegación y la Integración de los Estados Independientes Americanos en el Sistema Internacional, inProblemas de la For-mación del Estado y de la Nación en Hispanoamérica* (1984), 247. See also Horacio D. Rosatti, "Los Tratados Bilaterales de Inversion, el Arbitraje Internacional Obligatorio y el Sistema Constitucional Argentino," *Revista Juridica La Ley* (October 15, 2003): 67–198.

natural resources, the "socialization" of corporate losses, the "insulation" of regulatory risk, and the "repatriation" of capital to wealthy, industrialized countries.[42]

With these impacts in mind, scholars have also investigated how international investment law affects investment decisions. For example, authors have examined how foreign investment inflows, stock, and outgoing profit flows in the neoliberal period—roughly the twenty-fve-year period after the collapse of the Berlin Wall. Some authors conclude that the basic tenet of the dependency thesis still holds today. There is a huge and underreported transfer of surplus value out of the continent, thanks partly to trade and investment agreements.[43] One implication is that the legal regimes created by international law might support powerful economic interests, whether national or not, that often fail to reinvest profits in the region. Hence, scholars have also questioned the appropriateness of such a legal approach to generate innovation and research and development (R&D) in the region.[44] This transfer of knowledge is often considered necessary for economic prosperity.

In response to some concerns with international investment, scholars have suggested new models, including new approaches to international investment dispute settlement.[45] In the current reform process in UNCITRAL, many Latin American states have relied on interdisciplinary work to frame positions that attempt to transform the system.[46] Other scholars have developed and proposed using a new business environment index with indicators more concerned with the problems in the region. These new models, in part, question the basic economic principles—and their interpretation by law and economic scholars—that are institutionalized in economic agreements, especially BITs.[47]

[42] Nicolás M. Perrone, "Local Communities, Extractivism and International Investment Law: The Case of Five Colombian Communities," *Globalizations* 19, no. 6 (2022): 837–853, https://doi.org/10.1080/14747731.2022.2035494.

[43] Andy Higginbottom, "The Political Economy of Foreign Investment in Latin America: Dependency Revisited," *Latin American Perspectives* (May 2013): 184–206.

[44] Claudio Bravo-Ortega, "Exploring the Interaction between Intellectual Property Rights, Human Capital and R&D Expenditures: Are There Implications for Developing Countries?" *International Journal of Technological Learning, Innovation and Development* 5, no. 3 (2012): 237–266.

[45] For an analysis of some approaches to foreign investment in the region during the period 2004–2012, see María José Luque Macías, "Current Approaches to the International Investment Regime in South America," in *European Yearbook of International Economic Law* (New York: Springer, 2013) 285. María José Luque Macías, "Reliance on Alternative Methods for Investment Protection through National Laws, Investment Contracts, and Regional Institutions in Latin America," in *Shifting Paradigms in International Investment Law. More Balanced, Less Isolated, Increasingly Diversified* (Oxford: Oxford University Press, 2016) 291.

[46] See discussion in Anthea Roberts and Taylor St. John, "UNCITRAL and ISDS Reform: What to Expect When You're Expecting," *EJILTalk*! (blog), October 5, 2022.

[47] Alvaro Santos, "Labor Flexibility, Legal Reform and Economic Development," *Virginia Journal of International Law* 50 (2009): 43–106.

Trade and IP

Recent scholarship on international trade seems more concerned with how the current international trading system contributed to the transfer of technology that might improve R&D in the region. This scholarship often assumes that the pace of economic integration and innovation may activate a virtuous cycle of social and economic development—that is, faster integration leads to more efficient global value chains that lead to more income for workers. For example, some scholars argue that innovation is a central parameter in developing a knowledge-based economy. However, the author observes that Latin America has failed to use the international trading system to improve its economic performance and to overcome its social and financial problems.[48] One point of contention is whether international trade deals sufficiently increase the business participation of Latin American producers in world trade and the development of knowledge in the region (e.g., filling patent applications by national companies).

The impact of regional alternatives to the global trading system dominated by industrialized nations has likewise served as the focus of interdisciplinary research. For instance, Porter questions a rigid global order that fails to achieve consensus that benefits smaller, less influential economies.[49] Like his work, others study the cases of the MERCOSUR, the Andean Community, the Union of South American Nations (UNASUR), and the Bolivarian Alternative for the Americas (ALBA) as direct challenges to the US-led regional integration and neoliberalism.[50] Some of these studies have compared exclusively Latin American options with the NAFTA and the Dominican Republic–Central America Free Trade Agreement (CAFTA-DR)—which include the United States—assessing their impact on different social, political, and economic indicators, including prices of new goods and services.[51] Some of these pieces identify how domestic politics in the region have realigned because of trade policy. Yet, most of these

[48] Rodrigo Fuentes-Solís, De la Fuente-Mella Hanns, and Ana María Vallina-Hernández, "Analysis of the Internationalization and Value Chain Activities in Chilean Enterprises" *Contemporary Economics* 16, no 1 (June 9, 2022): 88–105, 2022, SSRN: https://ssrn.com/abstract=4132240.

[49] Patrick Porter, *The False Promise of Liberal Order: Nostalgia, Delusion, and the Rise of Trump* (New York: Polity, 2020).

[50] Rafael A. Porrata-Doria, Jr., "ALBA and UNASUR: Back to the Future?" *Santa Clara Journal of International Law* 20 (2022): 1; Karen J. Alter and Laurence R. Helfer, *Transplanting International Courts: The Law and Politics of the Andean Tribunal of Justice* (Oxford: Oxford University Press, 2017); Larry Catá Backer and Augusto Molina, "Cuba and the Construction of Alternative Global Trade Systems: ALBA and Free Trade in the Americas," *University of Pennsylvania Journal of International Law* 31, no. 3 (2010): 679, 698.

[51] J. S. Blum, "The FTAA and the Fast Track to Forgetting the Environment: A Comparison of the NAFTA and the Mercosur Environmental Models as Examples for the Hemisphere," *Texas International Law Journal* 35, no. 3 (2000): 435–458; M. White, C. Salas, and S. Gammage, *NAFTA and the FTAA: A Gender Analysis of Employment and Poverty Impacts in Agriculture* (Washington, DC: Women's Edge Coalition, 2003).

studies conclude that the degree of export diversification with these alternatives is limited. Moreover, the effects on welfare remain disappointing, especially compared to the international integration pattern followed by East Asian economies.[52]

The relationship between international trading and financial systems has remained largely unexplored in Latin American scholarship. However, some have offered hints that trade and investment inducements by the United States (after World War II and the fall of the Berlin Wall) may have had a role in capital flight from Latin America.[53] And others assessed both short- and long-run effects of trade and monetary policies on the business cycle linkages between the Latin American bloc and the four largest economies in the world (namely, the United States, the Euro area, Japan, and China). The general assessment is that the international trading system has not sufficiently created the conditions to retain capital that can be reinvested to incentivize R&D and generate a virtuous development cycle.[54]

Finance

Contrastingly, the role of international financial institutions and the relationship between the regulation of financial markets and the politics and macroeconomics in Latin America have resulted in important interdisciplinary work.[55] One area of particular interest is how Wall Street (as a proxy for US economic interests) and international financial institutions react to political events in the region. Key questions surround the effects of liberalization of the financial markets on economic growth and other commonly used indicators. For example, Iwasaki performed a meta-analysis of 233 analyses collected from 21 previous works and found some genuine empirical evidence of the growth-promoting effect of finance liberalization in the region.[56] It is unclear, however, if the effects result from changes in domestic law or changes imposed as conditions for financial support by international financial institutions, which is a concern of critics of the work of such international organizations.

[52] J. Romalis, "NAFTA's and CUSFTA's Impact on international Trade," *The Review of Economics and Statistics* 89, no. 3 (2007): 416–435; N. Chorev, *Remaking U.S. Trade Policy: From Protectionism to Globalization* (Ithaca, NY: Cornell University Press, 2007).

[53] John P. Tuman and Craig F. Emmert, "The Political Economy of U.S. Foreign Direct Investment in Latin America: A Reappraisal," *Latin American Research Review* 39, no. 3 (2004): 9–28.

[54] Guglielmo Maria Caporale and Alessandro Girardi, "Business Cycles, International Trade and Capital Flows: Evidence from Latin America," *Empirical Economics* 50, no. 2 (2016): 231–252.

[55] Carlos Santiso, "The Contentious Washington Consensus: Reforming the Reforms in Emerging Markets," *Review of International Political Economy* 11, no. 4 (2004): 827–843.

[56] Ichiro Iwasaki, "The Finance-Growth Nexus in Latin America and the Caribbean: A Meta-Analytic Perspective," *World Development* 149 (2022): 105692.

Key to the discussions of international finance and Latin America is the question of who influences the system. Armijo, for example, concludes that private foreign inflows, strongly promoted by Western-led multilateral actors like the Organisation for Economic Co-operation and Development (OECD) and the World Bank, during the 2010s, may have a negative influence on the region.[57] For the author, excessive dependence on private securities markets funded by globally mobile capital often undercuts the achievement of other valued societal goals, such as reducing inequality and ensuring democratic accountability. This can be read as support for the diversification of finance but, even more important, for the development of regional institutions able to withstand the negative influence of traditional financial power centers.

Following a recent trend in the diversification of financing, the influence of Chinese lending in Latin America has been a growing concern. Kaplan et al. looked at the unconditional lending practices of China. This question partly emerged because of the heavily criticized conditionalities imposed by the World Bank (and others) in its lending operations.[58] The author employs a comparative case study analysis of two of China's largest debtors—Brazil and Venezuela—before and after the introduction of Chinese credit. The main finding is that budget deficits increase as Chinese state-to-state financing accounts for a larger share of total external public financing. This, in a way, helps to explain the conditions under which nations veer away from governance models that stress the importance of a reduced fiscal deficit and competitive exchange rates—two of ten elements of the Washington Consensus.[59]

Business and Human Rights

Finally, efforts have also been made to study the connections between the business activities promoted by international economic law and human rights. Scholars have recognized the parallel goals toward which international economic law and human rights law strive. For example, the Ruggie Guiding Principles of Business and Human Rights, derived from an academic endeavor, reiterate the human rights duties that apply to all states, international organizations, and business enterprises, "regardless of their size, sector, location, ownership and

[57] Leslie Elliott Armijo, Daniel C. Tirone, and Hyoung-kyu Chey, "The Monetary and Financial Powers of States: Theory, Dataset, and Observations on the Trajectory of American Dominance," *New Political Economy* 25, no. 2 (2019): 174–194.

[58] Stephen B. Kaplan, "Banking Unconditionally: The Political Economy of Chinese Finance in Latin America," *Review of International Political Economy* 23, no. 4 (2016): 643–676.

[59] Carlos Lopes, "Economic Growth and Inequality: The New Post-Washington Consensus," *RCCS Annual Review* 4, no. 4 (2012).

structure."[60] The Guiding Principles reflect the general effort to understand how states and non-state actors may be implicated when commercial activities conflict with human rights and how to address some of these conflicts.

Latin American scholars have been especially interested in highlighting how human rights law interacts with the protections that apply exclusively to Indigenous peoples—this is partly the result of the robust development of the law and the practice of Indigenous rights in the region. In other words, within international human rights law, international Indigenous human rights are specific commitments that protect and empower Indigenous peoples, who tend to be especially susceptible to the effects of multinational corporations (in extractive sectors) doing business in the region. Scholars have denounced treaties encouraging foreign direct investment (FDI) by granting special rights to foreign investors (and an arbitration process outside normal, national courts to enforce such rights).[61] In this context, ethnographic studies have helped to open alternative discussions on the effect of international economic law by highlighting, with particular examples, some of the failures of multilateral institutions like the World Bank in creating more equal societies.[62] Works of this nature have also helped to import concepts like "consultation," "shared benefits," or "culturally appropriate procedures" into the mainstream debates of international economic law.

IV. Interdisciplinarity and Latin American International Law

The stakes of international economic law are too important to leave to lawyers and legal professionals. Their expertise is necessary but insufficient. Given the gaping differences in approaches, some may question whether interdisciplinary work leads to a dead end and thus call for a return to legal formalism.[63] However, problem-solving requires reflexive conceptual work and the study of the law-in-action. Each interdisciplinary approach provides essential tools for doing that, developing and applying international economic law in light of its promise and for understanding and responding to its pathologies, complicities, and limits.

[60] John Ruggie, "Report of the Special Representative of the Secretary-General on the Issue of Human Rights and Transnational Corporations and Other Business Enterprises: Guiding Principles on Business and Human Rights: Implementing the United Nations 'Protect, Respect and Remedy' Framework," *Netherlands Quarterly of Human Rights* 29, no. 2 (2011): 224–253.

[61] Lorenzo Cotula, "(Dis)integration in Global Resource Governance: Extractivism, Human Rights, and Investment Treaties," *Journal of International Economic Law* 23, no. 2 (2020): 431–454.

[62] S. James Anaya and Sergio Puig, "Mitigating State Sovereignty: The Duty to Consult with Indigenous Peoples," *University of Toronto Law Journal* 67 (2017): 435.

[63] M. Koskenniemi, "Law, Teleology and International Relations: An Essay in Counterdisciplinarity," *International Relations* 26 (2012): 3–34.

The stakes are also too important to leave interdisciplinary encounters to topics, issues, and problems of concern primarily to scholars and policymakers in traditional centers of economic and political power. Hence, the survey of the interdisciplinary literature helps us identify how the case of Latin American international interdisciplinary scholarship has contributed to refocusing the field in a broader direction and what its plausible implications for the study of law in the region are more generally. Here, I conclude with two reflections.

The Effect of Interdisciplinarity on IEL

Interdisciplinary legal scholarship can have a significant impact on the field of international law in several ways. First, it can help broaden the scope of legal research: interdisciplinary legal scholarship allows researchers to draw upon insights and methodologies from other fields, such as psychology, economics, sociology, and political science, to analyze legal issues from multiple perspectives. This broadening can enable a more comprehensive understanding of legal and policy problems. From this perspective, Latin American encounters with interdisciplinary IEL have questioned the usefulness of international investment law as a tool for economic growth and development, particularly its utility for local and Indigenous communities affected by the adverse effects of investments in some sectors. It has also broadened the scope of contestation against multilateral organizations like the WTO, often perceived as tilted in favor of powerful nations from the Global North. Finally, it has also helped to temper the criticism of some legal regimes like international finance and to slow the enthusiasm for regional alternatives to the current multilateral organizations.

The interdisciplinary scholarship has also contributed by creating new hypotheses, legal theories and approaches that draw upon insights from related fields. For example, in part, based on my work drawing from sociology, international arbitrators are now seen as an essential part of the power structures that shape the law and the arbitration outcomes of international investment law in the region. The same process can help theorize complex legal issues that cannot be fully understood through a single discipline or strict legal analysis. For example, understanding the impact of financial regulation requires insights from both economics and political science. In the region, the work of Gregory Shaffer has helped to theorize alternative models of economic development by looking at the engagement of Brazil (or China) and Brazilian interests with other nations and multinational organizations.[64]

[64] Gregory Shaffer et al., "The Trials of Winning at the WTO: What Lies Behind Brazil's Success," *Cornell International Law Journal* 41 (2008): 383, 384–385; Gregory Shaffer, *Emerging Powers and the*

Finally, interdisciplinary legal scholarship can enhance the relevance of legal research by making it more applicable to real-world problems. For example, multidisciplinary research on the effects of trade liberalization on the growth of R&D can inform policymakers and practitioners on how to reduce dependency on foreign technology and financing—or find ways for more autochthonous mechanisms to enhance economic growth. Interdisciplinary legal scholarship can provide a richer and more nuanced understanding of legal problems, leading to more effective and just legal solutions. LAIL and its encounters have facilitated the exploration of alternatives to the current global economic order and provided some tools, albeit limited, to compare the experiences of other regions within this field of international law.

The Effect of IEL on the Method

I conclude with a more general point regarding the effect of IEL interdisciplinarity on LAIL methods and approaches.

In Latin America, legal positivism was seen as breaking with the traditional legal systems inherited from colonialism and creating new legal orders based on reason, logic, and the needs of the modern state. Legal positivism provided a framework for legal scholars to analyze and critique the existing legal systems and propose legal reforms and new institutions. The study of international law was no exception.

Also, in the region, legal positivism was often associated with developing the civil law tradition, which is based on written codes and interpreting those codes by judges and administrative (and other) authorities. This tradition emphasized the importance of legal rules and formal procedures. The object of study tended to be the law (substantive and procedure), without much regard to the "extra-legal" factors such as institutions, lawyers, political authorities, and so on, that shape and affect the making, application, interpretation, and enforcement of the law. In this sense, positivism was fitting for the regional political systems in the region that limited democratic engagement. Today, legal positivism continues to be a dominant school of thought in the region, albeit decreasing, despite criticism and debate, particularly around issues of justice, morality, and the role of the law in modern societies.

The interdisciplinary encounters of IEL have contributed to moving legal scholarship about law away from strict legal analysis and to recognizing the importance of the role of law in modern, globalized societies. The new methods

World Trading System: The Past and Future of International Economic Law (Cambridge: Cambridge University Press, 2021).

adopted tend to emphasize the importance of understanding the social, political, and economic context in which legal decisions are made, including increased interdependency and cultural convergence. Hence, the interdisciplinary encounters belong to legal realism, where the law is not a set of abstract rules or principles but rather shaped by the individuals and institutions involved in its creation, interpretation, and application.

This move in the study of law is significant because it challenges the notion that law is objective and impartial and highlights the role of power, money, people, and politics in shaping legal decisions. It encourages scholars and practitioners to consider the social, political, and economic consequences of legal decisions and to work toward creating a more just and equitable legal system. Perhaps because of the obvious ways in which IEL mirrors the structural imbalances between different countries, interdisciplinarity has been common as a way to challenge international law. It is also possible that interaction with a global community of scholars made these encounters more common. In my view, the effect of the method is perhaps the most critical contribution of IEL to the study of international law in Latin America

Yet, the encounter between IEL and LAIL has contributed to a more important sociopolitical realization. The vertical, hierarchical form of authority that nobility and elites used for social control since the foundation of the nation-state became less useful. Such old forms of authority demanded compromises but enabled a Criollo elite to exercise power—the Colonial Law of Alvarez. In newer societies, a more horizontal, less hierarchical form of authority emerged. The new age that arose, as evidenced by the interdisciplinary encounters, was never wholly divorced from such power structures. But our modern societies have changed. The demand for better products, better services as well as more rights, including human rights, has made more apparent the realization that international law is a part cause, part effect of a changing culture. The method is an important conduit for that, and IEL might have contributed—albeit at the margins—to a change.

V. Conclusion

Interdisciplinary IEL scholarship has been a mechanism to "imagining alternatives" to the current global economic order where Latin America plays only a marginal role.[65] It has also been a site to challenge an excessively doctrinal view of the law in general and international law in particular, opening a broader view of how the law is shaped by the actors involved in its creation and

[65] Perrone, "¿Un espacio para pensar alternativas?"

application. Perhaps because the stakes of international economic law are essential, interdisciplinary research of the region and by scholars of the region has been a growing phenomenon, impacting the approach to studying law in the area. As the conditions continue to change and the sophistication of the scholars in the regions grows, interdisciplinary IEL has the potential to make LAIL more influential worldwide as a way to contest the sociopolitical aspects and cultural assumptions of international law.

8

Law and Development in/from Latin America

*Mariana Mota Prado**

I. Introduction

While international development policies encompass a global effort to enhance human capabilities, raise standards of living, and increase individual and collective welfare worldwide, there are many challenges to the universal aspirations of development as a field of study. One is the end goal of development: should we assume that every society aspires to achieve the same goals? Cultural relativists will answer this question in the negative. Others argue that there could be universal aspirations (e.g., economic growth), but strategies to pursue these common objectives should be contextual. Therefore, the goals may be universal, but policies are designed locally. A third view is that development goals and policy recommendations are universal (e.g., protection of individual property rights promotes economic growth).[1]

Law and development scholarship is also mired in similar debates.[2] Since its inception, influential scholars have debated whether it is possible to adopt universalistic assumptions, considering how the social-political-historical-cultural context is relevant for the success of legal reforms.[3] More recently, by embracing the importance of context, some law and development scholars have struggled

* I am grateful to the comments and suggestions of the editors of this volume, and other contributors. I am indebted to Ashna Hudani and Foti Vito for excellent research assistance. All remaining errors are mine.

[1] The field of international development, broadly defined, and the field of economic development have until recently been strongly influenced by claims of universality and internationalism. H. W. Arndt, *Economic Development: The History of an Idea* (Chicago: University of Chicago Press, 1989); Gerald Meier, *The Biography of a Subject: An Evolution of Development Economics* (Oxford: Oxford University Press, 2004). For the more recent literature that—at least partially—challenges these claims to universalism and internationalism, see Abhijit Banerjee and Esther Duflo, *Poor Economics: A Radical Rethinking of the Way to Fight Global Poverty* (New York: Public Affairs, 2012); Abhijit Banerjee and Esther Duflo, *Good Economics for Hard Times: Better Answers to Our Biggest Problems* (New York: Public Affairs, 2019).

[2] Mariana Mota Prado, "What Is Law and Development?" *Revista Argentina de Teoría Juridica* 11, no.1 (2010), https://ssrn.com/abstract=1907298; Mariana Mota Prado and Michael J. Trebilcock, *Advanced Introduction to Law and Development* (2nd ed., Cheltenham, UK: Edward Elgar, 2021).

[3] David Trubek and Marc Galanter, "Scholars in Self-Estrangement: Some Reflections on the Crisis in Law and Development Studies in the United States," *Wisconsin Law Review* 1974, no. 4 (1974): 1062–1102; John Henry Merryman, "Comparative Law and Social Change: On the

Mariana Mota Prado, *Law and Development in/from Latin America* In: *Latin American International Law in the Twenty-First Century*. Edited by: Alejandro Chehtman, Alexandra Huneeus, and Sergio Puig, Oxford University Press. © Oxford University Press 2025. DOI: 10.1093/9780197754016.003.0008

with the opposite question: considering the need for locally adapted solutions and the importance of context in assessing and defining problems, are there enough shared understandings or generalizable concepts that allow us to sustain any claims to universality that would allow scholars to call this a unified and coherent field of study?[4] Or, has law and development scholarship disintegrated into silos by emphasizing the importance of context.[5]

These law and development debates have much in common with the findings of Anthea Roberts' book, *Is International Law International?* Through careful research, Roberts shows how international law is very diverse globally.[6] While such findings may be counterintuitive for a field that claims or aspires to be universal, it is unlikely that similar findings would alarm most law and development scholars. Yet, exploring the complexities of defining what is "local" and what is "international" about law and development seems relevant.[7] To do so, this chapter uses three case studies of contributions to law and development that were conceived, created, or perfected in Latin America to identify different ways in which "local" ideas, insights, and policies may interact with the existing international development paradigm and international development institutions, and how such interactions vary in nature and over time. The case studies are loosely associated with the conceptual framework offered by Roberts to describe the interaction between the local and the universal in international law: *difference, dominance,* and *disruption.*[8]

The first case study is related to dependency theory, which was developed in the 1950s and 1960s by Latin American economists and challenged the then-prevailing theories of economic development. Dependency theory has influenced many developing nations worldwide and was adopted as a theoretical

Origins, Style, Decline, and Revival of the Law and Development Movement," *American Journal of Comparative Law* 457, no. 3 (1977): 457–491, https://doi.org/10.2307/839690.

[4] Michael Trebilcock, "Between Universalism and Relativism: Reflections on the Evolution of Law and Development Studies," *University of Toronto Law Journal* 66, no. 3 (2016): 330–352, https://doi.org/10.3138/UTLJ.3622.

[5] David Trubek, "Law and Development: Forty Years After: Scholars in Self-Estrangement," *University of Toronto Law Journal* 66, no. 3 (2016): 301–329, https://doi.org/10.3138/UTLJ.3671.

[6] Anthea Roberts, *Is International Law International?* (Oxford: Oxford University Press, 2017).

[7] The expression "law and development" may refer to either a field of research, populated primarily by academics and scholars, or a field for practice. These two fields often operate in silos and have little dialogue with each other. Mariana Mota Prado, "Book Review: *The Futility of Law and Development: China and the Dangers of Exporting American Law* by Jedidiah J Kroncke (New York: Oxford University Press, 2016)," *Asian Journal of Comparative Law* 13, no. 1 (2018): 197–202, https://doi.org/10.1017/asjcl.2018.2; Jedidiah J. Kroncke, "Author's Response to the Book Review of *The Futility of Law and Development*," *Asian Journal of Comparative Law* 13, no. 1 (2018): 202–205; Michael Charles Leach, "A Kaleidoscope of Meaning Fragments: Understanding the Rule of Law Paradoxes in International Development" (doctoral dissertation, University of Tilburg, 2021). Yet, the case studies in this chapter illustrate moments in which there is a dialogue between scholars, policymakers, and practitioners.

[8] Roberts, "Is International Law International?"

framework in many developed countries. The second case study explores the work of Peruvian economist Hernando de Soto on the protection of property rights and bureaucratic reforms. De Soto's work became highly influential in international development circles. The third case study is related to conditional cash transfers (CCTs). In the mid-1990s and early 2000s, Brazil and Mexico adopted policy experiments in social welfare, and CCT programs have now been adopted in most countries of the region and elsewhere. Not only have CCTs been embraced by international development institutions as a promising development strategy, but their scientific assessment has influenced meaningful discussions in international circles on how to conduct policy experimentation.

II. Difference in Law and Development: Dependency Theory

Dependency theory has had a significant influence on academic and policy circles in Latin America and other countries. Emerging in the mid-1960s from a transnational network of theorists with its epicenter in Chile, dependency theory became the dominant viewpoint in Latin American countries in the 1970s. The theory reached worldwide influence during that decade, significantly contributing to the fields of political economy, sociology, political science, history, and cultural criticism.[9]

Dependency theory holds that the relationship between the "periphery" of less developed countries (LDCs) and the "core" of more developed, industrialized countries has worked to the detriment of the former.[10] Rooted in economic history, the theory was initially conceptualized in the late 1960s to account for Latin America's continuing underdevelopment by the *dependentistas*, as the dependency theorists and followers were often called.[11] Dependence indicates a relational process where the economies of LDCs are conditioned by the development and expansion of the developed economies to which they are subordinated.[12] It is characterized by a high infiltration of foreign capital, dependence on capital goods and technology from developed countries, and the exploitation of the productive capacities of LDCs in favor of the international

[9] Clara I. Ruvituso, "From the South to the North: The Circulation of Latin American Dependency Theories in the Federal Republic of Germany," *Current Sociology* 68, no. 1 (2020): 22–40, https://doi.org/10.1177/0011392119885170.

[10] James C. W. Ahiakpor, "The Success and Failure of Dependency Theory: The Experience of Ghana. International Organization," *International Organization* 39, no. 3 (1985): 535–552, https://doi.org/10.1017/S0020818300019172.

[11] Ibid.

[12] Ramón Grosfoguel, "Developmentalism, Modernity, and Dependency Theory in Latin America," *Nepantla: Views from South* 1, no. 2 (2000): 347–374.

division of labor.[13] In large part, dependency theory was a response to modernization theory. Often espoused by domestic actors from developed nations and replicated by some Latin American thinkers during the 1960s and 1970s,[14] modernization theory assumed that each country was an independent unit that slowly develops through stages.[15]

According to dependency theory, the technology, machinery, and finance that LDCs import from developed countries contribute to underdevelopment because, among other factors, the world exchange system allocates to LDCs the production of raw materials and labor-intensive processed goods for export at low prices.[16] Developed countries export relatively capital- and skill-intensive goods to LDCs at excessively high prices while extracting the surpluses from their investments in LDCs, resulting in a continually unequal exchange.[17] Notably, this is exacerbated by their currencies also participating unequally in international markets.[18] In situations where world demand for the traditional exports of LDCs is low, LDCs are forced to take on significant foreign debt due to their continued dependence on goods and technology imported from developed countries.[19] In tandem with this unequal trade relationship, LDC elites are said to match the cultural and taste preferences of developed countries, ultimately reinforcing underdevelopment while accumulating large profits.[20]

Some Latin American scholars also proposed a version of dependency theory that divided the world into three: the core, periphery, and semiperiphery. This division is associated with Immanuel Wallerstein's world-system theory,[21] but the relationship between the two is unclear. While some scholars consider

[13] Arno Tausch, "Globalisation and Development: The Relevance of Classical 'Dependency Theory' on the World Today," *International Social Science Journal* 61, no. 202 (2010): 467–488, https://doi.org/10.1111/j.1468-2451.2011.01786.x.

[14] Modernization theory was in line with Western and Soviet models of development during the 1960 and 1970s. See Cristóbal Kay, "Modernization and Dependency Theory," in *The Routledge Handbook of Latin American Development*, ed. Julie Cupples, Marcela Palomino-Schalscha, and Manuel Prieto (London: Routledge, 2018), for a discussion of Latin American thinkers who replicated and modified modernization theory instead of dependency theory.

[15] Grosfoguel, "Developmentalism, Modernity"; and Michael Niblett, "The 'Catastrophic Consciousness of Backwardness': Culture and Dependency Theory in Latin America and the Caribbean," *New Formations* 103 (2021): 113–133, https://doi.org/10.3898/newf:103.07.2021.

[16] Ahiakpor, "Success and Failure."

[17] Ibid.

[18] Tausch, "Globalisation and Development."

[19] Haldun Gulalp, "The Eurocentrism of dependency theory and the question of 'authenticity': a view from Turkey," *Third World Quarterly* 19, no. 5 (1998): 951–961, https://doi.org/10.1080/01436599814118.

[20] David S. Randolf, "Philippine Underdevelopment and Dependency Theory," *Philippine Sociological Review* 28, no. 1/4 (1980): 81–87, https://www.jstor.org/stable/23892107.

[21] Motolani Agbebi and Petri Virtanen, "Dependency Theory—A Conceptual Lens to Understand China's Presence in Africa?" *Forum for Development Studies* 44, no. 3 (2017): 433, https://doi.org/10.1080/08039410.2017.1281161.

world-systems theory an offshoot of dependency theory,[22] others warn against confusing it with dependency theory.[23] In any event, the distinction tried to provide a more nuanced description of LDCs: "newly industrializing countries" such as Brazil, Mexico, Hong Kong, South Korea, Spain, Portugal, and Yugoslavia may have been considered part of the semiperiphery,[24] as these countries had a higher degree of autonomy.[25] Under these analytical distinctions, a country was considered part of the semiperiphery if it was able to develop its economic system (i.e., produce its own capital goods) but was still being subordinated to the central economies in the international capitalist system (e.g., further progress blocked by the reluctance of foreign corporations to transfer technology). Dos Santos described this distinction as whether a country could achieve an "articulated" economy, arguing that absolute autonomy was not attainable by dependent countries as long as the world system was interdependent.[26] Other scholars embraced this distinction between the periphery and semiperiphery based on the concept of subimperialism proposed by Ruy Mauro Marini.[27] For instance, in his analysis of Brazil after the military coup of 1964, Marini argued that Brazil engaged in military spending and used its large economy, geography, and population to exploit weaker countries and gain concessions from the core regarding access to technology and export markets.[28] Military spending also served to stimulate a small industrial sector.

There are conflicting views about the descriptive and prescriptive nature of dependency theory. On the one hand, it appears as though many *dependentistas* were primarily concerned with identifying the sources of development problems in Latin America[29] rather than advocating for specific policies. For instance, Stokes criticized Cardoso and Faletto's seminal *Dependency and*

[22] See, for example, James Mahoney and Diana Rodríguez-Franco, "Dependency Theory," in *The Oxford Handbook of the Politics of Development*, ed. Carol Lancaster and Nicolas van de Walle (Oxford: Oxford University Press, 2018), 22–42.

[23] See, for example, James A. Caporaso, "Dependency Theory: Continuities and Discontinuities in Development Studies," *International Organization* 34, no. 4 (1980): 605–628, https://doi.org/10.1017/S0020818300018865.

[24] Ibid.

[25] See, for example, Grosfoguel, "Developmentalism, Modernity," citing Fernando Henrique Cardoso and Enzo Faletto, *Dependency and Development in Latin America* (Berkeley: University of California Press, 1979); Kay, "Modernization," citing Theotonio Dos Santos, "The Structure of Dependence," *The American Economic Review* 60, no. 2 (1970): 231–236.

[26] Theotonio Dos Santos, *El nuevo carácter de la dependencia*, Centro de Estudios Socioeconómicos (CESO), Universidade de Chile (1968); see also Theotonio Dos Santos, "La crisis de la teoría del desarrollo y las relaciones de dependencia en America Latina," *Boletin del CESO* 3 (1968).

[27] Ruy Mauro Marini, "A dialética de dependência" (1973), in *Ruy Mauro Marini: Vida e Obra*, ed. Roberta Transpadini and João Pedro Stedile (São Paulo: Expressão Popular, 2005).

[28] Subimperialism was rejected by other scholars such as José Serra and Fernando H. Cardoso, "Las Desventuras de La Dialéctica de La Dependencia." *Revista Mexicana de Sociología* 40 (1978): 9–55. See Kay, "Modernization," 24.

[29] Mahoney and Rodríguez-Franco, "Dependency Theory."

Development in Latin America (1979)[30] for "not provid[ing] a base for policy recommendations . . . or even to propose solutions."[31] On the other hand, by highlighting the imperialist and asymmetrical relations between LDCs and developed countries, some theorists argued that the former's dependence could only be overcome with changes to international relations, governance structures, and foreign policy.[32] In line with this, earlier formulations of dependency theory argued in favor of import substitution industrialization (ISI),[33] but this view was adopted by a limited number of scholars (known as *cepalistas* due to their affiliations with CEPAL [Comisión Económica para América Latina y el Caribe, UN Economic Commission for Latin America and the Caribbean]). Most *dependentistas* were critical of ISI, as discussed in further detail below, as discussed in further detail below.

At least one dependency theorist made specific policy recommendations. Miguel S. Wionczek proposed that Latin America could

> (1) come up with sensible plans for sharing investment projects among countries within the major economic cooperation blocs; (2) regulate foreign investment in such a way that it is permitted on a selective basis, complementary to the long-term interests of socioeconomic development of the recipient countries; and (3) in a similar manner, establish legal provisions enabling Latin America to acquire technology in all of its multivariate forms on a more favorable basis. Furthermore, Latin America should channel much more effort into her own scientific and technological efforts, which includes necessary changes in the education system. Also, Wionczek hints at the possibility of diluting the traditional sources of dependency by establishing stronger economic ties with Australia, Japan, and Canada.[34]

[30] Cardoso and Faletto, *Dependency and Development*. See also Fernando Henrique Cardoso, "Dependency and Development in Latin America," *New Left Review* 74 (July/August 1972): 83–95.

[31] Charles J. Stokes, "Book Review: D*ependency and Development in Latin America* by Fernando Henrique Cardoso, Enzo Faletto and Marjory Mattingly Urquidi (Berkeley: University of California Press, 1979)," *Journal of Economic Literature* 18, no. 2 (1980): 598–600.

[32] Tausch, "Globalisation and Development"; and Dos Santos, "Structure of Dependence."

[33] See Mahoney and Rodríguez-Franco, "Dependency Theory," 8: "dependency theory was closely linked to economic policy within Latin America, specifically the policy of import substitution industrialization (ISI) that began after the Great Depression and took off in the 1950s and 1960s. Advocates of ISI suggested that the position of the Latin American economies in the world economy as food and raw material exporters was disadvantageous, industrialization was necessary for development, and the achievement of industrialization required protecting local industries by replacing imports from the advanced countries with the domestic production of manufactured products. The remedy involved a package of policies that included protective tariffs, preferential import exchange rates for industrial raw materials, public financial support for favored industries, and direct state participation in certain (often 'heavier') industries."

[34] Richard C. Bath and Dilmus D. James, "Dependency Analysis of Latin America: Some Criticisms, Some Suggestions," *Latin American Research Review* 11, no. 3 (1976): 8–9, https://doi.org/10.1017/S0023879100030284. Citing Miguel S. Wionczek, "The Pacific Market for Capital, Technology, and Information and Its Possible Opening for Latin America," *Journal of Common*

Wionczek's work shows a direct connection between dependency theory and law and development at the domestic and international levels.

While the theory acquired significant international prominence, there were significant differences in how it was formulated worldwide. The version of dependency theory conceived by Latin American scholars focuses on both internal and external forces, including the interactions between the two.[35] In addition to highlighting imperialist relationships and unequal trading relations, Latin American scholars emphasized the role of elites, corporate actors, and asymmetrical relations between social classes as important elements of the theory.[36] When dependency theory developed in Latin America, it was as much of a critique of internal class politics as it was of the international order.[37] However, when scholars in the United States adopted dependency theory, the emphasis on the domestic structure of dependency was largely lost as English-speaking scholars overstated the importance of external forces.[38] Due to a lack of access to influential Latin American works, the version of dependency theory adopted by English-speaking scholars focused on international capitalism, leaving the impression that domestic elements were merely by-products of the global factors driving underdevelopment.[39] As the domestic structure of the theory was continually neglected, dependency came to mean high reliance on trade, outside markets, and foreign technology.[40] In countries identified as underdeveloped outside Latin America, their versions of dependency theory sometimes introduced or highlighted particular units of analysis. For instance, the version of the dependency theory adopted in Ghana emphasized structures of colonialism,[41] and the version of the dependency theory adopted in Turkey emphasized the national struggle for liberation.[42]

Considering these differences, some scholars have argued that it is impossible to conceive of dependency as one single theory. Instead, one should discuss dependency theories in the plural rather than the singular.[43] They contend that dependency theory emerged in many forms, even among Latin American scholars. For instance, Kay argues there are two main camps among Latin American theorists: those influenced by a structuralist position (focused on

Market Studies 10, no. 1 (1971): 78–95; and "Un punto de vista latinoamericano sobre los problemas de ciencia y tecnologia," *Comercio Exterior* 22, no. 4 (1972): 346–349.

35 Caporaso, "Dependency Theory."
36 Ibid.
37 Niblett, "Catastrophic Consciousness."
38 Caporaso, "Dependency Theory."
39 Ibid.
40 Ibid.
41 Ahiakpor, "Success and Failure."
42 Gulalp, "Eurocentrism."
43 Kay, "Modernization."

achieving more equitable relations between the core and periphery) and those rooted in Marxist theories (focused on achieving transition to socialism).[44] When discussing the intellectual history of the theory, modern scholars do acknowledge the various writings of theorists across regions and periods.[45] In summary, for some, dependency theory arguably has a conceptual integrity that can be traced back to its origins in Latin America, but the differences that have arisen from its intellectual history and international circulation stand in contrast with the possibility of discussing it as a single theory.

In contrast, some scholars have suggested that different versions of dependency theory can be brought under one umbrella, given their common denominators and local construction in Latin America. To account for the differences between versions of dependency theory conceived by Latin American scholars and the versions adopted outside the region, these scholars argue that the international circulation of dependency theory resulted in "misunderstandings" of the original theory.[46] In this sense, dependency theory should be, and is, centered on the common conceptual approach of the *dependentistas*: underdevelopment was not a preexisting, natural state of LDCs but a result of a historical process of unequal integration into the global capitalist system.[47] As outlined by Caporaso, this single form of the theory incorporates a set of general ideas about the global capitalist system and specific factors relevant to individual countries.[48]

Dependency theory is more than a critique of intellectuals of the Global South to the prevailing development paradigm formulated in the Global North. In addition to offering a critique of the modernization theory of American scholars in the early 1960s, dependency theory also offered a critique of the neodevelopmentalist ideology of the CEPAL and the orthodox Marxism of the Latin American communist parties.[49] The neodevelopmentalist view of CEPAL maintained that LDCs could reach prevailing levels of welfare by simply reproducing the evolution followed by more developed countries.[50] Dependency theorists criticized the ISI strategy, wherein Latin American countries imposed tariffs to restrict the imports of consumer goods and promote domestic industrialization instead.[51] ISI was based on neomercantilism and economic nationalism (primarily associated with Raúl Prebisch and his work with CEPAL).[52] ISI led Latin American countries to import more capital goods in the early 1950s,

[44] Kay, "Modernization."
[45] Tausch, "Globalisation and Development"
[46] Ruvituso, "From the South to the North."
[47] Ibid.
[48] Caporaso, "Dependency Theory."
[49] Grosfoguel, "Developmentalism, Modernity."
[50] Claudio Katz, *Dependency Theory after Fifty Years: The Continuing Relevance of Latin American Critical Thought* (Leiden, The Netherlands: Brill, 2022).
[51] Grosfoguel, "Developmentalism, Modernity."
[52] Ibid.

increasing trade deficits and dependence on foreign technology, machinery, and finance.[53] In response, dependency theory helped make sense of these counter-productive effects and provided a novel way of understanding how the global capitalist system produces underdevelopment in Latin America.[54]

Dependency theory was arguably most influential in countering the view that Latin American countries needed to overcome their so-called archaic, traditional, and feudal structures to become developed, industrialized countries.[55] According to the different ideologies upheld by CEPAL, Latin American communist parties, and modernization theorists, Latin America was supposed to be lagging behind the United States and Europe because of its "archaic" structures.[56] As part of the political and theoretical struggle against these "time distancing" views, dependency theory examined how commercial classes tied to the export sector and the industrial bourgeoisie in Latin American countries also participated in the global capitalist system, producing underdevelopment.[57] The Marxist strand of dependency theory supported the view that the bourgeoisie were unreliable allies to dismantle the global capitalist system and that efforts to achieve this goal in Latin America should be focused on building socialism at the nation-state level.[58] The structuralist strand also critiqued how a dominant class maintained control of the productive process in nationally controlled economies, arguing that the extent to which the national bourgeoisie could control external relations shaped their prospects for development.[59]

Dependency theory is perhaps best known for being the first conceptual approach from "within the South" that significantly influenced the social sciences.[60] However, it also influenced political parties and some governments in Latin America, most notably that of Salvador Allende in Chile, whose socialist government was overthrown in 1973.[61] At its peak influence during the 1970s, the theory was "harmonically increasing the voice of the Third World" and characterized as the dominant viewpoint of many countries identified as underdeveloped.[62] Notably, historical and sociological research on the circulation

[53] Ibid.
[54] Ibid., 361 ("The main difference between the developmentalist ideas of *cepalistas* and *dependentistas* was that for the former, autonomous national development could be achieved within capitalism, while for the latter, it could not be achieved under the capitalist world-system.")
[55] Ibid.
[56] Ibid.
[57] Ibid.; and Caporaso, "Dependency Theory."
[58] Grosfoguel, "Developmentalism, Modernity."
[59] Mahoney and Rodríguez-Franco, "Dependency Theory," citing Cardoso and Enzo Faletto, *Dependency and Development*.
[60] Ruvituso, "From the South to the North."
[61] Kay, "Modernization."
[62] Rıdvan Turhan, "The Effect of Dependency Theory on Discussions of 'Underdevelopment' in Turkey," in *Philosophy of Globalization*, ed. Concha Roldan, Oscar D. Brauer, and Johannes Rohbeck (Boston: Walter de Gruyter, 2018), 269–286.

of the Latin American dependency theory underscores how its global dissemination was not limited to "South-South" mobility but also spread from the Global South to the Global North.[63] While the Latin American conception of dependency theory was largely misconstrued by scholars in the United States (as discussed above), greater access to Latin American works in countries such as Germany[64] and Turkey resulted in its relatively faithful adaptation elsewhere (e.g., Ghana[65] and the Philippines[66]).

The theory's demise started with the economic crisis of the 1980s, the "defeats" of the left in Latin America under military dictatorships, and the rise of neoclassical theories (e.g., Chicago School of Economics) and neoliberal policies advanced by World Bank and International Monetary Fund (IMF) structural adjustment programs.[67]

III. *Dominance* in Law and Development: De Soto's Property Rights and Bureaucratic Reforms

Hernando de Soto is a Peruvian economist whose ideas became notorious in development circles in the 1990s and 2000s. The basic premise of his analysis is that law matters. As he states, "the legal system may be the main explanation in the difference in development that exists between industrialized countries and those that are not industrialized."[68] According to de Soto, law is central in promoting private-sector investment and growth. Based on this premise, he articulated two central ideas. First, the high costs of formalizing entrepreneurial activity (multiple legal requirements, protracted approval processes, and corruption in public administration) lead to informality, which has social and private costs. Second, the lack of formalization of property rights in developing countries leads to inefficient allocation of resources and lower levels of economic growth. These two ideas have influenced development policies by creating an agenda for business regulation and property rights reforms. The ideas align with a school of thought that argues that institutions are central to development (captured in the mantra "governance matters"), which became influential in development circles starting in the 1990s.[69]

[63] Ruvituso, "From the South to the North."
[64] Ibid.
[65] Ahiakpor, "Success and Failure."
[66] Randolf, "Philippine Underdevelopment."
[67] Kay, "Modernization"; Ruvituso, "From the South to the North."
[68] Hernando de Soto, *The Other Path: The Invisible Revolution in the Third World* (New York: Basic Books, 1989), 185.
[69] For an overview of these ideas, see Prado and Trebilcock, *Advanced Introduction*, Chap. 3.

In his book, *The Other Path: The Invisible Revolution in the Third World*,[70] he claims that entrepreneurs stay in the informal sector due to the high costs of formalization. High levels of informality not only lead to inefficiency but also entail various social and private costs: avoiding taxes, legitimate building code, environmental, health and safety, and labor protection regulations while entailing costs and suboptimal scale because of lack of limited liability, lack of access to formal credit and insurance markets, costs of concealment, and excessive reliance on limited relational networks of suppliers, customers, and investors, given lack of access to the formal legal system.

De Soto's second idea largely reflects the importance of property rights in contemporary thinking on economic development. His book *The Mystery of Capital: Why Capitalism Triumphs in the West and Fails Everywhere Else* argues that strong protection for private property rights is the key factor in explaining the economic success of the developed world and the economic stagnation of many developing countries. He argues that, due to the lack of formal property titles, "the total value of the real estate held but not legally owned by the poor of the Third World and former communist nations is at least $9.3 trillion." De Soto calls this untapped wealth "dead capital."[71]

These ideas have influenced politicians, policymakers, and international organizations worldwide.[72] The concern with the high costs of formalization, for instance, was the primary source of inspiration for the annual World Bank's *Doing Business Reports*, which catalogued and compared time, costs, and complexities in performing many routine bureaucratic and legal activities in 185 countries (developed and developing).[73] The report has recently been canceled due to a corruption scandal,[74] but until its cancellation, it produced a ranking of bureaucratic performance in different countries. Yearly, the reports measured costs, complexity, and delays in performing a range of business functions, including starting a business, obtaining construction permits, securing electricity, registering property, obtaining credit, protecting investors, paying taxes, trading across borders, enforcing contracts, resolving insolvency, and hiring and

[70] de Soto, *The Other Path.*

[71] Hernando de Soto, *The Mystery of Capital: Why Capitalism Triumphs in the West and Fails Everywhere Else* (New York: Basic Books, 2000), 35.

[72] Cora Fontana, "Hernando de Soto on Land Titling: Consensus and Criticism," *plaNext - Next Generation Planning* 3 (2016): 36–48.

[73] Valeria Perotti, "Chapter 22: The World Bank's Doing Business Indicators," presented at the Mont Pelerin Society 2020 Special Meeting, hosted by Hoover Institution, 2020 https://www.hoover.org/sites/default/files/research/docs/mps_perotti.pdf. See also Simeon Djankov, "The Doing Business Project: How It Started: Correspondence," *Journal of Economic Perspectives* 30, no. 1 (2016): 247–248, https://doi.org/10.1257/jep.30.1.247.

[74] Fernanda G. Nicola, "Scandal Involving World Bank's 'Doing Business' Index Exposes Problems in Using Sportslike Rankings to Guide Development Goals," *The Conversation*, October 15, 2021, https://theconversation.com/scandal-involving-world-banks-doing-business-index-exposes-problems-in-using-sportslike-rankings-to-guide-development-goals-169691.

firing workers. The reports assumed that, in many countries, a wide range of burdensome legal and bureaucratic requirements constrain business formation and expansion. The reports also compared countries against each other, using an indicator to summarize each country's performance in all the dimensions listed here.

The inaugural report, launched in 2005, made extensive reference to de Soto's work:

> In *The Mystery of Capital*, Hernando de Soto exposed the damaging effects of heavy business regulation and weak property rights. With burdensome entry regulations, few businesses bother to register. Instead, they choose to operate in the informal economy. Facing high transaction costs to get formal property title, many would-be entrepreneurs own informal assets that cannot be used as collateral to obtain loans. De Soto calls this "dead capital." The solution: simplify business entry and get titles to property. But many titling programs aimed at bringing assets into the formal sector have not had the lasting impact that reformers hoped for. Doing Business in 2005 helps explain why. While it is critical to encourage registration of assets, it is as important—and harder—to stop them from slipping back into the informal sector and to use their formal status to gain access to credit.[75]
>
> In 1986 Hernando de Soto published *The Other Path*, using a time-and-motion study to show the prohibitive obstacles to establishing a business in Peru. De Soto's research team followed all necessary bureaucratic procedures in setting up a one-employee garment factory in the outskirts of Lima. It took 289 days and $1,231 for the business to legally start operations. Doing Business is a time-and-motion study which measures, across 145 countries, the obstacles faced by an entrepreneur performing standardized tasks: starting a business; hiring and firing workers; obtaining business licenses; getting credit; registering property; protecting investors; enforcing contracts; and closing down a business.[76]

His work on the formalization of property rights also had a significant effect on development programs. The idea has prompted several nations, besides de Soto's native Peru, to promote land titling programs (e.g., Egypt, Tanzania, and

[75] The World Bank, "Doing Business in 2005: Removing Obstacles to Growth," published by the World Bank, the International Finance Corporation, and Oxford University Press, 2015, https://www.doingbusiness.org/content/dam/doingBusiness/media/Annual-Reports/English/DB05-FullReport.pdf.

[76] Ibid.

the Philippines). It has revived interest in formalizing property rights among the United States Agency for International Development (USAID), Inter-American Development Bank (IADB), and the World Bank.[77] In other cases, de Soto's idea did not put formalization of title in the agenda but changed its justification and focus. For instance, in the case of the World Bank, the formalization of title was part of the agenda since the 1970s, but due to de Soto's ideas, it became part of an "enabling approach," which can be described as "a strategy that started a shift from doing something for the poor to enabling them to do something for themselves."[78] In line with this "enabling approach" on law and property, in 2005, the United Nations Development Programme (UNDP) established the Commission on Legal Empowerment of the Poor, co-chaired by former Secretary of State Madeleine Albright and Hernando de Soto. De Soto's ideas inspired the Commission, but its mandate goes beyond land titling and bureaucratic reforms.[79] Indeed, the 2008 Report entitled *Making the Law Work for Everyone* touts four development pillars: property rights, access to justice, business rights, and labor rights.[80] The idea of "legal empowerment of the poor" was also embraced by the World Bank.[81]

Interestingly, while de Soto's ideas were highly influential worldwide, they received special attention in the United States. As Fontana describes:

> George Bush Sr., for instance, declared in 1989 that "the economist Hernando de Soto helped us to understand a global economic phenomenon . . .," while Bill Clinton in 2002 claimed that "the most promising anti-poverty initiative is the one promoted by the great economist, Hernando de Soto." Time Magazine placed de Soto in the top five in their rankings of Leaders of the New Millennium in 1999, and in 2004, the magazine positioned him among the Hundred Most Influential Personalities of the Year rank. Cato Institute awarded him the Milton Friedman Prize for Advancing Liberty in 2004 and the Economist the Innovation Award in 2006.[82]

[77] Fontana, "Hernando de Soto on Land Titling."

[78] Ibid.

[79] Jan Michiel Otto, "Rule of Law Promotion, Land Tenure and Poverty Alleviation: Questioning the Assumptions of Hernando de Soto," *Hague Journal on the Rule of Law* 1 (2009): 173–195, https://doi.org/10.1017/S1876404509001730.

[80] United Nations Commission for Legal Empowerment of the Poor, "Making the Law Work for Everyone: Report," Vols. I and II (2008), https://digitallibrary.un.org/record/633970?ln=en and https://digitallibrary.un.org/record/633966?ln=en.

[81] Hassane Cissé, "Legal Empowerment of the Poor: Past, Present, Future," *The World Bank Legal Review* (2012): 31–44, https://doi.org/10.1596/9780821395066_CH03.

[82] Fontana, "Hernando de Soto on Land Titling."

More importantly, de Soto seems to have articulated the connection between "open markets" and "open societies,"[83] connecting democracy with economic growth in ways that helped shape the US foreign policy.[84]

While there is consensus around how influential de Soto's ideas have been in development circles (especially international development institutions headquartered in the United States, such as USAID, IADB, and the World Bank), there are disputes around their originality.[85] These critics argue that rather than bringing something new to the table, de Soto was simply the right person in the right place at the right time: a Peruvian economist articulating preexisting ideas in a way that was especially fitting for the neoliberal agenda that came to prevail in development circles in the 1990s.[86] In contrast with these criticisms, some argue that de Soto's work is unique and original. While acknowledging that de Soto's general assumptions and claims may not be entirely new, those defending him argue that there was methodological originality in gathering data to measure the magnitude of well-recognized development challenges.[87] In line with this interpretation, the 2009 Doing Business Report indicates that de Soto has created an innovative way of mapping obstacles to entrepreneurship by creating time and motion indicators.[88] Others argue that he has contributed to framing, not to the policy proposals per se. While there were concerns with the formalization of title and informal entrepreneurs, these had not been framed as strategies to "empower" the poor.[89]

[83] See, for example, Hernando de Soto, "The Secret to Reviving the Arab Spring's Promise: Property Rights," *The Wall Street Journal*, February 26, 2013, http://online.wsj.com/article/SB10001424127887324162304578302403519972088.html; and Hernando de Soto, "The Free Market Secret of the Arab Revolution," *Financial Times* (last accessed August 16, 2015), https://www.ft.com/content/653fab0e-0a00-11e1-85ca-00144feabdc0.

[84] Kate Geoghegan, "Neoliberalism and Democracy Promotion: Hernando de Soto and US Foreign Policy," in *The Reagan Administration, the Cold War, and the Transition to Democracy Promotion*, ed. Robert Pee and William Michael Schmidli (Cham, Switzerland: Springer International, 2018), 137–159.

[85] Alan Gilbert, "On the Mystery of Capital and the Myths of Hernando de Soto: What Difference Does Legal Title Make?" *International Development Planning Review* 24, no. 1 (2002): 1–19, https://doi.org/10.3828/idpr.24.1.1; and Ray Bromley, "A New Path to Development? The Significance and Impact of Hernando de Soto's Ideas on Underdevelopment, Production, and Reproduction," *Economic Geography* 66, no. 4 (2016): 328–348, http://www.jstor.org/stable/143968.

[86] Otto, "Rule of Law Promotion."

[87] Martin Andersson and Daniel Waldenström, "Hernando de Soto: Recipient of the 2017 Global Award for Entrepreneurial Research," *Small Business Economics* 49 (2017): 721–728.

[88] The World Bank, "Doing Business 2009: Comparing Regulation in 181 Economies," published by the World Bank and the International Finance Corporation, https://openknowledge.worldbank.org/server/api/core/bitstreams/04e270fc-e6d6-58f6-bbd8-9c546e40c616/content ("The Doing Business project encompasses two types of data. The first come from readings of laws and regulations. The second are time and motion indicators that measure the efficiency in achieving a regulatory goal (such as granting the legal identity of a business). Within the time and motion indicators, cost estimates are recorded from official fee schedules where applicable. Here, Doing Business builds on Hernando de Soto's pioneering work in applying the time and motion approach first used by Frederick Taylor to revolutionize the production of the Model T Ford. De Soto used the approach in the 1980s to show the obstacles to setting up a garment factory on the outskirts of Lima.")

[89] Fontana, "Hernando de Soto on Land Titling."

There has also been much debate about the results of reforms proposed by de Soto. Empirical studies show that the formalization of property titles often does not generate the benefits predicted by de Soto.[90] A series of studies analyzing the formalization of titles in Ghana, Namibia, and Indonesia, for instance, did not increase the security of tenure in these nations.[91] In contrast, some studies suggest that de Soto's proposals have led to positive results in urban titles in Latin America. Empirical studies in Argentina and Mexico indicate that strengthening property rights in slums seem to have increased investment, as predicted by de Soto.[92] Further, there is research showing that there may be variations within a country: results seem to be weaker or nonexistent in contexts in which there is an informal property rights system or where a culture of formality does not exist; these can vary from city to city in the same country, as shown by studies in Ecuador and Mexico.[93]

Despite being deeply embedded in Latin America, de Soto's proposals were embraced and touted by international development institutions as a global policy. Those supporting this universalization pointed out that rapid and intense urbanization, leading to a significant portion of the population living in urban areas, is not exclusive to Latin America. Also, having large numbers of people living in urban slums is not exclusive to the region; it is also a pressing issue in Africa, Asia (especially in China and India), and the Middle East.[94] However, while the problem seems common, the solution proposed by de Soto has not succeeded everywhere. As Otto concludes:

> Although De Soto's theories may prove to be right in certain areas under certain conditions, most of the case studies concluded that in reality such conditions remained unfulfilled. Thus, De Soto's theories seem to be based on mistaken assumptions about the context of legalization projects which, according to our

[90] Geoffrey Payne, Alain Durand-Lasserve, and Carole Rakodi, "The Limits of Land Titling and Home Ownership," *Environment and Urbanization* 21, no. 2 (2009): 443–462, https://journals.sagepub.com/doi/pdf/10.1177/0956247809344364.

[91] Otto, "Rule of Law Promotion."

[92] Erica Field, "Property Rights and Investment in Urban Slums," *Journal of the European Economic Association* 3 (2005): 279–290, https://www.jstor.org/stable/40004971. See also Sebastian Galiani and Ernesto Schargrodsky, "Effects of Land Titling on Child Health," *Economics and Human Biology* 2 (2004): 353–372, https://ssrn.com/abstract=1814746 (indicating that land security increases labor outside of the home, and children's health).

[93] Paavo Monkkonen, "Where Do Property Rights Matter More? Explaining the Variation in Demand for Property Titles across Cities in Mexico," *World Development* 88 (2016): 67–78, https://doi.org/10.1016/j.worlddev.2016.07.013; Jean O. Lanjouw and Philip I. Levy, "Untitled: A Study of Formal and Informal Property Rights in Urban Ecuador," *The Economic Journal* 112, no. 482 (2002): 986–1019, https://doi.org/10.1111/1468-0297.00067.

[94] Hannah Ritchie and Max Roser, "Urbanization," *OurWorldInData.org* (September 2018; updated 2024), https://ourworldindata.org/urbanization.

preliminary field data, often did not hold. Some such assumptions are related to a given country's legal system itself, while others have to do with the law's political, administrative, economic or social contexts.[95]

Last, but not least, de Soto is also criticized for embracing neoliberal assumptions that have further increased inequality in the region and that have not necessarily helped promote economic growth in his native Peru (or elsewhere). More specifically, influenced by de Soto's work, Peru has adopted property rights reforms that emphasized individual property rather than the collective title (undermining traditional Indigenous peoples' rights) and promoted the efficient use of property in a way that often favored large business owners in agrobusiness and the extractive sector.[96] De Soto's proposals also seem attractive to certain elite groups because they offered a response to demands for radical property redistribution programs formulated by the Peruvian Marxist guerrilla group, the Shining Path (*Sendero Luminoso*).[97] In summary, even in de Soto's native Peru, the results of the proposed reforms have been disappointing.

IV. Disruption in Law and Development: Conditional Cash Transfers in Brazil and Mexico

Conditional cash transfer (CCT)is a social policy that provides regular payments for low-income families based on conditions (e.g., keeping their children in school and taking them for regular health checkups).[98] Designed to reduce poverty and promote human development,[99] CCTs are "perhaps the most remarkable innovation in welfare programs in developing countries over the past few decades." [100] This innovation was created in Brazil and Mexico in the mid-1990s. From that point, the diffusion of the program was fast: by 2008, twenty-seven countries had adopted a form of CCT, and by 2015, sixty-three countries in the

[95] Otto, "Rule of Law Promotion."

[96] Helena Alviar Garcia, *Legal Experiments for Development in Latin America: Modernization, Revolution and Social Justice* (Oxford: New York: Routledge, 2021), 46.

[97] Timothy Mitchell, "How Neoliberalism Makes its World: The Urban Property Rights Project in Peru," in *The Road from Mont Pèlerin: The Making of the Neoliberal Thought Collective*, ed. Philip Mirowski and Dieter Plehwe (Cambridge, MA: Harvard University Press, 2015), 404.

[98] The term was coined by the International Poverty Center, a joint project of the United Nations Program for Development (UNDP) and a state-owned think tank in Brazil, Instituto de Pesquisas Econômicas Aplicadas (IPEA).

[99] Ministério do Desenvolvimento Social e Combate à Fome, *Evolução dos Recursos dos Programas de Transferência de Renda,* Caderno SUAS, ano 3, no. 3, Brasília: 2008, n.4, https://www.mds.gov.br/webarquivos/publicacao/assistencia_social/Cadernos/Suas_Evolucao_Recursos_III.pdf.

[100] Nur Cahyadi et al., "Cumulative Impacts of Conditional Cash Transfer Programs: Experimental Evidence from Indonesia," *American Economic Journal: Economic Policy* 12, no. 4 (2020): 88–110, https://doi.org/10.1257/pol.20190245.

world had adopted a program of this type.[101] While the programs themselves were an important innovation, the Latin American countries that spearheaded these programs decided to scientifically assess the impact of these programs using the experimental design that set up the gold standard in medical sciences. This has facilitated their rapid diffusion around the region and the world.

CCTs are similar tounconditional cash transfers in offering an immediate poverty alleviation measure, but they are distinct from unconditional transfers due to the conditionalities.[102] More specifically, in the programs created in Brazil and Mexico, CCTs require families to invest in their children's health and education. These conditionals, known as human capital investments, are designed to reduce intergenerational poverty. The health-related conditions may start before birth with prenatal care and may include a requirement that trained midwives or doctors perform delivery; once the child is born, there are requirements for immunizations and regular health checkups. The education-related conditionalities are school enrollment and regular attendance in classes.[103] Such conditionalities are designed to break intergenerational poverty cycles by enhancing future opportunities for the younger generations in poor families.[104] Their focus is on the demand-side constraints to public services; that is, even if education and health services are offered, individuals may not use them. The cash transfer offers an incentive for potential users to modify their behavior.[105]

Brazil and Mexico were pioneers in this innovation.[106] In Brazil, national policy debates about CCTs started in the late 1980s, influenced by the provisions regarding social assistance included in Brazil's 1988 Constitution (which marked the country's transition from a military dictatorship to a democratic regime) and by concerns with the structural causes of poverty, instead of its symptoms.[107] Local governments implemented the first two programs in January 1995: the

[101] Francesca Bastagli et al., "Cash Transfers: What Does the Evidence Say? A Rigorous Review of Impacts and the Role of Design and Implementation Features," *Overseas Development Institute*, 2016, https://cdn.odi.org/media/documents/11316.pdf.

[102] David Coady and Samuel A. Morley, *From Social Assistance to Social Development: Targeted Education Subsidies in Developing Countries* (Washington, DC: Peterson Institute for International Economics, 2003).

[103] Nur Cahyadi et al., "Cumulative Impacts."

[104] Ariel Fiszbein et al., "Conditional Cash Transfers: Reducing Present and Future Poverty: World Bank Policy Research Report," *World Bank*, 2009, https://openknowledge.worldbank.org/handle/10986/2597; Alan De Brauw et al., "The Impact of Bolsa Família on Schooling," *World Development* 70 (2015): 303–316.

[105] Kathy Lindert et al., "The Nuts and Bolts of Brazil's Bolsa Família Program: Implementing Conditional Cash Transfers in a Decentralized Context," *World Bank*, 2007, https://documents1.worldbank.org/curated/en/972261468231296002/pdf/398530SP1709.pdf.

[106] Bangladesh adopted the Food for Education Program (FFE) in July 1993. While some authors consider this the first CCT program implemented in the world, others do not. The exclusion is because the benefit is not provided in cash; the government provided monthly food rations contingent on the family's income and having one primary-school-age child attending school. Lindert et al., "Nuts and Bolts."

[107] Ibid.

Federal District, where the capital Brasília is located, launched the "Bolsa Escola" program (providing monthly payments for poor families that kept their children enrolled in school), and the city of Campinas, in the state of São Paulo, launched the "Programa de Garantia da Renda Mínima Familiar" (Minimum Family Income Program), which targeted families in extreme poverty with school-age children, based on education and health-based conditionalities.[108] These two pilot programs were adopted by many municipalities in Brazil, and in 2001 the Federal Government transformed "Bolsa Escola" into a national program. In 2003, the national "Bolsa Escola" program was merged with three other national welfare programs (Bolsa Alimentação, Programa Cartão Alimentação, and Auxílio Gás) to create the now famous "Bolsa Família" program.[109]

In the same year that Brazilian municipalities implemented the first versions of the program, 1995, Mexico's federal government started contemplating a CCT associated with attendingregular appointments in health clinics.[110] In 1996, the Mexican government sent a delegation to Brazil to visit several municipal "Bolsa Escola" programs, and those designing the program added school attendance as another condition.[111] In 1997, Mexico's federal government launched its own federal-level CCT program, Programa de Educación, Salud, y Alimentación (Progresa), renamed "Oportunidades" in March 2002.

The CCT programs created in Brazil and Mexico were significant policy innovations to promote human development, which is measured according to the United Nations' Human Development Index, comprising three dimensions: wealth, education, and health.[112] In addition, CCT programs are in line with neoliberal assumptions, which informed the economic-centered concept of development adopted by the Bretton Woods institutions, such as the World Bank and the International Monetary Fund.[113] More specifically, CCTs seem compatible with the assumption that there is a perceived distortion in the value that poor parents place on human capital investments given their

[108] Natasha Borges Sugiyama, "The Diffusion of Conditional Cash Transfer Programs in the Americas," *Global Social Policy* 11, no. 2–3 (2011): 250–278, https://doi.org/10.1177/146801811142.

[109] Ministério do Desenvolvimento Social e Combate à Fome, *Evolução dos Recursos dos Programas de Transferência de Renda,* Caderno SUAS, ano 3, no. 3, Brasília: 2008, 12, https://www.mds.gov.br/webarquivos/publicacao/assistencia_social/Cadernos/Suas_Evolucao_Recursos_III.pdf.

[110] Santiago Levy, *Progress against Poverty: Sustaining Mexico's Progresa-Oportunidades Program* (Washington, DC: Brookings Institution Press, 2006), 34.

[111] Ibid.

[112] United Nations Development Programme, "Human Development," https://hdr.undp.org/about/human-development.

[113] A. C. P. B. Boiadjian, Os programas de transferência de renda em países específicos da América Latina e no Brasil. Dissertação (Mestrado em Economia Política)—Pontifícia Universidade Católica de São Paulo, São Paulo, 2009. See also Luísa de Azevedo Nazareno and Ana Maria Nogales Vasconcelos, "Transferências Condicionada De Renda: Origens, Fundamentos E Tendências Recentes Na África Subsaariana," *Boletim de Economia e Política Internacional | BEPI |* no. 19 (Jan./Apr. 2015): 77–78.

long-term nature. The transfers are presumed to correct this distortion by providing an immediate incentive for parents to attend to the health and education of their children. While there are no claims that CCTs will eliminate poverty or promote economic growth, these transfers are deemed to contribute positively to these efforts.[114]

These CCT programs also started a new trend in impact evaluation of development policies by using independent scientific assessment of the results, often based on experimental or quasi-experimental methods.[115] The first generation of the Mexican CCT program used experimental methods (randomized controlled trials) to inform program design and expansion. PROGRESA expanded incrementally, having eleven phases between 1997 and 2000. As explained by one of the architects of the Mexican CCT program, Santiago Levy, an economist who was deputy minister of the Mexican Ministry of Finance and Public Credit from 1994 to 2000,[116] CCTs were randomly assigned to some localities. This randomization occurred in each expansion phase when policymakers took advantage of implementation obstacles (e.g., limited resources) to generate control and test groups. Through randomized implementation, it was possible to measure observable differences between localities. By December 2000, when control localities started receiving benefits, researchers could measure the program's impact by contrasting income, health, and education indicators between 1997 and 2000.[117]

Similarly, Brazil has taken advantage of constraints that prevented the policies from being implemented simultaneously throughout the country to assess results. Unlike its Mexican counterpart, however, Brazil used quasi-experimental methods, which means that the control group is generated by statistical matching. At the beginning of the national program in 2001, three municipalities receiving the benefits were compared with three municipalities not yet receiving the benefits. Still, the benefit allocation was not randomized, as in Mexico.[118] After that, the program was implemented nationally but in a decentralized fashion. The variation in implementation across municipalities created an opportunity for rigorously measuring the program's impact.[119]

114 Levy, *Progress against Poverty*.

115 Marie Gaarder, "Conditional Cash Transfer Programmes: Opening the Black Box, Introduction," *Journal of Development Effectiveness* 2, no. 1 (2010): 1–5, https://doi.org/10.1080/19439341003655007.

116 United Nations Development Programme, "Santiago Levy" (last accessed April 30, 2023), https://www.undp.org/latin-america/santiago-levy.

117 Laura B. Rawlings and Gloria Rubio, "Evaluating the Impact of Conditional Cash Transfers: Lessons from Latin America," World Bank Policy Research Working Paper, 2003, http://hdl.handle.net/10986/18119.

118 Rawlings and Rubio, "Evaluating the Impact."

119 Alain de Janvry, Frederico Finan, and Elisabeth Sadoulet, "Evaluating Brazil's Bolsa Escola Program: Impact on Schooling and Municipal Roles," University of California at Berkeley, 2006, http://are.berkeley.edu/~esadoulet/papers/BolsaEscolaReport6-6.pdf.

The rigorous evaluation of these programs not only helped demonstrate the value of these programs but also influenced the diffusion process as international institutions and countries were reassured by the results observed in other countries and also embraced the idea that their own attempts at implementing such programs should be measured and carefully evaluated.[120]

V. Conclusion

These three case studies partially illustrate complex interactions between "the local" and "the international" in law and development. Interestingly, each case study discussed in this chapter speaks to a different phase of the intellectual history of international development and potentially different ways in which "local" ideas interact with "international" paradigms.

First, it originated in Latin America, where dependency theory challenged the existing liberal paradigm on economic development in the 1960s and 1970s. It offered an alternative theory of economic development that paid much more attention to the role played by domestic and international institutions than the prevailing economic theories at the time. It also challenged linear theories of growth and modernization theory, pointing to the unique challenges faced by developing nations and proposing a different framework as the basis for international development discourse.

Second, in the 1980s and 1990s, a period in which international development institutions started to embrace the idea that "governance matters" by including a series of institutional concerns (such as property rights and bureaucratic reforms) in their agendas.In contrast with the first case study, there is a precise alignment between the local, i.e. the work of de Soto, primarily based on information and experiments conducted in Peru, and the agenda then embraced by international development institutions. This led to the dominance of de Soto ideas in international circles.

Third, there is a turn to human development and policy experimentation on the international agenda in the 2000s. Here, the Latin American innovation of assessing CCT policies may illustrate trailblazing; that is, local ideas creating a new (methodological) agenda in international circles and disrupting existing practices.

[120] Benjamin Davis et al., "Evaluating the Impact of Cash Transfer Programmes in Sub-Saharan Africa," International Policy Center for Inclusive Growth, One Pager, no. 146, 2012, http://goo.gl/mMo0YU.

9

Technoscientific Thought and International Law in Latin America

René Urueña

I. Introduction

Ideas about science and technology (i.e., "technoscientific imaginaries") provide a framework for thinking about the relationship between the state, markets, and society. By doing so, they provide a crucial underpinning for the role that law is expected to play in a particular context by policymakers, civil society, and the private sector.[1] In Latin America, though, this connection between technoscientific imaginaries and the law has been little explored, as it is often believed that technology is inherently foreign to the region and that, consequently, the role of law, and particularly international law, is merely to facilitate Latin American access to foreign technology. Indeed, the region is often understood as a passive importer of science and technology, with very little agency when engaging with technological developments beyond finding the capital to either import them as goods or to develop them locally.[2]

Yet, the role of technology in economic development has been a dominant theme in Latin America since the 1950s. Deeply original thought about science and technology has emerged in the region, which greatly contributed to the underlying rationale for the intervention of law in the region's economy. In particular, Latin American technoscientific thought has provided a normative horizon

[1] The idea that technology emerges independently from the law has been put into question. First, it is now clear that technology and law are co-produced, in the sense that "the ways in which we know and represent the world are inseparable from how we choose to live in it." Sheila Jasanoff, "The Idiom of Co-Production," in *States of Knowledge: The Co-Production of Science and Social Order*, ed. Sheila Jasanoff (London: Routledge, 2004).

[2] See, for example, James H. Street and Dilmus D. James, "Closing the Technological Gap in Latin America," *Journal of Economic Issues* 12 (1978): 477, 479. More recently, Rodrigo Arocena and Judith Sutz, "Desigualdad, Tecnología e Innovación En El Desarrollo Latinoamericano," *Iberoamericana* 1 (2001): 29. Such black-boxing is also present in the more heterodox accounts of technology in the región. See, for example, Mario Cimoli and Gabriel Porcile, "Productividad y Cambio Estructural: El Estructuralismo y Su Diálogo Con Otras Corrientes Heterodoxas," in *Neoestructuralismo y corrientes heterodoxas en América Latina y el Caribe a inicios del siglo XXI*, ed. Alicia Bárcena and Antonio Prado (Mexico City: CEPAL, 2015).

René Urueña, *Technoscientific Thought and International Law in Latin America* In: *Latin American International Law in the Twenty-First Century*. Edited by: Alejandro Chehtman, Alexandra Huneeus, and Sergio Puig, Oxford University Press. © Oxford University Press 2025.
DOI: 10.1093/9780197754016.003.0009

for thinking about what international law *should* do to facilitate Latin America's economic development.

This chapter maps this rich tradition of Latin American technoscientific thought, exploring the role that, in such tradition, international law can play in the creation, accumulation, and distribution of economic resources. To that effect, the first three sections of the chapter introduce three distinctively Latin American ways of thinking about science and technology, in roughly chronological order: first, the idea that the region is a technological desert, moving then to Raul Prebisch's structuralism of the 1950s, and, finally, to the Latin American Thought on Science, Technology and Society movement ("*Pensamiento Latinoamericano en Ciencia Tecnología y Sociedad*," PLACTS) of the 1970s. In each of these sections, the chapter explores the implicit theory of law that the respective approach entails and discusses the distributive impact that such an approach might have in its own terms. The final section concludes with a call to reconnect law and Latin American technological thought in Latin America.

II. Latin America as a Technological Desert

The belief that Latin America is a passive adopter of technology reflects a broader technoscientific imaginary, according to which scientific developments are subject to a process of diffusion from the center to the periphery. Most important in this mindset is the work of George Basalla in the 1960s, for whom there are three distinct phases in the diffusion of "Western European science" to places like Latin America: (1) the nonscientific society provides a source for European science (e.g., by providing samples or "native cultures"); (2) there is often a period of colonial science, and (3) the completion of the process of transplantation with a struggle to achieve an independent scientific culture in the periphery.[3]

This view was influential for twentieth-century Latin American scientific thought, which emphasized the important scientific contributions of the old Pre-Hispanic Empires Latin American but accepted the region's contemporary role as a passive adopter, and not a relevant producer, of "modern" technology. Thus, Eli de Gortari's 1963 "*La Ciencia en la Historia de México*," a seminal early contribution to Latin American technoscientific thought, opens by stating that "truth be told, since the time the ancient Mexicans were subject to the Spanish colony, our (i.e., Mexican) contributions to sciences have been scarce and, in many cases, were not timely known in other countries for lack of effective contact."[4]

[3] See George Basalla, "The Spread of Western Science," *Science* 156 (1967): 611.

[4] Elí de Gortari, *La Ciencia En La Historia de México* (1st ed., Mexico City: Fondo de Cultura Económica, 1963), 1. Despite its narrow approach to the region's scientific contribution, de Gortari's

Such was the general mindset in Latin America as the region sought to insert itself into international capitalism after World War II. The diffusion model of science and Latin America's passive role in that process was a good fit for an intellectual context in which Rostow's modernization theory was dominant. According to Rostow, "development" was a matter of following certain stages, and developing states require a push to "take off."[5] These were more than just theories in books. The geopolitical influence of Rostowian modernization theory was crucial for Latin-American technoscientific thought. As national security adviser to US President Kennedy, Rostow thought that Latin America was ripe to "take-off" if the United States would provide funds to promote a "decade of economic development" in the region.[6] This insight had critical implications for science. If, according to the prevailing view, the area lacked any accurate local technology, then the push to a Rostowian "take-off" had to include technological assistance for the region.

To do so, the first option was to bring in foreign experts to aid in technical assistance schemes, particularly under the UN's Expanded Programme of Technical Assistance (created in 1949), and technical assistance programs at the OAS.[7] However, by the late 1950s, such schemes were losing popularity: technical assistance seemed too shallow an intervention and lacked sustainability in the long term.[8] Facing the failure of technical assistance, a second option to solve the Latin American technology gap was to develop a local scientific community that could receive and sustain technological transplants from more "advanced" societies. This logic inspired the first UN Conference on the Application of Science and Technology for the Benefit of the Less Developed

book was still reviewed negatively by the famous US Latin Americanist Woodrow Borah for adopting too broad a definition of science. Foreshadowing what would become a common theme in the tension between Latin American scientific thought and its northern counterpart, Borah found de Gortari's definition of "science" was just too porous, as it included "technology, knowledge of environment and speculation about the nature of the world, religious beliefs, practice and education in medicine and the physical and life sciences, and even a scientific, i.e., Marxist, interpretation of general Mexican history." Woodrow Borah, "La Ciencia En La Historia de México, ed. Elí de Gortari," *Hispanic American Historical Review* 45 (1965): 164. Along a similar line as de Gortari's diffusionist logic was José López Sánchez, *Tomás Romay y el origen de la ciencia en Cuba* (2nd ed. rev., Havana, Cuba: Academia de Ciencias; Museo Histórico de las Ciencias Médicas "Carlos J Finlay," 1964).

[5] See generally W. W. Rostow, *The Stages of Economic Growth: A Non-Communist Manifesto* (3rd ed., Cambridge: Cambridge University Press, 1990).

[6] Michael E Latham, "Ideology, Social Science, and Destiny: Modernization and the Kennedy-Era Alliance for Progress," *Diplomatic History* 22 (1998): 199. As Latham recounts, Rostow was personally involved in explaining the modernization agenda as part of the administration's broader anti-communist strategy.

[7] See Samuel Guy Inman, "Technical Assistance in Latin America," *Current History* (pre-1986) Vol. 33, No. 192, (1957) pp. 105, 106–107.

[8] Ibid., 110–111. Along the same lines: Esha Shah, *Manifesting Utopia: History and Philosophy of UN Debates on Science and Technology for Sustainable Development* (Sussex, UK: University of Sussex, 2009), 8.

Areas (UNCSAT), which took place in Geneva in 1963 under the coordination of Brazilian biochemist Carlos Chagas Filho, at the time chairman of the UN Scientific Committee on the Effects of Atomic Radiation (and the son of the discoverer of Chagas disease).

The conference was an enormous affair, with 1,665 participants and ninety-six governments represented, of which only 16 percent belonged to "less developed areas."[9] The general feeling in Geneva in 1963 was one of a "science fair"[10]: mostly scientists giving papers, in which science was understood as a "global good,"[11] separate from concerns over economic developments, in which "less developed areas" were understood to have very little to contribute and much to learn from more advanced scientific communities.[12]

A key conclusion of the conference was the importance of national scientific systems in less developed areas. For Latin America, this meant a connection of technoscientific thought with, on the one hand, the official modernization thinking dominant at the time and, on the other, the geopolitics of the moment. First, the push for establishing national science systems closely followed modernization's developmental phases. It promoted the diffusion of the European postwar model when European states institutionalized and professionalized their own science and technology national system.[13] Moreover, the development of national scientific programs was one of the dimensions prioritized by the US government's Alliance for Progress in its effort to contain communism in the region. As we have seen, Rostow was an important player in providing the intellectual rationale for the Alliance. More specifically, a Latin American Science Board, composed of fifteen US scientists, was established in the United States as an advisory body to the Coordinator of the Alliance for Progress.[14] The Board was solely funded by USAID and thus fully reflected the State Department's policies, as opposed to, for example, the African Science Board, which was funded by several sources and was thus relatively more independent from State Department policy.[15] Such priorities meant that countries friendly to the United States received more funds to develop their scientific community: for example, despite having only 4.2 percent of Latin America's higher

[9] Klaus-Heinrich Standke, "Science and Technology in Global Cooperation: The Case of the United Nations and UNESCO," *Science and Public Policy* 33 (2006): 627, 634.

[10] Ibid.

[11] Shah, *Manifesting Utopia*, 8

[12] Standke, "Science and Technology," 636.

[13] See Hernán Thomas, Renato Dagnino, and Amílcar Davyt, "El Pensamiento En Ciencia, Tecnología y Sociedad En Latinoamérica: Una Interpretación Política de Su Trayectoria," *Redes* 3 (1996): 13, 19.

[14] Frederick William Ulbricht, "Science, International Relations, and the Policy Process" (master's thesis, American University, 1965), 81 (on file with the author).

[15] Harrison Brown and Theresa Tellez, *International Development Programs of the Office of the Foreign Secretary* (Washington, DC: National Academy of Sciences, 1973), 5.

education enrollment in 1960, Colombia (an ally of the Alliance for Progress under President Alberto Lleras[16]) captured 17 percent of Ford Foundation scholarships in the region (1960–1979), and 22.3 percent of Academic and Professional Programs for the Americas (LASPAU) scholarships (1965–1984). In contrast, Argentina had 31.8 percent of the enrolled population in the region yet received only 8.6 percent of Ford Foundation scholarships and just 0.6 percent of LASPAU scholarships.[17]

Law and Modernization in the Technological Desert

In this context, characterized by the diffusion model of science, Rostowian modernization, and Cold War anti-communism, law and legal reasoning were not the focus of the scientists' interests, nor was technology a focus point for lawyers in the region. This was not exceptional, as jurists were happy to leave development policies to other experts in the developmental state in the 1950s.[18] However, the law did provide the background norms where the promotion of a local scientific community (or of technical assistance) would occur. On the one hand, international law provided the underlying regional inter-American vocabulary that would serve not only the modernization dimension of the Alliance for Progress but also the specific organizational infrastructure for technical assistance programs and the OAS. Domestic law, in turn, provided the regulatory and legislative framework for creating domestic scientific systems that would receive technical support and serve as possible local scientific partners. Thus, reflecting the same mindset that inspired the UN conferences, several Latin American states created national science systems in the 1950s, with specialized agencies in each country, all in line with the expansion of the domestic administrative state in the region: Brazil (CNPq, 1951—following the recommendation of a scientific commission created by President Dutra in 1949), Argentina (CONICET, 1958), and later on in Chile (CONICYT, 1966), Colombia (Colciencias, 1968), and Mexico (CONACyT, 1970), among others.

[16] See Carlos Caballero Argáez, "Alberto Lleras Camargo, Cuba y la Alianza para el Progreso," in *Alberto Lleras Camargo y John F. Kennedy: Amistad y política internacional*, ed. Carlos Caballero Argáez et al. (Bogota, Colombia: Universidad de Los Andes, 2014).

[17] Daniel C. Levy, *To Export Progress: The Golden Age of University Assistance in the Americas* (Bloomington: Indiana University Press, 2005), 64. LASPAU (originally the "Latin American Scholarship Program of the American Universities") was not itself a donor but rather a nonprofit mechanism affiliated with Harvard University, which was, in the 1960s and 1970s, funded mainly by the State Department, particularly through AID and the United States Information Agency (USIA). See ibid., 44.

[18] See David Kennedy, "The 'Rule of Law,' Political Choices, and Development Common Sense," in *The New Law and Economic Development: A Critical Appraisal*, ed. Alvaro Santos and David M. Trubek, 104–105 (Cambridge: Cambridge University Press, 2006).

In this context, Latin American international lawyers proved to be a different beast. Besides creating international organizations like the OAS, and despite the apparent disconnection between law and technoscientific thought, international lawyers acted within their own scientific imaginary, different from the mindset described earlier. In contrast to the idea that Latin America was just a passive adopter of knowledge prevailing at the time, by the 1950s, Latin American international lawyers were at the end of a collective effort to codify international law. In particular, this collective project sought to highlight the possibility of a distinctively "American" contribution to the discipline—a concern that had dominated international legal scholarship in the region from the late nineteenth century.[19] For all its multiple layers and internal tensions, the "American" international law debate had at its core the idea that the "science" of international law was produced in Europe and, perhaps less prominently, in the United States. However, Latin American international lawyers did not perceive themselves as passive recipients of such expertise. Instead, they believed that their work had the quality and distinctiveness to be considered an original and significant contribution to universal international law and that their role was to persuade these centers of intellectual prestige of that fact.

Indeed, their intervention reproduced the technoscientific imagery that was dominant at the time. However, Paris, Geneva, Washington, and The Hague were still at the center of knowledge production, and Latin America was still on the periphery. In this sense, it reinforced the idea of Latin America as scientifically inferior.[20] However, even if their relevant audience was in the center and not on the periphery, these lawyers' self-perceived role was distinctively active, mobilizing their own knowledge and professional prestige to highlight their original contribution, thus partially subverting the consensus that seems

[19] See Arnulf Becker Lorca, "International Law in Latin America or Latin American International Law—Rise, Fall, and Retrieval of a Tradition of Legal Thinking and Political Imagination," *Harvard International Law Journal* 47 (2006): 283, 299–304; Arnulf Becker Lorca, *Mestizo International Law: A Global Intellectual History 1842-1933* (Cambridge: Cambridge University Press, 2014), 305–352

[20] Arnulf Becker Lorca has argued that one of the key players in the "American" international law effort, Chilean Alejandro Álvarez, in fact participated in a subaltern consciousness influenced by Latin American modernist authors like José Martí, José Enrique Rodó, and Rubén Darío. Arnulf Becker Lorca, "Alejandro Álvarez Situated: Subaltern Modernities and Modernisms That Subvert," *Leiden Journal of International Law* 19 (2006): 879. However, this literary framework hardly implies a questioning of belief of the overall centrality of Europe and the United States for the discipline of international law as "scientific" knowledge. Instead, it seems to be part of Alvarez's claim for the difference within the universalism of international law. Thus, while Martí and, in particular, Rodó and Darío did put forward a Latin Americanist mindset that decentered the United States and Europe, the audience that mattered for Álvarez was in Washington, The Hague, and particularly Paris, where he lived and was active in the solidarist approach to international law. See Juan Pablo Scarfi, *The Hidden History of International Law in the Americas: Empire and Legal Networks* (Oxford: Oxford University Press, 2017), 61–62, 74–85, distinguishing between Álvarez "literary habitus" (the modernists) and his "legal habitus"—the legal audience.

to dominate the UN scientific conferences and the OAS technical assistance programs existing at the time,

Latin American Structuralism, and the Effort to Manage the Distributive Effects of Technology

As international law became more specialized and new universal organizations became protagonists, the American international law movement declined, and with it, the idea that the region had something to offer the discipline as distinct knowledge.[21] In turn, the emphasis on fostering a domestic scientific community remained, though this time with a more specific focus on development. In 1964, the OAS organized its Conference on Policy and Planning Science and Technology, while UNESCO organized in Santiago de Chile what would be the first of seven Conferences on the Application of Science and Technology to the Development of Latin America (CASTALA), both of which would emphasize the need for an explicit science policy, led by scientist and technologists, targeting economic development.[22]

These conferences took place in the intellectual context of Latin American structuralist thinking. As is well known, between the 1940s and 1960s, a group of economists active in the United Nations Economic Commission for Latin America and the Caribbean (ECLAC) developed a robust (and radically original) body of work that sought to account for the role of Latin America in the global economy, and to propose the appropriate role that the state should play in the economy—most notably, through the work of Argentinean economist Raul Prebisch (1901–1986). For structuralists, poverty was not an anomaly but was closely connected with the expansion of industrialized countries. They rejected the Rostowian modernization approach that economic development is a process with evolutive "phases," where underdevelopment is a necessary first step; instead, "underdevelopment" was, for structuralists, a manifestation of the very same process that creates development.[23]

Structuralism was skeptical that comparative advantage normatively justified free trade, instead arguing that trade was structured around the divide between

[21] See Luis Eslava, Liliana Obregón, and René Urueña, *Imperialismo y Derecho Internacional* (Bogota, Colombia: Siglo del Hombre Editores, 2016), 64–65.

[22] Pablo Kreimer and Hernán Thomas, "Un poco de reflexividad o ¿de dónde venimos? Estudios sociales de la ciencia y la tecnología en América Latina," in *Producción y uso social de conocimientos: Estudios de sociología de la ciencia y la tecnología en América Latina* (Bernal, Argentina: Universidad Nacional de Quilmes, 2004).

[23] On structuralism, see generally Ricardo Bielschowsky, "Sesenta Años de La CEPAL: Estructuralismo y Neoestructuralismo," *Revista Cepal* (2009): 173. In English, a good introduction is Cristobal Kay, "The Latin American Structuralist School," in *International Encyclopedia of Human Geography*. Rob Kitchin and Nigel Thrift, 159 (New York: Elsevier, 2009).

the center and the periphery. Taking advantage of its privileged access to capital, the center specialized in high-productivity industrial sectors ("manufactures"), while the periphery specialized in primary-sector production (mainly agriculture and mining). Given this "structure" (hence the movement's name), free trade between the center and periphery would never allow the latter to develop because it systematically benefits the former, specifically through the decline of the periphery's terms of trade (i.e., the decline of the ratio between the price per unit of exports and imports of a country). Due to this decline, the more the periphery traded with the center, the less manufactured units it could "buy" with each of its primary units, thus reinforcing its "underdeveloped" status.

For structuralists, industrialization was the only way out of this process, mainly through import substitution, which made them keenly interested in technology. ECLAC played a key role in positioning this idea. From 1950 to 1963, Prebisch was ECLAC's Executive Secretary (before moving on to UNCTAD, as we will see in the next section). During his mandate, and until the 1970s, ECLAC became a hub for a vibrant community of scholars and policymakers who rejected the intellectual strategy of transplanting to Latin America models produced in (and for) Europe or the United States but were instead invested in developing their original theories to explain the region's role in the global economy.[24] For these structuralists, the center/periphery division partially emerged due to technology, which was necessary for structuralists because it significantly improved productivity.[25] However, technology was not, in and of itself, the solution to Latin America's development challenges. The problem lies in the context of the deployment of technology and its distribution to, and within, the periphery—a structuralist stance that sharply contrasted with the idea that technology was primarily context-neutral and that Latin America was a technological desert, which made technical assistance and domestic scientific communities a priority.

Structuralists argued that technological advances were adopted in all sectors in the center with the industrial revolution, but its diffusion was uneven in the periphery. There, new technologies were imported to improve productivity in the primary sector to export to the center.[26] In contrast, new technologies were not available for subsistence sectors in the periphery (i.e., those not focused on exports), which created a dual economy: outside the export economy, a considerable pre-capitalist sector of low productivity survives without access to technology, producing a permanent surplus of labor. This huge surplus of labor

[24] Ricardo Bielschowsky, "Evolución de Las Ideas de La CEPAL," *Revista CEPAL* 10 (1998): 1; Ricardo Bielschowsky, "Sesenta Años de La CEPAL: Estructuralismo y Neoestructuralismo," *Revista Cepal* (2009): 173.

[25] See Cristóbal Kay, "Estructuralismo y Teoría de La Dependencia En El Periodo Neoliberal," *Nueva Sociedad* 158 (1998): 100.

[26] Cristóbal Kay, "Teorías Latinoamericanas Del Desarrollo," *Nueva Sociedad* 113 (1991): 101.

keeps, in turn, wages low and prevents the periphery from accumulating capital to achieve its own technological progress. This is partly because the export sector's productivity gains are mainly transferred to the center.[27]

Structuralism, Technology, and the Law

Despite their focus on technology, structuralists were not naïve techno-optimists. The answer was not to merely transfer technology to the periphery. In Prebisch's view, countries in the center could accumulate capital and invest it in technology, thus reducing the need for labor and improving the return on capital. The problem was that Latin America lacked access to that capital, which meant that labor freed by technology would have nowhere to go, as other sectors (particularly outside exports) simply lacked the capital to absorb them. In that event, the impact of technological improvement in Latin America would be, in fact, negative—unless capital was redistributed to expand production and not only productivity by reducing the need for labor.[28]

For Prebisch, Latin America needed to put technology to a different use than the center: instead of improving productivity by reducing the amount of labor needed, the goal should be to maximize the production by capital unit.[29] This insight is key, as it shows that technology is not neutral but is somewhat wholly dependent on the context of its deployment. But for this to happen, a national industry had to be developed, which would ,in turn, build technology adjusted to the Latin American context and would also consider in its deployment the underlying problem of the potential reduction of the need for labor.

In this context, law played a dual role. On the domestic side, the law had to go beyond creating an administrative structure to foster national scientific communities. More than that, the law should first create the regulatory framework for import substitution, particularly taxes on exports of the primary sector and tariffs for industrial goods, so that native technology emerges. On the international side, in turn, the law had to create the conditions for import substitution as a domestic policy to work. This view was influential in the United Nations Conference on Trade and Development (UNCTAD), with Prebisch as its founding secretary-general (1964–1969). UNCTAD sought to put forward an alternative view to the integration of the "Third World" to international markets, different from the free trade model of the GATT 1947. From the perspective of our discussion on technology, a crucial goal of this mindset was that

[27] Ibid.
[28] Raúl Prebisch, *Problemas Teóricos y Prácticos Del Crecimiento Económico* (Mexico City: CEPAL, 1952), 9–10, 36–51.
[29] Ibid., 86.

the economies on the periphery, like Latin America's, would be able to access capital and hence develop the technology for industrialization it needed, and not only the technology that the center was willing to transfer to improve the former's export sector. To access this amount of capital, structuralists saw no option but to rely on the existing primary industry and transform international trade terms in commodities and agricultural products—and UNCTAD was an excellent platform to look for such results. Reflecting this approach (that went beyond structuralism), UNCTAD was critical of the general application of the most favored nation principle to all international trade (as reflected in Article 1 of the GATT) and instead pushed for a general system of preferences that would allow preferential access to affluent markets by poor states and strived to create a Commodity Price Stabilization Fund.[30] A system of preferences, and a stabilization fund, would allow a more stable source of currency for developing countries, thus allowing access to capital that, for structuralists, was the key for accessing technology and therefore breaking the dualist character of Latin American economies.

Structuralists techno-imaginaries contributed to the rationale for the role that law was to play in Latin America concerning international trade. And, as importantly, they also provided the rationale for its domestic role: the law had created the legislative and administrative means necessary to redistribute resources and manage the negative effect of technology, which risked deepening the gap between the periphery's local and subsistence sector (particularly concerning land, which occupied much of Prebisch's reflection on technology).[31] To that effect, tax policy, land titling, and labor regulations could be used so that the workforce displaced by technological advancement was again absorbed in another sector—a problem that is not relevant in the center, where the law had to play a different role with regards to technology.

III. New Technoscientific Imaginaries: The "Pensamiento latinoamericano en ciencia tecnología y sociedad"

Structuralism's import substitution strategy proved to be less successful than promised. Even after adopting it, Latin America grew even more dependent on foreign trade and technology, which triggered a set of critiques and new ideas on trade and development in the late 1960s and 1970s known as "*Dependentismo*." While building on the center/periphery construct, *dependentistas* rejected

[30] Antony Anghie, "Legal Aspects of the New International Economic Order," *Humanity: An International Journal of Human Rights, Humanitarianism, and Development* 6 (2015): 145, 148.

[31] For example, in Prebisch, *Problemas Teóricos y Prácticos*, 87.

structuralism's notion of an advanced "pocket" of industrial production within the periphery. Ultimately, for structuralists, the goal was to expand that pocket through import substitution via the careful expansion of technology—with the caveats discussed above. But, for *dependentistas*, there was no such dualism: all the periphery was already integrated into global capitalism and was kept dependent precisely by that process. *Dependentistas* thus complemented structuralism external analysis with their own exploration of the internal sociopolitical dynamic of the region, which helped explain its lack of economic development.[32] Thus, *Dependencia y Desarrollo en América Latina*, the groundbreaking 1969 study of Brazilian Fernando Henrique Cardoso and Chilean Enzo Faletto, linked the internal dynamics of Latin America with external forces and rejected the idea that dependency was just the domestic reflection of imperialism.[33]

In the context of our discussion of technology, a key insight from *dependentismo* (and an important difference with structuralism) was that, for them, capitalism created a particular kind of local elite in the periphery (what Frank calls the *comprador*, or *lumpenbourgeoisie*, class[34]). This class adopts the center's consumption patterns, manages the periphery's technology and process of exploitation, exports its products, and then uses the surplus to buy from the center. This creates a "development of underdevelopment,"[35] in which global trade will never increase productivity in the periphery. *Dependentisimo* rejected the structuralist idea that industrialization could ultimately lead to the beneficial integration of the periphery into world trade. By extracting resources and rents from the periphery (i.e., from poor countries, like Latin America), the center (rich economies, like North America and Europe) accumulated the capital that underdeveloped the former. No amount of industrialization would ever be able to reverse this dynamic.

The profound conceptual transformation reflected by *dependentismo* was equally important in technological thinking in Latin America. In the 1960s and 1970s a group of technologists such as Argentinians Jorge Sábato (1924–1983)[36],

[32] For the critique, I'm following Alfredo Saad-Filho, "The Rise and Decline of Latin American Structuralism and Dependency Theory," in *The Origins of Development Economics: How Schools of Economic Thought Have Addressed Development* (London: Zed Books, 2005).

[33] Fernando Henrique Cardoso, *Dependencia y desarrollo en América Latina: ensayo de interpretación sociológica* (3rd ed., Mexico City: Siglo Veintiuno Editores, 1971).

[34] See Andre Gunder Frank, *Lumpenburguesía, lumpendesarrollo: dependencia, clase y política en Latinoamérica* (1st ed., Bogota, Colombia: Editorial la Oveja Negra, 1970).

[35] Andre Gunder Frank, "The Underdevelopment of Development," *Monthly Review* 18 (1966): 17.

[36] Jorge was in fact Ernesto Sábato's nephew. Ernesto (1911–2011) is well-known for his fiction (*El Túnel* (1948), *Sobre Héroes y Tumbas* (1961), and *Abaddón, el Exterminador* (1974)) but first trained as a physicist and worked at the Curie Laboratory in Paris. In parallel with *El Túnel*, Ernesto Sabato's first essays are a technoscientific reflection on the diminished role of the self as a cog in the machine (most importantly, in *Hombres y Engranajes* (1951). This genre of existentialist, and more literary, technoscientific thought is not often taken up when the history of Latin American science and technology studied is told.

Amílcar Herrera, and Oscar Varsavsky, among others, mounted a strong critique of both the idea of Latin America as a mere adopter of technological advances and of structuralism's approach to import substitution, which never really triggered local technological innovation by the private sector and instead focused on its few innovations in the recently created national scientific institutions.[37] This body of work came be known as the *Pensamiento latinoamericano en ciencia tecnología y Sociedad*.[38] PLACTS scholars concentrated on the political challenges of innovation and explicitly connected scientific policy with the *dependentista* consensus of the time.[39] They rejected a linear model of innovation and instead argued that scientific developments derived from a dialectic process between policymakers, scientists, and the industry.[40]

While it is impossible to summarize the range of PLACTS work here, there were at least three key insights that implied a break from the notion of Latin America as a mere adopter of technology, with important implications for the role of law in the region.[41]

The first insight was the realization that states had, in fact, two scientific policies: one was the explicit policy, as expressed in official documents and carried out by the system of scientific institutions created as an expression of the Rostowian modernization and technology-transfer mindset. However, there was a second implicit policy, which reflected the actual policy choices of the respective society.[42] Latin America's failed scientific development was not an anomaly because it was not the result of a poorly implemented technological policy (which could be solved, for example, through technology transfers). The region's technological dependence was, in fact, an efficient implementation of the region's implicit technological policy determined, according to PLACTS

[37] See Thomas et al., "El Pensamiento En Ciencia," 18–19.

[38] PLACT work took distinct shape with the publication of *El Pensamiento latinoamericano en la problemática ciencia-tecnologiá-desarrollo-dependencia* (1975), a volume of collected essays featuring much of the new thinking of technology emerging from Latin America at this time. See Jorge A. Sábato (ed.), *El Pensamiento latinoamericano en la problemática ciencia-tecnología-desarrollo-dependencia* (Barcelona: Editorial Paidós, 1975).

[39] Kreimer and Thomas, "Un poco de reflexividad o ¿de dónde venimos?" 13 In fact, Jorge Sábato's seminal text was originally called "Science, Technology, Development, *and Dependency*." See Jorge A. Sábato, *Ciencia, tecnología, desarrollo y dependencia* (1st ed., San Miguel de Tucumán, Argentina: Editorial de la Universidad Nacional de Tucumán, 1971). The "dependency" part was dropped in later editions.

[40] Thomas et al., "El Pensamiento En Ciencia," 20.

[41] For more on PLACT's innovations, see Rosalba Casas Guerrero, "Conocimiento, Technologia Desarrollo En America Latina," *Revista Mexicana de Sociología* 66 (2004): 255; Pablo Kreimer and Hebe Vessuri, "Latin American Science, Technology, and Society: A Historical and Reflexive Approach," *Tapuya: Latin American Science, Technology and Society* 1 (2018): 17, 22–25; Thomas et al., "El Pensamiento En Ciencia," 20–25; Kreimer and Thomas, "Un poco de reflexividad o ¿de dónde venimos?" 14–18.

[42] See Amílcar O. Herrera, "Los Determinantes Sociales de La Política Científica En América Latina: Política Científica Explícita y Política Científica Implícita," *Desarrollo Económico* 13 (1973): 113.

technologist Amílcar Herrera, "by a structure of underdevelopment that is largely conditioned by the way these countries are inserted in the international system."[43]

For Herrera, the lack of scientific development in Latin America was usually (and incorrectly) chalked up to a combination of three variables: its culture (the region lacked entrepreneurial dynamism and an educated workforce), the structure of its economy (it was too reliant on primary goods and low-skill labor-intensive activities (i.e., the structuralists' "dualist" model), and, finally, its institutions (the region's public sector was corrupted and inefficient). Given this diagnosis, technology policy (including technology transfers) was supposed to work as an external factor that moved Latin America out of its inertia and cultural complacency, triggering cultural, economic, and institutional change.[44]

But, of course, it did not. Why? For PLACTS scholars, it was not true that Latin American culture, structure of production, or institutions notably failed—or at least, not more failed than those in other countries with much more scientific innovation.[45] The key was the "national project": the objectives that national elites chose and invested their resources in achieving.[46] While states in the center had a "national project" that demanded scientific innovation, Latin American states had national projects that dated back to the postcolonial era and sought to protect the position of local elites that were dependent on the center, as their income depended on exporting, while dominating local populations—none other than Frank's *lumpenbourgeoisie* class. In this Latin American "national project," technology is a luxury of few or a mechanism to reinforce the local elites' integration into the center (and hence their ability to exert domination at the domestic level). There is, thus, no demand for local technology that explains Latin America's relative lack of scientific development.

PLACTS's second critical insight was that import substitution and other industrialization strategies only perpetuated the periphery's technological dependency on the center. Changing that dynamic required the realization that technology was a social process (and not just a technical matter) deeply embedded in the respective social and cultural context, particularly the specific

[43] Ibid., 118.

[44] Ibid., 118–121.

[45] Herrera's cultural argument is based on racial tropes which seem revealing of the racial politics of Dependentismo and progressive economic policy in the region at the time. For Herrera, "Latin America, unlike other underdeveloped regions of the world, is a product of European conquest, colonization and immigration. In some countries—such as Uruguay and Argentina—the population is almost entirely of European origin, but even in those with a high percentage of Indigenous populations, the dominant classes, as well as the basic cultural patterns, are also distinctly European." And concludes: "[I]t can be affirmed that at the present time—except for small, very localized exceptions, which do not alter the general picture—there is, strictly speaking, no indigenous culture in the region." Ibid., 122.

[46] Ibid., 128.

needs of society. Structuralists might have been aware of the importance of context for technology. However, for PLACTS scholar Jorge Sábato, nations needed to go further: instead of focusing on technology as a means to productivity (as was the case with structuralists), policy should strive for "innovation"—that is, "the incorporation of knowledge—either one's own, or other's—to generate or modify a productive process."[47] To do so, fostering better interaction between the state, technoscientific institutions (like the university), and the industry was crucial, forming the famous "Sábato Triangle" paradigm for scientific policymaking in Latin America.

Finally, PLACTS's third key insight came from its more radical reading of the global political economy of scientific knowledge, beyond industrialization. Oscar Varsavsky, perhaps the most critical and prescient of PLACTS scholars, saw how technological development in Latin America depended not on the industrial titans in the center but on global centers of academic prestige—typically, universities and research institutes, particularly in the United States.[48] Latin America lacked its own "scientific style." Instead, it adopted it wholesale from the United States: its scientific culture continued colonialism by prioritizing the business interests of the center and, perhaps more importantly, by studying problems considered important by scientific centers in the United States but were of little relevance for their own countries.[49] This process implied an "internal brain drain,"[50] in which the best and the brightest of Latin America invest their time, effort, and scarce resources in work for the consumption of the conference circuit in the United States and Europe, moving those resources away from the region's own challenges.

These challenges implied that a fundamental transformation of the productive structure was needed if Latin America was to overcome its technological dependency. Beyond mere technology transfer or import substitution, PLACTS technologists like Amílcar Herrera believed that the national project had to be transformed. The protection of the privileges of the exporting elites (or its import substitution equivalent) had to be eliminated, not just reformed. That would require

[47] Jorge Sábato and Natalio Botana, "La ciencia y la tecnología en el desarrollo futuro de América Latina," *Revista de la Integración—INTAL* 1 (1968): 15, 19. Sábato is writing this six years before the publication of Freeman's seminal book on innovation. See Christopher Freeman, *The Economics of Industrial Innovation* (New York: Penguin, 1974).

[48] Oscar Varsavsky, *Ciencia, política y cientificismo* (1st ed., Piedros, Argentina: Centro Editor de América Latina, 1969).

[49] Ibid., 23.

[50] Xavier Polanco, "La Ciencia Como Ficción," in *Historia y contexto en el perfil de la ciencia en América Latina*, ed. J. J. Saldaña (Mexico City: Cuadernos de Quipu, Sociedad Latinoamericana de Historia de la Ciencia y la Tecnología, 1987).

at least the radical redistribution of income in favor of the popular classes in order to create a true mass market; the change in agriculture, with the destruction of the latifundia and the introduction of modern methods of production; the rupture of external dependence, with the consequent abandonment of the role of producers of raw materials or manufactured goods which the developed countries are not interested in producing; and the complete restructuring of the state, to give it the strength and self-sufficiency it should have in the process which requires the nationalization and control of the strategic elements of development.[51]

PLACTS and the Law

PLACTS scholars emphasized the political implications of technology, which implied an implicit understanding of the role that law and legal reasoning should play in achieving technological transformation in Latin America. PLACTS scholars were critical of both free markets and the import substitution model, and the role of law in perpetuating Latin American technological dependency can also be read in reference to these two frameworks.

In the free trade model, the law was complicit in Latin America's technological dependency. International economic law kept barriers to trade low, thus providing local elites access to export markets. In turn, international commercial law gave local elites access to the center's technology through exclusive international contracts. Domestic law, in turn, established labor regulations that allowed the easy movement of low-paying workers from and to the export sector, thus facilitating the adoption of new technologies from the center that dislocated workers. Finally, domestic law established the legal entitlements that protect the local elite's access to land and property, preventing other possible local elites from accessing or taking over by force that same export-oriented technology. In all, the law allowed local elites to maintain their privileges and domination of the local economy.

However, the situation would not have been much better on the import substitution side. In that model, international economic law establishes tariffs, quantitative restrictions, and other tools of protectionism, which seek to create a domestic market for the products of infant industries. In turn, domestic law establishes the network of legal relations and entitlements that differentiate between the industrial sector (i.e., the industry now supplying the domestic market

[51] Herrera, "Los Determinantes Sociales de La Política Científica En América Latina."

with import-substituted goods) and the subsistence sector, which remains despite the import substitution strategy. By doing so, the law provides local elites with control over technology imported from the center—only now, that technology is used to supply the domestic market. However, this local elite has no incentive to innovate because their focus is on using technology to improve productivity, eventually creating the problem of displaced low-skill labor. At best, the role of the law should be, as discussed above, to manage the consequences of this displacement through domestic regulation and distribution. In this context, law was the mechanism through which local elites perpetuated their connection with the center, hence blocking local technologies' development.

However, law could also be the tool that provided the mechanisms for the coordination of the different actors of technological innovation. In PLACTS's mindset, the law could also play a constructive role in reducing Latin America's technological dependency. Law provides the tools of state planning in the economy, which is key for innovation. Most importantly, domestic administrative law offers the regulatory machinery for coordinating the state, the academy, and the industry. Such coordination also required an active role of public enterprises, which would streamline the innovations and introduce them in the markets. Sábato, for example, was president of what was at the time the public power corporation *Servicios Eléctricos del Gran Buenos Aires* (SEGBA), from which he tried to spin off an *Empresa Nacional de Investigación y Desarrollo Eléctrico* (ENIDE), which was supposed to apply corporate practices to the creation of knowledge in the electric sector—an activity that was, to Sábato's mind, different from both research and engineering.[52] That project was never implemented and Sábato left public service in 1971[53]; however, the desired role of state enterprises implicit in PLACTS' view of technology would have a legal framework that complemented the planning role of the state and, going beyond structuralism's import substitution model, would allow these enterprises to operate at arm's length from the state, interacting with the other two actors of Sábato's triangle—the state and the academic community.[54]

[52] Jorge A. Sábato, "ENIDE: ¿Ingeniería o investigación?" *Ciencia Nueva* (1971): 12.

[53] See Oscar Galante and Manuel Marí, "Jorge Sábato y El Pensamiento Latinoamericano En Ciencia, Tecnología, Desarrollo y Dependencia," *Ciencia, Tecnología y Política* 3 (2020): 1, 6.

[54] While, as far as I have been able to gather, Sábato did not focus on the role of intellectual property in his view of "innovation," one can see the similarities between his vision of ENIDE and transnational corporate structuring in which a subsidiary is created solely to own the intellectual property of the corporation and, as its most valuable asset, is located in a low-tax jurisdiction. This "knowledge only" entity seems to be exactly what Sábato had in mind—of course, for purposes different from tax-planning.

International law and PLACTS

International law could also contribute to technological innovation. As PLACTS scholars were making their contribution, developing countries coalesced around the idea of a new international economic order (NIEO)—an unparalleled effort, until today, of changing the deep structures of international trade and investment.[55] As we can see, PLACTS scholars seemed not to be too interested in the NIEO. However, technology was crucial for the NIEO, which prioritized as one of its principles to give developing nations "access to the achievements of modern science and technology, and promot(e) the transfer of technology and the creation of indigenous technology for the benefit of the developing countries in forms and in accordance with procedures which are suited to their economies"[56]—including the right of access of all nations to universal heritage technology.

Such an emphasis on technology transfer was vital in the context of the NIEO. NIEO's Programme of Action called for a code of technology transfer,[57] an initiative taken up by UNCTAD.[58] This line of work eventually led to a draft UNCTAD Code of Conduct on the Transfer of Technology, which was discussed in 1977, but the negotiations stalled due to a division among states in the South,[59] and the initiative was ultimately abandoned.[60]

Regardless of this political failure, it is doubtful that PLACTS scholars would have found such a code useful for their policy objectives. PLACTS scholars were skeptical of decontextualized technology transfer without further local development. In particular, the NIEO seems to have envisioned a technology transfer focused on states: from states and, particularly, transnational corporations in the North to states in the South. But this kind of technology transfer, which seemed to reflect a structuralist mindset, would simply reinforce the position of local elites (even if those elites were close to the state) who would still be able to leverage

[55] See generally Anghie, "Legal Aspects of the New International Economic Order."

[56] UN Declaration on the Establishment of a New International Economic Order, G.A. Res. 3201 (S-VI), 6 Spec. U.N. GAOR (Supp. No. 1) at 3, U.N. Doc. A/9559 (1974), para. 4

[57] Programme of Action on the Establishment of a New International Economic Order, G.A. Res. 3202 (S-VI), 6 Spec. U.N. GAOR (Supp. No. 1) at 5, U.N. Doc. A/9559 (1974).

[58] Since its inception, UNCTAD has emphasized "technology transfer." In its first 1964 meeting, the conference recommended that "[c]ompetent international bodies (. . .) explore possibilities for adaptation of legislation concerning the transfer of industrial technology to developing countries, including the possibility of concluding appropriate international agreements in this field." *Proceedings of the United Nations Conference on Trade and Development*, A.IV.26 Annexes 57, U.N. Doc. E/CONFA6/141, vol. I.

[59] Pedro Roffe, "Transfer of Technology: UNCTAD's Draft International Code of Conduct," *The International Lawyer* 19 (1985): 689.

[60] On the history and aftermath of the Code, see Pedro Roffe, Surendra J. Patel, and Abdulqawi Yusuf, *International Technology Transfer: The Origins and Aftermath of the United Nations Negotiations on a Draft Code of Conduct* (Dordrecht, The Netherlands: Kluwer Law International, 2001).

their access to this newly transferred technology to perpetuate their positions of power, thus hindering the improvement of technology in Latin America.

Latin American approaches to the NIEO at the time (even those coming from the ECLAC) seemed to have adopted a much less critical view than PLACTS scholars, understanding technology as neutral in terms of sociopolitical context, mostly related to access capital.[61] Perhaps, despite obvious intellectual and institutional common ground between PLACTS and the NIEO, Latin American technologists needed to see the latter as a helpful institutional venue for achieving their goals.[62]

Despite PLACTS's scholars' skepticism, some doctrinal reforms proposed by the NIEO seem to reflect the kind of international legal tools needed for Latin American technological development from a PLACTS perspective. For example, the NIEO's focus on private actors was in line with PLACTS' view that technology is held by transnational corporations that, in turn, license its use to local elites in the periphery, bolstering their privileges. That is, PLACTS scholars were aware that, as a matter of international technology policy, the state had to be disaggregated, and the corporation had to be considered—all of which have been in line with the NIEO.

However, other NIEO proposals relied on a view of technology that, for PLACTS scholars, could have seemed hopelessly limited by a structuralist/import substitution mindset. For example, permanent sovereignty over natural resources, an article of faith for the NIEO, was a way to reinstate state control over the resources characteristic of Latin American participation in global capitalism. While taking control of such resources from multinational corporations was (and is) indeed crucial in terms of self-determination, this change of control does nothing to change the place of exploiting natural resources as the "national project" of Latin America. This national project simply reproduces the structuralist's view of an export economy that should be controlled by elites close to the government and, ultimately, reproduces also the mindset of Latin America as an exporter of primary goods and importer of technology—either

[61] Pedro Sampaio Malán, "Los Países Latinoamericanos y El Nuevo Orden Económico Internacional," *Revista de la CEPAL* (1980): 71, 81–83.

[62] Pedro Malán presented his views on Latin America and the NIEO in a meeting organized by the ECLAC in Washington, DC, in late June 1979. Ibid. In that same meeting, Mexican technologist Miguel S. Wionczek discussed UNCTAD's draft Code of Conduct at length, as well as its importance for the NIEO. Also in the room was Jorge Sábato, who presented a paper on Latin American technology from a PLACT perspective, which was published right between Malán's, and Wionczek's contributions in *Revista CEPAL* (directed at the time by Raul Prebisch). Not once does Sábato mention the NIEO in his remarks. See Jorge A. Sábato, "Desarrollo Tecnológico En América Latina y El Caribe," *Revista de la CEPAL* (1980): 87; Miguel S. Wionczek, "Las Principales Cuestiones Pendientes En Las Negociaciones Sobre El Código de Conducta de La UNCTAD Para La Transferencia de Tecnología," *Revista de la CEPAL* (1980): 101.

via voluntary technology transfer (as the one foreseen in the UNCTAD Code), or via the nationalizations of corporate assets in the territory of the periphery.

Perhaps the most precise legal expression of this tension was the NIEO's proposal of rules allowing host states to require foreign investors to train local personnel in technology and to promote local research and development. Similarly, under the NIEO, host states would have been allowed to restrict fearing investors' proprietary rights over technologies in joint investment with local undertakings.[63] As the NIEO faltered, though, its approach to technology became less influential. In its place, contemporary investment rules imposed strict restrictions on investment performance requirements for investors—and, specifically, on host states' power to impose technology transfer requirements on foreign investors.[64]

Ultimately, though, the NIEO-style of explicit engagement with the politics of technology became less frequent in the following years in Latin America for at least two reasons. First, the region moved toward a development model structured around trade liberalization, privatization and attracting foreign investment.[65] As Cimoli and Katz explain, in this new developmental common sense, domestic and foreign investors moved toward industries featuring low domestic knowledge generation, which limited local R&D and engineering activities.[66] This new reality led to major changes in national scientific and innovation systems in the region, moving their focus away from the development of local technology.[67] Thus, the policy-relevant discussions regarding regulation of (and for) technological innovation moved away from domestic developmental policy and into intellectual property law.[68] In particular, after the creation of the World Trade Organization and its TRIPS (Trade-Related Aspects of Intellectual

[63] Chantal Thomas, "Transfer of Technology in the Contemporary International Order," *Fordham International Law Journal* 22: (1998): 2096, 2107–2108.

[64] See generally David Collins, "Performance Requirement Prohibitions in International Investment Law," in *Handbook of International Investment Law and Policy*, ed. Julien Chaisse, Leïla Choukroune, and Sufian Jusoh (New York: Springer 2021). However, the underlying issue that informed the NIEO's approach is far from settled. At the time of writing, the United States and the European Union have often accused China of imposing "forced technology transfers" on foreign investors wanting to do business there, which violated both World Trade Organization law and international investment law. See Qian Yin, "Forced Technology Transfer Performance Requirement in International Investment Agreements—A Chinese Perspective," *Journal of Intellectual Property Law and Practice* 17 (2022): 114.

[65] John Williamson, "What Washington Means by Policy Reform," in *Latin American Adjustment: How Much Has Happened?*, ed. John Williamson (Washington, DC: Institute for International Economics, 1990).

[66] Mario Cimoli and Jorge Katz, "Structural Reforms, Technological Gaps and Economic Development: A Latin American Perspective," *Industrial and Corporate Change* 12 (2003): 387.

[67] Jorge Katz, "Market-Oriented Reforms, Globalization and the Recent Transformation of Latin American Innovation Systems," *Oxford Development Studies* 32 (2004): 375.

[68] For example, Theodore A. Khoury and Mike W. Peng, "Does Institutional Reform of Intellectual Property Rights Lead to More Inbound FDI? Evidence from Latin America and the Caribbean," *Journal of World Business* 46 (2011): 337.

Property Rights) agreement, the question of policy for technological innovation in the region became less a matter of dependency and the development of technologies and more a question of how to better signal to foreign investors a robust protection of their intellectual property rights, so they would be interested in deploying their proprietary technology in Latin America.[69] Ultimately, while the question of innovation continued to be discussed in the region, the key policy question concerned intellectual property protection.

This important change in the developmental common sense was accompanied by the fact that Science and Technology Studies (STS) became more professionalized in the region, radically changing the kind of technoscientific thought considered prestigious by technologists. In fact, much of the work reviewed in this chapter would not withstand the expert gaze of this new scholarly context. As Kreimer puts—"many illuminating texts like Varsavsky's read more like essays with a heavy dose of intuition than the rigorous research that would later be required."[70] Particularly since the 1990s, as more programs emerged and STS scholarship became more specialized, more researchers in the region joined international professional networks.[71] With that, a historical line of research in Latin American STS began to take form—for example, with the creation of *Quipu: Una Revista Latinoamericana de la Historia de las Ciencias y la Tecnología* in 1984. But, at the same time, the interest in contemporary, policy-relevant, and distinctly Latin American technoscientific thinking seems to have decreased in the 1990s and 2000s, while the influence of conceptual frameworks developed by prestigious institutions in the North increased.[72]

IV. Conclusion: Reconnecting law and Latin American technological thought

PLACTS represented an exceptional convergence of original technoscientific thinking and economic policymaking in the region. Building on both a forceful rejection of the idea that Latin America is a technological wasteland and a sustained critique of structuralist import substitution policy, PLACTS scholars developed a technological vocabulary specifically geared toward progressive

[69] See, for example, the discussion in Carlos M. Correa, "Harmonization of Intellectual Property Rights in Latin America: Is There Still Room for Differentiation," *New York University Journal of International Law and Politics* 29 (1996): 109.

[70] Kreimer and Vessuri, "Latin American Science, Technology, and Society," 30

[71] Kreimer and Thomas, "Un poco de reflexividad o ¿de dónde venimos?"

[72] Vessuri Hebbe, "La Actual Internacionalización de Las Ciencias Sociales En América Latina: ¿vino Viejo En Barricas Nuevas?" in *Estudio social de la ciencia y la tecnología desde América Latina*, ed. Antonio Arellano Hernández and Pablo Kreimer (Bogota, Colombia: Siglo del Hombre, 2011). Kreimer and Vessuri, "Latin American Science, Technology, and Society," 30–31.

policies and economic development, which featured a particular (yet often implicit) idea of what the law was doing to sustain Latin America's technological dependency and what it could do to help overcome it.

The Washington Consensus implied a shift in Latin America toward a mindset of technology as a problem of foreign investment and intellectual property and the concurrent depoliticization of science and technology studies. However, such a wave seems to be shifting now on two fronts. On the one hand, Latin America STS scholars have been active in developing both conceptual frameworks and particular case studies that move beyond the idea of Latin America as a passive adopter of "imported magic," as a seminal collected volume on Latin American STS has recently put it.[73] In this effort, technology and innovation are again seen as a political undertaking, complete with normative choices and reflective of underlying ideologies—all of which follow the well-established PLACTS tradition.[74]

Much of this new STS work in the region has found, in national and international legal practice, a site to explore the construction of technoscientific knowledge in Latin America fruitfully.[75] In turn, legal scholars working on the region have also moved to consider how technoscientific thinking interacts with the law in a specifically Latin American context. Boaventura de Sousa Santos, for example, has been active in pointing out both the epistemological blind spots in the technological common sense underlying neoliberalism and the ways to recover Indigenous knowledge that have been obscured by Western universalism—a move he has called "cognitive decolonization."[76] In my own work, I have explored how the use of "new technologies" (particularly algorithmic decision-making) might reinforce Latin American problems of social exclusion and discrimination.[77] More focused on the normative effects of technoscientific artifacts, Daniel Quiroga-Villamarín has adopted an STS framework to explore expanding the particular form of governance that organizes deeply integrated supply chains. "More than a mere box," Quiroga-Villamarín

[73] Eden Medina et al., *Beyond Imported Magic: Essays on Science, Technology, and Society in Latin America* (Cambridge, MA: MIT Press, 2014).

[74] Underscoring this continuity, see Rosalba Casas and Tania Pérez-Bustos, eds., *Ciencia, Tecnología y Sociedad En América Latina: La Mirada de Las Nuevas Generaciones* (Asociación Latinoamericana de Estudios Sociales de la Ciencia y la Tecnología (ESOCITE), 2019).

[75] For example, the case studies found in Casas and Tania Pérez-Bustos, ibid., include work on water rights, intellectual property of seed, the right to health, and how the Colombian Congress and the Colombia-Korea Free Trade Agreement as non-human actors are intertwined in the process of co-production. On the idiom of co-production (with cases outside Latin America), see Jasanoff, "The Idiom of Co-Production."

[76] Boaventura de Sousa Santos, *The End of the Cognitive Empire: The Coming of Age of Epistemologies of the South* (Durham, NC: Duke University Press, 2018), 120–136.

[77] René Urueña, "Regulating the Algorithmic Welfare State in Latin America," *German Law Journal* (2023); Rene Urueña, "Autoridad Algorítmica: ¿cómo Empezar a Pensar La Protección de Los Derechos Humanos En La Era Del 'Big Data'?" *Latin American Law Review* 1 (2019): 123.

argues, "the container contains a sociotechnical imaginary of global governance, in which law, rights, and regulation play a salient role."[78] Tackling the same question from an infrastructural point of view, Alejandro Rodiles has compared the UN Sustainable Development Goals with China's Belt and Road Initiative as expressions of "infrastructural developmentalism," exploring the varied ways in which each of such infrastructure projects implicitly organizes a particular of form global regulation around it.[79]

This kind of work seems promising in that it emphasizes that technology is not universal but is deeply connected to a particular site—with important distributive implications. As technology travels (i.e., as it emerges and is dispersed, copied, transformed, imposed, or rejected across different geographical sites), it influences and is influenced by legal vocabularies that account for multiple sites of "innovation"—a standard process of co-production that occurs through international law, among others transnational regulatory regimes. International law provides an overarching global narrative of transnational process technological innovation in multiple sites (e.g., by creating legal structures such as the UNCTAD's Technology Transfer Code, or the TRIPS regime), at the same time creating a vocabulary for domestic or regional initiatives of technological innovation (like structuralism, or PLACTS).

That international law should play such multiple and contradictory roles regarding technology does not come as a surprise. This is particularly true in Latin America, a region subject to intense international regulation that, at the same time, is traditionally perceived as technologically vacant. However, these two dimensions of the Latin American experience might be, in fact, two sides of the same coin: it is because of its particular form of integration into global capitalism, executed through intense international regulation, that Latin America appears technologically uninteresting. But alternative arrangements *are* possible, and the deep tradition of Latin American thought discussed in this chapter can be a place to start.

[78] Daniel R. Quiroga-Villamarín, "Normalising Global Commerce: Containerisation, Materiality, and Transnational Regulation (1956–68)," *London Review of International Law* 8 (2020): 457, 459.

[79] Alejandro Rodiles, "Infrastructural Developmentalism and Its Many Types of Global Law: A Comparative Look at the UN Sustainable Development Goals and China's Belt and Road Initiative," *London Review of International Law* (2022): lrac017.

10

Critical Approaches to International Law in Latin America

George Rodrigo Bandeira Galindo[*]

I. Introduction

The critical international legal thinking as a kind of scholarship related to intellectual movements associated with the "newstream"[1] or "new approaches to international law" (NAIL)[2] took some decades to flourish in Latin America.

* University of Brasilia, Brazil.

[1] The label "newstream" is often associated with scholars influenced by the thinking of David Kennedy—including Martti Koskenniemi, who acknowledges Kennedy's academic support and describes his work "as the most significant contribution to international legal scholarship by a contemporary lawyer." Martti Koskenniemi, *From Apology to Utopia: The Structure of International Legal Argument* (Cambridge: Cambridge University Press, 2005), xv (reissue with a new epilogue). Since the early 1980s, Kennedy has been engaged in a project to think about the foundations of international law in new terms, especially by scrutinizing its historical origins and showing how it is engulfed in a structure of constant repetition that bars or makes it difficult to make significant changes. David Kennedy, "A New Stream of International Legal Scholarship," *Wisconsin International Law Journal* 7 (1989): 2. A much more detailed account of the newstream project can be found in Deborah Cass's insightful article describing it as a set of conceptual, methodological, and strategic challenges against mainstream thinking in international law. See Deborah Cass, "Navigating the Newstream: Recent Critical Scholarship in International Law," *Nordic Journal of International Law* 65 (1996): 341–383.

[2] Although significantly influenced by Kennedy's writings, NAIL literature is more eclectic, encompassing scholars relying on several different approaches, such as postcolonialism, feminism, gender studies, law and society, and race theory. Due precisely to that, characterizations—including those proposed by Kennedy—tend to broaden the specter of NAIL literature. Thus, for Kennedy and Tennant, writing in 1994, NAIL can be characterized as "scholarly work that aims to rethink the foundations of international law and to respond to recent trends in political, social, and legal theory." David Kennedy and Chris Tennant, "New Approaches to International Law: A Bibliography," *Harvard International Law Journal* 35 (1994): 418 (this article compiles the views of different scholars at that time engaged with NAIL on their experience on a conference that gathered them together; the pictures are interestingly different on what they repute as the meaning of NAIL). Several years later, Kennedy again relied on a broad idea to characterize NAIL: "those who seek 'new approaches' to international law today do share a common impulse. An impulse to step back from contemporary common sense about the nature of global order and the available paths for reform, as well as a recognition that despite decades of careful study, we still lack a good picture of how we are governed at the global level." David Kennedy, "Preface," in *New Approaches to International Law: The European and the American Experiences*, ed. José María Beneyto and David Kennedy), vii (The Hague, The Netherlands: T.M.C. Asser Press, 2012). It is fair to say, however, that this new characterization relies more on the epistemological dimension of the critique, in the sense that those scholars rely on the idea of how knowledge is understood and applied in international law. Other general accounts inevitably fall into that broad definition of NAIL, such as the excellent bibliography compiled by Thomas Skouteris, "New Approaches to International Law," in *Oxford Bibliographies.*

George Rodrigo Bandeira Galindo, *Critical Approaches to International Law in Latin America*
In: *Latin American International Law in the Twenty-First Century.* Edited by: Alejandro Chehtman, Alexandra Huneeus, and Sergio Puig, Oxford University Press.
DOI: 10.1093/9780197754016.003.0010

Although it is possible to identify excellent scholarship of Latin American international lawyers adopting a critical vein since the end of the 1990s and the beginning of the 2000s,[3] its impact on a broader scale in the mainstream thinking in the region can more easily be found only in the second part of the 2000s decade and in the 2010s.[4]

Without a doubt, critical international legal thinking also took some years to be taken seriously in European and North American intellectual circles.[5] However, for some reason, that phenomenon was even slower in Latin America. It is possible to identify at least two reasons for the difference in speed.

First, and specifically for international law, recent studies—some of them grounded on good empirical research and relying on TWAIL (Third World approaches to international law) literature[6]—have shown that legal education in

International Law, ed. Anthony Carty (2012), https://www.oxfordbibliographies.com/view/document/obo-9780199796953/obo-9780199796953-0012.xml.

[3] For example, in an article of the late 1990s, Mickelson reclaimed a Latin American tradition as part of a Third World tradition in international law. See Karin Mickelson, "Rhetoric and Rage: Third World Voices in International Legal Discourse," *Wisconsin International Law Journal* 16 (1998): 353–419. Also worth mentioning are the works of Liliana Obregón, who, since the beginning of the 2000s, was engaged, in a creative way, in the history of international law in Latin America, or Jorge Esquirol's critical reflections on the internationalization of arguments in Colombia's peace process. See, e.g., Liliana Obregón, "Forgotten 19th Century: New History of Latin American International Law," *The Hague Yearbook of International Law* 13 (2000): 27–32; Jorge L. Esquirol, "Negotiating Colombia's Peace Process: Disagreements of International Law," *Leiden Journal of International Law* 13 (2000): 495–569. Starting in the 1990s, scholars involved in the LatCrit movement became increasingly interested in international legal issues. See, e.g., Elizabeth Mathilde Iglesias, "International Law, Human Rights, and LatCrit Theory," *University of Miami Inter-American Law Review* 28 (1997): 39; Elizabeth Mathilde Iglesias, "Mapping Intersections of Critical Race Theory, Postcolonial Studies and International Law," *Proceedings of the American Society of International Law* 93 (1999): 225; Berta Esperanza Hernandéz-Truyol, "Crossing Border lands of Inequality with International Legal Methodologies—The Promise of Multiple Feminisms," *German Yearbook of International Law* 44 (2001): 113; Carmen G. Gonzalez, "Beyond Eco-Imperialism: An Environmental Justice Critique of Free Trade," *Denver University Law Review* 78 (2001): 979–1016; Carmen G. Gonzalez, "Institutionalizing Inequality: The WTO Agreement on Agriculture, Food Security, and Developing Countries," *Columbia Journal of Environmental Law* 27 (2002): 433.

[4] This can be extracted from the opposition between an almost absence of Latin American international lawyers in early bibliographies, such as that of Kennedy and Tennant, "New Approaches to International Law," and the growing presence of those scholars in more recent ones, such as those made by James Gathii, focused on TWAIL. See James Thuo Gathii. "TWAIL: A Brief History of Its Origins, Its Decentralized Network, and a Tentative Bibliography," *Trade Law and Development* 3 (2011): 26–64; James Thuo Gathii, "The Promise of International Law: A Third World View," *American University International Law Review* 36 (2021): 377–477. The problem with those bibliographies, it must be said, is that they are generally English-centered, not properly encompassing works in Spanish or Portuguese.

[5] The history of the penetration of critical international legal thinking into international law's mainstream is retold in Fleur Johns, "Critical International Legal Theory," in *International Legal Theory: Foundations and Frontiers*, ed. Jeffrey Dunoff and Mark A. Pollack (Cambridge: Cambridge University Press, 2022), 144–150. Such an influence is also recognized by scholars who lean more toward the mainstream. See Andrea Bianchi, *International Law Theories: An Inquiry into Different Ways of Thinking* (Oxford: Oxford University Press, 2016), 150–156.

[6] See, for example, Laura Betancur Restrepo and Enrique Prieto-Ríos, "Educación del derecho internacional en Bogotá: un primer diagnóstico a partir del análisis de los programas de clase y su

the region is embedded in normativism and an orthodox doctrinal reading of the discipline. In this way, the general attitude of the teacher (and the student) of international law is often of the reproducer of a specific kind of cultural hegemony.[7] There is a certain level of Eurocentrism in education, which is not open enough to the region's reality. International legal education in Latin America has not always been reticent to adopting a critical vein, contesting the status quo of law, and reflecting upon the political, cultural, and economic context in which the region is inserted.[8] However, the fact remains that international legal education—because of its firm reliance on providing students mainly "the knowledge of the rules of the game" and hardly "space for critique or the possibilities of transformation"[9]—has played an active and vital role in slowing the widespread critical conceptions of international law in the region.

Second, in most of its varieties, critical literature in international law is based on the idea that to rethink the foundations of international law, the scholar must look beyond the confines of law as a discipline.[10] The reliance on interdisciplinarity is therefore necessary in critical international legal thinking. Some prominent scholars, such as Koskenniemi and Orford, became skeptical of dialogues of certain kinds of international lawyers with international relations theorists[11] and

relación con las epistemologías de no conocimiento," *Revista Derecho del Estado* 39 (2017): 53–89 (on Colombia). See Adriane Sanctis Brito and Salem Hikmat Nasser, "Ensinar direito internacional no Brasil: panorama de uma prática e seus desafios," *Revista Derecho del Estado* 39 (2017): 119–135; and Douglas de Castro, "Ensino e Pesquisa do Direito Internacional no Brasil: Reflexões de uma reprodução europeia," *Revista Direito, Economia e Globalização* 2 (2022): 1–26 (on Brazil). Worth mentioning, although more theoretical in its scope, is Luis Eslava, "The Teaching of (Another) International Law: Critical Realism and the Question of Agency and Structure," *The Law Teacher* 54 (2020): 368–384.

[7] See Paolo Andrea Acosta Alvarado, "REDIAL e Imperialismo y derecho internacional. Oportunidad para la reflexión," *Revista Derecho del Estado* 39 (2017): 8 (this is the introductory article of a special issue of the *Revista Derecho del Estado* devoted to the topic "Legal Education and International Law"). It is important to note, however, that legal culture in Latin America is not exclusive to the passive position. Latin Americans often reappropriated foreign doctrines with adaptations to local contexts. See Diego Eduardo López Medina, *Teoría impura del derecho: la transformación de la cultura jurídica latinoamericana* (Bogota, Colombia: Legis, 2004). See also Jorge L. Esquirol, *Las ficciones del derecho latinoamericano* (Bogota, Colombia: Siglo de Hombre, 2014) (on how fictions about the law in Latin America are complexly involved in the dynamics of reception and creation).

[8] As aptly demonstrated by Carvalho's study, focusing on the debates of the Conferences of Latin American Law Schools throughout the 1950s, 1960s, and 1970s. Fabia Fernandes Carvalho Veçoso, "História e crítica em direito internacional na América Latina: revisitando discussões pretéritas sobre ensino jurídico na região," *Revista Derecho del Estado* 39 (2017): 91–117.

[9] Paola Andrea Acosta Alvarado et al., "Rethinking International Legal Education in Latin America: Reflections toward a Global Dialogue," December 7, 2022, https://twailr.com/rethinking-international-legal-education-in-latin-america-reflections-toward-a-global-dialogue/ (also available in Spanish and Portuguese).

[10] See Cass, "Navigating the Newstream," 362–365.

[11] Martti Koskenniemi, "Law, Teleology and International Relations: An Essay in Counterdisciplinarity," *International Relations* 26 (2012): 3–34.

historians.[12] Among many Latin American international lawyers, some suspicion about interdisciplinarity resides in the fact that several kinds of legal positivism were carefully heard and applied in legal circles of the region. In this context, the so-called Austinian challenge—on the existence of international law *qua* law—was taken as one that should be vigorously tackled. That is why a significant part of Latin American international legal scholarship has focused on how the international legal obligation emerges, as exemplified by works concentrating on sources of international law.[13] Only recently, different circles of international lawyers have felt a more intense need for interdisciplinarity after some decades.

This chapter will focus on only two strands of critical international legal scholarship in Latin America: TWAIL and legal pluralism. These two strands have caught the attention of international lawyers in the region in powerful ways.

Before continuing, clarification is needed. In the last few years, it has become increasingly challenging to provide a unified idea about the objectives of TWAIL. Since the first works that provided coherence to this intellectual movement (such as those of Mutua,[14] Chimni, and Anghie[15]) at the beginning of the 2000s, much has been written under the label of TWAIL. One of the targets of this chapter is to scan how Latin American authors have understood the central tenets of TWAIL and how they have applied them to explain international law in the region. It is possible, however, to depart from a recent account of Gathii, an influential TWAILer, for whom TWAIL aims to formulate a critique both to the politics as well as to the scholarship in international law on the assumption that international law has contributed to the marginalization and domination of Third World peoples. TWAIL is also searching for ways for Third World peoples and countries to overcome such a situation of marginalization and domination.[16]

[12] Anne Orford, *International and the Politics of History* (Cambridge: Cambridge University Press, 2021).

[13] See René Urueña, "Introducción: El poder y los límites del derecho internacional en la sociedad global," in *Derecho Internacional: Poder y límites del derecho en la sociedad global*, ed. René Urueña (Bogota, Colombia: Ediciones Uniandes, 2015), x. I realized some emphasis, like that on sources, on what respects international legal literature written in Portuguese, what includes Brazil. See George R. B. Galindo, "International Law in Portuguese," *Oxford Bibliographies. International Law*, ed. Anthony Carty (Oxford: Oxford University Press, 2021), December 7, 2022, https://www.oxfordbibliographies.com/view/document/obo-9780199796953/obo-9780199796953-0224.xml.

[14] Makau Mutua, "What Is TWAIL?," *American Society of International Law Proceedings* 94 (2000): 31–38.

[15] B. S. Chimni, "Third World Approaches to International Law: A Manifesto," in *The Third World and International Order: Law, Politics and Globalization*, ed. Antony Anghie (Leiden, The Netherlands: Martinus Nijhoff, 2003), 47–73; Antony Anghie and B. S. Chimni, "Third World Approaches to International Law and Individual Responsibility in Internal Conflicts," *Chinese Journal of International Law* 2 (2003): 77–103. One of the most recent outstanding contributions to TWAIL literature is certainly Antony Anghie, "Rethinking International Law: A TWAIL Retrospective," *European Journal of International Law* 34 (2023): 7-112.

[16] James Thuo Gathii, "The Agenda of Third World Approaches to International Law (TWAIL)," in Dunoff and Pollack, *International Legal Theory*, 153–154.

It is possible to observe a focus on how international law is embedded in a political context and in which a hierarchy of peoples and states is relevant. International legal scholarship is also part of that context; it reproduces hierarchical relations. It is also noteworthy to realize a particular concern in developing an agenda to advance substantial changes in international law. The idea that power and knowledge are essentially entangled[17] in international legal scholarship, practices, and institutions opens the possibility of overcoming a strict division between theory and practice, where the critique can pave the way for deep transformations.

On the other hand, many current scholars associated with legal pluralism do not consider it a variant of critical legal thinking.[18] Legal theorists—such as Günter Frankenberg and Gunther Teubner—are a relevant source of inspiration for what legal pluralists scholars are doing nowadays.[19] Although legal pluralists use different tools of analysis, they share some common denominators (formal and informal, public and private, national, transnational, or international) that should be recognized and require theorizing their normativity to understand the global order better.[20]

Latin America is an excellent field of research for the interaction between different normativities. One topic for an in-depth investigation is the interactions between Indigenous and state legal orders. However, another chapter of this book is already dedicated to Indigenous peoples. Apart from the fact that Indigenous peoples have been the focus of good TWAIL research among Latin American legal scholars—mentioned below (see section II)—it seems more appealing to highlight emergent literature on the existence of a specific Latin American international law. What instigates those scholars—focused on an intellectual

[17] An inescapable reference to the relationship between knowledge and power is, of course, Michel Foucault. See, e.g., Michel Foucault, *Power/Knowledge: Selected Interviews and Other Writings, 1972-1977* (New York: Vintag Books, 1980). A good picture of how Foucault influenced David Kennedy's writings is provided by Samuel Moyn, "Knowledge and Politics in International Law," *Harvard Law Review* 129 (2016): 2164–2189. Chimni shows how David Kennedy played a pivotal role in the formation of TWAIL (and has also been influenced by it). See B. S. Chimni, *International Law and World Order: A Critique of Contemporary Approaches* (Cambridge: Cambridge University Press, 2017), 246–357.

[18] Altwicker and Diggelmann state that approaches such as "'global legal pluralism' appears in some sense as a sort of reaction to CIL [Critical International Law] insights into the relativity of knowledge about law." However, the authors see relevant contact points between this approach and critical international law. See Tilmann Altwicker and Oliver Diggelmann, "What Should Remain of the Critical Approaches to International Law? International Legal Theory as Critique," *Schweizerische Zeitschrift für internationales und europäisches Recht* 24 (2014): 90–93.

[19] See Kennedy and Tennant, "New Approaches to International Law," 442–443, 457.

[20] Nico Krisch, "Global Legal Pluralism," in Dunoff and Pollack, *International Legal Theory*, 240–243. See also Peer Zumbansen, "Transnational Legal Pluralism," *Transnational Legal Theory* 1 (2010): 141–189 (relying on TWAIL literature). In Latin America, Nicolás Perrone has used legal pluralistic tools to understand international investment law. See Nicolás Perrone, "International Investment Law as Transnational Law," in *Oxford Handbook of Transnational Law*, ed. Peer Zumbansen (Oxford: Oxford University Press, 2020), 291–314.

historical perspective—is understanding how such specificities operate and interact with the global dimension of international law. In this way, identifying regional international law in Latin America would be essential to understanding how pluralism operates in international law. Thus, I take the idea of legal pluralism in a broader sense to embrace the scholarship involved in trying to understand the notion of specificity in Latin American international law, which is a relevant part of understanding the existence of a specific normativity in international law in the region.

This chapter is divided into two parts. First, I address projects in the region associated with TWAIL. In the second part, the issue of legal pluralism is presented through the treatment of the subject of a regional Latin American international law. Some concluding remarks end the chapter.

It is important to note that this chapter does not try to be exhaustive. I aim only to provide some samples to show how many international lawyers in the region have been attempting to think of international law "out of the box."[21]

II. TWAIL in Latin America

As mentioned earlier, starting in the second half of the 2000s, especially in the 2010s, many Latin American scholars became involved with TWAIL. Initially, this literature was almost exclusively in English. After some years, pieces in Spanish, Portuguese, and, to a smaller extent, French mushroomed in the region.

This literature concerns both general questions—related, for example, to conceptual and historical issues—and those of a more specific dimension, such as human rights, international economic law, jurisdiction and sovereignty, international environmental law, and sources of law. Also, as highlighted earlier, the topic of international law teaching was the focus of international lawyers in the region.

It is beyond doubt that colonial experiences in the region were very distinct from those in Africa, Asia, and Oceania due to the independence of most Latin American countries in the nineteenth century. However, many today feel that if Latin America paved the way to future formal decolonization, it also anticipated many of the problems that the Third World as a whole would face.[22] This is one of the main reasons why many Latin American international legal scholars today show openness to TWAIL.

[21] David Kennedy, "When Renewal Repeats: Thinking Against the Box," *NYU Journal of International Law and Politics* 32 (2000): 334–500.

[22] Luis Eslava, "The Developmental State: Independence, Dependency and the History of the South," *Revista Derecho del Estado* 43 (2019): 59.

My perspective on some of those studies is that they should be taken seriously not only by the mainstream in international law, including in Latin America, but also by different circles of TWAIL or TWAIL-related international legal scholarship—especially those that have no access to literature written in Spanish or Portuguese.

General Questions

Conceptual Questions

Latin American scholars have tried to face difficult conceptual international legal questions under the premise that international law has contributed to the marginalization and domination of Third World peoples. Many of them exerted much effort to recalibrate TWAIL to focus on neglected theoretical or methodological aspects or to understand TWAIL as an intellectual movement. Also, some aim to disseminate TWAIL literature in the region following innovative and interdisciplinary perspectives.

Concerning the last kind of writing, it is noteworthy that, since the beginning of the 2010s, TWAL literature has been noticed, although in a cursory way.[23]

In 2013, I attempted to introduce, in Portuguese, the central tenets of TWAIL. I was astonishd that Brazilian international legal academia, despite Brazil's position as a highly unequal country, did not pay close attention to projects such as TWAIL. I presented some issues emphasized by TWAIL literature, such as history, the role of the state, culture, language of rights, and resistance.[24]

Later, pertinent book reviews[25] and good translations of prominent TWAIL scholars in Spanish and Portuguese[26]—some with insightful

[23] Juan Francisco Lobo Fernández, "Adiós a Westfalia: Hacia la 'constitución' de un derecho cosmopolita," *Estudios Internacionales* 167 (2010): 62.

[24] George R. B. Galindo, "A Volta do Terceiro Mundo ao Direito Internacional," *Boletim da Sociedade Brasileira de Direito Internacional* 119–124 (2013): 46–68.

[25] Adriane Sanctis, "América Latina em continuidades e rupturas," *Revista de Direito Internacional* 14 (2017): 258–259; Fabrício José Rodrigues de Lemos and Laura Madrid Sartoretto, "Resenha do livro Imperialism, Sovereignty and the Making of International Law, de Antony Anghie," *Revista de Direito Internacional* 15 (2018): 306–308; Gabriel Antonio Silveira Mantelli, "Quem tem medo do pós-colonial no direito internacional? Uma resenha de 'Decolonising international law: development, economic growth and the politics of universality' de Sundhia Pahuja," *Revista de Direito Internacional* 15 (2018): 484–488; Karine de Souza Silva, "O direito das nações de Charles Alexandrowicz e a crítica ao eurocentrismo no direito internacional," *Esboços* 28 (2021): 591–599.

[26] Antony Anghie, "La evolución del derecho internacional: realidades coloniales y poscoloniales," in *Imperialismo y Derecho Internacional*, ed. Antony Anghie, Martti Koskenniemi, and Anne Orford, 95–126 (Bogota, Colombia: Siglo de Hombre, 2016) (translation of Antony Anghie, "The Evolution of International Law: Colonial and Postcolonial Realities," *Third World Quarterly* 27 (2006): 739–753). This book contains an excellent introductory study that includes a topic on Anghie's scholarship: Luis Eslava, Liliana Obregón, and René Urueña, "Imperalismo(s) y Derecho(s) Internacional(es): Ayer y Hoy," in Anghie et al., *Imperialismo y Derecho Internacional*, 11–94. See

comments—appeared and helped make TWAIL literature more visible and well-known in the region.[27]

Such comprehensive visibility has led to good research on complex and intricate conceptual questions that are controversial for TWAILers in the region and throughout the world. In this vein, Ramina diligently collected several positions on conceptualizing TWAIL and found many commonalities.[28] Mantelli and Sanchez Badin made essential efforts to highlight perspectives with common aims but usually seen as separate, such as decolonialism and TWAIL.[29] Dal Ri Jr., Biazi, and Zimmermann found connections between TWAIL and critical theory tradition in Latin America,[30] and Afonso excavated the differences between TWAIL generations.[31]

Also noteworthy were the efforts of Fernanda Cristina de Oliveira Franco and others to make TWAIL speak to the needs of Indigenous peoples in Latin

also B. S. Chimni, "Abordagens terceiro-mundistas para o Direito Internacional: Um Manifesto," *Revista de Direito Internacional* 15 (2018): 41–60 (translation of Chimni, "Third World Approaches to International Law"). The same translation was reedited in *Direito Internacional: Leituras Críticas*, ed. Michelle Ratton Sanchez Badin, Fábio Costa Morosini, and Arthur Roberto Capella Giannattasio (Brasilia: Almedina Brasil, 2019), 33–70, with comments by Bruno Pegorari, Fernanda Cristina de Oliveira Franco, and Lucas da Silva Tasquetto, "Comentário ao Capítulo 1: Abordagens Terceiro-Mundistas ao Direito Internacional (TWAIL); um Manifesto," in Ratton Sanchez Badin et al., *Direito Internacional: Leituras Críticas*, 71–84. See also Sundhya Pahuja, "A Pós-Colonialidade do Direito Internacional—Abordagens Pós-Coloniais e Descoloniais no Direito Internacional," in Ratton Sanchez Badin et al., *Direito Internacional*, 85–100, with comments by Fernanda Frizzo Bragato and Gabriel Antonio Silveira Mantelli, "Comentário ao Capítulo 2: 'A Pós-Colonialidade do Direito—Abordagens Pós-Coloniais e Descoloniais no Direito Internacional," in Ratton Sanchez Badin et al., *Direito Internacional*, 101–112. More recently, see Tatiana Cardoso Squeff and Gabriel Pedro Moreira Damasceno, *Direito Internacional Crítico* (São Paulo: Arreas Editores, 2022) (containing translations and original TWAIL-related pieces).

[27] Studies that aim to present a specific topic through the lenses of different international legal theories are paying growing attention to TWAIL. See, e.g., María Helena Carbonell Yánez, "Teorías relativas al cumplimiento del derecho internacional público," *Anuario Mexicano de Derecho Internacional* 21 (2021): 487–491; Zlata Drnas de Clément, *Los Paradigmas Ideológicos y la Concepción del Derecho Internacional* (Buenos Aires: UNAM, 2020), 120–125. Insightful analyses also treat TWAIL as a particular methodology to address a given issue. See, e.g., José Manuel Luque González, "Hacia una reconsideración del prohibicionismo de las drogas en el derecho internacional desde el Tercer Mundo" (PhD diss., Universitat de Barcelona, 2017) (on the prohibition of drugs), and Patrícia Barros, *Saúde Global e Organização Mundial da Sáude: Uma perspectiva crítica a partir do direito internacional* (Brasilia: Lumen Juris, 2020) (on global health, especially in the context of pandemics).

[28] Larissa Ramina, "Framing the Concept of TWAIL: 'Third World Approaches to International Law'," *Justiça do Direito* 32 (2018): 5–26.

[29] Gabriel Antonio Silveira Mantelli and Michelle Ratton Sanchez Badin, "Repensando o Direito Internacional a partir dos estudos pós-coloniais e decoloniais," *Prima F@cie* 17 (2018): 1–33.

[30] Arno Dal Ri Jr., Chiara Antonia Sofia Mafrica Biazi, and Taciano Scheidt Zimmermann, "O Direito Internacional e as Abordagens do 'Terceiro Mundo': Contribuições da Teoria Crítica do Direito," *Revista da Faculdade de Direito da UFPR* 62 (2017): 61–81.

[31] Henrique Weil Afonso, "A questão desenvolvimentista na segunda metade do século XX: um olhar desde as TWAIL (Third World Approaches to International Law)," *Quaestio Iuris* 12 (2019): 101–124.

America—a criticism that had been raised before against TWAIL.[32] From the perception that Third World states and Indigenous peoples have been victimized by the colonial process, Franco helped clarify that TWAIL needs to get closer to Indigenous peoples and Latin American social reality.[33]

From the perspective of the relationship between constitutional and international law, Alvez Marin realized the potentialities of TWAIL for addressing Indigenous water rights in Chile. Since TWAIL aims to envisage international law beyond the dimension of the nation-state, such would be an essential lesson to constitutional law—inverting the traditional influence of constitutional law in international law—especially considering Indigenous peoples' worldviews on property issues.[34]

Attentive to the fact that TWAIL must avoid falling into a logic that reproduces exclusions, Frisso has proposed a connection between TWAIL, decolonial theory, and feminism to find ways to tackle international law's "overall unidimensional construct of woman." TWAIL literature would be in a good position since adopting the term "Third World" rejects an essentialized perspective of women, considering their differences within and among states.[35]

From the point of view of TWAIL methodology, besides finding points of contact with theoretical movements, such as decolonial theory, some have tried to envisage similitudes between TWAIL and the Annals School (*École des Annales*) because of the centrality both pose in history to the explanation of different social phenomena.[36] In the United States, Hernández-López has made many efforts to build solid bridges between TWAIL and LatCrit theory: both interrogate law and history to understand how injustice is produced; both realize in law a potential to conceal injustice but also to achieve justice.[37]

[32] See Amar Bhatia, "The South of the North: Building on Critical Approaches to International Law with Lessons from the Fourth World," *Oregon Review of International Law* 14 (2012): 131–175 (focused not on Latin America, but on Indigenous peoples in Canada).

[33] Fernanda Cristina de Oliveira Franco, "Oportunidades e desafios das TWAIL no contexto latino-americano a partir de perspectivas dos povos indígenas ao direito internacional," *Revista de Direito Internacional* 12 (2015): 226–244.

[34] Amaya Álvez Marín, "Constitutional Challenges of the South: Indigenous Water Rights in Chile: Another Step in the 'Civilizing Mission,'" *Windsor Yearbook of Access to Justice* 33 (2016): 87–110. See also Amaya Amaya Álvez Marín and Arnulf Becker Lorca, "Los pueblos originarios y la práctica del derecho internacional en Chile: nuevos horizontes ante el debilitamiento de los legados del autoritarismo," *Revista Derecho del Estado* 39 (2017): 21–52.

[35] Giovanna Maria Frisso, "Third World Approaches to International Law: Feminists' Engagement with International Law and Decolonial Theory," in *Research Handbook on Feminist Engagement with International Law*, ed. Susan Harris Rimmer and Kate Ogg (Cheltenham, UK: Edward Elgar, 2019), 479–498.

[36] Roberto Luiz Silva and Thiago Ferreira Almeida. "L'influence de l'ecole des annales sur l'approche du tiers-monde du droit international (TWAIL)," *Latin American Journal of Development* 4 (2022): 108–128.

[37] Ernesto Hernandez-Lopez, "Global Justice, History, and Law: Between FELA's Teachers Teaching 'Nonsense' and Bob Marley's 'Small Axe' for a Big Tree," *California Western International Law Journal* 42 (2012): 265--284.

Regarding the problematic issue of the periodization of TWAIL into generations, I argue that TWAIL should not be divided into two generations—the first chronologically situated during the decolonization years and the second starting from the 1990s onward. Instead, TWAIL should be seen as a continuum in a tradition of international legal scholarship.[38]

Freitas's analysis of the relationship between colonialism and the state's very existence is a significant attempt to refresh the dimension of memory in the TWAIL project. For him, through memories of suffering, it is possible to denaturalize law and poverty to reveal their inner constitutive relation.[39]

In 2011, Eslava (with Pahuja) identified TWAIL not precisely as a method but as a "political grouping of strategic engagement with international law, defined by a commonality of concerns."[40] Such an idea gives the proper dimension of how TWAIL needs to foster a strong engagement between law and politics. This can be shocking due to the influence of positivism in the region. Departing from three conceptions about the role of lawyers in society (conservation, reform, and revolution), Eslava and Pahuja associate TWAILers with the fourth position, which is molded by an impetus to resist the harmful effects of international law and a continuous will to reform it.[41] Resistance and reform, in this sense, would mean the belief that international law can be a locus to operate changes in the world.

The authors also urge TWAILers to supplant the divide between the international and national as well as the public and the private dimensions to reach the "materiality" of international law and focus on spaces different from those reputed as traditional in the discipline. In this way, they should engage in topics that could reveal, for example, what happens in international criminal courtrooms, how international NGOs influence the creation and the application of international law in international and domestic dimensions, and how international institutions impose reforms in domestic law.[42]

Using a legal ethnographic method, Eslava discussed, in a later book, how the government decentralization process in a city like Bogotá, by empowering local jurisdictions, reflects the priorities and aims of international financial institutions and erodes the divide between international and national

[38] George R. B. Galindo, "Splitting TWAIL?" *Windsor Yearbook of Access to Justice* 33 (2016): 37–56.

[39] Lucas Daniel Chaves de Freitas, "Direito Internacional, descolonização, desenvolvimento: uma releitura da ideia de Estado a partir das TWAILs (Abordagens Terceiro-Mundistas do Direito Internacional)," *Revista Videre* 14 (2022): 68–94.

[40] Luis Eslava and Sundhya Pahuja, "Between Resistance and Reform: TWAIL and the Universality of International Law," *Trade, Law and Development* 3 (2011): 103–130.

[41] Ibid., 110–122.

[42] Ibid., 122–128. Regarding history, see Luis Eslava, "The Materiality of International Law: Violence, History and Joe Sacco's The Great War," *London Review of International Law* 5 (2017): 49–86.

dimensions.[43] How illegal neighborhoods in Bogotá were integrated into the official order employing international norms and standards is an excellent example of how a "global administration"—although often invisible—operates in ways reminiscent of older forms of domination, such as colonization.[44]

Some Latin American scholars have also proposed specialized fields of research within TWAIL with the support of other approaches. Following—just as Eslava does—an ethnographical approach, Mantelli advances the idea that the discourse on development is structural to present international law, and resistance is essential to understanding it.[45]

History

Like in TWAIL's literature, history has been central to the reflections of Latin American international lawyers engaged in TWAIL.

Since at least 2014, Afonso has been involved in original research regarding the relationship between historiographical methods, notably the Cambridge School's contextualism and its relationship to the making of postcolonial histories. Almost simultaneously with Orford's vigorous defense of anachronism in international legal history,[46] Afonso pointed out the limits of separating past and present. For him, searching for the other should be one of the main merits of postcolonial histories in international law.[47]

In later writings, Afonso developed his ideas on anachronism further and stressed the role of memory in historiographical research and the problems of narratives teleologically oriented toward progress, with a firm reliance on TWAIL literature.[48]

One of the most important publications in TWAIL's engagement with history—*Bandung, Global History, and International Law*—presents an excellent account of the Latin American region and how the states were brought to the table and integrated into the history of the Third World. Obregón's study in that volume shows that although Latin American countries were not formally invited to the Bandung Conference (except as observers), anti-imperialist movements in

[43] Luis Eslava, *Local Spaces, Global Life: The Everyday Operation of International Law and Development* (Cambridge: Cambridge University Press, 2015).

[44] Ibid., 190–208.

[45] Gabriel Antonio Silveira Mantelli, "Maps and Encounters: Postcolonial Approaches to international Law and Development" (master's thesis, FGV, Escola de Direito de São Paulo, 2019).

[46] See, e.g., Anne Orford, "On International Legal Method," *London Review of International Law* 1 (2013): 166–197. More recently, she systematized and expanded her positions in Orford, *International and the Politics of History*.

[47] Henrique Weil Afonso, *A Reconstrução Histórica da Diversidade no Direito Internacional* (Rio de Janeiro: Lumen Juris, 2015). This book is originally a doctoral dissertation dated 2014.

[48] Henrique Weil Afonso, "Passado, presente e contexto à luz da historiografia do Direito Internacional," *Direito & Práxis* 7 (2016): 169–199; Henrique Weil Afonso, "A era da humanidade: reflexões para a história do direito internacional," *Revista de Direito Internacional* 13 (2016): 235–262.

the region managed to find alliances with Bandung participants in the following years.[49] Sandoval's contribution is in the form of a dialogue with the legal theorist Oscar Correas. That piece addressed essential aspects of a TWAIL perspective in contact with decolonial theory, such as human rights and Indigenous Peoples.[50] Carvalho acutely emphasizes the ambivalence of Brazilian universalism—close and far from the Third World—in her contribution to the volume, explaining how that ambivalence affects international legal scholarship in the country even today.[51]

General accounts of the so-called historiographical turn or "turn to history" in international law have paid much attention to TWAIL literature. For Barreto, one of the merits of TWAIL histories is its emphasis on the state's role in colonialism and private companies.[52] Olivares Jatib and Pérez Godoy stress TWAIL's historic contribution to unveiling the Eurocentric character of international law—which plays a strategic and functional role in fostering the geopolitical and economic interests of powerful states.[53] Ramina and Nunes, by praising the active role of TWAIL in that "turn," urge more scholarly contributions from Latin American international lawyers, including integrating inputs from decolonial theory.[54] By analyzing that "turn" regarding international criminal law, Quintana highlights TWAIL's contribution in challenging the logic of continuity and evolution displaced in the "textbook narratives."[55]

Also noteworthy is some scholars' interest in excavating past international lawyers' legacies. Morosini and Leichtweis's study on Celso de Albuquerque Mello—an author whose scholarship, written entirely in Portuguese, was very attached, especially in the 1960s and the 1970s, to the agendas of the Third World—is an excellent example of this kind of study.[56] Another meaningful

[49] Liliana Obregón, "Latin America during the Bandung Era: Anti-Imperialist Movements vs. Anti-Communist States," in *Bandung, Global History, and International Law: Critical Pasts and Pending Futures*, ed. Luis Eslava, Michael Fakhri, and Vasuki Nesiah (Cambridge: Cambridge University Press, 2017), 232–246.

[50] Germán Medardo Sandoval Trigo, "The Bandung Conference and Latin America A Decolonial Dialogue with Oscar Correas," in Luis Eslava et al., *Bandung, Global History, and International Law*, 263–275.

[51] Fabia Fernandes Carvalho Veçoso, "Bandung in the Shadow: The Brazilian Experience," in Luis Eslava et al., *Bandung, Global History, and International Law*, 411–428.

[52] José Manuel Barreto, "Visiones Eurocéntricas y Terceromundistas de la Historia del Derecho Internacional: La Crisis del Paradigma Estado-Céntrico," *Estudios Sociales* 59 (2020): 32–34.

[53] Oscar Olivares Jatib y Fernando Pérez Godoy, "Historia y Derecho Internacional," *Revista de Estudios Histórico-Jurídicos* 40 (2018): 153–158.

[54] Larissa Ramina and Laura Maeda Nunes, "História e Transformação no Direito Internacional na América Latina: A virada decolonial e a virada historiográfica," *Revista Brasileira de Direito Internacional* 6 (2020): 80–99.

[55] Francisco José Quintana, "América Latina y la Historiografía del Derecho Penal Internacional," *Estudios Sociales* 59 (2020): 63–87.

[56] Fabio Morosini e Matheus Liechtweis, "Um TWAILer entre nós? Desvendando as contribuições de Celso Duvivier de Albuquerque Mello para o direito internacional (crítico) no Brasil," in *Direto Internacional no Brasil: Pensamento e Tradição*, vol. 2, ed. George R. B. Galindo (Rio de Janeiro: Lumen Juris, 2021), 377–420.

analysis is Quintana's article on the role of a semi-peripheral jurist such as Jorge Castañeda in reshaping international organzations law.[57]

Specific Questions

Many TWAIL analyses of Latin American international lawyers have focused on specific topics of the discipline both from a theoretical and practical perspective.

Sovereignty and Jurisdiction

In a significant study on the US Supreme Court *Boumedine v. Bush* case, Hernández-López shows how the coupling of arguments based on international and constitutional law has facilitated the authority of Great Powers and, consequently, denied sovereignty to states and populations in the Third World. Hence, questions related to *habeas corpus* jurisdiction in places like Guantánamo can adequately be studied through notions like informal empire.[58]

More recently, Madeira da Silva demonstrated how the frontier-making process in some Latin American states during the Amazon rubber boom of the late nineteenth century and the beginning of the twentieth century is an excellent example of how private actors influence and make international law, putting a strict divide between international and national law in question.[59] This is so because the relationship between the nation-state and international law is indeed co-constitutive, as shown by Eslava and Pahuja.[60]

Environment

By referring to historical arguments grounded in inputs from TWAIL literature, Carmen Gonzalez has advanced relevant readings of international environmental law coupled with international economic law and human rights, making explicit the link between the economic differences among states and the responsibilities for environmental degradation. She shows that intragenerational reasoning is needed alongside an intergenerational rationale, considering the differences between the Global North and the South.[61] She is also cautious about

[57] Franciso-José Quintana, "Small Powers, International Organizations and the Role of Law: Jorge Castañeda's Views from Mexico," *European Journal of International Law* 34 (2023): 319-344.

[58] Ernesto Hernández-López, "Boumedine v. Bush and Guantánamo, Cuba: Does the 'Empire Strike Back'?" *SMU Law Review* 62 (2009): 117–200.

[59] Filipe Antunes Madeira da Silva, "The Conquest of the Devil's Paradise: International Law, Frontier-Making and Capitalist Power" (doctoral dissertation, Insitut d'études politiques de Paris, 2022).

[60] Luis Eslava and Sundhya Pahuja, "The Nation-State and International Law: A Reading from the Global South," *Humanity* 11 (2020): 118–138.

[61] Carmen G. Gonzalez, "Bridging the North-South Divide: International Environmental Law in the Anthropocene," *Pace Environmental Law Review* 32 (2015): 407–434.

enthusiasm for environmental human rights due to their potential for political abuse.[62]

Some studies aim to scrutinize principles such as the previous consultation in projects that may harm the environment, arguing that they are only a formality to legitimate the domination over local communities, not addressing their actual needs,[63] and reproducing the coloniality of power.[64] Others have stressed that solutions proposed for the possible disappearance of states due to climate change are a renewal of the civilizing mission since a concept of sovereignty that is necessarily coupled with statehood is paradoxical.[65]

Human Rights

Critique of human rights has long engaged international lawyers from the region. However, the spread of TWAIL perspectives on human rights is a more recent phenomenon that often comes in deep dialogue with other critical perspectives, such as decolonial theory, which was formulated and flourished under the banner of the region's specificities.

The first vital effort to disseminate TWAIL literature on the topic was the book edited by Barreto, *Human Rights from a Third World Perspective*. Some Latin American scholars contributed to the book, and Barreto's chapters show a clear attachment to TWAIL, like in the centrality he provides to the need to rewrite the history of international law through the perspective of individuals and peoples who suffered from colonization.[66]

The work of Merino on the self-determination of Indigenous peoples in Latin America, although departing from other theoretical frameworks, such as decolonial theory, makes use of the TWAIL literature to understand how the imaginaries of international law set limits on multinational state drawings but also makes it possible for peoples to fight for self-determination.[67]

[62] Carmen G. Gonzalez, "Environmental Justice, Human Rights, and the Global South," *Santa Clara Journal of International Law* 13 (2015): 151–195.

[63] Douglas de Castro, "O ressurgimento de formas antigas de exploração dos recursos naturais: A ontologia colonial do princípio da consulta prévia," *Veredas do Direito*, 16 (2019): 343–365.

[64] Jimena Sierra-Camargo, "La importancia de decolonizar el derecho internacional de los derechos humanos: el caso de la consulta previa en Colombia," *Revista Derecho del Estado* 39 (2017): 137–186

[65] Luís Paulo Bogliolo Piancastelli de Siqueira, "Mudanças climáticas e o desaparecimento de Estados: O paradoxo pós-colonial das respostas do direito internacional," in *Migrações, deslocamentos e direitos humanos*, ed. George R. B. Galindo (Brasilia: IBDC, 2015).

[66] See José-Manuel Barreto, "Introduction: Decolonial Strategies and Dialogue in the Human Rights Field," in *Human Rights from a Third World Perspective: Critique, History and International Law*, ed. José-Manuel Barreto (Cambridge: Cambridge Scholars, 2013), 1–43, and José-Manuel Barreto, "Imperialism and Decolonization as Scenarios of Human Rights History," in Barreto, *Human Rights from a Third World Perspective*, 140–171. The influence of TWAIL is clearer in his later writings: e.g. José Manuel Barreto, "Estrategia para descolonizar los derechos humanos," *Opción* 25 (2019): 815–860.

[67] Roger Merino, *Plurinacionalidad y autodeterminación indígena en América Latina* (Lima, Peru: IWGIA, 2022), 16–51.

Also, on the issue of self-determination, Sandoval questions, through a TWAIL perspective, how the principles of colonialism still influence self-determination since the idea of the nation on which it relies does not open enough space, for example, to the claims of Indigenous peoples.[68]

Bragato and Silveira Filho face the problematic (but essential) issue of the role of local élites in human rights violations perpetrated by transnational corporations.[69]

Very relevant is the study of García-Del Moral, which takes the idea of resistance in TWAIL literature to understand how activists in Mexico have used international human rights law tools to protect women from femicide.[70] This kind of research aims mainly to give a transformative dimension to TWAIL through the means available under current international law.

Resistance is the core idea Ramina envisages from different human rights perspectives that TWAIL scholars have provided. Such resistance needs to stimulate the revision of the inner structures of the rights-based discourse, which are essentially Eurocentric.[71]

Some studies use TWAIL literature to focus on how certain human rights conventions may counter the North-South unequal relations. Still, the lack of ratifications by some northern states has made them almost empty letters.[72]

Sources

Some Latin American scholars have tried to use TWAIL tools to understand how given doctrines of positive international law have been interpreted and applied detrimentally to Third World states. That is the case of Del Negro's insightful article on coercion as a cause for the invalidity of treaties. The author shows how International Law Commssion's Special Rapporteurs, such as Humphrey Waldock, made efforts to restrict the scope of what would be Article 52 of the Vienna Convention on the Law of Treaties (VCLT) to the threat or the use of force—following a logic reminiscent of the system of capitulations. He also points out how the Third World states tried to include other forms of coercion—such as economic and political pressure—during the Vienna Conference on the Law of Treaties but were unsuccessful. An outstanding achievement of the article

[68] Germán Medardo Sandoval Trigo, "La libre autodeterminación de los pueblos en el siglo XXI: Una aproximación de la historia del colonialismo y el neo-colonialismo desde los pueblos del tercer mundo en el derecho internacional," *Revista de Direito Internacional* 15 (2018): 90–104.

[69] Fernanda Bragato and Alex Sandro da Silveira Filho, "The Colonial Limits of Transnational Corporations' Accountability for Human Rights Violations," *TWAIL Review* 2 (2021): 34–58.

[70] Paulina García-Del Moral, "Feminicidio: TWAIL in Action," *AJIL Unbound* 110 (2016): 31–36.

[71] Larissa Ramina, "TWAIL—'Third World Approaches to International Law' and Human Rights: Some Considerations," *Revista Investigações Constitucionais* 5 (2018): 261–172.

[72] Mariana Magliolo, "La (des)protección de los trabajadores migrantes en la lógica Norte-Sur," *Revista Jurídica de la Universidad de Palermo* 19 (2021): 203–222.

is to provide concrete possibilities for TWAILers to widen the scope of Article 52 by interpreting the VCLT.[73]

Grounded on decolonial theory with essential insights from TWAIL literature, Squeff shows that colonialism was built not only on dimensions such as power and knowledge but also on the lack or bare effective participation of Third World states in the crafting of international legal norms—the so-called coloniality of doing. For her, reputing soft law as a source of international law per se would allow those states that were traditionally rejected from the norm-creating process to be heard.[74] In many senses, such a project actualizes the emphasis Third World scholars and states put on acts of international organizations to build a new international economic order (NIEO).[75]

Yip and I focused on how power relations influence the formation of customary international law detrimentally to Third World states. Specifically, we analyzed three elements in the debate about customary international law (acceleration of custom, the role of international organizations, and persistent objector) to exemplify its undemocratic bias.[76]

III. Legal Pluralism

A new generation of international lawyers in the region has been devoted to original research on the relationship between Latin America and universal international law. Most of them are concerned with finding specificities in the international legal discourse developed in Latin America through excellent historical legal research, as shown in section I.

The search for specificities in Latin American discourse on international law goes beyond finding specific rules or a given legal order to be applied in the region to encompass sociological, political, and cultural consequences of conceiving a "Latin American (or American) International Law." Thus, international law should be seen through pluralistic lenses since the region offers a rich and complex history of engagement with international law. In general terms, those scholars are concerned with finding legal pluralism through international legal history with a critical perspective.

[73] Guilherme Del Negro, "The Validity of Treaties Concluded under Coercion of the State: Sketching a TWAIL Critique," *European Journal of Legal Studies* 10 (2017): 39–60.

[74] Tatiana Cardoso Squeff, "Overcoming the 'Coloniality of Doing' in International Law: Soft Law as a Decolonial Tool," *Revista Direito GV* 17 (2021): 2–31.

[75] See Mohammed Bedjaoui, *Towards a New International Economic Order* (Teaneck, NJ: Holmes & Meier, 1979), 193–220.

[76] George R. B. Galindo and César Yip, "Customary International Law and the Third World: Do Not Step on the Grass," *Chinese Journal of International Law* 16 (2017): 251–270.

With her work on a Creole consciousness in Latin America, Obregón showed an inner contradiction in how international law was thought of in the region. The Creole élites were eager to be integrated into civilization, making their legal systems resemble the European ones—and expurgating other forms of legal organization, considered barbaric and inferior, such as those of Indigenous peoples and descendants of enslaved Africans. At the same time, they envisaged Latin American states as a distinct form of civilization that should complement (without contesting) the European one. Such consciousness can be identified in the works of many nineteenth-century jurists.[77]

Especially at the beginning of the twentieth century, the idea of a Latin American (and later an American, embracing the United States) international law emerged from a Creole consciousness, paying no regard to the diversity that remained in the region and the violence that lay upon any attempt to find a common origin for the region. That is why, for Obregón, the invocation of a Latin American international law emerges more from geopolitical, economic, and strategical elements related to the hemispheric and world scenario than from a shared historical identity.[78]

Obregón's significant contribution to understanding international law discourse in Latin America is making the region aware of what has been left behind through a history of more than two centuries. Such awareness is essential to a more plural and just international law.

Obregón's work is complemented by narratives demonstrating how Latin Americans appropriated European concepts to oppress Indigenous peoples. Pérez Godoy shows how Chilean intellectual élites recreated in a local dimension the so-called dynamic of difference—opposing civilized and uncivilized nations—to annex territories from the Mapuche nation and to declare war against neighbor states.[79] His research shows that the concept of civilization—instrumental to dividing peoples in international law—was also deployed among Latin American states in their mutual relations and domestic legal systems.

The original work of Becker Lorca is more concerned with the interactions between Western and non-Western states, what he calls the "center" and the "periphery." This interaction creates a mestizo international law—an international

[77] Liliana Obregón, "Completing Civilization: Creole Consciousness and International Law in nineteenth-century Latin America," in *International and Its Others*, ed. Anne Orford (Cambridge: Cambridge University Press, 2006), 247–264. Creole consciousness' contradiction "basically means that the region's elite often assume themselves as being part of the metropolitan centre (as descendants of Europeans) while at the same time challenging the centre with notions of their own regional uniqueness (as natives of America)." Liliana Obregón, "Between Civilisation and Barbarism: Creole intervention in international law," *Third World Quarterly* 27 (2006): 817.

[78] Liliana Obregón, "¿Para qué un derecho internacional latinoamericano?," in Urueña, *Derecho Internacional*, 29, 47–50.

[79] Fernando Pérez Godoy, "The Co-creation of Imperial Logic in South American Legal History," *Journal of the History of International Law* 21 (2020): 485–517.

law with hybrid origins from the encounter of the West and the non-West.[80] Latin America, as a semiperipheral region—with a certain level of autonomy—was an essential part of building current international law. Despite its complexities, codifying international law in the American continent, which gained traction, especially in the first three decades of the twentieth century, successfully established a formal definition of statehood through the Montevideo Convention on Rights and Duties of States, 1933. That represented a significant achievement in international law from a universal perspective since the convention clashed with the idea of the standard of civilization in statehood.[81]

Becker Lorca also trailed the Latin American legal tradition by assessing different and influential contemporary textbooks published in the region. However, historical considerations did not escape his attention, especially concerning the existence of American international law. For him, the debate unveils two sensibilities. The regionalist sensibility (in defense of American international law) was antiformalist, especially by blurring the limits between law and politics and showing their connection to the "psychology of American peoples." The universalist sensibility (against American international law) supported a distinction between law and politics by submitting the latter to a formal legal process. Despite those differences, both were politically oriented and did not restrict the role of the international lawyer to a professional neutral space.[82]

Avoiding the perils of depoliticization seems to be one of the main contributions of Becker Lorca's reflection on Latin America in international law. Both the project of codifying international law on the American continent and the debate on American international law express the self-awareness of international lawyers of the region of the social, cultural, and political conditions in which they are inserted.

American international law was the focus of Scarfi's book *The Hidden History of International Law in the Americas*. Scarfi is more concerned about the politics behind legal institutions and legal scholars. For him, American international law of the first decades of the twentieth century was the product of US hegemony over the region, primarily through the creation of the American Institute of International Law and the work of James Brown Scott and Alejandro Álvarez. The ideal of pan-Americanism was thus a way for the United States to implement its informal empire, reflected in the institution of continental organizations such as the Organization of American States (OAS) and human rights

[80] Arnulf Becker Lorca, *Mestizo International Law: A Global Intellectual History 1842-1933* (Cambridge: Cambridge University Press, 2014), 15, 22–24.

[81] Ibid., 305–352.

[82] Arnulf Becker Lorca, "International Law in Latin America or Latin American International Law—Rise, Fall, and Retrieval of a Tradition of Legal Thinking and Political Imagination," *Harvard International Law Journal* 47 (2006): 283–306.

bodies. In Scarfi's narrative, the law is engulfed by US hegemony and informal empire, demonstrating how apparent political interests create specificities (like American international law).[83]

Excavating a Latin American sensibility has been one of the main aims of Carvalho's scholarship. An excellent example of this is her research on how Drago formulated his famous doctrine. Carvalho does see the Drago Doctrine as one that was accommodated in the grammar established by the Monroe Doctrine, a by-product of a regional sensibility that allowed space for US imperialism in the region.[84] She, Sanctis de Brito, Roriz, and Barros have been original also in trying to understand a Latin American (regional) sensibility through its opposite, a universal sensibility, especially that advocated by the Brazilian jurist Manuel de Sá Vianna, who refuted the existence of an American international law.[85] Such research leads us to be aware that it is not the recurrence of the idea of a universal international law that makes one inattentive to local circumstances.[86] Besides that, it is not a regional or universal sensibility that will bring emancipation to Latin America but the politics in which those sensibilities are embedded.

The specificities of Latin America in international law have also been studied through the lens of human rights. Obregón,[87] Lorca,[88] and Scarfi[89] have aptly realized how previous debates about the existence of American international law, its codification, and the role of the United States were essential to the drafting of instruments such as the American Declaration of the Rights and Duties of Man

[83] Juan Pablo Scarfi, *The Hidden History of International Law in the Americas: Empire and Legal Networks* (Oxford: Oxford University Press, 2017).

[84] Fabia Fernandes Carvalho Veçoso, "Resisting Intervention through Sovereign Debt: A Redescription of the Drago Doctrine," *Third World Approaches to International Law Review* 1 (2020): 74–92; Fabia Fernandes Carvalho Veçoso, "Intervención, deuda externa y la conformación del orden espacial en América Latina," *Estudios Sociales* 59 (2020): 41–62.

[85] Adriane Sanctis de Brito, Fabia Fernandes Carvalho Veçoso, and João Henrique R. Roriz, "'Seremos julgados': revisitando o debate entre Álvarez e Sá Vianna sobre a regionalização do Direito Internacional na América Latina," in *Direito Internacional Atual*, ed. Liliana Lyra Jubilut (Maastricht, The Netherlands: Forense Juridica, 2014), 287–315; Patrícia Ramos Barros and Fabia Fernandes Carvalho, "A Brazilian Universalist: Manuel Alvaro de Souza Sá Vianna and international law in Brazil in the early twentieth century," *Latin American Law Review* 1 (2022): 1–17; Patrícia Ramos Barros e Fabia Fernandes Carvalho Veçoso, "Universalismo à Brasileira: Manuel Alvaro de Souza Sá Vianna e o direito internacional no Brasil no começo do século XX," in *Direto Internacional no Brasil: Pensamento e Tradição*, vol. 1, ed. George R. B. Galindo (Rio de Janeiro: Lumen Juris, 2021), 333–366.

[86] Jorge Esquirol, "Latin America," in *The Oxford Handbook of the History of International Law*, ed. Bardo Fassbender and Anne Peters (Oxford: Oxford University Press, 2012), 565–566.

[87] Liliana Obregón, "The Universal Declaration of Human Rights and Latin America," *Maryland Journal of International Law* 24 (2009): 94–98.

[88] Arnulf Becker Lorca, "Human Rights in International Law: The Forgotten Origins of Human Rights in Latin America," *University of Toronto Law Journal* 67 (2017): 465–495.

[89] Juan Pablo Scarfi, "Pan-American Human Rights: The Legacy of Pan-Americanism and the Intellectual Origins of the Inter-American Human Rights System," in *The New Pan-Americanism and the Structuring of Inter-American Relations*, ed. Juan Pablo Scarfi and David M. K. Sheinin (New York: Routledge, 2022), 138–162.

as well as the creation of institutions such as the Inter-American Commission of Human Right and the Inter-American Court of Human Rights. Making this connection through history is essential for understanding how the idea of specificity of Latin America gains space in contemporary debates on international legal issues, including in the Inter-American Court of Human Rights case law.[90]

Finally, the specificity of international law has also been approached through the perspective of influential scholars of the region. Studies on Alejandro Álvarez show the ambiguities of his project of American international law in the context of his professional life as a scholar and judge well inserted in universal academic and professional institutions.[91]

IV. Conclusion

I aimed to present how international legal scholarship in Latin America has been engaged in many creative ways with critical international legal theory, specifically on what concerns TWAIL and a variant of legal pluralism that focuses on the specificities of the engagement of Latin America with international law. TWAIL-related literature in the region has aptly addressed intricate and complex conceptual and historical issues, as well as specific ones, including those of a more technical dimension. Contesting, understanding, and reinterpreting the legacy of Latin American international law has been the main contribution of the scholars focused on the region's specificities from an international legal perspective.

This chapter has extended at least two relevant messages in the scholarship presented. First, there is a general call for critical international legal theory to pay growing attention to Latin America and its legal history. Regarding TWAIL, it is noteworthy that postcolonial theory, initially designed for the contexts of Asia and Africa, only poorly addresses colonialism as practiced in Latin America. This is reflected in the need many critical international lawyers of the region feel to embrace TWAIL with inputs from theories developed in the region, such as decolonial theory. This is even more evident in the legal pluralism literature that generally aims to demystify common sense about Latin America, scrutinizing the idea of Latin American international law, showing how politics affected the crafting of international legal norms and institutions, and making evident that

[90] See, e.g., Fabia Fernandes Carvalho, "O critério inter-americano sobre anistias: absolutismo de direitos humanos?," *Revista Derecho del Estado* 35 (2015): 3–26.

[91] See Arnulf Becker Lorca, "Alejandro Álvarez Situated: Subaltern Modernities and Modernisms that Subvert," *Leiden Journal of International Law* 19 (2006): 879–930; Jorge L. Esquirol, "Alejandro Álvarez's Latin American Law: A Question of Identity," *Leiden Journal of International Law* 19 (2006): 931–956; Liliana Obregón, "Noted for Dissent: The International Life of Alejandro Álvarez," *Leiden Journal of International Law* 19 (2006): 983–1016.

the region was not simply a receptacle of ideas developed in the Global North.[92] Second, there is an implicit message that by also writing in Spanish, Portuguese, and French, critical international legal scholarship must advance multilingualism in international law in the face of the predominance of the English language. Several power-related implications come from assuming English as the *lingua franca* of the discipline, and those implications strongly harm scholars from countries that do not have English as a mother tongue.[93] It is uncoherent to adopt a critical attitude, losing sight of how criticism takes shape.

The potentiality of critical approaches to international law in Latin America is immense. Nevertheless, critical approaches to international law might not lead Latin American international lawyers to superiority regarding other methods, such as finding the "true" argument about international law. On the contrary, critical approaches should lead to self-criticism and the consciousness that the necessary project is biased and should be subject to constant renegotiations about its very foundations.

[92] Articles published in a recent special issue of the Journal of the History of International Law on the 75th anniversary of the Bogotá Conferece (with contributions of Lixinski, Perrone, Quintana, Uriburu, Carvalho, and Galindo) continue this effort of showing the complexities and the original character of the contribution of the region to international law. See "Bogotá at 75", Journal of the History of International Law 25 (2024): 499-648.

[93] See Odie Ammann, "Language Bias in International Legal Scholarship: Symptoms, Explanations, Implications and Remedies," *European Journal of International Law* 33 (2022): 821–850. This is a good account of the issue, but unfortunately, it does not adequately address the impact of that bias on North-South relations. With such perspective, but not treating the language bias issue thoroughly, see Daniel Bonilla Maldonado, "The Political Economy of Legal Knowledge," in *Constitutionalism in the Americas* (Studies in Comparative Law and Legal Culture), ed. Colin Crawford and Daniel Bonilla Maldonado (Cheltenham, UK: Edward Elgar, 2018), 29–78. A more balanced account is provided by Justina Uriburu, "Between Elitist Conversations and Local Clusters: How Should we Address English-centrism in International Law?," *Opinio Juris,* December 7, 2022, http://opiniojuris.org/2020/11/02/between-elitist-conversations-and-local-clusters-how-should-we-address-english-centrism-in-international-law/.

11

Feminisms and International Law in Latin America

The Dispute over Protection of Women's Rights in the Inter-American Human Rights System

Ana Micaela Alterio

I. Introduction

The relationship between feminism and law goes back a long way. For example, the "Declaration of the Rights of Women and of the Citizens" written by Olympe de Gouges in 1791 challenged the exclusionary understanding of the newly enshrined legal equality.[1] Since then, it has had multiple and diverse developments, to the point that today, feminist studies are considered one of the richest sources of critical legal theory.

Part of the multiple challenges that feminism has posed to law is centered on its assumptions. The principles of universality, abstraction, objectivity, neutrality, and the public-private divide, to mention but a few, have been controversial when it comes to women and have been revealed to be paradoxical.[2] In fact, as I discuss in this chapter, who is the "legal subject" of law is a matter of controversy.[3] These reflections have permeated the field of international law[4] and, in Latin America, they have been enriched by decolonial, intersectional, ecological, anticapitalist, and other approaches[5] to generate their own developments, catalyzed in relation to grass-roots social movements.

[1] See Anne Lagerwall and Agatha Verdebout, "Olympe de Gouges. Beyond the Symbol," in *Portraits of Women in International Law: New Names and Forgotten Faces?*, ed. Immi Tallgren (Oxford: Oxford University Press, 2023), 56–65.

[2] See Joan Wallach Scott, *Only Paradoxes to Offer. French Feminists and the Rights of Man* (Oxford: Oxford University Press, 1996).

[3] See Stéphanie Hennette and Ruth Rubio-Marín, eds., *The Cambridge Companion to Gender and the Law* (Cambridge: Cambridge University Press, 2023); Fina Birulés, *Entreactos. En torno a la política, el feminismo y el pensamiento* (Madrid: Katz Editores, 2015), 18.

[4] See, for example, Dianne Otto, "Feminist Approaches of International Law," in *The Oxford Handbook of the Theory of International Law*, ed. Anne Orford and Florian Hoffmann (Oxford: Oxford University Press, 2016), 488–504.

[5] See, for example, Giovanna Maria Frisso, "Third World Approaches to International Law: Feminists' Engagement with International Law and Decolonial Theory," in *Research Handbook*

Ana Micaela Alterio, *Feminisms and International Law in Latin America* In: *Latin American International Law in the Twenty-First Century*. Edited by: Alejandro Chehtman, Alexandra Huneeus, and Sergio Puig, Oxford University Press. DOI: 10.1093/9780197754016.003.0011

Thus, feminists in Latin America have had their own imprint.[6] Although they have used and dialogued with the mobilization and the academic work of feminists from the Global North, the women of the region have organized themselves around their particular experiences, established their priorities, and thought and acted situationally as inhabitants of two colonized territories: their bodies and Latin America. From this double condition of subalternity, they established relations with the law and the state.

Throughout the twentieth century, these relations were intensely affected by the dictatorships suffered in the region and then by the renewed hope in democracy, constitutionalism, and human rights.[7] In this context and up to the present day (thanks in part to the "constitutionalization of international law"[8]), the Inter-American Human Rights System (IAHRS) has been a central interlocutor for human rights movements, including feminists fighting for the recognition of women's rights. It is worth mentioning that these rights found a specific (albeit partial) normative reception in the IAHRS only in 1994, with the Inter-American Convention on the Prevention, Punishment and Eradication of Violence against Women (Belém do Pará Convention)[9] and had to wait until the twenty-first century to be received in the jurisprudence of the Inter-American Court of Human Rights (IACtHR).[10] Since then, and especially since 2009, the

on Feminist Engagement with International Law, ed. by Susan Harris Rimmer and Kate Ogg (Cheltenham, UK: Edward Elgar, 2019), 479–498.

[6] See Isabel Cristina Jaramillo Sierra, "Latin American Feminist Legal Theory. Taking Multiple Subordinations Seriously," in *Routledge Handbook of Law and Society in Latin America*, ed. Rachel Sieder, Karina Ansolabehere, and Tatiana Alfonso, 111 (London: Routledge, 2019).

[7] See Marta Rodriguez de Assis Machado, Ana Luiza Villela de Viana Bandeira, and Fernanda Emy Matsuda, "Law, Gender, and Social Movements in Latin America. Moral Negotiations and Uneven Victories in Feminist Legal Mobilization," in *Routledge Handbook of Law and Society in Latin America*, ed. Rachel Sieder, Karina Ansolabehere and Tatiana Alfonso (London: Routledge, 2019), 358. The relations between feminism and law have been very different; put simply, they marked a rupture between the so-called autonomous feminists (the "historical" feminists or those of the "utopian") very critical of "this democracy," North American imperialism and the "*NGOnization* of the feminist movement," and the so-called "institutional" feminists (or those of "the possible") who bet on law (and the state) as tools for change. See Jules Falquet, "Las 'feministas autónomas' latinoamericanas y caribeñas: veinte años de disidencias," *Universitas Humanistica* no. 78 (2014): 39–63.

[8] *See* Eduardo Ferrer Mac-Gregor, "El control difuso de convencionalidad en el Estado Constitucional," in *Formación y Perspectivas del Estado en México*, ed. Héctor Fix Zamudio y Diego Valadés (Mexico City: IIJ, El Colegio Nacional, 2010), 151–188, esp 169.

[9] Although even before the American Convention on Human Rights was signed, there were developments such as the Inter-American Commission of Women (CIM), these did not have binding force. See Enzamaria Tramontana, "Hacia la consolidación de la perspectiva de género en el Sistema Interamericano: avances y desafíos a la luz de la reciente jurisprudencia de la Corte de San José," *Revista IIDH* 53 (2011): 141–181.

[10] Patricia Palacios Zuluaga criticizes the "delay" of the ISHR in the reception of gender-sensitive cases in "The Path to Gender Justice in the Inter-American Court of Human Rights," *Texas Journal of Women and the Law*, 17, no. 2 (2008): 227–295. However, I relativize the "delay" because I believe that the courts should not take a vanguard role in recognizing rights but rather receive the constructions that the different social actors are developing. In this sense, they can help strengthen

IACtHR has incorporated the analysis of women's human rights and the gender perspective as central to its decisions, becoming a fundamental voice for the delimitation of its scope at the regional and local levels.[11]

Beyond the debates on the *real* impact that the IACtHR's pronouncements have on the states and on the lives of women,[12] it could be said that feminist movements have celebrated them and used them strategically to advance their local struggles. Particularly noteworthy are the legal developments on violence against women promoted by the *Maria da Pehna v. Brazil* case before the Inter-American Commission of Human Rights,[13] those related to the concept of femicide, pushed by the *Campo Algodonero v. Mexico* judgment,[14] the advances in the area of abortion unlocked in part with the pronouncement in *Artavia Murillo v. Costa Rica*,[15] the collaboration for the advancement in the recognition of the rights of LGBTIQ+ persons, first established in *Atala Riffo v. Chile*,[16] and especially, with Advisory Opinion (AO) 24/17,[17] among others.

Today, the jurisprudence of the IACtHR is also playing a fundamental role in shaping the scope of the feminist critique of the idea of the legal subject. In particular, the IACtHR has pronounced itself on how to identify (or define) a "woman" as a subject of specific human rights protection and, more specifically, on the possibility of recognizing trans women as women. This again calls into question the very assumptions of the normative systems of human rights protection as binary.

and legitimize the claims of the groups, avoiding violent counteroffensives when there is no solid social base to tackle them. Reviewing women's mobilizations in Latin America shows that their strength varies significantly from country to country. The support that the IACtHR can provide in receiving social demands in terms of rights helps to strengthen women in countries where mobilization is still scarce and the normative reception is weak—countries for which the judgments of the IACtHR are "avant-garde" or very "advanced."

[11] See Mariano Fernández Valle, "Las temáticas de género en la jurisprudencia interamericana," in *Violencias contra las mujeres. Relaciones en contexto*, ed. Silvina Álvarez and Paola Bergallo (Brussels: Didot, 2020), pp. 297–332. Isabel Jaramillo Sierra called "Radical Feminism *a la Latina*" the way in which some Latin American feminist legal scholarship has confronted the tension between a well-established transnational canon and the local using international human rights law in local arenas. See Jaramillo Sierra, "Latin American Feminist Legal Theory," 111, 115–118.

[12] Paulina García-del Moral, "The 'Formally feminist State': A Potential New Player in the Inter-American Human Rights System?" *AJIL Unbound* 113 (2019): 365–369.

[13] *Maria da Penha v. Brazil*, Case 12.051, Inter-Am. Comm. H.R., Report No. 54/01, OAE/Ser. L/V/II.111, doc. 20, rev., at 704 (2000) (Inter-American Commission on Human Rights [hereinafter IACHR].

[14] *González et al. ("Cotton Fields") v. Mexico*, Preliminary Objection, Merits, Reparations, and Costs, Inter-Am. Ct. H.R. (ser. C) No. 205 (November 16, 2009).

[15] Since the interpretation of ACHR art. 4 had become an obstacle to advancing such legalization in Argentina, for example. *Artavia Murillo et al. ("In vitro fertilization") v. Costa Rica*, Preliminary Objection, Merits, Reparations, and Costs, Inter-Am. Ct. H.R. (ser. C) No. 257 (November 28, 2012).

[16] *Atala Riffo and Daughters v. Chile*, Merits, Reparations and Cost, Inter-Am. Ct. H.R. (ser. C) No. 239 (February 24, 2012).

[17] Advisory Opinion OC-24/17, Requested by the Republic of Costa Rica, Inter-Am. Ct. H.R. (ser. A) No. 24 (November 24, 2017).

However, unlike in previous cases, this time, the IACtHR's position has not been peacefully received but has intensified a radical controversy that divides feminism. Feminists are discussing the possibilities and limits of a system of human rights protection that has been designed for "men" (first[18]) and "women" (later[19]) as closed, all-encompassing, and exclusive sexual categories, and they disagree. This disagreement has been expressed in the IACtHR judgment *Vicky Hernández et al. v. Honduras*,[20] and then in the Advisory Opinion 29/2022 on "Differential approaches with respect to certain groups of persons deprived of their liberty."[21]

In this chapter, I concentrate on this latter question. I first explore the arguments referred to by the IACtHR judges, which reflect the internal debate among feminists in the region. Then, I undertake a theoretical reflection on who embodies the political subject of feminism and how attempts have been made to translate that subject into a legal category. From there, I show the discrepancies in interpreting these legal categories. Finally, I end the chapter with a brief reflection on the kind of contribution that a progressive (feminist and Latin American) vision of law is making to international human rights law, as well as to our legal systems.

II. The IACtHR Ruling in *Vicky Hernandez et al. v. Honduras*," and Its Partial Dissents

On March 26, 2021, the IACtHR decided *Vicky Hernández et al. v. Honduras*. The State of Honduras was condemned for the murder of Vicky Hernández, a sexual worker, trans woman, HIV-positive, and prominent human rights defender, in the city of San Pedro Sula while a curfew was in force in the country. The judgment states that the coup d'état that took place in Honduras on June 28, 2009, had generated a context of exacerbated violence against LGBTIQ+ people.

Although mentioning the coup d'état may suggest facts that are particular to the case at hand, the truth is that LGBTIQ+ people suffer systematic violence in the region.[22] This fact has led the IACHR to issue several reports and

[18] The Declaration of the Rights of *Man* and of the Citizen.

[19] The first specific international document is the "Convention on the Political Rights of Women" (UN, 1952), although the strong impulse for the real equality of women was given with the United Nations world conferences on women. The first conference was held in Mexico (1975), which led to the creation of the Convention on the Elimination of All Forms of Discrimination against Women (CEDAW) in 1980.

[20] *Vicky Hernández et al. v. Honduras*, Merits, Reparations and Cost, Inter-Am. Ct. H.R. (ser. C) No. 422 (March 26,2021).

[21] Advisory Opinion OC-29/22, Requested by the Inter-American Commission on Human Rights, Inter-Am. Ct. H.R. (ser. A) No. 29 (May 30, 2022).

[22] And in the world. See the Observatory of murdered trans people, with figures between 2008 and 2021. https://transrespect.org/es/map/trans-murder-monitoring/

recommendations to states.[23] Within this group, *trans* people[24] live in a situation of extreme vulnerability, an example of which is the fact that their life expectancy is thirty-five years.[25] Vicky Hernández was twenty-six years old when she was murdered.

The Court did not name her murder a "transfeminicide"[26] but a homicide based on gender expression or identity and applied the Belém Do Pará Convention on Violence against Women to condemn Honduras.[27] This is the first time an international court has applied a women-specific convention to a transgender woman, and this was the cause of the controversy within and outside the Court. While most of the judges held that to trigger instruments of enhanced protection such as the Inter-American Convention on the Prevention, Punishment and Eradication of Violence against Women, the category "woman" is not linked to genitalia,[28] there were two notable dissents. One by Judge Elizabeth Odio Benito and the other by Judge Eduardo Vio Grossi. Both the ruling and the partial dissent of Odio Benito attempt to "clarify" the concepts of "sex" and "gender" in an antithetical way, with consequences that are fundamental in the understanding of human rights protection systems.

According to the majority, when the Convention refers to "violence against women based on their gender" (Article 1), it refers to a system of patriarchal domination rooted in gender stereotypes that includes violence experienced by people who defy gender norms, as trans women do.[29] So much so that the Court continues, in Article 9, the Convention calls on states to take into account "the vulnerability of women to violence by reason of, among others, their race or ethnic background, or their status as migrants, refugees or displaced persons." It further explains that this list of factors is not *numerus clausus*, and that gender

[23] See, for example, IACHR, *Violence against Lesbian, Gay, Bisexual, Trans and Intersex Persons in the Americas* (November 12, 2015). Do coas/ser. L/V/II re.2 Doc 36

[24] "Trans" is an umbrella term that encompasses people who do not identify with the sex attributed at birth; it is a political category that corresponds to that subject that transcends the binary and transits genders. Diana Maffía and Alba Rueda, "El concepto de travesticidio/transfemicidio y su inscripción en el pedido de justicia por Diana Sacayán," in *Miradas feministas sobre los derechos,* ed. Diana Maffia, Patricia Laura Gómez, and Aluminé Moreno (Buenos Aires: Jusbaires, 2019), 165–188, 183.

[25] See IACHR, *Violence against Lesbian, Gay, Bisexual, Trans and Intersex Persons in the Americas* (2015), which indicates that 80 percent of transgender persons die before the age of thirty-five, ¶¶ 16, 15, https://www.oas.org/en/iachr/reports/pdfs/violencelgbtipersons.pdf (last visited June 26, 2024).

[26] There is a discussion about the proper terminology for naming a femicide of a *trans* woman. See Blas Radi and Alejandra Sardá-Chandiramani, "Travesticidio/transfemicidio: Coordenadas para pensar los crímenes de travestis y mujeres trans en Argentina," *Boletín del Observatorio de Género* (2016). https://www.aacademica.org/blas.radi/14 (last visited June 26, 2024).

[27] Inter-American Convention on the Prevention, Punishment and Eradication of Violence against Women ("Convention of Belem Do Para"), June 9, 1994, OAS.

[28] *Vicky Hernández,* Inter.-Am. Ct. H.R., ¶ 129: "sex and gender should be perceived as being part of constructed identity that is the result of the free and autonomous decision of each person and without this having to be subject to their genitalia," quoting OC-24/17 ¶ 94.

[29] Ibid., ¶ 128

identity can contribute in an *intersectional way* to the vulnerability of women who suffer gender-based violence.[30]

But this was not the understanding of the minority of the Court. The only woman judge at the time, Elizabeth Odio Benito, departed from the majority decision regarding the application of the Belém do Pará Convention because, in her opinion, the regional instrument does not apply to the facts of the case.[31] For the judge, there was a confusion between the concepts of sex (biological)[32] and gender (social and hierarchical construction) that equates sex with gender identity[33] and, consequently, "on the basis of this substitution, erase the feminine sex with all its biological properties and mix everything up in a single subjective and self-proclaimed category."[34] However, she continued, feminism as a political theory and social movement aims at eradicating inequality between *men and women* in all social structures; therefore, the central subject of feminism (and, in this case, the violence against women due to being women) is *women* and the specific oppression they suffer."[35] Her argument ended by stating that if the

[30] Ibid., ¶ 129. With similar citations to the IACHR. IACHR, *Violence against Lesbian*, ¶ 52, 46; CEDAW Committee, *General Recommendation No. 35 on gender-based violence against women*, updating *General Recommendation No. 19* (July 26, 2017), CEDAW/C/GC/35, ¶¶ 9, 12, and the Mechanism for Follow-up of the Convention MESECVI, *Practical Guide for the Implementation of the System of Progress Indicators for the Measurement of the Convention of Belém do Pará* (February 2015), technical sheet 5.7, 32.

[31] In addition, Judge Odio Benito expressed another dissent on the obligation that the majority judgment assigns to the state, on the one hand, to enact a "gender identity" law that allows changing the registered sex of trans persons without proof of a change, and on the other hand, to require statistics on the violence suffered by these persons, considering them impossible to comply with simultaneously. *Partially Dissenting Opinion of Judge Elizabeth Odio Benito, Vicky Hernández et al. v. Honduras*, Merits, Reparations and Cost, Inter.-Am. Ct. H.R. (ser. C) No. 422, ¶ 3 (March 26, 2021). I will not dwell on this point.

[32] For the judge, biological sex is supported by science and is defined by anatomical, genetic, and physiological traits of men and women; "never a social construct or even less a subjective matter or a feeling." Ibid., ¶ 8. Thus, discrimination against women because they are women is "linked to the reproductive function and responsibility as carers of the whole family group." Ibid., ¶ 9.

[33] Gender identity, on the other hand, would be for the judge "a feeling that can change even from one day to the next." Ibid., ¶ 12.

[34] Ibid., ¶ 5.

[35] Ibid., ¶ 15. Similarly, the partially dissenting vote of Eduardo Vio Grossi, considers that when the Convention speaks of women, it does not include "*trans* women" because according to the Vienna Convention on the Law of Treaties, "A treaty shall be interpreted in good faith in accordance with the ordinary meaning to be given to the terms of the treaty in their context and in the light of its object and purpose." Ibid., ¶ 4. None of these elements would support a different interpretation. Therefore, he believes promoting the reform or extension of protection would be necessary by signing new international instruments (ibid., ¶ 33). Odio Benito also calls for the creation of specific instruments in *Partially Dissenting Opinion of Judge Elizabeth Odio Benito*, Advisory Opinion OC-29/22 (May 30, 2022), 3, but, as Zuluaga puts it, attempting the path of establishing specific instruments of protection may allow states not to ratify them, to ratify them with reservations, or even to commit themselves to obligations that are much more diffuse (or weaker) than those already contemplated in the American Convention on Human Rights for all persons, which can have disastrous political effects for the invocation of these rights at the local level. "The path of gender justice in the Inter-American Court of Human Rights," *Texas Journal of Women and the Law* 17, no. 2 (Spring 2008): 227–295 (point VII, 1). Furthermore, in my opinion, this path not only ignores the current international context that would make it impossible to think of the formulation, signature, and ratification of a treaty

subject of feminism is replaced by "a strange and confused variable of subjective identities," the negative impact on decades of feminist struggle and theory would be predictable: "[N]ot only feminism would disappear, but also the theory of human rights that is also based on *objective and scientific categories,* rather than on feelings or self-perceptions."[36]

Odio Benito reaffirmed the point in her partially dissenting vote for Advisory Opinion 29/22. There, again, referring to the need to make reasonable accommodations for trans women deprived of liberty (chapter VII of the AO), the judge opposed that they should be received "in detention centers for women and live with them in the same spaces." This is because she claims—without evidence—there are "frequent and painful cases of violations and pregnancies suffered by women in detention caused by *these transexuals who enjoy absurd privilege*."[37] This does not mean that the judge, as well as other representatives of this position, does not consider that LGBTIQ+ people suffer systematic discrimination and violence, but that, for her, such violence has a different cause and, therefore, must be protected in a differentiated way and not through the specific mechanisms for biological women.[38]

As can be seen in her votes, the antagonism with the majority position of the IACtHR has to do with the identification of the political subject (which she calls "central") of feminism and, consequently, of the subject of protection of the mechanisms of reinforced guarantees. As I will try to show, how to understand the whole system of human rights protection and its consequences depends on how this dispute is "resolved."

This discussion, which a few decades ago was only found among a very conservative sector of societies that refused—and still refuses—to recognize the concept of gender,[39] has recently found its entry into self-proclaimed feminist

on the rights of transsexual persons but is also indifferent to the consequences of its position, because while this specific protection arrives, it accepts that persons not expressly named but who find themselves in situations of vulnerability lack adequate protection.

[36] *Partially Dissenting Opinion of Judge Elizabeth Odio Benito,* ¶ 15 (emphasis added).

[37] *Partially Dissenting Opinion of Judge Elizabeth Odio Benito*, Advisory Opinion, 3 (emphasis added).

[38] Judge Elizabeth Odio Benito makes this explicit in ¶¶ 17, 19, 21, 39, and 41 of her partially dissenting opinion in *Vicky Hernández*, and on page 3 of her partially dissenting opinion in OC 29/22.

[39] This sector, linked to religious expressions, vindicates biological sex as binary and as the only possible reality, and considers gender a "disrespect to the rules of nature imposed by divine transcendence." From there, it attacks progressive sectors for wanting to impose a "gender ideology," thus obstructing the possibility of sex education in schools, legislation that recognizes gender identities, equal marriage, and the rights associated with free sexuality such as access to contraceptive methods and abortion, among others. Dora Barrancos, *Historia mínima de los feminismos en América Latina* (Mexico City: El Colegio de México, 2020), 251–258.

movements, dividing them into two irreconcilable positions that are reflected in the judgment.[40] On the one hand, those self-ascribed as "radical" feminists (TERFs[41]) who defend the need to distinguish biological women, by their *sex*, from any other gender; to be able to recognize the subject protected by the regulations of reinforced rights for women, affirmative action measures, sexual segregation policies in sports, bathrooms, prisons, and so on; and all those who take into account sexual difference to achieve material equality.

For this movement, reflected in the dissenting opinion of Odio Benito, *gender*, as an analytical category, has served and serves to understand the social, cultural, legal, and political structures of oppression that mandate specific roles or behaviors to people based on their sex (natural and binary), but not as an individual expression of identity. Hence, gender identity, not being fixed and subject to the free choice/disposition of the person, would not allow anchoring a specific protection system and would lead to the dissolution of the current mechanisms for the protection of women ("the erasure of women"), due to the lack of a specific subject.[42]

On the other hand, there are inclusive feminists.[43] They share a conception of *sex* as a historical, dynamic, and nonbinary category and advocate for an understanding of the political subject of feminism in relational terms, as a matter of social hierarchy, and not in biological, static, or inherent terms.[44] In addition, they make visible the reality of intersex people from the very materiality of the

[40] This is not the only sharp division found in feminisms, which from their origins have been marked by pluralism, but it could be said that today it is the most polarizing and virulent transversal split. For a succinct reconstruction of feminisms in Latin America, see Ana Micaela Alterio and Alejandra Martínez Verástegui, "Introducción. Algunas notas en torno a los debates sobre los feminismos en América Latina," in *Feminismos y Derecho. Un diálogo interdisciplinario en torno a los debates contemporáneos*, ed. Ana Micaela Alterio and Alejandra Martinez Verástegui (Mexico City: SCJN, 2019), XIII–XLV.

[41] Trans exclusionary radical feminists. The term "radical" is misleading since radical feminists (paradigmatically Catharine MacKinnon) historically distinguished themselves from the so-called liberals by claiming a total transformation of the patriarchal system, not solvable through the simple formal inclusion or extension of the rights already recognized in the existing legal systems, but through structural and transformative approaches. For MacKinnon's position on the issue under analysis, see "Exploring Transgender Law and Politics," https://signsjournal.org/exploring-transgender-law-and-politics/ (last visited June 26, 2024), where she embraces an inclusionary approach.

[42] In this line of thought, we find Amelia Valcárcel, Alda Facio, or Andrea Medina, who presented their points at the Forum "Aclaraciones necesarias sobre las categorías Sexo y Género," organized by CEIICH, UNAM (March 24, 2022). https://www.youtube.com/watch?v=EpiyXz1fO-8 (last visited June 26, 2024).

[43] This includes a wide variety of feminisms such as transfeminism, queer feminism, decolonial feminism, intersectional feminism, afro-feminism, post-humanist feminism, and xenofeminism, among others.

[44] See Siobhan Guerrero Mc Manus, "Sujeto(s) del Feminismo," in *Enciclopedia Crítica del Género. Una cartografía contemporánea de los principales saberes y debates de los estudios de género*, ed. Norma Blazquez Graf et al. (Cambridge, MA: Arpa, 2023) 291–300.

body (sex), who have been historically ignored, pathologized, and subjected to processes of "normalization" to fit into the binary artifice.[45] For this group, with which the majority of the IACtHR positions itself, the term "gender" not only refers to the social, cultural, political, and legal construction that systematically disciplines and hierarchizes sexed bodies but also has an individual identity and expressive manifestations.[46]

In what follows, I would like to advance arguments favoring the latter understanding. In my opinion, the concern for the "erasure of women" expressed by Judge Odio Benito in conjunction with a certain feminist current is not only not empirically sustained but is based on mistaken, conservative, reifying, and, therefore, static conceptions of the political subject and the systems of protection that arise as a consequence of their mobilizations.

III. Gender, the Political Subject of Feminism, and Its Legal Translation

A few decades ago, feminists adopted the concept of gender to account for the social relations of power based on the differences that distinguish the sexes.[47] The term is included in the Belém do Pará Convention, which was applied in the *Vicky Hernández* case.[48] As an analytical category, "gender" served to make visible that the social overvaluation of the masculine, which naturalizes the association between power and masculinity and the consequent subordination of everything related to the feminine, is not due to natural or biological differences but to an ideology or set of shared beliefs about what people are or should be.[49]

[45] See Anne Fausto-Sterling, "The Five Sexes. Why Male and Female Are Not Enough," *The Sciences* 33, no. 2 (March–April 1993): 20–24, https://doi.org/10.1002/j.2326-1951.1993.tb03081.x (last visited June 26, 2024).

[46] See *Yogyakarta Principles—Principles on the application of international human rights law in relation to sexual orientation and gender identity* (March 2007). Exponents of this idea at the Forum "Historia y Política del Cuerpo Sexuado," organized by Postgraduate UNAM (April 1, 2022), https://www.youtube.com/watch?v=gCns_Ii0nAs (last visited June 26, 2024).

[47] Joan Scott, "Gender: A Useful Category of Historical Analysis," *The American Historical Review* 91, no. 5 (1986): 1053–1075.

[48] "Article 1: For the purposes of this Convention, violence against women shall be understood as any act or conduct, based on gender, which causes death or physical, sexual or psychological harm or suffering to women, whether in the public or the private sphere." According to Dianne Otto, gender language in international human rights law was only accepted by states at the 4th World Conference on Women in Beijing in 1995. Dianne Otto, "International Human Rights Law: Towards Rethinking Sex/Gender Dualism and Asymmetry," in *The Ashgate Research Companion to Feminist Legal Theory*, ed. Margaret Davies and Vanessa Munro (London: Routledge, 2013), 197–215, at 203.

[49] See also Tatiana Alfonso and Micaela Alterio, "Judicialización de DESCA y desigualdades estructurales: el caso de la desigualdad de género ante la SCJN," in *Manual sobre justiciabilidad de los Derechos económicos, sociales, culturales y ambientales*, Vol. II, ed. Christian Courtis (Mexico City: SCJN, 2021), 1075.

We call this ideology "patriarchy," and it explains the systematic discrimination suffered by women and all those who do not conform to gender mandates and are therefore perceived as socially inferior. In the words of Latin American feminist Julieta Paredes,

> Gender, being a relational category, is always revealing the position of inferiority assigned by patriarchy to women. We want to make it clear that gender is not a descriptive category or attributive category, nor is it deterministic in essence . . . Gender from our theoretical reconceptualization is a relational political category of denunciation, of an unjust, oppressive, and exploitative relationship that men establish with women for the benefit of the system of oppressions that is patriarchy, currently colonial-neoliberal patriarchy.[50]

Feminists fight against this system of patriarchal domination to overcome gender as an unjust historical reality.[51] They have had to build a feminist identity that is "the condition of possibility for women to constitute themselves as subjects and to collectively articulate the political struggle."[52] In other words, feminism needed the sexed entity "woman" as a pre-political subject to become aware of her situation of gender oppression to become a "political subject" and, from there, an engine for social change.

As Rosa Cobo explains, feminist identity "must be understood instrumentally as the foundation of the struggle against oppression, but never as the entrenchment in difference or the exaltation of an essence. . . . *Identity is above all the result of a political choice*."[53] Hence, the feature of this identity is its provisional and contingent character,[54] since what is of interest is to dismantle that system of hierarchies and patriarchal ideology that operates culturally and socially and that places certain people in *situations* of vulnerability, not because they are intrinsically or naturally vulnerable, but because their social position is one of disadvantage.[55]

[50] Julieta Paredes, *Hilando fino. Desde el feminismo comunitario* (Monterrey, Mexico: El Rebozo Palapa Editorial, 2013), 62, accessed June 26, 2024, https:// sjlatinoamerica.files.wordpress.com/2013/06/paredes-julieta-hilando-fino-desde-el-feminismo-comunitario.pdf. All the translations are mine.

[51] Ibid., 66.

[52] Rosa Cobo, "Democracia paritaria y sujeto político feminista," *Anales de la Cátedra Francisco Suárez* 36 (2002): 41.

[53] Ibid., 41 (emphasis is mine).

[54] For Spivak, the category "woman," for example, at the *descriptive* level, implies a unifying, artificial and strategic understanding that, at the *transformative level*, seeks to destroy the mechanics that construct the profile of the category itself in which a collective consciousness has situationally developed. Gayatri Chakravvorty Spivak, "Estudios de la Subalteridad. Deconstruyendo la Historiografía," in *Estudios PostColoniales, ensayos fundamentales*, ed. Sandro Mezzadra (Madrid: Traficantes de Sueños, 2008), 33–68, 45.

[55] Tatiana Alfonso and Micaela Alterio, "Judicialización de DESCA y desigualdades estructurales." See Roberto Saba, *Más allá de la igualdad formal ante la ley ¿Qué les debe el Estado a los grupos desaventajados?* (Mexico City: Siglo XXI, 2016), 31.

The point is that generating this feminist identity or identifying its features has not been a simple task and even less a peaceful one. The problem of identifying "women" has been raised in different contexts, from the feminist methodology that tried to recover "the experience" of women to show how these experiences have been made invisible in social organization and to recover it to the identification of the problems of "women" that should be addressed in a differentiated way, and even to the "representation" of women in democratic systems, among other issues.

In her famous 1851 speech, *Ain't I a woman?*, Sojourner Truth presented the inconsistencies of a definition of woman that did not include her.[56] Monique Wittig explains that a lesbian is not a woman because a woman only makes sense from a binary and heterosexual construction. A lesbian is a "savage"; she is something disruptive, a fugitive from her class that seeks the destruction of the same class.[57] Kimberlee Crenshaw, highlights how identity-based politics have been a source of strength and community sense-making, but, in turn, have contributed to reducing or ignoring intragroup differences, creating outcomes that only favor the dominant members of each group. In her words, "intersectionality might be more broadly useful as a way of mediating the tension between assertions of multiple identity and the ongoing necessity of group politics."[58] Angela Harris, from Afro-feminism, further criticizes "essentialism" in the definition of woman. That is, she challenges the idea that "something" makes us women, which is permanent, linked to our anatomy, and can be isolated and described independently of other realities of experience.[59] Latin American feminists also assert that "there is no such thing as 'woman' in general [for] this masks, for example, hegemonies of class, race, generation, sexual options."[60] As a more recent example, post-humanist feminists attempt to dismantle hierarchical relations between subjects, including at the center of feminism those

[56] See bell hooks, *Ain't I a woman, black women and feminism* (London: Routledge, 2015).

[57] Monique Wittig, *La pensée straight* (Balland, 2001), quoted by Jules Falquet, *Breve reseña de algunas teorías lésbicas* (Mexico City: Fem-e-libros, 2004), 29.

[58] Kimberlee Crenshaw, "Mapping the Margins: Intersectionality, Identity Politics, and Violence against Women of Color," *Stanford Law Review* 43, no. 6 (1991): 1241–1299, at 1296. Now, as Crenshaw continues, "to say that a category such as race or gender is socially constructed is not to say that that category has no significance in our world." Ibid. The problem, then, is not the existence of the category but the concrete values with which we associate them, and how these values promote and create social hierarchies. "[A] strong case can be made that the most critical resistance strategy for disempowered groups is to occupy and defend a politics of social location rather than to vacate and destroy it" (ibid., 1297) "it must be recognized "that the organized identity groups in which we find ourselves in are in fact coalitions, or at least potential coalitions waiting to be formed" (ibid., 1299).

[59] Angela P. Harris, "Race and Essentialism in Feminist Legal Theory," *Stanford Law Review* 42, no. 3 (February 1990): 581–616. The danger of essentialism for the author is in embracing the old belief, used against women for so long, that anatomy is destiny. Ibid., 585.

[60] Paredes, *Hilando fino*, 68.

who have had to fight for the fundamental right to be considered and treated as human.[61]

But the difficulty of identifying the political subject of feminism and its demands does not exhaust the problem posed. The issue becomes even more complex when we try to translate these political demands into law. Although feminists have converged (not without resistance[62]) in creating instruments for the specific protection of "women's" rights, their scope and interpretation are linked to the struggles and situations of injustice that gave rise to them and which they seek to remedy. Situations and struggles whose identification, as we have already seen, is controversial. So, in the attempt to establish a legal category that names, makes visible, and understands the group that has suffered patriarchal oppression to develop appropriate mechanisms to combat it, an intrinsically open, multiple, and unstable social-political phenomenon is reduced, simplified, and petrified.[63]

That is why using the term "woman" or, instead, the overlapping of different subjects and planes of reality in a single category "woman" generates so much dispute. The word "woman" is being used at the same time (1) in the *pre-political* arena to name the biological female (or *cis* woman as a fact[64]) who may or may not be a feminist, who may or may not be in a particular situation of discrimination; (2) in the *political arena* to identify the subject of feminisms that makes visible gender oppression in its various manifestations and fights to eliminate patriarchal ideology (which does not include all *cis* women, but at the same time goes beyond *cis* women)[65]; and finally (3) in the *legal system* it becomes a category that refers to an empirical referent for the adjudication of rights and special

[61] And to nonhuman subjects. See Emily Jones, *Feminist Theory and International Law* (London: Routledge, 2023), 15. Also Rosi Braidotti, *Posthuman Feminism* (Cambridge: Polity Press, 2022).

[62] See Otto, "International Human Rights Law," 199.

[63] On the point, see Noelia Igareda González and Marta Cruells López, "Críticas al derecho y el sujeto 'mujeres' y propuestas desde la jurisprudencia feminista," *Cuadernos Electrónicos de Filosofía del Derecho* no. 30 (2014): 1–16.

[64] The identification of the pre-political subject, or the categorization of biological bodies, is also highly contested. That I state it as "fact" does not mean that it is self-evident. I will not dwell on these disputes because it is not the subject of the present chapter, but for an approach, see Lu Ciccia, *La invención de los sexos, cómo la ciencia puso el binarimo en nuestros cerebros y cómo los feminismos pueden ayudararnos a salir de ahí* (Mexico City: Siglo XXI, 2022).

[65] Jaya Ramji-Nogales addresses this issue specifically in the context of international law in "Revisiting the Category 'Women,'" in *Research Handbook on Feminist Engagement with International Law*, ed. Susan Harris Rimmer and Kate Ogg (Cheltenham, UK: Edward Elgar, 2019), 240–252. Here the author poses whether to use the term "women," "feminism," or "gender" as a basis for political mobilization, and strategically chooses women "to speak to a broader audience." She is conscious of the risks and difficulties of "build[ing] alliances with women who hold perspectives that subtly undermine or clearly oppose inclusion of diverse voice"—taking inclusion as the objective of mobilization in international law (ibid., 250), but she concludes that "[t]hough not perfectly inclusive, the category 'women' can be defined beyond cisgender identity to include transwomen, cross-dressing men and other queer folk who may be viewed by society as fitting into the category 'women'. Given that this is a theory of inclusion, 'women' must be defined broadly" (ibid., 251).

protections but is not identical to it.[66] In addition, it is configured as a "suspect classification" that serves to presume that a differentiation based on it is a priori unconstitutional because it is discriminatory.[67]

In other words, "woman" as a legal category allows for a "shortcut" in judicial reasoning. It operates as a "proxy" that facilitates the identification of a case of discrimination without having to prove that discrimination occurs in every singular situation because it is structural.[68] But, as a proxy, it is under- and overinclusive and establishes a presumption that can be defeated. That it is under- and overinclusive means that although it is presumed that the empirical referent suffers the situation of oppression or that a differentiation based on sex-gender is discriminatory against women, it may happen that a woman is not in a situation of gender discrimination in a particular case, and that, on the contrary, another person who does not identify *theirself* as a woman is.[69] In such cases, the adjudication of the legal consequences (remedies) will have to be based on the reasons that gave rise to the protection or differentiation, discarding the use of the "shortcut" or proxy, or reinterpreting it (if it is still valid).[70]

This is what the IACtHR rightly does in the case of *Vicky Hernández*, consistent with the understanding of the prohibition of discrimination as rooted in nonsubordination and a conception of substantive equality.[71] The legal

[66] Stéphanie Hennette Vauchez and Ruth Rubio-Marín, "The Political Subject," in *The Cambridge Companion to Gender and the Law*, ed. Stéphanie Hennette and Ruth Rubio-Marín (Cambridge: Cambridge University Press, 2023), explain that in 1793 France, there were three different categories under which voters were listed: men, women, and children, where the first column effectively listed heads of household (including widows should they maintain an independent household), and servants (including male servants) were in fact registered as women. This proves that "[m]en and women were not defined in biological terms for the purpose of assessing their political subjectivity, but rather based on their independent/dependent status in a society structured around the patriarchal family as the basic societal pillar." Ibid., 341.

[67] I agree with Stéphanie Hennette and Ruth Rubio-Marín, "From Law and Gender to Law as Gender—The Legal Subject and the Co-production Hypothesis," in *The Cambridge Companion to Gender and the Law*, ed. Stéphanie Hennette and Ruth Rubio-Marín (Cambridge: Cambridge University Press, 2023), that "the legal subject, the human person that the law deals with, is not a 'natural' entity imposing its subjectivity onto legal rules and categories, but an artificially constituted one instead, and that law is a key instrument in this constitutive act." Ibid., 12.

[68] Saba, *Más allá de la igualdad formal ante la ley*, 83.

[69] Assuming sex-gender discrimination is structural would seem to imply that the category can be underinclusive (because it does not include people who suffer the same discrimination but who do not identify themselves as women) but never overinclusive (all women would always be in such a situation). But I consider that it can also be overinclusive in the consideration of specific cases since I understand that situations of oppression are relational.

[70] A similar discussion, within the framework of American antidiscrimination law, is raised by Kenji Yoshino with respect to the "discrete and insular minority" standard used to create strict scrutiny with respect to race and later extended to sex, alienation, national origin, and nonmarital parentage. The author proposes to refine the standards, formulating them more flexibly in relation to factors that allow for a presumption of a person's vulnerability. Thus, "it will enable a better civil rights jurisprudence not just for us, but for other groups—foreseen and unforeseen—that are to come." Kenji Yoshino, "The Gay Tipping Point" *UCLA Law Review* 57 (2010): 1544.

[71] It is worth noting that substantive equality is a multidimensional concept that also pursues the accommodation of difference to achieve structural change. This means that equality should not

argument for the justification of differentiated measures for certain subjects (belonging to groups listed—in a non-exhaustive manner—in Article 1 (1) of the American Convention on Human Rights—the "suspect classification") is that there are *factual* inequalities that enable (and oblige) special protection measures aimed at overcoming them.[72] These measures are aimed at members of groups that have historically suffered such disadvantages and are therefore in a situation of vulnerability.[73]

Let me illustrate this discussion through a concrete example. Taking violence as a paradigmatic case of discrimination against women, the debate on the justification of adopting differentiated measures for certain subjects arose in the *Maria da Penha v. Brazil* case.[74] When in 2006, Brazil enacted Law 11.340 to protect women from domestic and family violence, its constitutionality was challenged before the Supreme Court of Justice. As Rodriguez de Assis Machado and Mota Prado report, some lower courts had ruled that the fact that the law protected *only women* and not men violated the principle of equality.[75] The Brazilian Supreme Court rejected this claim, taking up the notion of substantive equality and stating that "the Law was designed to mitigate a situation of social and cultural discrimination and would be required for as long as the situation persisted in the country."[76]

mean exact conformity but "to respect and accommodate difference, removing the detriment but not the difference itself." Sandra Fredman, *Discrimination Law* (Oxford: Oxford University Press, 2012), 30. This means that in some cases, *cis* and *trans* women will not be able to be treated in the same way, but again, these cases will have to be very well justified. For an argument in this sense, see Graham Mayeda, "Who do you think you are? When Should the Law Let You Be Who You Want to Be?" in *You've Changed. Sex Reassignment and Personal Identity*, ed. Laurie J. Shrage (Oxford: Oxford University Press, 2009), 194–216.

[72] See Verónica Undurraga, "Transformative Gender Equality in the Inter-American System of Human Rights," in *Frontiers of Gender Equality. Transnational Legal Perspective*, ed. Rebecca Cook (College Park: University of Pennsylvania Press, 2023), 237–258.

[73] These interpretations are highly disputed. On the one hand, from the conservative position that recently achieved the declaration of unconstitutionality of affirmative action measures before the SCOTUS based on an interpretation of equality in a formal sense and under an anticlassification criterion of suspect categories. See *Students for Fair Admissions, Inc. v. President and Fellows of Harvard College*, No. 20-1199; *Students for Fair Admissions, Inc. v. University of North Carolina et al.*, No. 21-707 (2023), https://www.supremecourt.gov/opinions/22pdf/20-1199_hgdj.pdf (last visited June 26, 2024). For an account of these divergent positions and their ideological background, see Jack M. Balkin and Reva B. Siegel, "The American Civil Rights Tradition: Anticlassification or Antisubordination? *University of Miami Law Review* 58, no. 9 (2003): 9–34. On the other hand, there is also a sector of feminism that fears that the establishment of special protection measures may end up consolidating the very situations they wish to combat instead of destroying them (victimization). Otto, "International Human Rights Law."

[74] *Maria da Penha v. Brazil.* This was the first case in which the Inter-American Commission on Human Rights applied the Convention of Belém do Pará.

[75] Marta Rodriguez de Assis Machado and Mariana Mota Prado, "Institutional Dimensions of Gender Equality: The *Maria da Penha* Case," in *Frontiers of Gender Equality. Transnational Legal Perspectives*, ed. Rebecca Cook (College Park: University of Pennsylvania Press, 2023) pp. 384–405, 394–5.

[76] Ibid., 396.

Following this logic, it is understandable why, if the claim for the extension of the effects of the Belém do Pará Convention were to come from a *cis* man (who does not belong to a group that structurally suffers gender violence and is not in a situation of social vulnerability) *ceteris paribus* it would have no basis except from a notion of formal equality. On the other hand, if we show that *trans* people suffer de facto gender-based violence to a similar or greater degree than *cis* women, the claim for including them in the special protection system designed to combat such violence would be justified, since the distinction in treatment based on sex-gender (between *cis* and *trans* women) would not be based on factual inequality between them, and would constitute a form of discrimination.

IV. The Dispute over the Interpretation of Legal Categories by feminism as a Conclusion

Against this background, the dissenting votes of Judge Odio Benito defy the logic behind the legal establishment of rights and special protections for some subjects known to be in a situation of vulnerability and the antisubordination paradigm that sustains the legal provision of so-called suspicious classification.[77] In her votes, especially the one issued in the *Vicky Hernandez* case, Odio Benito insists on a positionaccording to which the subject of protection for the law is the "woman" *qua* "female," by *the mere fact of being a woman.*[78] Nevertheless, this interpretation is not only regressive in the face of the rights achieved by feminism,[79] but also conservative of a binary gender system,[80] oppressive for those who challenge it and who also suffer patriarchal discrimination. Her interpretation does not seek to understand the situation of subordination based on gender structurally but to establish characteristics as "inherent" to some people (individually) and, from there, to draw legal consequences.[81]

[77] See Balkin and Siegel, "The American Civil Rights Tradition."

[78] IACtHR, *Partially Dissenting Opinion of Judge Elizabeth Odio Benito*, ¶ 9.

[79] That seek to eliminate gender differentiations. As Gloria Steinem expressed: "*A gender-equal society would be one where the word 'gender' does not exist: where everyone can be themselves.*"

[80] By binary gender system is meant the construction of sex-gender as two opposing and exhaustive categories: masculine and feminine; male and female. For some feminists, this system is not only factually wrong but also problematic and dangerous. It is problematic in that it naturalizes these categories, invisibilizing or excluding other identities. It is dangerous because it can rely on other false binaries such as public/private, personal/political, universal/particular, equality/difference, and can solidify hierarchies of power and identity. Rebecca Kuperberg and Haley Norris, "Are Quotas Feminist? A Theoretical Approach" (June 8, 2017) (unpublished manuscript), https://ecpr.eu/Events/Event/PaperDetails/33157 (last visited June 26, 2024).

[81] When it should be the other way around. Since sex regulation is a legal and not a medical matter, recognition of gender identity should not depend on the opinions of medical science, which cannot determine the scope of fundamental rights. Sara Bengtson et al., "Christine Goodwin v the United Kingdom," in *Feminist Judgments in International Law*, ed. Loveday Hodson and Troy Lavers (Oxfordshire, UK: Hart, 2019) at 181, 185.

On the contrary, an interpretation faithful to the causes that gave rise to the codification of special rights and protections must be progressive, situated, open, and possibilistic.[82] That is why the categories on which it is based must be "explicitly tentative, relational and unstable."[83] A human rights protection system has to comprehend how social hierarchies operate in different contexts and historical moments to recognize people who are suffering different oppressions and, at the same time, try to dismantle the set of stigmas, prejudices, stereotypes, and violence that are operating against them and that maintain such a situation of domination.[84]

In this sense, *cis* ("biological") and *trans* women suffer patriarchal gender violence. And although the manifestations of such violence are not identical (not even among *cis* women), the system that produces them is the same and is the one that both feminists and international instruments for the protection of rights fight against. This was the understanding of the IACtHR in the judgment examined here, which, following an evolutionary interpretation,[85] uses the Belém do Pará Convention to identify the type of violence and to advance a comprehensive response for those who are in a situation of suffering it while recognizing intersectionality and moving away from a binary conception of gender.[86] This interpretation is the one that maximizes the protection and guarantee of rights, being the most favorable to the individual (according to the pro personae principle of interpretation).[87]

Thus, the significant contribution of the judgment of the IACtHR in *Vicky Hernández v. Honduras*, in line with inclusive feminism, is that it makes it possible to overcome the limits presented by the normative systems of the protection of rights. If not interpreted progressively, these systems can hinder the emancipatory claims of those who do not "fit" perfectly into their assumptions, even when they suffer the vulnerabilities foreseen. Independence of the subject of legal protection from the political struggle that gave rise to it would frustrate the dismantling of a system of oppression that reinvents itself every day.

By contrast, a progressive, intersectional, and nonessentialist interpretation accepts that the political subject who fights for human rights (in any of its

[82] See Robin West, *Progressive Constitutionalism* (Durham, NC: Duke University Press, 1994) 216, 275–276.
[83] Harris, "Race and Essentialism in Feminist Legal Theory," 586.
[84] Fredman, *Discrimination Law*, esp. 28 et seq.
[85] This was the understanding of the IACtHR, *Vicky Hernández*, esp. ¶ 133.
[86] Ibid., ¶ 69.
[87] As Undurraga points out, quoting IACtHR, in *Atala Riffo*, gender "must be interpreted in the perspective of the most favorable option for the individual and the evolution of fundamental rights in contemporary international law." Undurraga, "Transformative Gender Equality in the Inter-American System of Human Rights," 244.

manifestations, including the feminist) will always be dynamic and "emergent" and, consequently, that the law and the positivized rights will be in the rearguard of the struggles for recognition and, therefore, subject to questioning and a permanent need for change.[88] Hence the need for this type of evolutionary interpretation of positivized rights, one that is responsive to the interpellation that feminisms are making to legal systems (including those of international protection).

The fact that the majority of the IACtHR has followed this interpretation is a significant step forward for inter-American human rights law, but also for the understanding of the law itself, from below, in a feminist and transformative perspective.[89] In this sense, it challenges the rest of the national and international legal systems to adapt to the historical moments in which they operate and strengthens the transformative agenda proposed by inclusive feminisms—a transformation that, if taken seriously, will shatter the stability of legal systems as we know them: essentialist and anchored in the hierarchization of binary sexual difference.

As Harris highlights, while "[e]ssentialism is intellectually easy, because the dominant culture is essentialist," represents "emotional safety" for those who embrace it, and, above all, offers women "the opportunity to play all-too-familiar power games both among themselves and with men," it is at the expense of the possibility of social transformation.[90] On the contrary, a feminist agenda must necessarily leave these "comfortable places," be inclusive, and advance transformative interpretations that ultimately have the potential to collapse the entire legal system anchored both in the conception of the masculinist subject and in the binary artifice of sex-gender, which maintains and reproduces gender violence in all its dimensions. The challenge is not a minor one. It implies destabilizing basic assumptions of law; it forces us to rethink legal categories, methodologies of adjudication, and remedies to achieve the objectives of social justice and equality, but even more, it invites us to imagine a world without hierarchies, that is, without gender.

[88] Enrique Dussel, *Hacia una filosofía política crítica* (Brussels: Desclée de Brouwer, 2001), 151–152.

[89] As Balakrishnan Rajagopal, *International Law from Below. Development, Social Movements and Third World Resistance* (Cambridge: Cambridge University Press, 2003) 271, shows, "The place-based praxis of social movements has emerged as an important site of re/formulation and transformation of the space-based global legal discourse."

[90] Harris, "Race and Essentialism in Feminist Legal Theory," 605–606.

12
Democracy, Legitimacy, and Authority in International Courts

Roberto Gargarella

I. Introduction

If, for more than two centuries, local courts have faced difficulties justifying their legitimacy and authority within a democracy, international courts face the same kind of difficulties but multiplied. There are serious problems of justification, as in the first case, but now aggravated. I shall explain in Section II below what the democratic problem is, and why it is particularly serious in the case of international courts. Subsequently, I shall critically examine issues related to the legitimacy and authority of international courts. I am interested in showing, in this regard, that the dominant models concerning the relationship between international tribunals and local authorities are deeply flawed. For the critical examination of this and other questions, I shall adopt, as an evaluative viewpoint, the perspective of a dialogical or conversational conception of democracy.[1]

II. The Democratic Problem

The *democratic problem* faced by local and international courts arises from the place these tribunals occupy in the interpretation of democratic norms. The problem could be presented as follows. First, the Constitutional and Conventional norms we are considering here must be interpreted at the time of their application and enforcement. This is so both because of the difficulties inherent in the "natural" (and "technical") language used by the law (subject to ambiguities, vagueness, gaps, etc.) and due to the general character and value content of many of the main concepts to which our constitutions and treaties are committed (i.e., "dignity," "equality," and "freedom of expression").

[1] Roberto Gargarella, *The Law as a Conversation Among Equals* (Cambridge: Cambridge University Press, 2022); Mark Tushnet, "Dialogic Judicial Review," *Arkansas Law Review* 61, no. 2 (2009): 205.

Roberto Gargarella, *Democracy, Legitimacy, and Authority in International Courts* In: *Latin American International Law in the Twenty-First Century*. Edited by: Alejandro Chehtman, Alexandra Huneeus, and Sergio Puig, Oxford University Press.
DOI: 10.1093/9780197754016.003.0012

Second, in the context of plural and democratic societies, the task of legal interpretation triggers profound, reasonable, and perhaps insoluble controversies. These controversies relate to what Jeremy Waldron aptly described as "the fact of disagreement" (which is, as John Rawls would say, a reasonable disagreement between reasonable people, not a disagreement of whim or lack of understanding). In other words, in the framework of our democratic and "multicultural" societies, the fact is that we will routinely face very profound and perhaps unresolvable disagreements about the appropriate or "just" way to interpret the existing law.[2]

The third point in this story is the one that "triggers" the democratic problem referred to. The democratic problem emerges when an elite of judges—who, to begin with, are not democratically elected or democratically removed from office (i.e., by regular vote)—comes to occupy the decisive place in the resolution of such interpretative controversies. As a result, everything that is legally important ultimately comes to depend on how those officials interpret the law (i.e., one possible interpretation of the right of "liberty" may require the enforcement of an abortion law, but another possible reading of the same term may require the repeal of that law). In short, if—within a democratic society marked by the "fact of disagreement"—it is not the citizens themselves, or their political representatives, who finally interpret and decide what the law is. That community may, in fact, become dominated by a few or governed heteronomously. This is so since the effective content of its most important norms depends on (comes under the control of) what is finally decided by a small group of public officials, who are not democratically elected by the citizenry or politically accountable to it. This result, it seems clear, is highly questionable from many points of view, including one particularly relevant in the context of this text, namely, *democratic self-government.* In fact, as members of a democratic community, we have reason to assume that our rules and institutions aim to facilitate or make such self-government possible (which is denied, in fact, when we lose control and decision-making over everything that matters to us).

In the previous lines, I briefly introduced the "democratic problem," trying to explain the reasons for its emergence. At this point, I would like to mention, also briefly, a normative issue, bound to play a crucial role in the argument advanced in this chapter. I refer to how to define the idea of "democracy"—what conception do we have of it, when we speak of a "democratic problem." Thinking correctly about this problem can take us too far, so—in what follows—I will content myself with just saying the following. The idea of democracy that seems to lie behind many of our institutions and many of our studies on such institutions is a simple idea (perhaps a too simple or simplistic idea) that reduces democracy

[2] John Rawls, *Political Liberalism* (New York: Columbia University Press, 1993); Jeremy Waldron, *Law and Disagreement* (Oxford: Oxford University Press, 1999).

to *majority rule*. In its crudest form, this view reduces democracy to periodic elections. However, in some more sophisticated (less common versions), it may also refer to other fundamental liberal components of democracy, such as due process and freedom of expression.[3] This conception—let me call it *dominant* or *minimalist* conception—is too simple, but it suffices to understand most of the discussions that take place on the matter: why we speak of a "countermajoritarian difficulty,"[4] why certain forms of exercise of judicial review can be deemed "offensive" for democracy,[5] or why international organizations in general, and international courts in particular, are affected by a democratic problem.

In any case, I believe that this dominant conception of democracy, although adequately descriptive of our prevalent practice, does not deserve to be the one that guides our critical reflections on the matter. For this reason, I will present a summary of an alternative vision about how to define "democracy," which I consider more plausible and, at the same time, compatible with many of our most meditated considerations on the issue: *a dialogic perspective*. I understand that in a democratic community, the public decisions that affect it must result from profound agreements among citizens, which require "conversation among equals."[6] By this, I mean inclusive public debates, in which "all the potentially affected" are involved as much and as intensely as possible.[7] This is both for *reasons of authorship or self-government* (in a democracy, we must be, in a relevant or nontrivial sense, the "authors" of the decisions and rules that are to be applied to us) and, for *epistemic reasons*, linked to the impartiality or justice of the decision at stake.[8] To achieve those ends, we must implement an interactive process (of democratic dialogue) among the decision-makers or between the decision-makers and their constituents. It is for these reasons, as I understand it, that we consider—in general and in principle—the decisions of political bodies to be more democratic—and thus more legitimate in democratic terms—than the decisions of the courts. That is also why we believe that something important happens, in terms of the legitimacy of the decision, when the citizenry intervenes in some relevant way in constructing that decision. It is also for this very reason—I assume—that,

[3] Robert Dahl, *Polyarchy* (New Haven, CT: Yale University Press, 1972).

[4] Alexander Bickel, *The Least Dangerous Branch: The Supreme Court at the Bar of Politics* (New Haven, CT: Yale University Press, 1962).

[5] Waldron, *Law and Disagreement*.

[6] Gargarella, "The Law as a Conversation."

[7] Jurgen Habermas, *Between Facts and Norms* (Cambridge, MA: MIT Press, 1996); Jon Elster (ed.), *Deliberative Democracy* (Cambridge: Cambridge University Press, 1998); Carlos Nino, *The Ethics of Human Rights* (Oxford: Oxford University Press, 1991).

[8] I assume here, with John Stuart Mill or Robert Dahl, that each individual is the "best judge" of his own interests. Therefore, the intervention of each of them is fundamental to ensure that the decision made is not unduly biased in favor of some or against others—or in ignorance of their claims and their value. John Stuart Mill, *On Liberty* (London: Dover Publications, [1859] 2003); Robert Dahl, *Democracy and Its Critics* (New Haven, CT: Yale University Press, 1989).

when faced with certain fundamental decisions for the community, we resort to plebiscites.[9]

Of course, as is often the case, the picture is much more complex than the one just presented. One could argue, for instance, that it is unfair to suggest that members of the judiciary lack (entirely) democratic legitimacy to make the decisions they do. It may be fairer to say that their "democratic credentials" are considerably weaker than those of political officials (I will return to this point later). In addition, one could argue that achieving a "correct," "fair," or "proper" interpretation of the law (for the moment, I will take these terms as synonyms) does not exclusively require democratic legitimacy in the interpreter: several other competences (technical skills, personal honesty, etc.) are also needed. This is true. However, I am trying to stress that we must be able to answer the democratic challenge. And this is so because the core of our public disagreements (e.g., how to define the precise meaning of, or requirements derived from, the constitutional requirement of "equality" in a case concerning social rights) is usually moral (linked to the deep agreements we have, or can reach, on the matter) rather than technical. And it is we ourselves—democratic citizens in a multicultural community—who must have a crucial role in resolving such disagreements.[10]

III. On the (Particularly Weak) Democratic Legitimacy of International Tribunals

In the previous section, I referred to the "democratic critique" of the role of courts in interpreting the law. In this section, I shall suggest that this "democratic problem" becomes stronger when referring to international courts than to local courts. More precisely, I shall maintain that international tribunals confront particularly serious problems in regard to *democratic legitimacy*. Now, before going into the details of my view, let me make two clarifications. The first is that, in what follows, when I refer to international courts, I will be thinking basically of the Inter-American Court of Human Rights, although my argument will also be applicable—I assume—to other tribunals, such as the European Court of Human Rights, as I will try to demonstrate.

[9] For example, Brexit, the Colombian Peace Treaty, etc. See Alviar and Betancur, chapter 27, in this volume).

[10] Likewise, the idea that, in our societies, judges retain the "final" interpretation of the content of law can also be challenged. One of the best responses to a common version of the democratic argument—the critique of the "counter-majoritarian nature of judicial review"—was the one offered by Robert Dahl and, more recently, by Barry Friedman. Robert Dahl, "Decision-Making in a Democracy: The Supreme Court as a National Policy-Maker," *Journal of Public Law* 6 (Fall 1957): 279, 293–294; Barry Friedman, "Dialogue and Judicial Review," *Michigan Law Review* 91 (1993): 577.

The second clarification is conceptual and relates to the definition of the idea of "democratic legitimacy."[11] It seems clear that, to carry out the evaluative task that I propose and determine whether a group of judges or a particular tribunal lacks democratic legitimacy, many factors must be taken into consideration. Indeed, these factors include different elements that are directly related to the specific features of the judicial process and—more significantly perhaps—the personal qualities of the judges: their honesty, their technical capacities, their geographical origin (i.e., what country they are from), some of the features of their identity (i.e., race, gender), and so on. But here, I shall assume that the "democratic legitimacy" of the courts is related to different "dialogic" elements that we may also want to consider.

Thus, we may reasonably demand that the tribunal be more directly related to the community where the case occurred. For instance, we may want those judges to know the details of the case intimately, and also to know what the community feels about it. In addition, it may also be important for all of us—members of a democratic community—that these judges, like all of us, "carry" the weight of their decisions. It would be a problem, in this sense, if the judges could simply "impose" a "difficult" political mandate and then disregard the consequences of their actions, which will fall exclusively on the shoulders of the affected community. More specifically, it may be relevant, from this perspective, that the mandate be "constructed" in a two-way "process" of conversation between the members of the court and the affected community. To put it differently, from this perspective, it would be considered a serious problem, which would affect the legitimacy of the mandate, if it was adopted by a distant "elite of experts" and thus (came to be seen as) "*imposed from above*." In sum, from the perspective of the "dialogic" view that I defend, making "democratically legitimate" decisions may require a *process of construction*, based on the *frequent, continuous interaction* of citizens and public authorities, which should be conducive to the formation of deep and broad social agreements.

Now, when we examine how international tribunals are organized, how their members are chosen, what requirements are established as indispensable to reach the magistracy, what the procedures for evaluating a case are, and so forth, the legitimacy problems that affect those international courts become apparent.

[11] Max Weber, a crucial reference in legitimacy studies, provided an essentially "descriptive" definition of the term, which he basically related to the beliefs or faith of the participants in a certain political regime, based on which they accept the decisions of the authority. Weber famously alluded to three fundamental sources of legitimacy: tradition, charisma, and rationality (of the law). This view differs from the "normative" approaches to the term, which I will be thinking about here. This, in particular, in relation to the positions advocated in his works by John Rawls, where the American philosopher associates the idea of (political) legitimacy with the justification (or not) in the use of the coercive powers of the State. John Rawls, *A Theory of Justice* (Cambridge, MA: Harvard University Press, 1971).

I would suggest that, at the international level, there seems to be a strong neglect of everything related to the question of democratic legitimacy (the democratic legitimacy of its members, of the process, of the decision to be taken, etc.): as if the "democratic problem" were not too important, or as if the questions related to democratic legitimacy could easily be dissolved. Apparently, for the courts, the problem in question is resolved by ensuring rigorous compliance with the rules of due process and/or by securing certain technical and personal qualities in the magistrates (as if such attributes were determinant for the achievement of impartiality, within the framework of plural societies). Probably for such reasons, both international courts require their members to be distinguished by their personal, technical, and moral qualities ("jurists of the highest moral authority," as stated in Article 4 of the Statute of the Inter-American Court of Human Rights). In addition, and also relevant for our purposes, both courts want all, or almost all, of the countries in the region affected by their decisions to have a "representative" on the court(!). Note, in this respect, that the American court is composed of seven judges proposed by the member states (where no country can have more than one judge on the court), while the European court is composed of several judges identical to that of the states parties to the Convention: one for each of them. These facts alone are interesting because they suggest the presence of an (interesting but surprising) argument. According to this argument, the impartiality or justice of a judicial decision appears to be decisively tied to the rules of due process in force and some personal characteristics of the judges (their honesty, their technical capacity, etc.), including, in a prominent way, their country of origin.[12] The point is important for our purposes: it seems to be very common, within the community of international lawyers, to consider the (geographical) "closeness" of judges to citizens—the (physical) *distance* that exists between the tribunal and the affected community—to be fundamental; in fact, it is sometimes a sufficient condition to ensure the impartiality of the court.

Reflecting upon the relevant "legal standing," the standing necessary to call the accused to account for what he did, Antony Duff has reached a point similar to the one I want to stress here. For him, only the relevant community, in his words, "the relevant public," the relevant "we" has such standing. The legitimacy of a process that calls someone to answer for their alleged wrongdoings becomes thus dependent both on the procedural fairness of the judicial process and on the court's democratic authority to call the offender to answer. In other words, it does not suffice to have fair and well-prepared judges who follow all the

[12] All of this seems counterintuitive, at least concerning the usual ways in which the law is publicly thought of and justified: we are usually told that our legal "luck" or "destiny," as citizens, depends (and must depend) on what the law "says" rather than on the "will" of anyone, including the will of whoever reads it. This—this "nondependence" on anyone's (discretionary) will—is what we traditionally call "rule of law."

traditional rules of due process (rights to the lawyers, guarantees to the accused, etc.): it also matters to know who those judges are, whether they belong or not to the affected community, whether they are part of the "relevant we," whether the tribunal has strong ties with the community with which it interacts, and so forth. A crucial question in this respect is, in Duff's words, the following: "I might be guilty, but who are you to try me?"[13] Notably, Duff developed this view in contrast to the idea that any state or international organization could judge violations committed in other states, as long as a *champagne-quality due process* is put in place.[14] Against what authors like David Luban maintained, Duff replied that the fairness of the process is essential but that it is also essential for the process to be conducted by those who have the authority to do it (I will return to the question of democratic authority in Section VI below).[15]

IV. Comparing the Democratic Legitimacy of National and International Courts

At this point, we can compare national courts with international courts regarding their democratic legitimacy. Of course, national courts function differently in different countries. Depending on the case, the members of each of those courts may be elected by different procedures (some through indirect systems, others directly by the citizenry), and those magistrates may remain in office for various periods as well (e.g., some for life, others for the duration of their "good conduct," and others for fixed terms of about ten years). However, and in relation to the (thickness of the) "link" that relates courts and the affected community, one finds immediately some critical differences between national and international tribunals. Usually, the citizens of a democratic community have reasons to recognize themselves as much more linked to the judges of their community than to the judges of an international court (in other words, the link with such judges may be weak, but still much more intense than the bond that relates them to the judges of an international court). These (national) judges belong to the same culture; they participate in the same political debates; and they tend to be directly or personally affected by their decisions. In sum, for obvious and perhaps nowadays unavoidable reasons (e.g., the absence of formal institutions for

[13] Antony Duff, "I Might Be Guilty, but You Can't Try Me: Estoppel and Other Bars to Trial," *Ohio State Journal of Criminal Law* 1 (2003–2004): 245–259.

[14] David Luban, "A Theory of Crimes Against Humanity," *Yale Journal of International Law* 29 (2004): 85.

[15] Antony Duff, "Authority and Responsibility in International Criminal Law," in *The Philosophy of International Law* (New York: Oxford University Press, 2010), 589–604, 590. In his view, the adulterer's wife (or maybe his Church) can have the relevant *standing* for reproaching him for his conduct, but not his neighbors, even if they managed to organize a fair process.

global democratic governance), judges of international courts enjoy much less democratic legitimacy than judges of local courts.

One possible reply would say that the above criticism—on the weak democratic legitimacy of international tribunals—is based on ignorance of the effective dynamics of the creation and application of international law, and on the underestimation of the local processes that give authority, and thus legitimacy, to the decisions of international bodies. Victor Abramovich, for example, an expert in international human rights law and former member of the Inter-American Commission, acknowledges the relevance of some of the criticisms that are endorsed here, as well as other similar ones.[16] However, he refers to the existence of a broader practice through which local communities express their political and democratic agreement with the decisions made by international courts.[17] Thus, for him, an "effective practice" of interaction (not dialogic, as he acknowledges) exists between local authorities and international courts, which would help build the latter's legitimacy. For example, a country proposes and appoints its own member to the international tribunal, and it is responsible for the political approval and enforcement of human rights treaties such as those that the cited tribunals guard, and its own judicial (and, eventually, political) organs tend to support, explicitly or implicitly, with their decisions, the decisions of the international tribunals.

Now, despite its importance, this view also seems vulnerable from different sides. To begin, the fact that my country, for example, nominates—or, in the best case, appoints—a member of the international tribunal of the case says little or nothing interesting about the effective link that unites my community of belonging (not to say, "oneself, as a citizen") with the international tribunal of the case. It may well happen, of course, that some members of the current government of my country (a government that, perhaps, I do not support or directly repudiate) select a candidate that ends up occupying a (minority) position within an international court.[18] However, it seems odd to derive, from those

[16] Víctor Abramovich, "Editorial," *Nueva Doctrina Penal* B (2007): 1–18.

[17] He admits, for example, the lack of publicity of the decisions of international organizations; the insufficient participation of local actors in this field; or the existing deficit in the critique and systematization of international doctrine. However, he finally resists those views, by stating that such criticisms tend to be based on ignorance of the dynamics of the creation of international law, and on the underestimation of local processes tending to give greater weight to such international jurisdiction. Abramovich can support his position—and, in part, he does so—by invoking decisions, at different levels, that would mark the political commitment of the local community to what international tribunals decide.

[18] I refer to this, not to mention what the dimension of the problem is, if one thinks about that idea of "voice," in the terms (even if they are ideal and abstract) in which that idea is thought, from positions more seriously committed to a crucial ideal that is omnipresent here: the ideal of democratic self-government. I mean, the idea of democratic self-government appears completely frustrated if one thinks about it the way Jean Jacques Rousseau thought about it, when he said that the law should speak with our own voice. Jean-Jacques Rousseau, *The Social Contract* (London: Wordsworth, [1762] 1998); or—more contemporaneously—if one considers, as Antony Duff does, that self-government

facts, the conclusion that a citizen of my country has, in a nontrivial sense, a "voice" within that international tribunal. We can say similar things about all the other elements that Abramovich highlights in his analysis as forming an essential part of the "actual practice" of our societies—an essential part of the interaction between international courts and local authorities.

Before concluding this section, let me add the following. From the standpoint of the dialogic perspective that I defend, it seems clear that the practical possibilities of (conversation) interaction between local citizens and international tribunals are much lower than those that may eventually occur at the regional level. This claim may be supported, at least provisionally, by numerous impressionistic facts, such as the following: almost no citizen of our countries even knows the names and faces of the "international judges" who have jurisdiction over them, nor do they know anything about how those magistrates are selected, nor do they know anything about how that tribunal works, and they have not even—perhaps—ever heard about the very existence and jurisdiction of such tribunals. All of this is so for various reasons, which are more acute or serious at the international level. Among those reasons, I would mention the following two: first, citizens encounter significant obstacles to reaching an international tribunal,[19] and second, on those unusual occasions when they do get to the court, they lack the appropriate institutional means to interact with their international judicial authorities (challenge them, question them, talk to them, correct them). The difficulties of the case—let me put it in these terms—are extremely serious in terms of democratic self-government (and all of this—to make matters worse—when judges have so much discretion in the face of such demands, and so much time to respond to them, in the exceptional cases that they do so).

V. From Democratic Legitimacy to the Authority of International Courts: The "Deference" and the "Interference" Approach

In the previous section, we looked primarily at some debates on the democratic legitimacy of international tribunals. I examined rather contrasting (or, at least, different in a relevant sense) approaches to the question. Some of these views tie

is not realized when an important part of the community has reason to believe that "the voice of the law (the voice through which the community speaks to it) to its members in the language of shared values) finds it an alien voice that is not and could not be theirs." Antony Duff, *Punishment, Communication, and Community* (Oxford: Oxford University Press, 2001), 195–196.

[19] There seems to be widespread agreement, within the literature, about the seriousness of these difficulties for acceding to international courts.

the idea of legitimacy too closely to the *formal characteristics of the legal process, and—more significantly—to the personal characteristics of the court's members* (their country of origin, their honesty, their technical knowledge, etc.). By contrast, other approaches—like the one I argue for here—consider that the legitimacy in question relates, above all, to a *process of democratic construction or dialogue* between the international court and the affected community (and thus challenges the legitimacy of international tribunals, because of the kind of neglect or disengagement they display, in that respect). In all cases, however, the connection between such (normative) *conceptions of legitimacy* and *the authority assigned to, demanded, or recognized in the tribunals* becomes apparent. This is precisely the point I want to stress here: we are interested in reflections on the democratic legitimacy of international tribunals because we know that their greater or lesser legitimacy has an impact (it must have an impact) on the authority they have (and thus on the tribunals' right to demand respect for their decisions, and also on the reasons citizens have for adhering to or questioning the value or justification of such decisions).

At present, two contrasting approaches coexist regarding the authority of international courts in relation to local courts and public officials. One approach seems prevalent in the European context, while the other appears to be still dominant at the level of the Inter-American Court. Let me then distinguish between these two divergent views on the authority of international tribunals.

The first approach, which I am going to call the *Deferential approach*, maintains that—in principle and as a general rule—the European Court must assume a "deferential" role with local authorities. This view, as we shall see, appears in line with the predominant doctrine on the "margin of appreciation." On the other hand, I will refer to a different approach—the *Interfering approach*—that, for various reasons, attributes to international human rights courts the power to severely challenge the decisions adopted by the local political authorities. As we shall see, many reasons explain these two contrasting approaches, which are so different. However, there is one reason that, in addition to being very important, occupies a central place within the concerns of this article, namely, the democratic argument, understood according to the dominant or minimalist conception of democracy.[20] Let me then briefly present these two approaches.

[20] Another element that should not be dismissed, at the time of explaining the prevalence of the "interfering" approach in Latin America, relates to the influence of "traditional" legal doctrines—of an elitist type—(doctrines linked to "natural law" or of "Thomist" roots). These doctrines—I assume—contributed to "detach" the legal authority of the courts from any democratic consideration. Carlos Nino, *Introducción al Análisis del Derecho* (Buenos Aires: Ariel, 1983).

Let me first explore the deferential approach, which I will relate to the margin of appreciation doctrine. I would say that this principle came to confront and respond to the difficulties that appear in international legal systems characterized by multiple and overlapping authorities—situations of institutional pluralism. In those contexts, this alternative approach provides a prima facie case for deference to judicial lower-level authorities (typically, the authority of member states' institutions) to honor the value of federalism.

In Europe, the margin of appreciation doctrine resulted from an extended fear of member states against the centralization of powers.[21] The doctrine is concerned with the exercise of jurisdiction by the European Court of Human Rights. Developed by the European Court of Human Rights, it establishes a methodology for judicial scrutiny of decisions by national authorities. It requires judges to have a certain degree of deference toward decisions of local authorities. According to its rationale, national authorities should enjoy certain discretion in executing their international law obligations.[22]

The European Court developed the contours of the margin of appreciation doctrine in the case *Handyside v. the United Kingdom*,[23] where it stated:

> [I]t is not possible to find in the domestic law of the Contracting States a uniform conception of morals. The view taken by their respective laws...varies from time to time and from place to place . . . By reason of their direct and continuous contact with the vital forces of their countries, State authorities are in principle in a better position than the international judge to give an opinion on the exact content of these requirements as well as on the "necessity" of a "restriction" or "penalty" intended to meet them.

The Court also maintained that, in its decisions on the matter, it would consider a diversity of factors, including the nature of the right in place, the sensitivity of the issue, the aims pursued by the norm, and the existence and evolution of a European consensus concerning the topic.[24] Also, in *The Sunday Times v. The United Kingdom*,[25] the Court manifested that the margin of appreciation required "a just balance between the protection of the general interest of the

[21] Federico Fabbrini, "The Margin of Appreciation and the Principle of Subsidiarity: A Comparison," iCourts Working Paper Series, no. 15 (2015), https://ssrn.com/abstract=2552542.

[22] In this way, also, judges recognize the existence of "normative flexibility," thus preserving "a significant zone of legality within which states are free to operate." Yuval Shany, "Towards a General Margin of Appreciation Doctrine in International Law?" *European Journal of International Law* 16, no. 5 (2005): 907–940, 910.

[23] 5493/72 [1976] ECHR 5 (December 7, 1976).

[24] See also No. 44362/04 *Dickson v. The United Kingdom* [2007] ECHR §78.

[25] No. 6538/74 [1979] ECHR § 61, A30.

community and the respect due to fundamental human rights while attaching particular importance to the latter."

Trying to justify the adoption of this doctrine, the Court offered different reasons, including the fact that the states are primarily responsible for the protection of the rights defined by the European system and the idea that, in controversial issues concerning fundamental rights, local authorities are better situated to give due weight to relevant factors and decide how to deal with conflictive situations.[26]

Let us now explore the meaning and implications of the interfering approach, which is still enormously influential in Latin America. To examine the topic, it may be worth paying attention to a few basic facts concerning the origins and development of the Inter-American Human Rights System (IAHRS) in the region.

The IAHRS emerged in 1948 with the enactment of the Organization of American States (OAS) Charter, which defined the creation of the Inter-American Commission of Human Rights and the American Declaration on the Rights of Man and Citizen. The Commission began to function only after more than a decade (in 1959). The OAS would establish the Inter-American Court only in 1978, to enforce the provisions of the Inter-American Convention on Human Rights. Since the 1970s and for many years, the IAHRS, and the Commission in particular, appeared as a direct response to the wave of extreme authoritarianism and massive human rights crimes that dominated the region at the time.[27]

Experts tend to agree about how to organize and examine the system's evolution. This periodization would first show a long period when the IAHRS was fundamentally dedicated to responding to the brutality of the military regimes that prevailed within the region. Jorge Contesse, for example, considers that this first period began in 1978, "with the entry into force of the (Inter American Court), and ended around 1990, as the authoritarian regimes of member states lost power."[28] For him, "addressing non-democratic member states, the Inter-American Court established itself as a locus for rights protection and political integrity."[29] Decisive in this period was the very first decision of the Court, which

[26] Marisa Iglesias Vila, "Una Doctrina del Margen de Apreciación Estatal Para el CEDH: En Busca de un Equilibrio entre Democracia y Derechos en la Esfera Internacional," in *Derechos Humanos: Posibilidades Teóricas y Desafíos Prácticos*, Marisa Iglesias et al., 7 (Buenos Aires: Libraria, 2014).

[27] Alexandra Huneeus, "Courts Resisting Courts: Lessons from the Inter-American Court's Struggle to Enforce Human Rights," *University of Wisconsin Law School Legal Studies Research Paper Series*, no. 1168 (2011).

[28] Jorge Contesse, "Subsidiarity in Inter-American Human Rights Law," *Seminario en Latinoamérica de Teoría Constitucional y Política* (2015), 10 (manuscript on file with author), https://law.yale.edu/sites/default/files/documents/pdf/SELA15_Contesse_CV_Eng.pdf.

[29] Ibid.; see also Víctor Abramovich, "From Massive Violations to Structural Patterns: New Approaches and Classic Tensions in the Inter-American Human Rights System," *Sur International*

appeared in the case *Velásquez Rodríguez*, where the Court declared that Honduras had violated several provisions of the American Convention through an act of forced disappearance.[30]

The point is particularly important because this initial period defined the profile and general attitude of the Court and the character of the IAHRS. Contrary to what has been the common rule in Europe, the Court and the inter-American system, in general, assumed from the beginning an *interfering* or *interventionist* rather than a *deferential* position toward national governments. Its mission—it assumed—required strong interventions and declarations toward authoritarian regimes rather than a passive or complacent disposition. Those dispositions partially changed in subsequent years, but the general presumption seems to still be very much in line with this original approach.[31]

VI. Rejecting Pure Interfering or Deferential Approaches: The Depth and Breadth of Democracy

I believe the deferential and interfering approaches are both problematic, particularly if we examine them from a committed democratic perspective. Herein, I will adopt a dialogic standpoint for doing that critical analysis. However, before turning to it, I want to state the following. In the context of international tribunals discussed above, it is not unusual for cases and complaints related to the question of democracy to emerge. In other words, the democratic issue is not alien to the discourse of the international legal community or to the decisions of international courts. However, this situation does not deny that, in general, the

Journal of Human Rights 11 (2009): 6; Ariel Dulitzky, "The Inter-American Human Rights System Fifty Years Later: Time for Changes," *Quebec Journal of International Law*, special edition (2011): 127–164; Huneeus, "Courts Resisting Courts."

30 *Velásquez Rodríguez v. Honduras*, Judgment, Inter-Am. Ct. H.R. (ser. C) No. 4 (July 29, 1988).

31 In effect, and after the end of the Latin American authoritarian political wave, the IAHRS began to transcend the limits set during the first period. It was then assumed that it was time to go beyond the mere "protection" of human rights: it was now necessary to begin "promoting" those rights. Shortly afterward, these new commitments began to expand still more, to include, for instance, the defense of minority groups (typically, members of indigenous communities) whose rights were not adequately guaranteed by the new democracies. Contesse, "Subsidiarity in Inter-American Human Rights Law," 11–15; Dulitzky, "The Inter-American Human Rights System Fifty Years Later." These gradual political changes called, unquestionably, for a new profile and attitude in the Commission and the Court: What role should these institutions play when the political context in which they acted changed in the way it did? How were they supposed to decide when democratic, rather than dictatorial, governments characterized the region's landscape? Had the time arrived—as some doctrinaires suggested—for the IAHRS to adopt a deferential approach, as the one prevailing in Europe? These questions are now on the table, even though the general orientation of the system seems to be still related to its initial, interfering approach.

treatment these courts give to the democratic question tends to be quite superficial. This fact seems true both in Latin America[32] and in Europe.[33]

Not surprisingly, this rather superficial understanding of democracy is expressed in the deferential and interfering approaches. If anything explains their adoption, both in Europe and in Latin America, it is the minimalist reading of democracy that is assumed as obvious in each of these cases. This minimalist conception explains, first, why the idea of a margin of appreciation was so vigorously defended in Europe. In short, Europeans defended that view because they assumed that all European states that were part of the Union were democratic. The minimalist view also explains why the opposite tended to occur in Latin America. In short, Latin Americans defended the interfering approach because, at one point in history (when the Inter-American Court began to function), nondemocratic or authoritarian governments seemed to be present all around the region.[34]

[32] For instance, the Inter-American Court suggested that it would consider arguments related to the democratic principle in cases like *Yatama v. Nicaragua*, which was the first case decided by the court concerning democracy and political rights. More recently—and just to mention a few examples—the above approach also provided support to several decisions of the IACHR court, such as those aimed at protecting judicial independence from undue political interference (as in the *Apitz Barbera* or *Reverón Trujillo* cases in Venezuela, or *Quintana Coello* or *Camba Campos* in Ecuador); decisions such as those that proposed a broad interpretation of the rights of political participation (in cases such as *Castañeda Gutman*, related to popular participation through consultations, referendums, and plebiscites); or decisions such as those that affirmed a robust reading of freedom of expression, particularly protective of political criticism (in cases such as *Ríos, Perozo or Granier*, linked to restrictions on the media in Venezuela). See *Yatama v. Nicaragua*, Judgment, Inter-Am. Ct. H.R. (ser. C) No. 127 (2005); *Castañeda Gutman v. Mexico*, Judgment, Inter-Am. Ct. H.R. (ser. C.) No. 184 (2008); *Apitz Barbera et al. v. Venezuela*, Judgment, Inter-Am. Ct. H.R. (ser. C) No. 182 (2008); *Reverón Trujulli v. Venezuela*, Judgment, Inter-Am. Ct. H.R. (ser. C) No. 197 (2009); *Quintana Coello et al. v. Ecuador*, Judgment, Inter-Am. Ct. H.R. (ser. C) No. 266 (2013); *Camba Campos et al. v. Ecuador*, Judgment, Inter-Am. Ct. H.R. (ser. C) No. 268 (2013); *Ríos et al. v. Venezuela*, Inter-Am. Ct. H.R. (ser. C). No. 194 (2009); *Perozo et al. v. Venezuela*, Inter-Am. Ct. H.R. (ser. C), No. 195 (2009); *Granier et al. v. Venezuela*, Judgment, Inter-Am. Ct. H.R. (ser. C) No. 293 (2015).

[33] Similarly, the democratic principle played a certain role in the elaboration of the European doctrine in the area. Recall, for example, the criteria invoked by the European Court to give content to the notion of "margin of appreciation." The tribunal claimed that it was necessary to defer to decisions by state members, given their "direct and continuous contact with the vital forces of their countries." Seemingly, this geographical proximity put "State authorities . . . in a better position than the international judge to give an opinion on the exact content" of a particular right. On some occasions, the European Court made more reasonable but unduly brief and marginal references to the democratic principle. For example, see *Karatas v. Turkey*, App. No. 23168/94 [1999] IV Eur. Ct. H.R. 81, at 120 (Joint Partly Dissenting Opinion of Judges Wildhaber, Pastor Ridruejo, Costa and Baka).

[34] According to some scholars, it is time for Latin America to change its dominant view in the area, moving from the prevalent interfering paradigm—which was appropriate in times of widespread authoritarianism—to a more deferential one. For Jorge Contesse, for example "the principle of subsidiarity provides both a theoretical and practical foundation to determine how much authority a state should be granted in the regulation of human rights affairs." Contesse, "Subsidiarity in Inter-American Human Rights Law," 24. Below, I shall claim that the option for a different, now opposite, approach of this kind is also wrong.

Let me now turn to the dialogic democratic perspective and try to evaluate both models—the deferential and the interfering—from this standpoint. This dialogic perspective suggests that we ought to focus our attention on how the democratic decision-making *process* worked—or, more precisely, how the "conversation between equals" advanced and to what degree. For instance, it demands we pay attention to the degree of "thickness" of the public conversation developed in the decision-making process, in its different aspects: social inclusion, public deliberation, transparency, equality, and so on. Not surprisingly, this perspective rejects the "fixed" and "all-or-nothing" positions that both the deferential and interfering approaches seem to assume. Again, from this approach, what matters is something else: not, for example, to define whether the country that passed the examined law—say, Italy or Guatemala—is a democratic country, but whether decision X, taken at such a time in place, by country C, was the result of a transparent, inclusive construction process, and so on (or not).

What role should international monitoring bodies assume in relation to local authorities, according to such a dialogic approach? As a general principle, oversight bodies should be respectful (deferential) to the decisions of each democratic community —in case they were dealing with (legal decisions passed by) actual democratic countries. This should be so, however, to the extent that such decisions effectively reflect the outcome of a "conversation among equals" (inclusive public discussion processes). By contrast, international tribunals should adopt a different position—closer to the interfering approach—in the case that the country in question is an authoritarian, nondemocratic, or weakly democratic country (one where the opposition is persecuted, freedom of expression is limited, political protests are repressed, etc.).

For such reasons, in my view, neither deferential nor interfering approaches are sufficiently persuasive, particularly in their more demanding or purest forms: they want to set fixed instructions for situations that deserve varying regulations—a more flexible approach—depending on specific circumstances. Compared to those views, I suggest, the democratic approach would seem more justifiable and reasonable in what it demands from courts. It proposes they approach different situations differently, paying particular attention to contextual variations. In particular, the dialogic approach requires us to focus on the depth and breadth of the social agreement behind each international conflict at stake. Let me clarify and illustrate my claim by taking two examples, one related to the Latin American context and the other associated with the European context.

One interesting Latin American case relates to the Amnesty Law passed in Uruguay. More precisely, I am referring, first, to the Amnesty offered by Uruguay's government as a response to the horrendous crimes committed by the last Uruguayan dictatorship during the 1970s—and also to the *Gelman* case (*Gelman v. Uruguay*), where the Inter-American Court challenged that legislative decision—a decision that, we should note, was ratified not just once but twice by the Uruguay citizenry, through two properly held popular consultations.[35] On that occasion, the Inter-American Court invalidated Uruguay's sovereign decision and dismissed the value of those two popular consultations (or, more precisely, the value of that remarkable process of collective discussion) in strong terms.[36] Concerning the two popular consultations held in Uruguay, for instance, it maintained:

> The fact that the Expiry Law of the State was approved in a democratic regime and further ratified or supported by the citizenry on two occasions, namely, through the exercise of direct democracy, does not automatically or by itself grant legitimacy under International Law. The participation of the public in relation with the law, . . ., should be considered, as an act attributable to the State that give rise to its international responsibility.[37]

Immediately afterward,[38] the Court elaborated and clarified its position on the matter by affirming:

> The bare existence of a democratic regime does not guarantee, *per se*, the permanent respect of International Law, including International Law of Human Rights, and which has also been considered by the Inter-American Democratic Charter. The democratic legitimacy of specific facts in a society is limited by the norms of protection of human rights recognized in international treaties, such as the American Convention.

What made the Inter-American Court's decision so objectionable, in that case, was the way the tribunal simply ignored the presence of a deep and ample social agreement concerning the questioned Amnesty Law in Uruguay. For those of us who defend the strong democratic character of that agreement, that law reflected an exceptional situation, worthy of deep respect: the Uruguayan people, collectively, had established their view on an extremely difficult topic after a

[35] I am referring to the law adopted in Uruguay, granting an amnesty to those involved in grave human rights violations during the military period. The discussion around the pardons included not only people in the streets, articles in favor and against the decision published in the leading newspapers, and debates on the TV, but also—and most significantly—two direct popular consultations carried out by the Uruguayan government. The first of them was conducted in April 1989 by referendum (as mandated in paragraph 2 of Article 79 of the Uruguayan Constitution). The second was held on October 25, 2009, through a general plebiscite (as described in subparagraph A of Article 331 of the Uruguayan Constitution), which put to popular vote a projected constitutional reform that would have nullified Articles 1–4 of the Expiry Law.

[36] *Gelman v. Uruguay*, Judgment, Inter-Am. Ct. H.R. (ser. C) No. 221 (2011).

[37] Ibid., ¶ 238.

[38] Ibid., ¶ 239.

careful, detailed, and widespread debate. In conclusion, the Inter-American Court should have made a different decision on the case, not because Latin American countries like Uruguay were now living in a new, postauthoritarian, democratic era, but rather because the decision under scrutiny was the result of a strong process of democratic deliberation. In other words, the Inter-American Court should not now adopt a blind rule of deference to guide its actions in the new democratic era. By contrast, it should keep its eyes open and pay special attention to those decisions, like the one under discussion in *Gelman*, where a democratic community produced an exceptionally democratic agreement.

Let us now move to the second example from the European context. I shall focus on a polemical and important case, namely, the case *Lautsi v. Italy*.[39] On that occasion, the European Court determined that the Italian regulation that established the mandatory presence of a crucifix in public schools, a regulation that dated from the 1920s, which was the fascist period in Italy, did not violate the rights of Mrs. Lautsi to educate her children according to their convictions. Among other arguments, the Court maintained that even though the Convention's requirements on religious freedom prohibited different kinds of indoctrination by member states, the presence of crucifixes in state-school classrooms was not in itself sufficient "to denote a process of indoctrination on the respondent State's part" thus establishing a breach of Article 2 of Protocol n. 1." Also, and more fundamentally, the Court relied on the doctrine of the "margins of appreciation," to claim that Italy's preference for a particular religion was related to the country's traditions and identity. Accordingly, the Court maintained that it would respect the state's decisions concerning the organization of the school environment—including, for instance, the place to be reserved for religion (again, as far as those decisions did not lead to a form of indoctrination). Crucifixes on the wall were thus described as "an essentially passive symbol."

Against what the European Court maintained in that case, there were many reasons for challenging the authority of the Italian regulation. Most crucially, some of these reasons were directly related to the democratic principle. For instance, one could reasonably claim, with Marisa Iglesias, that "the Italian regulation (had) a week democratic pedigree . . . coming from the 1920s fascist period . . . (had not) been confirmed by the legislature, nor assessed by Italy's constitutional court."[40] When we consider these facts, it makes little sense to invoke the "margin of appreciation" doctrine, as the European Court did, to defer to the democratic authority of member states. The democratic character of that regulation was, in fact, under question in the case.

[39] *Lautsi et al. v. Italy*, App. No. 30814/06, [2011] Eur. Ct. H.R.
[40] Iglesias, "Una Doctrina del Margen de Apreciación Estatal Para el CEDH," 32.

To put it briefly, my question would be the same for both the Latin American and European cases: Why should we allow, say, the deferential paradigm to prevail in those contexts? It would make sense to favor that paradigm in situations characterized by profound democratic agreements or, to be more realistic, in specific cases where we deal with ample and deep democratic agreements.[41] But we should not simply assume that stable democracies decide their fundamental problems in ways that are respectful, in a relevant way, of the democratic will of its members. One could suggest that what tends to prevail, both in Latin America and Europe, is the opposite, namely, elite agreements based on limited or absent public deliberation.

There is a continuum between the two: weakly democratic and strongly democratic decisions. Therefore, we should be prepared to focus on the *democratic pedigree* of the decision at stake, mainly by paying attention to the level of inclusion and discussion behind the decision under study.[12]

This more fine-tuned approach—it should be noted—relates to the one presented by Robert Spano, Judge of the European Court of Human Rights, in his article "Universality or Diversity of Human Rights? Strasbourg in the Age of Subsidiarity,"[42] written in response to another article, "The Universality of Human Rights," also presented by a member of the European Court, Lord Hoffman, in 2009.[43] In his initial text, Lord Hoffman admitted the importance of the existing concerns related to the weak legitimacy and democratic deficit of the international tribunals.[44] In response to those fears, Spano proposed a "qualitative and democracy-enhancing approach" to be applied in implementing the principle of subsidiarity and the margin of appreciation doctrine.[45]

[41] However, there are two kinds of issues that—I submit—would merit a very special, careful and separate scrutiny, namely, (1) procedural issues, that is, issues related to the "basic rules of the democratic game" (John Ely, *Democracy and Distrust* (Cambridge, MA: Harvard University Press, 1980); and (2) issues related to private morality. Both issues have usually been under attack in our very imperfect democracies. Consequently, we need to be always alert concerning, first, the attempt of prevailing authorities to perpetuate themselves in power through the manipulation or violation of the basic rules of the democratic game (i.e., by changing the basic rules of the game, while playing the game, without reaching first a broad agreement with the opposition forces). Second, we need to be attentive concerning the attempt of prevailing authorities to enforce one comprehensive view thus affecting the individuals' right to follow the dictates of their own conscience on issues of personal morality (religion, sexuality, etc.).

[42] Robert Spano, "Universality or Diversity of Human Rights? Strasbourg in the Age of Subsidiarity," *Human Rights Law Review* 14 (2014): 487–502.

[43] I want to thank Marisa Iglesias and Oscar Parra Vera for calling my attention to these views.

[44] As he put it, "If one accepts . . . that human rights are universal in abstraction but national in application, it is not easy to see how in principle an international court was going to perform this function of deciding individual cases, still less why the Strasbourg Court was thought a suitable body to do so." Lord Hoffman, "The Universality of Human Rights," *Judicial Studies Board Annual Lecture* (2009): 11.

[45] Spano, "Universality or Diversity of Human Rights," 497. In support of this approach, Spano relied on different cases decided by the European Court, such as *Animal Defenders International v. United Kingdom* (App. No. 48876/08 [2013] ECHR Reports).

In sum, what matters for a dialogical conception of democracy is to determine whether the community at stake respected the rules of the (dialogic) democratic procedure at the time of creating and enforcing the norm under analysis. This conception wants to define whether the norm at stake has been—and to what extent—the product of a broad, transparent, and inclusive public debate. As a result, for this view, the judicial analysis of the validity of that law has to become dependent on the "degree" of the democratic agreement contained in the norm: more or less intense and drastic, according to the depth and extent of the agreement on which it is based. As I understand it, this is the perspective that a dialogical conception of democracy would suggest in relation to the place and role of international tribunals.

VII. Final Words

In this text, I examined the "democratic problem" that affects international courts in a unique way. I did so, particularly by adopting a conception of democracy as "dialogue between equals." I also argued that said "democratic problem" affects the democratic legitimacy of the judges of international tribunals and their decisions. I also showed how these problems of democratic legitimacy undermine the authority of these courts and impact their relationship with local political and legal authorities. Finally, I referred to the two prevailing models regarding the relationship between international tribunals and localauthorities: the deference model and the interference model. As I argued, none of these approaches, relatively fixed and inflexible, is defensible if one analyzes them from a "dialogic" perspective such as the one defended in this article.

13

Positivism and Latin American Developments in International Law

Ximena Fuentes

I. Introduction

International law governs the relations between sovereign states. The concept of sovereignty plays a central role in the international legal system. It is sovereignty that explains many of the features of international law, where power operates in a decentralized manner when creating legal rules. From this perspective, the international community can be described as the aggregation of states protecting their autonomy, the right of each political community to decide on its own, without external interference, about its political and economic destiny.

In the international community made up of sovereign states, none of them is legally empowered to impose rules on others. For this reason, the creation of legal norms in the international legal system depends greatly on the consent of states to be bound. This means that extensive interaction between states will be left without legal regulation. Aware of the negative consequences of the absence of norms in essential areas needing regulation, states have accepted that, alongside treaties, state practice might also be a valid source of international obligations. Hence, states' behavior might be transformed into law. These two sources of international law, treaties, and customs can be described as "created" international law.

This description of how international law works may be labeled a positivist understanding of the international legal system. The Permanent Court of International Justice (PCIJ) endorsed this view in the *Lotus* case (*Turkey v. France*, 1927):

> International law governs relations between independent States. The rules of law binding upon States therefore emanate from their own free will as expressed in conventions or by usages generally accepted as expressing principles of law and established in order to regulate the relations between these co-existing independent communities or with a view to the achievement of common aims. Restrictions upon the independence of States cannot therefore be presumed.[1]

[1] *S.S. "Lotus" (Turkey v. France)* [1927] P.C.I.J. (ser. A) No. 10, 18 (1927).

Ximena Fuentes, *Positivism and Latin American Developments in International Law* In: *Latin American International Law in the Twenty-First Century*. Edited by: Alejandro Chehtman, Alexandra Huneeus, and Sergio Puig, Oxford University Press.
DOI: 10.1093/9780197754016.003.0013

The PCIJ thereby adopted a positivist perspective, in its voluntarist version,[2] that emphasizes the role of the free will of states and makes no relevant distinction between treaties and customary law. Indeed, the latter is described as "usages generally accepted as expressing principles of law," as if the Court thought that customary law was a sort of tacit agreement.

However, in what appears to contradict the voluntarist perspective evidenced in the passage quoted above, the *Lotus* decision also states that the international legal system recognizes the existence of certain fundamental principles, such as the respect for the territorial integrity of states, limiting state action as a matter of principle, without need of an immediate link to the state's consent. The relevant paragraph states: "Now the first and foremost restriction imposed by international law upon a State is that—failing the existence of a permissive rule to the contrary—it may not exercise its power in any form in the territory of another State."[3]

In this period, the prohibition of the use of force had not yet become a rule of customary law, and the annexation of territory was a typical result of war. Therefore, it appeared somehow contradictory with its voluntarist view of international law that the PCIJ declared the existence of a fundamental principle of territorial integrity.

The fact is that more than a hundred years before this dictum, the voluntarist school of thought in Germany already knew about the connection between positivism and self-imposed limitations on state action. It seems that the self-limitation thesis was at the center of the elaboration of the concept of the *Rechstaat*.[4] Georg Jellinek developed this concept, and Stephen Neff has explained that "[t]he idea of autolimitation grew out of the philosophy of Kant, for whom voluntary adherence to rules of law or ethics was seen as the highest form of moral conduct."[5] On this basis, territorial integrity, as a restriction that international law would impose on state conduct irrespective of explicit or tacit consent, may be described as a constitutional norm that states must assume as a basic pillar of the international legal system. Among these principles of a constitutional character, Louis Henkin, in addition to the already mentioned principle of territorial integrity, has included the sovereign equality of states, state autonomy, and *pacta sunt servanda*.[6]

Nevertheless, even if there might be a consensus on many of these basic principles, that does not mean that there is no room for controversies. Indeed,

[2] Stephen Neff, *Justice among Nations. A History of International Law* (Cambridge: Harvard University Press, 2014), 236.

[3] *S.S. "Lotus" (Turkey v. France)*, 18.

[4] Neff, *Justice Among Nations*, 240.

[5] Ibid., 240.

[6] Louis Henkin, *International Law: Politics and Values* (Den Haag, The Netherlands: Kluwer Law International, 1995), 31.

even this "rule of law approach" to international law leaves the question of who is vested with the authority to ascertain the content of the alleged basic constitutional principles of the international legal system. The idea of the rule of law might work well in a democratic society within a state, in which the domestic political community would have established institutions to ascertain the "sovereign will." But, international relations between sovereign states are far distant from the political intercourse that takes place within democratic societies. Within the international community, there are few institutional limits for the dominant position that powerful states hold in the determination of the content of the basic principles of the international legal system. This holds not only in relation to the so-called constitutional principles of the international legal system but also with regard to the identification of customary international law.

Aware that powerful states are better positioned to create and determine the content of international law, Latin American states have, from time to time, shown a preference for an approach that views international law as a system of "created" rules. In this context, scholars of Third World Approaches to International Law (TWAIL) have viewed customary law with skepticism. In this vein, B. S. Chimni considers that customary international law "reveals the foundational role of the interests of European states, European legal consciousness, and European social and political theories in the making of modern international law."[7] The role of political and economic power in the international legal system is undeniable, as well as the fact that developing states have had multiple failed attempts to create new customary international law.[8] Nevertheless, against all the odds, Latin American states have not abandoned the belief that they can contribute to creating new international rules. The truth is that in some instances, they have been successful; in others, they have failed. This chapter explores instances of Latin American state practice that show the influence of positivism in their strategies to develop new principles and rules of international law in the following areas:

1. The *uti possidetis* principle to protect their territorial integrity when becoming independent states in the nineteenth century.
2. The Calvo Doctrine as a legal response to overcome the asymmetry of power between the United States and Europe, on the one hand, and Latin America, on the other.

[7] B. S. Chimni, "Customary International Law as Third World Perspective," *American Journal of International Law* 112 (2018): 4, https://doi.org/10.1017/ajil.2018.12.

[8] George Rodrigo Bandeira Galindo and César Yip, "Customary International Law and the Third World: Do Not Step on the Grass," *Chinese Journal of International Law* 16, no. 2 (2017): 251ff, https://doi.org/10.1093/chinesejil/jmx012.

3. Their attempts to transform the aspirations of Latin American states into law through codification. The experience of the Pan-American conferences.
4. The contribution of Latin America to the creation of the exclusive economic zone.

II. *Uti possidetis*

Once they declared independence, the challenge for Latin American states was to consolidate their sovereign status and prevent European powers from reestablishing title to unoccupied territories in Latin America. For this purpose, Latin American countries arrived at an agreed solution that served two essential objectives: (1) to avoid entering into a debate about the legitimacy of the boundaries of the newly born states, which would have started a never-ending debate about the historical, ethnical, or religious basis of a "just" title over territory, and (2) to stop European countries' attempts to recover territories based on the occupation of *terra nullius* territories.[9] The agreed solution was the creation of the *uti possidetis* rule.

Uti possidetis appeared on the legal stage as a provision included in international declarations, bilateral treaties, and the constitutions of the newly created Latin American states. Therefore, *uti possidetis* was conceived as a legal rule that forbade the acquisition of territory by occupying lands deemed *terra nullius* and excluded opening a debate about the justice or injustice of inherited boundaries.[10]

The history of international law concerning the acquisition of territory shows that many of the relevant principles and rules were developed when Europeans colonized "new territories" located in far distant "discovered" continents. The discovery of America by Europeans prompted a debate about the legal basis of the acquisition of territory by the Spanish Crown of lands that, at the time, were occupied by non-European human beings. The Spanish, English, French, and Dutch colonizers, among others, were faced with the question of the legal title for acquiring the new territories. Priests, philosophers, and lawyers advising their respective kings and queens found the answer in the "law of discovery," a set of natural law principles and rules duly studied and explained to the decision makers by their legal counsels. The law of discovery, duly sanctioned by the Pope in Papal Bulls, stated that European rulers were authorized to acquire

[9] Malcolm Shaw, "The Heritage of States: The Principle of Uti Possidetis iuris today," *The British Year Book of International Law* 67 (1996): 97.
[10] Ibid., 98.

the territory occupied by non-Christian settlers.[11] A later version of this natural law rule was developed by Francisco De Vitoria. He conceded that the Pope had no right to take away the property rights held by the Indigenous population. However, if Indigenous people refused to respect the natural law rights of free transit, free trade and commerce, and unrestrained exploitation of minerals and other natural resources, then Spain could fight a just war against the natives and as a result acquire their land.[12] In his *Political Writings*, De Vitoria stated:

> [A]s I proved above (1.1-6), the barbarians possessed true public and private dominion. The law of nations, on the other hand, expressly states that goods which belong to no owner pass to the occupier. Since the goods in question here had an owner, they do not fall under this title.[13]

Nevertheless, De Vitoria was able to find a way to sustain the claim that the Spanish Crown had a right to acquire territories in the new continent, even though Indigenous inhabitants occupied them:

> My first conclusion on this point will be that the Spaniards have the right to travel and dwell in those countries, so long as they do no harm to the barbarians, and cannot be prevented by them from doing so.[14]
>
> . . .
>
> My fifth proposition is that if the barbarians attempt to deny the Spaniards in these matters which I have described as belonging to the law of nations (ius gentium), that is to say from trading and the rest, the Spaniards ought first to remove any cause of provocation by reasoning and persuasion, and demonstrate with every argument at their disposal that they have not come to do harm, but wish to dwell in peace and travel without any inconvenience to the barbarians. And they should demonstrate this not merely in words, but with proof. As the saying goes, "in every endeavour, the seemly course for wise men is to try persuasion first" (Terence, Eunuchus 789). But if reasoning fails to win the acquiescence of the barbarians, and they insist on replying with violence, the Spaniards may defend themselves, and do everything needful for their own safety. It is lawful to meet force with force.[15]
>
> . . .

[11] Robert Miller, Lisa LeSage, and Sebastián López Escarcena, "The International Law of Discovery, Indigenous Peoples and Chile," *Nebraska Law Review* 89, no. 4 (2010): 833, https://digitalcommons.unl.edu/nlr/vol89/iss4/6.

[12] Ibid., 846.

[13] Francisco De Vitoria, *Political Writings* (Cambridge: Cambridge University Press, 1991), 264–265.

[14] Ibid., 278.

[15] Ibid., 281–282

> The conclusion is evident enough: if it is lawful to declare war on them, then it is lawful to exercise to the full the rights of war. And is confirmed by the fact that all things are lawful against Christians if they ever fight an unjust war; the barbarians should receive no preferential treatment because they are unbelievers, and therefore can be proceeded against in the same way. It is the general law of nations (ius gentium) that everything captured in war belongs to the victor, as stated in the laws De captiuis and Si quid in bello (Digest XLIX. 15. 28 and 24), in the canon Ius gentium (Decretum D.l. 9), and more expressly still in the law Item ea quae ab hostibus (Institutions II. 1. 17), which reads: 'in the law of nations, anything taken from the enemy immediately becomes ours, even to the extent that their people become our slaves."[16]

In the competition between England and Spain to identify a better title to acquire the territories in the American continent, the former developed an interesting theory that allowed it to apply the doctrine of discovery to places where the power of Spain was not materially present. This seems to be the origin of the *terra nullius* theory.[17] Under this theory, even if Spain had already applied the doctrine of discovery to the American continent under the authority of the Pope's Bulls, material occupation of territories not physically under the control of Spain would trump the mere legal title granted by the Pope.

During the early nineteenth century, Spanish colonies declared their independence from the Spanish Crown, and the newly created countries faced an important decision regarding the definition of the expanse of their sovereign territories. Insofar as the governing elites were the descendants of the European conquerors who had taken lands from the Indigenous populations, there was no intention to question the doctrine of discovery. However, it was unclear whether this doctrine would trump the *terra nullius* theory under which nonoccupied territories could be lost and become the property of whoever exercised positive acts of territorial control. As the newly created countries did not have material control over the whole territory that, in theory, belonged to Spain, the *terra nullius* argument threatened the newly created states' territorial integrity. Indeed, much of their territory was still unknown and beyond their material control. In this context, Simón Bolivar proposed to transform the administrative boundaries used by Spain to delimit its former *Vicerreinatos*, *Capitanías Generales*, *Audiencias*, and *Obispados*, into the international boundaries of the newly created Latin American states. This was the origin of the *uti possidetis* principle.[18]

[16] Ibid., 283.

[17] Miller et al., "The Law of Discovery," 849.

[18] Carlos Parodi, *The Politics of South American Boundaries* (Westport, CT: Praeger, 2002), 5.

The principle of *uti possidetis* was included in the constitutions of many of the new independent Latin American states: Nueva Granada, 1811 and 1832; Ecuador, 1830 and 1843; República de Colombia 1819, 1821, and 1830; Venezuela, 1830; México 1824 and 1843; Honduras, 1825 and 1839; Nicaragua, 1838; and Costa Rica, 1848.[19] Under the *uti possidetis* rule, a claim of territorial title by foreign countries in Latin America was null and void.

The experience of the creation of the *uti possidetis* rule is a case of successful positivism in Latin America. *Uti possidetis* became a general principle of law, which was applied later in the process of decolonization of Africa. In this regard, the International Court of Justice Chamber in the *Burkina Faso/Mali* case stated:

> [T]he principle [of *uti possidetis*] is not a special rule which pertains solely to one specific system of international law. It is a general principle, which is logically connected with the phenomenon of the obtaining of independence, wherever it occurs. Its obvious purpose is to prevent the independence and stability of new States being endangered by fratricidal struggles provoked by the challenging of frontiers following the withdrawal of the administering power.[20]

III. The Calvo Doctrine

As discussed, the approach of European countries to the acquisition of territory in the newly discovered regions of the American continent is one example of the imperialistic approach that is at the basis of certain principles and rules of international law. The law of state responsibility, particularly the rules on state responsibility for injury to aliens, is also linked to the colonial order established by European countries. In this context, the general view is that an injury to an alien is a cause of action to claim international responsibility from the host state. An injury to an alien was seen as an injury to the state itself. Unfortunately, the rule was also used to justify the use of force.

In 1758, Emmerich De Vattel wrote:

> Whoever uses a citizen ill, indirectly offends the state, which is bound to protect this citizen; and the sovereign of the latter should avenge his wrongs, punish the aggressor, and if possible, oblige him to make full reparation: since otherwise the citizen would not attain the grand end of the civil association, which is safety.[21]

[19] Samuel Durán, *Uti Possidetis. Doctrina Latinoamérica* (Concepción, Chile: Editorial Universidad de Concepción, 1977), 61–72.

[20] *Frontier Dispute (Burkina Faso/Republic of Mali)*, 1986 I.C.J. 565.

[21] Emer De Vattel, *The Law of Nations* (Indianapolis, IN: Liberty Fund, 2008), Book II, para. 71.

More than 150 years later, the Permanent Court of International Justice reasoned on the same basis, stating that:

> By taking up the case of one of its subjects and by resorting to diplomatic action or international judicial proceedings on his behalf, a State is in reality asserting its own rights—its right to ensure, in the person of its subjects, respect for the rules of international law.[22]

Protests against wrongdoings against nationals were communicated by the state of the foreigner's nationality through diplomatic channels. This explains the name of the international law institution devised to channel the respective diplomatic note of protest: diplomatic protection.

Latin American states resented how diplomatic protection was used by the United States and European countries, challenging the enactment of domestic legislation when it affected the interests of foreigners. Given the evident differences in political, economic, and military power between Latin American countries, on the one hand, and the United States and Europe, on the other, it was clear that diplomatic protection was seen as a form of intervention in the domestic affairs of the host state. In the case of the nonpayment of international debts, the intervention of the foreign state sometimes led to war.

In 1868, Carlos Calvo, an Argentine diplomat and jurist, wrote that diplomatic protection contradicted the sovereign equality between states and that the use of force for collecting the payment of international debts was not warranted by international law. It has been said that two military interventions by European countries in Latin America inspired Calvo to develop a legal strategy to restrict diplomatic protection and guarantee that the decisions of local judicial bodies were binding and final: the French armed intervention in the Rio de la Plata in 1845 and 1850 and the intervention in Mexico in 1861.[23]

As summarized by Lillich, Calvo's position was:

> first, sovereign States, being free and independent, enjoy the right, on the basis of equality, of freedom from interference by other States, whether that interference be through force or diplomacy, and second, aliens being entitled only to those right and privilege accorded nationals, must seek redress for grievances exclusively in local courts.[24]

[22] *Mavrommatis Palestine Concessions (Greece v. UK)* (Jurisdiction), P.C.I.J. (ser. A) No. 2, 12 (1924).

[23] Francisco Bello, "La responsabilidad internacional del Estado. Doctrinas Calvo y Drago," *Revista de Ciencias Jurídicas* no. 16 (1970): 11.

[24] Richard B. Lillich, *International Law of State Responsibility for Injuries to Aliens* (Charlottesville: University Press of Virginia,1983), 4.

Calvo has been described as a leading figure in the empirical tradition of positivism.[25] Indeed, the debate regarding the validity of the Calvo Clause can be described as a clash between natural and positive law. As explained by Stephen Neff, states opposing the Calvo Clause invoked an "inherent right" of states to bring claims on behalf of their nationals for injuries inflicted by the host state.[26] What did amount to an injury triggering the international responsibility of the host state was not determined by treaty or by customary law but by a basic standard of "civilization." In the words of Elihu Root:

> The rule of obligation is perfectly distinct and settled. Each country is bound to give to the nationals of another country in its territory the benefit of the same laws, the same administration, the same protection, and the same redress for injury which it gives to its own citizens, and neither more nor less: provided the protection which the country gives to its own citizens conforms to the established standard of civilization.
>
> There is a standard of justice, very simple, very fundamental, and of such general acceptance by all civilized countries as to form a part of the international law of the world. The condition upon which any country is entitled to measure the justice due from it to an alien by the justice which it accords to its own citizens is that its system of law and administration shall conform to this general standard. If any country's system of law and administration does not conform to that standard, although the people of the country may be content or compelled to live under it, no other country can be compelled to accept it as furnishing a satisfactory measure of treatment to its citizen.[27]

The colonialist approach contained in Root's words is undeniable. As Schmitt reminds us, "civilization" as a standard to outlaw and punish certain conducts was used in the past to exterminate Indigenous populations and nothing prevents this natural law argument from being applied to other "uncivilized" conducts, such as the nonpayment of international loans:

> Pufendorf (De jure naturae et gentium, VIII, 6, #5) quotes approvingly Bacon's comment that specific peoples are "proscribed by nature itself," e.g., the Indians, because they eat human flesh. And in fact the Indians of North America were then exterminated. As civilization progresses and morality rises,

[25] Neff, *Justice Among Nations*, 228.

[26] Ibid., 277.

[27] Elihu Root, "The Basis of Protection of Citizens Residing Abroad" (Opening address by Hon. Elihu Root, president of the American Society of International Law, at the fourth annual meeting of the Society, in Washington, April 28, 1910), *American Journal of International Law* 4, no. 3 (1910): 521–522, https://doi.org/10.2307/2186238.

> even less [harmful] things than devouring human flesh could perhaps qualify as deserving to be outlawed in such a manner. Maybe one day it will be enough if a people were unable to pay its debts.[28]

By the late nineteenth century, it was difficult to speak of a universal practice of protection of aliens based on a minimum standard of treatment. Latin American states looked at this rule as the imposition of a policy undertaken by the Great Powers (Europe and the United States) to assure, to use the words of Alejandro Alvarez, "unduly for their citizens who came to those countries a specially privileged situation."[29]

Latin American countries responded by promoting the conclusion of treaties stating that claims by foreigners should be brought to the competent domestic tribunals, leaving diplomatic protection for the exceptional case of a denial of justice.[30] The Calvo Clause was part of this policy, consisting of the inclusion in any contract accorded between the foreigner and the host state of an explicit waiver regarding recourse to the diplomatic protection of the state of their nationality. Few states accepted these treaties, and in the long term, as explained by Shea, they ceased to be in force.[31]

The Calvo Doctrine might not have been successful in its objective of restricting diplomatic protection and terminating the privileged position of US and European foreigners in Latin America, but it is an interesting example of how Latin American states attempted to create new law, leaving aside the dictates of natural law. During the twentieth century and even today, Latin America has shown that from time to time it is necessary to revive the Calvo Doctrine to challenge the unique legal position gained by foreign investors and the disconnection that they sometimes show with the social requirements of the country in which they operate. The rise of investment treaties and investor-state arbitration in the 1990s made it patently clear that investors succeeded in obtaining a privileged position to foreign investment interests in the host states. The response to this state affairs in Latin America has meant the rejection of investor-state arbitration by some states, such as Bolivia, Ecuador, and Venezuela. In this vein, Article 422 of the 2008 Constitution of Ecuador states that "[t]reaties or international instruments where the Ecuadorian State yields its sovereign jurisdiction to international arbitration entities in disputes involving contracts or trade between the State and natural persons or legal entities cannot be entered into."[32]

[28] Carl Schmitt, *The Concept of the Political*, trans. George Schwab (New Brunswick, NJ: Rutgers University Press, 1976), 54, n. 23.

[29] Alejandro Álvarez, "Latin America and International Law," *American Journal of International Law* 3, no. 2 (1909): 300, https://doi.org/10.2307/2186127.

[30] Ibid., 307. Few states accepted these treaties.

[31] Donald Shea, *The Calvo Clause* (Minneapolis: University of Minnesota Press, 1955), 24.

[32] Text in https://pdba.georgetown.edu/Constitutions/Ecuador/english08.html.

In its turn, Article 366 of the 2009 Constitution of the Plurinational State of Bolivia reads as follows: "All foreign companies operating in the oil and gas sector are subject to the sovereignty of the State and under no circumstances will a foreign tribunal be recognized nor can international arbitration or diplomatic interventions be resorted to."[33] In addition, the ICSID (International Centre for Settlement of Investment Disputes) Convention has been denounced by Bolivia (2007),[34] Ecuador (2009),[35] and Venezuela (2012). In the context of UNCITRAL, Working Group III on Investor-State Dispute Settlement Reform, Latin American states have put forward various proposals for improving the functioning of a system with which they are not at ease.[36]

IV. Codification of International Law at the Pan-American Conferences

The origins of pan-Americanism can be traced back to Simón Bolivar's desire for unity between the new Republics of Latin America. In 1826, he convened the Panama Conference, the purpose of which was to consolidate a Pan-American Assembly of Plenipotentiaries vested with the power to serve as "a point of contact in times of common danger, be the faithful interpreter of their public treaties when difficulties occur and judges, arbiters and conciliators in their disputes and differences."[37] The ultimate aim was establishing a supranational entity between Latin American States.

The outcome of the Panama Conference of 1826 was the proposal of a Treaty of perpetual Union, League, and Confederation between the Republics of Colombia, Central America, Peru, and the United Mexican States, establishing a General Assembly composed of two Ministers Plenipotentiary from each party, with the following functions:

[33] Text in https://pdba.georgetown.edu/Constitutions/Bolivia/bolivia09.html.

[34] See https://icsid.worldbank.org/news-and-events/news-releases/denunciation-icsid-convention.

[35] See https://icsid.worldbank.org/news-and-events/news-releases/denunciation-icsid-convention-ecuador. However, in August 2021, the new government of Ecuador decided to return to ICSID. Nevertheless, Article 422 of the Constitution continues in force and the Constitutional Court of Ecuador has not changed its view that Investor-State Dispute Settlement clauses remain unconstitutional, irrespective of Ecuador's decision to return to the ICSID Convention (Decision 2-23-TI/23, July 28, 2023, regarding the constitutionality of the Ecuador-Costa Rica Trade Association Agreement dated March 1, 2023).

[36] Christian Carbajal Valenzuela and Arthur Tochetto dal Piva, "Latin America's Perspective on the Reform of the Investor-State Dispute Settlement Mechanism," in *The Elgar Companion to UNCITRAL*, ed. Rishi Gulati, Thomas John, and Ben Köhler, 116–138 (Cheltenham, UK: Edward Elgar).

[37] *British and Foreign State Papers*, vol. X, 743.

(1) To negotiate and conclude between the powers it represents all such treaties, conventions, and arrangements as may place their reciprocal relations on a mutually agreeable and satisfactory footing.
(2) To contribute to the maintenance of a friendly and unalterable peace between the confederated powers, serving them as a council in times of great conflicts, as a point of contact in common dangers, as a faithful interpreter of the public treaties and conventions concluded by them in the said assembly, when any doubt arises as to their construction, and as a conciliator in their controversies and difficulties
(3) To endeavor to secure conciliation or mediation on all questions which may arise between the allied powers, or between any of them and powers foreign to the confederation.
(4) To adjust and conclude during the common wars of the contracting parties with any powers foreign to the confederation such treaties of alliance, concert, subsidies, and contributions as shall hasten its termination.[38]

Despite the efforts of Bolívar, only Colombia became a party to the Panama Treaty of 1826. The time was not ripe for inter-American political coordination, but at least the leaders demonstrated that they were aware of the need to act together against their common enemies. In 1826, the enemy was Spain. The United States did not yet appear as a threat to Latin American state's political independence. On the contrary, at that time, the United States was seen as a protecting power. Indeed, three years before the Panama Conference, on December 2, 1823, President Monroe delivered its seventh State of the Union Address, explaining the foreign policy to be followed by the United States in the American continent and making clear that European countries should not interfere with the independence of the newly created Latin American states:

> with the Governments who have declared their independence and maintained it, and whose independence we have, on great consideration and on just principles, acknowledged, we could not view any interposition for the purpose of oppressing them, or controlling in any other manner their destiny, by any European power in any other light than as the manifestation of an unfriendly disposition toward the United States.[39]

Of course, there were good reasons to look at this policy of the United States with skepticism. However, the Monroe Doctrine, generally speaking, was well

[38] *Inter American Conference. Reports of Committees. Discussion Thereon*. Vol. IV. Historical Appendix. The Congress of 1826 Panama and Subsequent Movements toward a Conference of American Nations. Washington, DC, 1890, 184.

[39] Text in www.archives.gov/milestone-documents/monroe-doctrine.

received by Latin American states.[40] It was only when it became clear that the United States was the hegemonic power in the region that Latin American countries began to realize that their destiny was inextricably linked to the relationship they could establish with the big neighbor from the north. Both Latin America and the United States understood the hegemonic position of the latter could be a source of tension in the future.

Pragmatism led the United States to counter the anti-imperialist sentiments that its hegemonic position could trigger in Latin American countries. Thus, from 1899 onward, the United States initiated a diplomatic strategy that involved its active participation in the organization, financing, and promotion of the Pan-American conferences. The strategy also involved the creation of the American International Law Institute.[41] According to Scarfi, the Pan-American conferences "played a key role in the construction and consolidation of US hemispheric hegemony."[42] In his view, "American international law and Pan-Americanism were 'gentle civilizers' of US hegemony in the Americas, since the US legal and political model was deployed by the AIIL as the standard of civilization for the Western Hemisphere."[43]

From the point of view of Latin American countries, the experience of the Pan-American conferences shows that Latin American states believed that by agreeing on recommendations, declarations, and treaties among themselves and between them and the United States, they could not only strengthen their cooperation in various topics, but they could also contribute to putting limits on the power of the United States. Aware of their lack of political, military, and economic power, Latin American countries might have thought that the Pan-American conferences allowed them to create rules that would govern the relations between each other and, more importantly, between them and the United States. In particular, Latin American states focused on foreign intervention in their domestic affairs. In the context of the Pan-American conferences, codifying the law was not a mere legal exercise but a deeply political task. For the United States, codification of certain principles through the conclusion of inter-American treaties could help increase and cement its political and economic influence on Latin American countries.

The first Pan-American conference took place in 1889 in Washington, DC. Of course, given its past efforts to resist the abusive use of diplomatic protection, it did not come as a surprise that Latin American countries attempted to restrict the application of this institution. However, despite the efforts, Latin

[40] Juan Pablo Scarfi, *The Hidden History of International Law in the Americas* (Oxford: Oxford University Press, 2017), 5.
[41] Ibid., xviii.
[42] Ibid., 33.
[43] Ibid., xix.

American countries could not get the United States to accept restrictions on protecting US nationals and US interests. During this First Pan-American Conference, a resolution was adopted regarding diplomatic claims, establishing that foreigners have the same civil rights as the nation's citizens, and that they can exercise those rights in the same manner as the citizens. It declared, furthermore, that the American nations have not recognized in favor of foreigners any other obligations and responsibilities than those which by their laws they have toward their own citizens. As expected, the delegation of the United States refrained from voting on this declaration. The text of the proposed resolution read as follows:

> Claims and Diplomatic Intervention
> The International American Conference recommends to the Government of the countries therein represented the adoption, as principles of American international law, of the following:
> (1) Foreigners are entitled to enjoy all the civil rights enjoyed by natives; and they shall be accorded all the benefits of said rights in all that is essential as well as in the form or procedure, and the legal remedies incident thereto, absolutely in like manner as said natives.
> (2) A nation has not, nor recognizes in favor of foreigners, any other obligations or responsibilities than those which in favor of the natives are established, in like cases by the constitution and the laws.

Concerning the principle of nonintervention, it must be borne in mind that in 1901, the US Congress passed the Platt Amendment, containing eight conditions under which the United States would end its military occupation of Cuba. This occupation resulted from the war between Spain and the United States.[44] Under the Platt Amendment, Cuba was forbidden to enter into any international treaty that would compromise Cuban independence or allow foreign powers to use the island for military purposes. The United States reserved its right to intervene in Cuban affairs to maintain "a government adequate for the protection of life, property, and individual liberty." The Platt Amendment required Cuba to conclude a treaty with the United States, making these conditions binding and including them as part of the Cuban Constitution (this was the eighth condition).[45]

Some Latin American delegates to the Pan-American conferences did not regard the Platt Amendment as a breach of the principle of nonintervention. A case in point is the position adopted by Chilean delegate Alejandro Álvarez. Scarfi has

[44] US Department Archive, https://2001-2009.state.gov/r/pa/ho/time/ip/86557.htm.
[45] Ibid.

commented that, though Álvarez was in favor of nonintervention as a basic rule to regulate the relations among states, he was willing to accept exceptions: "The first was when one state conceded to another one the right to intervene; the second, when one state sought to collect a public debt and the debtor state acted in bad faith; and the third, when the life or property of nationals residing or located in another state were at stake."[46] Scarfi added:

> By these concessions, Alvarez made room for the three varieties of standardized US interventions in Latin America, exemplified by the institutionalization of a right to intervene in Cuba under the Platt Amendment (1901) (case 1), the case of US intervention in the Dominican Republic (1904) to assure the payment of debts and to establish a system of customer receivership, as well as other interventions in Central America and the Caribbean through dollar diplomacy for collecting debts (case 2), and the interventions invoking the right to protect US lives and property, as well as US corporations, during political disorders in Central America, the Caribbean, and Mexico, as was the case of US military occupation of Cuba from 1906 to 1909 in the context of the collapse of President Tomás Estrada Palma's regime and the subsequent establishment of localized armed landings there in 1912 for the protection of US lives and property rights (case 3).[47]

During the Second Inter-American Conference, the seventeen states attending the meeting negotiated a treaty on the rights of aliens. The treaty would allow diplomatic protection only in the exceptional situation of denial of justice.[48] Only seven states ratified it.[49] A resolution regarding public debts was also negotiated, banning the collection of debts by force. Again, not all signatory states from Latin American ratified.[50] Scarfi also observed that "the principle of non-intervention was neither stated nor defended as a principle of American international law in the first two meetings of the American Institute of International Law."[51] By the time of the Fifth Pan-American Convention in 1923, there was no longer a debate about intervention on behalf of the rights of aliens. The United States had been successful in opposing the establishment of an absolute principle of non-intervention, and in 1928, the Department of State published a Memorandum on the Monroe Doctrine, written by Undersecretary of State J. R. Clark, putting

[46] Scarfi, *The Hidden History*, 54.
[47] Ibid., 54.
[48] *The Inter-American Conferences of American States 1889-1928* (Oxford: Oxford University Press 1931), 91.
[49] Ibid., 90. Argentina, Chile, Costa Rica, Dominican Republic, Haiti, Mexico, Paraguay, Peru, the United States, and Uruguay did not ratify.
[50] Ibid., 135.
[51] Scarfi, *The Hidden History*, 54.

forward the traditional view that the Monroe Doctrine worked for the benefit of Latin American countries. But Latin American states persevered, and the 1933 Montevideo Convention on the Rights and Duties of States included the principle of nonintervention in the following terms:[52]

> Article 4
> The fundamental rights of States are not susceptible of being affected in any manner whatsoever.
>
> Article 8
> No State has the right to intervene in the internal or external affairs of another.
>
> Article 9
> The jurisdiction of states within the limits of national territory applies to all the inhabitants. Nationals and foreigners are under the same protection of the law and the national authorities and the foreigners may not claim rights other or more extensive than those of the nationals.

According to Becker Lorca, Article 8 did not lay existing law but created new law.[53] It is interesting to underline that the United States ratified the Montevideo Convention on 13 July 1934.

V. The Creation of the Exclusive Economic Zone

For centuries, the sea was seen as a geographical area where anyone could navigate and fish freely, as the ocean belonged to nobody (*res communis*). But, Spain and Portugal decided to divide the new continent and the Atlantic Ocean into areas of influence along the geographical meridian located one hundred leagues west of Cape Verde Islands. The 1494 Treaty of Tordesillas was one of the first attempts to control vast areas of the sea beyond the coastal waters.[54] According to Grotius, the title of occupation—the sole basis to claim sovereignty or ownership—was not applicable on the high seas.[55] In his famous *Mare Liberum*, Hugo Grotius explained his arguments for the freedoms of the seas. In his view, the ocean, the same as the air, is *res communis*:

[52] U.N.T.S. Registration No. 3802.

[53] Arnulf Becker Lorca, *Mestizo International Law* (Cambridge: Cambridge University Press, 2014), 309.

[54] Ann Hollick, *U.S. Foreign Policy and the Law of the Sea* (Princeton, NJ: Princeton University Press, 1981), 5.

[55] Hugo Grotius, *Commentary on the Law of Prize and Booty* (1604-1605), Liberty Fund e-books, 2.

> The air belongs to this class of things for two reasons. First, it is not susceptible of occupation; and second its common use is destined for all men. For the same reasons the sea is common to all, because it is so limitless that it cannot become a possession of any one, and because it is adapted for the use of all, whether we consider it from the point of view of navigation or of fisheries.[56]

Before entering the eighteenth century, the views about the rules that govern the activities of states in the sea were based on natural law. *Mare liberum* was founded on arguments from natural law. The opposing view, *Mare claustrum*, was also based on natural law, stating that the sea could also be appropriated.[57]

During the eighteenth century, states accepted the notion of the freedom of the high seas, and the concept of territorial sovereignty applied to an offshore area close to the coast, the latter limited to the area in which the coastal state could exercise effective control. The cannon-shot rule of Cornelius Van Bynkershoek is the best known of these rules about the extent of the territorial sea. But, alongside the cannon-shot rule, states were already thinking about other criteria that could justify the exercise of sovereign powers beyond the cannon-shot rule. As a method of delimitation of the territorial sea, the space between the coast and the horizon was used in England and Scotland.[58] In Scotland, for example, they used the land-kenning rule to claim exclusive jurisdiction *over* fisheries. As reported by Fulton, "the extent of a land-kenning was stated to be fourteen miles."[59] Others pleaded for recognizing a rule based on the importance of fisheries for coastal populations. In this line, Sarpi, an Italian jurist, considered that the breath of the territorial sea should take into account the requirements of the population of the coastal state.[60] In turn, Scandivian countries favored a four-mile limit.[61] Despite the existence of different rules to determine the breadth of the territorial sea, by the end of the eighteenth century, the cannon-shot rule was the most accepted.[62] Still, the fact that some states put forward other relevant criteria to determine the outer limit of the territorial sea shows that they were open to abandon the prescriptions of natural law, enacting domestic laws and entering into international agreements establishing a different rule, more beneficial to their interests. In the context of the neutrality of the United States in the war between Great Britain and France, the United States declared that the extent of its territorial sea

[56] Hugo Grotius, *The Free Sea* (1609), Liberty Fund e-books, 28.

[57] John Selden, *Mare Claustrum* (1635) (Clark, NJ: LawBook Exchange, reprinted), 42 ff.

[58] T. W. Fulton, *Sovereignty on the Sea* (London: Wiliam Blackwood and Sons, 1911), 545. Text in: Gutenberg.org.

[59] Ibid.

[60] Ibid.

[61] Yoshifumi Tanaka, *The International Law of the Sea* (3rd ed., Cambridge: Cambridge University Press, 2019), 27.

[62] Fulton, *Sovereignty on the Sea*, 577.

extended to one marine league from the coast, more or less equivalent to three nautical miles.[63]

The debate about extending the territorial sea shows the transition between the natural and the positive law approaches. A positive law perspective on international law, which considers norms to be the result of the will of sovereign states, allowed the creation of new legal regimes on the sea based on the various state interests involved. Latin American states not only adopted the one-marine-league/three-mile rule for the territorial sea but also enacted domestic rules regarding a contiguous zone. The 1855 Chilean Civil Code drafted by Andrés Bello stated:

> Article 593. The contiguous sea to the distance of a marine league counted from low-water line is a territorial sea appertaining to the national domain; but the right of police in all matters concerning the country and the observance of the custom laws extends to the distance of four marine leagues counted in the same manner.

Ecuador (1857), El Salvador (1860), Argentina (1869), and Honduras (1880) followed Chile in extending the application of their jurisdiction beyond the one-marine-league rule.[64] Argentina went even further when, in 1907, it declared a fishing zone under the control of the state of ten nautical miles from the coast.[65] Uruguay followed the same trend in the Estuary of the Rio de la Plata.[66]

During the twentieth century, the extension of the territorial sea was a cause of tension between states. The Hague Conference for the Codification of International Law, under the auspices of the League of Nations, was the first intergovernmental attempt to codify the law of the sea.[67] Some countries favored the three-mile rule, among them Chile. However, the majority of Latin American states attending the conference expressed their view in favor of a six-mile extension.[68] Brazil, Colombia, Cuba, and Uruguay were among the states declaring twelve miles of territorial sea.[69] The contiguous zone was also a cause of vigorous debate.[70] Therefore, the conference was not able to show a positive result concerning the territorial sea.

[63] Ibid., 577.

[64] Farouk Brimah, "Latin American States and the Law of the Sea" (Master's thesis, Eastern Illinois University, 1976), 15.

[65] Fulton, *Sovereignty on the Sea*, 662.

[66] Ibid., 662.

[67] Tanaka, *The International Law of the Sea*, 26.

[68] Jesse Reeves, "The Codification of the Law of Territorial Waters," *American Journal of International Law* 24, no. 3 (1930): 492.

[69] Ibid., 492.

[70] Ibid., 492.

World War II would bring considerable changes to the law of the sea. In 1945, the United States decided to transform the existing international law of the sea using a unilateral declaration: the Truman Proclamation on the Continental Shelf. Ann Hollick reported that in the 1930s, President Franklin D. Roosevelt was already willing to extend coastal jurisdiction, defying the then-existing international law.[71] She mentioned three examples of this predisposition toward the enlargement of maritime areas under the control of the coastal state: (1) the 1935 anti-smuggling legislation covering an area of more than fifty miles from the coast; (2) the 1939 US proposal in the context of an inter-American conference of a zone of neutrality extending more than three hundred miles from the coast,[72] and (3) Roosevelt's suggestion to close the sea area along the coast of Alaska to all fishing from third countries.[73] It is not clear whether or not President Roosevelt was aware that unilateral action by the United States could have a regime-creation effect.[74]

On September 28, 1945 President Truman signed "Proclamation 2667—Policy of the United States With Respect to the Natural Resources of the Subsoil and Sea Bed of the Continental Shelf." The US decision to lay claim by means of a unilateral declaration to the continental shelf was mainly based on geological, economic, national security, and conservation reasons.[75] Unilateral declarations cannot create obligations on third parties, and it is unclear whether or not the United States wanted this precedent to be followed by other states. What is known is that on April 30, 1945, President Truman was advised in a Memorandum by the acting Secretary of State and the Secretary of Interior that "[t]he right of other countries to establish similar conservation zones off their shores in accordance with the same principles is conceded."[76] However, based on the scant historical record, Hollick concludes that "the extent of Truman's recognition of the international consequences of the proclamation is . . . difficult to determine."[77]

Ann Hollick criticized the strategy set by the State Department regarding the decision to enlarge the continental shelf area under exclusive US control. She thought it would have been preferable to negotiate with other states instead of planning a unilateral action. Indeed, in her view, the Truman Proclamation legitimized unilateral action concerning the enlargement of maritime zones,

[71] Hollick, *U.S. Foreign Policy*, 20.

[72] Ibid., 20. This neutrality zone was adopted in the Inter-American Conference: The Panama Declaration of 1939. Text in www.oas.org/sap/peacefund/VirtualLibrary/FirstMeetingConsultation/Declarations/Declaration%20of%20Panama.pdf.

[73] Hollick, *U.S. Foreign Policy*, 20.

[74] Ibid., 35.

[75] Ibid., 48.

[76] *Foreign Relations of the United States, Diplomatic Papers, General: Political and Economic Matters* 1945, II, 1504. Text in https://history.state.gov/historicaldocuments/frus1945v02/d774.

[77] Hollick, *U.S. Foreign Policy*, 51.

as happened two years later, in 1947, when Chile and Peru proclaimed the two hundred nautical miles zone:

> An assessment of the Truman Proclamation in terms of these objectives is not favorable. The continental shelf proclamation was perhaps the least harmful of the proclamations. Indeed, the 1958 Geneva Convention on the Continental Shelf reflects the wide acceptance of this proclamation by the international community. The very fact of acceptance, however, raises questions as to the unilateral approach adopted by the United States. The absence of foreign protests and the subsequent wide emulation of the continental shelf policy suggest that U.S. goals could have been accomplished through multilateral means.

Had the US government proceeded on a multilateral, negotiated basis to lay claim to its offshore resources, the ensuing rash of unilateral coastal state claims might not have occurred. At least the United States would have had a firmer basis from which to protest the extensive claims of others—particularly the coastal states of Latin America. These claims have contributed to continuing conflict and uncertainty in the law of the sea. In its short and long term consequences, therefore, it is difficult to make a case supporting the Truman Proclamations. "The explanation for the proclamations, since it cannot be found in the merits of U.S. offshore policy, must be sought in the decision-making process that led to them."[78]

On June 23, 1947, President Gabriel González Videla, of Chile, issued a presidential declaration in which Chile claimed sovereignty over the continental shelf and the superadjacent waters up to a distance of two hundred nautical miles.[79] Peru replicated this action in its Supreme Decree No. 781 of August 1, 1947. Costa Rica (1948),[80] El Salvador (1950),[81] and Honduras (1951)[82] also proclaimed a two hundred-mile zone through national decrees. In 1952, a treaty between Peru, Chile, and Ecuador was concluded, claiming a two hundred-nautical-miles maritime zone (Declaration of Santiago).[83] Colombia adhered to this treaty in 1979. In 1966, Argentina enacted Law 17.094, establishing the two hundred-nautical-miles Argentine Sea. Mexico did so in 1975. In 1973, the Inter-American Juridical Committee declared that "the sovereignty or jurisdiction of a coastal State extends . . . up to a maximum distance of 200 nautical miles."[84] The

[78] Ann Hollick, "U.S. Oceans Policy: The Truman Proclamations," *Virginia Journal of International Law* 17 (1976): 25.

[79] Text in Laws and Regulations on the Regime of the High Seas, vol. I (ser. B/1) (1951).

[80] Decree 116.

[81] 1950 Constitution of El Salvador, Art. 7.

[82] Legislative Decree 25 of 1951.

[83] U.N.T.S. Registration No. 14758.

[84] 12 ILM (1973), 711.

position of Latin American states gained momentum with the decolonization of Africa and Asia. As explained by Attard:

> The OAU also played a crucial role. In December 1971, it passed a resolution which endorsed a recommendation of the Scientific Council for Africa that African States should extend their territorial waters to 200 n.m, establishing a 212 n.m non pollution zone, and create a restricted national fishery zone in the 12 n.m. belt adjacent to the territorial-sea baselines. It was held that the 212 n.m. limit would thus constitute the national economic limit in the oceans and seas surrounding Africa.[85]

In contrast to the experience of the continental shelf maritime zone, which in the lapse of thirteen years became customary law, codified in the 1958 Geneva Convention on the Continental, the two hundred-mile zone had to wait for thirty-five years to be included in the 1982 United Nations Law of the Sea Convention.

Having examined the contribution of Latin American state practice to the creation of new principles, rules, and institutions of international law, the conclusion should be that positivism has been an ally in the efforts of Latin America to challenge the existing international legal paradigms in furtherance of the interests of its peoples. Positivism considers that legal norms are posited by those having the power to create law. In contrast to the natural law perspective, positivism holds that law results from a decision by an entity with such law-creating power. International law governs the relations between sovereign states, but it lacks a sovereign legislative authority. Since their establishment as sovereign states, Latin American countries have understood that their lack of political, economic, and military power might be compensated with active participation in creating international rules, believing that new regulations may help them in their path to development.

[85] David Joseph Attard, *The Exclusive Economic Zone in International Law* (Oxford: Oxford University Press, 1987), 21.

PART III
INSTITUTIONS AND PRACTICE

14

The Latin American States and the Peaceful Settlement of Disputes before the International Court of Justice

Toward Confidence as the Contemporary Pattern

Eduardo Valencia-Ospina and Giovanny Vega-Barbosa

I. Introduction

The analysis of the relationship between Latin American states[1] and the International Court of Justice (hereinafter Court or ICJ) is not novel in international legal literature.[2] Research on this subject has produced important pieces objectively describing the relevant *ratio decidendi* and *obiter dictum* in the jurisprudence of the ICJ involving or confronting Latin American states.[3] Academic work in this area has also sought to highlight the contributions of Latin American diplomacy and scholarship to the development of the Statute of the World Court (hereinafter Statute),[4] its

[1] For the purposes of this chapter, the term "Latin American states" includes all thirty-three member states comprising, at present, the Group of Latin American and Caribbean Countries (GRULAC), one of the five UN regional groups.

[2] Eduardo Valencia-Ospina and Justina Uriburu, Bogotá Pact (1948), *Max Planck Encyclopedia of International Law,* para. 20. See also Paula Wojcikiewicz Almeida and Jean-Marc Sorel (eds.), *Latin America and the International Court of Justice: Contributions to International Law* (London: Routledge, 2016).

[3] Paula Wojcikiewicz Almeida et al., *A Latin American Guide to the International Court of Justice Case Law* (Cambridge: Cambridge Scholars Publishing, 2016); María Teresa Infante, "*Peru v. Chile:* The International Court of Justice Decides on the Status of the Maritime Boundary," *Chinese Journal of International Law* 13, no. 4 (2014): 741–762; Giovanny Vega-Barbosa, "The Admissibility of Outer Continental Shelf Delimitation Claims Before the ICJ Absent a Recommendation by the CLCS," *Ocean Development & International Law* 49, no. 2 (2018): 103–117; Peter Tomka, "The Role of the International Court of Justice in World Affairs: Successes and Challenges with Special Reference to OAS Members States and the Pact of Bogotá," *Lecture Series of the Americas*, April 10, 2014, https://www.oas.org/en/media_center/press_release.asp?sCodigo=E-145/14 (last accessed August 22, 2021).

[4] Eduardo Jiménez de Aréchaga, "The Compulsory Jurisdiction of the International Court of Justice under the Pact of Bogotá and the Optional Clause," in *International Law at a Time*

Eduardo Valencia-Ospina and Giovanny Vega-Barbosa, *The Latin American States and the Peaceful Settlement of Disputes before the International Court of Justice* In: *Latin American International Law in the Twenty-First Century*. Edited by: Alejandro Chehtman, Alexandra Huneeus, and Sergio Puig, Oxford University Press. DOI: 10.1093/9780197754016.003.0014

jurisprudence,[5] or international law generally.[6] Significantly, Latin American international lawyers have recently focused on the relationship between Latin American states and the ICJ for, *inter alia*, elucidating "what the Latin American cases have to tell us about the role of the Court in the resolution of international disputes in the region" and, further, to identify the reasons that explain the increasingly active role that the ICJ is playing in the resolution of disputes between Latin American states.[7]

The historically favorable disposition of Latin American states toward peaceful settlement and, more specifically, toward binding adjudication is usually substantiated based on two prominent examples. First, the establishment in 1908 of the Central American Court of Justice by Nicaragua, El Salvador, Honduras, Guatemala, and Costa Rica.[8] Second, the Optional Clause as a basis for the ICJ's jurisdiction, which was discussed at the very first session of the Assembly of the League of Nations upon the initiative of the Brazilian diplomat Raoul Fernandez.[9] In any case, the commitment of Latin American states to the principle of the peaceful settlement of disputes can be traced further back to 1876, when Argentina and Paraguay submitted to arbitration their dispute regarding the territory between the Pilcomayo and Verde rivers.[10]

Nevertheless, it has also been advanced that Latin American states have been historically reluctant to accept the effects of rulings by the ICJ and that the

of Perplexity: Essays in honour of Shabtai Rosenne, ed. Yoram Dinstein and Mala Tabory, 356 (Dordrecht, The Netherlands: Martinus Nijhoff, 1989).

[5] Juan José Quintana, "The Latin American Contribution to International Adjudication: The Case of the International Court of Justice," *Netherlands International Law Review* 39, no. 1 (1992): 127–154. See recently Manuel Becerra Ramírez, *Casos de América Latina ante la Corte Internacional de Justicia: Fronteras, conflictos armados, derechos humanos y medio ambiente* (México City: UNAN, 2022).

[6] Wojcikiewicz Almeida and Sorel, *Latin America and the International Court of Justice*; Arnulf Becker, "International Law in Latin America or Latin American International Law? Rise, Fall, and Retrieval of a Tradition of Legal Thinking and Political Imagination," *Harvard International Law Journal* 47, no. 1 (2006): 283–305; F. V. Garcia-Amador, "The Latin American Contribution to the Development of the Law of the Sea," *American Journal of International Law* 68, no. 1 (1974): 33–50; Alan T. Leonhard, "Regional Particularism: The Views of the Latin American Judges on the International Court of Justice," *Miami Law Review* 22 (1967–1968): 674–685.

[7] Ximena Fuentes, "Latin American States and the International Court of Justice, in *Litigating International Law Disputes, Weighing the Options*, ed. Nataly Klein, 79–81 (New York: Cambridge University Press, 2014). See also C. Leah Granger, "The Role of International Tribunals in Natural Resources Disputes in Latin America," *Ecology Law Quarterly* 34 (2007): 1313–1317.

[8] Ana Elizabeth Villalta, *La Contribución de América al Derecho Internacional*, 65, http://www.oas.org/dil/esp/59-94%20Villalta%20def.pdf (last visited August 22, 2021).

[9] Shabtai Rosenne, "12. The Compulsory Jurisdiction (Optional Clause)," in *The Law and Practice of the International Court, 1920-2005*, Vol. 1, 702 (Leiden, The Netherlands: Martinus Nijhoff, 2006). Other scholars underline that the first proposal in this regard was made by Max Huber, who, as a delegate of the Swiss Federal Department of Foreign Affairs, represented Switzerland in the Second Peace Conference, which took place at The Hague in 1907. See Dietrich Schindler, "Max Huber—His Life," *European Journal of International Law* 18, no. 1 (2007): 81–95, at 88.

[10] Fuentes, "Latin American States and the International Court of Justice," 79.

Statute has been used as a mechanism to circumvent *res judicata* and final settlement. In this regard, it has been observed that many of the cases brought by Latin American states before the ICJ typically concerned past disputes already settled by treaties in force or by awards validly rendered.[11] The critique on the alleged revisionist approach of Latin American states is not new. More recently, it has been argued that territorial clauses in Latin American constitutions have been construed to resist the application of ICJ Judgments.[12]

Against this background, this chapter aims to add to the existing literature by critically analyzing the historical practice of Latin American states toward the Court. The authors' main proposition is that such practice represents a complex evolutionary process leading to the confidence currently shown by states in the Court's jurisdiction and powers. For convenience, the authors assess the practice of Latin American states before the World Court by distinguishing three relevant periods. The first period is characterized by timid yet important expressions of trust in the jurisdiction of the ICJ and is followed by a quarter of a century of absentia. The authors suggest that this second period can be explained by a mixture of unique factors, including the Cold War, the specific nature of the processes and events taking place in Latin America at that time, and the historical preference of Latin American states to settle highly sensitive matters within the region through arbitration. The final period is characterized by confidence in the Court as an effective instance for the peaceful settlement of the most important international legal disputes. The authors identify confidence as the defining contemporary feature describing the relationship between Latin American states and the Court, notwithstanding isolated expressions of discontent in the immediate aftermath of a judgment and initial—albeit not definitive—decisions not to appear as respondents before it.

The results of the authors' research also demonstrate that proceedings before the ICJ have historically served the purpose of long-term reconciliation by, *inter alia*, opening the doors for direct settlement of a dispute even just weeks before the commencement of oral proceedings in a case. A plea must, therefore, be made here for Latin American states to approach the Statute of the ICJ in good faith and for the Court to exercise its jurisdiction to its fullest[13] while providing guarantees of judicial predictability and final resolution.

[11] Ibid., 81.

[12] See Walter Arevalo, "Resistance to Territorial and Maritime Delimitation Judgments of the International Court of Justice and Clashes with 'Territory Clauses' in the Constitutions of Latin American States," *Leiden Journal of International Law* 35, no. 1 (2021): 1–24. See also Walter Arevalo, "Constitutions Challenging the International Court of Justice's Jurisdiction to Adjudicate Territorial Disputes in Latin America," *ZaöRV* 82 (2022): 425–448.

[13] This is almost a truism since the Court has consistently expressed that it "must not exceed the jurisdiction conferred upon it by the Parties, but it must also exercise that jurisdiction to its full extent." *Continental Shelf (Libyan Arab Jamahiriya/Malta), Judgment*, 1985 I.C.J. 23, ¶ 19. More recently. *Territorial and Maritime Dispute (Nicaragua v. Colombia), Judgment*, 2012 I.C.J. 624, 671, ¶ 136.

To avoid speculative reasoning, the authors have availed themselves of concrete examples of state practice and *opinio juris*, including declarations by high-ranking officials, domestic legislation, treaties, and direct conduct vis-à-vis the ICJ. This approach extends to analyzing isolated and poorly documented expressions of discontent by Latin American states in the immediate aftermath of ICJ's Judgments and initial, yet not definitive, decisions not to appear as respondents in proceedings before the Court.

For convenience, this chapter is divided into three sections, which chronologically follow three successive stages of the relationship of Latin American states with the ICJ. The first covers the period from 1946 to 1958, the second covers the period from 1959 to 1983, and the third covers the period between 1984 and today. Finally, we draw a brief conclusion.

II. 1946 to 1958: The Genesis of a New Relationship

As illustrated by the General List of the Court,[14] the most distinguishing feature in the first years of operation of the ICJ was the reduced number of cases brought before it, either using an Application[15] or through any of the other authorized forms for the institution of proceedings (i.e., Special Agreement[16] or *Forum Prorrogatum*[17]).

In this initial period of justifiable skepticism, Peru and Colombia filed before the ICJ a Special Agreement to refer to the Court a dispute, the proceedings on which could be instituted on the application of either of the parties. In this manner, both states authorized the ICJ to pronounce itself on the scope and content of one of the most emblematic contributions of Latin American legal culture to public international law: diplomatic asylum.[18] Their dispute concerned

[14] At the time of writing this chapter, the General List of the ICJ confirms the existence of thirty cases brought before the ICJ involving Latin American states as the two parties to a case or only as the applicant. Six of those cases have been discontinued; the remainder were judicially resolved except for four, which are still pending.

[15] Rules of the International Court of Justice (1978), adopted on April 14, 1978, and entered into force on July 1, 1978, amendment entered into force on April 14, 2005, art. 38(1)

[16] Ibid., art. 39(1).

[17] Ibid., art. 38(5).

[18] As underlined by a Latin American author, the very existence of a Special Agreement to submit a case before the Court "evidences that each of the parties possesses such an interest and, further, that this is recognized by the other party. In such cases, it is highly unlikely that the Court would feel inclined to question this common will." Juan José Quintana, *Litigation at the International Court of Justice* (Leiden, The Netherlands: Brill Nijhoff, 2015), 15. The most recent instance of a submission to the Court using a Special Agreement by Latin American states is the case concerning *Guatemala's Territorial, Insular and Maritime Claim (Guatemala/Belize)*. See Special Agreement dated December 8, 2008, and Protocol to the Special Agreement dated May 25, 2015, https://www.icj-cij.org/en/case/177/institution-proceedings (last visited August 22, 2021). Previously, El Salvador and Honduras had signed a Special Agreement to submit to the Court the case concerning *Land, Island and Maritime Frontier Dispute (El Salvador/Honduras: Nicaragua intervening)*. See Special

the interpretation and application of regional treaties on extradition and asylum and "the principles of American international law on asylum" concerning the Peruvian political leader Victor Raúl Haya de la Torre. The relevance of Colombia and Peru's decision to submit such an unusual case to the Court must not be underrated as it is an unequivocal expression of trust. Just as important was the confirmation of such trust in the aftermath of the Judgment. Indeed, on November 20, 1950, the same day the decision was rendered, Colombia filed a request for interpretation.[19] Oliver J. Lissitzyn recalls that after the Judgment was issued, Colombian spokesmen criticized the decision as having been adopted chiefly by European judges unfamiliar with Latin American conditions.[20] Beyond typical expressions of discontent, the meaningful evidence in this instance is Colombia's decision to request an interpretation and the party's well-documented compliance with the Judgment.[21]

This early position toward the ICJ, though restrained, still contrasts with the position adopted by the Latin American states regarding the Court's predecessor, the Permanent Court of International Justice (PCIJ). Although twelve declarations were made in the Americas recognizing its compulsory jurisdiction, eight of them for an indefinite term, the PCIJ knew of no case between Latin American states.[22] In fact, its only case involving a Latin American State was the *Case Concerning the Payment in Gold of Brazilian Federal Loans Contracted in France*,[23] instituted by means of a Special Agreement entered into between France and Brazil.

The PCIJ, whose establishment had been provided for in Article 14 of the Covenant of the League of Nations, was nevertheless not a part of the League, with which it kept a close relationship as regards the election of Judges by the Assembly and the Council. The hesitation to appear before the PCIJ becomes, thus, significant, especially when looking closely at the factors that, at that moment, could have justified the perception of the PCIJ as a friendly, familiar, and reliable forum for Latin American states. First, Latin American states had clearly diverged from US policy and attitude toward the League of Nations, of

Agreement dated December 11, 1986, htpp://www.icj-cij.org/docket/files/75/6541.pdf (last visited August 22, 2021).

[19] Application instituting proceedings and Special Agreement dated August 31, 1949, https://www.icj-cij.org/en/case/7/institution-proceedings (last visited August 22, 2021. See also *Haya de la Torre (Colombia v. Peru)* case, *Judgment of 13 June 1951*, 1951 I.C.J. 71.

[20] Oliver Lissittzyn, *The International Court of Justice: Its Role in the Maintenance of Peace and Security* (New York: UN Studies, 2008), 84.

[21] For a critical approach to the decision of the ICJ in the asylum case, see Alona E. Evans, "The Colombian-Peruvian Asylum Case: Termination of the Judicial Phase," *The American Journal of International Law* 45, no. 4 (1951): 755–762.

[22] Antonio Cançado Trindade, *The Construction of a Humanized International Law—A Collection of Individual Opinions (1991-2013)* (Leiden, The Netherlands: Martinus Nijhoff, 2015), 526.

[23] PCIJ, Series A No. 15, Series C. No. 16-IV.

which they had decided to become members precisely for the very same reason explaining the US decision to opt out:[24] the recognition and emphasis that the League placed on the principle of legal equality of states and on guarantees in favor of State sovereignty.[25] In this regard, it is worth quoting the December 19, 1919, declaration of the then President of Nicaragua Emiliano Chamorro, according to whom the League had the potential to promote international justice "through the recognition of identical rights to each and every nation, without smallness militating against any one enjoying its full sovereignty."[26]

Second, the proportionally larger number of Latin American members of the League of Nations secured for them a more influential role in the international organization, thus contributing to developing in them an increasing sense of confidence and reliability in its related work. It should be recalled that of the final fifty-seven members of the League, nineteen were Latin American states, which made for 33 percent of the total membership.[27]

Third, Article 25 of the Statute of the PCIJ, as amended on September 14, 1929,[28] authorized it to be constituted, as it was effectively done in some cases, with a quorum of nine judges. This possibility could have enhanced the comfort for Latin American states, as the proportion of sitting Latin American judges would have increased.[29] This situation can be evinced in the *Case Concerning the Payment in Gold of Brazilian Federal Loans Contracted in France*, where the

[24] Marc Erick Williams succinctly explains the reasons preceding the US reservations against the League of Nations, even though President Woodrow Wilson had been its leading advocate. First, the collective security system was deemed to be triggering a risk of surrendering US war-making authority to an international authority. Second, the possibility of standing on equal footing vis-à-vis small Latin American states was conceived as a threat to the preeminence of the United States in the region. Third, the emphasis on sovereignty could have limited US capacity to exert regional influence under the Monroe Doctrine. Marc Eric Williams, *Understanding US–Latin American Relations. Theory and History* (New York: Routledge: 2012), p. 124.

[25] Miriam Cohen, "Latin America and the Permanent Court of Justice," in *Latin America and the International Court of Justice: Contributions to International Law*, ed. Paula Wojcikiewicz Almeida and Jean-Marc Sorel, 50–60, 53 (London: Routledge, 2016). See also R. Russel and J. G. Tokatlian, "Grand Strategy," in *Routledge Handbook of Latin American in the World*, ed. J. Dominguez and A. Covarubias, (London: Routledge, 2014), 58–73, p. 63.

[26] Williams, *Understanding US–Latin American Relations*, 125.

[27] This stands, of course, in sharp contrast with the current proportional participation of Latin American states vis-à-vis the rest of the world in the United Nations, a factual situation that has not prevented them from appearing before the Court on numerous occasions and with more frequency in recent years.

[28] Article 25 as amended read as follows: "The full Court shall sit except when it is expressly provided otherwise. Subject to the condition that the number of judges available to constitute the Court is not thereby reduced below eleven, the Rules of Court may provide for allowing one or more judges, according to circumstances and in rotation, to be dispensed from sitting. Provided always that a quorum of nine judges shall suffice to constitute the Court." This text is essentially reproduced in Article 25 of the ICJ Statute.

[29] In *Concerning the Payment in Gold of Brazilian Federal Loans Contracted in France*, only eight Judges were present (Anzilotti [President], Huber [Vice-President], Loder, De Bustamante, Altamira, Oda, Pessoa, Hughes).

Court was composed of eight Judges, two of which were Latin American,[30] plus a judge ad hoc.[31] Moreover, Judge José Gustavo Guerrero from El Salvador held the presidency of the Court from 1936 to 1942.

The identified first relevant period in the ICJ finishes with the application submitted by Honduras on July 1, 1958, by virtue of the Agreement concluded in Washington on July 21, 1957, by the foreign ministers of Honduras and Nicaragua, "with regard to the procedure to be followed in presenting to the International Court of Justice the dispute between Honduras and Nicaragua concerning the Arbitral Award made on 23 December 1906 by His Majesty the King of Spain."[32]

This latter case is sometimes invoked as evidence that the ICJ has been historically instrumentalized in challenging the finality of awards and the validity of treaties in force. This is sometimes referred to in informal academic settings as a revisionist approach by Latin American states in its interaction with the Court. But there is ample room for a less pessimistic view. Indeed, changes in government may sometimes be accompanied by nationalistic speeches and a promise to regain what the replaced administration allegedly lost, a promise especially compelling when territory is concerned. Nevertheless, the consistent and prolonged respect for the rule of law by Latin American states has served as an effective guarantee against isolated and temporary instances of rejection or neglect. This is precisely what happened concerning the *Arbitral Award Made by the King of Spain on 23 December 1906*. While in this case Nicaragua attempted to challenge the validity of the award, the ICJ, relying upon the conduct of Nicaragua in the six years after the issuance of the award, concluded that "Nicaragua, by express declaration and by conduct [had] recognized the Award as valid."[33]

In the authors' view, this first period shows timid yet important expressions of trust in the work of the new Court. This is a milestone that must not be underestimated, mainly because, in that period, absolute skepticism might have been the more reasonable mindset.

III. 1959 to 1983: *Absentia*

After the filing of the application in the Arbitral Award case, the Latin American states remained absent from the ICJ for nearly twenty-six years. In this period,

[30] Epitacio Da Silva from Brazil (1923–1930) and Antonio Sanchez de Bustamante and Sirven from Cuba (1922–1942).

[31] The French ad hoc judge was M. Fromageot.

[32] http://www.icj-cij.org/docket/files/39/9171.pdf (last visited August 22, 2021).

[33] *Arbitral Award made by the King of Spain on 23 December 1906*, Judgment of November 18, 1960, 1960 I.C.J. 25. Nicaragua's conduct vis-à-vis the award has now become one of the textbook examples of the elements required to prove recognition.

between 1959 and 1983, twenty-one new disputes were listed in the General List of the ICJ between states of different continents.[34] As in the first period under scrutiny, mere quantitative considerations could lead the interpreter to assume that, at that time, Latin American states were still rather hesitant to submit their disputes to the ICJ. However, a closer look reveals that the lack of cases formally listed in the General List in this period could be a poor indicator.

On the one hand, it should be recalled that nearly in this same period, interstate relations at the universal and regional planes were greatly influenced, if not defined by the Cold War, by the geopolitical tensions between the two Great Powers, the United States and the Soviet Union and their allied European blocs, and by their impact on regional conflicts. During this period, several long-standing and important disputes were settled between Latin American states before arbitral tribunals. Arbitration of territorial disputes was, for a long time, the preference of Latin American states.[35] For purely illustrative purposes, it is worth mentioning the *Frontier Dispute* between Argentina and Chile, submitted to arbitration through a Special Agreement dated April 1, 1965 and settled on December 9, 1966.[36] Those two states followed the same mechanism in their *Dispute Concerning the Beagle Channel*. This time, Argentina and Chile entered into a Special Agreement dated July 22, 1971, thereby submitting to an Arbitration Tribunal composed of five sitting ICJ judges, a dispute regarding territorial and maritime boundaries and title to certain islands, islets, and rocks near the end of the continent, a dispute eventually being settled in 1977.[37] Although

[34] *Compagnie du Port, des Quais et des Entrepôts de Beyrouth and Société Radio-Orient (France v. Lebanon); Aerial Incident of 7 November 1954 (United States of America v. Union of Soviet Socialist Republics); Temple of Preah Vihear (Cambodia v. Thailand); South West Africa (Ethiopia v. South Africa); South West Africa (Liberia v. South Africa); Northern Cameroons (Cameroon v. United Kingdom); Barcelona Traction, Light and Power Company, Limited (Belgium v. Spain) (New Application: 1962; North Sea Continental Shelf (Federal Republic of Germany/Denmark); North Sea Continental Shelf (Federal Republic of Germany/Netherlands); Appeal Relating to the Jurisdiction of the ICAO Council (India v. Pakistan); Fisheries Jurisdiction (United Kingdom of Great Britain and Northern Ireland v. Iceland); Fisheries Jurisdiction (Federal Republic of Germany v. Iceland); Nuclear Tests (Australia v. France); Nuclear Tests (New Zealand v. France); Trial of Pakistani Prisoners of War (Pakistan v. India); Aegean Sea Continental Shelf (Greece v. Turkey); Continental Shelf (Tunisia/ Libyan Arab Jamahiriya); United States Diplomatic and Consular Staff in Tehran (United States of America v. Iran); Delimitation of the Maritime Boundary in the Gulf of Maine Area (Canada/United States of America); Continental Shelf (Libyan Arab Jamahiriya/Malta); Frontier Dispute (Burkina Faso/Republic of Mali).*

[35] The position was historically different with regard to the arbitration of economic disputes vis-à-vis foreign investors. Naon, Horacio A. Grigera, "Arbitration in Latin America: Overcoming Traditional Hostility (An Update)," *University of Miami Inter-American Law Review* 22, nos. 2+3 (Spring-Summer 1991): 203–258.

[36] UNRIAA, *Argentina-Chile Frontier Case, 9 December 1966*, Vol. XVI, 109–182.

[37] UNRIAA, *Dispute between Argentina and Chile concerning the Beagle Channel*, February 18, 1977, Vol. XXI, 53–264. While one party initially repudiated the award, the dispute was settled through mediation. M. C. W. Pinto "Recent inter-State Arbitration," in *International Arbitration: Past and Prospects. A Symposium to Commemorate the Centenary of the Birth of Professor J. H. W. Verzijl (1888-1987)*, ed. H. A. Soons, 83 (Dordrecht, The Netherlands: Martinus Nijhoff, 1989).

Argentina challenged the award as null and void, the dispute was immediately addressed peacefully, and attempts were made to resolve it through direct negotiation and, afterward, mediation of the Holy See. As a result, a *Treaty of Peace and Friendship* was signed between the parties at Vatican City on November 29, 1984, by which they "defined the boundary between the respective sovereignties over the sea, seabed and subsoil of the two countries in the sea of the southern zone."[38]

On the other hand, a careful examination of the subject matter of the disputes and the worldwide geographical distribution of states' participation in the ICJ in the years of Latin American *absentia* shows that cases among states from the same continent were only numerous in Europe,[39]six cases, and in Africa, four cases.[40] Notably, such cases predominantly dealt with territorial sovereignty and maritime delimitation matters. By their very nature, these types of affairs presuppose protracted and complex processes of negotiation. In Latin America, such processes had not yet been exhausted and would have rendered premature the institution of fresh proceedings before the ICJ. This consideration mirrors the most recent practice of Latin American states, which have had constant recourse to the Court to settle territorial and maritime disputes.[41]

It must be highlighted that the reuniting of Latin American states with the Court took place in 1984, concerning a situation that was a reflection of the Cold War, which at the time gravely threatened peace and security in the region. The referral of this situation to the Court also serves as a telling indicator that Latin American states had not definitively dismissed the ICJ as a proper forum for the peaceful settlement of the most complex and serious disputes, such as those involving the use of force.

[38] See UNRIAA, *Dispute between Argentina and Chile*, Vol. XXI, 55.

[39] The cases resulted in the following judgments: *Barcelona Traction, Light and Power Company, Limited*, Judgment, 1970 I.C.J. 3; *North Sea Continental Shelf cases (Federal Republic of Germany/Denmark; Federal Republic of Germany/The Netherlands) North Sea Continental Shelf*, Judgments, 1969 I.C.J. 3; *Fisheries Jurisdiction (United Kingdom v. Iceland)*, Merits, Judgment, 1974 I.C.J. Reports 3; *Fisheries Jurisdiction (Federal Republic of Germany v. Iceland)*, Merits, Judgment, 1974 I.C.J. 175; *Aegean Sea Continental Shelf (Greece v. Turkey)*, Judgment, 1978 I.C.J. 3.

[40] The cases resulted in the following judgments: *South West Africa Cases (Ethiopia v. South Africa and Liberia v. South Africa) South West Africa*, Second Phase, Judgments, 1966 I.C.J. 6; *Continental Shelf (Tunisia/Libyan Arab Jamahiriya)*, Judgment, 1982 I.C.J. 18; *Frontier Dispute (Burkina Faso/Republic of Mali)*, Judgment, 1986 I.C.J. 554.

[41] The most recent example is the submission, via Special Agreement, of *Guatemala's Territorial, Insular and Maritime Claim (Guatemala/Belize)*. See Special Agreement dated December 8, 2008, and Protocol to the Special Agreement dated May 25, 2015, https://www.icj-cij.org/en/case/177/institution-proceedings (last visited August 22, 2021). Before that, Costa Rica filed an application on January 16, 2017, instituting proceedings against Nicaragua regarding the *Land Boundary in the Northern Part of Isla Portillos*, https://www.icj-cij.org/en/case/165/institution-proceedings (last visited August 22, 2021). These proceedings were joined with those instituted by Costa Rica against Nicaragua on February 25, 2014, concerning a maritime delimitation both in the Caribbean Sea and in the Pacific Ocean, https://www.icj-cij.org/en/case/157/institution-proceedings (last visited August 22, 2021).

On April 9, 1984, Nicaragua filed an application concerning the alleged participation of the United States in military and paramilitary activities in its territory and against its territorial integrity and political independence.[42] Two years later, in 1986, Nicaragua again resorted to the Court to peacefully settle a controversy with its neighboring states, Costa Rica[43] and Honduras,[44] regarding alleged border and transborder armed actions.

The inception thus effected of a third new period (1984–present), is also of special relevance for two reasons. First, it constituted the starting point of a trend among Latin American states to bring their interstate disputes before the Court—in the understanding that recourse to the Court does not amount to an unfriendly act—in order to bolster reconciliation and direct settlement. Second, it marked the regularization of recourse to Article XXXI of the American Treaty on Pacific Settlement of Disputes[45] (the Pact of Bogotá).

Both reasons are addressed here in the next sections.

The ICJ as a Friendly Scenario for Understanding and Reconciliation

In parallel with the submission of the application by Nicaragua in the *Border and Transborder Armed Actions* case with Costa Rica and during the written stage of the proceedings, several instances of diplomatic negotiation took place among the five states of Central America. As a direct consequence of these negotiations and during the time limit for the submission of the Counter-Memorial by Costa Rica, the Court was informed of the signing of a treaty entitled "*Procedimiento para establecer una paz firme y duradera en Centroamérica*" (Procedure to establish a firm and long-lasting peace in Central America), also known as the "Esquipulas Agreement II," signed on August 7, 1987, in Ciudad de Guatemala by the five Central American states.[46] Subsequently, through a communication addressed to the Registrar, Nicaragua formally requested the discontinuance of the proceedings.

[42] *Military and Paramilitary Activities in and against Nicaragua (Nicaragua v. United States of America)*, Application instituting proceedings, http://www.icj-cij.org/docket/files/70/9615.pdf (last visited August 22, 2021).

[43] *Border and Transborder Armed Actions (Nicaragua v. Costa Rica)*, Application of July 25, 1986, instituting proceedings, http://www.icj-cij.org/docket/files/73/10703.pdf (last visited August 22, 2021).

[44] *Border and Transborder Armed Actions (Nicaragua v. Costa Rica)*, Application of 28, July 1986, instituting proceedings, http://www.icj-cij.org/docket/files/74/9663.pdf (last visited August 22, 2021).

[45] Bogotá, April 30, 1948, United Nations, 30 U.N.T.S. 55.

[46] *Border and Transborder Armed Actions (Nicaragua v. Costa Rica)*, Order of August 19, 1987, 1987 I.C.J. 5.

The inverse process has also taken place among Latin American states—that is, their participation in protracted and complex direct negotiations to reach agreement to submit a controversy to the ICJ. In this sense, it bears mentioning that the controversy in the case concerning the *Land, Island and Maritime Frontier Dispute (El Salvador/Honduras: Nicaragua intervening)* was submitted to the ICJ through a Special Agreement in compliance with the General Treaty of Peace, signed in Lima on October 30, 1980. As expressly recognized in the Treaty, the submission of the dispute to the Court was made possible due to the mediation of the former Peruvian president and former president of the ICJ, Mr. José Luis Bustamante y Rivero.[47]

In line with this trend, the institution of proceedings in the case concerning the *Dispute regarding Navigational and Related Rights* between Costa Rica and Nicaragua was preceded by the Tovar-Caldera Agreement, by which Nicaragua and Costa Rica agreed, respectively, that during the term of direct negotiations, Nicaragua would maintain unchanged, for three years, its status with regard to its Declaration of acceptance of the compulsory jurisdiction of the Court, and, in the same period, Costa Rica would abstain from instituting proceedings before the ICJ or before any other authority with respect to the treaties in force between the parties.[48]

The suitability of litigation before the ICJ to secure or strengthen friendly ties, which had temporarily weakened but not broken, finds a most eloquent example in the case concerning *Aerial Herbicide Spraying*. A claim against Colombia was brought before the Court through an application filed by Ecuador on March 31, 2008,[49] pursuant to Article XXXI of the Pact of Bogotá. In relation to this case and its discontinuance, in his speech of July 22, 2014 before the International Law Commission, the then president of the International Court of Justice, Judge Peter Tomka, said:

> The proceedings were instituted by Ecuador in 2008. The Court had already invested considerable energy in preparing for the case, in particular as regards the processing and assessment of the voluminous evidentiary record and the procedure regarding the deposition of witnesses. The proceedings were

[47] *Special Agreement concluded at Esquipulas (Guatemala) on 24 May 1986 between the Republic of El Salvador and the Republic of Honduras for the submission to the Decision of the International Court of Justice of a dispute between the two States*, jointly notified to the Court on December 11, 1986, http://www.icj-cij.org/docket/files/75/6541.pdf (last visited August 22, 2021).

[48] *Dispute regarding Navigational and Related Rights (Costa Rica v. Nicaragua)*, Application instituting proceedings, 8, http://www.icj-cij.org/docket/files/133/8268.pdf (last visited August 22, 2021).

[49] Application instituting proceedings, http://www.icj-cij.org/docket/files/138/14474.pdf (last visited August 22, 2021).

> ultimately discontinued given that the Parties reached an agreement to settle their dispute, just three weeks prior to the date in which the hearings before the Court on the merits were scheduled to commence. *That said, both Parties praised the Court for the time, resources and energy it had devoted to the case, and acknowledged that reaching a settlement would have been difficult, if not impossible, but for the involvement of the Court*"[50] (emphasis added).

As correctly pointed out by President Tomka, just weeks before the initiation of the oral rounds in the case, on September 12, 2013, the agent of Ecuador, by referring to Article 89 of the Rules of the Court, informed the registry that Ecuador and Colombia had entered into an agreement dated September 9, 2013, "that fully and finally resolve[d] all of Ecuador's claim against Colombia," and therefore, notified the Court of their wish to discontinue the proceedings in the case. Subsequently, the agent of Colombia informed the Court that his government had no objection to the discontinuance of the case.[51]

The Pact of Bogotá

The invocation of Article XXXI of the Pact of Bogotá before the ICJ was first made by Nicaragua on July 1, 1958 when instituting proceedings against Honduras concerning the Arbitral Award Made by the King of Spain on 23 December 1906.[52] Subsequently, concerning the border and transborder military activities of the "contras" in and against Nicaragua, the Pact was invoked on July 28, 1986, as the basis of jurisdiction against Honduras and against Costa Rica,[53] and as a basis of responsibility against Costa Rica.[54]

These milestones mark the start of the frequent use of the Pact of Bogotá before the ICJ. Its invocation in seventeen of the twenty-one cases between Latin American states recorded since 1984 in the General List of the Court[55] indicates its importance for the pacific settlement of regional disputes. Moreover, the content of Article XXXI of the Pact of Bogotá is in itself an acknowledgment of the favourable disposition of Latin American states toward the ICJ. Indeed, while no equivalent clause is to be found in comparable treaties adopted in other regions

[50] Peter Tomka, "Speech of the President of the International Court of Justice, at the sixty-sixth session of the International Law Commission," July 22, 2014, 9, https://www.icj-cij.org/en/statements-by-the-president (last visited August 22, 2021).

[51] *Aerial Herbicide Spraying* (*Ecuador v. Colombia*), Order of September 13, 2013, 2.

[52] https://www.icj-cij.org/en/case/39/institution-proceedings (last visited August 22, 2021).

[53] https://www.icj-cij.org/en/case/74/institution-proceedings.

[54] https://www.icj-cij.org/en/case/73/institution-proceedings.

[55] As of August 22, 2021).

in the world, Article XXXI reproduces, within the American context,[56] the content of Article 36, paragraph 2 of the Statute of the Court.

It is also noteworthy that since 1984, in every case in which the Optional Clause was used as the basis for intra-Latin American litigation, Article XXXI of the Pact of Bogotá was invoked concurrently. Such a conduct or procedural strategy is illustrative of the belief among Latin American states that Article XXXI is a valuable tool to secure a decision by the Court on the merits of a case. The Pact of Bogotá also allows for an enhanced expectation by Latin American states that disputes will be settled definitively. Indeed, while Article 60 of the Statute of the ICJ enshrines finality as one of the essential features of the Court's judgments and as an inherent limitation deriving from its judicial function, the ICJ will always bear in mind, when settling disputes between American states, that the Pact of Bogotá develops Article 27 of the Charter of American states, according to which " a special treaty will establish adequate means for the settlement of disputes and will determine pertinent procedures for each peaceful means such that no dispute between American States may remain without definitive settlement within a reasonable period of time."

The invocation of the pact gave rise to complex objections to the jurisdiction of the Court.[57] In this sense, the simultaneous invocation of the Optional Clause and Article XXXI of the Pact of Bogotá allowed the Court, *inter alia*, to clarify its jurisprudence on the relationship between these bases of jurisdiction and, in particular, on the independent character of each separate recognition of compulsory jurisdiction.[58]

In this context, it is appropriate to underline that preliminary objections must be deemed a reasonable and legitimate exercise of the rights conferred upon states by the Statute of the Court and the Pact of Bogotá. Moreover, in some situations, preliminary objections under the Pact of Bogotá played a substantive role in protecting states' established rights. For example, in the case concerning *Territorial and Maritime Dispute*, Colombia invoked Article VI of the Pact of Bogotá[59] to challenge the jurisdiction of the Court to pronounce over

[56] As explained by one of the authors: "Article XXXI provides for the compulsory jurisdiction of the ICJ in terms that reproduce the wording of the optional clause in Article 36 (2) ICJ Statute . . . except that is limited, *ratione personae*, to the American States Parties to the Pact.", Eduardo Valencia-Ospina and Justina Uriburu, Bogotá Pact (1948), *Max Planck Encyclopedia of International Law* ¶ 19.

[57] Under Article 79 of the Rules of the Court, the filing of a preliminary objection constitutes a right of the state which, as recognized by the Court in its Order of December 13, 1989 in the case concerning *Aerial Incident*, can be exercised even before the filing of the memorial by the applicant. *Aerial Incident of 3 July 1988 (Islamic Republic of Iran v. United States of America)*, Order of December 13, 1989, 1989 I.C.J. 134.

[58] *Border and Transborder Armed Actions (Nicaragua v. Honduras)*, Jurisdiction and Admissibility, Judgment, 1988 I.C.J. ¶¶ 34, 36.

[59] "ARTICLE VI. The aforesaid procedures, furthermore, may not be applied to matters already settled by arrangement between the parties, or by arbitral award or by decision of an international court, or which are governed by agreements or treaties in force on the date of the conclusion of the present Treaty."

the sovereignty of some islands, cays, and other maritime formations expressly recognized under its sovereignty by a treaty in force between Nicaragua and Colombia—*The Esguerra-Barcenas Treaty of 1928*. In this case, after recalling that it is a right of the party to have its preliminary objections decided at the preliminary stage of the proceedings and before entering into the merits,[60] the ICJ stated: "That matter has been settled by the Treaty. Consequently, Article VI of the Pact is applicable on this point and therefore the Court does not have jurisdiction over the three named islands."[61]

The considerations referred to above are relevant to assessing the efficacy of the Pact of Bogotá itself. Indeed, while the material value of the Pact has been subject to doubts due to a reduced number of ratifications, fourteen in total, a pragmatic approach reveals one significant conclusion: the Pact of Bogotá has achieved and continues to achieve the pacific settlement function for which it was envisaged.

Considering the above, the authors posit that the period of absentia should not necessarily be construed as demonstrative of a complete and definite dismissal of the Court as an effective means of peaceful dispute settlement. Even though, as the authors have pointed out, objective data suggest that arbitration, a historical favorite for the settlement of territorial disputes, remained a more attractive means for disputes that unfolded at that time. In any case, one cannot fail to note that, before 1984, the ICJ was not generally regarded as the ideal means to settle the most critical disputes. The successful invocation of the Pact of Bogotá in 1984 becomes, therefore, central to the visible transition in the Latin American states' perception of the Court. That the Latin American states have found more comfort in the Pact of Bogotá than in any other basis for the invocation of the Court's jurisdiction can be attested by the fact, previously underlined, that since 1984, in every case in which recourse to the Optional Clause was the basis for intra-Latin American litigation, Article XXXI of the Pact of Bogotá was invoked concurrently.

IV. 1984 until Today: Confidence in the ICJ for the Settlement of the Most Important Disputes

This section provides quantitative and qualitative evidence that the last period under analysis, namely, 1984 until today, represents a consolidation of the confidence of Latin American states in the ICJ and of their trust in its jurisdiction. Yet,

[60] *Territorial and Maritime Dispute (Nicaragua v. Colombia)*, Preliminary Objections, 2007 I.C.J. ¶ 51.

[61] Ibid., ¶¶ 88, 90.

as was shown before, this current attitude is not to be taken for granted; it is the consequence of a complex evolutionary process, including a long period when the Court was not perceived as the most suitable means for the settlement of the most important controversies.

Since 1984, twenty-six new cases have been instituted by Latin American states,[62] and only six cases have been discontinued.[63] Significantly, sixteen of those instances, dealing with the jurisdiction of the Court over intra-Latin American state disputes, have been activated in the new millennium,[64] a number

[62] *Military and Paramilitary Activities in and against Nicaragua (Nicaragua v. United States of America); Border and Transborder Armed Actions (Nicaragua v. Costa Rica); Border and Transborder Armed Actions (Nicaragua v. Honduras); Land, Island and Maritime Frontier Dispute (El Salvador/Honduras: Nicaragua intervening) (El Salvador v. Honduras)*; Vienna Convention on Consular Relations (*Paraguay v. United States of America*); *Territorial and Maritime Dispute between Nicaragua and Honduras in the Caribbean Sea (Nicaragua v. Honduras); Territorial and Maritime Dispute (Nicaragua v. Colombia); Application for Revision of the Judgment of 11 September 1992 in Land, Island and Maritime Frontier Dispute (El Salvador/Honduras: Nicaragua intervening) (El Salvador v. Honduras); Avena and Other Mexican Nationals (Mexico v. United States of America); Dispute regarding Navigational and Related Rights (Costa Rica v. Nicaragua); Status vis-à-vis the Host State of a Diplomatic Envoy to the United Nations (Commonwealth of Dominica v. Switzerland); Pulp Mills on the River Uruguay (Argentina v. Uruguay); Aerial Herbicide Spraying (Ecuador v. Colombia); Maritime Dispute (Peru v. Chile); Certain Questions concerning Diplomatic Relations (Honduras v. Brazil); Certain Activities Carried Out by Nicaragua in the Border Area (Costa Rica v. Nicaragua); Construction of a Road in Costa Rica along the San Juan River (Nicaragua v. Costa Rica); Obligation to Negotiate Access to the Pacific Ocean (Bolivia v. Chile); Question of the Delimitation of the Continental Shelf between Nicaragua and Colombia beyond 200 nautical miles from the Nicaraguan Coast (Nicaragua v. Colombia); Alleged Violations of Sovereign Rights and Maritime Spaces in the Caribbean Sea (Nicaragua v. Colombia); Maritime Delimitation in the Caribbean Sea and the Pacific Ocean (Costa Rica v. Nicaragua); Land Boundary in the Northern Part of Isla Portillos (Costa Rica v. Nicaragua); Guatemala's Territorial, Insular and Maritime Claim (Guatemala/Belize); Dispute over the Status and Use of the Waters of the Silala (Chile v. Bolivia); Arbitral Award of 3 October 1899 (Guyana v. Venezuela).*

[63] See *Border and Transborder Armed Actions (Nicaragua v. Costa Rica)*, Order of August 19, 1987; *Border and Transborder Armed Actions (Nicaragua v. Honduras)*, Order of May 27, 1992; *Vienna Convention on Consular Relations (Paraguay v. United States of America)*, Order of November 10, 1998; *Status vis-à-vis the Host State of a Diplomatic Envoy to the United Nations (Commonwealth of Dominica v. Switzerland)*, Order of June 9, 2006; *Certain Questions concerning Diplomatic Relations (Honduras v. Brazil)*, Order of May 12, 2010; *Aerial Herbicide Spraying (Ecuador v. Colombia)*, Order of September 13, 2013.

[64] *Territorial and Maritime Dispute (Nicaragua v. Colombia); Dispute regarding Navigational and Related Rights (Costa Rica v. Nicaragua); Pulp Mills on the River Uruguay (Argentina v. Uruguay); Maritime Dispute (Peru v. Chile); Aerial Herbicide Spraying (Ecuador v. Colombia); Certain Questions concerning Diplomatic Relations (Honduras v. Brazil); Certain Activities Carried Out by Nicaragua in the Border Area (Costa Rica v. Nicaragua); Construction of a Road in Costa Rica along the San Juan River (Nicaragua v. Costa Rica); Obligation to Negotiate Access to the Pacific Ocean (Bolivia v. Chile); Question of the Delimitation of the Continental Shelf between Nicaragua and Colombia beyond 200 nautical miles from the Nicaraguan Coast (Nicaragua v. Colombia); Alleged Violations of Sovereign Rights and Maritime Spaces in the Caribbean Sea (Nicaragua v. Colombia); Maritime Delimitation in the Caribbean Sea and the Pacific Ocean (Costa Rica v. Nicaragua); Dispute over the Status and Use of the Waters of the Silala (Chile v. Bolivia); Land Boundary in the Northern Part of Isla Portillos (Costa Rica v. Nicaragua); Arbitral Award of 3 October 1899 (Guyana v. Venezuela); Guatemala's Territorial, Insular and Maritime Claim (Guatemala/Belize).*

with no parallel in other regions.[65] This number accounts for approximately 34 percent of the cases brought to the Court since 2000.

The results are also impressive from a qualitative standpoint. Indeed, while preserving a long tradition of bringing sovereignty and boundary disputes before the ICJ, Latin American states have enriched the docket with far-reaching cases concerning, *inter alia*, navigational rights, the environment, diplomatic relations, transnational watercourses, the obligation to negotiate, traditional or subsistence fishing rights, and allegations about the threat or use of force and the law of the sea. For example, the referral of complex cases concerning maritime delimitation, including beyond two hundred nautical miles, has enabled the Court to maintain its traditionally paramount role in this area.[66] The initiatives of Latin American states in seizing the Court with novel disputes have been commended by the late Brazilian Judge Antonio Cançado-Trindade, emphasizing the opportunity that the Court has thus been given to pronounce on the human dimension underlying interstate disputes.[67] That Latin American states have felt confident to submit this new generation of cases before the Court is also a consequence of the Court's own disposition to deal substantively with contemporary global concerns that transcend basic bilateralism.[68]

Against those quantitative and qualitative demonstrations of reliance and confidence in the Court's work in the new era, some recent academic work describing a supposedly growing resistance to judgments of the ICJ by Latin American states, including the alleged "weapon[ization]" of Constitutional territorial clauses, cannot go unnoticed.[69] Such work raises awareness about an aspect of the relationship between states and the ICJ not dealt with in this chapter: compliance in the broadest sense.[70] But for present purposes, it suffices

[65] Since 2000, the ICJ has been seized of three cases between states from Africa, eight between states from Asia, and eight between states from Europe.

[66] *Question of the Delimitation of the Continental Shelf between Nicaragua and Colombia beyond 200 Nautical Miles from the Nicaraguan Coast (Nicaragua v. Colombia)*, Preliminary Objections, Judgment, 2016 I.C.J. 100.

[67] For a summary by Judge Cançado-Trindade see *Alleged Violations of Sovereign Rights and Maritime Spaces in the Caribbean Sea (Nicaragua v. Colombia)*—Counterclaims, Declaration of Judge Cançado-Trindade, ¶¶ 9–20.

[68] Rosalyn Higgins, "Themes and Theories," in *Selected Essays, Speeches and Writings in International Law* (Oxford: Oxford University Press, 2009); Christian J. Tams and James Sloan (eds.), *The Development of International Law by the International Court of Justice* (Oxford: Oxford University Press, 2013). Ulrich Fastenrath et al. (eds.), *From Bilateralism to Community Interest: Essays in Honour of Judge Bruno Simma* (Oxford: Oxford University Press, 2011).

[69] Arevalo, "Resistance to Territorial and Maritime Delimitation Judgments of the International Court of Justice," 8. Arevalo defines resistance as "an opposition process specifically focused on the judgments of the International Court by a recipient State that, facing a judgment that does not meet its legal or factual expectations, performs oppositional behaviours that may affect its full implementation but not the final and binding nature of the judgment or the institutional existence of the Court."

[70] Although this is a matter on which the Latin American states are certainly not the ones that should bear the heaviest burden or criticism. Their readiness to enthusiastically access the Court when others deliberately dismissed any source of jurisdiction or decided to employ the threat or the

to observe that the most notable of the few examples of the so-called resistance to ICJ judgments are—admittedly—not examples of noncompliance.

The preceding notwithstanding, since the Nicaragua versus Colombia saga has been chosen to illustrate the academic thesis in question, some brief, more detailed considerations need to be made to place the issue in its proper perspective. This is greatly helped by the outcome of the case between those two states concerning *Alleged Violations of Sovereign Rights and Maritime Spaces in the Caribbean Sea,* on which the ICJ delivered its merits judgment on April 21, 2022. In this respect, it must be emphasized that, despite criticism by Colombian high-level officials in the aftermath of the 2012 Judgment in the Territorial and Maritime Dispute, as well as a suggestion of nonappearance in further ICJ proceedings, and the recourse to the Constitutional Court to seek the proper interpretation about the relationship between certain provisions in the Pact of Bogotá and the Colombian constitutional territorial provision, Colombia's subsequent and definitive practice is consistent with its positive historical attitude toward the ICJ. In fact, Colombia's agent expressly stated that Colombia was satisfied with the Judgment of April 21, 2022.[71]

In this connection, it must be recalled that Colombia learned from the ICJ in 2007 that the maritime boundary it had historically defended was not opposable to Nicaragua under international law and was, thus, made aware that implementation issues would certainly arise out of the fact that the boundary the ICJ then denied was nonetheless domestically perceived as constitutionally rooted. Nevertheless, Colombia only denounced the Pact of Bogotá five years later, on November 27, 2012. In so doing, Colombia must have assumed that all disputes vis-à-vis Nicaragua and other states in the region had been definitively settled by the ICJ and expressed its determination to settle new regional disputes through negotiations before assessing the need to consent again to the jurisdiction of the Court. Colombia's expectation was defeated when Nicaragua brought an application on the issue concerning the continental shelf beyond two hundred nautical miles.[72] However, the fact remains that because Colombia's consent to

use of force—the genuine instances of weaponization—or other forms of unilateral action not only validates but facilitates academic work that focuses specifically on compliance with ICJ judgments in the Americas. Cf. the recent Application of Germany against Italy dated April 29, 2022, in *Questions of jurisdictional immunities of the State and measures of constraint against State-owned property (Germany v. Italy).*

[71] https://caracol.com.co/radio/2022/04/21/internacional/1650539378_667636.html (last visit May 14, 2022).

[72] Colombia opposed the *res judicata* preliminary objection against Nicaragua's application of September 16 concerning maritime delimitation beyond two hundred nautical miles, considering that this claim had been decided in the 2012 Judgment. See *Question of the Delimitation of the Continental Shelf between Nicaragua and Colombia beyond 200 Nautical Miles from the Nicaraguan Coast (Nicaragua v. Colombia),* Preliminary Objections, Judgment, 2016 I.C.J. 100. For a Latin American approach to the judgment and its contribution, see Mateo Sarzo, Res judicata, "Jurisdiction ratione materiae and Legal Reasoning in the Dispute between Nicaragua and Colombia before the

the Pact of Bogotá remained valid for one year after denunciation following the November 19, 2012, Judgment, the ICJ was entitled to exercise jurisdiction over Nicaragua's 2013 applications, including the allegation of breaches to those maritime rights and spaces declared to be Nicaraguan in the 2012 Judgment.

Moreover, while Colombia's defense before the ICJ in the *Alleged Violations of Sovereign Rights and Maritime Spaces in the Caribbean Sea* case referred to the interpretation of its constitutional territorial clause in connection with the issue of implementation, it did so only in parallel with both a recognition of the Court's jurisdiction and the finality of its judgments.[73] In other words, Colombia presented the Court with its domestic implementation issues, thereby implicitly allowing the ICJ to rule on this matter definitively, something the Court avoided doing in its 2022 Judgment. In fact, the Court had been formally asked by Nicaragua in its submissions to "adjudge and declare that [. . .] Colombia must ensure that the decision of the Constitutional Court of Colombia of 2 May 2014 or of any other National Authority will not bar compliance with the 19 November 2012 Judgment of the Court."[74] The Court, without discussing it, summarily dismissed Nicaragua's submission in operative paragraph (8) of the judgment.

Not only has Colombia recognized the binding character of the 2012 Judgment,[75] but it has also enriched the contents of the later dispute by bringing counterclaims related to essential aspects of its domestic and foreign agenda, *inter alia*, the traditional fishing rights of the Raizal people of the San Andrés Archipelago and a long-standing objection to Nicaragua's baselines.[76] This action was praised within the Court since it "enable[d] the ICJ to have a better knowledge of the dispute at issue that it has been called to adjudicate upon."[77]

In the case concerning the *Arbitral Award of 3 October 1899 (Guyana v. Venezuela)*, Venezuela's vice president formally indicated to the Court that "Venezuela had decided not to participate in the proceedings." In any event, it must be underlined that, on April 12, 2019, the Minister of People's Power for Foreign Affairs of Venezuela, while confirming Venezuela's decision not to

International Court of Justice," *The Law & Practice of International Courts and Tribunals* 16, no. 2 (2017): 224–244.

[73] See *Alleged Violations of Sovereign Rights and Maritime Spaces in the Caribbean Sea (Nicaragua v. Colombia)*, CR 2021/18, Agent, ¶¶ 10, 11.

[74] *Alleged Violations of Sovereign Rights and Maritime Spaces in the Caribbean Sea (Nicaragua v. Colombia)*, Reply of Nicaragua, Submission 1(2), 191.

[75] See *Alleged Violations of Sovereign Rights and Maritime Spaces in the Caribbean Sea (Nicaragua v. Colombia)*, CR 2021/14, Co-Agent, ¶¶ 3, 5.

[76] *Alleged Violations of Sovereign Rights and Maritime Spaces in the Caribbean Sea (Nicaragua v. Colombia)*, Counter-Memorial of the Republic of Colombia, November 17, 2016, ¶¶ 2.1, 2.9–2.11.

[77] *Alleged Violations of Sovereign Rights and Maritime Spaces in the Caribbean Sea (Nicaragua v. Colombia)*, Order of November 15, 2017, Declaration of Judge Cançado-Trindade, ¶ 5.

participate in the written proceedings, stated that "out of respect for the Court," it would provide it "in a later timely moment, with information in order to assist [it] in the fulfilment of its [duty] as indicated in Article 53.2 of its Statute." In fact, on November 28, 2019, Venezuela filed a memorandum entitled "Memorandum of the Bolivarian Republic of Venezuela on the Application filed before the International Court of Justice by the Cooperative Republic of Guyana on March 29th, 2018" which contained considerations on jurisdiction and admissibility. In a letter dated February 10, 2020, Venezuela informed the Court that it did not intend to attend the oral hearings on the question of jurisdiction. On December 18, 2020, the ICJ issued a judgment that it had jurisdiction to entertain the dispute.[78] Notably, more recently, Venezuela has appointed an agent in this case, and on June 7, 2022, it filed preliminary objections to the admissibility of the application. By Order of 13 June 2022, the Court fixed the time limits within which the Co-operative Republic of Guyana may present a written statement of its observations and submissions on the preliminary objections raised by the Bolivarian Republic of Venezuela's application. Hence, Venezuela has thus given definite proof that it remains consistent with the prevailing conteporary approach of Latin America to the Court.

The foregoing is clear evidence that, notwithstanding instances of alleged "resistance," confidence and reliance remain the most prominent characteristics of the contemporary relationship of the states of Latin America with the Court.

V. Conclusion

As cited by the Argentinean jurist Hugo Caminos, Argentine Judge Jose María Ruda, the last Latin American president of the ICJ, eloquently affirmed that

> el factor más importante en el éxito de la Corte, es la confianza de los Estados en ella. La confianza . . . es un concepto que proviene etimológicamente de *fides*, que significa fe . . . [;] es la trayectoria de una conducta la que da fe en el valor que buscan los Estados en los jueces internacionales. Y ese valor es indudablemente su independencia, su objetividad, su convicción de poder decir no o de poder decir sí, sin estar influido, ni por su nacionalidad ni por su raza, ni por sus ideas políticas, sino por su apreciación objetiva de los hechos y de la aplicación, también objetiva, de la norma jurídica que se considere vigente.[79]

[78] *Arbitral Award of 3 October 1899 (Guyana v. Venezuela)*, Jurisdiction of the Court, Judgment, 2020 I.C.J. 455.

[79] Hugo Caminos, "José María Ruda (1924-1994)," in *Liber Amicorum in Memoriam of Judge José María Ruda*, ed. Calixto A. Armas Barea et al. (The Hague, The Netherlands: Kluwer Law International, 2000), xxxix–xl.

We hope that this chapter has demonstrated that "confidence" is the most prominent contemporary feature to describe the relationship between Latin American states and the ICJ. The Court is now trusted by those states with the resolution and settlement of their most important disputes. Confidence and trust are also evident in the type of controversies they have brought before the Court, which include contemporary questions such as those involving the environment and the rights of the individual.

Notably, the current moment is by all accounts to be praised and cherished, as it is the positive result of a complex evolutionary process, including a long period when Latin American states did not perceive the Court as the most suitable forum to settle their most significant disputes. The acknowledgment of the road thus followed should send a message for Latin American states to make reasonable and responsible use of the Statute and the Pact of Bogotá, and for the Court to exhaustively exercise its jurisdiction to meet the expectations of finality that every state holds when submitting a case to the principal judicial organ of the United Nations.

15

International Humanitarian Law in Latin America

The Role of Truth Commissions

Elizabeth Salmón

I. Introduction

In international humanitarian law (IHL), there is no central authority in charge of qualifying a situation of violence and determining whether or not it is an armed conflict. As a result, there is a margin of uncertainty about the actors recognizing themselves as parties to a conflict. Notably, it must be emphasized that the parties are not required to declare the existence of an armed conflict for it to exist and for IHL to be mandatorily applicable. This means that when a specific situation meets the constitutive elements of the definition of armed conflict, the parties must apply the rules of IHL.

It has been a frequent practice among Latin American states to deny the existence of an armed conflict, even when applying IHL. This chapter describes the role that Truth Commissions have fulfilled by classifying a violent situation as a noninternational armed conflict (NIAC), filling the role, to a certain extent, of a body that makes such a determination. Such qualification by an entity with legitimacy, in the absence of recognition by the states themselves, makes it possible to open the debate on the periods of abuse, provide legal clarity, and deal with the crimes committed in said contexts.

II. The Role of Truth Commissions in Latin America in the Classification of Situations of Violence and Applicability of IHL

There is no normative definition, conventional or customary, of NIACs. A NIAC occurs, according to the classic definition in the *Tadić* case before the International Criminal Tribunal for the former Yugoslavia (ICTY), whenever there is "protracted armed violence between governmental authorities and

Elizabeth Salmón, *International Humanitarian Law in Latin America* In: *Latin American International Law in the Twenty-First Century*. Edited by: Alejandro Chehtman, Alexandra Huneeus, and Sergio Puig, Oxford University Press. © Oxford University Press 2025. DOI: 10.1093/9780197754016.003.0015

organized armed groups or between such groups within a State."[1] In consequence, if it is verified that a specific situation of violence complies with the following two elements—organization of the parties and intensity of the hostilities between the aforementioned actors—the logical consequence should be that the state classifies the situation as a NIAC without major inconvenience and subsequently applies IHL.

Throughout the twentieth century, the Latin American population has been immersed in NIACs of varying intensity. To analyze the position of the States regarding the application of IHL in relation to the NIACs that have occurred in their territories, the I have chosen to begin in 1949, considering that the four Geneva Conventions of 1949 were adopted on August 12 of that year.[2] Since that year, approximately forty-eight situations of violence have developed in Latin America that have reached the threshold to be considered NIACs, following the Uppsala Conflict Data Program.[3]

However, not all Latin American states have recognized the configuration of a NIAC. In fact, it is possible to identify two stages regarding the position of the states in recognizing a NIAC in their territory: first, a stage of reluctance to officially accept that a NIAC has occurred, and second, the creation of transitional justice mechanisms, which led to the qualification of the NIAC by certain Truth Commissions. These stages were present, for example, in the cases of Guatemala and Peru.

Concerning the first stage, it is worth asking what reasons prevented the Latin American states from recognizing the existence of a NIAC in their territory. We will see later that states usually fear that the classification of a violent situation as a NIAC would elevate the position of the armed groups and have them recognized as belligerents. This fear arises even though the most basic norms of IHL clearly establish that their application does not alter the status of the parties. Thus, Article 3, applicable to all NIACs, states that its application "shall not affect the legal status of the Parties to the conflict." This is because the article aims to protect the victims of conflicts for humanitarian reasons.[4]

[1] IT-94-1-T *Prosecutor v. Dusko Tadic aka "Dule" (Decision on the Defence Motion for Interlocutory Appeal on Jurisdiction)* [1995] International Criminal Tribunal for the former Yugoslavia, ¶ 70.

[2] I am referring to the "Geneva Convention for the Amelioration of the Condition of the Wounded and Sick in Armed Forces in the Field" (Convention I), "Geneva Convention for the Amelioration of the Condition of the Wounded, Sick and Shipwrecked Members of Armed Forces at Sea" (Convention II), "Geneva Convention relative to the Treatment of Prisoners of War" (Convention III), and "Geneva Convention relative to the Protection of Civilian Persons in Time of War" (Convention IV).

[3] For specific information regarding armed conflicts in Latin American countries, refer to the Uppsala Conflict Data Program website hosted by the Department of Peace and Conflict Research of Uppsala University: https://ucdp.uu.se/exploratory.

[4] Elizabeth Salmón, *Introducción al Derecho Internacional Humanitario* (Lima, Peru: IDEHPUCP and ICRC, 2016), 127.

In a second stage, as mentioned above, transitional justice processes are given way. In this regard, we understand transitional justice as the political transition process faced by societies emerging from periods of violence in which serious human rights violations have been committed and in which national reconciliation is sought.[5]

It is worth remembering that transitional justice has been understood to include both judicial and extrajudicial mechanisms,[6] such as the prosecution of the perpetrators, truth-seeking, reparation to victims, and institutional reform—which refers to fundamentally changing the institutions responsible for human rights violations.[7]

As part of the truth-seeking component, Truth Commissions have been created to establish official truth and give victims a voice in public discourse.[8] In Latin America, at least eleven countries have Truth Commissions[9] that have helped in national processes to transition from dictatorial regimes and NIACs.

For the development of this section, I have selected five of the most notorious Truth Commissions in Latin America established in the transitional justice processes of Argentina, Chile, El Salvador, Guatemala, and Peru. Additionally, I have considered the Commission for the Clarification of Truth, Coexistence and Non-Repetition in Colombia as a case in which the state recognized the existence of a NIAC before both the creation of the commission and the issuance of its final report.

[5] See United Nations Security Council, "The Rule of Law and Transitional Justice in Conflict and Post-Conflict Societies (S/2004/616), Report of the Secretary-General submitted to the Security Council," August 23, 2004, 4, where "transitional" is defined as "the full range of processes and mechanisms associated with a society's attempts to come to terms with a legacy of large-scale past abuses, in order to ensure accountability, serve justice and achieve reconciliation."

[6] Human Rights Council, "Annual Report of the United Nations High Commissioner for Human Rights and Reports of the Office of the High Commissioner and the Secretary-General. Analytical Study on Human Rights and Transitional Justice (A/HRC/12/18)" (August 6, 2009), accessed May 11, 2022, https://documents-dds-ny.un.org/doc/UNDOC/GEN/G09/149/18/PDF/G0914918.pdf?OpenElement, 4.

[7] Paul Van Zyl, "Promoting Transitional Justice in Post-Conflict Societies," in *Transitional Justice: Handbook for Latin America*, ed. Félix Reátegui (Brasília: Brazilian Amnesty Commission, Ministry of Justice of Brazil; International Center for Transitional Justice, 2011), 50.

[8] Ibid., 48–49.

[9] I am referring to the truth commissions of the following countries: Argentina, Brazil, Chile, Colombia, Ecuador, El Salvador, Guatemala, Honduras, Paraguay, Peru, and Uruguay. In October 2021, the Mexican government created a truth commission to investigate the period of police and military repression known as the "*Guerra Sucia*" (Comisión para el Acceso a la Verdad, el Esclarecimiento Histórico y el Impulso a la Justicia de las violaciones graves a los derechos humanos cometidas de 1965 a 1990). This commission has not yet submitted a final report on its findings.

III. Cases in which the Existence of an Armed Conflict Is Not Addressed: Argentina and Chile

The first two cases are related to contexts of transition from extremely repressive dictatorial regimes. In these cases, the Truth Commissions did not address the possibility of an armed conflict and the consequent application of the IHL. As I describe in the next section, the absence of such qualification might be explained, to a certain extent, by the limitations of their mandates and, mainly, by the disproportionate nature of the repression.

Argentina's National Commission on Disappearance of Persons (*Comisión Nacional sobre la Desaparición de Personas*, or CONADEP)

Between 1976 and 1983, Argentina was immersed in a period of military dictatorship in which serious human rights violations were committed.[10] The repression was directed mainly at left-wing armed movements such as the Montoneros and the People's Revolutionary Army (*Ejército Revolucionario del Pueblo*, or ERP); however, the limited armed resistance of these groups was quickly subdued, and most of the political violence was carried out by the state.[11]

After returning to democracy, in 1983, President Raúl Alfonsín created CONADEP through Decree No. 187 to clarify the facts related to the forced disappearance of persons during the dictatorship.[12] After nine months of work, on September 20, 1984, the CONADEP delivered its final report to the president of the Republic under the title "Never Again" (*Nunca Más*).[13]

In its final report, CONADEP stated that until that moment, 8,960 people continued to be in a situation of forced disappearance.[14] However, that figure

[10] Ministry of Culture of Argentina, "¿Qué es la CONADEP?" (December 15, 2020),accessed May 26, 2022.

[11] Lorena Balardini, "Argentina: Regional Protagonist of Transitional Justice," in *Transitional Justice in Latin America: The Uneven Road from Impunity towards Accountability*, ed. Elin Skaar, Jemima Garcia-Godos, and Cath Collins (New York: Routledge, 2016), 51.

[12] National Executive Branch of Argentina, "Decree No. 187/1983," Argentina.gob.ar (December 19, 1983), accessed May 26, 2022, https://www.argentina.gob.ar/normativa/nacional/decreto-187-1983-263505/texto.

[13] MERCOSUR Institute of Public Policies on Human Rights, "CONADEP (Comisión Nacional sobre la Desaparición de Personas)" (2019), accessed May 26, 2022, http://atom.ippdh.mercosur.int/index.php/conadep-comision-nacional-sobre-la-desaparicion-de-personas.

[14] Ministry of Culture of Argentina, *El Nunca más y los crímenes de la dictadura*, (Buenos Aires: Ministerio de Cultura de la Nación, 2021), accessed May 26, 2022, https://librosycasas.cultura.gob.ar/wp-content/uploads/2022/02/Nunca-Mas_Digital_2021-1.pdf, 211.

was not considered definite, and today, the figure most frequently mentioned, including by the government, is 30,000.[15]

Chile's National Truth and Reconciliation Commission

In Chile, the transitional justice process also took place after a dictatorial regime. In this case, on September 11, 1973, the armed forces overthrew an elected socialist government and seized power; for the next seventeen years, a right-wing regime led by Augusto Pinochet ruled.[16] It is estimated that between September 1973 and December 1989, at least 3,216 people were killed or forcibly disappeared, and 38,254 more survived political imprisonment and torture.[17]

Through Supreme Decree No. 355 of 1990, the first National Truth and Reconciliation Commission (*Comisión Nacional de Verdad y Reconciliación*, or CNVR) was created. The first article of CNVR established that its purpose would be to "contribute to the global clarification of the truth about the most serious violations of human rights committed in recent years":

> For these purposes, serious violations shall be understood as the situations of disappeared, executed and tortured detainees resulting in death, in which the moral responsibility of the State appears to be compromised and due to acts of its agents or persons at its service, as well as kidnappings and attacks against the life of people committed by individuals under political pretexts.[18]

The CNVR issued its initial report in 1991. Subsequently, work was carried out by new commissions such as the National Corporation for Reparations and Reconciliation or the National Commission on Political Imprisonment and Torture; these commissions expanded the number of victims and investigated acts not initially considered under the mandate of the CNVR.[19]

The cases of Argentina and Chile share some important features. In both, the mandates assigned to the Truth Commissions were restricted to a list of acts, excluding several others that were potentially committed in those contexts.[20]

[15] Ibid., 12.

[16] Cath Collins and Boris Hau, "Chile: Incremental truth, late justice," in Skaar et al.,126–127.

[17] Ibid., 127.

[18] Executive Branch of Chile, "Decreto Supremo No. 355 que Crea la Comisión Verdad y Reconciliación," Instituto Nacional de Derechos Humanos (April 25, 1990), accessed May 26, 2022, https://bibliotecadigital.indh.cl/bitstream/handle/123456789/179/ds355.pdf?sequence=1&isAllowed=y.

[19] Collins and Hau, "Chile: Incremental Truth, Late Justice," 128–129.

[20] Priscilla B. Hayner, "Truth Commissions: A Schematic Overview," *International Review of the Red Cross* 88, no. 862 (June 2006): 8, 10, https://international-review.icrc.org/articles/truth-commissions-schematic-overview.

The list included, in the Argentine case, forced disappearances, and, in Chile, in addition, executions, torture resulting in death, kidnappings, and attacks on life under certain circumstances. In the second, however, there have been new commissions to deal with some of the crimes originally excluded.

Regarding the application of IHL, it can be mentioned that the commissions did not rule on the question of whether at any time there had been an armed conflict—Argentina, with the Montoneros or the ERP, and Chile, even initially, between state forces and the military faction of Augusto Pinochet, Toribio Merino, and Leigh Guzman. In the Argentine case,[21] the state has also pointed out that it is necessary to emphasize the responsibility of the state and that, therefore, it is not appropriate to refer to state actions as a "dirty war," since that expression "gives the idea of two equal sides that face each other."[22]

On the other hand, the Chilean Truth Commission did not recognize the existence of a NIAC as such. However, in the *Almonacid* case, the Inter-American Court affirmed that a NIAC broke out during the coup d'état and remained active after 1979. The Supreme Court agreed with this view,[23] although in a loosely inconsistent way.[24]

IV. Cases of Recognition of NIAC by Truth Commissions: El Salvador, Guatemala, and Peru

Three Latin American Truth Commissions were created in post-conflict contexts: El Salvador, Guatemala, and Peru. Although their mandates did not explicitly mention IHL, the three entities qualified the conflict to interpret and carry out their mandates.

[21] Two armed conflicts took place in Argentina but were not analyzed by the truth commission. The first is the international armed conflict against the United Kingdom over *Las Malvinas* (April 1982). The second, noninternational in nature, was identified by the IACHR in the post-authoritarian period, specifically on January 23 and 24, 1989, after the attempted seizure and recovery of the military barracks in *La Tablada* (see Case 11.137 *Juan Carlos Abella v. Argentina*, Inter-Am. Comm'n Rep. No. 55/97, ¶¶ 327–329) (1998).

[22] Ministry of Justice of Argentina, "Recomendaciones para el tratamiento mediático responsable sobre la dictadura cívico-militar y el proceso de Memoria, Verdad y Justicia" (2021), accessed May 26, 2022, https://www.argentina.gob.ar/sites/default/files/2021/04/recomendaciones-dictadura_0.pdf, 4.

[23] The first case in which the Chilean Supreme Court recognized an armed conflict is Rol 559-2004 (2006). This position was later restated in the Rol 6188-2006 (2007) and Rol 1489-2007 (2007) cases and continued to be mentioned in jurisprudence in 2007, 2008, and 2009.

[24] For a more detailed discussion on this, refer to Catalina Fernández Carter, "La aplicación de los Convenios de Ginebra en ausencia de un conflicto armado: El caso de la dictadura militar chilena," *IUS ET VERITAS* 63 (2021): 46–50, where the author criticizes the position of the Chilean Supreme Court in this regard.

The Commission on the Truth for El Salvador

The Mexico Agreements signed on April 27, 1991, between the representatives of the Salvadoran government and the Farabundo Martí National Liberation Front (*Frente Farabundo Martí para la Liberación Nacional*, or FMLN) provided for the creation of the Commission on the Truth for El Salvador (*Comisión de la Verdad para El Salvador*). These agreements were included, in turn, in the Peace Agreement ("Chapultepec Agreement") of July 15, 1992.[25]

The commission was created to investigate the "serious acts of violence"[26] that took place in the armed conflict between 1980 and 1991 and which claimed around seventy-five thousand lives.[27] To identify which facts were within the framework of its mandate, the commission had to begin by defining the "serious acts of violence." In this regard, in its final report of March 15, 1993, it specified that "serious acts of violence" do not exist in a "normative vacuum" but must be analyzed based on "certain relevant principles of law."[28]

The commission referred to IHL and pointed out that not all violations of the rights recognized in human rights instruments constituted serious acts of violence. On the contrary, it specified that the classification of the severity of each act of violence would be based on the catalog of nonderogable rights mentioned in the human rights treaties that legally bind the state.[29]

Regarding IHL, the commission indicated that the principles contained in the treaties that regulate this branch of public international law and to which the state was a party applied to the Salvadoran conflict. The Commission noted the following:

> Although the armed conflict in El Salvador was not an international conflict as defined by the [Geneva] Conventions [of 1949], **it did meet the requirements for the application of article 3 common to the four Conventions.** That article defines some fundamental humanitarian rules applicable to non-international

[25] Thomas Buergenthal, "The United Nations Truth Commission for El Salvador," *Vanderbilt Journal of Transnational Law* 27, no. 3 (October 1994): 498–499, https://scholarship.law.vanderbilt.edu/vjtl/vol27/iss3/1/.

[26] Commission on the Truth for El Salvador, "From Madness to Hope: The 12-Year War in El Salvador. Report of the Commission on the Truth for El Salvador," United Nations Security Council (S/25500) (1993), 11, accessed May 11, 2022. https://documents-dds-ny.un.org/doc/UNDOC/GEN/N93/209/27/IMG/N9320927.pdf?OpenElement.

[27] Buergenthal, "The United Nations Truth Commission for El Salvador," 502.

[28] Commission on the Truth for El Salvador, "From Madness to Hope," 20.

[29] Ibid., 11.

armed conflicts. The same is true for Protocol II Additional to the Geneva Conventions, relating to the protection of victims of non-international armed conflicts [...]

Without going into those provisions in detail, **it is clear that violations** -by either of the two parties to the conflict- **of common Article 3 and of the fundamental guarantees contained in Additional Protocol II**, especially if committed systematically, **could be characterized as serious acts of violence for the purposes of the interpretation and application of the Commission's mandate.** (Emphasis added)[30]

It is possible to note that for the commission, it was relevant to classify the situation of violence as a NIAC since this allowed it to affirm, first, that the basic norms of the IHL that govern the NIAC were applicable. Bearing in mind that such norms contain fundamental guarantees and basic humanitarian rules, their violation effectively gives rise to "serious acts of violence" within the meaning of its mandate. In other words, it was helpful for the commission to resort to IHL to strengthen its position that the facts it had decided to analyze reached a sufficient level of "seriousness."

An interesting contribution from the commission, although unrelated to the qualification of the conflict, is that it concluded that the FMLN indeed had an obligation to repair; the FMLN, in turn, provided reparations, but as a political party in power, not as a rebel group.[31] This is important because it supports the notion that the scope of the obligation to redress under IHL is increasingly widening: it extends not only to states but also to other actors,[32] in this case, to nonstate armed groups.

Guatemala's Commission for Historical Clarification

For thirty-six years, between 1960 and 1996, Guatemala experienced one of the longest NIACs in Latin America.[33] It is estimated that two hundred thousand people were killed or disappeared. In addition, some 1.5 million people were displaced by the conflict.[34] The main parties to the conflict were the government

[30] Ibid., 21.

[31] Elizabeth Salmón and Juan Pablo Pérez-León, "Reparation for Victims of Serious Violations of International Humanitarian Law: New Developments," *International Review of the Red Cross* 104, no. 919 (June 2022): 1332, https://international-review.icrc.org/articles/reparation-for-victims-of-serious-violations-of-ihl-new-developments-919.

[32] Ibid., 1343.

[33] Jemima García-Godos and Luis Raúl Salvadó, "Guatemala: Truth and Memory on Trial," in Skaar et al., 204.

[34] Commission for Historical Clarification, *Guatemala: Memory of Silence. Report of the Commission for Historical Clarification Conclusions and Recommendations* (1999), 17, 30 accessed May 11, 2022, https://hrdag.org/wp-content/uploads/2013/01/CEHreport-english.pdf.

and the Guatemalan National Revolutionary Unit (*Unidad Revolucionaria Nacional Guatemalteca*, or URNG), which brought together several insurgent organizations.[35] However, in this case, 93 percent of the violations considered fell on the Guatemala.[36]

As part of the transitional justice process, the *Comisión para el Esclarecimiento Histórico* (CEH) was established with the Oslo Agreement of June 23, 1994, signed between the government and the URNG.[37] One of the purposes assigned to CEH was "[t]o clarify with all objectivity, equity and impartiality the human rights violations and acts of violence that have caused the Guatemalan population to suffer, connected with the armed conflict."[38]

In its final report of February 24, 1999, the CEH stipulated the expression "acts of violence" as acts that included actions or omissions related to the internal armed conflict and that constituted an infraction of the internal legal order, IHL and the international human rights law (IHRL) normative system.[39]

After that, the CEH confirmed that the situation of violence experienced in Guatemala constituted a NIAC in the following terms:

> 1687. The concept of non-international conflict or internal armed conflict is applied to armed clashes between government forces and armed and organized opposition groups, when these clashes take place within the territory of a State. This last requirement was fully met in Guatemala, since the armed conflict took place within its territorial limits and, precisely because of this factor, it acquired non-international characteristics.[40]

The CEH then affirmed the existence of an armed conflict. Although some points of its qualification of the conflict can be seen as debatable,[41] it is essential

[35] García-Godos and Salvadó, "Guatemala: Truth and Memory on Trial," 221.

[36] Commission for Historical Clarification, *Guatemala: Memoria del Silencio*, 324.

[37] Ibid.,15.

[38] United Nations General Assembly and Security Council, "The situation in Central America: procedures for the establishment of a firm and lasting peace and progress in fashioning a region of peace, freedom, democracy and development" (A/48/954 and S/1994/751) (July 1, 1994), accessed May 11, 2022, https://documents-dds-ny.un.org/doc/UNDOC/GEN/N94/263/35/PDF/N9426335.pdf?OpenElement, 13.

[39] Commission for Historical Clarification, *Guatemala: Memoria del Silencio*, 1662.

[40] Ibid., 311.

[41] On this point, it is understood today that if a NIAC crosses the borders of the territory of a state, it does not automatically lose its noninternational character—as happens with spillover conflicts. This is because although common Article 3 applies to NIACs that arise in the territory of "one" of the High Contracting Parties, it is accepted that the hostilities that spill over will be considered part of the same NIAC (Dapo Akande, "Classification of Armed Conflicts," in *The Oxford Guide to International Humanitarian Law*, ed. Ben Saul and Dapo Akande (Oxford: Oxford University Press, 2020), 42) as long as the armed forces of another state do not intervene (Dieter Fleck, "The Law of Non-International Armed Conflicts," in *The Handbook of International Humanitarian Law*, ed. Dieter Fleck (Oxford: Oxford University Press, 2013), 582).

to highlight that before the classification made by the CEH, the Guatemalan State did not consistently recognize the existence of a NIAC. On the contrary, the CEH mentioned that, in an article in the Military Journal (*Revista Militar*) from 1982, the Guatemalan Army itself went so far as to point out that its High Command recommended "the observance of the laws of war with regard to the civilian population."[42] Nevertheless, it added that "in no way it is being accepted that there is a situation of war in the national territory."[43]

Likewise, the classification of the situation as a NIAC and the consequent application of IHL served as the basis for the CEH to state in its conclusions that the state agents had committed acts prohibited by common Article 3, such as "attacks against life and bodily integrity, mutilation, cruel treatment, torture and torment, the taking of hostages, attacks on personal dignity, and particularly humiliating and degrading treatment, including the rape of women."[44]

The CEH did not stop at this point. Although it emphasized that according to its mandate it did not fulfill a judicial role, it did refer to the commission of genocide against Indigenous communities[45] and war crimes. Regarding this last point, the CEH noted that the actions of state agents in "the commission of forced disappearances during the armed confrontation constitute[d] serious violations of human rights and breaches of international humanitarian law; therefore, the State is the author of war crimes."[46]

In short, the CEH qualified the situation as a NIAC to give content to the "acts of violence" concerning the armed conflict, referring to violations of IHL norms. In turn, this served as the basis for affirming that the Guatemalan State would be the "author of war crimes."

The Peruvian Truth and Reconciliation Commission

The armed conflict in Peru took place between 1980 and 2000. In this conflict, government forces mainly clashed against the "Peruvian Communist Party 'Shining Path'" (*Partido Comunista del Perú—Sendero Luminoso*, or PCP-SL), which had decided to start a "people's war" against the state.[47] Likewise, the State confronted the Túpac Amaru Revolutionary Movement (MRTA).[48] The estimated death toll of the conflict amounts to 69,280 people.[49]

[42] Commission for Historical Clarification, *Guatemala: Memoria del Silencio*, 311.
[43] Ibid., 311.
[44] Commission for Historical Clarification, *Conclusions and Recommendations*, 37.
[45] Ibid., 38–41.
[46] Commission for Historical Clarification, *Guatemala: Memoria del Silencio*, 412.
[47] Truth and Reconciliation Commission, *Comisión de la Verdad y Reconciliación. Informe Final*, vol. I (Lima, Peru: CVR, 2003), 54.
[48] Ibid., 69.
[49] Ibid., 53.

Unlike the commissions of El Salvador and Guatemala, which emerged from peace agreements and received significant international support, the Peruvian Truth and Reconciliation Commission (Comisión de la Verdad y Reconciliación, or CVR) was created by an internal decree issued by the interim president of the Republic and published on June 4, 2001.[50] The CVR was installed on July 13, 2001,[51] and presented its final report on August 28, 2003.[52]

The decree that created the CVR established that it would be in charge of clarifying the process, the facts and responsibilities for the terrorist violence, and the violation of human rights that occurred between May 1980 and November 2000.[53] Likewise, Article 3 of the same norm established that the CVR would focus its work on the following acts, as long as they are attributable to terrorist organizations, state agents, or paramilitary groups: (1) assassination and kidnapping, (2) forced disappearances, (3) torture and other serious injuries, (4) violations to the collective rights of the Andean and native communities of the country, and (5) other crimes and serious violations of the rights of individuals.[54]

The CVR's mandate did not expressly include violations of the IHL in its material scope. The CVR identified that this was probably because, for some sectors, the allusion to IHL generated concern as "indicating the existence of an armed conflict could indirectly imply the attribution of belligerent status to subversive groups."[55] Consequently, the CVR noted that it would have to identify the "most appropriate legal bases to classify the criminal acts attributed to subversive organizations."[56]

In line with this, in its final report, the CVR expressly classified the situation of violence that Peru faced between 1980 and 2000 as a NIAC by stating the following:

> [T]he facts examined—tens of thousands of people killed in a context of armed violence and several thousand others wounded or maimed—can only be explained by the existence of an internal armed conflict governed without a doubt by common Article 3 aforesaid.[57]

[50] Presidency of the Council of Ministers of Peru, "Supreme Decree No. 065-2001-PCM. Creation of the Truth Commission," Comisión de la Verdad y Reconciliación (June 4, 2001), accessed May 11, 2022, http://www.cverdad.org.pe/ingles/lacomision/cnormas/normas01.php. The CVR was created by Supreme Decree No. 065-2001, modified by Supreme Decree No. 101-2001-PCM

[51] Presidency of the Council of Ministers of Peru, "Supreme Decree No. 101-2001-PCM. Modification of the denomination of Truth Commission to Truth and Reconciliation Commission," Comisión de la Verdad y Reconciliación (August 31, 2001), accessed May 11, 2022, http://www.cverdad.org.pe/ingles/lacomision/cnormas/normas01.php.

[52] Truth and Reconciliation Commission, "TRC Final Report was made public on August 28th 2003 at noon," Comisión de la Verdad y Reconciliación (August 28, 2003), accessed May 11, 2022.

[53] Presidency of the Council of Ministers of Peru, "Creation of the Truth Commission".

[54] Ibid.

[55] Truth and Reconciliation Commission, *Informe Final*, tome I, 24.

[56] Ibid., 24.

[57] Ibid., 204.

It is worth mentioning that the express qualification of the situation of violence as a NIAC made by the CVR has not been officially endorsed by the Peruvian State. In fact, the official documents of the Peruvian government currently use expressions such as "the violence unleashed by terrorist groups"[58] or "the period of violence 1980-2000"[59] to refer to the armed conflict.

In sum, in the cases of the three Commissions that recognized the existence of an armed conflict, the mandates did not include explicit references to IHL violations, as they did with respect to human rights violations. In the cases of El Salvador and Guatemala, the mandate used similar expressions to refer to acts of violence that later had to be linked to violations of IHL by truth commissions. In the case of Peru, a more detailed list of acts was included, but again armed conflict was not mentioned in the decree that created the Truth and Reconciliation Commission.

This omission could be explained by the reluctance of states to recognize the existence of an armed conflict due to the erroneous assumption that such recognition might imply granting a belligerent status or legitimizing the armed groups in question.[60] It is, in turn, different from what happened with Argentina and Chile, where state repression was so acute and disproportionate to the insurgency that the mere mention of the word "war," as in the case of the "dirty war" in Argentina, would seem to justify the acts of the state. Therefore, it is automatically ruled out.

V. When Conflict Is Recognized without the Need for a Commission: Colombia

Unlike previous cases where the Truth Commissions concentrated their efforts to search for the truth, in Colombia, the effort has been multifaceted.[61] There

[58] This expression was used, for example, in the intervention of the Permanent Representative of Peru before the Sixth Committee of the United Nations General Assembly in its 72nd session in 2017. Throughout the entire intervention, the NIAC category was not used to qualify the 1980–2000 period. See Permanent Mission of Peru before the United Nations, "Intervención del Embajador Gustavo Meza-Cuadra Velásquez Representante Permanente del Perú ante la Sexta Comisión de la Asamblea General de las Naciones Unidas" (speech, Sixth Committee of the General Assembly, 72nd session, New York, October 2, 2017), https://www.un.org/en/ga/sixth/72/pdfs/statements/int_terrorism/peru.pdf

[59] This expression is used, for example, on the website of the Place of Memory, Tolerance and Social Inclusion (*Lugar de la Memoria, Tolerancia e Inclusión Social*), which is a space of the Peruvian Ministry of Culture to commemorate what happened between the years 1980 and 2000. See Place of Memory, Tolerance and Social Inclusion, "Quiénes Somos," Ministry of Culture of Peru, accessed February 22, 2024, https://lum.cultura.pe/el-lum/quienes-somos.

[60] Alonso Gurmendi Dunkelberg, *Conflicto armado en el Perú: la época del terrorismo bajo el derecho internacional* (Lima, Peru: Universidad del Pacífico, 2019).

[61] Nelson Camilo Sánchez León, Jemima García-Godos, and Catalina Vallejo, "Colombia: Transitional Justice before Transition," in Skaar et al., *Transitional Justice in Latin America*, 260.

have been multiple attempts to establish Truth Commissions: those with somewhat fragmented and limited functions—such as the Truth Commission on the Palace of Justice events; or with very broad objectives; with high government participation—such as the National Commission for Reparation and Reconciliation created in 2005—and little involvement of civil society.[62]

On November 24, 2016, the National Government of Colombia and the Revolutionary Armed Forces of Colombia-People's Army (*Fuerzas Armadas Revolucionarias de Colombia—Ejército del Pueblo*, or FARC-EP) signed the "Final Agreement to End the Armed Conflict and Build a Stable and Lasting Peace," after fifty years of armed conflict. With this agreement, the Integral System of Truth, Reparations, Justice and Non-repetition was established.[63] This system, in turn, includes the Commission for the Clarification of Truth, Coexistence and Non-Repetition (CEV) as the component of truth. The CEV issued its final report in June 2022, after the Colombian Constitutional Court extended its original three-year mandate.[64]

Regarding recognizing the armed conflict, in May 2011, Juan Manuel Santos, then president of the Republic, affirmed the existence of an armed conflict in that state.[65] Such recognition came after years of conflict. In this case, for example, opposition figures constantly protested against classifying the situation of violence as an armed conflict and instead resorted to calling the situation exclusively a "terrorist threat."[66] However, it can be said that this "occasional flirting" with the idea of denying the existence of an armed conflict contrasts with the general rule where "[a]ll of the branches of government have continuously acknowledged the validity of IHL, be it through laws, military manuals, ministerial decrees or judicial decisions."[67]

In consequence, the CEV no longer had to deal with the task of classifying the situation of violence as an armed conflict. The prior recognition of the situation

[62] Gina Kalach Torres, "Las comisiones de la verdad en Colombia," *Revista Jurídica Mario Alario D´Filippo* 8, no. 16 (2016): 120, https://doi.org/https://doi.org/10.32997/2256-2796-vol.8-num.16-2016-1534.

[63] Presidency of the Republic of Colombia, Office of the High Commissioner for Peace, *Acuerdo Final para la Terminación del Conflicto y la Construcción de una Paz Estable y Duradera* (Bogotá, Colombia: Oficina del Alto Comisionado para la Paz, 2018).

[64] Commission for the Clarification of Truth, Coexistence and Non-Repetition, "Sobre la decisión de la Corte Constitucional de extender el periodo de la Comisión" (October 1, 2021), accessed May 11, 2022, https://comisiondelaverdad.co/actualidad/comunicados-y-declaraciones/sobre-la-decision-de-la-corte-constitucional-de-extender-el-periodo-de-la-comision.

[65] United Nations, "Colombia: ONU encomia reconocimiento de existencia de conflicto armado" (May 10, 2011), accessed May 26, 2022, https://news.un.org/es/story/2011/05/1217101.

[66] BBC, "Colombia decide si reconoce la existencia de un conflicto armado," BBC News Mundo (May 11, 2011), accessed May 26, 2022, https://www.bbc.com/mundo/noticias/2011/05/110511_colombia_impliaciones_reconocimiento_conflicto_armado_jrg.

[67] Marcela Giraldo Muñoz and Jose Serralvo, "International Humanitarian Law in Colombia: Going a Step Beyond," *International Review of the Red Cross* 101, no. 912 (November 2019): 1122.

as an armed conflict was reflected in the CEV's mandate. Thus, in accordance with Article 11 of Decree 588 of 2017, the CEV had the mandate to clarify and promote the recognition of

> 1. Practices and events that constitute serious violations of human rights and grave breaches of International Humanitarian Law (IHL), in particular those that reflect patterns or are massive in nature, that took place during the armed conflict, as well as the complexity of the contexts and territorial dynamics in which they happened.[68]

The CEV, in its final report, then had the opportunity to expand on the violations of IHL and the context in which they were committed. In this regard, it should be remembered that according to Article 4 of Decree 588 of 2017, the activities of the CEV "will not be judicial in nature, nor will they be used for criminal charges before any jurisdictional authority" and that the information that it receives or produces may not be transferred by it to judicial authorities to be used to attribute responsibilities in judicial proceedings or even "to have probative value."

This aligns with the nonjurisdictional nature of commissions. However, this does not mean that truth commission reports do not have undeniable legal consequences.[69] As will be addressed in section VI, the final report of the Colombian CEV could have an evidentiary or interpretative nature in the petitions that reach the inter-American human rights system.[70] In other words, although it will no longer be necessary for the CEV to substantiate in detail the existence of an armed conflict in Colombia, its final report may ultimately be useful in proving other facts about the context of the armed conflict. This, in addition to the other three functions related to the right to truth, the establishment of state responsibility, and the granting of reparations.

[68] Presidency of the Republic of Colombia, "Decreto 588 de 2017, 'Por el cual se organiza la Comisión para el Esclarecimiento de la Verdad, la Convivencia y la no Repetición,'" *Comisión de la Verdad* (April 5, 2017), accessed May 26, 2022, https://comisiondelaverdad.co/images/decreto-588-de-2017-comision-verdad-mandato-funciones.pdf.

[69] Elizabeth Salmón, "Las Comisiones de la Verdad y la jurisprudencia de la Corte Interamericana de Derechos Humanos. ¿Hacia la parajudicialización de las Comisiones de la Verdad?," in *La verdad nos hace libres. Sobre las relaciones entre filosofía, derechos humanos, religión y universidad*, ed. Miguel Giusti, Gustavo Gutiérrez, and Elizabeth Salmón (Lima, Peru: Fondo Editorial PUCP, 2015), 291.

[70] Juan Carlos Lucero Rojas, *Efectos jurídicos del análisis de contexto presentado en los informes finales de la Comisión de la Verdad ante la Corte Interamericana de Derechos Humanos, una proyección para la situación colombiana* (Bogotá: Universidad Externado de Colombia, 2019), 36–37.

VI. The Role of Truth Commissions' Reports in the Inter-American Human Rights System

Despite the nonjudicial nature of truth commissions, their final reports and findings carry important evidentiary weight about the events investigated by each commission. In the inter-American system for the protection of human rights, for example, the Inter-American Court of Human Rights has used reports from truth commissions in fifty-six judgments as of November 2022.

The Inter-American Court's use of the reports of the truth commissions gives them a special character, which I have called "parajudicial," since they serve to fulfill the jurisdictional role of the Inter-American Court.[71] The functions that the reports have fulfilled in the judgments of the Court can be classified as follows: (1) the establishment of the facts that constituted the violation of a right, (2) the affirmation of the right to the truth as a right belonging to the legal heritage of individuals and society, (3) the use of the reports to establish the responsibility of the State, and finally (4) to grant a reparation.[72]

The first time that the Inter-American Court used the reports of the regional truth commissions to establish the facts and the context in which the violation of a right occurred was in the case of *Bámaca Velásquez v. Guatemala*. Thus, with regard to the NIAC of Guatemala, the Court pointed out that "the Army had the practice of torturing the guerrillas they captured, which was proved very exactly in . . . the reports prepared by both the Commission for Historical Clarification and the REMHI [Recovery of the Historical Memory]," as well as in the testimonies received.[73]

In fact, the Court tends to give the reports "conclusive weight, "particularly in the 'context' section of its judgements."[74] For instance, in the *Almonacid* case, it stated that "the information on the events described in subparagraph b(i) was entirely gathered from three official reports," including the report of the Chilean National Truth and Reconciliation Commission.[75]

Regarding El Salvador, the Court had already recognized the existence of an armed conflict in the case of the *Serrano-Cruz Sisters*.[76] Later, in the *Contreras*

[71] Salmón, "Las Comisiones de la Verdad y la jurisprudencia de la Corte Interamericana," 292.

[72] Ibid., 294.

[73] *Bámaca-Velásquez v. Guatemala*, Merits, Inter-Am. Ct. H.R. (ser. C) No. 70, 65, ¶ 145.d (2000).

[74] Álvaro Paúl, "Evidence: Inter-American Court of Human Rights (IACtHR)," in *Max Planck Encyclopedia of International Procedural Law* (Oxford: Oxford University Press, June 2018), accessed May 26, 2022, https://opil.ouplaw.com/view/10.1093/law-mpeipro/e3429.013.3429/law-mpeipro-e3429?rskey=6WXxLo&result=1&prd=MPIL.

[75] *Almonacid-Arellano et al v. Chile*, Preliminary Objections, Merits, Reparations and Costs, Inter-Am. Ct. H.R. (ser. C) No. 154 , 26, ¶ 82 (2006).

[76] *Serrano-Cruz Sisters v. El Salvador*, Merits, Reparations and Costs, Inter-Am. Ct. H.R. (ser. C) No. 120, 7, 29 (2005).

case, it went further and established the context of the facts "based principally on the Report of the Truth Commission for El Salvador."[77]

In *Cruz Sánchez et al. v. Peru*, the Court indicated that it would use the final report of the CVR "as a fundamental part of the proof of the political and historical context contemporary to the facts."[78] Likewise, it described the Peruvian armed conflict based on that final report.[79]

As can be seen, in cases regarding Guatemala, El Salvador, and Peru, where states had not recognized the existence of a NIAC, the Inter-American Court has affirmed the context of armed conflict based on the findings of the truth commissions. Precisely, the Inter-American Court believes it is necessary to establish not only the immediate context of the moment in which the violation of a right occurred, but also the possible repetition of such practices.[80] The reports of the truth commissions allow the Court to understand the reality of a society in the period of the facts of the case.

VII. Final Considerations

Although the application of IHL depends on the fact that certain objective requirements are configured in practice and not so much on the willingness of the parties to an armed conflict to recognize its existence, recognition of a NIAC allows for a broad debate on the consequences of the periods of violence and the paths to follow in transitional justice processes. In addition to the crucial role that truth commissions in Latin America have played in building an official truth, they have played an essential role in introducing IHL norms in Latin American societies.

It might be relevant to consider the implications of the government's outright recognition of the existence of an internal armed conflict. In strict legal terms, and regarding the application of the IHL norms, there is no difference between government recognition, a declaration by an official truth commission, and lack of any official recognition. As already mentioned, IHL norms do not require such recognition to be applicable.

However, there can be a difference in political will and the adoption of the necessary policies to bring about legal accountability. Official recognition can lead to a more proactive involvement by the government, such as allocating

[77] *Contreras et al. v. El Salvador*, Merits, Reparations and Costs, Inter-Am. Ct. H.R. (ser. C) No. 232, 17, ¶ 40 (2011).

[78] *Cruz Sánchez et al. v. Peru*, Preliminary Objections, Merits, Reparations and Costs, Inter-Am. Ct. H.R. (ser. C) No. 292, 41, ¶ 139 (2015).

[79] Ibid., 42, ¶ 140.

[80] Salmón, "Las Comisiones de la Verdad y la jurisprudencia de la Corte Interamericana," 295.

the necessary resources to a special judicial system, strengthening security guarantees for civil rights defenders, facilitating access to official classified information, and so on. However a question remains regarding the implications of a definition of armed conflict by a truth commission when the government has been reluctant to offer such recognition. Whether this situation will modify the government's approach or reaffirm its preceding reluctance is a matter for further analysis that exceeds the limits of this chapter.

Furthermore, there are other challenges concerning the definition of a NIAC, a notion of vital relevance to clarify the legal regime applicable in a situation of violence. In the current circumstances surrounding Latin American countries, the challenge emerges from organized crime and the possibility of considering that there is a NIAC when a criminal gang, a drug cartel, or any other illegal organization defies government forces.

The growth of organized crime in the Latin American region[81] has turned into a normalization of state of emergency declarations across the region and a militarization of security responses. To fight against organized crime in this context, governments have adopted a narrative of "war" against crime that puts in question the constitutive criteria established by case law and practice to identify an armed conflict.[82] For instance, Mexico has been conducting a "war on drugs" against drug cartels since 2006; however, the government has not adduced IHL or qualified the situation as an armed conflict. Most recently, Ecuador declared the existence of a NIAC against criminal organizations and ordered the armed forces to conduct military operations applying IHL. The latter has raised questions about the resort to IHL to increase the level of force a state can use, particularly lethal force, in contexts that are not typically considered NIACs. This issue demands further discussion and clarification of the basic notions of IHL and the possibilities of adapting IHL to Latin American circumstances and needs.

[81] According to the United Nations Office on Drugs and Crime (UNODC), the Americas region registers the highest homicide rate in the world, and, in particular, Latin America and the Caribbean show a prevalence of homicidal violence by organized crime. For example, in 2022, Ecuador doubled the homicide rate registered in 2021, an increase that can be attributed to transnational and local criminal groups. By contrast, El Salvador has shown a recent decline in homicides as a result of antigang policies and the implementation of a state of emergency since March 2022. See UNODC, "Global Study on Homicide 2023: Homicide and Organized Crime in Latin America and the Caribbean," 2023, https://www.unodc.org/documents/data-and-analysis/gsh/2023/GSH_2023_LAC_web.pdf.

[82] See Pablo Kalmanovitz, "Can Criminal Organizations Be Non-State Parties to Armed Conflict?" *International Review of the Red Cross* 105, no. 923 (June 2023): 618–636, https://international-review.icrc.org/sites/default/files/reviews-pdf/2023-06/can-criminal-organizations-be-non-state-parties-to-armed-conflict-923.pdf.

16

The Dynamic Relationship between Latin American Legal Professionals and International Law

Two Contemporary Examples

*Manuel A. Gómez**

I. The Long-Standing Importance of International Law in Latin America: From Classroom to Courtroom

This chapter addresses the interplay between Latin American legal professionals and international law. It shows how the expansion of international law into certain areas has incited changes in the legal professions. Cognizant of the vastness and complexity of this topic and the limited space allotted for this chapter, the changes are illustrated through vignettes of two interesting—and so far, overlooked—regional developments that have deepened during the last two decades and have already had an impact on specific segments of the legal professions and the practice of international law in the region. The first development is the rise of an international dispute resolution legal community, a fast-growing segment still dominated by elite practitioners representing clients in high-stakes multijurisdictional disputes for which international law is central. This includes, for example, claims filed in US courts on behalf of Ecuadorean and Peruvian Indigenous peoples, Guatemalan farmers, Colombian displaced persons, or, conversely, multinational US corporations in domestic courts of Latin American countries before arbitral tribunals regarding investment and other treaty violations, and in US courts for other illicit conduct occurred abroad. The second development looks at a different subset of legal professionals: law students. It focuses on expanding clinical legal education to contemporary international law-related areas. Latin American legal clinics have

* I would like to thank Alejandro Chehtman, Alexandra Huneeus, and Sergio Puig for the invitation to participate in this volume, and to the coauthors and colleagues who provided valuable comments and feedback during workshops and academic conferences where I presented earlier versions of this work.

Manuel A. Gómez, *The Dynamic Relationship between Latin American Legal Professionals and International Law* In: *Latin American International Law in the Twenty-First Century*. Edited by: Alejandro Chehtman, Alexandra Huneeus, and Sergio Puig, Oxford University Press. © Oxford University Press 2025.
DOI: 10.1093/9780197754016.003.0016

served the dual purpose of giving law students chances to improve their learning by participating in real cases while contributing to facilitate international access to justice to benefit traditionally excluded rights holders.

The chosen period—the first two decades of the twenty-first century—is significant because it has been marked by a series of events that have affected Latin American societies. These include reconfiguring regional and global alliances and integration strategies, political upheavals, institutional crises, corruption scandals, changes in trade and investment policies, environmental disasters, and humanitarian crises. These events have also influenced Latin American legal professionals and, by extension, international law practice in the region. The recent transformations of Latin American legal professionals, both internally and in their relationship with society, have been the subject of extensive academic commentary,[1] professional publications,[2] and frequent mainstream media coverage.

Unsurprisingly, lawyers are the subset of legal professionals who have garnered the most significant attention. At least two reasons might help explain why. First, lawyers are the most numerous and visible group compared to the other categories of legal professionals. Second, lawyers are the professional legal actors who seem to have the most frequent contact with the rest of society, partly because they receive preferential treatment from the state and partly because legal practice is often treated like a "monopoly."[3] In this regard, and despite the trend toward facilitating access to justice, many national laws still require ordinary citizens to be formally represented by a lawyer whenever they need to interact with the official legal system. In addition to their typical professional occupation of serving as the conduit between the state and the rest of society, lawyers are often involved in other activities such as policymaking, civil rights activism, and diplomacy, which make up a significant portion of the practice of

[1] See, e.g., Manuel A. Gómez, "Evolution of Latin American Lawyers over Three Decades: 1990-2020," in *Lawyers in 21st Century Societies*, vol. 2, ed. Richard Abel et al. (London: Hart, 2022); Manuel A. Gómez, "Legal Professionals in Latin America in the 21st Century," in *Handbook of Law and Society in Latin America*, ed. Rachel Sieder, Karina Ansolabehere, and Tatiana Alfonso (London: Routledge, 2019); Manuel A. Gómez, "Innovaciones en la educación jurídica latinoamericana y políticas públicas en tiempos de globalización," in *La Educación Legal como Política Pública en América Latina*, ed. Gorki Gonzales Mantilla (Lima, Peru: Palestra Editores, 2018), 99–118; Manuel A. Gómez and Rogelio Pérez-Perdomo (eds.), *Big Law in Latin America and Spain: Globalization and Adjustments in the Provision of High End Corporate Legal Service* (London: Palgrave-Macmillan, 2017); Manuel A. Gómez, "Political Activism and the Practice of Law in Venezuela," in *Cultures of Legality: Judicialization and Political Activism in Latin America*, ed. Javier Couso, Alexandra Huneeus, and Rachel Sieder (Cambridge: Cambridge University Press, 2010); Rogelio Pérez-Perdomo, *Latin American Lawyers: A Historical Introduction* (Stanford, CA: Stanford University Press, 2006).

[2] See, e.g., *LatinLawyer*, https://latinlawyer.com/; *LexLatin*, https://lexlatin.com/; *The Latin American Lawyer*, https://thelatinamericanlawyer.com/; *Chambers Latin America*, https://chambers.com/legal-guide/latin-america-9.

[3] Gómez, "Evolution of Latin American Lawyers over Three Decades."

international law. In this sense, lawyers are also the legal professionals who are among the most relevant to the field.

Interestingly, contemporary legal education is still oriented toward preparing future lawyers to practice law in their own jurisdiction and not elsewhere. This is despite significant efforts to infuse law school curricula with more international and comparative law content[4] and formal attempts by governments to facilitate professional mobility through the mutual recognition of certificates and degrees obtained.[5] For example, someone who goes to law school in Costa Rica will take courses mainly relevant to that country's legal system and, upon graduation, will be expected to practice law there. Legal practice has also been traditionally treated as a fiercely guarded national monopoly. As a result, national governments, either directly or through professional associations, set the standards regarding the education and training, licensing, and oversight of lawyers and other legal professionals in their territory.

The formal entry to the legal profession is commonly preceded by several years of formal study at a national university capped by the conferral of the academic title of *abogado*, *licenciado en derecho*, or *advogado*, depending on the country. In Latin America, only Brazil requires a qualifying professional exam to obtain a practicing license;[6] other countries require an internship or practical experience. These are some of the requisites still in place throughout Latin America, where, like most of continental Europe and other countries that follow the civil law tradition, law is offered as an undergraduate degree. In terms of curricular contents, the courses commonly found at Latin American law schools tend to focus on traditional areas such as constitutional law, civil and criminal law, commercial law, administrative law, and international law (private and public).

In recent years, Latin American law schools—usually elite—have witnessed the addition of a growing number of transnational courses that offer substantive content, practical skills, and interdisciplinary approaches to contemporary legal practice.[7] Law schools encourage students to become more involved in international competitions in arbitration, human rights, and public international

[4] Gómez, "Innovaciones en la educación jurídica latinoamericana y políticas públicas en tiempos de globalización," 99–118.

[5] UNESCO, Regional Convention on the Recognition of Studies, Diplomas and Degrees in Higher Education in Latin America and the Caribbean, July 19, 1974, and July 13, 2019. https://www.unesco.org/en/legal-affairs/regional-convention-recognition-studies-diplomas-and-degrees-higher-education-latin-america-and-0.

[6] M. da G Bonelli and P. Fortes, "Brazil: Fragmentary Development, Democratisation, and Globalisation," in *Lawyers in 21st-Century Societies. Volume 1: National Reports*, ed. R. L. Abel et al. (London: Hart, 2022).

[7] Manuel A. Gómez, "Beyond Borders and Across Legal Traditions: The Transnationalization of Latin American Lawyers," in *Oxford Handbook of Transnational Law*, ed. P. Zumbansen(Oxford: Oxford University Press, 2021), 1093–1108.

law. Legal clinics have also expanded their offerings to focus on international human rights, public international law, and international trade, and universities are devoting resources to teach competencies in transnational lawyering skills.[8]

Regarding the study of international law, it is worth noting that its inclusion in the curricula of Latin American law schools can be traced back to the post-independence reforms of the nineteenth century that viewed legal education as the foundation of future government officials and political leaders of the nascent republics.[9] Despite some curricular transformations and innovations implemented more recently across law schools in the region, international law has remained a critical subject that every graduate must have. When international law was incorporated into the curriculum, no one thought of it as a stepping stone for those who wanted to become "international lawyers," practice before international tribunals, or advise international organizations.

International law has always been considered necessary for a proper generalist legal education. It has been traditionally offered alongside other subjects, such as Contracts and Constitutional Law, with no expectation other than to prepare those bound to practice law in their own country. Despite the recent trend among Latin American law schools to strengthen their international and comparative curricular offerings, international law is still viewed as a foundation course, or group of courses, that any future lawyer is expected to master. Even graduates from a small regional Latin American law school will indeed have taken at least one public international law course. At some of the most innovative and globalized law schools, the international law-related offering is much more robust and explicitly oriented toward giving future lawyers a competitive edge. Nevertheless, even at the most basic level, the international law literacy of an average Latin American law graduate is probably greater than that of the average law graduate from a US law school where international law courses are generally offered only as elective subjects for upper-level students.

In addition to the traditional placement of international law within Latin American law school curricula as one of the foundation courses, the production of international law-related works by Latin American scholars and practitioners has always been prolific and influential. From Andrés Bello's seminal treatise *Principios de Derecho Internacional* (Caracas, 1837), which was popular among Latin American law schools for many years, to more recent works by Hildebrando Accioly, Alberto Ulloa, L. A. Podestá Costa, José María Rida, and Eduardo Jiménez de Aréchaga,[10] among many others; the intellectual contribution of

[8] Gómez, "Innovaciones en la educación jurídica latinoamericana y políticas públicas en tiempos de globalización," 99–118.

[9] Rogelio Pérez-Perdomo, "La educación jurídica y los sistemas de justicia," in *Los Actores de la Justicia Latinoamericana*, ed. L. Pásara, (Spain: Ediciones Universidad Salamanca, 2007), 41–56.

[10] Antonio Augusto Cançado Trindade, "Los aportes latinoamericanos al derecho y a la justicia internacionales," in *Doctrina Latinoamericana del Derecho Internacional*, vol. 1, ed. Antonio Augusto

Latin Americans to international law is well known. Luis María Drago, Carlos Calvo, Carlos Tobar, Genaro Estrada, Rui Barbosa, Epitacio Pessoa, Alejandro Álvarez, Lafayette Rodrigues, Gustavo Guerrero, and F. V. García Amador are just a few names in a long list of Latin American lawyers, scholars, and judges who helped develop, shape, transform, and put into practice critical international law concepts not just in the region but also globally. They and their successors created schools of thought, strengthened institutions, and fostered younger generations of internationalists that remain relevant today. Thanks to this foundation, the body of work attributed to Latin American scholars and practitioners devoted to international law is more robust than ever.[11]

Section II describes a general demarcation of the contours and intragroup features of Latin American legal professionals that considers the quintessential national character of Latin American legal professions and the difficulty of mapping out the international law practitioners in the region. The section also calls attention to the growth of the international law practice field in the area. Section III delves into a description of the international dispute resolution field and its impact on Latin American lawyers. Section IV shifts attention to legal education by describing the expansion of clinical programs to expose future lawyers to issues that affect internationally protected rights in areas such as human rights and climate change. This section also explains how legal clinics contribute to facilitating access to justice for vulnerable and otherwise disenfranchised groups and also help to change the mindset of future Latin American lawyers and their role in society.

II. The Growth of International Law Practitioners in Latin America

Occupation and title are usually the two elements that make up a profession. If we apply such concepts to the legal professions, "occupation" would refer to any activity that is related to the functioning of the official legal system through the performance of a role that demands expertise, familiarity, and training. A typical occupation for a lawyer, for example, would be representing a client in court, before a state organ, or advising them in a legal transaction. The typical occupation for a judge, on the other hand, would be to adjudicate legal matters by applying the relevant laws and enforcing their own decisions. The second element, "title,"

Cançado Trindade and Alfredo Martínez Moreno (San José, Costa Rica: Corte Interamericana de Derechos Humanos, 2003).

[11] See Sergio Puig, in this volume, on interdisciplinarity in Latin American international law.

is a formal validation that signals that someone has expertise vis-à-vis the rest of society and proves that a person is qualified to perform a professional occupation. In the case of legal professionals, a title —lawyer, judge—is usually conferred upon the individual by a state agency or a university delegated by the state or another authority.

The conferral of a title attests that a person has met specific requirements, such as attending a formal educational program. In addition to obtaining a title, some jurisdictions, like Brazil, require those who want to practice law to take a qualifying exam. As a result, the title of lawyer would be a requirement—albeit not sufficient—for practicing law in that country. Additionally, not all those who earn a title automatically become employed as lawyers or are otherwise engaged in the practice of law. There are many government officials, activists, executives, policy advisors, and so on, who have obtained a legal education and a title but have not joined a bar association or practiced law in the traditional sense. Others might have engaged in the practice of law intermittently or for a limited time, which may cause them to be considered legal professionals by some but not by others. Furthermore, since the requisites to be designated a legal professional and to be allowed to engage in a specific professional legal occupation vary by country, it is difficult to generalize and, therefore, to ascertain the population of legal professionals and to classify them correctly.

In addition to the nuances that need to be considered regarding who can be counted as a legal professional, there are national variations in the methods for collecting, assessing, and disseminating demographic data on legal professionals. In most Latin American countries, data regarding legal professionals tend to be incomplete or publicly unavailable. The region has no tradition of compiling and disseminating statistics on law graduates, unlike the United States or some European countries.[12] Therefore, it is difficult to get an accurate snapshot of the population of legal professionals regionally and, in some cases, even by individual country.

In the case of those engaged in international law practice, the issue of counting and studying legal professionals becomes a bit more complicated for two reasons. First, having a title and a license to practice law tends to be a requirement for domestic practice only. While some international organizations and courts may demand qualifications for those nominated to serve, other roles, such as appearing as counsel, agent, or advocate before an international court or tribunal, do not require a license to practice law. Precisely on this point, an empirical study of lawyers that acted before the International Court of Justice (ICJ) between 1999 and 2012 revealed that the legal teams appearing on behalf of states before the ICJ in contentious proceedings often involved non-nationals and other persons (e.g.,

[12] Gómez, "Legal Professionals in Latin America in the 21st Century."

law professors) who were not necessarily licensed to practice law.[13] Furthermore, Articles 42 and 43 of the ICJ Statute allow high-ranking diplomats—who may or may not be legal professionals—to represent parties before the Court, thus expressly permitting nonlawyers to act in those legal proceedings.[14] Being able to establish who makes up the legal teams appearing before certain international organizations or tribunals might be a way to get a snapshot of a certain category of legal professionals involved in international law, but it would certainly be incomplete if we want to get a sense of who makes up the entire population.

As for the second reason, international law practice is often intertwined with activities like diplomacy, political strategy advising, and lobbying, which do not fall within the traditional notion of legal practice in any country. The nature of the field requires professionals who possess a skill set that goes beyond interpreting and applying laws and offering traditional legal advice. Teams working on international law matters often involve legal professionals who, in addition to their traditional occupation, engage in nonlegal work. Conversely, nonlegal professionals are doing tasks that might be considered legal work under certain definitions and professional practice rules. As a result, at least regarding the professional actors involved, international law is a melting pot where lawyers and nonlawyers work together, thus creating an interesting dynamic that contributes to shaping the field, as we will explain in section IV. ~~later.~~

The difficulty of estimating the population of Latin American legal professionals working in international law does not diminish the value of researching the topic. Despite the lack of proper demographic data, no one would doubt that the international law field has grown in size and notoriety, which has also had an impact on the legal professions in the region. There are also some visible signs of growth in the international law field in Latin America. One is the increased importance of matters relevant to international law, ranging from human rights to foreign investment to climate change. This is evidenced by the number of cases in both local and international courts, by looking at the activities of international organizations, nongovernmental organizations, groups of activists, governments, and the private sector. Another indicator of the growing importance of the international law field is the changes in the legal services industry in terms of specialization, diversification, and geographical expansion.[15] One of the most salient examples is large and multiservice law firms,

[13] Shashank P. Kumar and Cecily Rose, A Study of Lawyers Appearing before the International Court of Justice, 1999–2012, *European Journal of International Law* 25, no. 3 (August 2014): 893–917, https://doi.org/10.1093/ejil/chu057.

[14] Statute of the International Court of Justice, Articles 42, 43, https://www.icj-cij.org/en/statute.

[15] Gómez, "Evolution of Latin American Lawyers over Three Decades."

which, during the last few decades, have strengthened their presence in different areas of legal practice, especially in international dispute resolution.[16]

Regarding this aspect, more global and regional law firms than ever before are increasingly brandishing their international law expertise and showcasing their involvement in relevant international law-related matters. Law firms have greatly invested in boosting their capacity because there is also a growing demand for legal services related to international law. As a result, the relevant practice groups have attained a higher stature within the firms' internal hierarchy, and their increasingly complex portfolio of legal matters, coupled with the arrival of sophisticated clients, has also begun to justify subdivisions of lawyers by teams of specialists that did not exist two decades ago. Nowadays, it is not uncommon for some of the largest global law firms to organize their international law practitioners into several highly specialized practice groups exclusively dedicated to handling a type of matter such as foreign corruption and white-collar crime, international disputes, sanctions, and ESG (environmental, social, and governance).

In the international dispute resolution arena, for example, law firms now have discrete teams of lawyers specialized in international commercial arbitration and mediation, investor-state arbitration, boundary disputes, international armed conflict, and climate litigation. Not too long ago, all those matters were handled by the same team composed by a handful of "international law generalists" without any specialized training. During the last two decades or so, as the field has become more specialized and there is growing demand, Latin American law schools have begun adding courses to their curricula and have fostered other methods of disseminating knowledge about these novel areas of practice, such as moot court competitions and legal clinics.

III. The Rise of International Dispute Resolution Lawyers in Latin America

International dispute resolution is a relatively young and thriving legal field. We can call it young because even though arbitration has existed since time immemorial,[17] and the largest arbitral institution in the world—the ICC Court of Arbitration—is more than one hundred years old,[18] the emergence of a

[16] Manuel A. Gómez and Rogelio Pérez-Perdomo, "Corporate Lawyers and Multinational Corporations in Latin America and Spain: 1990-2015," in Gómez and Pérez-Perdomo, *Big Law in Latin America and Spain*.

[17] Earl S. Wolaver, "The Historical Background of Commercial Arbitration," *University of Pennsylvania Law Review* 83 (1934): 132.

[18] Manuel A. Gómez, "After One Hundred Years of Solitude: The Re-Encounter of International Labor Protection and Arbitration," *Revista Derecho Social y Empresa* 13 (2020): 94–113.

discernable professional community did not occur until the late twentieth century. Arbitration has been long relied upon by states to sort out their differences, and the leading players have traditionally been public international law experts, many of whom hail from Latin America. The 1990s witnessed an aggressive endorsement of international arbitration by multilateral organizations and governments through various legal and judicial reform efforts, which provoked the adoption of domestic laws and the ratification of treaties that gave arbitration practical significance. This movement was particularly salient in Latin America because countries of the region were among the first beneficiaries of loans, aid packages, and institutional reform efforts led by the World Bank, the Inter-American Development Bank, and other similar organizations.[19]

The private sector obliged by promoting the launch of arbitral institutions through chambers of commerce and other trade organizations and by steering more disputes toward arbitration, especially the large-scale and complex ones. The potential created by arbitration alerted many Latin American legal professionals, and law firms began strengthening their capacity in that area. The growth of an arbitration legal community in the region was relatively easy partly because many Latin American elite lawyers had close connections with US and European practitioners—who were leaders in international dispute resolution. Additionally, it had become increasingly popular for Latin American lawyers to obtain LL.M. degrees from US law schools, which had already begun expanding their international and comparative course offerings. The return of these professionals after completing their foreign studies helped raise the bar in many jurisdictions and contributed to internationalizing the local legal communities.[20]

In 1996, when Ives Dezalay and Bryant Garth published their seminal book, *Dealing in Virtue*, which mapped the nascent international arbitration community, the field was made up by a handful of repeat players, primarily based in Paris, London, and perhaps New York. Two and a half decades later, every Latin American capital has a sizable community of international dispute resolution practitioners. Each country in the region has at least an arbitral institution, a domestic law providing for arbitration, several specialized firms, and law schools offering international arbitration courses and is a party to one or more international legal instruments facilitating the recognition and enforcement of foreign arbitral awards. In sum, international arbitration is a proper legal field that embodies an essential facet of international law. More importantly, it is an intellectual microcosm where institutions, rules, and actors interact.[21]

[19] Manuel A. Gómez, "All in the Family: The Influence of Social Networks on Dispute Processing," *Georgia Journal of International and Comparative Law* 36 (2008): 291.

[20] Gómez, "Evolution of Latin American Lawyers over Three Decades: 1990-2020."

[21] Dezalay and Garth, *Dealing in Virtue*. For a depiction of the arbitrators' interaction in investment arbitration, see Sergio Puig, "Social Capital in the Arbitration Market," *European Journal of International Law* 25 (2014): 387–424.

The social space occupied by this field involves professional and academic networks of participants from diverse backgrounds, experience, and skilled occupations. The community, which in Latin America has become particularly salient during the last two decades, comprises lawyers affiliated with global, regional, and domestic law firms; in-house counsel; independent arbitrators; judges; university professors; researchers; students; government officials; policymakers; and members of the business sector. The international arbitration field is also made up of an array of institutions that include arbitration centers, government agencies, international organizations, professional associations, and other corporate bodies. Finally, treaties, transnational norms, and domestic legislation govern the relationships between the actors, the institutions, and the rest of the legal complex.

At least five developments signal the current salience of the international arbitration field in Latin America. First, there has been an upsurge in enacting national laws and policies endorsing arbitration and international law instruments. Second, arbitral institutions, basically dispute resolution service providers, have taken a leading role in the administration of cases and the governance of the field. Third, law firms have fostered the specialization and bundling of international arbitration practitioners, who have, in turn, acquired their own professional identity as a professional community. Fourth, the Latin American international arbitration field—like any other academic or professional field—has given rise to a growing number of planned events (conferences, workshops, seminars, and congresses) to exchange ideas, disseminate knowledge, strengthen professional and academic networks, and contribute to the overall growth of this global community. Finally, universities and other educational institutions from different parts of the region have integrated international arbitration-related courses into their curricula. They are increasingly supporting student competitions in various languages, designed to strengthen their substantive knowledge, advocacy, and intellectual skills. A related development is the emergence of journals and other periodicals, casebooks, and legal commentaries. As we will explain in section IV, when describing the other important development that concerns this chapter, Latin American law schools have also expanded their clinical legal education offerings to help their students gain real-life advocacy and client interaction opportunities in international law matters.

The international arbitration field in Latin America is a melting pot of academics, legal practitioners, government officials, policymakers, financiers, representatives of international organizations, regional and nongovernmental organizations, activists, and stakeholders from different industries (e.g., quantum experts and technical experts). Arbitration is an old form of dispute resolution that can be applied to a broad universe of situations, from relatively insignificant disputes (in the economic sense) and labor/employment and tenant-landlord cases to complex investor-state disputes. Nevertheless, the archetypal conflicts in international arbitration stem from high-value, high-stakes, multijurisdictional, and large-scale legal disputes. As a result, the relevance of international law in this space is evident. Unsurprisingly, handling international arbitration cases necessitates a cadre of lawyers, arbitrators, institutions, and, obviously, clients with the economic capacity (or the ability to secure support) to withstand the fight. The transnational nature of arbitration often attracts individuals trained in different legal traditions who speak other languages and are specialized in a particular industry or sector (e.g., oil and gas, maritime, international trade, foreign investment, and international trade). To a certain extent, the general perception is that international arbitration is the "Rolls Royce" of dispute resolution.

Prominent Latin American arbitration practitioners sometimes work at the local branches of large multinational law firms, which have a sophisticated infrastructure—the resources and human power needed to handle large complex cases. Nevertheless, the "rock stars" in the field tend to practice at their own firms, which, in addition to being more agile and cost-efficient than their international competitors, give them more independence to join the leadership of international organizations and professional societies, act as government advisers, and pursue other activities in addition to their professional legal practice. Some examples of these practitioners are Claus von Wobeser from Mexico, Dyalá Jimenez Figueres from Costa Rica, Adriana Braghetta from Brazil, and Andrés Jana from Chile. Arbitration practitioners may perform different roles, the main ones being arbitrator and counsel or party representative. Those generally appointed as arbitrators are expected to carry out their duties with utmost impartiality and independence.

Paradoxically, it is not uncommon for international arbitration practitioners to alternate between their roles of counsel and arbitrator or even to perform both simultaneously (obviously, not in the same matter). Even though there is growing criticism within the international arbitral community about the so-called double-hatting phenomenon, few practitioners can afford the luxury of only accepting arbitrator appointments and not acting as counsel. Practicing attorneys are not the only prominent players in this field. Academics have increasingly joined the ranks as neutrals, advisers, counsel, and party- or tribunal-appointed legal experts.

In some areas of the law, there is a clear divide between practitioners and academics; that is, between those devoted to practice and those devoted to a purely intellectual pursuit. That is not necessarily the case of international arbitration. One of the interesting features of this field around the world—and not only in Latin America—is that its participants tend to have a foot in each world simultaneously. For example, some of the most widely known Latin American scholars who are part of the international arbitration field happen to be also Big Law partners who are very active in representing clients in high-stakes matters or deciding cases as arbitrators while they write and publish casebooks, law review articles, and book chapters.

On the other hand, some academics split their time between their scholarly pursuit and the role of arbitrator, counsel, or expert. As if it were not enough, many of these individuals are also frequent speakers at conferences held throughout the year in different parts of the world, thus confirming the high value of these events to their careers while boosting their legitimacy in the eyes of their peers. This dual nature of international arbitration is not confined to individuals who, as we have just explained, often wear two or more hats. The dual or hybrid nature of international arbitration affects the entire field, where both the practice-oriented and the academic-oriented goals go hand in hand. This may not be unique to the international arbitration field, but the salience with which such dual nature is manifested indeed stands out. A similar growth and specialization to the one just described for international arbitration has also occurred in nongovernmental organizations, advocacy groups, and law school clinics. The latter has had a significant impact in the international law field.

IV. Legal Clinics as Breeding Ground for International Law Practitioners in Latin America

Until a couple of decades ago, clinical legal education—in Latin America and other parts of the world—mainly focused on exposing students to real-life scenarios limited to matters affecting the local community, such as minor contracts and tenant-landlord disputes.[22] Nowadays, it is common for legal clinics to represent clients, or at least assist, in complex international cases before local courts, government agencies, the Inter-American Commission of Human Rights, and similar organs.

Latin American legal clinics are not a recent idea. The first vestiges in the region seem to go back to the programs developed by the Central University of Venezuela Law School and the Andrés Bello Catholic University, located in Caracas, Venezuela, during the 1960s. From the outset, the legal clinics aimed to expose students to receiving and handling real cases under the supervision of experienced instructors. This practical experience was generally accompanied by courses in which students were taught to write contracts and other valuable documents for the practice of the profession. This clinical model was designed as

[22] This section is largely built on the concepts discussed in Gómez, "Innovaciones en la educación jurídica latinoamericana y políticas públicas en tiempos de globalización," 99–118.

a reference for the student practices and internships offered by medical schools for many years.

In addition to carrying out valuable pedagogical work for the benefit of law students, traditional legal clinics have fulfilled an important social function because most of the cases they handle involve low-income people who cannot afford to pay attorneys' fees. The community approach was the one that defined the legal clinics in the first stage. In a more recent period, Latin American legal clinics broadened their spectrum to issues of greater social, political, and transnational relevance, such as representing victims for violations of their human rights; protecting other collective rights of social content, such as the right to a healthy environment, climate change, and consumer rights; and protecting against different forms of discrimination. Legal clinics have also joined transnational networks like Tradelab (cofounded by Sergio Puig, a Mexican professor), whose participants hail from law schools in Argentina, Brazil, Colombia, and Mexico (among others), engaged in practical education in topics related to international economic law.[23] This expansion of the role of Latin American legal clinics has been occurring simultaneously with the expansion of a global culture of protection of human rights, trade, and international law in general.

Today, most Latin American law schools have at least one legal clinic and are receiving more and more students. Even though the trend among contemporary Latin American legal clinics is to focus on issues considered to be of public interest and impact litigation, in some universities, the clinical offering has expanded to other areas such as labor law, criminal justice, and family law, in addition to maintaining the typical community focus of the 1960s and 1970s.

In countries like Colombia, legal clinics have been organized at the national level, which has contributed to increasing their visibility and impact on the communities where their work is directed. There are also some regional organizations such as the Latin American Network of Legal Clinics (LANLC), founded in 1996 and led by the Diego Portales University of Chile. LANLC has almost twenty member universities from Argentina, Chile, Colombia, Ecuador, Mexico, and Peru. More recently, the members of the LANLC have strengthened ties with North American universities, which constitutes another opportunity for the development of foreign language and comparative law proficiency.

The contributions of Latin American legal clinics to the development of the protection of human rights from an international law perspective in the region have been particularly relevant. The most active clinics in this regard are those at law schools in Argentina, Colombia, Chile, Mexico, Peru, and Costa Rica. The involvement of legal clinics in this field has generally occurred through the representation of matters before the constitutional courts of each of these countries,

[23] Tradelab, https://tradelab.org/clinics/ (last visited July 5, 2024).

the preparation of reports presented before national and international organizations, and training and dissemination activities for their students and the public. The legal clinics have also stood out for the presentation of briefs and requests for intervention in processes before the Inter-American Human Rights System and for their contribution to the activities of various nongovernmental organizations in the fight to protect fundamental rights.

The intervention of legal clinics in real cases of high social impact, which frequently require the involvement of professionals with various areas of knowledge, has also opened the doors to the interdisciplinary study of law in Latin America. Dealing with issues such as gender, race, and other types of discrimination; the protection of Indigenous communities; and the prosecution of serious international crimes has required that students and teachers who participate in the clinics interact with professionals from other disciplines in search of solutions that go beyond obtaining a judgment that puts an end to a dispute in court.

The most recent trend among public interest legal clinics operating in the region has been to use litigation to achieve change in public policy, legislation, and society in general. For this reason, it is increasingly common for legal clinics to collaborate with sociologists, anthropologists, economists, doctors, and professionals from other areas to design strategies and forms of intervention that effectively solve social problems and litigation in its traditional sense. Monitoring judicial processes continues to be an important task for Latin American legal clinics, but it is certainly not the only one they carry out.

In some cases, the interaction between law students and professors with members of other disciplines has exceeded the sporadic collaboration of handling a specific case and has given rise to more permanent initiatives such as undergraduate and graduate courses and continuing education programs. Examples are the Interdisciplinary Seminar on Human Rights and Mental Health offered by the Blas Pascal University in Argentina and the Interdisciplinary Postgraduate Course in Environmental Law offered by the Faculty of Law of the Universidad Nacional del Nordeste, also in Argentina. Some law schools have promoted more ambitious long-term initiatives by sponsoring research centers. Two important examples are the Institute of Interdisciplinary Studies Richard Tovar Cárdenas of the Faculty of Law of the Externado University[24] and the Center for Interdisciplinary, Social and Humanist Studies (CIES, in Spanish) of the

[24] Instituto de Estudios Interdisciplinarios Richard Tovar Cárdenas, Universidad Externado de Colombia, https://www.uexternado.edu.co/instituto-de-estudios-interdisciplinarios/ (last visited July 5, 2024).

Faculty of Law and Social Sciences of the ICESI University,[25] both in Colombia. These entities combine research activities, teaching, and publications on contemporary topics that involve the intersection between law and social sciences. Additionally, some law schools, such as the Torcuato Di Tella University School of Law in Argentina, have openly expressed their support for an interdisciplinary legal approach throughout their curriculum by combining mandatory and elective courses both in law and on the intersection between law and economics, philosophy, history, and political science.[26]

Other examples of interdisciplinary collaboration that have gone beyond law schools can be seen in applied research projects conceived at the university level, such as the Interdisciplinary Initiative on Mapuche Conflict and Criminal Law of the University of Chile[27] or the Center for Interdisciplinary Studies Industrial and Economic Law (CEIDIE, in Spanish) from the University of Buenos Aires. Interdisciplinary legal research has also been effectively promoted outside the organizational structure of universities within the framework of academic institutions and researchers who work closely with them. One of the most successful examples in the region, considering its productivity and high impact, is the Center for Law, Justice, and Society Studies (DeJusticia)[28] based in Bogotá, Colombia. Finally, the interdisciplinarity of law has also been supported by regional organizations such as the Inter-American Institute of Human Rights[29] based in Costa Rica, which since 1983 has been teaching an interdisciplinary course on human rights.

As we have seen, although the interdisciplinarity of law has had a significant boom in the Latin American region, it still has a long way to go. The efforts that have been made up to now focus on issues of public interest or those related to the advancement of social policies. Interdisciplinarity, however, is a vast field that should also encourage opportunities for collaboration in other areas, such as international trade, banking, and tax law. This would open other doors for students interested in these disciplines and help consolidate the relationship between universities and the rest of society.

[25] Centro de Estudios Interdisciplinarios Jurídicos, Sociales y Humanistas, https://www.icesi.edu.co/unicesi/1458:centro-de-estudios-interdisciplinarios-juridicos-sociales-y-humanistas-de-icesi-estrena-portal-web (last visited July 5, 2024).

[26] Universidad Torcuato di Tella, Escuela de Derecho, https://www.utdt.edu/ver_contenido.php?id_contenido=280&id_item_menu=1045 (last visited July 5, 2024).

[27] Universidad de Chile, Iniciativa Interdisciplinaria en Conflicto Mapuche y Derecho Penal, https://uchile.cl/investigacion/programas-de-investigacion-domeyko/linea-sociedad-y-equidad/sujetos-y-actores-sociales/lineas-y-proyectos-de-investigacion/iniciativa-interdisciplinaria-en-conflicto-mapuche-y-derecho-penal (last visited July 5, 2024).

[28] DeJusticia, https://www.dejusticia.org/en/ (last visited July 5, 2024).

[29] Instituto Interamericano de Derechos Humanos, https://www.iidh.ed.cr/es/ (last visited July 5, 2024).

International Access to Justice in Latin America

Another door opened by Latin American legal clinics is access to justice (ATJ), especially regarding matters that transcend national borders and affect otherwise excluded populations or the state itself. It was precisely the idea of facilitating ATJ that stimulated the promotion of arbitration and mediation in the 1990s, and what prompted multilateral agencies to include them as critical components of their judicial reform agendas. Furthermore, contemporary constitutions, including some from Latin America, generally mention ATJ as a fundamental right of the citizens and a duty of the state toward them. This role of the state as a guarantor of ATJ is precisely what the traditional literature has assumed.[30] Such assumption should come as no surprise if we consider that the justice system called upon to protect legal rights is the archetypal state monopoly at the service of its people, especially those deemed marginalized, excluded, or disenfranchised. As a result of the different crises that have affected Latin America during the last two decades, states have been pressured to address the legal needs of refugees, asylum seekers, labor migrants, Indigenous peoples, and other vulnerable populations. Government actors have also been pressured to protect their citizens from exposure to a growing number of man-made and natural disasters and climate change-related harms. Such a situation has renewed the need to guarantee ATJ domestically and internationally.

The need to guarantee ATJ at the international level is reflected in several key legal instruments ranging from the Universal Declaration of Human Rights,[31] the International Covenant on Civil and Political Rights,[32] and the Hague Convention on International Access to Justice of 25 October 1980[33] and the United Nations Principles and Guidelines on Access to Legal Aid in Criminal Justice Systems of December 2012.[34] ATJ is generally understood in absolute terms. As a result, states are obligated to ensure ATJ regardless of their actual ability to do so. The reality, however, is that not all states possess the resources to effectively guarantee ATJ to all its citizens or to safeguard their own sovereign rights from the harmful conduct of other states, multinational corporations, or

[30] Mauro Cappelletti and Bryant Garth (eds.), *Access to Justice: A World Survey. A World Survey: Volume 1* (Amsterdam: Sijthoff, 1978).

[31] G.A. Res. 217 A, Universal Declaration of Human Rights (December 10, 1948), https://www.un.org/en/universal-declaration-human-rights/ (last visited December 12, 2022).

[32] G.A. Res., International Covenant of Civil and Political Rights (December 19, 1966) https://treaties.un.org/doc/publication/unts/volume%20999/volume-999-i-14668-english.pdf (last visited December 12, 2022).

[33] Hague Convention on International Access to Justice of October 25, 1980, https://www.hcch.net/en/instruments/conventions/full-text/?cid=91 (last visited December 12, 2022).

[34] United Nations, United Nations Principles and Guidelines on Access to Legal Aid in Criminal Justice Systems of December 2012, https://www.unodc.org/documents/justice-and-prison-reform/UN_principles_and_guidlines_on_access_to_legal_aid.pdf (last visited December 12, 2022).

other actors with greater political and economic strength and better legal representation. In this context, "a financially weak state, such as Timor Leste, may be in a similar position to a disenfranchised individual when it comes to asserting its legal rights."[35]

Treating states as rights holders that deserve due process and other guarantees has become especially salient in a transnational justice system where other international actors (e.g., multinational companies) with equal or more power than a state have become repeat players. The rights of states are separate and conceptually different from the rights of its citizens, but there is a connection between them. When, for example, a state with limited resources faces a potentially costly claim by a powerful foreign investor, the former may have to surrender to the investor's demands or accept less favorable settlement terms to end an otherwise costly dispute that might harm its citizens. In other words, the state might be forced to act in a way that prioritizes "investors' concerns over those of right holders in ways that indirectly undermine rights holders' access to justice."[36] Such power imbalance has become visible in investor-state dispute settlement (ISDS) and has prompted many calls for reform to balance things out.

In addition to the states, there are third-party rights holders, such as individuals and groups of citizens like Indigenous groups, who might be adversely affected by foreign investments. When disputes against governments arise, as frequently occurs in cases of infrastructure or manufacturing projects that have an impact on natural resources, the rights of these individuals or communities can be affected.

In this complex landscape of legal issues arising from contracts between states and foreign investors, human rights violations might occur because of humanitarian crises, large-scale environmental disasters, and other legal problems. For the victims, the only way to bring the issue to an ISDS (or any other tribunals) is with teams with adequate legal expertise and resources that many parties cannot afford. It is precisely in this situation where legal clinics play a crucial role. Since they have the potential to attract academics with the required intellectual prowess, practitioners with experience and connections, and students with interest and time availability, clinics may assemble first-rate legal teams that would be otherwise costly or very difficult to coordinate.

The international or regional impact of the work of legal clinics stems not only from their involvement in proceedings before supr-national courts, tribunals,

[35] Manuel A. Gómez, "A Frontier within Reach: Access to Justice of Small States through Crowd-Litigation-Funding (CLF)," in *Acesso à Justiça, Direito e Sociedade: Estudos em homenagem ao Professor Marc Galanter*, ed. Flávio Luis Yarshel et al.(São Paulo: Quartier Latin, 2022), 477–480.

[36] Columbia Center on Sustainable Investment, The International Investment Regime and Access to Justice, Roundtable Outcome Brief, September 2018, http://ccsi.columbia.edu/files/2018/09/CCSI-and-UNWGBHR-International-Investment-Regime-and-Access-to-Justice-Briefing.pdf (last visited December 12, 2022).

and similar organs. Even their work at the local level, on matters that mainly arise from alleged violations of domestic law, has an important effect on the practice of international law. This is particularly true if we consider that international instruments have also established the safeguard of fundamental rights, and the outcome of domestic cases often informs how international courts and other organs interpret and protect those rights. During the last decades, Latin American legal clinics have amassed incredible experience in pursuing impact litigation strategies in local courts on behalf of clients in vulnerable situations, migrants, disabled persons, Indigenous peoples, and persons subject to racial, gender, and other types of discrimination. Some examples include the amicus curiae intervention of the Public Interest Legal Clinic of Universidad del Rosario (Colombia) before the Inter-American Court of Human Rights in a matter involving gender identity and sexual orientation;[37] the *Baraona Bray v. Chile* case before the Inter-American Court of Human Rights, led by the Public Interest and Human Rights Clinic of the Diego Portales University (Chile);[38] and the amicus curiae intervention of the Legal Clinic for Disabled and Human Rights of the Pontifical Catholic University of Peru (Peru) in the case *María Inés Chinchilla v. Guatemala*.[39]

In addition to coordinating with regional peer institutions, legal clinics have also shared and disseminated their knowledge and experience through conferences, workshops, and joint research projects. One example is the Regional Congress of Legal Clinics held by the LANLC, whose last edition was hosted by Mexico's ITAM in August 2022.[40] Akin to what occurs with the international arbitration conferences described earlier, legal clinicians use their meetings not only to socialize and share professional experiences but to build and strengthen their professional networks. Furthermore, clinic directors and affiliated faculty are occasionally appointed to key roles such as UN Special Rapporteur on the Human Rights of Migrants,[41] which helps further reinforce the field.

[37] Amicus Curiae brief submitted on behalf of the Public Interest Legal Clinic of the Universidad del Rosario Law School, December 7, 2016, https://www.corteidh.or.cr/sitios/observaciones/costaricaoc24/14_clinica_juridica.pdf,

[38] CIDH acoge reclamación patrocinada por clínica jurídica UDP y condena al estado de Chile por violar la Libertad de expression, https://clinicasjuridicas.udp.cl/cidh-acoge-reclamacion-patrocinada-por-clinica-juridica-udp-y-condena-al-estado-de-chile-por-violar-libertad-de-expresion/.

[39] Amicus curiae brief submitted on behalf of the Legal Clinic for Disabled and Human Rights of the Pontifical Catholic University of Peru (Peru) in the case *María Inés Chinchilla v. Guatemala*, 2015, https://idehpucp.pucp.edu.pe/lista_publicaciones/amicus-curiae-presentado-ante-la-corte-interamericana-de-derechos-humanos-sobre-el-caso-maria-ines-chinchilla-vs-guatemala-sobre-personas-con-discapacidad-y-reclusion-en-centros-penitenciarios/ (last visited December 12, 2022).

[40] Instituto Tecnológico Autónomo de México, II Congreso Regional de Clínicas Jurídicas, https://eventos.itam.mx/es/evento/ii-congreso-regional-de-clinicas-juridicas (last visited December 12, 2022).

[41] Felipe González Morales, Report of the Special Rapporteur on the human rights of migrants (Office of the High Commissioner for Human Rights), https://www.ohchr.org/en/special-procedures/sr-migrants/felipe-gonzalez-morales (last visited December 12, 2022).

V. Conclusion

As this chapter has shown, the relationship between Latin American legal professionals and international law is long-standing and multifaceted. If we look at legal education, students from the region have been exposed to critical international law topics since the nineteenth century, which has not changed. The field has also benefited from the intellectual contributions of many prominent scholars and practitioners who have helped advance and transform international law both regionally and globally. Conversely, Latin American legal professionals have been impacted and shaped by expanding the international law field into new areas. The two legal communities analyzed in this chapter have the value of illustrating how the legal professions have reacted to and changed because of the increased importance of legal matters that transcend national borders.

The constantly evolving state of international law in the region has incentivized a new cadre of legal professionals who act on behalf of multinational corporations and states; similar actors in international arbitration cases; and legal clinics that assist victims of human rights violations, vulnerable communities, refugees, and others. A brief description of them does not offer an exhaustive snapshot of the entire landscape of Latin American legal professionals. Nonetheless, it has great value in showing us, with some detail, the porosity of the invisible line that purports to divide international and domestic legal practice.

17

Education in International Law in Latin America

Mónica Pinto

I. Introduction

In her book, Anthea Roberts submits that domestic legal systems differ, yet lawyers often assume that international law is universal.[1] She proposes that what counts as international law depends partly on how the actors concerned construct their understandings of the field and pass them on to the next generation.[2] She considers that a dynamic interplay between the centripetal search for unity and universality and the centrifugal pull of national and regional differences define the field of international law.[3] Roberts argues that the ideas and practices that characterize international law vary widely across countries and regions. This argument, however, is not new to Latin America, which has long taken pride in its regional exceptionalism in international law.

Anthea Roberts recalls Brian Garth and Yves Dezalay's statement on the faculties of law serving central roles in the reproduction of knowledge, governing elites, and the hierarchies among elites and expertise.[4] She moves forward considering that the "privileged status accorded to legal academics may partly reflect the influence of the civil law tradition on international law, as well as the absence of a general literature" and also supports her consideration in the fact that "academics are instrumental in shaping international law because they often engage in its practice as advisers to governments, counsel in disputes, judges and arbitrators, and members of expert bodies."[5]

[1] Anthea Roberts, *Is International Law International?*, (Oxford: Oxford University Press, 2017), xvii.

[2] Ibid., 2.

[3] Ibid., 3.

[4] Ibid., 28 (quoting Yves Dezalay and Brian G. Garth, *The Internationalization of Palace Wars. Lawyers, Economists, and the Contest to Transform Latin American States* (Chicago: University of Chicago Press, 2002), 5).

[5] Ibid., 28–29 (relying on Daniel Terris and Cesare Romano, *The International Judge: An Introduction to the Men and Women Who Decide the World Cases* (Oxford: Oxford University Press, 2007), 20.

Mónica Pinto, *Education in International Law in Latin America* In: *Latin American International Law in the Twenty-First Century*. Edited by: Alejandro Chehtman, Alexandra Huneeus, and Sergio Puig, Oxford University Press. DOI: 10.1093/9780197754016.003.0017

In fact, different authors put forward Latin American international law or international law in Latin America with different formulations. However, none of them assess the existence of true regional international law but instead the existence of peculiar readings of certain international law rules according to the region's interests and needs at different times. In fact, those theorists "were united by a vision of a shared community of practice of international law at the regional level."[6] There is a relevant bibliography on the contribution of Latin America to international law.[7]

The expression "Latin America," as used here, involves a mix of criteria stemming from geography, history, political sociology, and even language. In fact, Latin America describes a region of non-English-speaking countries, located to the south of the border between the United States and Mexico. As put by Carlos Calvo, the first to use the expression, all American nations were formerly colonized by Europe's Latin powers, including Haiti and Brazil.[8]

Latin American countries' relationship with international law developed very early, throughout the eighteenth century, while they were (mainly) European colonies. The law of nations was functional to the Emancipation in the nineteenth century. Arnulf Becker Lorca states that international law was an instrument in nation-building from 1810 to 1880.[9] In the last century, international law provided tools for Latin American republics to participate in the building of a developing international society and, then, in the new legal and political order established after World War II. In the second half of the twentieth century, after a wave of military rule, our countries started recovering democracy, and human rights played a vital role in that, both for the treatment of the past and in the design of the future. The twenty-first century opened to the questioning of certain institutions. It also shook the landscape of sustainable democracy with human rights and development. In such a time frame, three

[6] See Chehtman, Huneeus, and Puig, "Introduction to Latin American International Law," in this volume.

[7] Rafael De La Colina, "Principales problemas jurídicos del Sistema Interamericano," *VIII Curso de Derecho Internacional* (Comité Jurídico Interamericano, OEA, 1981), 181–220, at 185; Hugo Caminos, "The Latin American Contribution to International Law," *Proceedings of the 80th Annual Meeting of the American Society of International Law* 80 (1986): 157–161, at 157–158. Mónica Pinto et al., "Aperçu sur les systèmes juridiques de l'Amérique du sud," *Revue de droit international et de droit comparé, Bruxelles* 1–2 (1988): 105–133, at 124; Julio Barberis "Les règles spécifiques du droit international en Amérique latine," *Collected Courses of The Hague Academy of International Law* 235 (1992): 81–230, at 93; Claudio Grossman, "Latin American Contributions to International Law," *Proceedings of the American Society of International Law* 94 (2000): 45; Arnulf Becker Lorca, "International Law in Latin America or Latin America International Law? Rise, Fall and Retrieval of a Tradition of Legal Thinking and Political Imagination," *Harvard International Law Journal* 47 (2006): 283–306, at 284.

[8] V. De Mars, A. Geffroy, and C. de Mazade, "Essais et Notices," *Revue des Deux Mondes (1829-1971), seconde période* 41 (1862): 231–240, at 238.

[9] Becker Lorca, "International Law in Latin America or Latin America International Law?" 284.

political phenomena—decolonization, democracy, and globalization—became the driving force of specific changes in the way in which our countries rely on international law.

This chapter will deal with education in international law in Latin America throughout the nineteenth, twentieth, and twenty-first centuries. I will go through the positions and doctrines that Latin American jurists put forward and link them to the problems the region was facing at the same time. The education in international law and how it took place as formal education in law schools, the law curriculum, and textbooks will provide tools for the analysis of international law in Latin America.

II. The Colonial Rule (1492–1799)

Colonialism entails a migration phenomenon. The metropolis leads the political, economic, and legal migration, imposing a territorial regime, appointing its authorities, establishing the ways and means to obtain resources, and also establishing the necessary legal rules to that end. The metropolis either creates a specific legal order for its dependencies or extends some of its rules to those territories.[10]

Spain organized its territories in America as Viceroyalties, with a Viceroy heading each of them. The position is mentioned in the *Capitulaciones de Santa Fe*, an instrument signed by the Catholic Monarchy and Columbus in 1492.[11] Viceroys were the direct representatives of the Spanish monarchs in America. The Viceroy concentrated all branches of government: the executive (as captain general and governor), which included legislative capacities, and the judiciary (as president of the *Audiencia).*

The Viceroyalty of New Spain was established in 1535, covering the current territories of Central and North America. Its capital was in Mexico. The Viceroyalty of Peru was established in 1542, with its capital in Lima, covering all of South America except for the current territories of Panama and Venezuela. In 1717, the Viceroyalty of New Grenada, with its capital in Bogotá, was established to cover the current extension of Panamá, Colombia, Ecuador, and Venezuela. Last, the Viceroyalty of the River Plate was established in 1776 to cover Argentina, Bolivia, Brazil (southern part), Chile (northern part), Paraguay, and a portion of Peru and Uruguay. These territories were governed by the so-called

[10] Mónica Pinto, *El derecho internacional, Vigencia y desafíos en un escenario globalizado* (Buenos Aires: Fondo de Cultura Económica, 2004), 17–18.

[11] Capitulaciones de Santa Fe, https://www.unesco.org/es/memory-world/santa-fe-capitulations#:~:text=Las%20Capitulaciones%20de%20Santa%20Fe,de%20la%20toma%20de%20Granada (last visited June 26, 2024).

Leyes de Indias (India's law)[12] and specific legislation was adopted to cover different situations.

Different from the Portuguese Crown, which did not authorize the establishment of higher education institutions,[13] in the Spanish colonies the Catholic Church was the first institution to establish universities in Latin America, following the models provided by the Universities of Salamanca and Alcalá de Henares. The aim was to train missioners and prepare men for liberal professions. Different congregations managed those institutions, among them the Jesuits.[14] During that period, universities were established in the territories of what today are Argentina, Bolivia, Colombia, Cuba, Chile, Ecuador, Guatemala, México, Perú, Dominican Republic, and Venezuela. Most of them were confessional and royal institutions, like the Universities of San Marcos de Lima y México (1551), San Carlos de Guatemala (1676), and San Cristóbal de Huamanga y Charcas.

Nearly all of them taught natural law and the law of nations. Courses dealing with law topics included the study of norms and their practice. The teaching method was closer to what we nowadays know as a common law approach than that of a continental law system. In fact, students analyzed cases and drew conclusions. The "academy of jurisprudence" became a common feature in the region.[15]

Most law graduates obtained their degrees either in Spain or at the then well-known University of Chuquisaca—the *Universidad Mayor, Real y Pontificia San Francisco Xavier de Chuquisaca* was established in 1624 by the Jesuits. Others studied in Spain and came back to practice in their respective countries. A good number of those obtaining their law degrees in Chuquisaca led the revolutionary period that produced the emancipation of Spanish colonies, like Mariano Moreno (Argentina), Mariano Alvarez (Perú), and José Mariano Serrano (Bolivia), among others.

Brazil established its first law schools after its independence. In fact, the political and institutional changes in the recently independent Brazil were closely linked to the creation of the first two law schools in the country on August 11, 1827, in São Paulo and Olinda. In 1831, six men obtained their law degree at São Paulo.[16]

[12] "Recopilación de Leyes de los Reynos de las Indias," https://www.boe.es/biblioteca_juridica/publicacion.php?id=PUB-LH-1998-62 (last visited June 26, 2024).

[13] Diego Rafael Ambrosini, "A interiorização da metrópole: atores e instituições," in *Os juristas na Formação do Estado-Nação Brasileiro. Século XVI a 1850* (São Paulo: Quartier Latin, 2006) 242–250, at 231.

[14] Carlos Tünnermann Bernheim, "Breve historia del desarrollo de la universidad en América Latina," in *La Educación superior en el umbral del siglo XXI* (Caracas: Ed. CRESALC, 1996), 11–38, at 11–13.

[15] Abelardo Levaggi, "Bicentenario de la creación de la Academia Teórico-Práctica de Jurisprudencia de Buenos Aires," *Academia, Revista sobre Enseñanza del Derecho* 24 (2014): 237–247.

[16] Ambrosini, "A interiorização da metrópole: atores e instituições," 248–249.

III. Emancipation: International Law in the Building of the New States (1810–1880)

Latin American countries are former Spanish, Portuguese, and French colonies. Their emancipation took place in the first half of the nineteenth century. In fact, Latin America performed the first wave of decolonization. In that period, the group of those former colonies became known as "Latin America" or "Latin American Republics." As indicated above, Carlos Calvo was the first to use the expression. He included information and comments on Latin America in every piece he wrote and published, mainly in Paris.

Over almost a century, Latin American countries used international law as a tool to design common strategies against those who resisted their emancipation. They also created common rules, designed to be conventional rules but which became customary rules because of the deficit of ratification of common instruments, as evidenced in the *Asylum Case* (1950) between Peru and Colombia.[17]

Emancipation for Latin American countries started at the beginning of the nineteenth century when Napoleon imprisoned the King of Spain, whoowned the colonies in America. However, even when the great majority of the colonial rules could be set aside because of the clean slate doctrine,[18] the newly independent statesneeded to maintain some legal rules as their essential building blocks. The "imitation rule" (*la loi de l'imitation*) played a role in that sense. In fact, some rules that proved useful during *l'ancien régime* were deemed helpful in the new era. This also explains some of the features of the national and regional legal orders today.[19]

As most colonies did, Latin American countries ideologically repudiated those rules that they could not afford because of their colonial content but also pragmatically manipulated some, which they kept for a while and some forever.[20] International law had a definite role during this period. As Arnulf Becker Lorca argued, it was an instrument in the process of nation-building, especially

[17] *Colombian-Peruvian asylum*, Judgment of November 20, 1950, I.C.J. 266 (1950), *Dissenting Opinion by Judge Alvarez*, 290.

[18] International Law Commission, *Report to the General Assembly (Draft articles on Succession of States in respect of Treaties with commentaries 1974), 26th session*, 1974, 211: Most writers take the view, supported by state practice, that a newly independent state begins its life with a clean slate, except regarding "local" or "real" obligations. The clean slate is generally recognized to be the "traditional" view on the matter. It has been applied to earlier cases of newly independent states emerging either from former colonies (i.e., the United States and the Spanish American Republics) or from a process of secession or dismemberment (i.e., Belgium, Panama, Ireland, Poland, Czechoslovakia, and Finland).

[19] René Rodière, *Introduction au droit compare* (Paris: Dalloz, 1979), 11.

[20] R. A. Falk, "The New States and International Legal Order," *Collected Courses: The Hague Academy of International Law* 118 (1966): 1–103, at 10–11.

between 1810 and 1880.[21] Latin American countries had to establish the building blocks of their institutions and, at the same time, be aware of the new European situation and its consequences for themselves.

During the emancipation period, Simón Bolívar took political initiative and gathered representatives from the territories that belonged to the King of Spain. The threat of political intervention and the occupation of territory by the European powers was the uniting factor.

Alejandro Álvarez later recalled that "[t]he Latin States (sic) recognized the community of interests that existed between them, and, feeling that they were members of one great family of nations, desired to establish a political unity, a confederation, which would furnish them protection from the dangers of European intervention, show them the course to take in their new life, aid them in arriving at the best solution of their special problems, bind them together through mutual interests and obviate the conflicts that might arise between them."[22]

Moreover, Álvarez moved forward, stating:

> [The new States] organized their respective countries uniformly, subjecting them to a constitutional regimen whose principles and forms were republican, liberal and democratic. And this uniformity of views is so much the more worthy of note because in proceeding thus uniformly the statesmen of these new nations did so spontaneously and without any previous agreement of any kind whatsoever and in spite of the formidable reaction against those principles which at that time was being felt, above all in France.[23]

Both Julio Barberis and Hugo Caminos firmly stated:

> Two basic ideas inspired the development of international law in Latin America during the decolonization period: (1) creation of a confederation of nations of the Americas for consolidation and protection of newly won freedom and independence; and (2) adoption of a set of legal principles which would be in force between the emerging states. It was only to be expected that the newly independent Latin American countries would reaffirm their freedom, equality, and independence and at first would be confronting the European establishment.[24]

[21] Becker Lorca, "International Law in Latin America or Latin America International Law?" 284.

[22] Alejandro Álvarez, "Latin America and International Law," *American Journal of International Law* 3 (1909): 269–353, at 270.

[23] Ibid., 273

[24] Barberis, "Les règles spécifiques du droit international en Amérique latine," 93; Caminos, "The Latin American Contribution to International Law," 157–158; the same idea in De La Colina, "Principales problemas jurídicos del Sistema Interamericano," 185.

Until the Pacific War in 1883, the Spanish-speaking countries were dominant. Afterward, Brazil, Haiti, and the Caribbean countries joined the group, and by the end of the century, so did the United States while offering its capital city for the headquarters of the administrative office of the Pan-American Union.[25]

During the second half of the nineteenth century, some Latin American states, strongly influenced by the *Code Napoléon*, decided to codify the rules of the primary law branches. The codification became a generalized phenomenon. In fact, the codification movement was intense and covered the whole region; for example, Argentina adopted its Commercial Code in 1862 and its Civil Code in 1869; Bolivia implemented the *Code Napoléon* in 1830 and adopted its Commercial Code in 1834; Chile got its Civil Code in 1855 and its Commercial Code in 1865; both Colombia and Ecuador promulgated the Chilean Civil Code; Paraguay did the same with the Argentine Civil and Commercial Codes, among others.

The adoption of the codes had a direct impact on the law curriculum. Instead of dealing with and studying "cases," future law graduates had to be familiar with "rules," their drafting history, and their priorities. Accordingly, the law curriculum included the teaching of the codes. The practice had to be built. From there, we can trace back to the formalistic approach that prevailed in Latin America for long time.

In that context, international law remained one of the very few topics that had to be taught "in an ancient way," both in theory and in practice. In the last quarter of the nineteenth century, the idea that international law was an extensive and a complex subject began to grow. The predominant view pointed to international law as that noncodified field in which politics seemed to be more important than the rules. However, the subject was interesting, and Latin America produced many international law jurists.

IV. Latin America in International Society (1889–1945)

The twentieth century was very rich in conferences, legal products, and the development of education in international law. Indeed, several important doctrines were shaped during this period. In his *Droit international public, théorique et pratique,* published in 1887, Carlos Calvo discusses using force to recover public debt. He stated:

> In strict international law, the collection of debts and the institution of legal proceedings claiming for private debts do not justify *per se* the armed intervention

[25] De La Colina, "Principales problemas jurídicos del Sistema Interamericano," 188.

of governments and as European States invariably follow this rule in their reciprocal relations, there is no reason for them not to impose the same in their relations with the nations of the New World.[26]

These ideas were neither isolated nor rhetorical. The threat of intervention in Venezuela by three European powers in December 1902 provided flesh and bones to the statement of Argentine Luis María Drago. The so-called Drago Doctrine on the noncoercive enforcement of public debt (1902) was a public position by the Argentine government, through its Minister of Foreign Affairs Luis María Drago, regarding the gun-boat diplomacy of some European states.[27]

The question was debated at the Third Pan-American Conference (Rio de Janeiro 1906), which recommended that the Second Peace Conference at The Hague examine the question of the compulsory collection of debts and, in general, the best means to diminish conflicts of purely pecuniary origin among nations.[28] It finally led to the Drago-Porter Convention at The Hague Conference in 1907, which prohibited recourse to armed forces for the recovery of contract debts claimed from the government of one state by another government on behalf of its nationals.[29] Minister Drago published his government's position in the *American Journal of International Law* in 1907.[30] Its impact can be measured in the interest of international law literature on the doctrine.[31]

That same year, Ecuadorian Carlos Tobar proposed the nonrecognition of any government resulting from a *coup d'état*. This political position was also embodied in conventional rules in 1907 and 1923.[32] It became an effective

[26] Carlos (Charles) Calvo, *Le droit international. Théorique et Pratique, t.I* (4th ed., Paris: Guillaumin-Rousseau-Pédone-Lauriel-Marchal et Billard, 1887), 393: en droit international strict le récouvrement de créances et la poursuite de réclamations privées ne justifient pas de plano l'intervention armée des gouvernements, et que, comme les états européens suivent invariablement cette règle dans leurs relations réciproques, il n'y a nul motif pour qu'ils ne se l'imposent pas aussi dans leurs rapports avec les nations du Nouveau Monde.

[27] See Chehtman et al., "Introduction to Latin American International Law," in this volume.

[28] Amos S. Hershey, "The Calvo and Drago Doctrines," *American Journal of International Law* 1 (1907): 26–45, at 26.

[29] Barberis, "Les règles spécifiques du droit international en Amérique latine," 186–189.

[30] Luis Drago, "State Loans in Their Relation to International Policy," *the American Journal of International Law* (1907): 692–726. See also T. S. Woolsey, "Drago and the Drago Doctrine," *American Journal of International Law* 15 (1921): 558–559.

[31] Among others: Amos S. Hershey, "The Calvo and Drago Doctrines," *American Journal of International Law* 1 (1907): 26–45; Amos S. Hershey, "La Doctrine de Drago. Par H. A. Moulin, Professeur de Droit International Public à l'Université de Dijon (Paris: A. Pedone. 1908), xii, 368," *American Journal of International Law* 3 (1909): 772–776; William R. Manning, "La Doctrina Drago by Alfredo N.Vivot, Buenos Aires, Coni Hnos, 1911," *American Journal of International Law* 8 (1914): 172–275.

[32] Convention de Washington du 20 décembre 1907 (Costa Rica, Guatémala, Honduras, Nicaragua, Salvador), *Nouveau Recueil général des traités (Martens),* 3d ed. série, vol. III, 94; Convention de Washington du 7 février 1923 (Costa Rica, Guatémala, Honduras, Nicaragua, Salvador), *Nouveau Recueil général des traités (Martens),* 3d ed. série, vol. III, 102.

practice in the region, especially in the relationship among Central American states.[33] The United States refreshed it under the Wilson Doctrine and invoked it toward the governments of Carranza in Mexico (1917–1921) and Tinoco in Costa Rica (1917).[34]

In 1930, Mexican Foreign Affairs Minister Genaro Estrada instructed the diplomatic representatives that Mexico would no longer express recognition of new governments that come into power by *coups d'état* or revolution.[35] Philip C. Jessup informed of the existence of the so-called Estrada Doctrine in this way: "The reason for this new policy is the belief that recognition involves the assumption of a right to pass critically upon the legal capacity of foreign régimes, a right which is derogatory to the sovereignty of other states."[36]

In 1935, another Argentine foreign minister, Carlos Saavedra Lamas, obtained an armistice between the parties in the Chaco War and was, because of that, awarded a Nobel Peace Prize in 1936. He was the first Latin American receive a Nobel Prize. He also worked to establish the Saavedra Lamas Pact, the Anti-War Treaty of Non-Aggression and Conciliation.[37]

In his study of Latin American international law textbooks, Arnulf Becker Lorca explained:

> The reason for concentrating on textbooks is twofold. First, each Latin American country has a number of international law textbooks that have consolidated their hold on Latin American international legal thinking through numerous editions and extensive use in teaching and legal counsel at national universities and foreign relations offices. Second, textbooks express the professional common sense, the popular and tacit understanding about international law in the region, building up a national lore. Also, monographs devoted specifically to the question of a Latin American international law are rare. Often, they do no more than restate the history of Latin American international law for foreign audiences.[38]

However, Anthea Roberts nuances the above statement and points out the following:

[33] Charles Rousseau, *Droit international public*, vol. III (Paris: Sirey, 1977), 559–560.

[34] Louis Cavaré, *Le droit international public positif*, 3d ed., vol. I (Paris: Pédone, 1967), 360; Charles Rousseau, *Droit international public*, vol. III (Paris: Sirey, 1977), 562–567.

[35] "Estrada Doctrine of Recognition," *American Journal of International Law* 25 (1931): 203.

[36] Philip C. Jessup, "The Estrada Doctrine," *American Journal of International Law* 25 (1931): 719–723.

[37] Anti-War Treaty of Non-Aggression and Conciliation, Río de Janeiro, October 10, 1933, *American Journal of International Law* 28 (1934): 79–84.

[38] Becker Lorca, "International Law in Latin America or Latin America International Law?" 287.

> There are limits to relying on a study of textbooks. First, textbooks are not necessarily the only materials to teach students... Second, these books do not necessarily reflect how IL is practiced in the state concerned.... Third, the type of book that is commonly used may differ among states.[39]

International law jurists and professors, as well as politicians, made their views and positions known regarding specific Latin American issues and some other topics of international law. Charles Fenwick[40] summarized the international law literature in Latin America. He underlined Andrés Bello's *Principios de Derecho Internacional*, "an advanced treatise" written based on the author's experiences as a member of different Venezuelan delegations and as Minister of Foreign Affairs of Chile. In 1861, Carlos Calvo published *Collected Treaties and Other Diplomatic Acts of all Latin American States, from the Gulf of Mexico to the Cape Horn, from 1493 to the Present*, preceded by a study on the present situation of America; in 1868, he published his *Derecho internacional teórico y práctico de Europa y América*, and in 1887 its French version, *Droit international théorique et pratique*, in three volumes. Andrés Bello, a Chile and Venezuela national, published his *Derecho Internacional* in Santiago (Chile) in 1886. Again, Fenwick recalled *Le droit international américain* by Alejandro Álvarez, of Chile, published in Paris in 1910, in which Álvarez tried to define the field of inter-American relations and where he thought special rules should be applicable.[41]

One of the results of the the First Hague Peace Conference in 1899 was the establishment of an institutionalized method of solving international disputes through arbitration. Eighteen Latin American countries joined the Permanent Court of Arbitration before World War II and, accordingly, presented their lists for the members of the court.[42] Even when arbitration was the usual method for solving interstate disputes, only a few Latin American jurists sat as arbitrators, Luis María Drago in *The North Atlantic Coast Fisheries Case* (*Great Britain v. United States of America*), decided on September 7, 1910;[43] Cuban Gonzalo de Quesada in *The Orinoco Steamship Company Case* (*United States of America v. The Republic of Venezuela*) decided on October 25, 1910;[44] and Peruvian Manuel Alvarez Calderón in the *Canevaro Claims Case* (*Italy v. Peru*) decided

[39] Roberts, *Is International Law International?*, 33

[40] Charles Fenwick, *International Law* (3rd ed., New York: Appleton Century Crofts, 1952), translated into Spanish by María Eugenia I de Fischman (Buenos Aires, Editorial Omeba, 1963), 69.

[41] Ibid.

[42] Permanent Court of Arbitration (PCA), "Contracting Parties," https://pca-cpa.org/en/about/introduction/contracting-parties/ (last visited June 26, 2024).

[43] PCA, *The North Atlantic Coast Fisheries Case* (*Great Britain v. United States of America*), The Hague, September 7, 1910, https://pcacases.com/web/sendAttach/496 (last visited June 26, 2024).

[44] PCA, *The Orinoco Steamship Company Case* (*United States of America, v. Venezuela*), The Hague, October 25, 1910, https://pcacases.com/web/sendAttach/513 (last accessed June 26, 2024).

on May 3, 1912.[45] Both Gonzalo de Quesadâ and Manuel Alvarez Calderon were acting diplomats when they sat in those proceedings.

The preliminary test of institutionalization of the international society that was the League of Nations (1919) was joined by the establishment of the first permanent international tribunal, the Permanent Court of International Justice, in 1920, and outside the structure of the League. International law jurists and diplomats from the region became members of the Permanent Court of International Justice, such as Ruy Barbosa from Brazil, who was elected along with Antonio Sánchez de Bustamante y Sirvén from Cuba in the first panel. Barbosa was succeeded by Epitácio da Silva Pessoa, who served until 1930, when Francisco José Urrutia Olano from Colombia and José Gustavo Guerrero from El Salvador were elected. Sánchez de Bustamante y Sirvén and Guerrero resigned in 1945, allowing the new international organization that was created, the United Nations, to elect the judges of the new tribunal, the International Court of Justice

During this period and until World War II, international law was part of the mandatory curriculum of law schools in almost all public universities and the great majority of private ones in the region. The syllabus's content followed the evolution of international events and was taught mainly through lectures.

At the University of Buenos Aires Law School, from 1919 to 1946, Isidoro Ruiz Moreno was the head of a *cátedra*. During that long period, he also served in different positions at the Law School Board and from 1926 as the Legal Advisor at the Ministry of Foreign Affairs. In 1925, he established the Centre for International Law Studies, which became the Institute of International Law in 1935.[46] Revealing a pattern of cross-fertilization between academia and government service, it is said that Ruiz Moreno submitted a Project on International Public Debts to the American Institute of International Law in its session at Montevideo in 1927.[47]

In the first years of the twentieth century, in almost every Latin American country, an international law association or society was created to promote the study of international law and the gathering of practitioners and professors. Annual meetings and yearbooks are published in Spanish or Portuguese. As an illustration, the *Sociedade Brasileira de Direito Internacional* published its first

[45] PCA, *Canevaro Claim, Italy v. Peru*, The Hague, May 3, 1912, https://pcacases.com/web/sendAttach/516 (last visited June 26, 2024).

[46] Leopoldo Godio, "La enseñanza del derecho internacional en la Universidad de Buenos Aires: la cátedra de Isidoro Ruiz Moreno (1919-1946)," *La Facultad de Derecho de la Universidad de Buenos Aires hacia su Bicentenario*, ed. Tulio Ortíz and Luciana Scotti (Buenos Aires: Departamento de Publicaciones, 2019), 127–159, at 127–141

[47] Ibid., 146.

newsletter in 1915, while Ruy Barbosa was the president of that institution.[48] That same year, the Peruvian society was established.[49]

V. The New Legal and Political Order: Imitation; Contestation; Association (1945–1998)

The twentieth century revealed three different moments. First, Latin American countries looked to Europe for inspiration to set up their cooperation and integration agreements, perhaps without paying much attention to the difference in the contexts. Second, they took *avant-garde* positions regarding development and challenging some existing structures. The position was not successful at that time, but it posed the principles that later would be captured again through a different approach, for instance, in the field of environment. Third, they united to face the different crises that affected the continent, like the Malvinas War, the Central American crisis, and regional indebtedness, among others.[50]

The new legal and political order established with the adoption of the United Nations Charter in 1945 included an International Court of Justice, the successor of the PCIJ. For the election of its judges, both the General Assembly and the Security Council bore in mind that in the body as a whole, the representation of the primary forms of civilization and the principal legal systems of the world should be assured, as provided for in Article 9 of the Statute of the ICJ. In practice, those requirements translated into equitable geographical distribution in which Latin America got two judges.

As of today, twenty-three Latin American Judges have served at the Court,[51] and four of them as president: José Luis Bustamante y Rivero from Perú, who presided from 1967 to 1970, José Gustavo Guerrero from El Salvador, who had been judge at the PCIJ, acted as president at the ICJ from 1946 to 1949; Eduardo

[48] Academia Brasileira de Direito Internacional, Boletim, https://direitointernacional.org/publicacoes/ (last visited June 26, 2024).

[49] Sociedad Peruana de Derecho Internacional, http://spdi.org.pe/ /6 August 2022) (last visited June 26, 2024).

[50] Mónica Pinto et al., "Aperçu sur les systèmes juridiques de l'Amérique du sud," 125–130.

[51] Andrés Aguilar (Venezuela), 1991–1995; Ricardo Joaquín Alfaro (Ecuador), 1959–1964; Alejandro Alvarez (Chile), 1948–1955; Ernique Armand-Ugon (Uruguay), 1952–1961; José Philadelpho de Barros e Azevedo (Brazil), 1946–1951; Leonardo Nemer Caldeira Brant (Brazil) from 2022; José Luis Bustamante y Rivero (Peru), 1961–1970; Antonio Agusto Cançado Trindade (Brazil), 2009–2022; Levis Fernandes Carneiro (Brazil), 1951–1955; Roberto Córdova (Mexico), 1955–1964; Isidro Fabela (Mexico), 1946–1952; Juan Manuel Gómez Robledo (2024 – 2033); José Gustavo Guerrero (El Salvador), 1946–1958; Eduardo Jiménez de Aréchaga (Uruguay), 1970–1979; Lucio Manuel Moreno Quintana (Argentina), 1955–1964; Luis Padilla Nervo (Mexico), 1964–1973; Gonzalo Parra Aranguren (Venezuela), 1996–2009; Francisco Rezek (Brazil), 1997–2006; Patrick Robinson (Jamaica), from 2015; José María Ruda (1973–1991; Bernardo Sepúlveda Amor (Mexico), 2006–2015; José Sette Camara (Brasil), 1979–1988; Mohamed Shahabuddeen (Guyana), 1988–1997, https://www.icj-cij.org/en/all-members (last visited June 26, 2024).

Jiménez de Aréchaga from Uruguay, who chaired from 1976 to 1979; and José María Ruda from Argentina who presided from 1988 to 1991.[52]

In the 1960s, the new states emerging from the decolonization process under UN Resolution A/1514(XV) brought amazing changes to international society and the law regulating it: those new states became the Third World; they formed the so-called Non-Aligned Countries Movement and also gathered as the Group of 77 and became a negotiator of their common issues including how to achieve development. The UN Economic Commission for Latin America in Santiago (Chile) hosted Raul Prebisch and others who brought diverse literature regarding the issue of development, essentially, as Mariana Mota Prado shows in this book, literature that "provided a novel way of understanding how the global capitalist system produces underdevelopment in Latin America."[53] Latin American jurists developed doctrines and advanced their positions regarding development and underdevelopment and the new international economic order, which is discussed later. The declarations and positions regarding the extension of the national jurisdiction beyond the twelve miles, which gave birth to its predecessors and the exclusive economic zone itself, were also framed at that time. Written materials supported those debates. *Fondo de Cultura Económica* published authored books[54] as well as compilations (e.g. *Derecho Económico Internacional*), which gathered well-known intellectuals and academics like Jorge Castañeda, Marcos Kaplan, Eduardo Novoa Monreal, Eduardo White, Carlos Correa, and Alberto Székely, among others.[55]

In 1965, a group of states prompted the creation of an Institute for the Integration of Latin America and the Caribbean (INTAL) within the Inter-American Development Bank. INTAL'sw publications supported the debate and discussion on issues of development and integration. Since 1973, the OAS Inter-American Juridical Committee has been offering international law courses in August in Río de Janeiro, where it has its headquarters.[56] International law professors, diplomats, international civil servants, and politicians share their knowledge and experience with a classroom of younger colleagues. After the students satisfy different levels of evaluation, they receive attendance and pass certificates.

A common criticism from legal academia is that the teaching of international law has a Eurocentric approach, lacks an interdisciplinary method, and has a limited relationship with local problems. International law is perceived as a topic

[52] https://www.icj-cij.org/en/all-members (last visited June 26, 2024).

[53] Mariana Mota Prado, "Law and Development in/from Latin America,", chapter 8 in this volume.

[54] Francisco Villagrán, *Teoría general del derecho de integración económica* (San José, Costa Rica: Editorial Universitaria Centroamericana, 1969).

[55] *Derecho Económico Internacional* (Mexico City: FCE, 1976).

[56] Organization of American States, "Course on International Law," https://www.oas.org/en/sla/iajc/course.asp (last visited June 26, 2024).

for the *elites* and not one that affects the everyday life of an ordinary citizen.[57] Along the same lines, it is said that the tables of contents of Latin American textbooks , as the outward manifestation of the idea of international law, echo closely the core content of the great textbooks of the European tradition.[58]

At the same time, critics suggested that there were not many updated international law courses published in Spanish and Portuguese, so students missed important topics.[59] In 1970, Ernesto De La Guardia and Marcelo Delpech published *El Derecho de los Tratados y la Convención de Viena de 1969*,[60] which helped to advance Latin American positions at the Vienna Conference on the Law of Treaties. In fact, this book followed the trend of publishing national positions, which emerged from the Vienna Conference. In 1977, Moncayo-Vinuesa-Gutiérrez Posse published a volume dealing with sources of international law.[61] A couple of years later, José María Ruda, a judge at the ICJ, updated the treatise by Luis A. Podestá Costa.[62] That same year, Edmundo Vargas Carreño published *Introducción al Derecho Internacional*.[63] In 1981, Antonio Cançado Trindade published *Princípios do Direito Internacional Contemporâneo*.[64] With a view to improving the publication of written materials, the International Law Department of the OAS Secretary General Office produced written materials from 1999 to 2010.

Notably, the wave of authoritarian governments of the 1960s and the subsequent recovery of democracy in the 1980s had an impact on international law education. The fall of Brazilian President Joâo Goulart in 1964 was the take-off of a wave of autocracies. The military rule imposed by Humberto de Alencar

[57] Fabián Salvioli, "Algunas consideraciones sobre la enseñanza contemporánea del derecho internacional público," *Relaciones Internacionales, 2002*, vol. 11, https://revistas.unlp.edu.ar/RRII-IRI/article/view/1622 (last visited June 26, 2024); Alberto do Amaral Júnior et al., "Um novo modo de ensinar o Direito Internacional: a delicia de experimentar," https://www.google.com/search?q=amaral+jr+um+modo+de+ensinar&rlz=1C5CHFA_enAR801AR801&oq=amaral+jr+um+modo+de+ensinar&aqs=chrome..69i57.7266j1j7&sourceid=chrome&ie=UTF-8 (last visited June 26, 2024); Laura Betancur-Restrepo and Enrique Prieto-Ríos, "Educación del derecho internacional en Bogotá: Un primer diagnóstico a partir del análisis de los programas de clase y su relación con las epistemologías del no conocimiento" (The Teaching of International Law in Bogotá: A Preliminary Diagnosis, Departing from the Analysis of Syllabusses and its Relationship with the Epistemologies of not-knowing), https://revistas.uexternado.edu.co/index.php/derest/article/view/5039/6027.

[58] Becker Lorca, "International Law in Latin America or Latin America International Law?" 288.

[59] Jean-Michel Arrighi, "Para iniciar el debate sobre la metodología de la enseñanza," in *Jornadas de Derecho Internacional* (OEA Secretaría General, 2008), 173–178.

[60] Ernesto De La Guardia and Marcelo Delpech, *El derecho de los Tratados y la Convevción de Viena de 1969* (Buenos Aires: La Ley, 1970).

[61] Guillermo R. Moncayo, Raúl E. Vinuesa, and Hortensia D. T. Gutiérrez Posse, *Derecho Internacional Público*, vol. 1 (Buenos Aires: Zavalía, 1977).

[62] L. A. Podestá Costa and J. M. Ruda, *Derechos Internacional Público*, 2 vol. (Buenos Aires: TEA, 1979).

[63] Edmundo Vargas Carreño, *Introducción al derecho internacional* (San José, Costa Rica: Ed. Juricentro, 1979).

[64] Antonio Cançado Trindade, *Princípios do Direito Internacional Contemporâneo* (Brasilia: Editora de la Universidad de Brasilia, 1981).

Castelo Branco lasted until 1985; in 1966, a military government displaced Argentine President Arturo Humberto Illia and remained in office until 1973; in 1968, General Juan Velasco Alvarado replaced the President Fernando Belaunde Terry of Peru, and others followed. Military rule awarded relative weight to international law, "the rule of the weak." That situation prevailed until the 1980s.

The government of Argentina sworn in on December 10, 1983 was the first to resume democracy and also the first to adopt the existing human rights rules and to conceive the first policies to deal with the past. The way back to democracy—in Argentina, Uruguay, Brazil, Chile, and other countries—brought new international law developments into the region.[65] The measures taken to settle accounts with the past, the so-called transitional justice, amount to an important chapter in the region where international law played a crucial role. Alejandro Chehtman underlines that "the body of law developed to address gross human rights violations in Latin America has a genuine regional character."[66]

From the 1980s, democracies led to new approaches to international law. In countries like Brazil, the topic was back in the law curriculum after a break caused by military rule. Still in others, the law curriculum was reviewed and updated and, together with the mandatory course of international law, courses on international human rights law and other international law issues were offered.[67]

New publications brought fresh air to the law literature on international law. The *Anuario de Derechos Humanos* (Human Rights Yearbook),[68] which has been published since 2005 by the Center of Human Rights of the School of Law of the Universidad de Chile, at that time chaired by professor Cecilia Medina Quiroga, =became reference material in the field; *Tribuna Internacional* (International Tribune),[69] published by the Universidad de Chile since 2012, promoted the debate, analysis, and communication with a pluralist and scientific approach; in 2015 *Revista Brasileira de direito internacional* started publishing original essays and articles in an open-access regime, sponsored by the *Conselho Nacional de Pesquisa e Pós-graduaçao em direito*, among others.

[65] I worked that point in *L'Amérique latine et le traitement des violations systématiques des droits de l'homme*, Université Panthéon-Assas Paris II, Institut de Hautes Etudes Internationales, Coll. Cours et Travaux N°7 (París: Éditions .Pédone, 2007); "El tratamiento de las violaciones sistemáticas de derechos humanos del pasado reciente: El derecho y la experiencia de América Latina", XLII *Curso de Derecho Internacional*, Comité Jurídico Interamericano (OAS, 2016), 479–514.

[66] See Alejandro Chehtman, "Latin America as a Laboratory of Transitional Justice," chapter 21 in this volume.

[67] Beatriz Pallarés and Laura Aguzin, "El impacto y la evolución del derecho internacional en los programas de estudio de las facultades de derecho en Argentina," in *Jornadas de Derecho Internacional* (OAS Secretaría General, 2002), 431–446.

[68] Anuario de Derechos Humanos, https://anuariocdh.uchile.cl/ (last visited June 26, 2024).

[69] Revista Tribuna Internacional, https://tribunainternacional.uchile.cl/ (last visited June 26, 2024).

In 2013, a group of interested students at the Universidad Torcuato Di Tella, in Argentina, established *Revista Latinoamericana de Derecho Internacional,* which became the official publication of the SLADI (Sociedad Latinoamericana de Derecho Internacional/Latin American Society of International Law)[70]. They joined other publications like *Revista Peruana de derecho internacional,* which is in its seventy-first year.

Some comments indicate that law schools prepare their graduates mainly for local litigation. In that context, the teaching of international law has been perceived as superfluous.[71] Such criticism is very contextual because with globalization, international law issues have permeated the legal web applicable by local tribunals.

The judgment of the Inter-American Court on Human Rights in the *Velásquez Rodríguez v. Honduras,* in 1988, was the first judicial piece defining enforced disappearances vis-à-vis a national government. The growing influence of the Inter-American System on Human Right (IASHR) in Latin America translated into teaching special courses on the topic, different research programs, and published materials. In 1985, the University of Buenos Aires Law School was the first in Argentina to include a course on human rights in its curriculum and to offer International Protection of Human Rights as a seminar in the second cycle of studies.

Some books dealing with the main concepts and instruments of human rights law, authored by Eduardo Rabossi, Genaro Carrió, and others, and published by Eudeba (the University of Buenos Aires publishing house), helped law professors in their task. Other works followed: *Etica y Derechos Humanos* (Ethics and Human Rights) by Carlos Nino, published in 1984; "Aspectos actuales de la protección internacional de los derechos humanos" by Guillermo R. Moncayo, published in 1985 by the *Revista Jurídica de Buenos Aires*; *Los derechos humanos y las garantías* by Hortensia Gutiérrez Posse, in 1987; in 1993, *La denuncia ante la Comisión Interamericana de Derechos Humanos*; Susana Albanese's *Derechos Humanos. Estudio de Casos y Opiniones Consultivas* in 1997; and *Temas de Derechos Humanos.* Also in 1997, the Centro de Estudios Legales y Sociales, a relevant nongovernmental organization (NGO) in Argentina, edited *La Aplicación de los Tratados sobre Derechos Humanos por los Tribunales Locales,* which included chapters by almost the whole constituency of human rights activists. Ten years later, *La Aplicación de los tratados sobre derechos humanos en el ámbito local* updated content and added more authors.

[70] Revista Latinoamericana de Derecho Internacional (LADI), https://www.revistaladi.com.ar/index.php/revista-ladi (last visited June 26, 2024).

[71] Martín Bohmer, "Algunas sugerencias para escapar del silencio del aula," *Academia, Revista sobre Enseñanza del Derecho* 1 (2003): 13–34; Pallarés and Aguzin, "El impacto y la evolución del derecho internacional en los programas de estudio de las facultades de derecho en Argentina," 431–446.

Early in the democratic wave, in 1988, Rafael Nieto Navia published his *Introducción al Sistema Interamericano de Derechos Humanos*.[72] At the same time, Antonio Augusto Cançado Trindade published *A Proteção Internacional dos Direitos Humanos—Coletânea de Ensaios*.[73] In 1999, Carlos Eduardo de Abreu Boucault and Nadia de Araujo edited *Os direitos humanos e o direito internacional*, gathering Brazilian authors who dealt with both issues, such as Antonio Augusto Cançado Trindade, José Lindgren Alves, and Flavia Piovesan, among others.[74] Some of the significant topics of Latin American research in international law and its literature are the IASHR, Democracy-Elections, and Human Rights, Transitional Justice or how to deal with a past of systematic violations of human rights, and gender issues.

International supervision of free, fair, and periodic elections started in the 1980s. Both the Organization of American States (OAS) and CAPEL, a program created within the Inter-American Institute of Human Rights, took the lead in that field. Gender issues, the situation of women in society and their human rights, as well as other gender identities and sexual orientations, including the LGBTIQ+ communities, gave room to the adoption of new rules (e.g., egalitarian marriage) and the promotion of gender approaches and new insights into ancient rules. Moreover, in Argentina, during the debates on egalitarian marriage and abortion, law school deans and professors were invited to take the floor in Parliament.

VI. From Globalization to Current Times

More recently, globalization has produced the miracle of making international law popular among law practitioners. International trade and the World Trade Organization (WTO) regime, foreign investment arbitration, international human rights law, and international environmental law, among others, have become the specific fields of many practitioners and international law professors.

Notably, constitutional reforms envisaged from the 1990s brought a new legal scenario. International treaties were generally awarded a higher status than domestic rules, and international human rights treaties were awarded constitutional ranking in many countries. This internationalization of constitutional law brought international materials to the toolbox of almost every jurist. As an

[72] Rafael Nieto Navia, *Introducción al Sistema Interamericano de Derechos Humanos* (San José, Costa Rica: IIDH, 1988).

[73] Antonio Augusto Cançado Trindade, *A Proteção Internacional dos Direitos Humanos - Coletânea de Ensaios* (Rio de Janeiro: SBERJ, 1988).

[74] Carlos Eduardo de Abreu Boucault and Nadia de Araujo, *Os direitos humanos e o Direito Internacional* (Rio de Janeiro: Renovar, 1999).

illustration, Article 1 of the new Argentine Civil and Commercial Code, in force since 2015, provides that the Code should be enforced in light of the applicable rules in conformity with the national constitution and the human rights treaties binding for the republic. In fact, in recent years, law schools began offering different orientations to law students. At the University of Buenos Aires in 2010, research became an option for the students. Human rights clinics became a more frequent feature in university life.

During the last twenty years, teaching methods diversified through the inclusion of other experiences, which are the norm in US law schools, like moot courts. In 2019, before the pandemic, around ten Latin American states had their law students participating in moot courts, such as the Philip C. Jessup International Law Moot Court Competition or the Jean Pictet Competition. Latin Amrerican law schools offer the possibility to apply for a school team in areas such as international law, international human rights law (universal and regional systems), international humanitarian law, international criminal law, international commercial arbitration, foreign investment arbitration, environmental law, and local criminal law, among others.[75] Candidates enroll in specific courses and once elected prepare the given year's assignment. At present, there are also many moot courts organized in Spanish for the law schools of the region.[76]

In 2014, in Colombia, a group of faculty members launched a project called *Rethinking International Law Education in Latin America* (in Spanish REDIAL, *Repensando la Educación en Derecho Internacional en América Latina*). The project is grounded on the assumption that current teaching practices in the region put aside the rich Latin American tradition. International law is then introduced as a neutral, decontextualized, and depoliticized discipline, far from any useful tool for social change. REDIAL is a network and platform that facilitates dialogue in which scholars on the "periphery" share ideas from their experiences as such. The network allows for the exchange of experiences and projects and enables the articulation of debates about international legal education in Latin America and other regions of the Global South.[77]

The project identified the tendency toward classical Eurocentric teaching where the relationship to local issues is limited, creating disciplinary blind spots. Accordingly, the project concluded that what has prevailed to date is a European

[75] Leopoldo Godio, "Los programas de derecho internacional público: su evolución en la Facultad de Derecho de la Universidad de Buenos Aires desde 1955," *Academia, Revista sobre Enseñanza del Derecho* 26 (2015): 141–187. Also, Alejandro Chehtman, "Internationalisation, Globalisation and the Effect on Legal Education in Argentina," in *The Internationalisation of legal Education*, ed. Christophe Jamin and William van Caenegem (Cham, Switzerland: Springer, 2016), 37–46.

[76] The law school of the University of Buenos Aires participates in more than seven moot courts conducted in Spanish. http://www.derecho.uba.ar/internacionales/competencias-internacionales.php

[77] Betancur-Restrepo and Prieto-Ríos, "Educación del derecho internacional en Bogotá."

international law that has camouflaged itself as universal. International law in Latin America continues to privilege certain people and projects at the expense of most of the Latin American population. The project states it is a law that contributes to the maintenance of exclusion and violence, even in the face of strategic action to promote social transformation through a critical commitment to the language of international law in regard to Indigenous and Afro peoples, women, and LGBTQI movements. Following the dictates of the academic market and its intellectual extractivism deepens the disconnect between the academy and the Latin American context. Because of that, the project submits, the opportunity is lost to reflect and theorize in an original and situated way and to become a replicator of the dominant knowledge and sites of knowledge production.[78]

With globalization, Latin American law graduates became proficient in international law practices. They are associates and even partners in big law firms in the United States and Europe. They usually bring with them the experience of the continental system and a common law approach obtained through an LLM and the bar exam. The same can be asserted regarding legal officers in international tribunals, like the ICJ, regional courts, and administrative tribunals. Latin American law graduates are also arbitrators in commercial arbitration and foreign investment arbitration. As per the latest statistics published by ICSID (International Centre for Settlement of Investment Disputes), 12 percent of arbitrators appointed in the period 1966–2023 were Latin American nationals. Regarding those appointed in 2023, the figure rose to 16 percent. No gender disaggregated information is provided, but in general only 15 percent of all the appointees were women https://icsid.worldbank.org/sites/default/files/publications/ENG_The_ICSID_Caseload_Statistics_Issue 2024.pdf, (last visited November 29, 2024).

VII. Concluding Remarks

Latin America has been labeled the most unequal region in the world. It is also very unequal in its education in international law. Some of our law schools provide high-quality teaching and research while caring for our problems and shaping our views; others do not. From the more encyclopedic approach to the more rational approach, both coexist in the region; from the more Eurocentric approach to the one more focused on the Latin American region and its problems.

[78] Ibid.

Latin American publications, whose qualities are diverse, face many obstacles to updating. To keep our level and to be updated, we have to be bilingual. Managing the English language is the bottom line for anyone wishing to work in this field; speaking French, Portuguese, and German is an added value.

Having a professional career in international law, putting aside diplomacy, and being based in a Latin American country is not easy. As usual, it is twice as difficult for women. However, today, some professionals meet all the above criteria. That means it is not impossible.

18

Local Politics and Regional Rights

Reflections on Comparative International Law in the Americas

David Landau

I. Introduction

Since Anthea Roberts coined the term "comparative international law," comparative constitutional and international lawyers have worked together to study how domestic courts and other domestic institutions create and apply international law.[1] Latin America is a region in which domestic judiciaries are especially engaged with international human rights norms because of legal cultural shifts, changes in constitutional design that have helped to spread clauses requiring the incorporation of international human rights law into constitutional law, and changes in the doctrine and practice of the Inter-American Court.

Some scholars have called this increasingly thick dialogue between domestic courts and regional human rights institutions, and the consequent interchange between international human rights law and constitutional law, a new Latin American "ius commune."[2] The claim has considerable support as a common language of constitutional discourse. However, it is less accurate to the extent it suggests a convergence between constitutional systems and international human rights law. Local politics and other factors, such as conceptions of the judicial role, drive continuing divergence in the ways in which domestic systems tackle international legal issues.

This chapter examines the impact of domestic courts on the development of international human rights law by considering three important issues: (1) same-sex marriage, (2) social rights, and (3) prior consultation with Indigenous groups. In some ways, the three issue areas show a common pattern. In each area, much of the generative work to construct new norms comes from a set of leading domestic constitutional jurisdictions (often including the

[1] Anthea Roberts, "Comparative International Law? The Role of National Courts in Creating and Enforcing International Law," *International & Comparative Law Quarterly* 60, no. 1 (2011): 57.

[2] Armin von Bogdandy et al. (eds.), *Transformative Constitutionalism in Latin America: The Emergence of a New Ius Commune* (New York: Oxford University Press, 2017).

David Landau, *Local Politics and Regional Rights* In: *Latin American International Law in the Twenty-First Century*. Edited by: Alejandro Chehtman, Alexandra Huneeus, and Sergio Puig, Oxford University Press.
 DOI: 10.1093/9780197754016.003.0018

Colombian Constitutional Court). These "leading" domestic judiciaries are major protagonists of international human rights law in Latin America. In each case, the Inter-American Court enters the game as a relative latecomer, although its interventions can nonetheless be important in inducing new jurisdictions to take on an issue. Consensus can form where domestic political factors allow (as the same-sex marriage example shows), but often, domestic judiciaries will continue to engage an issue in wildly different ways (as demonstrated by social rights), or progress on the issue will stagnate despite the efforts of activists and the Inter-American Court (as shown by prior consultation).

Section II of this chapter briefly maps the landscape of comparative international law as it applies to human rights in Latin America. Section III gives three examples of comparative law in action, finding both common patterns and significant differences in the evolution of norms governing same-sex marriage, social rights, and Indigenous prior consultation. Section IV draws out the implications of the examples, focusing on the importance of leading jurisdictions as major players in the spread of international human rights norms and the factors that determine the impact of an Inter-American Court jurisdiction on the conversation between domestic courts. Section V concludes.

II. Mapping the Landscape of the Comparative International Law of Human Rights in Latin America

Important shifts in the past few decades have thickened regional engagement with international human rights norms. One of these is composed of changes in constitutional design and practice. Many countries have moved toward models of constitutionalism that give international human rights law a high constitutional status, as a mandatory guide to the interpretation of constitutional provisions, as a supraconstitutional norm, or as both. Incorporation clauses, for example, were added in Colombia in 1991, in Argentina in 1994, and in Mexico in 2011, during constitutional replacement or reform processes in each country.[3] Verdier and Versteeg observe that one important source of variation in the domestic application of international law stems from different national rules regarding the interface between domestic and international law.[4] To be clear, these differences persist in Latin America even on human rights, but they have shrunk

[3] Rene Urueña, "Domestic Application of International Law in Latin America," in *Oxford Handbook of Comparative Foreign Relations*, ed. Curtis A. Bradley, 565 (New York: Oxford University Press, 2019).

[4] Pierre-Hugues Verdier and Mila Versteeg, "International Law in National Legal Systems: An Empirical Investigation," in *Comparative International Law*, ed. Anthea Roberts et al., 209 (New York: Oxford University Press, 2018).

over time. The expectation that a domestic constitutional system ought to engage human rights and the jurisprudence of the Inter-American Court now seem to be firmly embedded in most countries in the region.

Moreover, these changes interact with shifts in the nature of constitutionalism, which swept throughout the region under the banner of the "new constitutionalism."[5] The changes associated with new constitutionalism are abstract and have not been operationalized in the same way across all countries. But, in general, they reflect shifts that have emphasized the rights provisions of constitutions as their heart. New constitutionalism has also fed changes in constitutional interpretation toward a style of reasoning where provisions are interpreted in light of broad constitutional principles, often using proportionality as a key adjudication tool. The new modes of constitutional interpretation are conducive to using international human rights law as a significant form of constitutional reasoning.

Finally, the inter-American system has exercised increasing influence over domestic constitutional law. The Inter-American Court issues more decisions and compliance reports than it once did, and those decisions touch on a broader range of issues. As I show below, the Court is often in dialogue with constitutional courts across the region on issues of human rights. Beginning in 2006, the Court developed its doctrine of conventionality control, which requires that national courts review domestic law for compliance with the American Convention on Human Rights and defer to the Inter-American Court as the "ultimate interpreter" of the Convention.[6]

These interrelated legal shifts, alongside parallel changes in politics and civil society, have tended to meld constitutional law and international human rights law closer, while making both a core discourse of constitutionalism. Some work has called this discourse—a combination of comparative and international human rights law—a constitutional *ius commune*.[7] The common goal of scholars who use this term is to advance a transformative conception of constitutionalism, one that aims to alter the historical forms of inequality, discrimination, and democratic deficits faced by countries in the region.[8] These efforts to

[5] Javier Couso, "The Transformation of Constitutional Discourse and the Judicialization of Politics in Latin America," in *Cultures of Legality: Judicialization and Political Activism in Latin America*, ed. Javier Couso, Alexandra Huneeus, and Rachel Sieder, 141 (New York: Cambridge University Press, 2010). Couso has also noted that the broad label "new constitutionalism" encompasses two very different constitutional traditions: a liberal tradition and a radical critique of liberalism. Javier Couso, "Latin American New Constitutionalism: A Tale of Two Cities," in *The Oxford Handbook of Constitutional Law in Latin America*, ed. Conrado Hübner Mendes, Roberto Gargarella, and Sebastián Guidi, 354 (New York: Oxford University Press, 2022).

[6] Ariel E. Dulitzky, "An Inter-American Constitutional Court? The Invention of the Conventionality Control by the Inter-American Court of Human Rights," *Texas International Law Journal* 50, no. 1 (2015): 45.

[7] von Bogdandy et al., *Transformative Constitutionalism*.

[8] Armin von Bogdandy and René Urueña, "International Transformative Constitutionalism in Latin America," *American Journal of International Law* 114, no. 3 (2020): 403.

constitute a regional *ius commune* might be seen as a descriptive project or an effort to conceptualize the shifts outlined below, as well as a normative effort to push regional human rights and constitutional law in a particular direction (see also chapter 25 in this volume).[9]

The mixture of constitutional and regional human rights law is leading to common discourse across many countries in the region; the same sets of ideas are in the air. But the idea of the *ius commune* as a *lingua franca* is quite different from the question of substantive convergence on human rights norms, much less human rights practices on the ground. There are of course overt challengers to the regime. The most prominent example in the region is Venezuela, which stated that it was withdrawing from the inter-American system after a dispute over a decision on judicial independence.[10] At a more granular level, compliance with Inter-American Court decisions has long been challenging, with executive, legislative, and judicial officials often resisting its orders, explicitly or implicitly.[11]

At any rate, focusing on the regional institutions of the inter-American system, in isolation, would miss an enormous amount of how human rights norms actually evolve in Latin America.[12] As the examples in section III highlight, the first judicial mover across many issues is not the Inter-American Court or Commission but domestic courts that do important work in shaping and applying international legal norms, often drawing from a broad mixture of constitutional law, regional human rights law, and other international legal norms. As such, the blending between the creation and enforcement functions of domestic courts is particularly apparent in Latin America.[13] Domestic courts often carry out a significant creative function, synthesizing and mutating multiple sources of law. These leading domestic tribunals play a key role in diffusing human rights norms across the region. The Inter-American Court, in contrast, is often involved later in the story, to varying degrees and with varying results, as dialogue spreads across the region.

Perhaps most interesting for our purposes is the open-textured nature of the regime itself, which allows for several different outcomes. In some cases, regional

[9] Alberto Coddou Mc Manus, "A Critical Account of Ius Constitutionale Commune in Latin America: An intellectual Map of Contemporary Latin American Constitutionalism," *Global Constitutionalism*, 22, no. 1: 111. See also Bordin and Paddeu, in this volume.

[10] Jorge Contesse, "Resisting the Inter-American Human Rights System," *The Yale Journal of International Law* 44, no. 2 (2019): 179, 206–208.

[11] Alexandra Huneeus, "Courts Resisting Courts: Lessons from the Inter-American Court's Struggle to Enforce Human Rights," *Cornell International Law Journal* 44, no. 3 (2011): 493.

[12] Bogdandy and Urueña, "International Transformative Constitutionalism."

[13] Roberts, "Comparative International Law?"

and domestic institutions seem to grapple to find a common position; in other cases, however, they do not. Section III stresses political factors in explaining divergent outcomes. That is not to say that these are the only factors. As I have explained elsewhere, other factors, such as enduring distinctions in conceptions of the judicial role or the details of judicial design, are also very important aspects of context.[14]

III. Comparative International Law and Human Rights in Action: Three Examples

This section explores the ways in which international human rights norms emerge and spread in Latin America. It highlights three examples of recent importance: (1) same-sex marriage, (2) socioeconomic rights, and (3) the right to prior consultation of Indigenous groups. The examples here are not meant to be exhaustive treatments of each of these issue areas but rather brief sketches to give readers a sense of the comparative evolution of international norms.

These three examples, drawn from disparate areas of human rights law, nonetheless show striking similarities along some dimensions. In each case, domestic courts play a protagonist's role in constructing and disseminating international norms, generally synthesizing domestic constitutional law with international law drawn from many different sources. As these norms spread through domestic jurisdictions, cases eventually tend to enter the inter-American system. In other words, the normative development of national courts often tends to feed the caseload of the Inter-American Court, rather than vice versa.[15] The interventions of the Inter-American Court, in turn, may have some power to shape the responses of domestic courts, for example by inducing latecomers to engage with the norms, or by reshaping existing interpretations. The outcomes depend heavily on differences in political factors on the ground, which modulate whether states move toward a common position or persists with a divergent one.

[14] David Landau, "Judicial Role and the Limits of Constitutional Convergence in Latin America," in *Comparative Constitutional Law in Latin America*, ed. Rosalind Dixon and Tom Ginsburg, 227 (Northampton, UK: Edward Elgar, 2017).

[15] This perspective is quite different from Alejandro Rodiles's interesting claim that the relationship between the Inter-American Court and the domestic judiciaries is more of a monologue and vertical relationship rather than a horizontal one. Alejandro Rodiles, "The Great Promise of Comparative Public Law for Latin America: Towards Ius Commune Americanum?" in *Comparative International Law*, ed. Anthea Roberts et al., 501 (New York: Oxford University Press, 2018). I argue that the Inter-American Court is utilizing ideas that largely originate from leading domestic judiciaries in the region.

Same-Sex Marriage: (Relative) Regional Consensus

Over the course of the past two decades, same-sex marriage rights have spread throughout Latin America.[16] There are various reasons for this shift, including changing cultural attitudes and the rise of civil society groups advocating for change.

Courts have played a key role in some countries in the region. In Colombia, the Constitutional Court recognized same-sex marital unions in fact in a 2007 decision and subsequently extended a range of property and similar benefits to same-sex couples.[17] In 2011, the Court held that there was still a "deficit of protection" for same-sex couples because they could not engage in marriage and exhorted the legislature to act.[18] After the legislature failed to pass a same-sex marriage bill, the Court finally legalized same-sex marriage throughout Colombia in 2016.[19]

In Mexico, judicial decisions legalizing same-sex marriage took time. In 2010, the Mexican Supreme Court upheld a Mexico City law legalizing same-sex marriage. Beginning in 2012, panels of the Supreme Court issued amparo judgments allowing same-sex couples to marry and, in the process, held state constitutional provisions defining marriage as between one man and one woman to be unconstitutional.[20] Because of the characteristics of the Mexican amparo, these judgments only bound the parties to the case (although an accumulation of five jurisprudential theses has a binding effect on the judiciary), and jurisprudence proceeded state by state. In 2015, the Court began issuing a broader thesis stating that *all* state bans on same-sex marriage were unconstitutional. Eventually, same-sex marriage was legal in every state of Mexico.[21]

The Colombian and Mexican decisions followed similar reasoning. They relied on a mix of nondiscrimination norms based on historical patterns of discrimination, liberty interests such as free development of personality, and a substantive conception of equality. They both also used the jurisprudence of the European Court of Human Rights to ground a broad, flexible, and substantive, rather than formal, conception of the family.

[16] Jason Pierceson, Andriana Piatti-Crocker, and Shawn Schulenberg (eds.), *Same-Sex Marriage in Latin America: Promise and Resistance* (New York: Lexington Books, 2012).

[17] Decision C-075 of 2007 (February 7, 2007) (Const. Ct. of Colombia), translated in Manuel Jose Cepeda-Espinosa and David Landau, *Colombian Constitutional Law* (New York: Oxford University Press, 2017), 87–91.

[18] Decision C-577 of 2011 (July 26, 2011) (Const. Ct. of Colombia), translated in Cepeda-Espinosa and Landau, *Colombian Constitutional Law*, 91–97.

[19] Decision SU-214 of 2016 (April 28, 2016) (Const. Ct. of Colombia), translated in Cepeda-Espinosa and Landau, *Colombian Constitutional Law*, 97–100.

[20] Amparo en Revision 581 of 2012 (Sup. Ct. Mexico).

[21] Amparo en Revision 376 of 2015 (Sup. Ct. Mexico).

Movement toward same-sex marriage also occurred in other key countries in the region. In Brazil, the judiciary legalized same-sex marriage nationally in 2013, and in Uruguay (2013) and Argentina (2010), legislatures passed laws creating same-sex marriage. However, in other countries, including Costa Rica (2006) and Chile (2011), courts rejected claims to recognize same-sex marriage. In Chile and Ecuador, legislatures created civil union regimes in 2015.[22]

In this context, in 2016, the Costa Rican government asked the Inter-American Court for an advisory opinion clarifying several LGBTQ issues, including the recognition of same-sex relationships. The Inter-American Court discussed the regional judicial decisions moving toward same-sex marriage. It used reasoning similar to that of domestic courts, including the broad, flexible conception of a family explicated by the jurisprudence of the European Court of Human Rights.[23] The Court concluded that there was an obligation on regional states to recognize and protect same-sex family ties without any discrimination. It held that this obligation could potentially be satisfied by "diverse types of administrative, judicial, and legislative measures to ensure the rights of same-sex couples" but also noted that the extension of marriage to same-sex couples would be the "most simple and effective way to ensure the rights derived from the relationship between same-sex couples."[24]

The Inter-American Court's decision, in turn, has proven impactful in galvanizing further developments in the region. In Costa Rica and Ecuador, high courts held that because the Inter-American Court decision was binding under domestic law, their constitutions must be interpreted in light of the decision. Thus, same-sex marriage was now required by their respective national constitutions.[25] In Chile, the Congress approved a law recognizing same-sex marriage in 2021, following a complex set of events involving a 2015 agreement of the Chilean government with the Inter-American Commission on Human Rights and pressure stemming from the advisory opinion and domestic court cases.[26] In Bolivia, the Court issued a 2022 decision recognizing same-sex civil

[22] For a summary of these developments, see Landau, "Judicial Role and the Limits of Constitutional Convergence."

[23] State Obligations Concerning Change of Name, Gender Identity, and Rights Derived from a Relationship Between Same-Sex Couples, Advisory Opinion OC-24/17, Inter-Am. Ct. H.R. (ser. A) No. 24 (November 24, 2017).

[24] Ibid., ¶ 218. For discussion, see Jorge Contesse, "The Inter-American Court of Human Rights' Advisory Opinion on Gender Identity and Same-Sex Marriage," *ASIL Insights* 22, no. 9 (July 26, 2018), https://www.asil.org/insights/volume/22/issue/9/inter-american-court-human-rights-advisory-opinion-gender-identity-and.

[25] Decision No. 11-18-CN of 2019 (Const. Ct. of Ecuador); Voto No. 2018-012782 (Sup. Ct. Costa Rica).

[26] Vanessa Romo, "Chile's Congress Approves Same-Sex Marriage by an Overwhelming Majority," *NPR* (December 7, 2021), https://www.npr.org/2021/12/07/1062261334/chile-same-sex-marriage.

unions, which also treated the advisory opinion as having an obligatory effect on the constitutional domestic order.[27]

This regional consensus has not been complete. In some countries, such as Peru, the status of same-sex couples remains in flux. Probably the most overt resistance to date has occurred in Panama, where the Supreme Court issued a 2023 decision holding that same-sex marriage was not a constitutional or human right and explicitly rejecting the Inter-American Court's advisory opinion as a "mutation" of the meaning of the Convention.[28] Nonetheless, the movement of domestic courts toward a consensus position, using similar reasoning across countries and recently guided by the advisory opinion of the Inter-American Court, has been impressive.

Socioeconomic Rights: The "Catalytic" Function of Domestic Courts

Latin America has long been a leader in the recognition of socioeconomic rights. The Mexican Constitution of 1917 was one of the first constitutions in the world, along with other pioneers like the Irish and Weimar constitutions, to include socioeconomic rights.[29] Over the course of the twentieth century, as I have explored in greater depth elsewhere, it is remarkable how virtually all constitutions written in the region, despite being drawn from a range of different constitutional and ideological traditions, have included socioeconomic rights. At least regionally, there seems to be a consensus that socioeconomic rights are part of constitutionalism.

Unsurprisingly, justiciability was slower to come. The innovative rights found in the 1917 Constitution were long held essentially nonjusticiable and were instead viewed mainly as political guidelines for the ruling party. But, over the latter part of the twentieth century and into the twenty-first, a tendency has also emerged to hold these rights justiciable. In most countries in the region, socioeconomic rights now seem to be judicially enforceable, at least to some degree. However, the region still has broad differences in the degree and nature of enforceability.

Courts in some countries have emerged as regional leaders on this issue. The Colombian Constitutional Court is probably the most visible. The 1991

[27] Decision 577 of 2023 (Const. Trib. of Bolivia).

[28] Juan Carlos Paz, "Corte Suprema de Panamá determina que no es inconstitucional la prohibición del matrimonio entre personas del mismo sexo," *CNN* (March 1, 2023), https://cnnespanol.cnn.com/2023/03/01/panama-matrimonio-mismo-sexo-corte-inconstitucional-orix/.

[29] Thomas Murray, "Socio-Economic Rights Versus Social Revolution? Constitution Making in Germany, Mexico and Ireland, 1917–1923," *Social and Legal Studies* 24, no. 4 (2015): 1.

Constitution contained a fairly complete list of socioeconomic rights, but the individual complaint mechanism found in the constitution, the *tutela*, was silent on whether it could be used to enforce those rights, merely stating that "fundamental" rights could be enforced via individual complaint.[30] The Court nonetheless immediately moved toward a position where it enforced those rights via *tutela* by linking them to other rights like the right to life and the right to human dignity. Later, it expanded on this connectivity doctrine by holding that some rights, such as the right to health, could be inherently fundamental, even without being linked to other rights.[31]

Over time, the Court began issuing a large number of *tutelas* on social rights, most prevalently the right to health.[32] But it has also become known for its creative, larger-scale interventions, which have drawn on international law. In 2004, for example, the Court issued a landmark judgment that declared a "state of unconstitutional affairs" involving the country's huge population of internally displaced persons (IDPs), who had been displaced during the country's long-running internal armed conflict.[33] The Court noted that while a law was on the books giving IDPs substantial rights, there was no coherent public policy surrounding the issue. The Court aggregated several *tutelas* brought by IDPs. Then it drew heavily on the UN's Guiding Principles on Internal Displacement and other sources to construct a set of rights to which IDPs were entitled, ranging from immediate assistance in healthcare, education, and job placement to longer-term issues like restitution of land. It issued a series of structural orders and maintained jurisdiction over the case, subsequently holding periodic public hearings, asking for follow-up reports from stakeholders, and issuing many follow-up orders over many years. In 2008, the Court issued a somewhat similar judgment involving the right to health, again drawing on international law and particularly the International Covenant on Economic, Social, and Cultural Rights and the General Comments written by the UN Committee on Economic, Social, and Cultural Rights.[34]

Other courts in the region have also become active in enforcing social rights. For example, the Brazilian Supreme Judicial Court has an extensive jurisprudence on the right to health, where it has granted treatments and other remedies to petitioners. This jurisprudence has been criticized for having unfair or even

[30] Const. of Colombia, art. 86 (1991). The constitution also provided a list of rights that were "immediately applicable," which generally excluded the social rights. Ibid., art. 85.

[31] Decision T-760 of 2008 (July 31, 2008) (Const. Ct. of Colombia).

[32] Pablo Rueda, "Legal Language & Social Change During Colombia's Economic Crisis," in *Cultures of Legality: Judicialization & Political Activism in Latin America*, ed. Javier Couso, Alexandra Huneeus, and Rachel Sieder, 25 (New York: Cambridge University Press, 2010).

[33] Decision T-025 of 2004 (January 22, 2004) (Const. Ct. of Colombia), translated in Cepeda-Espinosa and Landau, *Colombian Constitutional Law*, 179–186.

[34] Decision T-760 of 2008.

regressive distributive effects on the healthcare system, but the courts and the Congress have also taken measures to incorporate more scientific input into judicial decisions on these issues, potentially improving outcomes.[35] The Brazilian courts incentivized major changes in the availability of HIV medications, and the Costa Rican judiciary had a similar impact.[36] The Argentine courts have experimented in some cases with similar kinds of structural remedies as the Colombian courts, perhaps most notably in a case involving the environmental and socioeconomic effects of pollution on the Riachuelo River.[37]

The core point is that this bubbling of social rights jurisprudence, in quite different ways across countries, had an impact on the regional human rights system. By design, the inter-American system is not particularly conducive to the enforcement of social rights. The American Convention on Human Rights (1969) contains only one provision, Article 26, dealing directly with economic, social, and cultural rights, and this provision creates a general duty of "progressive realization" of a vague set of rights.[38] The first protocol of the Convention, the Protocol of San Salvador (1988), contains an extensive list of socioeconomic rights.[39] However, the text of the Protocol gives the Commission and Court the ability to hear claims over only two of its articles: the rights to unionize and the right to education.[40] In other words, the protection of social rights in the inter-American system has been marked by the same differences between civil and political rights on the one hand and economic, social, and cultural rights on the other, which have marked much of international law.

[35] For the critique, see Octavio Luiz Motta Ferraz, *Health as a Human Right: The Politics and Judicialisation of the Right to Health in Brazil* (New York: Cambridge University Press, 2021). For an accounting of the Supreme Judicial Court's efforts to improve the quality of judgments over time, see Costa Leite Borges, "Individual Health Care Litigation in Brazil through a Different Lens: Strengthening Health Technology Assessment and New Models of Health Care Governance" *Health and Human Rights Journal* 20, no. 1 (2018): 147.

[36] Costa Leite Borges, "Individual Health Care Litigation in Brazil"; Olman Rodríguez Loaiza et al., "Revisiting Health Rights Litigation and Access to Medications in Costa Rica: Preliminary Evidence from the Cochrane Collaboration Reform," *Health and Human Rights Journal* 20, no. 1 (2018): 79.

[37] Martin Sigal, Julieta Rossi, and Diego Morales, "Argentina: Implementation of Collective Cases" in *Social Rights Judgments and the Politics of Compliance: Making It Stick*, ed. Malcolm Langford, Cesar Rodriguez-Garavito, and Julieta Rossi, 140 (New York: Cambridge University Press, 2017).

[38] Organization of American States, American Convention on Human Rights, November 22, 1969, O.A.S.T.S. No. 36, 1144 U.N.T.S. 123, 9 ILM 99, art 26 ("The States Parties undertake to adopt measures, both internally and through international cooperation, especially those of an economic and technical nature, with a view to achieving progressively, by legislation or other appropriate means, the full realization of the rights implicit in the economic, social, educational, scientific, and cultural standards set forth in the Charter of the Organization of American States as amended by the Protocol of Buenos Aires.").

[39] Additional Protocol to the American Convention on Human Rights in the Area of Economic, Social, and Cultural Rights (Protocol of San Salvador), 1988, O.A.S.T.S. No. 69.

[40] Ibid., art. 19, sec. 6.

Nonetheless, the Inter-American Court has developed an increasingly aggressive social rights jurisprudence. Before 2017, the Court would at times protect social rights using other rights found in the Convention, such as the right to property (Article 21) and the right to judicial protection (Article 25), particularly in cases involving pensions and similar social benefits.[41] But, since 2017, the Court has begun to enforce Article 26 directly. In a landmark 2018 decision, the Court held that the right to health was an autonomous right protected by Article 26, and that Guatemala had violated the Convention because it failed to take measures to progressively develop the right to health cfor those in the country who were living with HIV .[42] Subsequently, the Court issued a series of decisions dealing with the right to health. For example, in another landmark case from 2021, the Court held that Chile had violated the right to health of a child with Leigh Syndrome, a catastrophic and long-term illness impacting a small percentage of newborns, when it allowed a private insurer to terminate the child's coverage because of the chronic nature of the disease.[43] The Court held that Chile had failed in its duty to adequately supervise the private insurer to protect the right to health, among other rights. Since 2018, the Court has also issued decisions involving healthcare in emergencies, healthcare for prisoners, healthcare for those with disabilities, healthcare in conjunction with employment, and healthcare during pregnancy.[44]

The Inter-American Court's flourishing interest in social rights, despite a relatively inauspicious textual base, seems to have been catalyzed by the ongoing work on social rights that has been done by several domestic courts within the region. The Inter-American Court, indeed, has been an impactful latecomer in this area. Unlike in the case of same-sex marriage, it is unlikely to crystalize a consensus among courts in the region. There remains far too much regional diversity in how social rights are enforced, which is fed by differences in conceptions of judicial role, the design of judiciaries, and politics. This diversity in how social rights are enforced is likely to continue. But the Court may put more pressure on relative outliers (i.e., states that are only weakly enforcing social rights). For example, its judgments may impact countries like Guatemala, which has weak traditions of judicial capacity and independence, or Chile, which has constitutional designs making it more difficult to judicialize social rights.

[41] *"Five Pensioners" v. Peru*, Inter-Am. Ct. H.R. (February 28, 2003).

[42] *Caso Cuscul Pivaral y otros v. Guatemala*, Inter-Am. Ct. H.R. No. 359 (August 23, 2018).

[43] *Vera Rojas y otros v. Chile*, Inter-Am. Ct. H.R. No. 439 (October 1, 2021).

[44] Luz Eliyer Cárdenas-Contreras, "La salud a la manera de la Corte Interamericana de Derechos Humanos: una exploración de la jurisprudencia, hasta 2021, a propósito del artículo 26 de la Convención Americana sobre Derechos Humanos," *Díkaion* 32, no. 1 (2023): 1, 15 tbl.3.

Prior Indigenous Consultation: Divergence and Resistance

The branch of international human rights law dealing with Indigenous communities has had great salience in Latin America. International Labour Organization (ILO) Treaty 169 (1989), the Indigenous and Tribal Peoples Convention, has been ratified by twenty-four states—fifteen are in Latin America and the Caribbean, including virtually every major state in the region with the exceptions of Uruguay, El Salvador, and Panama. At the heart of ILO 169 is a set of mandates to "consult" Indigenous populations whenever measures are undertaken that affect their core interests: "when legislative and administrative measures [are being considered] that may affect them directly," in cases involving exploitation of resources, or other development projects on Indigenous lands, and where changes are made to Indigenous "capacity to alienate their lands or otherwise transmit their rights outside their own community."[45]

Of course, these rights of prior consultation are only a small part of a much broader set of constitutional and international legal issues involving Indigenous groups. But they have emerged as a particularly important battleground, often pitting strengthening movements representing Indigenous autonomy and interests, on the one hand, against economic interests seeking to carry out resource-intensive projects, on the other. These fights have played out again and again in Latin America in recent years.

The Colombian Constitutional Convention was written by a process that included special provisions for Indigenous representation, and the 1991 Constitution included a transformative set of Indigenous rights. These include special rights to political representation, language, and legal and social autonomy, as well as a provision stating that the exploitation of natural resources on Indigenous territories must be "coordinated with the representatives of the respective communities."[46] The Court has also aggressively incorporated international law into the constitution, holding that international human rights treaties ratified by Colombia, including ILO 169, form part of the constitutional block and thus have constitutional rank.[47]

On this basis, the Court has issued a series of important decisions requiring consultation to be undertaken both for economic projects and for laws directly affecting Indigenous communities. These decisions have demanded that consultation meet high standards in terms of good faith; the community members who are consulted; the seriousness, length, and informed nature of the consultation; and ongoing opportunities to influence or modify the project. They have

[45] I.L.O. Convention No. 169 (1989), arts. 6, 7, 17.
[46] Const. Colombia, art. 330 (1991).
[47] E.g., Decision SU-123 of 2018 (Nov. 15, 2018) (Const. Ct. of Colombia).

also developed a broad definition of laws and administrative matters subject to consultation, including measures such as the General Forestry Law, the Rural Development Plan, and the government plan to fumigate illegal crops.[48] In a landmark 2011 case, the Court held that a series of infrastructure and economic projects in northern Colombia, including highway construction, electricity lines linking the country with Paraguay, and gold mining, violated the rights to prior consultation of the Embero-Katio community.[49] The Court in that case emphasized that rights to consultation are ongoing and require that Indigenous groups be able to intervene at different points during the life of a project. The Court evaded the question of whether prior consultation might amount to a right of veto by the affected community, emphasizing that the goal is achieving consensus but also noting that in at least some circumstances, the judge might need to insist on the consent of the impacted community before a project could proceed. This conclusion about the need for prior consent was reiterated in subsequent cases while avoiding the term "veto."[50]

This extensive line of jurisprudence of the Colombian Constitutional Court has arguably been one of its most impactful but also one of its most controversial. The economic projects affected by these requirements are often major in a resource-intensive economy, and both government actors and private economic interests have criticized the Court's jurisprudence on these grounds. Indeed, the government has called the prior consultation an "extortion mechanism."[51] Draft statutory laws governing prior consultation in 2016 and 2018 would have contradicted some of the Court's jurisprudence on issues like consent. However, these laws have not been enacted and the topic still lacks a governing statutory law. Commentators argue that inadequate or fraudulent consultations still run rampant.[52]

The landscape elsewhere in Latin America on this issue shows frequent engagement with ILO 169 and the issue of prior consultation, but also enormous divergence in its implementation, with no other country reaching the depth and breadth of engagement of Colombia. In Argentina, for example, courts have often avoided hearing cases on this issue, and scholarly work has found that few consultations have taken place.[53] In Brazil, the situation seems similar. The

[48] Cepeda-Espinosa and Landau, *Colombian Constitutional Law*, 259–270.

[49] Decision T-129 of 2011 (March 3, 2011) (Const. Ct. of Colombia).

[50] Decision C-389 of 2016 (June 27, 2016) (Const. Ct. of Colombia).

[51] Juan C. Herrera, "Binding Consent of Indigenous Peoples in Colombia: An Example of Transformative Constitutionalism," in *The Prior Consultation of Indigenous Peoples in Latin America: Inside the Implementation Gap*, ed. Claire Wright and Alexandra Tomaselli, 41, 53 (New York: Routledge, 2019).

[52] Ibid., 52–53.

[53] Marzia Rosti, "The Right to Consultation and Free, Prior, and Informed Consent in Argentina: *The Case of Salinas Grandes-Laguna de Guayatayoc*," in Wright and Tomaselli, *The Prior Consultation of Indigenous Peoples in Latin America*, 225.

government attempted to write a law regulating prior consultation through a consultative process between 2012 and 2014, but the effort failed, and it then wrote a series of decrees that critics have alleged were deficient, without holding consultations.[54] The Supreme Federal Tribunal (STF) has issued a few decisions ordering suspensions of projects and consultations in particular cases, but compliance with these decisions seems low.

In Mexico, the Supreme Court has issued several important decisions that hold economic projects inadequate because of a failure to consult and require the state to legislate on the issue.[55] Moreover, a state institution, the Consultation Council for the National Commission for the Development of Indigenous Peoples, has been charged with implementing consultations. But commentary has still found serious problems, such as a failure to hold consultations in necessary cases and deficiencies in procedure when consultations have been held.[56] In Chile, the government held several consultations on constitutional amendments, legislation, and regulation, including the process of consultation itself, but the legal framework remains incomplete, and the scope of consultation became a major issue of conflict during the failed 2022 constitutional drafting process.[57] In Peru, prior consultation processes were finally regulated by a 2011 law, although this law has been heavily criticized for its narrow definition of who needs to be consulted and how consultation will occur. In 2022, the Constitutional Tribunal issued a decision holding that rights to prior consultation were not fundamental constitutional rights; it reversed that position in 2023, while also adopting a narrow definition of "direct effects" necessitating consultation and exhorting the Congress to enact new legislation.[58]

The Inter-American Court has waded slowly into these waters. In *Saramaka Kichwa Indigenous People v. Ecuador*, the Court held Ecuador responsible for failing to consult before a massive oil exploitation process was undertaken.[59] It noted requirements that consultations be made before a project is commenced, in good faith, be accessible and effective, and based on adequate information, as well as taking into account the traditional ways in which the Indigenous peoples

[54] Charlotte Schumann, *Framing Prior Consultation in Brazil: Ethnographic Perspectives on Limits of Participation and Multicultural Politics* (Bielefeld, Germany: Transcript, 2018).

[55] E.g., Acción de Inconstitucionalidad 285 of 2020 (S. Ct. of Mexico).

[56] Anavel Monterrubio Redonda, "Institutional Scope and Limitations of the Right to Consultation and the Free, Prior, and Informed Consent of Indigenous Peoples in Mexico," in Wright and Tomaselli, *The Prior Consultation of Indigenous Peoples in Latin America*, 133.

[57] Mauricio Ávila Cárdenas, "¿Los pueblos originarios tendrán poder de «veto» para bloquear los futuros cambios a la Constitución?" *CIPER* (July 29, 2022), https://www.ciperchile.cl/2022/07/29/los-pueblos-originarios-tendran-poder-de-veto-para-bloquear-los-futuros-cambios-a-la-constitucion/.

[58] Decision 310 of 2023 (June 28, 2023) (Const. Ct. Peru).

[59] Inter-Am. Ct. H.R. No. 245 (June 27, 2012). *Saramaka Kichwa* relied on principles developed in *Saramaka People v. Suriname*, Inter-Am. Ct. H.R. No. 172 (Nov. 28, 2007).

have reached decisions. The Court also recognized that the *Saramaka Kichwa* people were holders of such rights under the Convention, an important shift in its jurisprudence.[60] Many of these standards were reiterated in *Comunidad Garífuna de Punta Piedra y sus Miembros vs. Honduras*.[61]

This sketch suggests significant engagement with the norms surrounding prior consultation throughout Latin America but also pervasive contestation over compliance with these norms, as well as over their very meaning and content. Moreover, the role of domestic judiciaries is ambiguous, and in many cases, they seem to be working to frustrate rather than advance support for the norms. Even when domestic judiciaries are pushing the right forward, on the ground, progress is extremely slow, hindered by hostile governments and private economic interests. The engagement of the Inter-American Court in this area has neither settled relative consensus (as in the case of same-sex marriage) nor even catalyzed significant further development (as in the case of social rights). The right to prior consultation seems mired in a morass, with progress being slow and difficult.

Some factors explaining these patterns might be found in ambiguities in the norms themselves. As scholars have noted, the regime of prior consultation has significant ambiguities involving when consultation must be undertaken, what it must look like, and whether and when "consent" (as opposed to mere good faith consultation) must be achieved.[62] But probably more important are the politics surrounding the area. In many Latin American countries, indigenous groups have become powerful actors in civil society, pushing constitutional and legal gains. However, the consultation issue tends to raise powerful opponents: the domestic and transnational economic interests pushing projects in resource-intensive economies, who usually tend to gain the strong support of governmental institutions.

IV. Implications

The examples in section III are meant to give readers a sense of how comparative international human rights law in Latin America tends to work. A set of leading jurisdictions constructs norms in a way that mixes domestic constitutional law with regional human rights norms and other sources of international human

[60] Juan Pablo Vismara, "Pueblos indígenas y derechos colectivos. La consulta previa como garantía esencial para el resguardo de los derechos indígenas. La nueva jurisprudencia de la Corte IDH," *Doctrina* 2, no. 2 (2013); 77, 97–98.

[61] Inter-Am. Ct. H.R. No. 304 (October 8, 2015).

[62] Claire Wright and Alexandra Tomaselli, "From the Implementation Gap to Indigenous Empowerment: Prior Consultation in Latin America," in Wright and Tomaselli, *The Prior Consultation of Indigenous Peoples in Latin America*, 279.

rights law. The task here has, at its core, a significant amount of what Roberts has called "norm creation."[63] The ideas expressed in these initial decisions tend to spread to other jurisdictions, carried by political groups and civil society actors who find the norms valuable instruments for their purposes.

At some stage, cases involving the new norms make their way up to the inter-American system, and in fact, this pressure can cause important shifts in the Inter-American Court's jurisprudence. On social rights, for example, the prevalence of social rights claims in the region is related to changes in the Court's jurisprudence that made social rights claims directly justiciable under Article 26 rather than needing to rely on other provisions like property or judicial protection as the source of protection. Likewise, on prior consultation, the Court moved toward a position that recognized and enforced the collective rights of Indigenous communities rather than merely the individual rights of its members. In both cases, rights that might have seemed to be at the periphery of the inter-American system were moved closer to the core. Thus, the norm creation of domestic courts has had a significant impact on the docket and jurisprudence of the Inter-American Court.

In turn, the interventions of the Court can play an important role in impacting the behavior of domestic courts. One role of the Inter-American Court seems to be incentivizing a broader range of domestic courts to engage with international norms. In the cases of same-sex marriage, prior Indigenous consultation, and social rights, the Inter-American Court's jurisprudence seems to be bringing some latecomers into the game. This may be because claimants can haul jurisdictions with limited engagement in front of the inter-American system. Or, as in the case of same-sex marriage, the decision may impel national courts to revisit the issue directly, to determine whether they are bound by the decision.

Finally, and perhaps most obviously, the result of this diffusion of jurisprudence varies heavily depending on the politics involved in a given issue area. Same-sex marriage is a topic where domestic courts, with the impactful intervention of the Inter-American Court, have crystallized something approaching a consensus. Leading jurisdictions like Colombia and Mexico developed the core reasoning, partly drawing on the jurisprudence of the European Court of Human Rights. The Inter-American Court's advisory opinion had a substantial impact on some jurisdictions that had previously avoided recognizing the right. On social rights, a near-regional consensus has developed that the rights should be justiciable, but crucial differences persist in the degree and method of enforcement. Indeed, no consensus exists on these questions in scholarly literature, either inside or outside Latin America. Finally, on prior consultation, the treatment of the issue by leading courts and, more recently, by the Inter-American

[63] Roberts, "Comparative International Law?"

Court, has induced more courts and political actors to engage with the issue. It is striking how difficult it has been to get jurisdictions to implement and enforce the right, given that it is expressly enshrined in ILO Treaty 169, which every major Latin American jurisdiction has ratified. However, in most countries in the region, political actors and even courts remain deeply resistant to the implementation of prior consultation. The resistance of governmental and private economic interests makes this situation seem likely to continue.

What implications might these patterns have for those interested in studying both comparative constitutional law and international human rights law in Latin America? First, the analysis suggests the importance of what I have called "leading courts"—domestic courts that tend to play the norm-creation function, which other national courts and the Inter-American Court itself then pick up. The identity of these courts is not an accident but instead seems to recur across issue areas. Indeed, it is notable that the Colombian Constitutional Court has seemed to play something like this role across all three issues (and several others). The power of leading courts is worth interrogating, particularly since their norm-creation function is highly creative and responsive to domestic politics.

Another interesting issue highlighted by this analysis is the impact of Inter-American Court interventions. These decisions can have a dramatic impact on the regional dialogue, but perhaps only in certain circumstances. Considering the Inter-American Court's role strategically, in light of underlying political and capacity concerns, is not new, but viewing it as a part of a much larger conversation among national contexts and courts provides a useful perspective. One obvious point concerns timing. The same-sex marriage advisory opinion played a crucial role in crystallizing consensus on the issue. But to play this role, it may have been wise to wait until major jurisdictions had already weighed in and outlined the core reasoning. A decision issued significantly earlier may not have had the same impact on the political context.

The Court's many recent decisions on social rights, particularly the right to health, likewise raise important questions about maximizing impact. This is an area, as noted above, where domestic courts have used many different means of enforcement. Some of these modes have been heavily criticized. In Latin America, the method of enforcement of the right to health where courts grant individual remedies to claimants when they are denied a treatment or medicine has been analyzed as having potentially problematic effects, since it may grant benefits to relatively privileged petitioners without fixing the underlying problems with the system.[64] The Court may be able to help guide best

[64] Motta Ferraz, *Health as a Human Right*; David Landau, "The Reality of Social Rights Enforcement," *Harvard International Law Journal* 53, no. 1 (2012): 189.

practices by pointing its remedies toward the underlying structural issues, as it has done elsewhere. In *Caso Cuscul Pivaral and others v. Guatemala*, the Court recognized that Guatemala was systematically failing to cover HIV medications and treatments for those with the disease.[65] Aside from requiring the payment of compensatory damages, the Court also ordered systemic changes within the healthcare system, both at the level of coverage and the level of supervision. It also stated that it would supervise full compliance with the decision. These structural approaches, repeated elsewhere and in other contexts involving social rights, may play an important role in guiding the regional conversation about social rights enforcement in productive directions.

V. Conclusion

This chapter has explored the comparative international law of human rights in Latin America. By describing three issue areas—same-sex marriage, social rights, and Indigenous prior consultation—it showed that domestic judiciaries play a critical role in developing these norms in ways that are often eventually taken up by the Inter-American Court of Human Rights. It also demonstrates that local political factors will likely lead to continued divergence in the interpretation of international human rights on the ground, as the examples of social rights and prior consultation highlight. Conceptualizing the Inter-American Court as a relative latecomer to many regional human rights debates and as an institution that is largely picking up norms that have already percolated locally in domestic judiciaries may help clarify the role of the Court and improve its interventions.

65 Inter-Am. Ct. H.R. No. 359 (August 23, 2018).

19

The Human Rights Institutions of Latin America

Jorge Contesse[*]

I. Introduction

This chapter addresses the human rights organizations of Latin America with a particular focus on two institutions, the Inter-American Commission on Human Rights and the Inter-American Court of Human Rights. The chapter discusses formal and informal institutional rules and explains two distinctive doctrines of Latin American international law: the incompatibility of self-amnesty laws with international law and the doctrine of conventionality control. The analysis of these doctrines is situated in the cultural and political context in which they have developed: one in which "the idea" of human rights first gave birth to a political and diplomatic project that eventually turned into a (regional) legal system that holds states accountable for their human rights violations. This system, the chapter argues, cannot be fully appraised without consideration of municipal law, as the human rights institutions of Latin America operate at both the national and international levels. The chapter briefly examines recent developments in the Inter-American Court's jurisprudence concerning the justiciability of social rights and democracy as an international legal obligation. The examination emphasizes a common law of human rights that promotes an active and even intrusive role for the Court, expanding its powers in areas not originally granted to the work of the regional human rights organizations. At a time of contestation toward supranational institutions, the chapter argues for a renewed commitment to take both legality and legitimacy seriously.

* For helpful comments and criticism, I am grateful to participants at the Biennial Conference of the Latin American Society of International Law, held in São Paulo, Brazil, in November 2023. I also thank Dante De La Pava and Nicholl Simmonds for providing excellent research assistance.

Jorge Contesse, *The Human Rights Institutions of Latin America* In: *Latin American International Law in the Twenty-First Century*. Edited by: Alejandro Chehtman, Alexandra Huneeus, and Sergio Puig, Oxford University Press. © Oxford University Press 2025. DOI: 10.1093/9780197754016.003.0019

II. Latin America and the Idea of Human Rights

Human rights as an idea are widely accepted in Latin America. Human rights are commonly understood as a beacon that guides states, civil society organizations, victims, and survivors of human rights violations. Therefore, a fundamental point to begin the analysis of human rights institutions in the region is to look at the origin of the Latin American idea of human rights—an idea that birthed a complex regional system for the protection of rights and fundamental liberties.

For some, the notion of human rights in Latin America can be traced back to the sixteenth-century writings of Bartolomé de Las Casas. Under this narrative, in Las Casas's writings lies the genesis of what we understand today as human rights. Las Casas—"the midwife of human rights," in the words of human rights scholar Paolo Carozza—was concerned about the treatment of Indigenous people at the hands of the Spanish Crown.[1] Las Casas's writings drew on philosophical and religious ideas, as well as his own experience as a missionary, to argue for the equality of Indians and their right to freedom.[2] For many, this way of understanding the interaction between Indians and Spanish colonists under systems of subjugation is the remote antecedent of what we would later understand as human rights.

Carozza also points to the influence of thinkers such as Jean-Jacques Rousseau on some of the independence leaders of Latin American countries, particularly Simón Bolívar. The region's revolutionaries saw the political theory that underpinned the American and French revolutions at the end of the eighteenth century as an important source to guide their own independence projects. The influence of the revolutions' theorists effectively served as a conceptual basis for many Latin American thinkers.[3] They promoted independence from the Spanish Crown and later pushed for less authoritarian institutional arrangements.[4] According to Carozza, they also saw in law "a pedagogical instrument for the

[1] Paolo G. Carozza, "From Conquest to Constitutions: Retrieving a Latin American Tradition of the Idea of Human Rights," *Human Rights Quarterly* 25 (2003): 281–313, https://scholarship.law.nd.edu/law_faculty_scholarship/581/.

[2] Carozza observes, "Las Casas' defense of the freedom of the Indians based on an internal appreciation of their values and beliefs has strong elements of what today we would regard as a defense of their cultural integrity and self-determination." Ibid., 295.

[3] See Roberto Gargarella, *Latin American Constitutionalism,1810-2010: The Engine Room of the Constitution* (New York: Oxford University Press, 2013).

[4] In Chile, for example, another religious man, Camilo Henríquez, was inspired by the writings of Jefferson and Paine to justify the right of the people to make their own laws. The influence of this school of thought is visible in recent instances, such as the constituent process promoted by former President Michelle Bachelet in 2015. In the presidential speech in which she announced the process, Bachelet relied on Henríquez to justify the need for a deliberative and participatory process outside the National Congress. See Jorge Contesse, "Constitutional Change from Afar," *Rutgers Law Review* 75 (forthcoming, 2024).

cultivation of virtue"[5] in ways that seem resonant with the contemporary jurisprudence of Latin American human rights institutions.

A common narrative in Latin American human rights law is that Latin American countries were early advocates for universal human rights *as law*, an idea that took shape in 1948 with the adoption of the Universal Declaration of Human Rights. Mary Ann Glendon popularized this narrative two decades ago in an article called "The Forgotten Crucible of the Universal Human Rights Idea."[6] Other human rights scholars, like Carozza and Kathryn Sikkink, have also explored Latin America's "protagonist" role in making the Universal Declaration.[7] Glendon, Sikkink, and Carozza argue that the Universal Declaration reflected the influence of Latin American countries, which only months earlier had adopted the American Declaration of the Rights and Duties of Man.[8] Following Michael Novak, Glendon points to the influence of Catholic thought upon Latin American countries and political elites as the key driver behind the promotion of social and egalitarian ideas.[9]

On the one hand, the canon understands that Latin America was "ahead" of the world's civilizational progress, as reflected in the American Declaration. On the other hand, the narrative suggests that such progress is a linear sequence of the international community's moral development—a sequence that gives birth to a regional *juridical* architecture, reflected in the inter-American human rights system. As a legal and not only political or diplomatic regime, Latin America's regional human rights institutions are tasked with overseeing how states comply with their international obligations from a legal point of view. Human rights regional institutions may thus find states to be "in violation" of their international (or, more precisely, *regional*) obligations and may, therefore, impose remedies in favor of individuals who are the victims of states' wrongful acts.

[5] Ibid..

[6] Mary Ann Glendon, "The Forgotten Crucible: The Latin American Influence on the Universal Human Rights Idea," *Harvard Human Rights Journal* 16 (2003): 27–39, https://journals.law.harvard.edu/hrj/wp-content/uploads/sites/83/2020/06/16HHRJ27-Glendon.pdf.

[7] Kathryn Sikkink, "Latin American Countries as Norm Protagonists of the Idea of International Human Rights," *Global Governance* 20 (2014): 389–404, https://www.jstor.org/stable/24526221; Paolo G. Carozza, "'They Are Our Brothers, and Christ Gave His Life for Them': The Catholic Tradition and the Idea of Human Rights in Latin America," *Logos: A Journal of Catholic Thought and Culture* 6 (2003): 81–84, https://scholarship.law.nd.edu/cgi/viewcontent.cgi?article=1889&context=law_faculty_scholarship ("Latin American proposals formed the first models on which the Universal Declaration of Human Rights was drafted."); and Sikkink and Jensen, in this volume.

[8] Ibid.

[9] Glendon, "The Forgotten Crucible," 34. Sikkink notes that "[t]he research showing the impact of Latin American countries on the inclusion of economic and social rights in the UDHR corrected a long-held belief that the economic and social rights in the UDHR were primarily the result of Soviet pressure." Sikkink, at 398. And Carozza observes that "Latin American delegates in general became the 'guardians' of the social and economic provisions of the draft declaration." Carozza, "From Conquest to Constitutions," 286.

Some, however, challenge this "linear narrative."[10] Quintana observes that human rights "initially played an important role, but they were predominantly employed as instruments in regional geopolitical and economic struggles rather than pursued as ends in themselves."[11] In contrast to the traditional canon, some scholars emphasize the geopolitical dynamics in which the countries of the region participated. These dynamics were (and still are, no doubt) dramatically determined by the relationship of Latin American countries with their northern neighbor, the United States. Guy Fiti Sinclair, for example, points out that "[d]espite (or perhaps as a consequence of) several interventions by the United States in Latin America, the interwar period . . . saw further development of the Inter-American system, with both hegemonic and counter-hegemonic effects."[12] Similarly, Arnulf Becker Lorca argues that it was "diplomatic protection," not a long tradition of commitment to human rights, that motivated Latin American states to elaborate human rights declarations in Latin America, first, and at the global level months later.[13] Whichever point of view is adopted, the result is the path toward a regional mechanism for the protection of rights. This mechanism, similar to the one Europe adopted in the early 1950s, is to this day administered by the region's human rights institutions: the Inter-American Commission and the Inter-American Court of Human Rights, on the one hand, and national courts, on the other. It is thus a truly transnational mechanism in which national and international bodies intervene in ways that generate both friction and complementarity and support and resistance, as I show in the following sections.

III. The Regional System for the Protection of Rights

After the adoption of the two human rights declarations in 1948, the transition to a legal system for the protection of human rights continued. In the universal system, the onset of the Cold War made it increasingly difficult to reach a consensus on a single international human rights treaty. As is well known, in 1966,

[10] See Francisco-José Quintana, "The (Latin) American Dream? Human Rights and the Construction of Inter-American Regional Organisation (1945-1948)," *Journal of the History of International Law* 25 (2023): 560–591, https://brill.com/view/journals/jhil/25/4/article-p560_5.xml.

[11] Ibid., 585.

[12] Guy Fiti Sinclair, "Between Functionalism and Hegemony: Regional International Organizations in the History of International Law," *International Organizations Law Review* 21 (2024): 65–86, at 71, https://brill.com/view/journals/iolr/21/1/article-p65_004.xml.

[13] Arnulf Becker Lorca, "Human Rights in International Law? The Forgotten Origins of Human Rights in Latin America," *University of Toronto Law Journal* 67 (2017): 465–495, at 476, https://www.jstor.org/stable/10.2307/90017183 ("when Latin American states decided to draft a declaration of the rights of man—at the Inter-American Conference on Problems of War and Peace in Mexico City—they neither recalled a tradition of rights inaugurated by Las Casas nor pictured a system of individual rights to be enforced by transnational movements against states.").

the international community was divided into two covenants that responded to the then-opposing interests of the West, led by the United States, and the East, led by the Soviet Union.

In Latin America, talk about the legalization of human rights also continued.[14] At the Tenth Inter-American Conference, held in Caracas, in 1954, states tasked the Council of the Organization of American States (OAS) "to continue studies on the *jurisdictional* protection of human rights human rights."[15] States expressly mandated the Council to analyze "the possibility of establishing an Inter-American Court to protect human rights."[16] Five years later, the Inter-American Commission on Human Rights was established at the Fifth Meeting of Ministers of Foreign Affairs, held in Santiago, Chile. In 1960, the OAS Council approved the Commission's Statute, and the Commission's inaugural seven members were elected to "promote" respect for human rights. In 1965, at another regional diplomatic meeting, Latin American states expanded the Commission's mandate to "protect" human rights by examining individual complaints and communicating with states to obtain information and make recommendations.[17] In 1967, states adopted the Buenos Aires Protocol to amend the Charter of the Organization of American States: the Commission was elevated to the status of an organ of the OAS, and states agreed to adopt "an inter-American convention on human rights" which would "determine the structure, competence and procedure of the Commission, as well as of the other organs other bodies responsible for such matters."[18] Two years later, OAS member states gathered in San José, Costa Rica, to adopt the American Convention on Human Rights. What had thus far been a diplomatic or "declarative" system for promoting and protecting rights became a regional *legal* system. The inter-American human rights system, as a regional legal system, was now born.

Toward the end of the 1970s, amid the pervasive grip of military dictatorships across the Southern Cone of Latin America, a pivotal moment unfolded as the American Convention on Human Rights was on the cusp of coming into force. During this tumultuous period, the Inter-American Commission on Human

[14] See Alexandra Huneeus & Mikael Rask Madsen, "Between Universalism and Regional Law and Politics: A Comparative History of the American, European, and African Human Rights Systems," *International Journal of Constitutional Law* 16 (2018): 136–160, at 140, https://academic.oup.com/icon/article/16/1/136/4995560 ("Latin American states were . . . loath to further legalize and institutionalize the human rights they declared.").

[15] See Manuel E. Ventura Robles, "El Sistema Interamericano de Protección de los Derechos Humanos," *Revista do Instituto Brasileiro de Direitos Humanos* 14 (2014): 257–280, at 258 (emphasis added), https://www.revista.ibdh.org.br/index.php/ibdh/article/view/275.

[16] Ibid.

[17] Ibid.

[18] Protocol of Amendment to the Charter of the Organization of American States (B-31) (February 27, 1967), art. 112(2) [hereinafter Protocol of Buenos Aires], https://oas.org/sap/peacefund/virtuallibrary/ProtocolBsAs/ProtocolBuenosAires.pdf.

Rights embarked on a visit to Argentina, which would ultimately catalyze a cascade of events that reverberated across the region.

The timing of the Commission's visit proved particularly significant against the backdrop of Argentina's oppressive military regime. The visit coincided with the growing momentum of civil society movements—both domestically and internationally—demanding accountability for human rights violations. It served as a powerful sign of international scrutiny, shedding light on the atrocities committed by an authoritarian regime. The Commission's presence in Argentina was a stark reminder of the regime's disregard for fundamental human rights principles. The culmination of this pressure, coupled with the regime's subsequent military defeat in the Malvinas—or Falkland—Islands War, would be the final blow to the Argentine military junta's grip on power.

In the broader context of the inter-American system, the Commission's actions underscored its emerging role as a beacon of democratic legitimacy. By leveraging its authority and international standing, the Commission effectively positioned itself as a potential force for change. In the early 1980s, as the tide slowly began to turn against authoritarianism, it became increasingly apparent that the Commission could serve as a linchpin in helping to dismantle regimes that systematically violated human rights. This realization marked a significant point, affirming the Inter-American Commission's pivotal role in upholding democratic principles and advancing human rights across the Americas.[19]

In the following decade, the Inter-American Commission slowly consolidated its legal authority by increasing its interaction with both civil society organizations and Latin American states. In parallel, the Inter-American Court began to issue advisory opinions on various issues that both states and the Inter-American Commission brought before the Court. In the absence of contentious cases submitted by the Inter-American Commission—as provided for in the American Convention—the Court used its advisory jurisdiction to increase its authority and influence.[20]

The changes in the region's political landscape also impacted the development of human rights protection mechanisms, from a rather diplomatic system to a

[19] Robert K. Goldman, "History and Action: The Inter-American Human Rights System and the Role of the Inter-American Commission on Human Rights," *Human Rights Quarterly* 31 (2009): 856–887, at 873, https://digitalcommons.wcl.american.edu/cgi/viewcontent.cgi?article=1027&context=facsch_lawrev.

[20] As Huneeus and Madsen note, "the Inter-American Commission was both mistrustful of the new court and jealous of its own role. It refused to refer cases for seven years, confining the Court's activity to requests for advisory opinions referred by states." Huneeus & Madsen, "Between Universalism and Regional Law," 146. The Court issued opinions in areas such as freedom of expression, suspension of rights in emergency contexts, and specific aspects of interpretation of the new regime. See Thomas Buergenthal, "Remembering the Early Years of the Inter-American Court of Human Rights," *New York University Journal of International Law & Politics* 37, no. 2 (Winter 2005): 259, 269–70, https://heinonline.org/HOL/P?h=hein.journals/nyuilp37&i=271.

model of individual petitions channeled through judicial processes. This change was possible because of the region's democratization process, which caused "an identity crisis" for the inter-American system.[21] The Commission, in particular, adjusted its practice in response to states' resistance to the Commission supervising whether *democratic* states complied with their international obligations. The Commission's power to review states' domestic legislation and the processing of individual complaints solidified its new role as a site of legal, not only diplomatic or political, debate. The language of rights was now consolidated as a legal language. With the Commission fully established and the Court beginning to adopt contentious decisions, the language of human rights began to establish itself as a radically legal practice. Now would come the turn of development at the national level and a growing and intense interaction between national courts and regional human rights institutions.

IV. International Law as Constitutional Law

At the end of the 1980s, many Latin American countries began transitioning to constitutional democracy. Many adopted new constitutions, while some reformed existing constitutions. States that experienced a "new constitutional beginning" and did so through new legal regulations made an explicit commitment to international human rights law. The new constitutions adopted at that time—e.g., Brazil in 1988, Colombia in 1991, and Peru in 1993—and the major constitutional reforms adopted in other countries, such as Chile in 1989 or Argentina in 1994, show a regional trend to render international human rights law part of constitutional law.[22] International law, particularly *human rights* law, became the "supreme law of the land."

In response to constitutional amendments, Latin American courts began to use international law extensively, incorporating international human rights norms in their reasoning. As I show in section V, this phenomenon would crystallize with the Inter-American Court's adoption of the doctrine of conventionality control, thus cementing the notion of Latin American international human rights law as constitutional law.

Among the examples worth considering is the decision of a Lima district court that invalidated the Peruvian amnesty law in the mid-1990s. In November 1991, a Peruvian death squad known as "Grupo Colina" irrupted into a local celebration in the Barrios Altos neighborhood, in Lima, Peru. Six heavily armed

[21] Huneeus & Madsen, "Between Universalism and Regional Law," 151.

[22] See Rodrigo Uprinmy, "The Recent Transformation of Constitutional Law in Latin America: Trends and Challenges," *Texas Law Review* 89 (2011): 1587–1609, https://corteidh.or.cr/tablas/r27168.pdf.

men forced fifteen attendees, including an eight-year-old boy, to lie down on the floor and shot them all. The government claimed that those killed were members of the Shining Path organization.

The massacre of Barrios Altos triggered a criminal investigation under the direction of Judge Antonia Saquicuray of the Sixteenth Criminal Court of Lima. In 1995, Judge Saquicuray's efforts to hold accountable the members of the Grupo Colina, however, faced a seemingly insurmountable obstacle: an amnesty law that the administration of Alberto Fujimori had jammed through the Peruvian Congress. The law granted amnesty to "all members of the security forces and civilians who had been accused, investigated, prosecuted or convicted, or who were carrying out prison sentences, for human rights violations." President Fujimori quickly promulgated the law, thwarting Judge Saquicuray's criminal investigation into those responsible for the Barrios Altos massacre.

But Judge Saquicuray did not back down. Instead, she issued a decision finding Article 1 of the amnesty law unconstitutional. Saquicuray relied on Peru's constitutional provisions incorporating international human rights instruments into the Constitution.[23] Never before had a district court used international human rights law in this way. Judge Saquicuray, after consulting a constitutional lawyer, concluded that the Peruvian Constitution allowed, by means of the diffuse control of constitutionality, to challenge a law directly invoking both the Constitution and international human rights treaties. In her words, "[t]here were no references on the subject of amnesties in the Inter-American Court, but there was the [American] Convention and the Constitution with diffuse control."[24] International law was unequivocally now part of Peru's domestic law.

Around the same time, the Constitutional Court of Colombia created one of its most consequential doctrines, known as the "block of constitutionality." According to the block of constitutionality doctrine, the court should consider not only the provisions of Colombia's Constitution but also the norms and principles of international human rights law. According to the Colombian Court, international human rights norms, "without appearing formally in the articles of the constitutional text, are used as parameters for the control of the constitutionality of laws," thus generating a single normative "block" to be used by the Constitutional Court.[25]

[23] *Ley de Amnistía 26.479*, Judgment (Disposición Cuarta Transitoria; Control Difuso) (June 16, 1995).

[24] Interview with Judge Antonia Saquicuray, Superior Court of Lima (July 26, 2023). Judge Saquicuray added: "I was a judge, I swore by the Constitution to deliver justice in accordance with the law."

[25] Constitutional Court of Colombia, Judgment C-225/95 (May 18, 1995). In this judgment, the Colombian Court examined the role that international humanitarian law, particularly the Second Geneva Convention, has in Colombian constitutional law.

A few years later, the Chilean courts—known for their reluctance to use international law and especially their acquiescence to the military dictatorship of Augusto Pinochet[26]—did the same with the self-amnesty law that Pinochet enacted in 1978. Resorting to the 1949 Geneva Conventions, the Chilean Supreme Court dramatically changed its case law, which had thus far rejected all efforts to hold accountable those responsible for serious human rights violations. The Chilean Court found that international law (in this case, international humanitarian law) took precedence over domestic law.[27] The Court's decision was crucial for opening the possibility that victims of the dictatorship could overcome the obstacle of the amnesty law. This novel doctrine was a direct way of combating impunity, made possible by the direct implementation of international human rights and humanitarian law.

These developments in the constitutional jurisprudence of various countries strengthened the authoritative and legal character of inter-American human rights norms. One may also note an aspect that is sometimes obscured but vital in how international law became a central part of domestic law in the region: the role of legal education. Legal education in Latin America, traditionally marked by the formalist legacy of European legal education, was also undergoing a process of change.[28] This change was driven, among other factors, by the work and influence of foreign organizations—such as the Ford Foundation—that funded the revision of law school curricula and the creation of a network of human rights legal clinics, thus giving an essential boost to a novel way of using the courts as actors of social change.[29] It thus became increasingly common to invoke international law before domestic courts, generating an impact not only on judges but also on public opinion: international law was no longer simply a set of norms and rules produced "out there." In line with the judicial doctrines explained above, international law became an integral part of the curriculum of some law schools that innovated in teaching and sought to leave behind the formalism characteristic of legal systems created in light of the French Civil Code.[30]

[26] See Lisa Hilbink, *Judges beyond Politics in Democracy and Dictatorship: Lessons from Chile* (New York: Cambridge University Press, 2007).

[27] Supreme Court of Chile, Criminal Chamber, Judgment No. 469-98 (September 9, 1998).

[28] See Jorge Contesse, "International Legal Scholarship in Latin America," *Virginia Journal of International Law* 64 (2024): 373–404, at 376, https://static1.squarespace.com/static/5f0a3654a47d231c00ccd14f/t/6609fa4ea22b5a4d519ce771/1711929934415/64.2+Contesse%2C+FINAL.pdf.

[29] Daniel Bonilla, "Legal Clinics in the Global North and South: Between Equality and Subordination," *Yale Human Rights & Development Law Journal* 16 (2013): 1–40, https://papers.ssrn.com/sol3/papers.cfm?abstract_id=2511370; Arturo J. Carrillo & Nicolas Espejo Yaksic, "Re-Imagining the Human Rights Law Clinic," *Maryland Journal of International Law* 26 (2011): 80–112, at 89, https://digitalcommons.law.umaryland.edu/cgi/viewcontent.cgi?article=1565&context=mjil.

[30] Lawrence M. Friedman & Rogelio Pérez-Perdomo, eds., *Legal Culture in the Age of Globalization: Latin America and Latin Europe* (Stanford: Stanford University Press, 2003).

V. Constitutional Law as International Law

The process by which international (human rights) law became increasingly important in Latin America was not only a product of internalization by national courts. The regional human rights institutions—particularly the Inter-American Court of Human Rights—progressively took on the role of a type of regional constitutional court. The interaction between national courts and the Inter-American Court of Human Rights delineated a new understanding of the close relationship between the two legal orders, domestic and international. How the Inter-American Court developed its increasingly influential jurisprudence is a critical element in understanding the role of international law, and of the Court in particular, in the development of Latin American law.

As explained in section IV, the Barrios Altos massacre served as the starting point of the Peruvian jurisprudence that placed international law in a preferential position. But this event also led to one of the most important decisions by the Inter-American Court: *Barrios Altos v. Peru*.[31] In this judgment, the Inter-American Court found Peru responsible for the lack of proper investigation and punishment of those responsible for the Barrios Altos massacre. Arguably, the decision's most important feature is the Court's holding that amnesty laws "lack legal effect" due to "the manifest incompatibility of self-amnesty laws and the American Convention on Human Rights."[32] Accordingly, the Court ordered Peru to reopen the criminal investigations into the Barrios Altos massacre.

The Inter-American Court's *Barrios Altos* judgment marked what would become a vital component of inter-American human rights case law: amnesty laws are incompatible with the American Convention. Beyond this holding, however, the claim that such incompatibility renders these laws "devoid of legal effect" is what seemingly turned the Inter-American Court into a sort of regional constitutional court, as declaring domestic laws inapplicable—or null and void—is typically a decision for *domestic* (i.e., "constitutional") courts, not *international* courts.[33]

In this context, reiterating the doctrine on the invalidity of self-amnesties, the Inter-American Court issued another landmark judgment in 2006: *Almonacid Arellano v. Chile*. In *Almonacid Arellano*, the Court created the doctrine of "conventionality control," according to which all national judges are directly bound to follow the norms of the Convention and the interpretations of the

[31] *Barrios Altos v. Peru*, Merits, Inter-Am. Ct. H.R. (ser. C) No. 75 (March 14, 2001).

[32] Ibid., ¶ 44.

[33] See Jorge Contesse, "The International Authority of the Inter-American Court of Human Rights: A Critique of the Conventionality Control Doctrine," *International Journal of Human Rights* 22 (2018): 1168–1191, https://doi.org/10.1080/13642987.2017.1411640.

Inter-American Court.[34] In the decision's most famous paragraph—paragraph 124—the Court declared:

> when a State has ratified an international treaty such as the American Convention, its judges, as part of the State, are also bound by such Convention. This forces them to see that all the effects of the provisions embodied in the Convention are not adversely affected by the enforcement of laws which are contrary to its purpose and that have not had any legal effects since their inception. In other words, the Judiciary must exercise a sort of 'conventionality control' between the domestic legal provisions which are applied to specific cases and the American Convention on Human Rights. To perform this task, the Judiciary has to take into account not only the treaty, but also the interpretation thereof made by the Inter-American Court, which is the ultimate interpreter of the American Convention.

Since then, there has been a growing understanding of the Court as a true regional constitutional court.[35] The separation between international and constitutional law progressively unravels, as the Court seems to understand national judges as genuine "inter-American judges."[36] The monist character of Latin American legal systems, which directly incorporate international law into domestic law, has been critical to the prominence of international jurisprudence at the domestic level. Added to this is the positioning of the Inter-American Court as a court that seeks to bind national courts directly, generating an intrusive jurisprudence in domestic affairs that further blurs the boundaries between domestic law and international law.

VI. A Latin American Common Law?

The increasing blurring of the lines that separate domestic and international law and the idea of national judges as international judges have an intellectual home in the "*ius constitutionale commune*" school of thought, originated at the Max Planck Institute in Heidelberg, Germany. The theory postulates that the Inter-American Court and Latin American states participate in a judicial

[34] *Almonacid Arellano v. Chile*, Preliminary Objections, Merits, Reparations and Costs, Inter-Am. Ct. H.R. (ser. C) No. 154 (September 26, 2006).

[35] See Laurence Burgorgue-Larsen, "La Corte Interamericana de Derechos Humanos como Tribunal Constitucional," in von Bogdandy et al., *Ius Constitutionale Commune en América Latina*, 421.

[36] Armin von Bogdandy and René Urueña, "International Transformative Constitutionalism in Latin America," *American Journal of International Law* 114 (2020): 403–442, at 416, https://doi.org/10.1017/ajil.2020.27.

dialogue that seeks to "transform" Latin American law and the region's structural inequalities.[37] The theory, which gives the Inter-American Court a core mission to do so, has Inter-American Court Judge Eduardo Ferrer Mac-Gregor as "one of [its] most prominent supporters."[38]

In the words of Armin von Bogdandy, the functions of the *ius constitutionale commune* "resemble those of a series of concepts, such as, for example, the new *Ius Commune* in Europe, the European *Ius Publicum* . . . the so-called law of humanity, cosmopolitan law, global law, world law, internal world law, transnational law or transconstitutionalism."[39] The list suggests that the school is normatively located on almost all possible grounds of authority—a feature that, as some have observed, makes it hard to characterize it clearly.[40] In addition, as has been said, a distinctive feature of the *ius constitutionale commune* is the idea that the inter-American human rights institutions have a "transformative mandate." It is unclear from where this mandate arises, given that the American Convention creates a court with the power to "rule that the injured party be ensured the enjoyment of his right or freedom that was violated [and that] that the consequences of the measure or situation that constituted the breach of such right or freedom be remedied and that fair compensation be paid to the injured party."[41]

The "transformative mandate" idea, however, is a fertile intellectual ground for the expansion of powers by praetorian means, that is, beyond the text of the Convention. As the inter-American human rights institutions break new ground in several areas—from anti-impunity to same-sex marriage to the right to water and a healthy environment—it is worth examining how the Inter-American Court materializes the idea of transformative law. The analysis is particularly relevant if we consider the inter-American system's transit from a model of diplomatic relations that sought to *promote* human rights to one in which states also entrusted human rights *protection* to regional institutions. Significantly, such

[37] Armin von Bogdandy et al. (eds.), *Transformative Constitutionalism in Latin America: The Emergence of a New Ius Commune* (Oxford: Oxford University Press, 2017).

[38] Alejandro Rodiles, "The Great Promise of Comparative Public Law for Latin America: Toward *Ius Commune Americanum*?," in *Comparative International Law*, ed. Anthea Roberts (New York: Oxford University Press, 2018), 501–524, 512.

[39] Armin von Bogdandy, "Ius Constitutionale Commune en América Latina: Una Mirada a un Constitucionalismo Transformador," *Revista Derecho del Estado* 34 (January-June 2015): 3–50, at 15-16, https://doi.org/10.18601/01229893.n34.01.

[40] See Alberto Coddou McManus, "A Critical Account of Ius Constitutionale Commune in Latin America: An Intellectual Map of Contemporary Latin American Constitutionalism," *Global Constitutionalism* 11 (2022): 110–138, https://doi.org/10.1017/S2045381721000125; Francisca Pou Giménez and Ana Micaela Alterio, "Book Review: *Transformative Constitutionalism in Latin America*" (blog), IACL, October 23, 2018, https://blog-iacl-aidc.org/blog/2018/10/21/book-review-transformative-constitutionalism-in-latin-america; Natalia Torres Zúñiga, *The Inter-American Court of Human Rights: The Legitimacy of International Courts and Tribunals* (New York: Routledge, 2023).

[41] American Convention on Human Rights Art. 63.1.

protection remained at the regional level. The past decades' development, however, with more intense interaction between domestic law and international law and the articulation of a notion of a Latin American common law, moves the transition from diplomacy to legality a step further by placing on international judges, not on states, the decision to change the rules of interaction between municipal law and international law.[42] In a context of increased rejection of supranational structures for the protection of rights, it is especially relevant to take seriously the virtues and problems of understanding human rights institutions as being charged with *transforming* the legal and social structures of the countries of the region.[43]

I briefly examine two areas that, in my view, exemplify the blurring of differences between domestic and regional jurisdictions and the Inter-American Court's expansion of powers: the justiciability of social rights and the role of international adjudication in assessing the democratic character of states. These two areas are important to consider because inequality and the lack of protection of social rights, as well as the fragility of constitutional democracy, are two prominent issues in the region—and they are issues that "define" the theory of transformative constitutionalism.[44]

Under the American Convention, social rights are not directly justiciable. The Convention contains only one general provision concerning social rights—Article 26—which directs states "to adopt measures" but does not include them among the justiciable rights.[45] In 1988, states adopted the Protocol of San Salvador on Economic, Social and Cultural Rights, where states included a comprehensive list of social rights as rights protected under inter-American

[42] A prominent example is a 2010 separate opinion by Judge Ferrer Mac-Gregor, where he expounds at length the notion of "conventionality control." At times, Judge Ferrer MacGregor's separate opinion reads more like legal doctrine than a judicial opinion, as it details how states—particularly, national judges—should adhere to the conventionality control theory. See *Cabrera García and Montiel Flores v. Mexico*, Inter-Am. Ct. H.R. (ser. C) No. 220 (November 26, 2010) (concurring opinion of Ferrer MacGregor, J.).

[43] I discuss some of the dynamics of resistance toward the inter-American human rights system in Jorge Contesse, "Judicial Interactions and Human Rights Contestations in Latin America," *Journal of International Dispute Settlement* 12 (2021): 271–290, at 271, https://doi.org/10.1093/jnlids/idab005.

[44] "In Latin America, transformative constitutionalism is defined by the challenges of widespread violence, social exclusion, extreme inequality, weak domestic institutions, due to phenomena such as hyperpresidentialism, a lack of judicial independence and corruption." See Armin von Bogdandy, "The Transformative Mandate of the Inter-American System—Legality and Legitimacy of an Extraordinary Jurisgenerative Process," *Max Planck Institute for Comparative Public Law & International Law*, MPIL Research Paper No. 2019-16 (2019): 1–19, at 1, https://papers.ssrn.com/sol3/papers.cfm?abstract_id=3463059.

[45] Organization of American States, American Convention on Human Rights art. 26, November 22, 1969, O.A.S.T.S. No. 36, 1144 U.N.T.S. 123: "The States Parties undertake to adopt measures, both internally and through international cooperation, especially those of an economic and technical nature, with a view to achieving progressively, by legislation or other appropriate means, the full realization of the rights implicit in the economic, social, educational, scientific, and cultural standards set forth in the Charter of the Organization of American States as amended by the Protocol of Buenos Aires."

human rights law. The Protocol of San Salvador provides for the justiciability of only two rights: the right to unionize and the right to education.[46] In a series of cases starting in 2017, however, the Inter-American Court has found that Article 26 of the American Convention is *directly* justiciable, even though the provision does not give the Court this power.[47] On the one hand, the majority opinion—originally promoted by former Judge Roberto Caldas and Judge Ferrer Mac-Gregor in a 2015 separate opinion—claims that despite the language of the Convention, under the *iura novit curia* principle, the Court may ex officio advance and expand the scope of social rights. Some members of the Court systematically dissent from this interpretation, with opinions that question the authority of the Court and warn about the risks of an expansive reading of Article 26.

The discussion on the justiciability of social rights is based on the idea of a "paradigm shift in jurisprudence," as announced by Judge Ferrer Mac-Gregor writing extrajudicially.[48] However, the Court's jurisprudential expansion, essentially based on the evolutionary interpretation of the American Convention, encounters resistance within the Court itself. Some members routinely criticize the doctrine as a departure from basic rules of treaty interpretation and as undermining the legitimacy of the inter-American system.[49] For the *ius constitutionale commune*, however, far from being a matter of concern that the Court interprets its powers in ways beyond the American Convention, this new jurisprudence represents "a new frontier in [the Court's] steadfast pursuit of its transformative mandate."[50]

[46] Organization of American States, Additional Protocol to the American Convention on Human Rights in the Area of Economic, Social and Cultural Rights, art. 19.6, November 14, 1988, 28 I.L.M. 156 (1989).

[47] Some scholars objected to the Court's expansive reading of its powers under Article 62 of the American Convention, which states that the Court has jurisdiction "on all matters relating to the interpretation or application of this Convention." See Oswaldo R. Ruiz-Chiriboga, "The American Convention and the Protocol of San Salvador: Two Intertwined Treaties: Non-Enforceability of Economic, Social and Cultural Rights in the Inter-American System," *Netherlands Quarterly of Human Rights* 31 (2017): 159–186, https://doi.org/10.1177/016934411303100203.

[48] Eduardo Ferrer Mac-Gregor, Mariela Morales Antoniazzi & Rogelio Flores Pantoja (eds.), *Inclusión,* Ius Commune *y justiciabilidad de los DESCA en la jurisprudencia interamericana: El caso Lagos del Campo y los nuevos desafíos* (Mexico City: Institute of Constitutional Studies of the State of Querétaro, 2018), at 15. The Court has reiterated this jurisprudential position in a number of cases, including *Poblete Vilches and Others v. Chile*, Merits, Reparations, and Costs, Inter-Am. Ct. H.R. (ser. C) No. 349 (March 8, 2018); *Cuscul Pivaral and Others v. Guatemala*, Preliminary Objections, Merits, Reparations, and Costs, Inter-Am. Ct. H.R. (ser. C) No. 359 (August 23, 2018); and *Indigenous Communities of the Lhaka Honhat Association (Our Land) v. Argentina*, Merits, Reparations, and Costs, Inter-Am. Ct. H.R. (ser. C) No. 400 (February 6, 2020).

[49] Former Judge Sierra Porto, for example, argued that the Court "uses the 'evolutive' interpretation to conceal a 'conventional mutation.'" *Lagos del Campo v. Peru*, Preliminary Objections, Merits, Reparations and Costs, Inter-Am. Ct. H.R. (ser. C) No. 340 (dissenting opinion of Sierra Porto, J.), ¶ 42 (August 31, 2017).

[50] Von Bogdandy and Urueña, "International Transformative Constitutionalism," 442.

As some have argued, the *ius constitutionale commune* doctrine's transformative impetus, far from correcting the inequalities prevailing in the continent, may prove counterproductive.[51] Verdugo claims that the doctrine's marked emphasis on the judicialization of human rights is "poorly suited to advance its egalitarian goals fully."[52] More significantly, the entire intellectual enterprise rests on the premise that the Inter-American Court is mandated to "transform" the law and, as a result, Latin American social structures. However, it is unclear *where* this mandate comes from, let alone *who* entrusted it to the Court. Since the Inter-American Court's source of authority is the American Convention—a treaty drafted by OAS states—only states can grant such a mandate. And it is highly dubious that Latin American states have done so. In any case, it does not seem advisable that, in the face of criticism of how it carries out its work, the Court should simply "double down."[53] In the words of former Judge Sierra Porto, "[I]t is not possible to create transformational law that runs counter to the law in force."[54]

The second example that highlights the problematic scope of the Latin American common law notion is the Court's understanding of its role as an international enforcer of democracy. In November 2020, the Inter-American Court issued an advisory opinion addressing the human rights obligations of states that have denounced the American Convention.[55] In a sweeping opinion, the Court declared that whenever a state denounces the American Convention, other states should "express any observations or objections deemed pertinent regarding denunciations that do not withstand scrutiny in light of the democratic principle and that undermine the inter-American public interest."[56] Of course, that states can issue such opinions is not something new or that the Court has invented. What is remarkable is that the Court's finding is situated in the context of understanding that "[t]he effective exercise of democracy in the Americas is an international legal obligation . . . [and] is *no longer solely a matter of domestic, internal or exclusive jurisdiction*."[57] This doctrine, which the Court first articulated in a contentious case against Venezuela, is based on the 2001 Inter-American

[51] Sergio Verdugo, "Is the Idea of a Latin American *Ius Constitutionale Commune* a Failed Promise?" *European Yearbook of Constitutional Law* 6 (forthcoming, 2025).

[52] Ibid.

[53] As von Bogdandy and Urueña note, the Court "tends to double down in the face of criticism." von Bogdandy and Urueña, "International Transformative Constitutionalism," 442.

[54] *Lagos del Campo v. Peru*, Preliminary Objections, Merits, Reparations and Costs, Inter-Am. Ct. H.R. (ser. C) No. 340 (dissenting opinion of Sierra Porto, J.), ¶ 48 (August 31, 2017).

[55] *Denunciation of the American Convention on Human Rights and the Charter of the Organization of American States and the consequences for State human rights obligations (interpretation and scope of articles 1, 2, 27, 29, 30, 31, 32, 33, 65 and 78 of the American Convention on Human Rights and 3(l), 17, 45, 53, 106 and 143 of the Charter of the Organization of American States)*, Advisory Opinion OC-26 (ser. A) No. 26 (November 9, 2020).

[56] Ibid., ¶. 71.

[57] Ibid., ¶ 72 (emphasis added).

Democratic Charter, which stipulates that "[t]he peoples of the Americas have *a right to democracy* and their governments have an obligation to promote and defend it" (Art. 1; emphasis added) and that "[t]he effective exercise of representative democracy is the basis for the rule of law and of the constitutional regimes of the member states of the Organization of American States" (Art. 2).[58] To be sure, the Charter does not grant any powers to the Court, which probably explains why the Court's advisory opinion resorts to states' collective (i.e., vague) obligations to protect democracy in the region.

More significantly, in a separate opinion, Judge Patricio Pazmiño Freire takes the idea of "the effective exercise of democracy" as a matter that falls under international jurisdiction one big step further. Judge Pazmiño Freire points out that the Court did not go far enough in this advisory opinion. In his view: "[G]iven the high and extreme volatility and radicalization of the political conflict in our countries . . . we should seek to rationalize, from a regulatory perspective, the solution of these conflicts. . . . The power to substantively analyze a denunciation should belong to the Inter-American Court and not to the [OAS] General Assembly."[59] For him, any state that seeks to withdraw from the American Convention should "be required to submit a petition for an advisory opinion . . . requiring the Court to analyze the compatibility of the denunciation with the instrument from which the State is seeking to withdraw."[60]

It is hard to imagine a more radical stance on the assumption of powers by the Court, as it is no longer only *with* or *over* states but even with and over the central political organ of the Organization of American States—its General Assembly. To be sure, Judge Pazmiño Freire's opinion is only a separate opinion and not the Court's. But just like the notion that Article 26 of the American Convention is a directly justiciable provision was first articulated in a separate opinion, Judge Pazmiño Freire's opinion could obtain more support from other members of the Court. It took only two years for two judges writing separately to persuade their colleagues and for that minority opinion to become the official position of the Court on the direct justiciability of social rights. The journey of human rights institutions in the region is one more step that may well generate similar interpretations in the future.

The two areas to which I have briefly referred—social rights and democracy as an international legal obligation—highlight two aspects that the idea of a Latin American common law seems to overlook. On the one hand, the idea forces us to question the correctness of the legal interpretations that the Court articulates. As an international court, the expectation of the reasonableness of

[58] The Court's first articulation of the doctrine is found in *San Miguel Sosa et al. v. Venezuela*, Merits, Reparations and Costs, Inter-Am. Ct. H.R. (ser. C) No. 348, ¶ 114 (February 8, 2018).
[59] *Denunciation of the American Convention* (dissenting opinion of Pazmiño Freire, J.) ¶ 15.
[60] Ibid., ¶ 18.

the Court's judgments is (as it should be) very high. But, it offends legality to ignore what the states decided when adopting the Convention and other subsequent instruments, such as the Protocol of San Salvador. On the other hand, as Judge Sierra Porto notes in his dissenting opinions, the praetorian expansion of powers affects the legitimacy of the Court as a supranational tribunal. In a context of resistance on the part of some states, it is essential for the Court to protect itself and to have what Laurence Helfer has called "survival strategies."[61] By amplifying only that which seems to push the transformative aim, the project of a Latin American common law may not only be intellectually problematic, as some have pointed out,[62] but counterproductive to the health of the inter-American system.[63] Today, it is necessary to protect the human rights institutions that the states decided to establish decades ago; this is the shared responsibility not only of states, which have often sought to weaken the system, but also of its leading actors—that is, the institutions and those who work with them and study them.

VII. Conclusion

In 1916, at the first meeting of the then newly created American Institute of International Law, jurists from different countries adopted a declaration stipulating that, "[i]nternational law is at one and the same time both national and international."[64] A century later, the one aspect of international law that reflects that idea is "inter-American" human rights law. Since the adoption of the American Declaration of the Rights and Duties of Man in 1948, and especially since the 1950s, with the creation of the Inter-American Commission on Human Rights, and later with the adoption of the American Convention on Human Rights in 1969, Latin American human rights institutions have been, are, and will continue to be an essential regional phenomenon of international law.

This chapter has analyzed how Latin America has articulated human rights law, from the origins of "the idea" of human rights to the establishment of the inter-American system to the distinctive forms of interaction and influence between international law and constitutional law. The chapter has shown that the idea of a Latin American common law of human rights—a notion that has

[61] Laurence R. Helfer, "Populism and International Human Rights Law Institutions: A Survival Guide," in *Human Rights in a Time of Populism: Challenges and Responses*, ed. Gerald L. Neuman (Cambridge: Cambridge University Press, 2020), 218–249.

[62] See Coddou, "A Critical Account of Ius Constitutionale Commune"; Giménez and Alterio, "Transformative Constitutionalism."

[63] See Sergio Verdugo, "Can the Idea of a Latin American Ius Constitutionale Commune a Failed Promise?," *European Yearbook of Constitutional Law* 6 (forthcoming).

[64] Elihu Root, "The Declaration of the Rights and Duties of Nations Adopted by the American Institute of International Law," *American Journal of International Law* 10 (1916): 211–221, at 213, https://doi.org/10.2307/2187520.

become highly influential in the past decade—is an example of the outer limits of the potential integration.

The impressive development of international human rights law in Latin America has made regional bodies critical players in protecting and promoting a shared language of rights. States, advocates, and scholars understand how important it is to preserve the authority of the Latin American human rights institutions as a project of Latin American transnational law. However, this project must ensure that the integration between national law and international law, while responding to common objectives—rule of law, democracy, social justice, and human rights—does not affect the norms and principles that make such integration possible. As Latin American countries have paid a high price when democracy has been at risk, it is imperative that Latin American international law can serve those values with full adherence to the norms and principles that make them possible in the first place.

PART IV
NEW DOCTRINES

20

Contributions of Latin America to International Law

Reparations for Human Rights Violations

Claudio Grossman Guiloff

I. Introduction

Latin America has played a significant role in developing the law of reparations for human rights violations. The concept of reparations was initially conceived in international law as a state obligation based on minimum standards of treatment of foreign nationals. This obligation developed further in the 1900s when individuals became subjects of international law. However, the specific content of this obligation was largely left to interpretation by the universal and regional human rights systems. This chapter examines Latin America's contribution to developing the obligation of full reparations.

The basic premise of reparations for human rights violations is restoring the situation that existed before the violation. That said, restoring only provides guidance because restoring a situation that no longer exists is impossible since the consequences of wrongdoing cannot be erased. Further, as this chapter will explain, human rights violations entail not only the reparations for individual harm but also the reestablishment of the rule of law as a whole. Accordingly, this chapter refers to the development of the concept of full reparations, including measures that directly impact the victims, society as a whole, and the rule of law.

II. Development of the Law of Reparations

Before analyzing reparations in the inter-American system, it is important first to explain the standards of protection that existed in international law on protecting people's rights prior to the development of human rights norms in the twentieth century (e.g., minimum standard and nondiscrimination). Traditionally, international law—construed as "positive international law," not as the pre-Westphalian natural law system—was exclusively defined as the law

Claudio Grossman Guiloff, *Contributions of Latin America to International Law* In: *Latin American International Law in the Twenty-First Century*. Edited by: Alejandro Chehtman, Alexandra Huneeus, and Sergio Puig, Oxford University Press.
DOI: 10.1093/9780197754016.003.0020

applicable to interstate relations. The past century has, however, brought about a growing interdependence among states in practically every field of human activity, especially after the establishment of the United Nations and the subsequent boom in international/regional organizations.[1] The international community moved from an international law model centered exclusively on states' rights and duties vis-à-vis one another to a richer landscape where the individual's relationship with the state and the state's obligations to the individual have become the objects of study.

Consistent with these developments in the international law landscape, reparations in international law primarily developed as an interstate concept—a duty owed to a state for a violation of the state's rights committed by another state. In classical positive international law, individuals were not considered subjects of international law and, thus, were not directly entitled to reparation for wrongdoing against them.[2]

Reparation for harm suffered by individuals began as an obligation owed to the state of the individual's nationality for violations by another state based on the minimum standard of treatment to foreign nationals as prescribed under international law. This included, among other rights, due process, principles of legality, and compensation for expropriated or confiscated property. Under the minimum standard theory, the state alone could decide whether to exercise diplomatic protection on the individual's behalf and whether to agree with other states on the content and scope of the reparation.[3]

Thus, since the beginning of judicial adjudication before international tribunals, it is a general principle of international law that breaching an international obligation involves an obligation to make reparation in an adequate form.[4] In 1928, in *Factory at Chorzów*, the Permanent Court of International Justice clearly articulated the content of this general obligation, noting that "reparation must, as far as possible, wipe out all the consequences of the illegal act and re-establish the situation which would, in all probability, have existed if that act had not been committed."[5] The 2001 Draft Articles on the Responsibility of States

[1] See generally P. K. Menon, "The International Personality of Individuals in International Law: A Broadening of the Traditional Doctrine," *Journal of Transnational Law & Policy* 1 (1992): 151.

[2] Under the previous interstate view, exercising diplomatic protection was understood as an assertion of the state's own rights rather than those of the individual victim: "By taking up the case of one of its subjects and by resorting to diplomatic action or international judicial proceedings on his behalf, a State is, in reality, asserting its own rights—its right to ensure, in the person of its subjects, respect for the rules of international law." *The Mavrommatis Palestine Concessions*, P.C.I.J. (ser. A) No. 2, 112 (1924).

[3] Ibid.

[4] *Factory at Chorzów (Germany v. Poland)*, Claim for Indemnity, P.C.I.J. (ser. A) No. 9, 21 (1927).

[5] See *Factory at Chorzów (Germany v. Poland)*, Judgment, P.C.I.J. (ser. A) No. 17, 125 (1928) (elaborating further that "[r]estitution in kind, or, if this is not possible, payment of a sum corresponding to the value which a restitution in kind would bear; the award, if need be, of damages for loss sustained which would not be covered by the restitution in kind or payment in place of it—such

for Internationally Wrongful Acts reiterated, and even crystallized, this principle by establishing that "[t]he responsible State is under an obligation to make full reparation for the injury caused by the internationally wrongful act."[6] Moreover, the International Court of Justice (ICJ), foreign investment tribunals, and other jurisdictional and quasi-jurisdictional international bodies have recognized this principle.[7] Suffice it to say that the idea that harm must be followed by a means of remedying that harm is well established in the international *corpus juris.*

While these standards and developments were taking place at the supranational level, Latin American legal scholars contributed their own additions to the international law theory on reparations. Indeed, Latin America was an active proponent of the principle of nondiscrimination as the applicable rule for remedies and reparations, as opposed to the minimum standard of treatment theory.[8] Further, Latin American states and jurists reacted against the theory of the minimum standard, which afforded protection only to foreigners, because it violated the principle of nondiscrimination by granting foreigners more protection than the nationals of the state. By the end of the nineteenth century, during a period in which Latin American states formally emerged as independent from the Spanish and Portuguese empires, Argentinian scholar Carlos Calvo presented a new thesis (later known as the Calvo Doctrine):

> Firstly, that the principle of indemnity and diplomatic intervention in favor of foreigners, for damages suffered in cases of civil war, has not been accepted by any nation in Europe or America. Secondly, that the governments of powerful nations who exercise or impose this so-called right, against relatively weak states, are committing an abuse of power and force which nothing can justify, and which is as contrary to their own legislation as it is to international practice and political expediency.[9]

Moreover, in the context of the International Law Commission's work, the contribution of Carlos Calvo to the development of international law has been

are the principles which should serve to determine the amount of compensation due for an act contrary to international law").

[6] Int'l Law Comm'n, *Draft Articles on Responsibility of States for Internationally Wrongful Acts,* U.N. Doc. A/56/10 (2001), arts. 12, 28, 31.

[7] James Crawford, *State Responsibility: The General Part* (Cambridge: Cambridge University Press, 2013), 481. *See Revue de droit international et de législation comparée* (1869).

[8] Neither the theory of nondiscrimination nor the minimum standard theory recognizes any international legal right for nationals of the state who engaged in the alleged rights violation. Instead, the law of human rights combined elements of both theories by recognizing an individual's rights (minimum standard theory) and expanding these rights to everyone without discrimination (nondiscrimination principle).

[9] Crawford, *State Responsibility,* 427.

acknowledged, for instance, in the *Report on International Responsibility* (1956) on the topic of state responsibility, by citing Calvo's thesis: "[a]liens who establish themselves in a country are certainly entitled to the same rights of protection as nationals, but they cannot claim any greater measure of protection."[10] Further, the third report on diplomatic protection (2002) noted that the Calvo Doctrine sought to outlaw all forms of diplomatic protection by invoking two principles: the sovereign equality of states, which prohibited foreign intervention, and the equality of nationals and aliens, which deprived aliens of their claim to privileged treatment.[11]

The notion of full reparation[12] was developed in Latin America by the reaction against mass and gross human rights violations that resulted from the military dictatorships that emerged on the continent in the 1960s. This reaction occurred within the framework of the inter-American system of human rights due to the mobilization of victims and nongovernmental organizations, the independent action of the inter-American system supervisory organs, the Inter-American Commission on Human Rights (IACHR) and the Inter-American Court of Human Rights (IACtHR), and the governments that provided support and legitimacy to the inter-American organs' decisions.

These organs, entities, and individuals primarily operated based on the American Convention on Human Rights (Pact of San José, Costa Rica) (American Convention), seeking reparations predominantly through interpreting Article 63 of said text. As noted by Pablo Saavedra Alessandri, the executive secretary of the IACtHR, the American Convention gave the Court jurisdiction to order states to make reparations for "the consequences of the measure or situation that constituted the breach of . . . [rights]." By granting this jurisdiction, the Court could dictate measures designed to address the victims' needs individually and collectively, as well as the structural problems originating from the violation. This ability to correct the sources of a human rights violation (e.g., the lack of proper legislation) creates the understanding that reparations have an *erga omnes* character. For example, Saavedra observed that this is the case when reparations include guarantees of nonrepetition.[13] Further, in applying American Convention Article 63(1), the IACtHR stated that violations of

[10] Int'l Law Comm'n, Report on International Responsibility by Mr. F.V. Garcia-Amador, Special Rapporteur, U.N. Doc. A/CN.4/96, 201-202, ¶¶ 145–150 (1956).

[11] Int'l Law Comm'n, Third report on diplomatic protection, by Mr. John Dugard, Special Rapporteur, U.N. Doc. A/CN.4/523 & Add.1, 76, ¶ 121 (2002).

[12] In practice, there is no consistent use of terms. Both "full reparations" and "integral reparations" have been used to refer to direct and indirect damages.

[13] Pablo Saavedra Alessandri, "Some Reflections Regarding the Structural Impact of the Decisions of the Inter-American Court of Human Rights," in *Ius Constitutionale Commune en América Latina: Textos Básicos para su Compensión*, ed. Armin von Bogdandy, Mariela Morales Antoniazzi, and Eduardo Ferrer Mac-Gregor (Munich, Germany: Max Planck Institute for Comparative Public Law and International Law, 2017), 464.

international obligations that cause harm necessitate "the obligation to make adequate reparations," and this necessity "reflects a customary norm" fundamental to the contemporary rules on state responsibility.[14] The Court has considered it a rule of customary international law and a principle.

The law of reparations developed within the inter-American system as a whole, which includes not only Latin America but also Canada, the United States, and the Caribbean countries. By ratifying the Charter of the Organization of American States, these states fall under the IACHR's jurisdiction. For the states that have not ratified the Pact of San José, the IACHR will apply the American Declaration on the Rights and Duties of Man adopted in 1948 in Bogotá. For the latter, Article XVIII provides:

> Every person may resort to the courts to ensure respect for his legal rights. There should likewise be available to him a simple, brief procedure whereby the courts will protect him from acts of authority that, to his prejudice, violate any fundamental constitutional rights.

While some observe that the application of this article has become customary law, for some states, IACHR decisions made under the American Declaration have only a recommendatory character.[15] However, this debate cannot simply be reduced to choosing between these two options. Instead, the nature of the violation and the content of the reparation could inform the normative value of the IACtHR's decisions (e.g., summary executions vis-à-vis restrictions to the right to appeal in certain circumstances). Second, the IACtHR decisions concerning reparations are unquestionably binding and require prior ratification of the American Convention and acceptance of the Court's jurisdiction. Therefore, states cannot excuse themselves from complying with the reparations issued by the IACtHR by relying on their domestic law.[16] Only Latin American countries and a handful of Caribbean countries have ratified the American Convention.[17]

[14] *Gonzales Lluy et al. v Ecuador*, Preliminary Objections, Merits, Reparations, and Costs, Inter-Am. Ct. H.R. (ser. C) No. 298, 92–93 (September 1, 2015).

[15] Pedro Nikken, "La Declaración Universal y la Declaración Americana. La formación del modern derecho internacional de los derechos humanos," *Revista del Instituto Interamericano de Derechos Humanos*, special issue (1989): 82.

[16] Claudio Nash Rojas, *Las Reparaciones ante la Corte Interamericana de Derechos Humanos (1988–2007)* (2nd ed., Santiago, Chile: Center for Human Rights, 2009), 34, in relation to *Velásquez Rodríguez. v. Honduras*, Judgment, Reparations, and Costs, Inter-Am. Ct. H.R. (ser. C) No. 7, ¶ 30 (July 21, 1989); *Godínez Cruz v. Honduras*, Judgment, Reparations, and Costs, Inter-Am. Ct. H.R. (ser. C) No. 8, ¶ 28 (July 21, 1989); *Bámaca Velásquez v. Guatemala*, Judgment, Reparations, and Costs, Inter-Am. Ct. H.R. (ser. C) No. 91, ¶ 39 (February 22, 2002); *Trujillo Oroza v. Bolivia*, Judgment, Reparations, and Costs, Inter-Am. Ct. H.R. (ser. C) No. 92, ¶ 61 (February 27, 2002).

[17] "Treaty Ratifications: American Convention on Human Rights," U.N.T.S., accessed February 7, 2023, https://treaties.un.org/pages/showdetails.aspx?objid=08000002800f10e1.

Within the inter-American system, the law of reparations facilitates the presentation of legal claims by and for individuals and nongovernmental organizations alleging human rights violations.[18] Third parties can present complaints, even without the victims' knowledge, or by IACHR initiative (*motu proprio*). As the late Judge A. A. Cançado Trindade of the ICJ and former IACtHR's chair noted, this right is the fundamental clause of the American Convention and the other human rights treaties that also call for it.[19] Within the inter-American system, the right to petition incorporates the victim's right to submit their own arguments and evidence when the court determines reparation, to access and obtain justice, and to plead autonomously.[20] This possibility for the victims to act autonomously in presenting their claims with regard to reparations developed jurisprudentially in proceedings before the IACtHR. During the first contentious case before the IACtHR, *Velásquez Rodíguez v. Honduras*, the victims' lawyers acted as members of the IACtHR's legal team with its approval but were allowed to fully present the position of the victims. Since then, a practice emerged that ultimately led to modifying the Court's statute wherein, once the IACHR brings a case to the IACtHR, the victim's lawyers may present their client's claims independently of the IACtHR's legal team.[21] The Court has also implemented the Inter-American Public Defenders to represent a victim who does not have legal representation or cannot pay for it.

Furthermore, the "right of individual petition" ensures that state parties respect their obligations, and that individuals can vindicate any violated rights. In addition to multiple opportunities for civil society to communicate with the supervisory organs (in particular, the IACHR), these possibilities create a domain for non-state actors' participation. When the American Convention is ratified, or under the American Declaration, individuals can thus present claims asserting that their protected rights were violated. However, only the IACHR can bring a case before the IACtHR or a state. Nevertheless, the IACHR will do so after consulting with the victims, and once the case is before the Court, the victims

[18] For the Western Hemisphere, individuals gained access to international justice in the early 1900s. In this system, reparations are referenced in the American Convention, art. 63; the Inter-American Convention on the Prevention, Punishment and Eradication of Violence Against Women (Convention of Belém do Pará), art. 7; the American Declaration on the Rights of Indigenous Peoples, art. XXX and XXXIII; and the Inter-American Convention on Protecting the Human Rights of Older Persons, art. 9. States that have not ratified the American Convention are subject to the jurisdiction of the IACHR by the singular fact that they ratified the Charter of the Organization of American States. The IACHR, in that case, applies the American Declaration on the Rights and Duties of Man.

[19] A. A. Cançado Trindade, *International Law for Humankind: Towards a New Jus Gentium*, vol. 1 (Amsterdam: Brill, 2006), 313 n. 1111.

[20] Ibid., 312; *Rules of the Procedure*, Inter-Am. Ct. H.R., art. 25.

[21] *See* Statute of the Inter-American Court of Human Rights, art. 44.

are entitled to direct representation.[22] These possibilities exist because victims' participation is central to protecting human rights.

Additionally, Latin America's role in developing the law of reparations is further demonstrated by the adoption of the norms concerning reparations generated in the inter-American system by organs such as the UN Committee Against Torture and the UN General Assembly Resolution 60/147: "Basic Principles and Guidelines on the Right to a Remedy and Reparations for Victims of Gross Violations of Human Rights Law and Serious Violations of International Humanitarian Law." Chile co-presented the joint draft resolution of the Basic Principles and Guidelines on behalf of forty-five delegations.[23] The preamble of the Basic Principles and Guidelines also endorses American Convention Article 25.

III. The Evolution of the Law of Reparation within the Inter-American System

In the Inter-American System of Human Rights, the notion of reparation includes "integral or comprehensive reparations," meaning reparations include restitution of the infringed right, satisfaction, rehabilitation measures, the search for truth and justice, and guarantees of nonrepetition, in addition to compensation for material and nonmaterial damages.[24] This broad notion of reparations differentiates the inter-American system, for example, from the European Human Rights System, in which reparations are generally left to the state alone and consist mostly of pecuniary compensation. In the African system, there has been a growing trend to follow the concept of integral reparations used within the inter-American system framework. Accordingly, the most extensive interpretation of the scope of reparations owed by violating states primarily derives from IACHR and IACtHR jurisprudence.

Integral or comprehensive reparation, therefore, goes beyond the classical reparation of the injury (material and immaterial) through economic compensation because it considers the injury and impact that a human rights violation produces in both an individual and a collective dimension. Thus, reparations are

[22] *Rules of the Procedure*, Inter-Am. Ct. H.R., art. 25.

[23] See General Assembly, Joint draft resolution submitted by Chile on behalf of forty-five delegations to the Third Committee, U.N. Doc. A/C.3/60/L.24 (2005).

[24] *See* Pablo Saavedra Alessandri, "40 Years Changing Realities. A Look at The Structural Impact of the Decisions of the Inter-American Court of Human Rights," in *Cumplimiento e impacto de las sentencias de la Corte Interamericana y el Tribunal Europeo de Derechos Humanos. Transformando Realidades*, ed. by Armin von Bogdandy et al. (Munich, Germany: Max Planck Institute for Comparative Public Law and International Law, 2019), 558–567.

oriented not only from a human being's economic perspective but also from a broader perspective and immersed in a world of social interaction.[25]

As introduced earlier, the law on reparations predated the inter-American system, as evidenced by the American Convention's inclusion of a definition of reparations in Article 63. However, the full scope of appropriate reparations for human rights violations was not fully developed until the late 1980s to early 2000s, when allegations of gross human rights violations in several Latin American countries, including Chile and Colombia, were addressed in IACHR and IACtHR jurisprudence. Thus, the principle of full reparations was developed through decisions of the IACHR and IACtHR. The role of the IACHR was particularly important prior to the creation and widespread utilization of the IACtHR, and because only the IACHR may bring cases to the IACtHR. The first contested case brought by the IACHR was *Ángel Manfredo Velásquez Rodríguez*, against Honduras, in 1986.

After the IACtHR was established, the IACHR continued to play a role by representing the interests of the victims before the IACtHR. Later, the Court's regulations were modified to allow victims to appear before the tribunal once a case is brought to the Court, therefore creating another avenue to present victim's views on the content of reparations. The pendulum on the law of reparations then moved from the IACHR, which was the final organ, to the IACtHR, which became the final decision maker.

Beginning in the 1980s, the inter-American system, particularly through the IACHR, started the process whereby reparations could not be restricted to pecuniary damages. During that time, gross and mass human rights violations occurred or were taking place. In responding to the victims' lawyers, the IACHR concluded that mere monetary compensation could not achieve the goal of satisfying the victims and their families, achieving justice, and ensuring the restoration of peace in society. Thus, in 1988, the IACHR first recommended reparations and monetary compensation in Case 9755 against Chile.[26] The IACHR also recommended that Chile compensate victims and their families for moral injury.[27]

A further development took place when the IACtHR, in *Velásquez Rodríguez*, considered "the seriousness of the crime of enforced disappearance [means] just compensation could not be limited to monetary aspects, but instead should include ethical redress" which incorporates the authority's public actions that "demonstrate the government's unequivocal condemnation" of enforced disappearances, "remembrance of the victims through public tributes," and

[25] Ibid., 610.

[26] *Annual Report of the Inter-American Commission on Human Rights, 1987-1988*, Inter-Am. Comm'n H.R., Case No. 9755, Report No. 01a/88, OEA/Ser.L/V/II.74 document 10 rev. 1 (1988).

[27] Case No. 9755, Report No. 01a/88, OEA/Ser.L/V/II.74 document 10 rev. 1.

investigation of the facts of the enforced disappearance and punishment for the perpetrators.[28] Notwithstanding the IACHR's view, the IACtHR only considered monetary compensation mandatory.[29] However, the IACHR's articulated view on reparations had allowed parties before the IACtHR to reiterate the expansive view of reparations, ultimately causing the IACtHR to embrace the view of full reparations.

Another development in the IACtHR law of reparations took place in *Aloeboetoe v. Suriname*. In the reparations phase, the Court required measures beyond monetary payments, ordering the state to reopen a school and provide effective education.[30] The Court also ordered the creation of a trust fund and a foundation. Then, in *Benavides Cevallos v. Ecuador*, the Court ordered the state to investigate human rights violations as part of the reparations the state must fully satisfy.[31] The Court continued on this trend by ordering broader measures of reparation such as obligations to reform legislation that violate human rights standards and the construction of public memorials.[32]

These modes of reparations are considered "measures of satisfaction and non-repetition."[33] Satisfaction includes, at a minimum, the state's obligation to publish the Court's ruling and publicly acknowledge its responsibility. Nonrepetition refers to institutional reforms intended to cease an ongoing or structural violation and to prevent future similar violations.[34] These measures have become tools for removing laws contrary to human rights and for helping states develop legislation and institutions that guarantee human rights.[35]

The satisfaction measures aim to repair nonmaterial damage (i.e., "the suffering and distress caused by the violation, such as the loss of values that are very significant for people and any non-pecuniary alteration"). They include both acts or works of public scope or repercussion, such as the transmission of an official message of condemnation of the human rights violations in question that aims to recognize what happened, recover the memory of the victims, acknowledge

[28] *Velasquez Rodriguez v. Honduras*, Inter-Am. Comm'n H.R., Case No. 7920, Res. No. 22/86 (April 18, 1986).

[29] *Velasquez Rodriguez v. Honduras*, Judgment, Reparations, and Costs, Inter-Am. Ct. H.R. (ser. C) No. 7, ¶¶ 13–14 (July 21, 1989).

[30] *Aloeboetoe v. Suriname*, Judgment, Reparations, Costs, Inter-Am. Ct. H.R. (ser. C) No. 15, 24 (September 10, 1993).

[31] *Benavides-Cevallos v. Ecuador*, Judgment, Merits, Reparations, and Costs, Inter-Am. Ct. H.R. (ser. C.) No. 38, 12–13 (June 19, 1998).

[32] *Suarez Rosero v. Ecuador*, Judgment, Reparations, and Costs, Inter-Am. Ct. H.R. (ser. C) No. 44, 18–19 (January 20, 1999).

[33] *Molina Theissen v. Guatemala*, Judgment, Reparations, and Costs, Inter-Am. Ct. H.R. (ser. C) No. 108, 37–38 (July 3, 2004).

[34] See also *Claude Reyes v. Chile*, Judgment, Merits, Reparations, and Costs, Inter-Am. Ct. H.R. (ser. C) No. 151 (September 19, 2006); *Mayagna (Sumo) Awas Tingni Community v. Nicaragua*, Judgment, Merits, Reparations, and Costs, Inter-Am. Ct. H.R. (ser. C) No. 79 (August 31, 2001).

[35] Alessandri, "Some Reflections," 502.

their dignity, provide comfort to their loved ones, or have high-ranking officials ask for public forgiveness.

The Court has also ordered that radio broadcasts be made with the content of the judgment (e.g., in the cases of *Rosenda Cantú and others v. Mexico, Tiu Tojin v. Guatemala, Sawhoyamaxa Indigenous Community v. Paraguay*, and the *Yakye Axa Indigenous Community v. Paraguaya*). In this last case, the Court ordered that the state transmit the judgment through the community radio in the Exet and Guarani languages.

Furthermore, in *Last Temptation of Christ (Olmedo Bustos and others)*, the IACtHR held that Chile's film censorship laws violated Chile's obligations in Article 2 of the Pact of San José and the right to freedom of expression in Article 13 of the Convention. Thus, "the State must modify its domestic legal system, within a reasonable period of time, in order to abolish prior censorship to allow the exhibition of the film *The Last Temptation of Christ*."[36] Accordingly, in June 2001, the Chilean National Congress approved the draft constitutional reform bill, which codifies the right to free artistic creation by replacing cinematographic censorship with a film rating system.[37]

The Court addressed the issue of amnesty laws in *Barrios Altos*, which dealt with the extrajudicial killings of fifteen persons and the violation of personal integrity of four other persons by members of the Peruvian army during the Alberto Fujimori administration. In 1995, Peru passed amnesty laws that exonerated the military, police forces, and civilians who participated in human rights violations between 1980 and 1995. According to the IACtHR,

> [s]elf-amnesty laws lead to the defenselessness of the victims and the perpetuation of impunity, and are therefore manifestly incompatible with the letter and spirit of the American Convention. This type of law impedes the identification of the individuals responsible for human rights violations, since it hinders the investigation and access to justice and prevents the victims and their families from knowing the truth and receiving the corresponding reparation.[38]

Since then, for example, in *19 Comerciantes v. Colombia* (2004) and *Gutiérrez Soler v. Colombia*, the Court established that this measure includes the obligation of the state to provide, free of charge, through its specialized health institutions (or those designated), the physical and psychological (or psychological and psychiatric; or dental) treatment required by the victims (or their family

[36] *Olmedo Bustos et al. v. Chile*, Judgment, Merits, Reparations, and Costs, Inter-Am. Ct. H.R. (ser. C) No. 73 (February 5, 2001).

[37] See Alessandri, "40 Years Changing Realities," 569.

[38] *Barrios Altos v. Peru*, Judgment, Merits, Inter-Am. Ct. H.R. (ser. C) No. 75, ¶¶ 42–43 (March 14, 2001).

members), including the necessary medications. The Court has determined that beneficiaries must be adequately informed throughout the process. In the case of *Familia Barrios v. Venezuela*, the Court ordered that treatment should be provided in places close to the residence. In the case of *Durand and Ugarte v. Peru*, the state committed to covering the costs related to lifelong health services for beneficiaries.

The IACtHR and IACHR have also considered measures of rehabilitation as a form of reparations. In *Palacio de Justicia v. Colombia*, the IACHR included measures of rehabilitation in the order of reparations, such as providing free, immediate, effective, and adequate medical, psychiatric, and psychological treatment to victims.[39] Moreover, in the category of "other reparations," the Commission requested that the IACtHR order the state to provide training to its security forces.[40]

As reflected in the jurisprudence discussed above, orders of reparations have varied throughout the years, culminating in an understanding that full and comprehensive reparations are necessary and cannot be merely monetary compensation. This was touched on *expressis verbis* in *Gonzales Lluy et al v. Ecuador*, where the IACtHR recognized that the duty of reparations means

> [t]he reparation of the harm caused by the violation of an international obligation requires, whenever possible, full restitution (*restitutio in integrum*), which consists in the re-establishment of the previous situation. If this is not feasible, as in most cases of human rights violations, the Court will determine measures to guarantee the rights that have been violated and to redress the consequences of the violations. Therefore, the Court has found it necessary to award different measures of reparation in order to redress the damage fully, so that, in addition to pecuniary compensation, measures of restitution, rehabilitation and satisfaction, and guarantees of non-repetition, have special relevance to the harm caused.[41]

In that case, the IACtHR ordered a plethora of reparations, including ordering the state to investigate, prosecute, and punish; measures of restitution, rehabilitation, and satisfaction; an education scholarship to the individual harmed; housing for the individual harmed; and guarantees of nonrepetition.[42]

[39] *Rodríguez Vera, et al. v. Colombia*, Judgment, Preliminary Objections, Merits, Reparations, and Costs, Inter-Am. Ct. H.R. (ser. C) No. 287, ¶¶ 194–195 (November 14, 2014).

[40] Inter-Am. Ct. H.R. (ser. C) No. 287, ¶ 198.

[41] *Gonzales Lluy et al. v. Ecuador*, Judgment, Preliminary objections, Merits, Reparations, and Costs, Inter-Am. Ct. H.R. (ser. C) No. 298, 93 (September 1, 2015). See also *Torture in International Law: A Guide to Jurisprudence* (Geneva, Switzerland: Association for the Prevention against Torture and Center for Justice and International Law, 2008), 111.

[42] Inter-Am. Ct. H.R. (ser. C) No. 298 (September 1, 2015).

Additionally, in *Villagrán Morales et al. v. Guatemala*, the IACtHR allowed the murdered natural persons and their next of kin to be named directly as injured parties;[43] found that the state violated human rights by allowing or failing to prevent their deaths; espoused that providing reparation to individuals harmed in this way is a principle of international law;[44] and ordered reparations including the payment of nonpecuniary and pecuniary damages,[45] legislative reforms,[46] performance of effective investigations to bring the individual perpetrators to justice,[47] transfer of victim remains to locations requested by the victims' families,[48] and the creation of an educational center in honor of the victims.[49]

In *Maldonado Vargas and Others v. Chile*, the Court held Chile responsible for failing to comply with its duty to adopt domestic legal provisions that guarantee victims an effective judicial remedy to review harmful convictions handed down by the courts. These convictions were imposed in 1974 and 1975, in criminal proceedings during Chile's military dictatorship, in which evidence and confessions were obtained through torture during the victim's detention. The Court ordered Chile to adopt appropriate legislative, administrative, or other measures to "make available to persons convicted by the war councils during the Chilean military dictatorship an effective mechanism to review and annul the sentences of conviction that were handed down in proceedings that may

[43] *Villagrán Morales et al. v. Guatemala*, Judgment, Merits, Inter-Am. Ct. H.R. (ser. C) No. 63, ¶¶ 65–66 (November 19, 1999).

[44] Ibid., ¶¶ 58–59.

[45] Ibid., ¶¶ 82, 93.

[46] Ibid., ¶ 98.

[47] Ibid., ¶¶ 99-101.

[48] Ibid., ¶ 102.

[49] Ibid., ¶ 103. Other examples of domestic reparation programs include "truth commissions," of which numerous instances provide rich and intensive practice in Latin America and Africa. The various truth commissions in South Africa, Guatemala, El Salvador, Haiti, and Panama have recommended extensive reparation programs. Conversely, Chile's program emphasized providing a wider variety of benefits and compensation awards. Inter-Am. Ct. H.R. (ser. C) No. 63, 4. Reparation for violations during the 1973 dictatorship included the creation of organizations dedicated to transparency and truth to provide reliable data on victims. Scholarships, bonuses, pensions, and maintenance were also provided to victims and their families. Additionally, because many people were exiled during the dictatorship, the National Office of Return was created to grant a customs exemption for exiles to pay a lower tax on goods brought into Chile. Finally, the right to petition for reparation was granted to victims and their relatives for actions against the state and against those responsible for crimes committed during the regime. This right has been utilized within Chilean jurisprudence. *See* Case No. 34057/2016 (Casación), Resolution No. 568956 de Corte Suprema, Sala Segunda (Penal) de 6 de Octubre de 2016. Further, truth commissions have demonstrated that legal obligations give rise to reparations and provide good examples of how reparation occurs during political transitions. Pablo De Greiff (ed.), *The Handbook of Reparations* (Oxford: Oxford University Press, 2006), 4. Chile and Argentina both provided compensation, rehabilitation, and services to the victims of dictatorships. Argentina had the earliest reparation program in a South American transition, and the reparation awards were generous. Ibid., 3. A series of reparation laws were passed between 1984 and 1985, and the National Commission on the Disappearance of Persons stated, "[n]orms should be enacted in order to provide economic assistance to the children and or family of the disappeared persons during the repression; scholarships, social assistance, and job positions." Ibid., 22.

have taken into account evidence and/or confessions obtained under torture."[50] As Pablo Saavedra Alessandri points out, the structural problem in *Maldonado Vargas* was that those who had been convicted due to evidence obtained by torture did not have a mechanism to review their convictions. While a formal mechanism for review existed in the Chilean legal system, it was an ineffective remedy because of the local court's restrictive interpretations.[51] In light of the IACtHR's ruling, the Chilean Supreme Court created a more flexible interpretation for review, which was an evolutionary interpretation that effectively protected rights—in this case, the right to an effective judicial remedy. Thus, the structural problem was resolved by annulling not only the case victim's convictions but also all the convictions of those in the same situation.[52]

Recently, in a 2008 report, "Principal Guidelines for a Comprehensive Reparations Policy," the IACHR established the principle that reparations should consist of measures designed to repair the effects of human rights violations.[53] The measure's nature and extent depend on pecuniary and nonpecuniary damages. Moreover, state reparations should result from an open and transparent dialogue and consultation process between civil society and state institutions.[54] The state must also play a primary role in guaranteeing victims' effective access to reparations, including the state's obligation to investigate and punish the persons responsible for human rights violations.[55] Last, in *Lhaka Honhat v. Argentina*, for the first time, the Court dealt with a violation of the right to a healthy environment based on American Convention Article 26. In considering the question of reparations, the Court ordered the creation of a "community development fund" to redress the harms caused.[56]

As a measure of nonrepetition, through its judgments, the Court ordered the responsible states to implement development programs in health, education, production, and infrastructure. These programs can be developed differently, such as creating a community development fund or through national budget public works.

To repair the victims of *Masacre Plan de Sánchez v. Guatemala* and *Masacres de Río Negro v. Guatemala*, respectively, the following programs were implemented

[50] *Maldonado Vargas et al. v. Chile*, Judgment, Merits, Reparations, and Costs, Inter-Am. Ct. H.R. (ser. C) No. 300, ¶ 170 (September 2, 2015).

[51] Alessandri, "40 Years Changing Realities," 580.

[52] Ibid., 580.

[53] Inter-American Commission on Human Rights, *Principal Guidelines for a Comprehensive Reparations Policy*, OAS Doc. OEA/Ser/L/V/II.131, ¶ 1 (2008).

[54] Ibid., ¶ 4.

[55] Ibid., ¶ 5.

[56] *See Indigenous Communities of the Lhaka Honhat (Our Land) Association v. Argentina*, Judgment, Merits, Reparations, and Costs, Inter-Am. Ct. H.R. (ser. C) No. 400, ¶¶ 337–342 (February 6, 2020).

through national budget public works: (1) study and dissemination of the Achí Maya culture in the affected communities through the Academy of Mayan Languages of Guatemala or another similar organization; (2) maintenance and improvements in the road communication system between the indicated communities and the municipal head of Rabinal; (3) sewer system and supply of drinking water; (4) provision of trained teaching personnel in intercultural and bilingual teaching in primary, secondary, and diversified education of these communities; and (5) establishment of a health center in the village of Plan de Sánchez with the appropriate personnel and conditions, as well as the training of the personnel of the Municipal Health Center of Rabinal to provide medical and psychological care to people who require this type of treatment.

In *Comunidad Indígena Yakye Axa v. Paraguay, Comunidad Indígena Xákmok Kásek. v. Paraguay*, and *Caso Comunidad Indígena Sawhoyamaxa v. Paraguay*, the Court considered it more appropriate to urge the state to provide, in accordance with the American Convention on Human Rights, directly and without the creation of a development fund, drinking water and medical and psychological care to members of the community, with particular attention to vulnerable groups, food delivery, installation of latrines, and access to education.

Also, the Court ordered the implementation of programs in health, education, production, and infrastructure through a community development fund. When studying the cases where the Court urged the responsible state to create a community development fund, some points can be highlighted. First, the state and members of the communities must choose a representative to ensure that the implementation of the fund is carried out in accordance with the community's needs. Second, in each repair that involves the establishment of a development fund, the Court ordered the community and the state to prepare an annual report to detail the progress of the projects and the state's investments.

From the jurisprudence of the Court, it can be concluded that many human rights violations result from the actions or omissions of state agents, such as members of the armed forces, police, judicial officials, and prison staff. Thus, the Court seeks to strengthen institutional capacities by training and education in human rights for public officials. Therefore, these measures aim to prevent the recurrence of events such as those that arose from the violations. The Court has also observed that "training, as a system of continuous education, should be extended over a significant period in order to fulfill [these] objectives."

Because training programs in international human rights law constitute a crucial factor for preventing further harm, measures must be adopted to ensure that national and international jurisprudence is effectively applied. In *Massacre of Dos Erres v. Guatemala*, the Court ordered this measure for members of the armed forces, judges, and prosecutors. The Court specified that mention should be made of other cases involving Guatemala and international human rights and humanitarian law instruments "specifically regarding serious human rights violations and access to justice components for victims."

By analyzing the facts and context in which violations occurred in some instances, the Court has found a lack of knowledge about protecting certain human rights in society, which could also affect their protection in that country. That is why, in some cases, the Court has also ordered the state to develop training or awareness campaigns for civil society. For example, in *Servellón García et al. v. Honduras*, the Court ordered a campaign to protect children and young people. In *González et al. ("Campo Algodonero") v. Mexico*, the Court ordered a gender awareness program, taking into account many instances of violence against women. The Court added that it is about repeating the norms and effectively analyzing the inequality of girls and women.

The developments in the law of reparations in the inter-American system show how the IACtHR gave a broader scope to the law of reparations since its first case—*Manfredo Velásquez*. As demonstrated above, this evolution resulted in a holistic concept of reparations, including satisfaction and measures of nonrepetition. This concept evolved essentially as a reaction to mass and gross violations of civil and political rights—including disappearances, summary executions, and torture—that took place in the region as a result of repression by dictatorial regimes.[57]

IV. Reparation in Other International Adjudicatory Bodies

Despite having a shorter trajectory than the Inter-American or European regional systems, the African Court of Human and Peoples' Rights has established a trend toward awarding reparation to individuals. In *Malawi African Association v. Mauritania* (2000), the Court recommended the government provide reparations to the victims.[58] Later, in *Mtikila v. Tanzania* (2013), the Court recognized its power to award reparations for human rights violations but declined due to inadequate evidence of the applicant's claimed losses

[57] The vanguard position adopted by the inter-American system in response to these violations has formed a basis to address economic, social, and cultural rights. See, e.g., *Aloeboetoe v. Suriname; Benavides Cevallos v. Ecuador; Gonzales Lluy et al. v. Ecuador; Masacre Plan de Sánchez v. Guatemala; Masacres de Río Negro v. Guatemala; Comunidad Indígena Yakye Axa v. Paraguay; Comunidad Indígena Xákmok Kásek v. Paraguay; Caso Comunidad Indígena Sawhoyamaxa v. Paraguay; Massacre of Dos Erres v. Guatemala; Servellón García et al. v. Honduras; González et al. ("Campo Algodonero") v. Mexico*(section II).

[58] See *Malawi Africa Association & Amnesty International, Ms Sarr Diop, Union interafricaine des droits de l'Homme and RADDHO, Collectif des veuves et ayants-Droit, Association mauritanienne des droits de l'Homme v. Mauritania*, Af. Comm'n Hum. & Peoples' Rts., Comm. Nos. 54/91, 61/91, 98/93, 164/97, 196/97 (May 11, 2000).

and expenses.[59] Finally, in *Zongo v. Burkina Faso* (2015), the Court ordered reparations for the applicants for the first time in the Court's history, including measures of satisfaction and guarantees of nonrepetition.[60] The Court relied heavily on decisions from the IACtHR and the Articles on State Responsibility to establish its authority to issue reparation.

The European Court of Human Rights (ECtHR) has long maintained a passive approach toward restitution by deferring to the state's discretion to redress a violation and determine the type of restitution provided.[61] Since 2004, however, the ECtHR has notably begun shifting its approach. Two cases can be marked as the start of this novel approach: *Assanidze v. Georgia* and *Ilascu v. Moldova and Russia*.[62] These cases involved the applicant's unlawful detention and a violation of the European Convention on Human Rights Article 5.[63] The ECtHR declared that a breach existed and requested the immediate release of the applicants, as continuing the unlawful detention would entail continuing the violation.[64]

At the international level, reparations in the International Criminal Court (ICC) jurisprudence, and as conceived within the Rome Statute, have also referred to the practice of the inter-American system.[65] Under Rome Statute Article 75, the ICC can issue an order for reparation. As of 2022, the Court has ordered reparations orders in four cases: *Lubanga* (2015), *Katanga* (2017), *Al Mahdi* (2017), and *Ntaganda* (2021). Moreover, the Ntaganda order modified the initial legal framework on reparations, as laid out in *Lubanga*, thus making the current framework more victim-centered.[66] For example, when calculating the imposition of monetary liability upon the accused individual, the Court considered the harm and damage suffered by the victims instead of considering the harm caused by the person in question.[67]

By placing victims at the center of the calculations for compensation, the ICC is shifting away from its previous paradigm. Thus, the modes of liability,

[59] See *Mtikila v. United Republic of Tanzania*, Reparations, Af. Ct. Hum. & Peoples' Rts., App. No. 011/2011 (June 13, 2014).

[60] See *Beneficiaries of Late Norbert Zongo et al. v. Burkina Faso*, Reparations, Af. Ct. Hum. & Peoples' Rts., App. No. 013/2011 (June 5, 2015).

[61] See "Pilot Judgments," European Ct. H.R., December 2022, https://www.echr.coe.int/documents/fs_pilot_judgments_eng.pdf.

[62] *Assanidze v. Georgia*, European Ct. H.R., App. No. 71503/01 (April 8, 2004); *Ilascu v. Moldova and Russia*, European Ct. H.R., App. No. 48787/99 (July 8, 2004).

[63] *See* App. No. 71503/01; App. No. 48787/99.

[64] *See* App. No. 71503/01; App. No. 48787/99.

[65] See, e.g., *Prosecutor v. Al Mahdi*, Reparations Order, Int'l Crim. Ct., Case No. ICC-01/12-01/15-236 (August 17, 2017), ¶ 85, n. 134; *Prosecutor v. Ntaganda*, Reparations Order, Int'l Crim. Ct., Case No. ICC-01/04-02/06-2659 (March 8, 2021), ¶¶ 48, 57, 61, 127–128, 230–231, 283.

[66] *See* ICC-01/04-02/06-2659, ¶¶ 28-103 (listing the reparation principles).

[67] Marina Lostal, "The Ntaganda Reparations Order: A Marked Step towards a Victim-Centered Reparations Legal Framework at the ICC," *EJIL: Talk!* (blog), May 24, 2021, https://www.ejiltalk.org/the-ntaganda-reparations-order-a-marked-step-towards-a-victim-centred-reparations-legal-framework-at-the-icc/.

gravity of crimes, and conditions for mitigation of punishment no longer play a role in calculating monetary compensation.[68] However, the shift to a victim-centered approach has vastly increased the calculated reparations. For example, in *Ntaganda*, the accused owed approximately US$30 million,[69] whereas in *Lubanga*, the maximum compensation requested was approximately US$10 million. Because the ICC handles the criminal responsibility of individuals and not that of states, the convicted person's inability to make reparations to their victims poses a significant problem—a problem that has only intensified with this novel victim-centric approach to reparations.

Committees and other international supervisory organs that have addressed the issue of reparations are also relevant. In 2012, the Committee against Torture issued General Comment No. 3, discussing the implementation of Article 14 of the UN Convention against Torture and Other Cruel, Inhuman or Degrading Treatment or Punishment (UNCAT). Article 14 details the right of victims of torture or cruel, inhuman, and degrading treatment to seek redress and receive compensation and rehabilitation.[70] According to the Committee, reparation is contained within the concept of redress, which also includes effective remedy.[71] Importantly, in agreement with the recent jurisprudence of the IACHR and IACtHR, the term "redress" includes the whole spectrum of measures, from restitution, satisfaction, and compensation to rehabilitation and guarantees of nonrepetition. General Comment No. 3 also includes the following key points: *restitution* means the victim is returned to their status prior to the violation; *compensation* means the victim is economically compensated for assessable pecuniary or nonpecuniary damage resulting from the violation; *rehabilitation* includes medical and psychosocial care, legal and social services, and the acquisition of new skills as required by any change of circumstances caused by the violation; *satisfaction and the right to truth* include effective measures to end any continuing violations and to both verify and publicize the facts of the violation; *guarantees of nonrepetition* means the state undertakes preventative efforts to combat impunity for violations; *victims* are persons individually or collectively harmed by the acts or omissions that constitute a violation of the Convention; and, last, *reparations vs. criminal proceedings* clarifies that compensation does not depend on the establishment of criminal liability.[72]

[68] ICC-01/04-02/06-2659, ¶ 98.

[69] Ibid., ¶ 247.

[70] Convention against Torture and Other Cruel, Inhuman or Degrading Treatment or Punishment, 1465 U.N.T.S. 85.

[71] United Nations Committee Against Torture and Other Cruel, Inhuman or Degrading Treatment or Punishment, General Comment No. 3—Implementation of Article 14 by States Parties, U.N. Doc. CAT/C/GC/3 (2012).

[72] CAT/C/GC/3, ¶¶ 2–5.

V. Reparations as the Right of the Victims

The inter-American system established that the right to reparations is not a benefit of the victim but a right that the victim can demand that the state fulfill.[73] Thus, the state must respond to these demands and provide comprehensive reparations in accordance with international law. Consequently, pursuant to the IACHR and IACtHR jurisprudence, states must implement reparations programs that include measures of satisfaction, guarantees of nonrepetition, and rehabilitation.

In General Comment No. 31, the Human Rights Committee clarified that, under Article 2 of the International Covenant on Civil and Political Rights, the adequate remedy obligation owed to individuals whose Convention rights are violated cannot be discharged if reparations are not issued.[74] Similarly, in its General Comment No. 3, the Committee against Torture clarified the state's obligations under UNCAT Article 14 for victims of Convention violations, including providing a full spectrum of measures amounting to full reparations of both a procedural and substantive nature.[75] Therefore, by centering the right around the victim rather than the state, individuals have both a substantive and procedural right to reparation under the international framework established by UNCAT concerning the prohibition of torture and other cruel, inhuman, or degrading treatment. This right to reparation was likewise explicitly mentioned in Article 24(4) of the recently adopted International Convention for the Protection for All People from Enforced Disappearances (ICPPED).[76] The UN General Assembly has also recognized the right to reparation in the *Basic Principles and Guidelines on the Right to a Remedy and Reparation*, which explains that victims of gross human rights violations have the right to "adequate, effective and prompt reparation for harm suffered," as well as "access to relevant information concerning violations and reparation mechanisms."[77]

Finally, for situations where several victims were subject to abuse, the law has established methods to satisfy the right of reparation accordingly with the State's resources. For example, in cases of transitional justice, the IACtHR usually requires the state to make reparations on a massive scale. Further, these reparations "must be understood in conjunction with other measures of truth

[73] Rojas, *Las Reparaciones*, 15.

[74] Human Rights Committee, CCPR General Comment No. 31—The Nature of the General Legal Obligation Imposed on States Parties to the Covenant, U.N. Doc. CCPR/C/21/Rev.1/Add.13, ¶ 16 (May 26, 2004).

[75] CAT/C/GC/3, ¶ 5.

[76] International Convention for the Protection against Enforced Disappearances, 2716 U.N.T.S. 3.

[77] General Assembly, Basic Principles and Guidelines on the Right to a Remedy and Reparation for Victims of Gross Violations of International Human Rights Law and Serious Violations of International Humanitarian Law, U.N. Doc. A/RES/60/147 (2006), ¶ 11.

and justice, provided that they meet a series of related requirements, including their legitimacy . . .; their adoption in good faith; the degree of social inclusion they allow; the reasonableness and proportionality of the pecuniary measures," amongst other criteria.[78]

VI. The Value of Reparations in the Inter-American System and the Question of Implementation

In Latin America, the great accomplishment of both the Court and Commission in the Inter-American Human Rights System is their ability to fill a vacuum by creating a normative framework with which we can require and demand compliance. The reparation system's regulatory mechanisms benefit both victims of harm by addressing said harm and other citizens of the state by resolving domestic structural shortcomings to protect human rights.[79] The IACtHR has also played a significant role in the development and evolution of human rights on the continent and human rights law more generally, as demonstrated by the impact of the Court's jurisprudential interpretations of the American Convention, by institutional transformation within states' machinery, and by the development of an institutional practice of integral reparations, particularly for guarantees of nonrepetition.[80]

After indicating original reparation measures, the Court requires states to submit an initial report on the decision's implementation within one year. Afterward, the Court monitors compliance by issuing orders, holding hearings, and conducting on-site procedures in the states' territory. The Court exercises this function by monitoring individual cases and joint monitoring of reparation measures ordered in cases against the same state. The joint monitoring mechanism allows the Court to have a greater impact by comprehensively addressing an issue common to several cases involving the same state. It also enables the Court to encourage discussions among the different victim representatives for each case. It allows more dynamic participation by the state officials responsible for implementing reparations at the domestic level.[81]

[78] *Afro-descendant Communities displaced from the Cacarica River Basin (Operation Genesis) v. Colombia*, Judgment, Merits, Reparations, and Costs, Inter-Am. Ct. H.R. (ser. C) No. 270, ¶ 470 (November 20, 2013). See, on the collective conception of reparations, the decisions of the IACtHR: *Operacion Genesis v. Colombia, Kichwa Indigenous People of Sarayaku v. Ecuador, Kaliña and Kokomo Peoples v. Suriname*, and *Maya Kaqchikel v. Guatemala.*

[79] Alessandri, "Some reflections," 468.

[80] Ibid., 501.

[81] Inter-Am. Ct. H.R., "2020 Annual Report," 59, accessed February 6, 2023, https://www.corteidh.or.cr/docs/informe2020/ingles.pdf.

Implementation of reparation measures takes time and can be quite challenging. Moreover, the statistics suggest that it is a daunting task. The latest IACtHR Annual Report, issued in 2020, illustrates the current status of implementation for the Court's orders of reparations. According to the report, 237 cases are in the compliance monitoring stage, which entails monitoring 1,231 reparation measures.[82] Because reparation measures can take many forms, some cases involve measures that are harder to implement than others. Similarly, some cases involve an order of multiple forms of reparations, while others involve only one. Further, even if numerous reparations measures have been executed, the Court keeps the case open until it considers that the involved state(s) have fully complied with the measures.[83]

Since 1986, the Court has considered only forty-two cases "in full compliance" with the indicated reparation measures.[84] This represents around one-sixth of the cases in the compliance monitoring stage. The geographic distribution of cases pending implementation are as follows: Argentina, twenty-three cases; Barbados, one case; Bolivia, four cases; Brazil, nine cases; Chile, eleven cases; Colombia, twenty-four cases; Ecuador, nineteen cases; El Salvador, seven cases; Guatemala, thirty-five cases; Honduras, thirteen cases; Mexico, ten cases; Nicaragua, two cases; Panama, three cases; Paraguay, eight cases; Peru, forty-eight cases; Dominican Republic, four cases; Suriname, three cases; Uruguay, three cases; and Venezuela, eleven cases.[85] Further, in 2020, the Court's monitoring mechanism addressed measures of reparation, including the obligation to investigate, prosecute, and punish gross human rights violations in fourteen cases against Guatemala; the identification, granting of property title, and delivery of lands to three indigenous communities in three cases against Paraguay; providing medical and psychological treatment to victims in nine cases against Colombia; guarantees of nonrepetition in two cases against Honduras concerning protection for human rights defenders, particularly environmentalists; and searching for the location of disappeared persons or the identification of remains in six cases against Colombia and eleven cases against Peru.[86]

However, the states have already complied with many, if not most, reparation measures for many pending cases. The Court is also continually developing

[82] Ibid.
[83] Ibid.
[84] Cases Filed by the Monitoring Compliance with Judgment (Only in Spanish), Inter-American Court of Human Rights, accessed February 6, 2023, https://www.corteidh.or.cr/casos_en_supervision_por_pais_archivados.cfm?lang=en.
[85] Cases at the Monitoring Compliance with Judgment Stage (Only in Spanish), Inter-American Court of Human Rights, accessed February 6, 2023, https://www.corteidh.or.cr/casos_en_supervision_por_pais.cfm?lang=en.
[86] Inter-Am. Ct. H.R., "2020 Annual Report," 59.

its *jurisprudence constante* for the law of reparations. Further, national human rights bodies and ombudsmen can foster compliance with reparation measures at the national level by involving national entities and organs in urging the corresponding public authorities to take specific actions or adopt measures to implement reparations.[87] The national judiciary's role should also be underscored because it can request the state's compliance with specific reparations ordered by the Court.[88] Moreover, the interest shown by academics, nongovernmental organizations, and other members of civil society are relevant to monitoring the implementation of measures of reparations since they contribute to the public debate regarding compliance with international norms.[89] Overall, when observed from the perspective of a long-term process, the Court has yielded encouraging results in terms of implementation as states appear to voluntarily implement the orders of reparations in good faith, in line with American Convention Article 68.

VII. Current Challenges of Populism in the Inter-American System and the Law of Reparations

Historically, international human rights legal institutions confronted authoritarian regimes that continually violated human rights. Today, however, these institutions must confront a new challenge: the threat that populist regimes pose to human rights and international human rights law institutions.[90] Democratically elected governments undermine the system's foundations through rhetoric presenting a Manichean vision of the political landscape. In so doing, these regimes often purport to speak in the name of the abstract concept of "the people," which is utilized to frame political and legal decisions as ones that must rightfully quash the power of an "evil" minority in favor of a "just" majority. Naturally, championing the rights of a specific subset of society—be it national, ethnic, racial, and so on—is incompatible with respecting the rights of minorities.[91] The inter-American system is particularly vulnerable, as populist political leaders have risen in Latin America in the past years,[92] and the fact that populist styles of discourse have deep roots in the histories of many states across the continent. It is, thus, important to analyze how populism poses a

[87] Ibid., 76.
[88] Ibid., 76.
[89] Ibid., 76.
[90] Laurence Helfer, "Populism and International Human Rights Law Institutions: A Survival Guide," in *Human Rights in a Time of Populism*, ed. Gerald L. Neuman (Cambridge: Cambridge University Press, 2020), 219.
[91] Ibid., 219.
[92] Venezuela, Ecuador, and Argentina are just a few states that have seen populist leaders, such as Hugo Chávez, Nicolás Maduro, Rafael Correa, Carlos Menem, and Cristina Kirchner.

threat to human rights, particularly to the international mechanisms created to protect them.

Populism is a political logic in which one leader unites the people and the existing order, which are separated by an internal frontier.[93] Ernesto Laclau argued that since populism is a political logic, it is a phenomenon that can occur in different historical contexts and opposite ideologies and, therefore, should not be associated with only right-wing or left-wing political groups[94]—what some political scientists have referred to as a thin-centered ideology. Moreover, whether a leader is a populist is determined in varying degrees depending on the context in which they act[95] particularly when it comes to their relations with traditionally powerful sectors of society and the media. The rise in populism over the last decades also points to a structural problem in the political sphere, one where the net trust that society has in the institutions of democracy has been eroded by systemic shocks (financial and political crises). According to Kenneth Roberts, the rise in populism is a response to the crisis of political representation.[96]

Populism conflicts with human rights in several ways. First, because populism is closely linked to nationalism, populist states are usually unwilling to accept criticism of, or inquiries into, their internal affairs, such as human rights.[97] Second, populist states are usually wary of globalism and often accuse international systems of violating the principle of noninterference in a state's internal affairs.[98] Third, while populist governments could be democratically elected, the rights of minorities and marginalized peoples are not a high concern for the majority who vote for them.[99] Interestingly, however, the rhetoric used by populist leaders has a tendency to present itself as being in favor of human rights, with the important caveat being that only the rights of a designated subset of the population ("el pueblo," "the silent majority," "the people") are deemed to be worthy of protection.[100]

In Latin American countries with the inter-American system, populist regimes seek absolute control by dismantling the institutions in charge of internal or domestic control and relying on a façade of democracy.[101] This causes

[93] Virginia Morales and Mercedes Barros, "Populismo y derechos ciudadanos: anotaciones sobre un vínculo errante," *Latinoamérica Revista de estudios Latinoamericanos* 67 (2018): 119, 122–123.

[94] Ibid., 122–123, in reference to Ernesto Laclau, "La Razón Populista," in *Fondo de Cultura Económica* (Mexico City: Casa Matriz, 2005).

[95] Ibid., 122–123.

[96] Kenneth Roberts, "Populism, Political Mobilizations, and Crises of Political Representation," in *The Promise and Perils of Populism*, ed. Carlos de la Torre (Lexington: University Press of Kentucky, 2014), 141.

[97] Marcelo Alegre, "Populismo y derechos humanos: ¿Agua y aceite?" *Yale Online Files* (2016): 16–17.

[98] Ibid., 16–17.

[99] Helfer, *Populism*, 222–223.

[100] Ibid., 222–223.

[101] Ibid., 224–225; Alegre, "Populismo," 19–20.

an increase in human rights violations, which in turn overwhelms the internal judiciary and forces victims to rely on international judicial systems.[102] Thus, the inter-American system becomes overloaded with cases from states where governments constantly criticize outsiders' interference and usually react by threatening to leave the system.[103] Being constantly threatened makes it difficult for the inter-American system to function strongly. Further, when populism corrupts and oversaturates the domestic judicial systems, these internal entities cannot play their vital role in assisting with the implementation of international decisions.[104] Therefore, it becomes easier for populist states to ignore international law and international courts.[105]

All of the above connects to the law of reparations, as the inter-American system faces populist regimes that, first, do not fully respect human rights; second, take all available measures to prevent the IACtHR from ordering reparation measures; and third, even when the Court can order said measures, challenge the Court's jurisdiction. The lack of implementation can create movements to challenge the legitimacy of a norm by claiming that it is not supported by state practice. Consequently, the issue of populism threatens states' implementation of the inter-American system's normative developments in a manner that fosters compliance and enforcement.

VIII. Conclusion

Since *Chorzów*, the law of reparations has come a long way. From the Calvo Doctrine in the late 1800s to the advancement of the concept of integral reparations in the context of the IACtHR, the inter-American system has played an important role in the law's development for the countries in Latin America and the Caribbean, and the international community as a whole. Through developing the law of reparations and the concept of integral reparation in its jurisprudence, the IACtHR's judgments aim to promote justice by providing an integral reparation that would satisfy the victims of human rights violations and to avoid repetition by requiring measures that reform the norms and institutions responsible for human rights violations.

[102] Helfer, *Populism*, 224–225; Alegre, "Populismo," 19–20.

[103] Helfer, *Populism*, 224–225; Alegre, "Populismo," 19–20.

[104] Helfer, *Populism*, 224–225.

[105] Ibid., 224–225. See *Expelled Dominican & Haitian Persons v. Dominican Republic*, Judgment, Preliminary Objections, Merits, Reparations, and Costs, Inter-Am. Ct. H.R. (ser. C) No. 282 (August 28, 2014). See also *Apitz Barbera et al. v. Venezuela*, Preliminary Objections, Merits, Reparations, and Costs, Inter-Am. Ct. H.R. (ser. C), No. 182, 66 (August 5, 2008); Alexandra Huneeus and René Urueña, "Treaty Exit and Latin America's Constitutional Courts," *AJIL Unbound* 111 (2018): 456–457.

Certainly, the road has not been easy. The IACtHR has faced, and must still face, significant challenges in implementing its decisions—challenges created, for example, by populist regimes in the region. Further, states do not always immediately comply with the Court's decisions on reparations, particularly those concerning the investigation and punishment of those responsible for the violations. This is a significant issue for some, since it could show the lack of state practice in implementing the Court's decisions. Compliance and the need to fully implement the Court's decisions remain relevant in assessing the impact and efficiency of the law of reparations. Nevertheless, by providing a legal basis supporting justice and transformation, the IACtHR gives vital support to victims' claims—as is reflected, for example, in the rejection of amnesty laws, the prohibition of discrimination, the rejection of *desacato* laws, and the protection of the right to freedom of expression and access to justice. That being said, full compliance remains a valid goal; ultimately, only full compliance will protect the system from erosion.

21

Latin America as a Laboratory of Transitional Justice

*Alejandro Chehtman**

I. Introduction

Latin America has been a scene of constant and radical innovation in the field of transitional justice.[1] The number, breadth, and constant pace of initiatives, ideas, and experiments on this issue are arguably unparalleled in any other part of the world. The region has seen several of the more ambitious and sophisticated institutional attempts at truth-seeking, accountability, reparations, and peace. Its influence in shaping responses to gross human rights violations both in other regions and at a global level is substantial and deep—albeit if sometimes unacknowledged. Landmark milestones include the first operative truth commission and the many developments obtained in subsequent models, the first trial of former heads of state for human rights violations, the development and diffusion of forensic anthropology to investigate massive human rights violations and the use of different techniques to determine filiation, the rights to "truth" and "identity," the conditioning penal benefits for truth (El Salvador), the revolutionizing of the law on remedies before international human rights bodies, as well as the domestic laws on reparations, among others.

This chapter embarks on the challenging task of mapping these key legal ideas and innovations, situating them in their context, and identifying the actors involved in their development. In doing so, it ultimately advocates three broader propositions. First, it argues that the body of law and institutions developed to address gross human rights violations in Latin America have a genuine regional character and that they are distinguished by certain key waves or movements of dominant strategies being implemented and influencing developments in other

* I have benefited from interviews and conversations with many colleagues and relevant actors including Victor Abramovich, León Arslanián, Gabriel Cavallo, Graciela Fernández Meijide, Marcelo Ferrante, Hernán Folgueiro, Manuel Garrido, Ricardo Gil Lavedra, María José Guembe, Manuel Iturralde, Nahuel Maysley, Rafael Mazzella, Luis Moreno Ocampo, Pablo Parenti, Nicolás Sissini, Catalina Smulovitz, Maco Somigliana, Patricia Tappatá, and Francisco Ugas Tapia, among many others.

[1] See, classically, Ruti Teitel, *Transitional Justice* (Oxford: Oxford University Press, 2002).

Alejandro Chehtman, *Latin America as a Laboratory of Transitional Justice* In: *Latin American International Law in the Twenty-First Century*. Edited by: Alejandro Chehtman, Alexandra Huneeus, and Sergio Puig, Oxford University Press. © Oxford University Press 2025. DOI: 10.1093/9780197754016.003.0021

countries. Second, this chapter reflects the legal and institutional innovations that were developed as well as the path dependency we see in this area, from the foundational attempts in the early 1980s. Third, it traces the origins of these developments to collaborations and cross-fertilization between victims and human rights organizations, members of the judiciary, and the academy. Indeed, it shows how ideas traveled within the region and beyond through particular figures and institutions. Finally, this chapter obliquely reflects the consolidation of international (human rights) law as a critical discourse within domestic legal systems in Latin America.[2]

The chapter unfolds as follows. Section II concentrates on the "foundational" period in which many of the initial experiments took place. Section III discusses efforts in truth-seeking conducted mainly in the 1990s. Section IV focuses on the consolidation of "anti-impunity" law in the late 1990s and 2000s. Section V revolves around the extension of this framework to peacemaking in the 2010s. Section VI concludes by identifying critical threads in this rich story.

II. Foundations

In the midst of the political violence in Latin America during the 1970s, many social movements began organizing around different issues, such as women's rights, ethnic rights, and the "new" vocabulary of human rights.[3] In Argentina, family members—mostly women—of victims of enforced disappearance began seeking information regarding their relatives (abducted by the military, typically tortured and killed, and whose bodies were disposed of and rarely found) to file *habeas corpus* petitions. To do this, they had to develop a way to interview victims' families, identify useful information, and hide the files and other information (which was sent to international organizations[4]). They further needed to vet those who approached them to avoid being infiltrated by the military

[2] See Alejandro Chehtman, "International Law and Constitutional Law in Latin America," in *Oxford Handbook of Constitutional Law in Latin America*, ed. Conrado Hubner Méndez et al. (Oxford: Oxford University Press, 2022), and Pablo Kalmanovitz, "The Enforcement of International Humanitarian Law in Latin America", in Jorge Contesse et al, *Comparative Enforcement of International Law* (London: Edward Elgar, forthcoming).

[3] See, e.g., Elizabeth Jelin, "Los derechos humanos y la memoria de la violencia política y la represión: la construcción de un campo nuevo en las ciencias sociales," *Cuadernos del ides* 2 (2003): 6.

[4] These organizations included the Service of Peace and Justice, the Permanent Assembly for Human Rights (APDH), the Ecumenical Movement for Human Rights and the Family members of disappeared and detained for political reasons, Mothers and Grandmothers of Plaza de Mayo, and the Center for Legal and Social Studies (CELS). Several exiles also created organizations outside Argentina, such as the Argentine Commission for Human Rights and the Argentine Centre for Information and Solidarity, which worked alongside transnational organizations such as Amnesty International.

intelligence services as well as by the non-state groups targeted by the military repression.[5] It was ultimately a matter of survival.

These organizations soon began systematizing this information. In 1977, they presented a *sui generis* administrative action before the Argentine Supreme Court requesting information about those "who had been detained but their whereabouts were unknown" (appropriately named "collective" habeas corpus).[6] They joined efforts among different organizations, and with trade unions, to develop the first comprehensive list of victims. The visit of the Inter-American Commission of Human Rights (IACHR) to Argentina in 1979 provided a further opportunity to find information regarding their loved ones and shed light on the repression. From the moment the visit was announced, these organizations embarked on a process of streamlining and systematizing testimonies concerning disappearances—critically, they began organizing information by topics ("disappeared adolescents," "families as victims of repression," "missing babies," etc.).[7] By the time the Commission visited Argentina, these organizations had gathered information regarding around five thousand persons who had disappeared.[8] In its final report, the Commission "essentially conveyed the information human rights organizations had provided."[9] The report, furthermore, constituted the first call in print for the government to "initiate the corresponding investigations, to bring to trial and to punish, with the full force of the law, those responsible" for human rights violations.[10]

The political situation in Argentina soon changed drastically. The military defeat in the Malvinas war in 1982 catalyzed the transition to democracy and allowed the incoming authorities to set the terms of the new regime and its treatment of the recent past. By this time, victims' organizations, rebranded as human rights organizations, began advocating openly for a process of legal accountability ("*juicio y castigo a todos los culpables*").[11] The military, in response, issued a directive stating that every action against a terrorist organization would be considered an act of service and thereby beyond punishment. Soon afterward, they considered this proclamation insufficient and passed a "self-amnesty law."[12]

[5] Graciela Fernández Meijide, *La Historia Íntima de los Derechos Humanos en la Argentina (a Pablo)* (Santa Fe, Argentina : Sudamericana, 2009), 47.

[6] Interview on file with author.

[7] Fernández Meijide, *La Historia Íntima*, 100.

[8] Marcos Novaro and Vicente Palermo, *La dictadura militar. Del golpe de estado a la restauración democrática* (Barcelona: Ediciones Paidos Iberica, 2003), 294.

[9] Interview on file with author.

[10] See Kathryn Sikkink, *The Justice Cascade: How Human Rights Prosecutions are Changing World Politics* (New York: W. W. Norton: 2011), 81. This was standard practice at the IACHR, which had advocated similar measures in its 1974 and 1977 reports on Chile under Pinochet, as well as in its 1979 reports on El Salvador and Haiti. Ibid., 82.

[11] Elizabeth Jelin, "La Política de la memoria: El movimiento de derechos humanos y la construcción democrática en la Argentina," in *Juicio, castigos y memoria: Derechos humanos y justicia en la política argentina* (Buenos Aires: Nueva Visión, 1995), 119–20.

[12] Act 22.924 (Boletín Oficial, September 27, 1983).

Raúl Alfonsín would be elected president in 1983. He had been a member of the *Asamblea Permanente por los Derechos Humanos* (APDH), a leading human rights organization, and had filed dozens of habeas corpus actions during the dictatorship. He was, indeed, the only candidate advocating criminal accountability as the adequate response to mass criminality. Alfonsín's program, articulated by a group of leading legal philosophers, including Carlos Nino and Jaime Malamud Goti, was based on three essential elements: (1) the removal of any legal obstacles to prosecutions, most relevantly the self-amnesty law; (2) the military would be tried by a military court—civilian courts would only have a supervisory role; and (3) justice would be selective. To that extent, they proposed three levels of responsibility: those who gave the orders, those who committed "excesses," and those who simply followed them—a majority of whom would not be part of the accountability response.[13] This differentiation—it was believed—would help drive a wedge between the upper and lower ranks in the military, thereby weakening the foreseen resistance. Any accountability process would have to secure democratic stability.

The first step was nullifying the amnesty law. The grounds for this finding referred centrally to the provisions in the Argentine Constitution on equality before the law (Section 16) and on the division of powers, prohibiting the vesting of "extraordinary powers or the total public authority" upon the Executive (Section 29).[14] As I discuss in section IV below, it would be another ten years until courts in Argentina and Perú, as well as the Inter-American Court of Human Rights (IACtHR) would advocate a similar position by reference to international law provisions. With self-amnesty out of the way, the administration ordered the prosecution of the leaders of armed organizations and the members of the military juntas, who were to be tried by military, through the Supreme Council of the Armed Forces (*Consejo Supremo de las Fuerzas Armadas*).[15] Although it reformed the Code of Military Justice, it gave civilian authorities only complementary jurisdiction over the crimes perpetrated by the military.

Victims' organizations, feeling betrayed by this strategy, began advocating for the creation of a parliamentary commission that would investigate human rights violations perpetrated by the armed forces during the dictatorship. Such a commission, they believed, would be best positioned to summon military officials and gather relevant evidence in military garrisons. Ultimately, it would be able to issue a public, political—even if not legal/criminal—condemnation of the

[13] Pablo Gerchunoff, *Raúl Alfonsín. El planisferio invertido* (Barcelona: EDHASA, 2022); Fernández Meijide, *La Historia Íntima*, 213.

[14] Argentine Supreme Court (CSJN), *Fallos* 247: 287. Incidentally, the Argentine judiciary had already invalidated other amnesties before, such as those granted by the *de facto* regime of Lonardi in 1955 (Decree-Law 63/55), on similar grounds. See further Federal Appeals Chamber for Criminal Matters, Division I, "Fernández y Argemi" (decision of 4/10/84).

[15] Decrees 157 and 158/83, issued on December 13, 1983.

crimes of the dictatorship. Seeking to block this initiative—as it was considered potentially destabilizing—Alfonsín announced the creation of what would become the CONADEP (*Comisión Nacional sobre la Desaparición de Personas*), arguably the first fully operational truth commission. To secure its independence (and deprive it of any legal powers), it would be led by public figures—writers, journalists, scientists, and artists—and function outside Congress as an ad hoc institution.[16]

The initial architecture of CONADEP was hardly promising: its goals were largely unclear (many believed it would be occupied with searching for missing persons), it was inadequately staffed,[17] the time frame provided was exceedingly short (six months), and, despite their reputation and credibility, its members overwhelmingly had no concrete experience in documenting human rights violations.[18] Nevertheless, things changed drastically when human rights organizations took the reins through the appointment of Graciela Fernández Meijide from APDH, and her recruiting staff from the different human rights organizations, bringing in the experience, knowledge, and trust built during the previous years with victims and their relatives—information was essentially collected from victims. CONADEP rapidly became a space of incessant work and innovation. They decided not to concentrate on the disappeared but rather those responsible for the disappearances (*desaparecedores*), the places where they had been held, and how the repression had operated. For this purpose, they developed the so-called "magnet" strategy: organized all relevant information and evidence around each clandestine detention center.[19] They were able to identify more than three hundred clandestine detention centers and gather evidence of the systematic nature of the repression. According to one of its key figures, CONADEP had become a "prosecution office."[20]

On September 20, 1984, only nine months after being established, CONADEP presented its report with evidence of almost ten thousand enforced disappearances.[21] They further drafted a list of individuals identified as perpetrators of the documented human rights violations. As they received orders from the Administration not to publish this list, CONADEP decided to include

[16] Many figures belonging to the civil society refused to take part in it as full members, including Nobel Peace prize winner Adolfo Perez Esquivel.

[17] The initial personnel were bureaucrats from the Argentine Ministry of the Interior, with neither interest nor expertise in the task at hand. They soon all resigned.

[18] Interview on file with author.

[19] Fernández Meijide, *La Historia Íntima*, 243.

[20] Interview on file with author.

[21] Carlos Acuña and Catalina Smulovitz, "Militares en la transición argentina: del gobierno a la subordinación constitucional," in *Historizar el pasado vivo en América Latina*, ed. Anne Pérotin-Dumon, 40 (Santiago, Chile: Centro de Derechos Humanos, Universidad Alberto Hurtado, 2007), 40.

their names among the testimonies in the final report.[22] Notably, the report already included recommendations regarding reparations.

Meanwhile, the criminal investigation against the three *juntas* had stalled before the Supreme Council.[23] The Alfonsín plan of having the military impart swift justice to the members of the juntas had failed. On October 4, 1984, only two weeks after the CONADEP Report was issued, the Federal Appeals Chambers recalled the files and unilaterally assumed the investigation.[24]

It is worth emphasizing several innovations that had lasting influence in subsequent prosecutions. First, the judges decided to assign responsibility for the investigation to the prosecutor's office in a civil law country with investigative judges. The prosecutor's office explicitly adopted a case selection strategy in the context of mandatory prosecutions.[25] Indeed, they decided to select a group of "paradigmatic" cases, ultimately 709. Second, to attribute the acts of their subordinate to the juntas' members, the prosecutor invoked the doctrine of co-perpetrator through an "organized apparatus of power," developed by German jurist Claus Roxin, some twenty years earlier.[26] This mode of liability allowed the court to treat as principals the direct perpetrators of the crimes and the members of the juntas giving the orders. This mode of attribution became enormously influential in the region and beyond. Third, the trial pioneeringly incorporated the testimony of forensic anthropologist Clyde Snow, who had worked with CONADEP. Finally, the Court decided to conduct an oral trial—in Argentina's federal judiciary, trials were written proceedings. In fact, the trial would be open to the public and the press and it would be videotaped in its entirety by the state TV station. Paradoxically, several of these innovations were justified by referencing the fact that the proceedings were conducted under the Code of Military Justice instead of the domestic criminal procedure code applicable before civilian courts.[27]

After five months of intense hearings, the court had received testimony in 281 of the 709 cases initially selected.[28] Given their concerns about reaching a verdict

[22] Interview on file with author. The penultimate version of the list was eventually leaked to the press and published a few weeks later.

[23] Marcelo Sancinetti and Marcelo Ferrante, *El derecho penal en la protección de los derechos humanos* (Munich: Max Planck Institute, 1999), 305.

[24] Act 23.049, § 10 empowered civilian courts to "take over" the investigation and adjudication in "unjustified delays or negligence in conducting the trial."

[25] The trial was constantly attended by the general public and members of civil society organizations. It was also televised daily, though without sound.

[26] The Court cited a 1970 translation as C. Roxin, "Sobre la autoría y participación en el derecho penal," in *Problemas actuales de las ciencias penales y la filosofía del derecho. En homenaje al Profesor Luis Jiménez de Asúa*, ed. E. Bacigalupo et al. (Buenos Aires: Pannedille, 1970), 55–70.

[27] For a more detailed account, see Alejandro Chehtman, "The Juntas Trial: Adjudicating on the Tightrope" in Frédéric Mégret et al (eds), Mass Trials for Mass Crimes (London: Hart, forthcoming).

[28] Ricardo Gil Lavedra, *La Hermandad de los Astronautas. El Juicio a las Juntas por dentro* (Madrid: Editorial Debate, 2022), 259.

quickly before the military could organize a backlash, they considered the evidence sufficient and brought the trial to a close. The Court arrived at a decision on December 9, 1985, convicting five of the nine *juntas'* members on trial. But a far more extensive justice process had been unleashed. CONADEP has already filed complaints regarding specific cases with investigative justices in different parts of the country. Furthermore, "Point 30" of the Court's decision ordered that all relevant high command officers be investigated, as well as those "with operative responsibility" for the relevant actions.

Alfonsín first sought to limit prosecutions and contain accountability efforts in his initial justice proposal. He first issued general instructions to military prosecutors, but the justices in the Federal Appeals Chamber who had been involved in the trials of the juntas threatened to resign, and these instructions were repealed.[29] Accordingly, the Administration decided to pay the political price of containing prosecutions by passing the Full Stop Act (*Ley de Punto Final*), which established a sixty-day closing deadline for investigations that failed to summon the indicted to defend themselves in early December 1986. Despite January being a judicial holiday for the courts, the new law generated an explosion of activity by victims, courts, and organizations of the civil society. By the end of the deadline, courts in different parts of the country had indicted more than three hundred high-level officers.[30]

A strong military backlash was imminent. In April 1986, Alfonsín faced the first armed rebellion by the *Carapintadas*, a group of middle-level officials in the military. In another one of the critical milestones of Argentine democratic history, Alfonsín met with the rebels and, on Easter Sunday, sent home a large crowd gathered in *Plaza de Mayo* (and several other public spaces in Argentina), with the ominous words: "the house is in order and there is no blood in Argentina." On April 19, the Democratic Compromise Act was signed among the main parties, reinstating the "duly recognition of the different levels of responsibility for conduct and acts in the past."[31] On June 4, 1987, de "Due Obedience" law was passed, establishing a presumption of innocence for those who lacked the capacity to design the policy or give orders.[32] Though this measure amounted to a comprehensive amnesty, when Alfonsín left office there was still a significant level of accountability, with many of the most responsible in prison. Nevertheless, the incoming Peronist government of Carlos Menem would complete the reversal of the accountability process by pardoning not only those who had been convicted

[29] Gerchunoff, *Raúl Alfonsín*, 178. Only judge Jorge Torlasco did in fact resign.

[30] See, *inter alia*, Horacio Verbistky, *Civiles y militares. Memoria secreta de la transición* (Buenos Aires: Editorial Contrapunto, 1987), 322.

[31] Cited in Acuña/Smulovitz, "Militares," 51.

[32] Alfonsín faced further military rebellions in September 1987 (Monte Caseros) and December 1988 (Villa Martelli). But there were no further concessions.

and sentenced but also those who were still under investigation or awaiting a decision.

The ensuing period has been aptly referred to as "the blackout" (*el apagón*). Nevertheless, important developments were taking place away from the public eye. First, the *Equipo Argentino de Antropología Forense* (EEAF), established in 1987 under the leadership of Clyde Snow, was able to carry out meaningful investigations unhindered, for "no one was paying any attention" to their work.[33] That same year, the Administration created the National Bank of Genetic Data (BNDG), the first of its kind in the world, a public institution that stored blood samples of individuals seeking their family members could test blood samples of a large number of possible victims.[34] In effect, the Argentine delegation further pushed for the inclusion of the right to identity in the Convention of the Rights of the Child.[35]

A whole new language and institutional framework were also emerging from the wreckage of these initial accountability efforts. In 1988, the IACtHR issued its first decision positing a "legal duty . . . to use the means at its disposal to carry out a serious investigations of violations committed within its jurisdiction, to identify those responsible, to impose the appropriate punishment and to ensure the victim adequate compensation," despite lacking any explicit textual basis for such a claim.[36] Perhaps less well-known is the 1989 decision by Judge Leopoldo Schiffrin authorizing the extradition of SS official Josef Schwammberger to Germany. He argued that his crimes were not subject to statutes of limitations on the grounds of the Argentine obligations under human rights treaties and the *jus cogens* character of the prohibitions involved.[37] These new language and ideas would have momentous implications.

III. Truth

By the late 1980s and through the 1990s, accountability was out of the question in almost every country in the region.[38] Chile passed an amnesty law in 1978

[33] Interview on file with author. See, further, Alejandro Chehtman, "Re-Constructing Criminal Accountability for Human Rights Abuses: Argentina 1990-2024", *Modern Criminal Law Review* 1(1) (2024), 64-94.

[34] Act 23.511.

[35] Articles 7 and 8 were informally referred to as the "Argentine Articles." See Kathryn Sikkink, "From Pariah State to Global Protagonist: Argentina and the Struggle for International Human Rights," *Latin American Politics and Society* 50, no. 1 (2008): 14.

[36] *Velázquez Rodríguez v. Honduras*, Inter.-Am. Ct. H.R. ¶ 174 (1988).

[37] Federal Appeals Chamber, La Plata (30/09/1989), at *J.A.* 27-XIII-1989.

[38] In Bolivia, after the return to democracy in October 1982, a "Responsibility Trial" (*Juicio de Responsabilidades*) was initiated in 1984 against those who led the last *coup d'état*. They were prosecuted both for domestic crimes and for genocide. The Supreme Court ultimately convicted

and was trying to navigate its transition, with Pinochet still in a position of power. Brazil passed an amnesty law in 1979, which is still on the books today. In Paraguay, Stroessner was deposed only in 1989, after a thirty-five-year rule. Nicaragua, El Salvador, Perú, and Guatemala adopted amnesty laws in 1989, 1993, 1995, and 1996, respectively.[39] Accordingly, transitional justice efforts focused on truth-seeking, and truth commissions gave victims a platform, and even public rehabilitation, while being considered far less destabilizing than prosecutions. For many, though, they were the only way toward accountability.

Uruguay was a forerunner and one of the most interesting examples of this approach. Soon after the return of democratic rule, victims began requesting investigations of crimes before domestic justices. Whereas military courts challenged the jurisdiction of civilian courts, the Supreme Court of Uruguay ultimately held the latter were entitled to proceed (with the dissent of the military judges).[40] By February 1985, the Uruguayan Congress was already discussing the creation of parliamentary commissions of inquiry, at the request of the left-wing *Frente Amplio*—mirroring the initiatives of victim groups in Argentina in the previous years. By July 1985, Congress issued a first report with twenty-nine cases of individual victims of enforced disappearance on Uruguayan soil between 1975 and 1978 and, by the end of 1985, a final report counted a total number of 164 Uruguayan nationals who had been victims of enforced disappearance in Uruguay, Argentina, Chile and Paraguay, foregrounding the findings of the Condor plan.[41]

The Parliamentary Commission further requested that the House of Representatives require the judiciary to prosecute these crimes. Two senators presented a bill conferring jurisdiction to the appeals chambers, fostering oral hearings, and suspending the statutory limitations during the period of military rule, citing the Nuremberg precedent. Nevertheless, one year later, on December 21, 1986, the Senate passed the Expiry Bill (*Ley de Caducidad de la Pretensión Punitiva del Estado*), and the House of Representatives followed suit only a few hours later. The next day, the Expiry Law was in force precluding all prosecutions for crimes perpetrated by the dictatorship.[42] On May 2, 1988, the Supreme Court

García Meza and others in 1993, nine years after the trial's initiation, in absentia, and with serious allegations about the lack of credibility of the verdict.

[39] Guatemala's did not cover genocide, torture, forced disappearances or crimes for which no statutes of limitations applied.

[40] Gianella Bardazano, "Cuando nos muramos todos' Interpretación, derechos y democracia en el Uruguay contemporáneo" (PhD diss., National University of the Litoral of Santa Fe), 115 (on file with author).

[41] Ibid., 116. On the Condor Plan, see Francesca Lessa, *The Condor Trials: Transnational Repression and Human Rights in South America* (New Haven, CT: Yale University Press, 2022).

[42] The National Pacification Law passed in 1985, pardoning all but sixty-five of the eight hundred political prisoners.

found that this amnesty was compatible with the Uruguayan Constitution.[43] Perhaps most notably, in April 1989, the law was subject to public consultation, and 56 percent of the votes were in its favor.[44]

Meanwhile, in 1990, Chile created the first Commission that included the word "truth" in its title.[45] The so-called Rettig Commission was given nine months to conduct its work. As the military refused to cooperate, much like CONADEP they started with the "extensive records of non-governmental organizations."[46] The Commission was innovative in that instead of focusing on systematic repression, it delivered detailed reports on each of the individual cases examined. Arguably, this approach contributed to the idea that each victim had a right to know the truth.[47] By contrast, it did not identify or name any perpetrators; nor did it seek to trigger prosecutions.[48] When its report was issued, Pinochet rejected it, claiming that the army had saved the freedom and sovereignty of Chile.[49] President Alwin, by contrast, issued a public apology.[50] This pronouncement, in turn, offered the victims a form of public rehabilitation after being consistently attacked and defamed as "enemies of the state."[51]

Only a few months later, the Truth Commission for El Salvador was formally set up in Mexico as a way out of an armed conflict. The agreement was secured under the active auspices of the Peruvian UN Secretary General, Javier Pérez de Cuellar, and even before the 1992 peace agreement (and any form of disarmament) could be secured. Unlike in previous cases, the members and staff of the Commission were foreigners, in an attempt to avoid accusations of bias or partiality toward any of the parties in the conflict.[52] Irrespective of its grounds, it had the unwanted implication of creating deep mistrust among the local civil society.[53] Previous experiences were brought in. Before starting work, the Secretariat met with Graciela Fernández Meijide, a key figure in CONADEP, to discuss organizational and procedural issues. It also contacted the lead

[43] Sentencia n. 184/88, *Detta, Josefina et al. Excepción de Inconstitucionalidad*, arts. 1, 2, 3 y 4 Ley no. 15848.

[44] J. L. Bruno, Referéndum uruguayo del 16 de abril de 1989, IIDH-CAPEl, 1989, 36.

[45] He resisted pressures to widen the scope of impunity provisions under Chilean law.

[46] Priscilla Hayner, *Unspeakable Truths. Transitional Justice and the Challenge of Truth Commissions* (London: Routledge, 2002), 48.

[47] Juan Méndez, "An Emerging 'Right to Truth': Latin-American Contributions," in *Legal Institutions and Collective Memories*, ed. S. Karstedt (London: Bloomsbury, 2009), 43.

[48] The few that remained open were stalled by the judiciary, still dominated by judges from the Pinochet era.

[49] Human Rights Watch, "Politics of Agreement" (July 1991), 32–33, https://www.hrw.org/report/1991/07/01/human-rights-and-politics-agreement/chile-during-president-aylwins-first-year.

[50] Méndez, "An Emerging," 43. A second truth commission was created to investigate cases of torture that had not resulted in the death of the victim.

[51] Teitel, *Transitional Justice*, 84.

[52] Mark Ensalaco, "Truth Commissions for Chile and El Salvador," *Human Rights Quarterly* 16, no. 4 (1994): 661.

[53] Interview on file with author.

investigator and the information technology person at Human Rights Watch to train the Commission's personnel on documenting atrocities, and on how to design and use a digital database. The Argentine EEAF was brought in to help investigate crimes in *El Mozote*. In contrast to the Argentine and the Chilean experiences, however, the Commission decided to concentrate on thirty-three emblematic crimes, which allowed them to strike a balance between the different factions.[54]

Crucial input for its work was, again, the testimonies and evidence collected for years by *Socorro Jurídico*, the leading local organization providing support to victims.[55] This Commission was the first to be conferred legal powers to access governmental facilities without prior notice and summon official documents and participants in the armed conflict, including members of the military. Nevertheless, the information it initially received from them was mostly useless. Accordingly, it devised a mechanism to "informally identify the whereabouts of alleged perpetrators," "contact them with broad information about their possible connection with alleged criminal acts, provide them with the possibility of correcting or rejecting the allegations," and "indicate that failure to respond would be openly indicated in the final report."[56] In response, many of them appeared before the Commission with their lawyers and provided relevant information. This mechanism, subsequently replicated in the Peruvian Truth Commission,[57] was arguably a first attempt at conditioning benefits to truth-telling. This feature later became a key, perhaps even standard, component of truth-seeking and accountability mechanisms in transitional justice processes.[58]

The final report—From Madness to Hope"—was pathbreaking in that it explicitly identified over forty senior state officials allegedly responsible for gross human rights violations. This "naming names" strategy, as it was later called, was considered crucial by those in the Commission given that the justice system was "in total disarray" and "could not be trusted" to conduct any genuine prosecutions.[59] Amid rumors of a coup, Congress passed a broad amnesty law just five days later.[60] Eager to reenter public life, members of the *Frente Farabundo Martí* did not object.[61]

[54] Teitel, *Transitional Justice*, 86.

[55] This collaboration required a slow process of trust-building—ecclesiastical authorities played a key role as facilitators—until they decided to share their records. Interview on file with author.

[56] Interview on file with author.

[57] Hayner, *Unspeakable Truths*, 138.

[58] In the mid-1990s, the South African Truth and Reconciliation Commission was created, with a novel approach that allowed it to grant amnesty from prosecution in exchange for truth and the power to issue subpoenas and name perpetrators.

[59] Interview on file with author.

[60] It also had some, though ultimately disappointing, effects in the United States.

[61] Méndez, "An Emerging 'Right to Truth,'" 44.

Guatemala established its Commission for Historical Clarification (1997) as a response to one of the bloodiest repressions in the region. This time, the Armed Forces made it clear that there would be no "naming names." The Commission included both national and foreign figures, and despite initial resistance, the human rights movement in Guatemala also ended up supporting its work.[62] It was the first Commission to find that the army had committed acts of genocide against the Mayan population of the Guatemalan highlands. It further indicated that the atrocities had been perpetrated with the knowledge or by order of the highest authorities, providing human rights organizations with a plausible basis to advocate prosecutions. Nevertheless, then President Álvaro Arzú refused to accept the report, embodying "the profound contempt that the political and economic establishment felt towards the victims of the conflict and the genocide narrative itself."[63] Unsurprisingly, the Commission's recommendations "mostly gather[ed] dust."[64]

In 2001, incoming Peruvian President Alejandro Toledo created a Truth and Reconciliation Commission.[65] This was the first truth commission to hold public hearings, and it did so throughout the country.[66] This had a direct impact on the quest for justice, as many victims openly demanded that perpetrators be punished. Furthermore, the Commission created a special unit focused on preparing criminal cases, formalizing a practice that can be traced as far back as CONADEP in the 1980s. Regarding the selection of cases, it indicated that it would concentrate on cases considered "explanatory" of the patterns of human rights violations.[67] Using statistical projections, it also used the relevant information to calculate the total number of victims who had been killed or disappeared during the conflict. It found that 75 percent of the victims were part of some Indigenous community and were from the poorest regions in Perú.[68] The Legal Team within the Commission identified almost two hundred perpetrators and recommended prosecution in forty-seven cases in a confidential report. Indeed, "the first public hearings . . . had made it obvious that criminal justice was one of the top priorities of the victims."[69]

[62] The information provided by two organizations was critical to the work of the Commission: the project of Recovery of Historical Memory of the Catholic Church's Human Rights office and the *Centro Internacional para Investigaciones en Derechos Humanos* (CIIDH).

[63] Roddy Brett, "Peace without Social Reconciliation? Understanding the Trial of Generals Ríos Montt and Rodriguez Sánchez in the Wake of Guatemala's Genocide," *Journal of Genocide Research* 18(2–3) (2016): 295.

[64] Naomi Roht-Arriaza, *The Pinochet Effect: Transnational Justice in the Age of Human Rights* (Philadelphia: University of Pennsylvania Press, 2005), ix–x.

[65] See Salmón, "International Humanitarian Law."

[66] E. González-Cueva, "The Contributions of the Peruvian Truth and Reconciliation Commission to Prosecutions," *Criminal Law Forum* 15, no. 1–2 (2004): 55–66.

[67] This approach was arguably a forerunner of that adopted by the Special Jurisdiction for Peace in Colombia in the 2010s. See section V in this chapter.

[68] Hayner, *Unspeakable Truths*, 37.

[69] González-Cueva, "The Contributions," 80.

Another institutional innovation in this area was truth trials in Argentina. In 1995, Adolfo Scilingo—an obscure officer in the Argentine Navy—recognized for the first time the existence of the death flights on prime-time TV and confessed his involvement in them. This explicit acknowledgment created a political storm. These events triggered many responses. The head of the Argentine Armed Forces, General Martín Balza, recognized the illegal repression and issued a public apology. Victims' organizations, such as H.I.J.O.S and Mothers of Plaza de Mayo, began resorting to *escraches*[70] against members of the military who had benefited from the amnesty and pardons. This form of protest entailed a demonstration of artistic, public denunciation of individuals responsible for human rights violations. One of the first examples was putting up street signs indicating information about the homes of those accountable for tortures and disappearances.[71]

Soon after the initial revelations, human rights lawyers requested the Federal Appeals Court in Buenos Aires—the court that had conducted the *Juntas* trial—to gather information concerning individual victims of enforced disappearance during the dictatorship, giving birth to truth trials. The legal basis of these requests was novel: both presentations invoked international human rights law. They resorted to Report 28/92 of the IACHR which recommended "that the Government of Argentina adopt the necessary measures to establish the facts and identify those responsible for human rights violations that occurred during the last military dictatorship."[72] They also referred to the duty to investigate enforced disappearance as long as the fate of the disappeared person is unknown, established by the IACtHR in its very first case *Velázquez Rodríguez v. Honduras* (1988). The legal architecture they sought was also new; they requested the use of judicial criminal proceedings to investigate and establish certain facts related to serious human rights violations, even if there was no possibility of calling the alleged perpetrators to account. A key, long-lasting innovation was articulating these petitions based on the newly coined rights to "truth" and to "mourning," later replicated in the European and African contexts and ultimately endorsed as a universal human right.[73]

A final, key breakthrough in this context came in regard to evidence: the development of a technique to scan and identify "old" fingerprints

[70] The word "escrache" comes from Buenos Aires slang and means to "shed light on what is hidden."

[71] This type of protest was designed by a collective group called *Grupo de Arte Callejero* (Street Art Group).

[72] Cámara Nacional de Apelaciones en lo Criminal y Correccional Federal (CCCF) (Argentina), Causa ESMA, Res. 1/95 (March 20, 1995). They also invoked the decision of the IACtHR in *Velázquez Rodríguez* and *Bámaca Velázquez*.

[73] Martín Abregú, "La Tutela Judicial del Derecho a la Verdad en la Argentina," *Revista IIDH* 24 (1996): 20 and Méndez, "An Emerging," 40.

and the development during this time of identification through mitochondrial DNA. Through a collaboration with the EEAF, this led to the identification of the remains of more than three hundred bodies and the restitution of the remains of more than fifty persons to their families. Among them, the Federal Appeals Court was able to identify the remains of Uruguayan citizens, who had been disappeared in Argentina in the context of the *Plan Condor*, as well as some of the founding members of Mothers of Plaza de Mayo and one of the French nuns who the military had kidnapped.[74] This work was also instrumental in the reignition of the accountability process a few years down the line.[75]

IV. Justice

The next move was toward accountability or, as has been often argued, toward establishing the anti-impunity paradigm of transitional justice. This section captures the primary dynamics, innovations that favored this trend, and some of its limitations and setbacks.

By the early 1990s, Chile had made very little progress in prosecuting crimes perpetrated during the Pinochet era. Yet soon, a continuous search for innovative ways to break through this cloak of impunity was unleashed. A 1994 decision by a first-instance judge was an early forerunner of this trend when it considered the crimes under Pinochet as crimes against humanity and war crimes, and thereby not subject to statutory limitations. Yet this decision was rapidly revoked by the Supreme Court. The investigation was subsequently transferred to the military jurisdiction and closed.[76] As elsewhere, this outcome was primarily the result of the amnesty law but can also be explained by the prominent place Pinochet still had in Chilean politics.[77]

By 1998, however, things began to change. This year saw a deep renovation of the Chilean judiciary (by the end of that year, "more than half the Supreme Court was made up of post-Pinochet appointees").[78] In this new context, civilian criminal judges began taking over military courts to investigate cases concerning grave human rights violations. Furthermore, in September 1998, the Supreme Court reversed how the amnesty law operated in practice. Under the new

[74] Horacio Cattani, "La llamada 'búsqueda de la verdad' por los tribunales federales de la Ciudad Autónoma de Buenos Aires," 14 (typescript on file with author). Some litigants were planning to use the investigation to bring the case before Spanish Judge Baltasar Garzón. Luciani et al., "Justicia, Historia y memorias," 277.

[75] For a detailed reconstruction, see Chehtman, "Reconstructing Criminal Accountability", 68–70.

[76] *Caso Bárbara Uribe & Edwin Van Yurick* (Appeals Court of Santiago, September 30, 1994).

[77] Among the relevant exceptions were the prosecution of the former director of Pinochet's secret police, the DINA, and his deputy for the killing of Orlando Letelier, which had occurred in Washington, DC, in 1975.

[78] Roht-Arriaza, *The Pinochet Effect*, 73.

regime, courts had to conduct a criminal investigation, including identifying the individuals responsible for the investigated offenses, to determine whether amnesty applied.[79] This innovation allowed for judicially determining key facts and made impunity increasingly costly.

The international context was particularly favorable to criminal accountability. The 1990s saw the (re)birth of international criminal justice as an institutional response to mass atrocity. The UN Security Council created the ICTY (International Criminal Tribunals for the Former Yugoslavia) and the ICTR (the International Criminal Tribunal for Rwanda) in 1993 and 1994, respectively, and brokered the creation of the Special Court for Sierra Leone in 1996. In July 1998, 148 states gathered in Rome and signed the ICC Statute.[80] The so-called anti-impunity agenda had become prevalent in the West. In this context, Latin American exiles and jurists initiated proceedings based on universal jurisdiction in states such as Spain, Italy, Germany, and France. As a result of one of these processes, on October 16, 1998, Augusto Pinochet was arrested by Scotland Yard at the London Clinic at the request of Spanish judge Baltasar Garzón on international crimes charges.

With Pinochet arrested in London, criminal "complaints against him multiplied" before Chilean courts.[81] Accordingly, in June 1999, several high-ranking military officials were indicted for the events of the so-called death caravan—a raid killing prisoners in different detention centers in the forty days following the 1973 coup.[82] Chilean courts thereby began circumventing the Chilean Amnesty Law, which applied only to crimes perpetrated between September 11, 1973, and March 10, 1978, by characterizing crimes for which the bodies had not been found as "kidnappings" and considering this crime a continuous offense.[83] Pinochet, nevertheless, could not yet be indicted because of his parliamentary immunity.

On March 11, 2000, Ricardo Lagos took office in Chile as the first Socialist President of Chile since Salvador Allende. His administration opened a negotiation instance ("*Mesa de Diálogo*") with the armed forces to gather information concerning the sites where victims of enforced disappearance had been buried. One of the outcomes of this dialogue was the request to appoint members of the judiciary to investigate this type of case. In 2001, with Pinochet back in the country, the Chilean Supreme Court appointed nine appeals court justices and fifty-one first-instance judges to concentrate on cases involving human rights

[79] Supreme Court of Chile, *Caso Pedro Poblete Córdova* (September 9, 1998).

[80] Interview on file with author.

[81] By the time he arrived back on March 3, 2000, there were more than sixty complaints (and two months later, more than one hundred). See Roht-Arriaza, *The Pinochet Effect*, 69.

[82] Cámara de Apelaciones de Santiago (Chile), Rol 2182-98.

[83] Suprema Corte de Justicia, Rol 49-98. By contrast, those crimes considered murders were dismissed on grounds of self-amnesty.

violations.[84] In 2004, the Supreme Court started using the "permanent" character of the kidnapping offense as the ground to circumvent statutory limitations and the amnesty decree.[85] This finding led, on the one hand, to the conclusion that there were no legal obstacles to prosecution as the crimes continued to be perpetrated. Yet, on the other hand, penalties imposed in Chile were considerably low—around two-thirds of all those convicted in this type of case did not serve any prison time. The reason for this was the "partial" application of statutory limitations.[86] Things would further change after the IACtHR decided against Chile in the *Almonacid Arellano* case.

Impunity measures were also being challenged in Argentina. In October 1996, after the Scilingo revelations, several victims sought to challenge the impunity by requesting the prosecution of what they termed a systematic plan for the illegal appropriation of minors who had been born in captivity during the 1970s dictatorship. This specific offense had not been included in the amnesty laws ("Final Stop" (art. 5) and "Due Obedience" (art. 2)) or in the pardons issued in the early 1990s. On June 9, 1998, a federal judge detained former junta member Jorge Rafael Videla for his responsibility in a plan to kidnap babies and alter their identities. A few weeks later, fellow junta member Emilio Massera, another key figure of the first military junta, was detained on similar charges.

However, there was an apparent legal obstacle to this type of prosecution: statutes of limitations applied to crimes that had been perpetrated almost twenty years before. In September 1999, in several influential decisions, the Federal Appeals Court in Buenos Aires argued, first—mirroring the argument of Chilean courts with regards to kidnapping—that given that the appropriation of minors had continued, the lapse required for the statutes of limitations to apply had not been exhausted. Furthermore, it argued that statutes of limitations did not apply to crimes against humanity such as "enforced disappearances."[87] As *jus cogens* rules, the Court further concluded, following Schiffrin's 1988 vote in *Schwambergger*, that these provisions could not be modified by treaties or domestic legislation.[88]

As noted, in the late 1990s, different legal arguments had slowly undermined impunity in Argentina. Domestic courts began truth trials and began prosecuting the military for unlawful appropriation of minors. As in Chile, they

[84] Observatorio de Justicia Transicional (Chile), *Principales hitos jurisprudenciales, judiciales y legislativos en causas de DDHH en Chile 1990-2023* (Santiago de Chile, 2023), 8.

[85] Supreme Court of Chile, *Miguel Ángel Sandoval Rodríguez* (November 17, 2004).

[86] See, e.g., Supreme Court of Chile, *Juan Luis Rivera Matus* (July 30, 2007).

[87] The Supreme Court had anticipated this reasoning in deciding the extradition of a Nazi official to Italy a few years earlier. See Corte Suprema de Justicia de la Nación, *Priebke*, Erlich s/ solicitud de extradición- causa N° 16.063/94 (1995), *Fallos* 318:2148.

[88] See, e.g., CCCF, "Videla, J.R. s/prisión preventiva" (September 9, 1999), "Suárez Mason y otros s/procesamiento" (September 9, 1999), and "Massera, Emilio—Exp. 30.514" (September 9, 1999), among several others.

had already invoked the "permanent" nature of the crime and international legal provisions to circumvent statutory limitations. But amnesty laws and pardons were still in force. A federal judge, Gabriel Cavallo, had a case of unlawful appropriation with—due to DNA sampling—conclusive evidence also about the enforced disappearance of the mother. After meeting with the victim—Claudia Victoria Poblete—by then a youngster in her twenties, he was confronted with the uncomfortable position of having to prosecute the people who had raised her but not those responsible for the disappearance and death of her mother. On March 6, 2001, in a pathbreaking decision, he removed the last remaining obstacle to prosecution by declaring null and void the Argentine Full Stop and Due Obedience Laws. This ruling was based on three critical considerations. First, following the IACtHR since *Velázquez Rodríguez*, states under the ACHR are obliged to investigate and prosecute serious human rights violations.[89] Second, offenses under investigation constituted crimes against humanity and, following the 1989 vote of Judge Schiffrin in the *Schwammberger* extradition case,[90] violations of *jus cogens* norms. As a result, they were not subject to statutory limitations. Finally, he argued that the acts under investigation violated the American Convention on Human Rights—anticipating for a week the IACtHR's decision in *Barrios Altos*—the International Covenant on Civil and Political Rights (ICCPRs), and the Convention against Torture and that they were unconstitutional and thereby null and void.[91]

After taking office on May 25, 2003, the Kirchner administration made prosecuting crimes perpetrated by the dictatorship one of its landmark public policies. In August of that year, the Argentine Congress conferred constitutional hierarchy to the Convention on the Non-Applicability of Statutory Limitations to War Crimes and Crimes against Humanity and it declared null and void the Full Stop and Due Obedience—amnesty—laws passed by the Alfonsín administration in the late 1980s.[92] Despite this declaration arguably having no concrete *legal* effects—under Argentine law Congress has no authority to void pieces of criminal legislation retroactively—it provided judges who wanted to proceed with the investigation of this type of crime with a strong political support. In

[89] Report 28/92 of the IACHR on Argentina had already found that the amnesty laws and pardons were incompatible with the ACHR since they deprived victims of a right to a judicial investigation directed to individualize and sanction those responsible.

[90] Federal Appeals Chamber, La Plata (Argentina) (30/09/1989), at *J.A.* 27-XIII-1989. This is, incidentally, one of the judges who, based on international legal provisions, authorized the truth trials in La Plata in 1998.

[91] Hernán Folgueiro, "Inconstitucionalidad de las Leyes de 'Punto Final' y 'Obediencia Debida.' Notas al fallo 'Simón' de la Corte Suprema de Justicia de la Nación," in *Derecho a la Identidad y Persecución de Crímenes de Lesa Humanidad* (Madison: University of Wisconsin Press, 2002), 70.

[92] Acts 25.778 and 25.779, respectively. Many believe that Congress had no authority under the Argentine Constitution to issue any such retroactive measure. Lavedra, *La Hermandad*, 76.

2005, the Argentine Supreme Court confirmed the Cavallo 2001 decision.[93] Several of its justices invoked the IACtHR's decision in *Barrios Altos*, signaling its binding character, as a strategy to overcome the fact that this same Court had decided in favor of the amnesty laws being compatible with the Argentine Constitution in 1987.[94] In 2007, the Argentine Supreme Court further found that the pardons issued by the Menem administration were unconstitutional and thereby null and void, allowing for all those freed to be reimprisoned.[95]

Peru was similarly joining the "anti-impunity" wave, but not without relevant setbacks and dissent. In April 1995, a prosecutor requested the opening of an investigation of crimes perpetrated in 1991 by military officials and Judge Antonia Saquicuray obliged. Yet, even before the Supreme Court could adjudicate on the matter, Fujimori's Congress passed an amnesty law precluding the investigation of human rights violations perpetrated during the conflict (Act 26.479). In this context, Judge Saquicuray, issued a revolutionary judgment, claiming that this amnesty was contrary to the Peruvian Constitution and thereby null and void. The specific argument was that the facts under investigation constituted crimes against humanity and, thereby, could not be the subject matter of a valid amnesty. A few days later, the Peruvian Congress passed a "clarificatory" law, avoiding the substance of the decision but indicating that the original amnesty could not be the object of a constitutional review by the judiciary (Act 26.492). The Superior Court of Lima ultimately upheld both amnesties as compatible with the Peruvian Constitution and its obligations under the human rights treaties. It declared judge Saquicuray's decision null and void, quashing the preliminary investigation.[96] It further ordered that Judge Saquicuray be investigated for her interpretation of the applicable laws.[97]

Yet the National Human Rights Coordinator brought the case of the extrajudicial killings in *Barrios Altos* to the IACHR in June of that year. The petition reached the IACtHR in June 2000. Despite the fact that Peru recognized its international responsibility in the case—*Barrios Altos v. Perú*—the IACtHR decided to issue an opinion on the merits of the case on March 14, 2001. In four brief paragraphs, the Court handed in what is arguably one of its most influential decisions to date, stating that amnesty laws were "manifestly incompatible with the aims and spirits" of the ACHR and as such were devoid of any legal effects (it also stated that victims had a right to truth).[98] After the IACtHR ruling,

[93] CSJN, *Case no 17.768, Simón Julio y otros, s/privación ilegítima de la libertad* (June 15, 2005). Before, it had adopted a similar doctrine in the extradition of Arancibia Clavel to Chile.

[94] CSJN, "Camps," *Fallos* 310:1162 (June 22, 1987).

[95] CSJN, "Mazzeo, Julio y otros," *Fallos* 330:3248 (July 13, 2007).

[96] See Jorge Contesse, in this volume.

[97] César Landa Arroyo, "Límites Constitucionales de la Ley de Aminstía Peruana," *Revista IIDH* 24 (1996): 68.

[98] *Barrios Altos v. Peru*, Judgment of March 14, Inter-Am. Ct. H.R. (ser. C) No. 75, ¶¶ 43, operat. 4, and 47–49, respectively (2001).

the Supreme Court of Peru considered this decision binding upon the Peruvian authorities, thereby opening the way for prosecuting the cases closed in 1995. In 2004, in its effort to overcome statutory limitations, the Constitutional Court of Peru further acknowledged the crime of enforced disappearance as a permanent offense.[99]

Trials against Peruvian military officials began in 2005. That same year, Fujimori was detained in Chile and extradited to Peru. In 2009, he was convicted and sentenced to twenty-five years in prison by a Special Chamber of the Peruvian Supreme Court for, among other charges, the Barrios Altos and La Cantuta Massacres. He was the first democratically elected head of state to be convicted for human rights violations in domestic courts of his own country. Although sentenced for domestic offenses such as homicide, assault, and kidnappings, the Court held that these acts constituted "also crimes against humanity" because of their systematic nature as part of a state policy of elimination of alleged members of an insurgent group.[100] Fujimori was considered responsible as a principal based on Roxin's idea of a perpetrator through the dominion of an organized apparatus of power first employed by the Argentine juntas trial chamber. Incidentally, before the beginning of the hearings, the Peruvian court met with the Argentine judges to discuss both organizational and substantive law issues.[101] Later, the Peruvian judiciary expanded the use of this mode of liability to Abimael Guzman, the leader of Shining Path, a non-state armed group, opening new ground.[102]

Uruguay also found ways to challenge impunity. As mentioned in section III, by the late 1980s, Uruguay had passed an expiry law, confirmed by the judiciary and by an unprecedented public consultation. Furthermore, the implementation of the expiry law gave priority to the executive. That is, it required that, upon receiving a criminal complaint, judges ask the executive whether the terms of the amnesty covered the relevant acts. Bardazano has suggested that for an extended period, the judiciary did not contest the executive's finding, even in cases where it seemed clear that the acts were beyond the specific terms of the expiry law.[103]

By the early 2000s, however, this general framework began to crumble. For one, Uruguayan courts began prosecuting cases against *civilian* officers involved in gross crimes, as they considered them not covered by the specific terms of

[99] This was particularly relevant given that enforced disappearance in Peru only became a crime in 1998. See Peruvian Criminal Code, art. 320.

[100] Supreme Court of Peru (2009), translated and published as "The Judgment against Fujimori for Human Rights Violations," *American University International Law Review* 25 (2010): 802.

[101] Interviews on file with author.

[102] See, e.g., Francisco Muñoz-Conde and Héctor Olásolo, "The Application of the Notion of Indirect Perpetration through Organized Structures of Power in Latin America and Spain," *Journal of International Crime Justice* 9 (2011): 130.

[103] Gianella Bardazano, "Cuando nos muramos todos," 177.

the law. As of 2005, moreover, the executive began to interpret the conditions established by the expiry law in a far more restrictive manner, allowing for the judiciary to proceed in several cases.[104] Perhaps most influentially, in 2006, the former de facto President Juan M. Bordaberry and his Foreign Affairs Minister Juan Carlos Blanco were prosecuted for four homicides. In 2007, former military President Gregorio Álvarez was prosecuted and detained for thirty-seven counts of homicides, after the executive determined that they were not covered by the expiry law. This new consensus could not be stopped. On October 19, 2009, the Supreme Court of Uruguay found the expiry law contrary to the Constitution of Uruguay and thereby null and void. Interestingly, before issuing this decision, the Court consulted both the executive power and Congress, and both issued opinions stating that the law was unconstitutional.

A critical consideration was, following the courts in Chile, Argentina, and Perú, the constitutional relevance of Uruguay's human rights obligations under the doctrine of the "constitutional block." It suggested that they are part of the Constitution insofar as they are rights "inherent to the human person that the international community recognizes."[105] Furthermore, the Supreme Court based its decision in the doctrine of Italian jurist Luigi Ferrajoli, stating that certain legal issues concerning fundamental rights are beyond the pale of majoritarian rule.[106] For these purposes, it cited the Argentine Supreme Court in *Simon* and *Riveros*, and the IACtHR in its decisions in *Barrios Altos*, *Almonacid Arellano*, and *La Cantuta*.

Notably, in October 2009, only six days after the Supreme Court's decision against the expiry law, a new public consultation was organized. Yet, as in 1989, the population voted to maintain the Expiry Act in force. This conundrum was ultimately resolved by the IACtHR, further pushing for prosecutions. In February 2011, it found that the expiry law was incompatible with the ACHR and, thereby, should be declared null and void.[107] As a result, in June, the executive decided to revert its previous opinions concerning the cases covered by the Expiry Act. This meant retroactively stating that prosecution of these acts was not precluded under the Expiry Act.[108] Furthermore, in October of that year, Congress passed—albeit by a majority of just one vote—an "Interpretive Act of the Expiry Act" establishing, in essence, that the prosecution of crimes of "state terrorism" initially covered by the Expiry Act was "reestablished." Furthermore,

[104] Gianella Bardazano, "Los efectos de la Ley: entre la amnistía de la tradición nacional y Nuremberg en la conciencia de la Humanidad," in *Ley de Caducidad: un tema inconcluso: momentos, actores y argumentos*, ed. A. Marchesi et al. (Montevideo, Uruguay: Ed. Trilce, 20132013), 166.

[105] SCJ, Sentencia no. 365/2009, ¶ III.8.

[106] SCJ, Sentencia no. 365/2009, ¶ III.3, citing Luigi Ferrajoli, *Democracia y Garantismo*, 55.

[107] *Gelman v. Uruguay*, Inter-Am. Ct. H.R. (2011).

[108] Bardazano, "Cuando nos muramos todos," 250.

it established that, insofar as these constitute crimes against humanity, they were not subject to statutory limitations.[109] Admittedly, this latter implication was repeatedly, albeit if inconsistently, questioned by the Supreme Court of Uruguay, which, under different compositions, refused to apply them.

During this period, the IACtHR made "national prosecution of gross, state-sponsored crimes a centerpiece of its regional agenda."[110] In 2000, the IACtHR recognized the right to truth as an autonomous right under the ACHR, despite the lack of any explicit reference to that effect, overturning a 1997 decision to the contrary.[111] This right was based on the right to justice, which had been incorporated in the American and Universal Declaration of Human Rights, and was likely based on the Latin American domestic provision on *amparo*.[112] Furthermore, the IACtHR linked this right to the state's duty to investigate as well as to prosecute and punish any serious human rights violations. After its groundbreaking decision in *Barrios Altos* (2001), the Court found that amnesty laws were incompatible with the ACHR in cases against Chile, Brazil, Uruguay, and El Salvador. In *Almonacid Arellano v Chile* (2006), the Court added to its analysis that the relevant offenses amounted to crimes against humanity and, as such, violated *jus cogens* norms—echoing Schiffrin's opinion in *Schwammberger* (1987), the Saquicuray 1995 decision, and the Cavallo 2001 decision—in order to bolster the claim that they were incompatible with the ACHR.[113] That same year, in *La Cantuta v. Peru* (2006), the Court clarified that amnesty laws regarding this type of offense lacked legal effects since their passing. Thereby, they did not require a separate, domestic act invalidating them.[114] It further stated that *non bis in idem* and *res judicata* principles were no obstacles to prosecution when the original decision resulted from a process that was not independent or impartial or did not respect basic due process guarantees (¶ 153). In *Gelman v. Uruguay* (2011), the Court further stated that even if the amnesty has "been approved in a democratic regime and ratified or supported by civil society in two

[109] Act 18.831/2011, §§ 1–3. Only to add that, in any event, the period in which the Expiry Act was in force should not be considered for the purposes of the statutory limitations analysis.

[110] Alexandra Huneeus, "International Criminal Law by Other Means: The Quasi-Criminal Jurisdiction of the Human Rights Courts," *American Journal of International Law* 107, no. 1 (2013): 1.

[111] *Castillo Páez v. Peru* (1997) ¶ 86. The IACtHR had rejected the notion of a right to truth as a discrete human right under the ACHR. It changed its mind in *Bámaca Velázquez v. Guatemala.*

[112] Kathryn Sikkink, "Latin American Countries as Norm Protagonists of the Idea of International Human Rights," *Global Governance* 20 (2014): 289–404.

[113] Fabia Fernandez Carvalho, "Whose Exceptionalism? Debating the Inter-American View on Amnesty and the Brazilian Case," in *Anti-Impunity in the Human Rights Agenda*, ed. Karen Engle et al (Cambridge: Cambridge University Press, 2016), 189.

[114] At ¶ 189. Cassese suggested that this may have been the first time that an international jurisdiction directly invalidates a domestic provision, obliging the state which dictated it to act as if it had never existed. See Antonio Cassese, "Y-a-t-il un conflict insurmontable entre souverineté des États et justice pénale internationale?" in *Crimes Internationaux et Jurisdictions Internationales*, ed. Antonio Cassesse and Mirellie Delmas-Marty (Paris: PUF, 2002), 16.

occasions, it is not automatically and by itself endowed with legitimacy under International Law."

The anti-impunity response consolidated in many countries during the following years. Since the decision of the IACtHR in *Almonacid Arellano*, accountability in Chile made significant progress, but sentences were considerably lenient compared with other parts of the region (and the gravity of the offenses). This resulted from the reasoning still including the partial application of statutory limitations. In December 2017, the Supreme Court of Peru found null and void a pardon issued on humanitarian grounds by President Pedro Pablo Kuzcinski to Fujimori. In Argentina, which had arguably the most comprehensive accountability process in the region (and the world), 1,025 individuals had been sentenced in 254 decisions (165 had been acquitted) by 2021. There were still 2,200 individuals under investigation, 21 ongoing trials, and another 73 waiting for their commencement date to be settled.[115] Furthermore, Argentine courts began investigating crimes perpetrated in other parts of the world on grounds of universal jurisdiction.[116]

The anti-impunity approach, which had become a critical element in the regional transitional justice process, has been criticized for being overly activist,[117] for not being sufficiently sensitive to the democratic pedigree of some of these amnesties (*re* Uruguay),[118] for not being sufficiently sensitive to context,[119] for not respecting the sovereignty of states under its jurisdiction,[120] or for not respecting the rights of the accused.[121] Ultimately, Brazil has been the only country that has openly defied the IACtHR. Although it created a National Truth Commission (November 2011),[122] the 1979 Amnesty Law passed by the

[115] See "A 45 años del golpe de Estado, suman 1025 las personas condenadas por crímenes de lesa humanidad en 254 sentencias," https://www.fiscales.gob.ar/lesa-humanidad/a-45-anos-del-golpe-deestado-suman-1025-las-personas-condenadas-por-crimenes-de-lesa-humanidad-en-254-sentencias/.

[116] Although Argentina had had a constitutional provision allowing courts to adjudicate crimes perpetrated abroad when perpetrated "against the law of nations" ("*derecho de gentes*") since the nineteenth century, it was the article on access to courts in the ACHR that was decisively used by domestic courts to establish its universal jurisdiction over international crimes. CCCF, Sala II, Causa N 29.275, September 3, 2010. See Alejandro Chehtman, "Strategic Approaches to Extraterritorial Jurisdiction in Latin America," *Extraterritoriality in International Law*, ed. Austen Parrish (London: Edward Elgar, 2023), 180–194.

[117] Gerald Neuman, "Import, Export and Regional Consent In the Inter-American Court of Human Rights," *European Journal of International Law* 19, no. 1 (2008): 101–123.

[118] Roberto Gargarella, "La democracia frente a los crímenes masivos: una reflexión a la luz del caso Gelman," *Revista Latinoamericana de Derecho Internacional* 2 (2015): 1.

[119] Fernandes Carvalho, "Whose Exceptionalism?" 186.

[120] Ezequiel Malarino, "Judicial Activism, Punitivism and Supranationalisation? Liberal and Anti-Democratic Tendencies of the Inter-American Court of Human Rights," *International Conference on Learning Representations* 12 (2012): 665–695.

[121] Fernando Basch, "The Doctrine of the Inter-American Court of Human Rights Regarding States' Duty to Punish Human Rights Violations and Its Dangers," *American University International Law Review* 28, no. 1 (2007): 195–229.

[122] President Lula da Silva proposed the creation of this commission in 2009 but had to drop it when members of the military threatened to resign.

military regime was confirmed (and broadened) by the democratically elected authorities in 1988, and remained in place even after the IACtHR's decision in *Gomes Lund* (2010).[123]

Furthermore, backlash and resistance were rampant in certain parts of the region. In 2013, the former head of state of Guatemala, Efraín Ríos Montt, was convicted by a domestic court of his own country for genocide and humanitarian crimes (a combination of crimes against humanity and war crimes). The prosecution and trial of Rios-Montt was the result of an innovative process of collaboration among different actors. The UN-sponsored International Commission against Impunity in Guatemala, created in 2006, promoted the creation of a team of local prosecutors and a high-risk court, a unit with a focus on macro-criminality, including international crimes, money laundering, and drug-trafficking. These new institutions enhanced domestic capacity and judicial independence, as embodied by the appointment of Claudia Paz y Paz as attorney general in 2010. Furthermore, NGOs like *Asociación para la Justicia y Reconciliación* and *Centro para Acción Legal en Derechos Humanos* were critical in promoting prosecutions and collecting evidence, including witness location, taking statements, finding and analyzing documentation, and commissioning experts reports, among other functions.[124] They mobilized over a hundred indigenous survivors who presented evidence before the Court. Rios-Montt was convicted to eighty years in prison. Nevertheless, only ten days after his conviction, the Constitutional Court ordered a retrial.[125] President Pérez explicitly stated that there had been no genocide in Guatemala and that the trial threatened the peace process, thereby consolidating impunity.[126]

V. Peace

The transitional justice framework was endorsed and reworked in Colombia as a path to peace. In 2003, after several attempts at a negotiated peace with Colombia's different non-state armed groups,[127] incoming President Alvaro Uribe reached an agreement with most of the right wing-paramilitary groups (e.g., *Autodefensas Unidas de Colombia*, or AUC). It was known as the Agreement

[123] *Gomes Lund et al. ("Guerrilha do Araguaia") v. Brazil*, Judgment of November 24, Inter-Am. Ct. H.R. (ser. C) No. 219, ¶¶ 200 and 201 (2010).

[124] Susan Kemp, "Guatemala Prosecutes former President Rios Montt: New Perspectives on Genocide and Domestic Criminal Justice," *Journal of International Criminal Justice* 12 (2014): 152.

[125] Rios Montt ultimately died before the retrial.

[126] Kemp, "Guatemala Prosecutes former President Rios Montt," 152.

[127] Between 1981 and 1997, there were seven attempts to reach a negotiated peace (usually including an amnesty) with different groups by presidents Turbay Ayala (Act 37/1981), Betacuncur (Act 35/1982), Barco Vargas (Act 77/1989), Gaviria (Decree 213/1991 and 1943/1991, and Act 104/1993), and Samper (Act 418/1997).

of Santa Fe de Ralito and was kept secret until ultimately leaked to the press in 2007. In it, paramilitary leaders agreed to a total cessation of hostilities and a gradual demobilization in the following two years in exchange for substantial benefits. A Bill of Penal Alternativity was sent to Congress, offering the AUC virtual impunity and full enjoyment of their wealth. However, under pressure from human rights and victims' organizations, certain political forces (including members of Uribe's party), and international actors (notably the United States and the United Nations), Uribe withdrew this proposal and replaced it in 2004 with the "Justice and Reparation" bill. After significant adjustments in Congress, it was passed as the "Justice and Peace Law" (Law 975 or JPL). The new framework sought to achieve a balance between facilitating peace and promoting the transitional justice agenda of truth, justice and reparations.[128]

This innovative framework bifurcated the justice response and integrated it with the search for truth and the aim of securing reparation for victims. It offered AUC members reduced sentences (a maximum of eight years) on the condition of a commitment to confess to the relevant crimes, provide reparation to victims, and continue to cooperate with the Colombian authorities in dismantling the armed group to which they belonged.[129] Those who did not accept these terms would be handled by the ordinary criminal jurisdiction under its standard proceedings and much more severe legal (sentencing) framework. Notably, in these proceedings Colombian courts also adopted Roxin's approach to indirect perpetration through an organized structure of power[130]—several Colombian magistrates traveled to Peru to discuss technical aspects of the Fujimori decision with their local counterparts.[131] In contrast to the approaches in Argentina and Chile, it decided to charge defendants for international crimes, such as crimes against humanity—as codified in Article 7 of the Rome Statute which had recently come into force.[132]

Despite granting substantial rights to victims, many still considered the law a disguised amnesty. In 2006, the Colombian Commission of Jurists, a leading human rights NGO, challenged the JPL before the Constitutional Court in proceedings involving several other national and international human rights organizations. The central claim was that the crimes perpetrated "could not be excluded from ordinary criminal punishment."[133] The Constitutional Court reviewed

[128] This framework contrasts with the "Democratic Security Policy," which provided harsh penalties for left-wing guerrillas.

[129] They must also avoid perpetrating new offenses.

[130] See, e.g., Unit of Human Rights, process No. 1556, May 14, 2005, 24 and Supreme Court, in Alvaro Alfonso García Romero, Supreme Court, Criminal Cassation Chamber, Decision No. 32805 (February 23, 2010).

[131] Interview on file with author.

[132] Constitutional Court of Colombia, Decision T-355/07, 23.

[133] Helena Alviar García and Karen Engle, "The Distributive Politics of Impunity and Anti-Impunity: Lessons from Four Decades of Colombian Peace Negotiations," in Engle et al., *Anti-Impunity*, 230.

this framework, and although it sustained its compatibility with the Colombian Constitution and its international human rights obligations, it demanded a "full" confession of any crimes as well as "full" disclosure of the groups' unlawful activities. Furthermore, the Court clarified that penalties, even if reduced, must be served in standard penitentiary establishments. The time spent at the "concentration zones" would not count toward the fulfillment of the sentence. It finally stated that demobilized AUC members would need to compensate their victims with their lawfully and unlawfully obtained assets.[134]

These measures "hardening" the JPL framework led to a breakup of the agreement with the AUCs and their leaders. Politicians associated with these groups began attacking the government, and the government exposed their links to these groups and prosecuted them. This political scandal, "*parapolitica*," ended up with more than forty members of Congress convicted on serious charges. The confrontation with AUC leaders further drew Colombian president Alvaro Uribe to extradite fourteen of the most prominent leaders to the United States on drug-related charges on May 12, 2008.[135] This policy silenced them, but at the same time, it thwarted the truth, justice, and reparations components of the JPL. It thereby helped undermine the JPL framework. Ultimately, these legal and political challenges meant that the JPL framework could process a small number of cases.[136] Of the more than thirty thousand paramilitaries demobilized, only five thousand were subjected to the JPL mechanisms—the rest benefited from a de facto amnesty. Furthermore, the onus of the investigations of hundreds of thousands of crimes rested solely upon the shoulders of the prosecutor's office.

By December 2015, the JPL framework had made some progress. Still, not nearly as much as expected: the number of perpetrators processed by the system amounted to 3.4 percent of the total list of AUC members who had accepted the terms of this transitional justice mechanism. The task, in any event, was enormous.[137] According to the Victims Record, as of September 2018, 8.7 million people had suffered serious human rights violations as a direct consequence of the armed conflict since 1985. Some 7.4 million were internally displaced, and 267,000 were killed. Disappeared victims amounted to 47,000, and child soldiers conscripted surpassed 7,500. Previous approaches to truth and accountability were not particularly helpful.

In 2012, under the presidency of Juan Manuel Santos, the strategy of the prosecutor's office changed and focused on macro-cases and a case prioritization

[134] Constitutional Court of Colombia, Decision C-370/06, 211.

[135] A total of thirty paramilitaries involved in JPL proceedings were extradited to the United States.

[136] By 2012, the Justice and Peace Tribunal had convicted only fourteen defendants. Andrés Bermúdez Liévano, *Los debates de La Habana: una mirada desde adentro* (Barcelona: Institute of Integrated Transitions, 2018), 228.

[137] See Verdad Abierta, "La Magnitud de los Crímenes develados por Justicia y Paz," https://verdadabierta.com/la-magnitud-de-los-crimenes-develados-por-justicia-y-paz/.

(instead, at least formally, of case selection). Although the total number of adjudicated cases remained low, this adjustment allowed the JPL authorities to elucidate and begin to shed some light on the structural patterns of criminality that characterized the AUC phenomenon. At the same time, a small number of cases were being prosecuted domestically, including, most relevantly perhaps, those of so-called false positives—murders perpetrated by state armed forces which were presented as war casualties—and certain forms of criminal offenses, periodically monitored by the ICC.[138]

In November 2012, President Santos began peace negotiations with FARC (Revolutionary Armed Forces of Colombia) in Havana, Cuba. These negotiations focused on six main issues: illegal drugs, victims' rights, agrarian development, the end of the conflict, political participation, and implementation, verification, and signature of agreements. One of the innovations in this negotiation was its emphasis on the provisions concerning the agreement's implementation. A second aspect was the direct participation of victims and minorities. In effect, sixty victims visited Havana—they included victims of different ethnicities, genders, geographical origin, and political allegiance. Women also had a prominent role in adopting gender-sensitive language in the agreement and proposing 120 positive measures for the implementation phase.[139] The Peace Agreement was finally signed on September 26, 2016, giving birth to an extraordinarily complex institution.

The parties in the negotiations sought a new strategy to secure the legal stability of the peace agreement, especially its critical provisions on reduced sentencing, political participation, and reparations. FARC had put the issue of alternative sentencing on the table from the beginning.[140] Stability was key for the success of the demobilization and disarmament processes, particularly in the light of the IACtHR's case law, the ongoing preliminary examination of the ICC, and, most notably, the experience of the agreement with the AUCs. Furthermore, stability was pursued through two main strategies: a short-term political strategy and a longer-term legal one. Politically, it was decided that the Agreement would need to be adopted by a general referendum to give it greater social legitimacy—a constitutional reform was envisaged and ultimately discarded.[141] This strategy failed, as a slight majority (43 percent of votes) of the Colombian population voted against the final agreement after a harsh campaign by the opposition to

[138] See, e.g., Interim Report of the Situation in Colombia issued by the ICC's Office of the Prosecutor in November 2012, https://www.icc-cpi.int/sites/default/files/2022-09/OTPCOLOMBIAPublicInterimReportNovember2012.pdf.

[139] This ended up being one of the main aspects of the campaign against the Agreement in the referendum (see below).

[140] Alviar and Engle, "The Distributive Politics," 232.

[141] The inspiration was the 1998 Good Friday Agreement between the United Kingdom, Ireland, and eight other actors.

President Santos. After (minor, essentially procedural) amendments,[142] the Final Agreement was subsequently adopted by Congress and later validated—at least in its main traits—by Colombia's Constitutional Court.

The legal strategy was complementary to the political one. As described in greater detail by Helena Alviar García and Laura Betancur-Restrepo in this volume,[143] the parties followed a two-pronged legal architecture to ensure this outcome. First, the Legal Framework for Peace passed by the Colombian Congress in 2012 to facilitate the negotiations included two transitory articles in the Constitution allowing for prosecutorial discretion as well as suspended or alternative sentencing. Second, the Colombian authorities decided to consider the peace agreement as a special agreement under international law, under the terms of common Article 3 to the Geneva Conventions.[144] This aspect sought to make this agreement only binding under international law, and not part of the Colombian domestic legal system.

Admittedly, by this time, the IACtHR's position vis-à-vis amnesties had started to change. The Court had acknowledged that "it is justified on occasions to issue laws of amnesty upon the cessation of hostilities in-non-international armed conflicts so as to allow for a return to peace," even if it immediately added that "this is not an absolute norm, insofar as there also exist in International Humanitarian Law an obligation for States to investigate and try war crimes."[145] In his concurrent opinion, Judge García Sayán further argued that

> [b]eyond what has been resolved in previous cases, the issue with amnesties and their relation to the duty to investigate and sanction grave human rights violations requires an analysis that provides adequate criteria for a trial of ponderance in contexts where tensions might arise between the demands of justice and the requirement of a negotiated peace within the framework of a non-international armed conflict.

He thereby concluded that in "certain situations of transition from an armed conflict to peace, it may happen that a State does not have the possibility of fully materializing, simultaneously, the different international rights and obligations it has contracted." In such context, it would be reasonable to ponder the different

[142] For instance, the possibility of foreign judges taking part in JEP was rejected.

[143] See, Helena Alviar García and Laura Betancur-Restrepo, "Strategic Uses of International Law in Peace Negotiations in Colombia", 552 and ff.

[144] See International Committee of the Red Cross, *Commentary on the First Geneva Convention: Convention (I) for the Amelioration of the Condition of the Wounded and Sick in Armed Forces in the Field*, 2nd ed., Geneva, 2016, para. 850, cited in Government of Colombia and FARC, Final Agreement to End the Armed Conflict and Build a Stable and Lasting Peace, Bogotá, 24 November 2016.

[145] *Masacres de El Mozote y lugares aledaños v. El Salvador*, Inter-Am. Ct. H.R. (2012).

rights in play, including "the degrees of justice to be reached" in pursuance of a lasting, "reciprocal tolerance and peace."[146]

Furthermore, the peace agreement created a whole new institutional architecture (the Comprehensive System of Truth, Justice Reparation and Non-repetition), which followed the JPL framework with an added degree of complexity. Indeed, this new system contains several "mechanisms" that seek to provide an "integral response" to the phenomenon of mass criminality. A truth commission operates as a space for victims to express their grievances and harms suffered in the context of public hearings, as in Chile. It is also more concerned with the process of providing for a "general catharsis" than solely in issuing a final report, as the first generation of truth commissions did.[147] Within its mandate, the Commission must also document instances of resilience, altruistic actions, and positive transformations in victims and their communities. The unit for seeking disappeared persons, in turn, is in charge of helping the families find their loved ones. Five commissions are charged with examining issues of special interest, such as ethnic, gender, territorial and environmental, political participation, and implementation. Notably, the Special Jurisdiction for Peace (hereinafter, SJP) is significantly funded by foreign donations, including the Post-Conflict Multi-Donor Fund and the Colombia in Peace Fund.

A tribunal for peace has three main chambers: a Chamber for Amnesty and Pardon created to examine on a case-by-case basis whether certain offenses (including murder and drug-trafficking) would be the object of amnesties on the grounds of their connection with political motivations; a Chamber for Defining Legal Situations, in charge of exempting from prosecution those individuals who, despite not acting with "altruistic," political motives, were not part of those bearing the greatest responsibility; finally, a Chamber for the Recognition of Responsibility for those with a decisive role in the perpetration of international crimes who, subject to the fulfillment of certain commitments—such as acknowledging their responsibility, providing truth and reparations—would be sanctioned, albeit with reduced penalties.[148] This system also has a unit responsible for investigations and prosecutions. Furthermore, sanctions are not to be served in standard prisons and are construed in restorative-reparative justice terms, offering an open-ended list of forms of public service, reparations, and other public engagements.[149]

[146] Separate concurring opinion by Judge Diego García Sayán, ¶¶ 4, 5, and 38.

[147] Bermúdez Liévano, *Los debates*, 252–253.

[148] They were calibrated along a few issues, such as how timely the recognition of responsibility was, how full were the truth and reparations offered, and so on. Those who refused to recognize responsibility, if found guilty in regular proceedings, would be sanctioned with harsher penalties, though still reduced because they had voluntarily abandoned the armed struggle. Ibid., 240.

[149] JEP, "Lineamientos en materia de sanción propia y Trabajos, Obras y Actividades con contenido Reparador–Restaurador" (April 14, 2020), https://www.jep.gov.co/Sala-de-Prensa/SiteAssets/Paginas/Conozca-Los-lineamientos-en-materia-de-sanci%C3%B3n-propia-y-Traba

Yet perhaps the main conceptual innovation in terms of the transitional justice framework is the focus on economic inequalities as one of the drivers of the conflict, and thereby as a key focal point for transitional justice. This agenda included three main topics: "access to land and formalization of property rights, development programs designed for regional differences, and the incorporation of agrarian reform in national plans."[150] FARC insisted on discussing broader political, economic, and social reform when Belisario Betancourt offered a general amnesty in exchange for peace in 1982.[151] Throughout the following years, Alviar and Engle indicate, "FARC's position on redistribution remained consistent."[152] Indeed, in the negotiations in Havana, they proposed to include within the framework of reparations the violation of economic, social, and cultural human rights. By contrast, the economic elites in Colombia were refractory of any strong political agenda. The Colombian Federation of Cattle Ranchers (Fedegán), for instance, was concerned that FARC's advocacy for agrarian reform would end in expropriations.[153] Ultimately, although what the parties agreed in Havana concerning social justice is hardly revolutionary, these debates and negotiations have the potential of bringing to the front a central aspect of the systematic violations of human rights perpetrated in Latin America that has remained outside the framework of transitional justice.[154]

VI. Coda

In recent years, the ICC closed its preliminary examination in Colombia. To the frustration of local civil society organizations, it opened two investigations in Venezuela. The Office of the Prosecutor further developed relevant forms of collaboration and technical assistance with local authorities in other countries, including Colombia and Argentina (vis-à-vis universal jurisdiction prosecutions). In El Salvador, the amnesty has been recently declared null and void to prosecute political opponents of the Bukele administration.[155] Between 2016 and

jos%2C-Obras-y-Actividades-con-contenido-Reparador---Restaurador/28042020%20VF%20Lineamientos%20Toars%20y%20SP.pdf.

[150] Alviar and Engle, "The Distributive Politics," 239.

[151] Ana María Bejarano et al., *Discusiones sobre la Reforma del Estado en Colombia: la fragmentación del Estado y el funcionamiento del Congreso* (Bogotá, Colombia: Colciencias, 2001), 26.

[152] Alviar and Engle, "The Distributive Politics," 224.

[153] Ibid., 238.

[154] Colombia still faces critical limitations in addressing the root causes of the conflict and the outstanding violence. See Manuel Iturralde, "Colombian Transitional Justice and the Political Economy of the Anti-Impunity Transnational Legal Order," in *Transnational Legal Ordering of Criminal Justice* (Cambridge: Cambridge University Press, 2020), 248.

[155] See the prosecution of the five water defenders from the Salvadorean NGO ADES Santa Marta, arrested on January 11, 2023, for conduct during the 1980–1992 civil war.

2019, high-level officers were prosecuted in Guatemalan courts for international crimes, including enforced siappearance, sexual violence and torture.[156] In October 2021, Mexico established a truth commission to address the period known as the "Dirty War" (*Guerra Sucia*).[157] Argentina convicted defendants for sexual offenses during the state repression. Despite its significant claim to innovation, the SJP in Colombia seems to be struggling to make progress with its justice components, and broader economic reparations have been scant. In 2022, the IACtHR further acknowledged the right to truth as a collective right in a democratic society in its *Integrantes y Militantes de Unión Patriótica v. Colombia* case (2022).[158] In short, the field of transitional justice is still very much alive in Latin America.

This chapter sought to trace the development of ideas, institutions, and policies developed in Latin America to address state violence and mass criminality and to pursue key aims such as consolidating democratic regimes. These include critical innovations in practical aspects such as interviewing victims, documenting violations, developing evidentiary techniques (such as forensic anthropology or concerning filiation), and innovating on the institutional framework such as the different approaches in the workings and outcomes of truth commissions and truth trials. They also cover developments to circumvent and overcome legal obstacles to accountability, such as the permanent nature of certain offenses, the nonapplicability of statutory limitations, and different forms of blanket amnesties and pardons. Furthermore, judicial and political actors have developed criteria and strategies to select and/or prioritize cases (including limiting proceedings to "paradigmatic" or "macro" cases, distinguishing between "levels" of responsibility). They also sought to develop legal ideas to modulate, contain, or limit the accountability response, including partial statutory limitations, exchanging benefits for truth, alternative penalties, "internationalizing" a peace agreement following a noninternational armed conflict, and restorative justice practices. They further sought to complement truth and justice with reparations and ultimately acknowledged that transitional justice should look far more closely at issues of structural inequality.

This extraordinarily rich and creative history was the result of virtuous interactions—often via collaboration but sometimes through confrontation—from key stakeholders, most notably victims/human rights organizations,

[156] J.M. Burt, "The Justice We Deserve: War Crimes Prosecutions in Guatemala", *Latin American Research Review* 56(1) (2021), 214–232.

[157] See *Comisión para el Acceso a la Verdad, el Esclarecimiento Histórico y el Impulso a la Justicia de las violaciones graves a los derechos humanos cometidas de 1965 a 1990*, https://comisionverdadyjusticia.segob.gob.mx/. As of the end of 2023, the Commission has not issued a public report and, by contrast, has complained about the lack of cooperation of Mexican authorities.

[158] The Court also avoided considering whether genocide can be perpetrated against "political" groups, as requested by the claimants, on the grounds that it lacked jurisdiction.

members of the judiciary, international tribunals, and academics, but also members of non-state armed groups and, in specific contexts, the military. By showing the relevant waves of truth, justice, and peace and how these innovations traveled, reappeared, and were adapted and transformed in different countries of the region, this chapter claims that this body of law has a genuine regional character. It also shows that the perpetual search for solutions to different problems (innovations) was marked by relevant forms of path dependency. Indeed, perhaps once established, this path dependency and the approaches it has ultimtately foreclosed deserve closer scrutiny.

22

The Racial Dimension of Latin American International Law

Maryluz Barragan Gonzalez

I. Introduction

Racism and racial discrimination are prominent features of Latin American societies and have had considerable influence on regional international law. This chapter uses the relationship between international law and racism in Latin America to explore the racial dimension of Latin American international law. To this end, I pose two guiding questions: How does international law relate to racial inequality in the region? In what ways does Latin American international law assist in the global struggle against racial discrimination?

The failure to guarantee the fundamental rights of Black communities is a common phenomenon in the region. It is predominately understood as a reality against which the law can do little. This perception is largely explained by the fact that after abolishing slavery, Latin American countries never used positive law (at least consistently) to maintain the regime of racial subordination that has existed since colonial times. This differs significantly from the cases of apartheid (South Africa) and Jim Crow laws (United States). Nevertheless, some regional dynamics have facilitated the consolidation of a racial and socioeconomic gap, such as informal social rules, denial of the social tensions derived from the idea of race and, consequently, the absence of hard national and international legal norms to confront the problem.

This chapter is divided into two parts. The first part is an introduction to the racial dimension of Latin American international law, proposing that the idea of race has been central to Latin American countries' international relations. Slavery—as one of the most critical legal and economic enterprises of colonization—was founded on the idea of racial subordination[1]. Based on slavery, mercantile relations were woven between European countries to ensure

[1] Adelle Blackett & Alice Duquesnoy, "Slavery is not a metaphor: U.S. prison labor and racial subordination through the lens of the ILO's Abolition of Forced Labor Convention". *UCLA Law Review*, *67* (May 2021): 1504-1568, https://www.uclalawreview.org/slavery-is-not-a-metaphor-u-s-prison-labor-and-racial-subordination-through-the-lens-of-the-ilos-abolition-of-forced-labor-convention/

Maryluz Barragan Gonzalez, *The Racial Dimension of Latin American International Law* In: *Latin American International Law in the Twenty-First Century*. Edited by: Alejandro Chehtman, Alexandra Huneeus, and Sergio Puig, Oxford University Press.
DOI: 10.1093/9780197754016.003.0022

the trafficking of African people to America, a project that directly involved the three continents. Later, the fight against slavery would become one of the first expressions of international cooperation manifested by signing international agreements to put an end to this barbaric practice, which in turn implied a humanization of international law.

In Latin America, however, racism as an ideology did not end with the legal abolition of slavery in the mid-19th century. Racism as an ideology is deeply rooted in our societies and constitutes a sort of "social contract" on the issue of race ("racial contract")[2] that influences the way we create and apply international legal instruments.[3] This consensus involves denying the existence of racism, approaching the problem by implementing negative or prohibitive obligations when it comes to racial discrimination, and resisting the establishment of positive obligations on states to reduce the socioeconomic gap that harms racialized groups.

The second part of this chapter presents two significant contributions of Latin American international law in the fight against racism and racial discrimination. On the one hand, there is the jurisprudential and dogmatic interpretation of ILO Convention 169 on the rights of Indigenous and Tribal peoples. Although Convention 169 is an instrument of international law produced by the International Labour Organization (a special agency of the United Nations), it has, in fact, been interpreted and developed primarily by the Inter-American Human Rights System and the constitutional courts of Latin American countries. This is explained by the fact that fifteen of the twenty-four countries that have ratified Convention 169 are Latin American. Regarding this instrument, the regional experience is decisive in understanding the content of the right to prior consultation of Indigenous peoples and Afro-descendant communities, one of the main prerogatives created by the Convention.

Another highly relevant aspect of Latin American international law is the historical reparations movement carried out by the Caribbean Community (CARICOM)[4] (officially formed in 1973 by the Chaguaramas Treaty). This platform has led the conversation in the region regarding reparations to compensate for the legacy of slavery and colonization. This conversation problematizes current international law and the relationship between European countries and their former colonies in Latin America (specifically, in the Caribbean). It

[2] Charles W. Mills, *The Racial Contract* (1st ed., Ithaca, NY: Cornell University Press, 1997).

[3] In this article I adapt to the Latin American context the notion of "racial contract" used by Christopher Gevers (2021) to demonstrate how the dynamics of "white racial supremacy" operate in international law.

[4] Christian Courtis, "Apuntes sobre la aplicación del Convenio 169 de la OIT sobre los pueblos indígenas por los tribunales de América Latina," *Sur International Journal on Human Rights* no. 10 (2009). https://www.corteidh.or.cr/tablas/r23739.pdf

proposes the return of public debts that Latin American countries paid to their colonizers so that they could be independent nations and recognize the current negative effects of colonization.

II. The Idea of Race in Latin American International Law

In this section, I will explain how the idea of "mestizaje" or racial mixing, has created a transnational ideological pact throughout Latin America. It has resulted in a sort of "racial contract," in the words of Charles W. Mills, which implies a "social contract" around racial relations in our society. This not only marks the agenda of Latin American international law but also contributes to the little salience given to racism and racial discrimination in the region despite being a structural problem shared by all Latin American countries. The systematic denial of racial conflicts will also be a distinctive feature of Latin American international law.

The first examples of Latin American international law appear during the period of independence from Spain and other former European metropolises in the 19th century. In these legal mechanisms, the idea of race was always present, albeit implicitly. Simón Bolívar's ideal was to create a regional confederation with its own specific legal system to be applied in the new nations.[5] The basic characteristics of this system included the design of permanent supranational bodies; recognition of the *uti possidetis iuris* principle or preferential trade relations between member countries; recognition of *social, cultural,* and *political homogeneity* and the incorporation of democratic, republican institutions; and *the abolition of slavery*.[6]

On the one hand, the sophism of *cultural homogeneity* implanted through the idea of mestizaje[7] has been fundamental in the construction of regional identity.[8] It is a constant denial of racial tensions and the reaffirmation of a single harmonious Latin American race: the mestizo race. This basic idea of regional identity was strategically constructed with the goal of leaving behind an immediate past of violence against Indigenous people and Afro-descendants (imposed by colonization) and preventing the latent threat embodied by the expansive eagerness

[5] Cesareo Gutiérrez-Espada, "Existe un derecho internacional latinoamericano?" in La idea de América en el pensamiento *ius* internacionalista del siglo XXI, ed. Yolanda Gamarra Chopo (Zaragoza, Spain: Universidad de Zaragoza, 2010), 87–105. https://dialnet.unirioja.es/servlet/articulo?codigo=4509908

[6] Ibid.

[7] The so-called myth of mestizaje is the denial of racial hierarchies in Latin America. The ideologist who consolidated this theory was the Mexican politician José Vasconselos (1882–1959) who, through his masterpiece "*La raza cósmica*" (1925), developed this narrative.

[8] Peter Wade, "Repensando el mestizaje," *Revista Colombiana de Antropología*, no. 39 (January–December 2003) 273–296, https://www.redalyc.org/pdf/1050/105018181009.pdf

of US domination.[9] Mestizaje is an ideology that denies interethnic antagonisms and exalts regional nationalism.[10] However—and aside from the celebratory eagerness of racial fusion—in Blackness, the stigma of dehumanization and the idea of white superiority, which people should aspire to, has always existed.

On the other hand, *enslavement* as an enterprise that was legal and widespread in the region is another central element in the international relations of the emerging Latin American countries and in the way they participated in the international community. This is so not only because America was one of the epicenters of the system of slavery, but also because it was through this system that European countries first began to consolidate their relations and collaboration. This cooperation manifested first in ensuring the transportation of enslaved people from Africa to the Americas and, later, in overthrowing the barbaric system they had built.

The dismantling of slavery in the Americas signified the humanization of international law. Spanish scholar Gregorio Peces Barba identified the fight against slavery as one of the first signs of international cooperation within the framework of human rights.[11] Between 1815 and 1880, more than fifty international agreements were reached in this regard,[12] the most relevant being the Declaration of the Powers on the Abolition of the Slave Trade (Vienna, February 8, 1815), signed by Austria, Spain, France, Great Britain, Norway, Portugal, Prussia, and Sweden; the Anglo-Spanish treaty to suppress the slave trade (1817); and the Treaty between Spain and Great Britain for the Abolition of the Slave Trade (1835). These instruments of international law stemmed mainly from the social demands of the American colonies. It is, therefore, no exaggeration to say that the humanization of international law is largely due to the demands for equality that emanated from the plantations of the American colonies. This is also why, as mentioned earlier, the abolition of slavery was one of the central issues for the independence movements in the region.

The slavery system, developed within the framework of European colonization in the Americas, marked a global racial regime that simultaneously became integrated into Latin American societies. Although formally this legal order no longer exists, dynamics that perpetuate racial hierarchies persist today. In Latin American region, this order is not implemented through positive law but rather through informal social rules that have allowed the racial subordination of Afro-descendant and Indigenous peoples to continue over time. Or as the scholar

[9] Jean-Pierre Tardieu, "El negro y la "raza cósmica" de José Vasconcelos (1925)," *Revista Boletín americanista*, Universidad de Barcelona no. 71 (2015–2012), 155–169, https://dialnet.unirioja.es/servlet/articulo?codigo=5503120

[10] Ibid.

[11] Gregorio Peces-Barba Martínez, *Curso de Derechos Fundamentales. Teoría Genera* (1st ed., Madrid: Agencia Estatal Boletín Oficial del Estado, BOE, 1995), 173.

[12] Ibid.

Tania Hernandez would put it, they became rules of customary law.[13] Both positive law (such as Jim Crow-USA or apartheid-South Africa regimes) and custom have been particularly effective in maintaining the global racial hierarchies that were established during the colonial era. Nevertheless, the absence of a racial legal regime with consistent positive law norms in Latin America has been very useful in denying the existence of racism in the region.

Apart from this, racism seems to have developed into a social consensus that is expressed through racial discrimination as a custom. In turn, this custom ends up normalizing the fact that millions of racialized people are not guaranteed a minimum standard of human rights.[14] Faced with this reality, it is helpful to review the analytical framework proposed by Charles W. Mills, a London philosopher of Jamaican origin, in his work *The Racial Contract* (1997). He argues that racism and racialization are not extraordinary, sudden phenomena that fracture politics in a liberal democracy that presents itself as neutral in the face of racial tensions. On the contrary, racism, colonialism, slavery, and reparations naturally stem from liberalism. The author emphasizes that the modern world developed through consensus on slavery and colonialism, and with this consensus, came a racial regime dominated by European countries.

The notion of "racial contract" is a valuable lens through which to examine the intersection of state power, international law, and racial discrimination.[15] In Latin America, we have our own subordinate "racial contract," which entails an implicit pact between countries to deny racial tensions in our societies or, at the very least, to deny their relevance. This is reflected in the limited focus of the regional international instruments designed to address this problem. This unspoken pact may also explain why—although formally illegal and in violation of human rights principles—societies of the region continue to perpetuate and propagate racism.

In the Latin American context, racism is perceived as an accidental as opposed to a structural problem and a domestic responsibility of each state. This approach is insufficient because it restricts and disincentivizes governments from developing strong measures against racial discrimination.[16] The prohibitive approach

[13] Tania K. Hernández, *La subordinación racial en Latinoamérica,* 1st. ed (Bogotá-Colombia: Editorial Siglo del Hombre, 2013).

[14] This is a serious problem, partly because of the number of victims it claims. One in five people in Latin America are of African descent, equivalent to about 20 percent of the total population. This reality is perceived by society and state institutions as something natural and inevitable, as a sort of manifest destiny, which complicates the demands of this social group to modify their realities. However, in this scenario, international legal instruments have been crucial in deploying some measures to protect their rights.

[15] Christopher Gevers' "Unwhitening the World: Rethinking Race and International Law," *UCLA Law Review* 67 (May 2021): 1652–1685, https://www.uclalawreview.org/unwhitening-the-world-rethinking-race-and-international-law/.

[16] Cristina Echeverri-Pineda, "Normas internacionales para afrodescendientes en América Latina: interacción entre movimientos sociales, Estados e instituciones internacionales," *Revista*

is common in the various instruments of international law related to Afro-descendants; however, it is unusual for these instruments to call for the recognition and positive obligation of states to eliminate racism and its consequences.

The second half of the twentieth century and the beginning of the twenty-first century saw the emergence of the main legal instruments on the subject.[17] The first was the International Convention on the Elimination of All Forms of Racial Discrimination, adopted in 1965. Consequently, the Committee on the Elimination of Racial Discrimination was created to oversee the implementation of the Convention. In the regional context, ILO Convention 169, also known as Indigenous and Tribal Peoples Convention, was perhaps the international instrument with the greatest normative force and crucial to the recognition of the rights of Afro-descendants. This Convention 169 includes the rights of self-determination, territorial rights, and prior consultation of Indigenous and Tribal communities.

More recently, at the regional level, the Inter-American Convention against Racism, Racial Discrimination and Related Forms of Intolerance (2013) was adopted.[18] From the very name of this convention, one can perceive a shift in approach to racial discrimination. The regional community was beginning to understand the structural nature of the phenomenon of racism. The low level of ratification of the Convention (2013) could be explained by the greater commitment required by this regional instrument, particularly with respect to positive obligations for states. In 2024, of the thirty-five countries in the region, only six have ratified this instrument. Although it may also be too early to conclude why so few countries ratified this instrument, the bigger commitment required of states seems a cogent explanation.

What is irrefutably true is that the frequently used prohibitive approach to racial discrimination has not had a major impact on racial equity in the region. For example, although progress has been made in reducing poverty and social inequality, there is still a marked deficit in guaranteeing the rights of Afro-descendants. This is demonstrated by the latest report on the subject published in 2021 by the United Nations, ECLAC (Economic Commission for Latin America and the Caribbean), and Universidade Federal do Pará (UFPA)

Colombia Internacional, no. 102 (2020): 139–164, http://www.scielo.org.co/scielo.php?pid=S0121-56122020000200139&script=sci_abstract&tlng=es

[17] Roberto Rojas Dávila, "Afro-descendants as subject of rights in international human rights law. The historical process of recognition and its challenges," *Sur International Journal on Human Rights* no. 28. (December 2018), https://sur.conectas.org/en/afro-descendants-as-subjects-of-rights-in-international-human-rights-law/

[18] Of the thirty-five countries in the region, only six have ratified the commitments acquired in the Inter-American Convention against Racism, Racial Discrimination and Related Forms of Intolerance, http://www.oas.org/es/sla/ddi/tratados_multilaterales_interamericanos_A-68_racismo_firmas.asp.

entitled "Afro-descendants and the Matrix of Social Inequality in Latin America. Challenges for Inclusion." This study develops relevant indicators to measure the social inequality faced by the Afro-descendant population in the region in terms of health, education, employment, political participation, and migration, among others. The study shows that ethnic and racial inequality continues to be a structural feature of Latin American societies and is an obstacle to the objectives of poverty reduction.[19] These inequality gaps between population groups are present even in Uruguay, which stands out for having the lowest poverty rates in the region.[20]

Racial inequality and Latin American international law intersect in at least the two aspects described above. First, international cooperation agreements on the abolition of slavery were influenced, among other factors, by the demands of enslaved persons in the early stages of forming Latin American states. This marks an important early milestone in the contribution of Latin America to the international law regime. Second, racism rooted in the colonial and enslavement eras continues to shape Latin American international law, constituting a true implicit "racial contract", in other words, a social consensus that marks race relations in the region. The low importance given to the deficit in the guarantee of the rights of Afro-descendant and Indigenous communities has prevented the development of instruments that create strong obligations on the part of states to address this problem. However, this has been changing gradually, as indicated by the content of the Inter-American Convention against Racism, Racial Discrimination and Related Forms of Intolerance.

III. Two Contributions of Latin American International Law in the Fight against Racism and Racial Discrimination

Other chapters in this book delve into a more philosophical discussion on the existence or absence of authentic Latin American international law. For the purposes of this section, we start from the assumption that Latin American international law exists. This assumption is based not only on the existence of a set of international norms aimed at regulating legal relations between countries of the region but also on the existence of significant contributions to global international law rooted in Latin American practice and experience. In terms of the fight against racism and racial discrimination as a global problem, the region has

[19] Comisión Económica Para América Latina y el Caribe–CEPAL, "Afrodescendientes y la matriz de desigualdad social en América Latina. Retos para la inclusión," Informe de Naciones Unidas (2020), 251. https://www.cepal.org/es/publicaciones/46191-afrodescendientes-la-matriz-la-desigualdad-social-america-latina-retos-la

[20] Ibid., 108.

made important efforts that have strengthened the current international legal framework and other efforts that have aimed to reconfigure international relations of some countries in the region vis-à-vis their former colonists.

The Inter-American Convention against Racism, Racial Discrimination and Related Forms of Intolerance (2013) is probably the most important contribution of regional international law in the fight against racism. However, because it is very recent, it may be premature to analyze its impact on the matter. For this reason, in this section I do not focus on this instrument but rather emphasize other regional experiences. First, I highlight ILO Convention 169. Although it is an instrument that emerged from an international body such as the United Nations, the content and scope of ILO 169 are marked by the Latin American experience. This is because fifteen of the twenty-three countries in which the Convention is applied are Latin American. Therefore, the rights doctrine recognized in the Convention has been mainly developed through the Inter-American Human Rights System and domestic courts. Next, I highlight the global movement for historical reparations. This movement consists of a strategy led by countries of the Caribbean subregion that seek recognition of enslavement and colonization as crimes against humanity that deserve reparations under the rules of international law.

ILO Convention 169, an Instrument of International Law Primarily Applied and Developed in Latin America

Convention 169 was adopted by the International Labour Organization (ILO) in 1989. It is the second binding international instrument on Indigenous and Tribal peoples, the first being Convention 107 of 1957. The ILO is one of the international bodies that has drawn the most attention to the situation of Indigenous and Tribal peoples. After independence, many countries continued to exploit a labor force of Indigenous and Afro-descendant peoples. They veiled this exploitation under supposed legal labor contracts that maintained this labor force in inhumane conditions. The ILO observed how, in many parts of the world, these communities were not guaranteed their rights compared to the rest of the population.[21] For example, in Latin America, this segment of the population continues to have the worst socioeconomic and labor indicators, which, together with discrimination based on ethnic or racial origin, radically aggravates income gaps.[22] This illustrates the continued importance of the ILO's international

[21] International Labour Organization, *Convention No. 169 concerning Indigenous and Tribal Peoples in Independent Countries. United Nations Declaration on the Rights of Indigenous Peoples*, 25th Anniversary Commemorative Edition (2014), https://www.ilo.org/wcmsp5/groups/public/---americas/---ro-lima/documents/publication/wcms_345065.pdf

[22] Ibid.

instruments in guaranteeing the rights of Indigenous and Tribal communities in Latin America.

Although Convention 169 is not explicitly characterized as an international instrument against racism and racial discrimination, in practice, it has become the most efficient tool for the defense of these groups in the region. This has been possible because, at its core, the Convention recognizes the deficit in protecting Indigenous and Tribal peoples' rights. The Convention has two basic postulates: the right of Indigenous and Tribal peoples to maintain and strengthen their own cultures, ways of life, and institutions, as well as their right to participate effectively in the decisions that affect them. These premises constitute the basis on which its provisions must be interpreted. The Convention does not merely declare the prohibition of discrimination on ethnic and racial grounds but recognizes rights that protect the autonomy of these peoples. This translates into the possibility of Indigenous and Tribal peoples deciding their own priorities regarding economic, social, and cultural development.[23]

As of 2024, Convention 169 has been ratified by twenty-four countries: Argentina, Bolivia, Brazil, Chile, Colombia, Costa Rica, Denmark, Dominica, Central African Republic, Ecuador, Fiji, Guatemala, Honduras, Mexico, Nepal, the Netherlands, Nicaragua, Norway, Paraguay, Peru, Venezuela, Germany, Spain, and Luxembourg. Of these, fifteen countries are Latin American, six are European, one is African, one is Oceanic, and one is Asian. This explains the great influence of Latin American international law in the substantive recognition of the rights contemplated in the Convention. The doctrinal evolution of the Convention in the Inter-American Human Rights System and the constitutional courts of the countries of the region is an international point of reference not only for United Nations bodies but also for other regional human rights systems.

How international law has been incorporated into the domestic law of the states in Latin America has been decisive for the substantive (not only formal) recognition of the Convention. The monist tradition has dominated the region, leading countries to incorporate duly ratified treaties into domestic law. In some countries, when incorporated into domestic law, human rights treaties are given the highest status in the hierarchy of norms. Through the mechanism referred to as the "block of constitutionality," international human rights norms enjoy the same legal status as constitutional law. Such is the case of Bolivia and Colombia, where judges, in their sentences, must protect the fundamental rights recognized internally and in human rights treaties, such as Convention 169.

Latin American governments, constitutional judges, and the Inter-American Human Rights System have determined the content of ILO Convention

[23] Ibid.

169.[24] Extending the prerogatives of Convention 169 to Afro-descendant communities is one of the significant developments in the region. In countries such as Colombia, the category of Tribal people also includes Afro-descendant communities, and therefore the rules of the Convention also apply to these communities. For this reason, it is also noteworthy that, due to the direct application of the rules of the ILO Convention 169, the defense of the rights of Afro-descendant communities in the region draws on the model of the defense of the rights of Indigenous communities. In contrast to the civil rights model in the United States, the defense of the rights of Black communities is not limited to the adoption of measures aimed at facilitating a process of assimilation to the majority society but rather recognizes a certain degree of autonomy and self-determination for some Black communities. Autonomy allows Black communities to preserve and develop their cultural identity without undermining the integrity of the national state.

CARICOM and the Movement for Reparations to Compensate for the Harms of Slavery and Colonization

The proposal that the legacy of slavery and colonialism be addressed in international law under a global reparative justice approach is perhaps one of the main contributions of Latin American regional law. The global movement for reparations is a strategy proposed and led mainly by Caribbean Community - CARICOM.[25] The claim is simple. According to international law, proven cases

[24] It may be insufficient to analyze international legal transformation based on treaties alone. Social movements also play an influential role. According to Echeverri-Pineda ("Normas internacionales para afrodescendientes en América Latina: interacción entre movimientos sociales, Estados e instituciones internacionales"), the case of Afro-descendant people is an example of this approach, since the international norms that protect this population are the product of intense activism on the part of transnational social movements or actors and their collaboration with international institutions. It has been precisely the legal mobilization of Afro-descendant social and human rights movements that has allowed for the consolidation of interpretations that guarantee the rights of Afro-descendant communities, even when the agreement is aimed primarily at Indigenous peoples.

[25] CARICOM is a community of countries founded in 1973 through the Treaty of Chaguaramas and is one of the oldest regional integration systems in Latin America and the world. It currently is comprised of Antigua and Barbuda, the Bahamas, Barbados, Belize, Dominica, Grenada, Guyana, Haiti, Jamaica, Montserrat, Saint Lucia, Saint Kitts and Nevis, Saint Vincent and the Grenadines, Suriname, and Trinidad and Tobago. It is a subregional integration system that has had very significant cooperation dynamics; economically, it is emerging as a common market; socially, it has made progress in the free movement of persons and social security; and politically, it has created a consistent organizational and regulatory structure (e.g., the Council on Foreign and Community Relations) that defines the relations between the community and other actors in the international system. Daniel Morales-Ruvalcaba, "La política exterior de las potencias latinoamericanas hacia la Caricom: los casos de Brasil, México, Colombia, Venezuela y Cuba," *Revista Colombia Internacional* no. 96 (2018), https://www.redalyc.org/journal/812/81257495004/html/.

of crimes against humanity must be repaired. Since slavery is a crime against humanity, it must be repaired by the descendants of the perpetrators in favor of the descendants of the victims. This is because the former continue to enjoy the privileges derived from the exploitation, and the latter continue to live the psychological, material, and social effects of it.

The issue of reparations is not new in international law. In the essay "Reparations for Slavery and Other Historical Injustices" (2003), US scholars Eric Posner and Adrian Vermeule provide a comprehensive overview of various historical reparations experiences. For example, France paid reparations to Germany after the Franco-Prussian War of 1872; Germany paid reparations to France after World War I, and the Soviet zone of Germany paid reparations to the Soviet Union after World War I; Iraq has paid and continues to pay reparations on account of the destruction it caused during the Gulf War. The common denominator of these reparations is that they have occurred in the context of armed conflicts, where the defeated countries must "repair" the damages caused to the victorious countries.

The most relevant case of reparations in which the beneficiaries are not the victorious powers but the victims come out of the Nazi Holocaust. After World War II, West Germany paid several billion dollars to Israel and to the victims, descendants, and organizations of Holocaust victims. The program emerged autonomously from the German political system, during the 1950s and 1960s, when Germany was no longer threatened by further physical or economic destruction. German leaders such as Konrad Adenauer believed that Holocaust reparations would persuade the international community that West Germany had left its Nazi past behind and could be trusted with political autonomy.[26]

The global reparations movement, led by CARICOM, shares this claim for victim compensation. However, the approach of the right to reparation for the effects of slavery and colonization is novel. This claim not only implies the reparation of an event more distant in time than the Holocaust but also the possibility of creating a precedent that can be used by nations in Africa or Asia where the negative effects of colonization are also being experienced. The latter would open up the possibility of profound changes in international relations at the global level.

There are various alternatives for reparations, including financial compensation, affirmative action, and public apologies.[27] In its Ten-Point Program,[28]

[26] Erik A. Posner and Adrian Vermeule, "Reparations for slavery and other historical injustices," *Columbia Law Review* 103, no. 3 (2003): 689–748, https://www.jstor.org/stable/1123721

[27] Ibid.

[28] CARICOM member states voted unanimously to seek reparations and demand: (1) an official apology from slave and colonial nations; (2) support for the repatriation of those who wish to resettle in Africa; (3) the creation of an Indigenous peoples development program; (4) support for cultural institutions such as museums and research centers that expose the colonialists' crime against humanity and affirm the humanity of Caribbean peoples; (5) the launch of public health programs

CARICOM proposes a combination of these and urges using "reparations as a development strategy." The goal of Caribbean nations is to use reparation payments to collectively alleviate the psychological, social, economic, and educational problems resulting from the crimes against humanity perpetrated by the slave trade, slavery, the genocide of Indigenous peoples, and the colonialism of European nations, which they see as the genesis of contemporary underdevelopment in Caribbean countries.

In general, the issue of historical reparations has been subject to a great deal of scrutiny and criticism[29], the most frequent of which are that: these are situations that happened a long time ago; it is impossible to know what economic benefit was obtained by the colonizing countries; there is an insufficient legal basis for making reparations claims; it is a matter of shared guilt because several African individuals and governments collaborated with the slave trade; at the time, slavery was a legal enterprise. All these critiques have been widely discussed and theoretically confronted since many of them were debated in the framework of Holocaust reparations. For instance, the formal legality of actions taken by the Nazi regime was not an excuse for refusing to make reparations to the victims of the Nazi regime.

In response to the central question of whether reparations in the Caribbean constitute a solid international legal case, Asian-born jurist Mari Matsuda has developed a typology that provides a good starting point for the discussion. Matsuda suggests that at least three conditions must be present: (1) the injustice must be well documented, (2) the victims must be an identifiable group, and (3) the members of the group must continue to suffer the effects of the harm.[30] All of these conditions are met in the case brought by CARICOM.

Perhaps one of the most dramatic and best-documented cases for reparations in the Caribbean is that of Haiti. By 1750, 77 percent of Haiti's population was enslaved, and by 1780, it was already 90 percent. This accelerated growth rate of slavery, coupled with the ideas of freedom that emerged in the French Revolution, which then spread rapidly to the colonies, increased the demands of the enslaved

to address the chronic diseases that afflict Caribbean people; (6) support for illiteracy elimination programs; (7) the building of "bridges of belonging" to reconnect Black Caribbean people with their African heritage through school and cultural exchange programs; (8) the development of reparative programs to overcome the psychological trauma of slavery and underdevelopment; (9) the transfer of the latest technology and scientific knowledge to the education of Caribbean youth; and (10) the reduction of domestic debt and the cancellation of international debt. Caricom 10 Points Plan for Reparatory Justice, 2014, https://caricom.org/caricom-ten-point-plan-for-reparatory-justice/

[29] Mari J. Matsuda, "Looking to the Bottom: Critical Legal Studies and Reparations", 22 Harv. C.R.-C.L. L. Rev. (1987): 323-374, https://scholarspace.manoa.hawaii.edu/server/api/core/bitstreams/d4d417a7-fff0-4aa0-b99c-636e27797043/content

[30] Hilary McD. Beckles, *Britain's Black Debt. Reparations for Caribbean Slavery and Native Genocide* (1st ed., Kingston, Jamaica: University of West Indies Press, 2013), 14.

population for equality. After an internal war, the French commissioners had no choice but to surrender and declare the emancipation of enslaved people in 1793, and the country declared its independence in 1804. But the case of Haiti is relevant not only because it was the first independent nation in Latin America but also because of the enormous debt it owed to France through a contract, which made further economic development impossible. The debt represented approximately 300 percent of Haiti's national income by 1825[31]. For this reason, they were forced to carry out multiple and disadvantageous renegotiations with French banks, which then traded part of the debts with US banks in the first half of the twentieth century. This debt was finally settled in 1950.

In Haiti, as one of the CARICOM member countries, a deep historical injustice persists because of the conditions Haiti underwent for its independence. For decades, the Haitian state has demanded the return of what was paid. This is not an ethically simple issue, but it is politically and materially feasible. In his most recent work, "A Brief History of Equality," French economist Thomas Piketty proposes a simple formula for calculating and paying the debt that would not have a large impact on France's finances since it would be about 1 percent of its total current public debt (equivalent to 300 percent of Haiti's current national income).[32] Indeed, it would be a relief for the Haitian state and a significant expression of global justice on the part of France.

CARICOM's demands make several interesting points. First, they are not limited to economic reparations but are comprehensive in nature. The issue of debt cancellation is only one of the demands. Additionally, the ten points challenge several of the rules of present-day international law. The demands are directed against an act that today would be qualified as a crime against humanity and continues to have consequences for its victims.

For instance, these claims test the fairness of key principles of international law on reparations, such as nonretroactivity, causation, and attribution.[33] First, given that enslavement was not a crime against humanity at the time it occurred, the question of historical reparation would imply an eventual retroactive application of international law. Although the prohibition of slavery existed in the domestic statutes of states, the direct prohibition in international law did not appear until 1926. Second, causation implies the connection or proximity of the harmful events to the harm caused to the victims, which requires some degree of assessment of remoteness, foreseeability, and proximity. Because of

[31] Thomas Piketty, *Una breve historia de la Igualdad*, ed./trans. Daniel Fuentes. (Barcelona: Ed. Ariel, 2021), 85–115.

[32] Ibid.

[33] Luke Moffett and Katarina Schwarz, "Reparations for the Transatlantic Slave Trade and Historical Enslavement: Linking Past Atrocities with Contemporary Victim Populations," *Netherlands Quarterly of Human Rights* 36, no. 4 (2018): 247–269, https://pureadmin.qub.ac.uk/ws/files/154492922/Final_Reparations_for_the_Transatlantic_Slave_Trade.pdf.

the enslavement period, causation poses another significant challenge to international legal theory. Finally, attribution is another burden of proof in international state responsibility. Normally, attributions of responsibility are against specific individuals or legal entities. However, in this case, the claim would be against the assets or wealth accumulated by the descendants of slavers to the detriment of the descendants of enslaved persons who today continue to experience the consequences of slavery.

Despite the theoretical and practical challenges involved in historical reparations claims, from the perspective of international law, these demands have the potential to be one of the important contributions of Latin American international law. They constitute demands for global justice that test current standards of state responsibility and their ability to respond to genuine tensions between countries.

IV. Conclusion

Delimiting the racial dimension of Latin American international law can be a theoretical challenge. This chapter aims to share some reflections from navigating sections of history and the primary instruments of international law against the backdrop of racism and racial discrimination. Emphasizing key points of our social and normative reality, it is possible to affirm that racism has had a distinct influence on how we create and apply Latin American international law.

One of the most striking issues in this field is the absence of rigorous analysis of the central legal structures of the colony, such as enslavement, and their current effects on Latin American societies.[34] These are silences replicated even in the critical currents of international law that study the impact of colonial relations on international norms. One possible explanation for this gap in research surrounding the racial dimension in this field may lie in the (un/conscious) recognition of cultural homogeneity (mestizaje) and the constant denial of racial tensions as one of the characteristics of Latin American societies (Latin American "racial contract"). Mestizaje continues to shape the agenda of Latin American international law and continues to act as a barrier to the development of decisive commitments in the fight against racism and racial discrimination.

At the regional level, the recent adoption of the Inter-American Convention against Racism, Racial Discrimination and Related Forms of Intolerance (2013), perhaps one of the most robust instruments with respect to state obligations

[34] Darril Li, "Genres of Universalism: Reading Race into International Law, with Help from Sylvia Wynter," *UCLA Law Review* 67 (May 2021): 1686–1719, https://www.uclalawreview.org/genres-of-universalism-reading-race-into-international-law-with-help-from-sylvia-wynter/

in this area, remains relevant. There are many expectations regarding the possibilities of effective implementation. But prior to this, applicable strategies have been developed, such as adopting and ratifying ILO Convention 169 (1989). This Convention has experienced sufficient implementation and constitutes the main international instrument for guaranteeing the rights of Indigenous peoples and Afro-descendant peoples in Latin America. This and the leadership in the construction of the international doctrine on reparations for the legacy of colonization and enslavement by CARICOM are both important developments of international law regarding racism and racial discrimination. The latter, although not yet showing tangible results, represents an important challenge to international standards regarding restorative justice.

23

Community of Practice and the *Ius Constitutionale Commune en América Latina*

Lina M. Céspedes-Báez, Enrique Prieto-Rios, and Mónica Mazariegos-Rodas

I. Introduction

Ius Constitutionale Commune en América Latina (ICCAL) is an academic concept that describes, explains, and fosters a particular instantiation of transformative constitutionalism in the region. It outlines the norms, institutions, and legal rationales deployed to operate such linkage, placing at the center of its conceptual endeavor, the Inter-American Human Rights System (IAHRS) and the national constitutional "openings" domestic regimes have established to facilitate the interplay with regional international law.[1]

ICCAL's transformative thrust involves a group of Latin American countries, multiple constitutions, and a regional international law system. As a transformative constitutional project, ICCAL seeks to achieve and promote human rights, democracy, and the rule of law and analyze how the region has embraced and implemented these constitutional normative values after the dictatorships gradually came to an end in the 1980s and at the beginning of the 1990s.[2]

As Juan C. Herrera points out, ICCAL is a term to name and rationalize the specific way in which the region has drawn connections between domestic and international law to spark transformation and tackle the inequality and

[1] Armin von Bogdandy, "Ius Constitutionale Commune en América Latina: Observations on Transformative Constitutionalism," in *Transformative Constitutionalism in Latin America: The Emergence of a New Ius Commune*, ed. Armin von Bogdandy et al., 27, 28 (Oxford: Oxford University Press 2017).

[2] Armin von Bogdandy et al., "Ius Constitutionale Commune en América Latina: A Regional Approach to Transformative Constitutionalism," in von Bogdandy et al., *Transformative Constitutionalism in Latin America*.

Lina M. Céspedes-Báez, Enrique Prieto-Rios, and Mónica Mazariegos-Rodas, *Community of Practice and the* Ius Constitutionale Commune en América Latina In: *Latin American International Law in the Twenty-First Century*. Edited by: Alejandro Chehtman, Alexandra Huneeus, and Sergio Puig, Oxford University Press.
 DOI: 10.1093/9780197754016.003.0023

exclusion that have mired it.[3]. ICCAL focuses on public law and its role in improving society. Particularly, it emphasizes the role courts and adjudication have in promoting positive transformation by applying Inter-American international law standards enshrined in the American Convention on Human Rights (ACHR) and developed by the Inter-American Court of Human Rights (IACtHR).

Several scholars have criticized ICCAL[4]. They have questioned its faith in law and lawyers to operate meaningful changes in society, doubted the existence of a common legal framework binding Latin American countries, and problematized the lack of a significant theoretical engagement with politics and democracy. Moreover, they have been adamant in challenging the top-down approach ICCAL proposes to address social justice issues in the region. Their concern is that ICCAL's version of transformation in Latin America emphasizes and aggrandizes the role high courts, specifically the IACtHR, and a legal scholar elite have in provoking change obscuring and minimazing the part played by social movements, grass-roots organizations, and ordinary citizens.

Despite all these criticisms, the idea of an *ius commune* in Latin America has favored the systematic analysis of the growing importance of international human rights law in the region and how it has been intertwined with adopting constitutions with robust charters of rights, strengthening of the role of the judiciary, and abandoning military dictatorships in the 1980s and 1990s.[5] ICCAL has been interested in tracking and understanding the strategic use of regional international law to inform the development of human rights, democracy, and the rule of law in a post-authoritarian context in Latin America. Without negating international law's colonial, hegemonic, and European roots, ICCAL strives to highlight how the region has appropriated and shaped it to make it speak to its reality.[6]

[3] Juan C. Herrera, "La Idea de un derecho común en América Latina a la luz de sus críticas," *International Journal of Constitutional Law* 19, no. 4 (2021): 1385.

[4] See for instance Carlos Arturo Villagrán and Fabia Fernandes Carvalho, "A Human Rights' Tale of Competing Narratives," *Revista Direito e Práxis* 8 (2017): 1603; Jorge Contesse, "Human Rights as Transnational Law," *AJIL Unbound* 116 (2022): 313; Roberto Gargarella, "The 'New' Latin American Constitutionalism. Old Wine in New Skins," in von Bogdandy et al., *Transformative Constituionalism in Latin America*, 211; Ana Micaela Alterio, "El Ius Constitutionale Commune Latinoamericanum y los desafíos de la judicialización de la política," *Estudios de Filosofía Práctica e Historia de las Ideas* 20 (2018): 1; Alejandro Rodiles, "The Great Promise of Comparative Public Law for Latin America: *Towards ius commune americanum*?" in Comparative International Law (Oxford: Oxford University Press, 2018) 501; Natalia Torres Zúñiga, "The Image of The Inter-American Court of Human Rights as an Agent of Democratic Transformation: A Tool of Self-Validation," *Araucaria Revista Iberoamericana de Filosofía, Política, Humanidades y Relaciones Internacionales* 23, no. 46: (2021): 483; Alberto Coddou McManus, "A Critical Account of Ius Constitutionale Commune in Latin America: An Intellectual Map of Contemporary Latin American Constitutionalism," *Global Constitutionalism* 11 (2022): 110.

[5] This does not mean that the authoritarian imprint and the influence of criminal networks and corruption have been washed away from Latin America.

[6] Herrera, "La Idea de un derecho común en América Latina a la luz de sus críticas," 1405.

The objectives of this chapter are threefold. First, it briefly describes the evolution and content of ICCAL. Second, it presents and addresses the criticism raised by different scholars against the ICCAL project. Third, it analyzes how Latin America's "communities of practice" have strategically appropriated and mobilized transformative constitutionalism's narratives and ways of interpreting the law to grant agency and guarantee the human rights of subalterns in the region. This chapter provides an overview of ICCAL by identifying its contribution to the study and development of international and constitutional law in Latin America, the criticisms to which it has been subjected, and its strategic uses by citizens to protect their rights.

II. ICCAL

Armin von Bogdandy and Mariela Morales Antoniazzi of the Max Planck Institute for International and Comparative Law (MPIL) in Heidelberg-Germany coined the term "ICCAL." The process behind its development began in 2009 when Mexican academic Jorge Carpizo Orozco invited German-based academics to a conference at the National University of Mexico (UNAM) in Mexico City to promote educational exchanges between Latin American academics and the MPIL. Other prominent academics working on comparative constitutionalism, such as Rodolfo Arango, Eduardo Ferrer Mac-Gregor, and Flavia Piovesan, also attended the conference.

ICCAL is shorthand for a particular manifestation of transformative constitutionalism in Latin America that seeks to foster democracy, the rule of law, and human rights in the region.[7] Using Latin was a solution to provide a readable term for all Latin American countries despite language differences. In addition, resorting to a Latin term was not entirely foreign to Latin American legal culture, which has prided itself on having its roots in Roman law. Also, the use of Latin expressions to name the synchronized development of international Inter-American law and constitutional law in the region was not entirely new. In the early 2000s, the German academic and lawyer Peter Häberle coined the term "ius commune americanum" to refer to a Latin American identity materialized in constitutional clauses that promote solidarity and cooperation in the region and the common framework of the Interamerican System of Human Rights.[8]

[7] von Bogdandy et al., "Ius Constitutionale Commune en América Latina."

[8] Peter Häberle and Markus Kotzur, *De la soberanía al derecho constitucional común: palabras clave para un diálogo europeo-latinoamericano* (Mexico City: Universidad Autónoma de México 2003), accessed July 25, 2023, http://ru.juridicas.unam.mx/xmlui/handle/123456789/9513.

The conceptual construction of ICCAL is based on Karl E. Klare's influential scholarly contribution titled "Legal Culture and Transformative Constitutionalism."[9] According to him, transformative constitutionalism is

> a long-term project of constitutional enactment, interpretation, and enforcement committed (not in isolation, of course, but in a historical context of conducive political developments) to transforming a country's political and social institutions and power relationships in a democratic, participatory, and egalitarian direction. Transformative constitutionalism connotes an enterprise of inducing large-scale social change through nonviolent political processes grounded in law.[10]

The use of the expression "*ius Commune*" is based on the concept conceived to refer to the gradual crystallization of a European system of law familiar to central and western Europe, except for England and the Scandinavian countries, from the late Middle Ages until the end of the eighteenth century.[11] This common European legal system developed under the influence of the reception of the law of the Roman Empire. "Roman law was taught at all law schools in Europe—for a long period it was even the only subject of academic legal training."[12] Thus, the appropriation of *ius commune* serves the purpose of underscoring the emergence and consolidation of a common legal tradition in Latin America rooted in the regional international law that is produced in the context of the IAHRS and the constitutional reforms Latin American countries have passed since the late twentieth century that gave prominence to human rights and opened domestic systems to the influence of international law norms.[13]

ICCAL is concerned with positive norms and the legal discourse that emerges from them. It also engages with how domestic law has opened to international law and participates in producing comparative constitutional discourse to promote democracy, the rule of law, and the protection of human rights.[14] The centrality of the inter-American system and international law is essential for the ICCAL project. It shares the vision César Sepúlveda, the architect of the Inter-American

[9] Karl E. Klare, "Legal Culture and Transformative Constitutionalism," *South African Journal of Human Rights* 14, no. 19 (1998): 146.

[10] Ibid., 150.

[11] Helmut Coing, "The Sources and Characteristics of the *ius commune*," *Comparative and International Law Journal of South Africa* 19 (1986): 483.

[12] Ibid.

[13] Armin von Bogdandy, "*Ius Constitutionale Commune* en América Latina: una mirada a un constitucionalismo transformador," *Revista Derecho del Estado* 34 (2015): 3.

[14] von Bogdandy et al., "Ius Constitutionale Commune en América Latina."

System, had about human rights as instruments for consolidating democracies and promoting peaceful cooperation among states.[15]

ICCAL has three main dimensions.[16] The first dimension is the analytical and ontological. It refers to ICCAL as a concept that describes and explains a specific legal phenomenon occurring in Latin America involving domestic constitutions and the IAHRS. The second refers to the normative agenda the project seeks to further, summarized in the consolidation of democracy, the strengthening of the rule of law, and the effective protection of human rights. The third refers to the academic dimension that supports the project and aims to promote comparative exercises and national and international legal academic production that enable the materialization of the promises of transforming constitutionalism.

ICCAL, as a project, seeks to describe, analyze, and promote the use of domestic and international public law to spur change in the region. It is grounded in and relies on the intersection of constitutional law and international law. Therefore, ICCAL is more than comparative constitutional law since it is invested in understanding how domestic high courts interact with the IAHRS, particularly, with the IACHR and the IACtHR.[17] In this form, ICCAL tracks innovations and advancements in the region's international human rights law and has the potential to become a crucial conceptual tool for tracing the uses of this intersection by different communities of practice.[18]

III. ICCAL Criticisms

Critiques against ICCAL are not new. The traction the term has acquired among scholars in fewer than two decades explains the interest in exploring and dissecting it. The intensity of the criticism could be interpreted as a marker of its success and potential for strengthening and expansion. Paraphrasing Juan C. Herrera, ICCAL has pointed out that "something" is happening in Latin America in terms of international and constitutional law that deserves examination.[19] Its irruption in the legal scholar landscape has turned it into "[t]he story that everyone reads" and to which everyone interested in that "something" has to react.[20]

[15] Alejandro Rodiles, "The Great Promise of Comparative Public Law for Latin America: Towards ius commune americanum?" in *Comparative International Law*, ed. Anthea Roberts et al. (Oxford: Oxford University Press 2018).

[16] von Bogdandy et al., "Ius Constitutionale Commune en América Latina."

[17] von Bogdandy, "*Ius Constitutionale Commune* en América Latina."

[18] Ibid.

[19] Herrera. "La Idea de un derecho común en América Latina a la luz de sus críticas," 1414.

[20] Carlos Arturo Villagrán Sandoval and Fabia Fernandes Carvalho Veçoso, "A Human Rights' Tale of Competing Narratives (Um Relato de Narrativas Rivais de Direitos Humanos)," *Revista Direito e Práx* 8, no. 2 (2017): 1603, 1613.

ICCAL criticisms could be grouped into four main categories: (1) ICCAL is a top-down elite project; (2) ICCAL flattens the diversity of Latin American constitutionalism; (3) ICCAL is not clear about the meaning of "transformative"; and (4) ICCAL is not straightforward about its political agenda A closer analysis of these critical approaches is an opportunity to determine precisely their contours, theoretical insights, and strategic deployments. Since 2009, the expansion of the group of scholars interested in studying ICCAL, whether they are critics or not, and its appropriation and deployment by activists and victims seeking to find redress for human rights violations have strengthened the concept. Mapping the main aspects of the critical perspectives toward ICCAL makes it possible to track what is happening in Latin America in international law. The following subsections summarize the main features of these critiques.

ICCAL Is a Top-Down Elite Project

Using Latin and affirming the existence of a common legal framework in Latin America, mirroring the expression that named the gradual consolidation of a common European legal culture between the twelfth and the fourteenth centuries, certainly exposes ICCAL to the suspicion of embodying a hegemonic and neocolonial enterprise. For instance, Alejandro Rodiles has indicated how ICCAL outlines a common legal background for Latin America, based on the IAHRS and the enactment of constitutions that enable the connection between the international and the domestic, echoing the proposal of the German constitutional law expert Peter Häberle who in the early 2000s explored the possibility of an *ius commune americanum* grounded on these premises.[21] Drawing on the confirmation of the contemporary existence of an *ius commune europaeum* entrenched in a shared legal past and the contemporary "commonality of fundamental rule-of-law principles across national constitutions in Europe,"[22] Häberle established that such a model could be transplanted to Latin America. Armin von Bogdandy and other scholars linked to the project have argued that ICCAL is a similar notion to *ius commune europaeum.*[23] However, von Bogdandy has underscored the transformative constitutional drive that has inspired the project. For this reason, although he points out the resonances between ICCAL and the *ius commune europaeum*, his emphasis lies in Karl E. Klare's conceptual reading of South Africa during the transition after apartheid.[24] Furthermore, other

[21] Alejandro, "The Great Promise of Comparative Public Law for Latin America," 507–508.
[22] Ibid., 506.
[23] von Bogdandy et al., "Ius Constitutionale Commune en América Latina," 4.
[24] Armin von Bogdandy, "Ius Constitutionale Commune Latinoamericanum Una Aclaración Conceptual," in *Ius constitutionale commune en América Latina. Rasgos, potencialidades y desafíos*, (Mexico City: Universidad Autónoma de México, 2014) 3.

scholars such as Pedro Salazar have argued that the expression *ius commune* is not exclusive to Europe but can be applied to describe the universalist aspiration of human rights and analyze regional trends toward building a common legal culture in regions like Africa or Latin America.[25]

Critical scholars have also stressed that ICCAL is a self-referential project that has emerged in an elitist environment. The MPIL, located in Heidelberg, Germany, has played a vital role in shaping the concept and structuring the academic community that is devoted to furthering it. Together with this institute, Latin American first-class universities participate in it, such as Universidad de los Andes or Rosario in Colombia and Universidad Autónoma de México, alongside IAHRS elites and prominent constitutional lawyers and scholars. Alberto Coddou McManus has expressed that ICCAL seems more like an academic collaboration platform than a real legal phenomenon that is taking place in the regions.[26] He foresees that the consensus that ties together ICCAL scholars might fade away as the network welcomes more members and diversity. Natalia Torres Zúñiga has affirmed that this group has created a narrative about transformative constitutionalism in the region, with the IACtHR as its leading figure, that only exists for the members of ICCAL. In a few words, she declares that an elite of lawyers and academics have created the reality they seek to describe and that ICCAL is an *ius commune* only for that community and not for the Latin American countries and population.[27] For that reason, she considers ICCAL to be self-referential and validating.

Furthermore, ICCAL has been accused of promoting a top-down approach to solving the issues that Latin America confronts. The idea that the IACtHR case law will meaningfully contribute to promoting and consolidating democracy, furthering the rule of law, redressing systematic human rights violations, and fixing poverty and exclusion is met with skepticism. It raises questions about the role of the people and democratic processes in addressing that situation. Micaela Alterio has pointed out how such an understanding of transformation gives precedence to lawyers, scholars, and high courts to the detriment of bottom-up approaches, politics, and democratic means.[28] She concludes that giving

[25] Pedro Salazar Ugarte, "La disputa por los derechos y el *Ius Constitutionale Commune*," in *Ius Constitutionale Commune en América Latina. Textos básicos para su comprensión. Colección Constitución y Derechos* (Mexico City: Instituto de Estudios Constitucionales del Estado de Querétaro, 2017), 109.

[26] Alberto Coddou McManus, "A Critical Account of *Ius Constitutionale Commune* in Latin America: An Intellectual Map of Contemporary Latin American Constitutionalism," *Global Constitutionalism* 11 (2022): 110, 117.

[27] Natalia Torres Zúñiga, "The Image of The Inter-American Court of Human Rights as an Agent of Democratic Transformation: A Tool of Self-Validation," *Araucaria Revista Iberoamericana de Filosofía, Política, Humanidades y Relaciones Internacionales* 23, no. 46 (2021): 483.

[28] Ana Micaela Alterio, "El Ius Constitutionale Commune Latinoamericanum y los desafíos de la judicialización de la política," *Estudios de Filosofía Práctica e Historia de las Ideas* 20 (2018): 1.

such preeminence to the judiciary does not support consolidating democratic regimes in the region, since they need to strengthen their political processes and develop their own constitutional identity.[29]

Although ICCAL scholars have repeatedly asserted that this *ius commune* is based on the horizontal dialogue between the IACtHR and domestic high courts, critics have contended that the regional court behaves as a first among equals and that the conventionality control has contributed to the idea of considering domestic high courts hierarchically inferior.[30] The lack of deference the IACtHR has shown to domestic courts has been considered another indication of the top-down approach that defines ICCAL. Ariel Dulitzky has referred to how the IACtHR has developed the doctrine of conventionality control to integrate the ACHR and decisions of the ICAtHR into domestic law and consider it at the top of the normative hierarchy, distorting the original conception of the inter-American system. He acknowledges that this court has started to cite domestic decisions that align with its precedent. However, he deems it a significant failure of this court, and another proof of this hierarchical positioning endorsed by the IACtHR, that it has not structured a "proper theory on the value of those Latin American precedents in interpreting the Convention."[31]

Jorge Contesse summarizes this critique when he states that the IACtHR "seems to understand national judges as genuine 'inter-American judges'" and that the ICCAL promotes an overreaching application of this Court's case law that creates conflict with member states and undermines the legitimacy of the IAHRS in the long run.[32] Roberto Gargarella has called attention to the importance of thinking seriously about the relationship between protecting human rights and furthering democracy. To do so, he has used as a point of departure the IACtHR decision *Gelman v. Uruguay*, which annulled the democratically approved amnesty law that impeded the investigation and prosecution of grave human rights violations committed during the 1970s and 1980s military dictatorship. Gargarella noted that this law was not only endorsed two times in popular referendums but also that Latin America had had, until the moment the decision was issued, "a long history of amnesty and pardon laws."[33] This practice undermined the IACtHR's rationale, claiming that such provisions were incompatible with the inter-American normativity. Gargarella's reasoning joins other

[29] Ibid.

[30] Ibid., 8, 13; McManus, "A Critical Account of *Ius Constitutionale Commune* in Latin America," 115; Torres Zúñiga, "The Image of The Inter-American Court of Human Rights as an Agent of Democratic Transformation," 490.

[31] A. E. Dulitzky, "An Alternative Approach to the Conventionality Control Doctrine," *AJIL Unbound* 109 (2015): 100, 103.

[32] Jorge Contesse, "Human Rights as Transnational Law," *AJIL Unbound* 116 (2022): 313, 316.

[33] Robert Gargarella, "Democracy and Rights in *Gelman v. Uruguay*," *AJIL Unbound* 109 (2015): 115, 116.

voices in warning against accepting a government of regional judges without considering the impact such an organization of power will have on democratic processes. As Alterio does, Gargarella cautions against any human rights protection scheme that assumes or leads to conclude that the majority rule is always "irrational or unreasoned."[34] Also, while he praises some of IACtHR's decisions, he underlines that it is not realistic that a regional court could trigger systematic changes since that court is far removed from the communities in need of human rights protection, it is not easily accessible, and its judges are not popularly accountable.[35]

ICCAL Flattens the Diversity of Latin American Constitutionalism

Critical literature has questioned the very base of the ICCAL project, pointing out that it is difficult to identify the common normative constitutional foundation that Latin America shares. Micaela Alterio considers that ICCAL endorses a liberal approach to human rights, democracy, and the rule of law that privileges individual rights, the protection of personal autonomy, and the establishment of strong high courts to realize the promises of these values and goals.[36] Even if several constitutions in the region adopt this liberal scheme, she reminds us that this ideal is far from being widely accepted in the region. Alterio offers as an example the Bolivian and Ecuadorian constitutions in which the rights of the communities have a preeminence foreign to the liberal model. Moreover, she mentions that constitutional principles such as self-determination and sovereignty are gaining traction in the region and shaping constitutions and constitutional practices. For her, it is essential to consider that constitutionalism in the region has developed in the context of US hegemony. That explains why some Latin American states strive to fashion constitutional regimes in stark contrast to US liberalism.

Alterio's point is connected to two broader criticisms of human rights and the Organization of American States (OAS). The former underscores that international human rights law is a creation of the Global North, developed with scarce Global South participation.[37] Specifically, it highlights how "human rights" was a term coined in the United States and then matured and refined in the context of the United Nations, an international organization established during the height

[34] Ibid., 118.

[35] Roberto Gargarella, "The "New" Latin American Constitutionalism. Old Wine in New Skins," in von Bogdandy et al., *Transformative Constituionalism in Latin America*, 211–234.

[36] Alterio, "El Ius Constitutionale Commune Latinoamericanum y los desafíos de la judicialización de la política," 7–8.

[37] Balakrishna Rajagopal, *International Law from Below* (Cambridge: Cambridge University Press 2003), 175.

of colonialism without a clear decolonial agenda.[38] The latter is related to the resistance the OAS has met throughout history for being considered by some Latin American countries an international organization established to serve US economic and security interests.[39]

Alberto Coddou McManus considers that ICCAL disregards the different constitutional ideas and debates that are taking place in Latin America to sustain the notion of an *ius commune*. He denounces that the project flattens the account of what is happening in the region, and that attitude undermines ICCAL's possibility of developing a robust normative proposal. According to his mapping of non-orthodox constitutionalism in the region, he identifies three schools of thought leading the debates around democracy and socioeconomic inclusion: Latin American neoconstitutionalism, new Latin American constitutionalism, and egalitarian-dialogic constitutionalism.

Rodiles identifies Latin American neoconstitutionalism with ICCAL since it advocates for detailed constitutional charters of rights and strong courts to achieve social and economic improvement. In contrast, new Latin American constitutionalism situates the people and direct democratic mechanisms as the epicenter of constitutional law at the expense of law and judges, vesting the executive branch with authority to realize "the constituent power's will."[40] Egalitarian-dialogic constitutionalism stems from a critical approach to neoconstitutionalism and new Latin American constitutionalism.[41] Although its representatives acknowledge the benefits of strong courts to further democracy, the rule of law, and human rights, they also warn against the elitism that impregnates this stance and the dangers of the cooptation of courts and litigation strategies by conservative agendas. To counteract these perils, its representatives advocate for rescuing the role of common people and social mobilization in devising and modifying the constitutional framework. However, they are also conscious of the part that the recourse to the voice of the people can play in the consolidation of authoritarian and hyperpresidential regimes.[42] Therefore,

[38] Samuel Moyn, *The Last Utopia* (Cambridge, MA: Belknap Press of Harvard University Press 2012), 49–50, 94–95.

[39] John C. Dreier, "The Organization of American States and United States Policy," *International Organization* 17, no. 1 (1963): 36–53; Liliana Obregón, "Latin America during the Bandung Era: Anti-Imperialist Movements vs. Anti-Communist States," in *Bandung, Global History, and International Law*, ed. Luis Eslava, Michael Fakhri, and Vsuki Nesiah (Cambridge: Cambridge University Press, 2017), 232, 235–237. See Organization of American States, "Note from the Permanent Mission of the Bolivarian Republic of Venezuela Enclosing a Copy of the Letter Denouncing the Charter of the Organization of American States (OAS) Pursuant to Article 143 and Initiating the Permanent Withdrawal of the Bolivarian Republic of Venezuela from the Organization. April 28, 2017," OEA/Ser. G CP/INF. 7707/17 (April 29, 2017), accessed August 31, 2023, http://www.oas.org/en/sla/dil/docs/a-41_note_venezuela_04-28-2017.pdf.

[40] McManus, "A Critical Account of *Ius Constitutionale Commune* in Latin America," 129.

[41] Ibid., 132–133.

[42] Gargarella, "The "New" Latin American Constitutionalism."

they insist on identifying and making visible "what is shared in common by the members of a certain polity"[43] to challenge liberal individualism and resist any instrumentalization by the executive power.

McManus draws attention to the resistance certain states and constituencies have shown to the IACtHR and how it undermines the idea of a common normative ground among Latin American states. His criticism echoes Carlos Arturo Villagrán and Fabia Fernandes Carvalho's contribution to the topic when they underscore that there is a "[t]he lesser known story" refuting ICCAL's, and it is one of domestic courts and governments rebelling against the IACtHR.[44] They explained how Guatemala's and Argentina's higher courts have resisted the idea that the inter-American regulation on human rights stands above domestic constitutions.[45] Additionally, they refer to the 2013 modification of the rules of procedure of the Inter-American Commission of Human Rights (IACHR) as an outcome of the backlash against the precautionary measures this body was issuing. After the IACHR began to order these measures without any explicit conventional basis or procedural rules, states like Brazil and Guatemala expressed their disagreement and resisted through different means (i.e., suspending monetary contributions to the organization or dubbing those measures as abusive).[46]

ICCAL Is Not Clear about the Meaning of "Transformative"

McManus indicates that ICCAL can be blamed for not approaching transformative constitutionalism critically and endorsing it without considering how contested this term is among constitutionalists.[47] Scholars have mainly criticized transformative constitutionalism's faith in the ability of high courts to produce meaningful socioeconomic improvements in society and the correlated weakening of other democratic mechanisms to do so, such as the legislative process.[48] McManus reiterates this critique, pointing out that the *transformation* that transformative constitutionalism proposes seems limited to

[43] McManus, "A Critical Account of *Ius Constitutionale Commune* in Latin America," 130–136.

[44] Villagrán and Fernandes Carvalho, "A Human Rights' Tale of Competing Narratives," 1603, 1617, 1622–1626.

[45] Recently, the Colombian Constitutional Court in a 5–4 decision established that the inter-American precedent has to be harmonized with the domestic constitutional block. See Judgement C-030-23 Colombian Const. Ct., 2023.

[46] Villagrán and Fernandes Carvalho, "A Human Rights' Tale of Competing Narratives," 1617–1622.

[47] McManus, "A Critical Account of *Ius Constitutionale Commune* in Latin America," 119.

[48] Erik Kibet and Charles Fombad, "Transformative Constitutionalism and the Adjudication of Constitutional Rights in Africa," *African Human Rights Law Journal* 17 (2017): 340; Sanele Sibanda, "Not Purpose-made—Transformative Constitutionalism, Post-Independence Constitutionalism and the Struggle to Eradicate Poverty," *Stellenbosch Law Review* 22 (2011): 482.

the production of judicial decisions that trump the outcome of legislative and executive decision-making.[49] Since ICCAL claims to be a transformative constitutionalism enterprise, its theoretical and normative tenets are open to this appraisal. In this fashion, Villagrán and Fernandes Carvalho have accused ICCAL of emphasizing IACtHR decisions that support their idea of transformation and commonality and sidelining the problematic tensions and backlashes between the IAHRS and member states and their courts. Natalia Torres Zúñiga advances a related retort in which she describes ICCAL as an academic project that selects certain IACtHR decisions and frames them as transformative without offering concrete evidence to sustain that claim.[50]

McManus has also made clear that a limitless call for transformation is at odds with the liberal constitutional project, which seeks to consolidate transformational gains and strengthen democratic mechanisms.[51] A constant state of transformation is an open invitation to the disruption of constituted power. If ICCAL's ultimate goal is to further democracy, human rights, and the rule of law, its emphasis on transformation from above does not contribute to sustaining the changes it fosters. Accordingly, transformative constitutionalism, therefore ICCAL, is trapped between two contradictory drives: one incentivizes alteration in the established state of affairs and the other seeks stability and institutionalization.

ICCAL Is Not Straightforward about Its Political Agenda

One of the most controversial tenets of ICCAL is that its representatives claim that the project is not linked to and does not further "a specific partisan agenda."[52] This overarching declaration of principle, which echoes legal formalist aspirations, has been nuanced to clarify that ICCAL openly pursues social and democratic change in Latin America to overcome the inequality and institutional weakness that are characteristic of the region.[53] Moreover, they argue that advancing democracy, human rights, and the rule of law can be a shared goal among conservatives, socialists, and liberals. Supporting this affirmation,

[49] McManus, "A Critical Account of *Ius Constitutionale Commune* in Latin America," 118.

[50] Villagrán and Fernandes Carvalho, "A Human Rights' Tale of Competing Narratives," 1617–1637; Torres Zúñiga, "The Image of the Inter-American Court of Human Rights as an Agent of Democratic Transformation," 483; Johanna Fröhlich, "Traces of Constitutional Reasoning in Latin America and the Caribbean—Regional Cosmopolitanism Without Backlash?" *International Journal of Constitional Law* (blog) (2020), accessed October 5, 202, 3https://www.academia.edu/43775166/Traces_of_constitutional_reasoning_in_Latin_America_and_the_Caribbean_Regional_Cosmopolitanism_without_backlash.

[51] McManus, "A Critical Account of *Ius Constitutionale Commune* in Latin America," 118–119.

[52] von Bogdandy et al., "Ius Constitutionale Commune en América Latina," 6.

[53] Ibid.

ICCAL's representatives recalled what happened in Europe after World War II, when different political forces united to accomplish these objectives. For that reason, they defend their "conceptual fuzziness,"[54] suggesting that not having a partisan normative stand facilitates the integration of diverse voices and strategies to attain those ends.

Critics of ICCAL have taken issue with these statements. Their objections intend to reveal that ICCAL certainly endorses a political agenda embodied in the objectives it pursues and the process it backs to do so. For them, the conjunction of ICCAL's descriptive and normative dimensions implies a political stance that ICCAL has been reluctant to acknowledge openly. Villagrán and Carvalho Veçoso contend that this conceptual fuzziness does not mean openness to a diverse set of political ideas but a tactic to advance ICCAL's universalistic legal vision in which some features of Latin America's legal and political thought are underscored and others are concealed.[55] For them, this universalistic approach obscures the resistance the IAHRS has faced in the region.

Alterio's point of departure to grapple with ICCAL's nonpartisan claim is to affirm that constitutional law is apolitical phenomenon.[56] Thus, if ICCAL endorses a common constitutional framework for Latin America, it is embedded in a political ideology whether it admits it or not. For her, ICCAL is a liberal democratic elitist project led by the IACtHR and domestic high courts. Echoing Villagrán and Carvalho Veçoso, she contends that this liberal model is far from being pacifically endorsed in the Latin American context. Torres Zúñiga considers ICCAL an expression of "the liberal paradigm of international law"[57] that has shaped a notion of global governance based on establishing international courts and has promoted a universalistic idea of democracy, human rights, and the rule of law.

Alterio and Giménez[58] and McManus[59] have called on ICCAL's representatives to openly embrace and develop their political agenda if they believe it is the best option to address Latin America's ailments. Even though ICCAL has recognized that political processes can enmesh the realization of its universalistic values, critics consider that that is not enough. For them, sidelining the issue of ICCAL's political underpinnings may be very well a strategy to sustain its

[54] Ibid., 7.

[55] Villagrán and Fernandes Carvalho, "A Human Rights' Tale of Competing Narratives," 1617–1637; Torres Zúñiga, "The Image of the Inter-American Court of Human Rights as an Agent of Democratic Transformation."

[56] Alterio, "El Ius Constitutionale Commune Latinoamericanum y los desafíos de la judicialización de la política."

[57] Natalia Torres Zúñiga, *The Inter American Court of Human Rights. The Legitimacy of International Courts and Tribunals* (London: Routledge 2023), 170.

[58] Ana Micaela Alterio and Francisca Pou Giménez, "Book Reviews," in von Bogdandy et al., *Transformative Constitutionalism in Latin America*, 415.

[59] McManus, "A Critical Account of *Ius Constitutionale Commune* in Latin America."

universalistic aspiration but also an expression of its unwillingness to engage in frank discussions about its plausibility.

IV. ICCAL and the Community of Practice

Answering the criticisms raised concerning ICCAL will allow its representatives to determine the concept's scope and limitations. Armin von Bogdandy and René Urueña have recently resorted to the concept of *community of practice* to grapple with some of those critiques.[60] Their work has focused on demonstrating that ICCAL is not an abstract fictitious conception but an organic practice of the law. Their deployment of the idea of a *community of practice* seeks to establish that the ICCAL project is not a top-down endeavor but one in which multiple actors participate to create knowledge and advance their agendas. Furthermore, it indicates that the meaning of transformation emerges from this social practice as an evolving, unstable, and contested notion constantly in the making but always striving to further democracy and the rule of law.

Von Bogdandy's and Urueña's objective is to make visible the set of different actors that employ inter-American human rights law to further their agendas and their role in ICCAL.[61] Their main point is to demonstrate how ICCAL involves a diverse group beyond inter-American judges and commissioners. . Following Bourdieu, Von Bogdandy's and Urueña assert that ICCAL names and depicts a *legal field* understood as a structure of forces in which different agents compete. Therefore, ICCAL denotes a "real-life phenomenon"[62] since it constitutes a "social practice."[63] In this way, the agents constitute a "community of experts"[64] who mobilize this field of law to promote the transformation they believe in and see embodied in the human rights mandate.

Drawing on Jean Lave and Ettiene Wegner's notion of *situated learning*, von Bogdandy and Urueña contend that these groups of people resorting strategically to the inter-American human rights law constitute a *community of practice*.[65] As they acknowledge, this term has been used before in international law. In 2010, Stephen Toppe and Jutta Brunnée applied it to approach the issue of international obligations. However, von Bogdandy and Urueña implement it

[60] Armin von Bogdandy and René Uruena, "Comunidad de Práctica en Derechos Humanos y Constitucionalismo Transformador en América Latina," *Anuario de Derechos Humanos*, special issue, 15; Armin von Bogdandy and René Uruena, "International Transformative Constitutionalism in Latin America," *American Journal of International Law* 114 (2020): 403.

[61] von Bogdandy and Uruena, "Comunidad de Práctica en Derechos Humanos y Constitucionalismo Transformador en América Latina."

[62] Ibid., 22 (translation by authors).

[63] Ibid., 22.

[64] Ibid., 22.

[65] Ibid., 22–23.

for a different purpose: to grasp how ICCAL manifests and evolves in the inter-American region. Situated learning underscores that the process of creating knowledge is social. A community of practice refers to an informal group of people tied together by shared goals and commitments and a common set of symbols, narratives, and languages.

International and national NGOs, grass-roots organizations, public servants, scholars, politicians, and inter-American judges and commissioners are some of the potential members of ICCAL's community of practice. For von Bogdandy and Urueña, the ICtHR is just another actor participating in the legal field. They insist that, although this court is central, that does not mean it is at the top of a pyramidal structure. They seem to propose that the ICtHR is at the center of a network structure.[66] The existence of such a community underscores that law is alive and that ICCAL is more than an abstract legal phenomenon happening in the enclosed space of remote national and international institutions.

In a few words, von Bogdandy and Urueña propose that balancing *agency* and *structure* in the context of ICCAL deploying the concept community of practice is possible.[67] ICCAL encompasses a legal structure and agents that mobilize it to attain their ends. They claim that the structure does not fatally prescribe the outcomes and that the agents contribute to its configuration and reconfiguration. In this fashion, the IACtHR is not the only relevant actor with such power. Likewise, they stress that the community of practice does not have a single, coherent project. It may group contradictory projects. However, a shared understanding of its endeavor and the legal tools it uses makes it a community of practice.

Even though von Bogdandy and Urueña do not offer a detailed description and analysis of the different groups and strategies that are grouped under the ICCAL's banner beyond the IACtHR and domestic high courts, they outline a research agenda to do so. One possible point of departure to develop it is to understand IACtHR's decisions as one more stage in constructing meaning in the legal field that ICCAL describes, not as its last and most meaningful step. Behind almost every IACtHR ruling is a story of mobilization and advocacy. These decisions are the product of a complex community of actors working together to make them possible. Shedding light on how this community works within the field contributes to furthering the understanding of ICCAL's intended scope.

Marginalized and discriminated against individuals and groups have strategically utilized the IAHRS framework to protect their rights and promote their ideas of fairness and democracy. The IACtHR docket can be read as an intense debate among different actors backed by political and advocacy activities

[66] Ibid., 24.
[67] Ibid., 23–24.

that occur inside and outside the court's legal space and time. Filing briefs and petitions before the IAHRS is neither the beginning nor the end of the social and political actions that enabled them. The following three cases illustrates how different individuals and groups understand and appropriate IAHRS , modifying, and translating human rights into practice.

In 2001, the Court protected the right to communal property of the Mayagna community Awas Tingni in Nicaragua over the lands they inhabited. Litigation before the IAHRS was just another step the community and other actors had taken to protect their land. Located in an isolated tropical forest on the Nicaraguan Atlantic coast, the Awas Tingi inhabited a territory coveted by the timber industry.[68] The lack of official titling imperiled their rights over ancestral land. The State of Nicaragua treated their land as public land and, based on that understanding, granted concessions in the 1990s.[69] The involvement of the World Wildlife Fund (WWF), a well-known international NGO, helped to provisionally stop industrial logging and engage the community in negotiations to reach an agreement to guarantee a sustainable approach to this activity. This organization provided funds to the University of Iowa's College of Law to legally support the community.

In 1994, the state, one logging company, and the Awas Tingni reached an agreement. As part of it, the Nicaraguan State committed to "definitively identify and title the Community's traditional lands" and abstain from any action that could undermine their claim to the territory.[70] However, the state was unwilling to comply with its part of the deal. At the same time it was participating in this negotiation, the state was granting another concession to a different company in a different part of the land the community alleged to be theirs. Supported first by the legal counsel of the University of Iowa and later by the Indian Law Center and the Indigenous Peoples Law & Policy Program of the University of Arizona James E. Rogers College of Law, the community tried to communicate with the government. After receiving no response from the state, they initiated legal actions. When they exhausted the domestic judicial channels, they resorted to the IAHRS.[71]

Their petition to the IACHR claimed that Nicaragua had violated,, their rights to property and cultural integrity among other rights stated in the petition. Bringing this case to this regional forum was not without its dangers. The inter-American regulation did not explicitly mention Indigenous rights, and, up

[68] Claudio Grossman and S. James Anaya, "The Case of *Awas Tingni v. Nicaragua*: A Step in the International Law of Indigenous Peoples," *Arizona Journal of International and Comparative Law* 19 (2020): 1.

[69] Ibid.

[70] Ibid., 3.

[71] Ibid.

to that point, IAHRS case law had not ruled on issues related to Indigenous communal property.[72] Litigation before the IACtHR demonstrated the support and involvement of indigenous and human rights organizations. The Assembly of First Nations, the National Congress of American Indians, the Mohawk Nation, the Human Rights Law Group, and the Organización de Síndicos Indígenas del Caribe Nicaragüense filed *amicus curiae* to strengthen the Awas Tingni case.[73]

The IACtHR delivered a ruling against Nicaragua for violating the community's right to property, among others. To do so, it employed a method of interpretation that it termed "evolutionary" to take into consideration international law developments on indigenous rights to expand the meaning of the right to property established in Article 21 of the American Convention on Human Rights.[74] In this way, the Court broadened the strictly liberal and individualistic concept of this right to include the collective dimensions of "communal property regimes of indigenous peoples as defined by their own customs and traditions."[75] Therefore, the Court's rationale adopted an interpretation of the right to property in which it indicated that the possession of the land by the Indigenous community was sufficient to obtain the formalization of its ownership. Furthermore, the decision underscored that domestic law must be in accordance to international law, hencestates cannot modify the international law understanding of the right to property to undermine Indigenous communities' claims to their ancestral lands.

This case paved the way for other claims relating to Indigenous peoples's right to communal property to be brought before the IAHRS. The litigation of the Sawhoyamaxa Indigenous Community against Paraguay is a case in point.[76] In that opportunity, the IAHRS dealt with the negligence of the Paraguayan State in recognizing and protecting the indigenous community's property right to their ancestral property. The state's behavior facilitated the appropriation by different private actors of their ancestral territories throughout the end of the nineteenth century and during the twentieth century, as well as the pauperization, displacement, and marginalization of their members.[77] The IACtHR decided in favor of the community based on the interpretation of the right to property outlined in the Awas Tingni case. Thus, it ordered the State of Paraguay to return the tenure

[72] Felipe Gomez Isa, "El derecho de los pueblos indígenas sobre sus tierras y recursos naturales: conflicto social y ambiental a la luz del caso Awas Tingni," *Revista del Programa de Investigaciones sobre Conflicto Social* 7 (2012): 93–99.

[73] Natalia Álvarez Molinero, "Del reconocimiento a la propiedad del derecho: el caso Awas Tingni vs. Nicaragua," *Papeles de cuestiones internacionales* 83 (2003): 167.

[74] *Community Mayagna (Sumo) Awas Tingni v. Nicaragua*, Inter.-Am. Ct. H.R. (August 31, 2001), ¶ 149.

[75] Grossman and Anaya, "The Case of *Awas Tingni v. Nicaragua*," 12.

[76] Sawhoyamaxa Indigenous Community v. Paraguay, Inter.-Am. Ct. H.R. (March 29, 2006).

[77] Ibid., ¶ 73.

of their ancestral land to the Indigenous community and recognize their formal property rights over them.

Civil society involvement has been essential to prepare and file the case and seek compliance with the decision of the Court. The NGO "Tierra Viva a los Pueblos Indígenas del Chaco" filed the petition before the IACHR and represented the victims before the IACtHR. In 2013, the International Network of Economic, Social and Cultural Rights (Red-DESC, after its name in Spanish) joined efforts to effectively implement the decision, given the state's failure to do so. Amnesty International has funded campaigns for this purpose.[78]

The case of the Colombian journalist Jineth Bedoya provides another opportunity to examine the different sets of actors and organizations that mobilize the regional human rights corpus to redress gross human rights violations, challenge discrimination against vulnerable groups, and position their agenda in the domestic and international fora. In 2000, Bedoya, a Colombian journalist, was reporting on the confrontations between paramilitary and gang members in one of the Colombian prisons. After receiving several threats and learning of the paramilitaries' resentment over her published newspaper articles, Bedoya visited the prison to interview one of them. At the entrance, a man kidnapped her. A group of men tortured and raped her for approximately ten hours.[79] The criminal investigation and prosecution against her aggressors were deficient. She had to testify several times and find the evidence to support her case.

The national press reported that she was brutally battered but shied away from informing that she had suffered sexual violence. This approach lasted until she decided to talk publicly about what had happened. In 2009, the Spanish NGO Oxfam Intermón invited her to present its campaign against sexual violence impunity in the context of the Colombian armed conflict. She accepted because she thought she needed to talk to encourage other women to do so.[80] Her decision triggered a mobilization and advocacy process, encouraging other women to join, speak, and seek justice.

Central to Bedoya's endeavor of making visible sexual violence against women in conflict and strengthening them to talk about their experience was her campaign *No es hora de callar* (It is not time to be silent),[81] journalism on the subject, alliances with national and international NGOs, and litigation of her case before

[78] Red-Desc, "Caso de la comunidad indígena Sawhoyamaxa versus Paraguay," accessed September 29, 2023https://www.escr-net.org/es/caselaw/2013/caso-comunidad-indigena-sawhoyamaxa-versus-paraguay.

[79] Bedoya Lima et al. vs. Colombia, Inter.-Am. Ct. H.R. (August 26, 2021).

[80] Liliana Rocío Chaparro Moreno, "'Pensé que era el momento de hablar'. La emergencia de la categoría de la violencia sexual en el conflicto armado como un problema público en Colombia, 1990-2008" (PhD diss., Universidad Nacional de Colombia, 2021).

[81] El Tiempo, "No es hora de callar," accessed October 5, 2023, https://www.eltiempo.com/multimedia/especiales/no-es-hora-de-callar/16598691/1/index.html.

the IAHRS. In 2011, the Colombian Fundación para la Libertad de Prensa (Foundation for Press Freedom) and the Center for Justice and International Law (CEJIL) filed a petition before the IACHR looking to hold the Colombian state responsible.[82] Several facts pointed to the collaboration of state officials and serious mishandling of the criminal investigation. In 2019, the IACHR submitted the case to the IACtHR. Strategic civil society actors from Colombia and other countries filed amicus curiae during the proceedings. Legal clinics from United States and Colombian universities, NGOs, networks, and coalitions supported her case. Also, *Cinco Claves* (Five Keys), the alliance she and other women and organizations established to advocate for victims of sexual violence during the peace negotiations with the Colombian guerrilla Revolutionary Armed Forces of Colombia (FARC, after its name in Spanish), filed a brief.

Bedoya's actions helped to position sexual violence against women in conflict as a public issue in Colombia. Her litigation before the IAHRS exposed the major failures of the state to prevent, investigate, and punish sexual violence against women in wartime contexts. It was also crucial to catalyze a civil society movement around this subject. In 2021, the IACtHR issued a decision on her case after two decades of denial of justice.[83] The Court concluded that Colombia was responsible for her human rights violations. According to the ruling, the state failed to comply with its reinforced due diligence duty since Bedoya experienced a heightened vulnerable position as a woman in the context of conflict and as a journalist reporting about it. Furthermore, the decision emphasized the "chilling effect" such a crime had on freedom of expression in the country, particularly for women journalists.[84]

These three cases illustrate the vital dynamics of ICCAL. They highlight the dynamic and vibrant engagement of diverse actors and organizations that strategically utilize the shared framework of Inter-American human rights law. By leveraging institutional mechanisms, these groups effectively safeguard their rights, pursue substantive equality, and contribute to the strengthening of democratic principles. More research is needed to grasp fully this dynamic and to determine its promises and dangers. An urgent and pending issue on the ICCAL agenda is the in-depth and systematic research of the mobilization of the IAHRS by organizations that could be considered illiberal, such as religious groups whose purpose is to limit the rights of the LGBT population or women. Likewise, it is imperative to acknowledge and analyze the strategic resistance some states deploy to the IAHRS, the poor record of compliance of the Court's decisions, the hurdles citizens face to file their cases, and the non-democratic way in which the

[82] Bedoya Lima et al. vs. Colombia.
[83] Ibid., ¶ 151.
[84] Ibid.

Court's judges are appointed. Focusing on success stories means telling partial stories. The ICCAL project has matured sufficiently and gained space in scholarly debates to take this step.

V. Conclusion

We closed this chapter with a brief analysis of three cases decided by the IACtHR to highlight the involvement of other actors beyond IAHRS officials to illustrate the vital dynamics of ICCAL. These cases speak of the intense and vigorous involvement of multiple actors and organizations that strategically s employ the shared framework and language of inter-American human rights law to further their understandings of democracy and equality. More research is needed to fully grasp this dynamic and determine its promises and dangers.

ICCAL offers a plausible narrative of what has been happening in Latin America in the last three decades regarding regional international law. It makes the region's contribution to this body of law visible and allows us to ask ourselves about the existence and new directions of a Latin American international law. In this sense, ICCAL could be considered part of the tradition and contributions of jurists such as Alejandro Álvarez and Luis María Drago and on what was once called Latin American international law.

Apart from addressing the appropriation and deployment of the language of inter-american human rights by illiberal movements and the rejection certain states profess toward the IAHRS, ICCAL has to explore seriously the tensions that potential legal pluralism poses to the idea of an *ius commune* in the region. In Latin America, different legal systems and visions converge—liberal, Indigenous, Afro-descendant—and ICCAL needs to grapple with this diversity beyond highlighting the instances in which the IAHRS offers adequate solutions for historically discriminated against communities and individuals. ICCAL has the opportunity to challenge the colonial legacies and acknowledge traditionally excluded populations' active role in shaping an *ius commune*. ICCAL has already gained theoretical robustness and traction to integrate and make sense out of instances in which a common language of inter-american human rights tells a tale of progress and realization of equality, and of those in which it fails to do so.

24

Maritime Delimitation in Latin America

María Teresa Infante Caffi

I. Introduction

This chapter addresses the evolution of maritime delimitation in Latin America and the Caribbean since the middle of the twentieth century to provide an overview of the process that integrated the new institutions of the law of the sea. This period has been marked by the establishment of extended maritime zones and the determination of questions involving access to marine resources, alleged historic rights, and the status of islands. The persistent interest in delimitation among the states of the region has not necessarily resulted in a common approach to the methodologies used for this purpose or in adherence to the United Nations Convention on the Law of the Sea (UNCLOS) and its dispute settlement mechanisms.

The second section of the chapter will deal with facts and events that have shaped the discussions about delimitation in the region, including the geographical and political impact of this phenomenon, and the laborious pathway to direct arrangements. The third section will discuss diplomatic and legal strategies underlying the practice of delimitation in Latin America, and the place and role of the autonomy of the parties vis-à-vis the delimitation decided by tribunals. Issues such as geostrategic preferences, geographical projections, and the stability of agreed lines will appear in this analysis. The fourth section will show the impact of judgments and arbitral awards in shaping the law of the sea, and its impact on the legal position of states, including nonparties to UNCLOS. At the same time, some delimitation issues have been linked to territorial disputes and influenced by the invocation of doctrines such as the doctrine of *uti possidetis*. This subject is discussed in the fifth section. Finally, the sixth section highlights the choices and preferences of states reflected in their agreements, as well as in the selection of dispute settlement procedures that empower a third actor to decide based on international law. The practice of Latin American and Caribbean states is rich in lessons in both senses.

María Teresa Infante Caffi, *Maritime Delimitation in Latin America* In: *Latin American International Law in the Twenty-First Century*. Edited by: Alejandro Chehtman, Alexandra Huneeus, and Sergio Puig, Oxford University Press. DOI: 10.1093/9780197754016.003.0024

II. Facts in a Regional Conversation

Geography, economy, human presence, politics, and law are among the criteria that have most frequently shaped the determination of maritime boundaries.[1] The maritime delimitation process appears to have been accelerated with the adoption of the exclusive economic zone of two hundred nautical miles and the legal definition of the continental shelf, extending up to two hundred nautical miles. There is also the emerging question relevant to the criteria set forth for the continental shelf in Article 76 of the UNCLOS: how an outer limit beyond two hundred nautical miles may impact maritime delimitation of adjacent or opposite coasts with neighboring states. The International Court of Justice had to give special consideration to this phenomenon in the case brought by Nicaragua against Colombia in 2013.[2] In 2022, in preparation for the hearings, the ICJ asked the parties to address questions regarding customary international law and the criteria for the determination of the limit of the continental shelf beyond two hundred nautical miles, as well as whether the state's entitlement to a continental shelf beyond two hundred nautical miles from the baselines from which the breadth of its territorial sea is measured may extend two hundred nautical miles from the baselines of another state.[3]

Latin American and Caribbean (Latin American) countries have been active participants in international legal and technical fora through which the general principles of the Law of the Sea, and particularly the rights and jurisdictions of coastal states, have been discussed. This was particularly visible during the Third United Nations Conference on the Law of the Sea that concluded in 1982.[4] Latin American countries, partisans of the equidistance line, or partisans of equitable principles tried to influence the outcomes of the discussions, first sitting with other states under the umbrella of Negotiating Group 7 (Commission II) and then upholding the final involvement of the president of the Conference. The choice of dispute settlement mechanisms was also part of the preferences for future rules.[5] A few Latin American states have made exceptions, under Article 298,

[1] A review of the main delimitation cases may be consulted in *International Maritime Boundaries*, published from 1993 up to 2020, with successive editions and updates. These series indicate the underpinnings of maritime delimitation discussions in Latin America and the Caribbean, including pending cases. Also, particularities related to the determination of maritime boundaries can be assessed in Latin America and the Caribbean (Latin America) like in any other region.

[2] Question of the delimitation of the continental shelf between Nicaragua and Colombia beyond two hundred nautical miles from the Nicaraguan Coast (*Nicaragua v. Colombia*), submitted in 2013 to the International Court of Justice.

[3] Ibid., 2022 I.C.J. Order (October 4).

[4] An account of the case law and the ensuing discussions at the Third UN Conference in Lucius Caflisch, "La délimitation des espaces entre Etats dont les côtes se font face ou sont adjacentes," in *Traité du Nouveau Droit de la Mer*, (Brussels: Economica, 1985), 397–426.

[5] UN Convention on the Law of the Sea, "Article 74. Delimitation of the exclusive economic zone between States with opposite or adjacent coasts," in *Commentary 1982 Online Publication* (Center for Oceans Law and Policy, University of Virginia) (Leiden, The Netherlands: Brill NV, 2014),

paragraph l(a) of UNCLOS, to the applicability of Section 2, Part XV on dispute settlement: Argentina, Chile, and Ecuador.

Already in the Declaration of Santo Domingo (1972), in preparation for the Third Conference on the Law of the Sea, Latin American participating states provided that the delimitation of the territorial sea should be "subject to an international agreement, preferably of a worldwide scope"; in the case of the patrimonial sea (terms used to designate the current exclusive economic zone (EEZ)), "the delimitation of this zone between two or more states, should be carried out in accordance with the peaceful procedures in the Charter of the United Nations."[6] Thus, there was a clear prospect to develop rules from a worldwide perspective and an appeal to the procedures enunciated by the UN Charter.

In Latin America, maritime delimitation processes have followed the evolution of the Law of the Sea as a global regime. Delimitation appears either as part of a long-term political cooperation process between the concerned states, as has been the case in the Southeastern Pacific coast,[7] or as the result of a sustained strategy to conclude agreements with relevant neighbors, as Colombia has done with Costa Rica (1984) (the delimitation of the Pacific Ocean boundary is in force), Panama (1976), Honduras (1986), Haiti (1978), Jamaica (1993), Ecuador (1975), and the Dominican Republic (1978).[8] In the framework of a Caribbean Conference on Maritime Delimitation, convened by Mexico, the 2005 Treaty of maritime delimitation between this country and Honduras, was adopted.[9] The treaty uses trijunction points with Belize and Cuba as the extreme points of the line.

Venezuela showed an inclination to conclude agreements with several neighboring countries some decades ago,[10] including with the Dominican Republic (1979), France (with Martinique and Guadeloupe, 1980), the Kingdom of the Netherlands (1978), Trinidad and Tobago (1990), and the United States (1978,

796–816; "Article 84. Delimitation of the continental shelf between States with opposite or adjacent coasts," in ibid, 948–985.

[6] Declaration of Santo Domingo, Doc. CCM/RC/5 (1972), *American Journal of International Law* 66 (1972): 918–920. The Declaration was supported by Colombia, Costa Rica, Dominican Republic, Guatemala, Haiti, Honduras, Mexico, Nicaragua, Trinidad and Tobago, and Venezuela. Barbados, El Salvador, Guyana, Jamaica, and Panama, abstained.

[7] Ann L. Hollick, "The Origins of 200-Mile Offshore Zones," *American Journal of International Law* 71 (1977): 494–500; Francisco García Amador, "The Latin American Contribution to the Development of the Law of the Sea," (1974) *American Journal of International Law* 68 (1974): 36–38.

[8] See Andreas Osthagen, *Ocean Geopolitics* (Cheltenham, UK: Edward Elgar, 2022), 58–69.

[9] Law of the Sea Bulletin, DOALOS, 65, 2007, 33.

[10] Kaldone G. Nweihed, "EZ (Uneasy) Delimitation in the Semi-enclosed Caribbean Sea: Recent Agreements between Venezuela and Her Neighbors," *Ocean Development and International Law* 8 (1980): 1–33. An account of the Law of the Sea situation in the Caribbean, in David Freestone and Clive Schofield, "The Caribbean Sea and Gulf of Mexico," in *The Oxford Handbook of the Law of the Sea*, ed. D. Rothwell et al., (Oxford: Oxford University Press, 2015), 672–700.

granting full effect to Aves island).[11] Also, the Mexico-Cuba Agreement in 1976 was the first bilateral delimitation between Latin American countries in the Middle American and Caribbean regions.[12] Venezuela and Great Britain are to be praised for the 1942 Treaty relating to the Submarine Areas of the Gulf of Paria, the first delimitation over the seabed and subsoil outside the territorial waters of the parties.[13] The 1990 Treaty on the Delimitation of Marine and Submarine Areas superseded the 1942 treaty and another one dated 1989.[14] The parties characterized the settlement as equitable.

And in 1973, Argentina and Uruguay concluded the Agreement relating to the Delimitation of the River Plate and the Maritime Boundary between the two countries, whereby a method to establish the lateral boundary is determined, following an equidistance line applicable to all effects, including the continental shelf boundary.[15] The Treaty provides for a common fishing zone for registered vessels of their flags, beyond twelve nautical miles, in a space delimited by arcs of circles whose points are in Punta del Este (Uruguay) and Punta Rasa del Cabo San Antonio (Argentina).

Further examples of direct settlement are the Agreements signed by Brazil and France in 1981 (on the delimitation between Brazil and the French Guyana)[16] and by Brazil and Uruguay in 1972.[17] In the last case, an approximate perpendicular line to the general direction of the coast was determined. And yet, alongside those precedents, unresolved disputes remain, for example, between Colombia and Venezuela regarding the Gulf of Venezuela,[18] a dispute that includes the status of islands, together with the relevant coasts and their maritime projections.

[11] See comments in Kaldone G. Nweihed, "Region II. Middle American and Caribbean Maritime Boundaries," in Jonathan I. Charney and Lewis M. Alexander (eds.), *International Maritime Boundaries* (The Hague, The Netherlands: The American Society of International Law, Martinus Nijhoff, 1993), 271–283. A critical point on this attribution is in Winston Anderson, *The Law of the Sea in the Caribbean* (The Hague, The Netherlands: Brill Nijhoff, 2022), 390.

[12] Kaldone G. Nweihed, "Cuba-Mexico, Report Number 2-8," in Charney and Alexander, *International Maritime Boundaries*, 565–576.

[13] League of Nations Treaty Series Vol. CCV, 1944–1946, No. 4829.

[14] https://www.un.org/Depts/los/LEGISLATIONANDTREATIES/PDFFILES/TREATIES/TTO-VEN1990SA.PDF. See "Trinidad and Tobago-Venezuela, Report No. 2-13(3)," in *International Maritime Boundaries*, The American Society of International Law, Brill NV, 2016), 685–689.

[15] 1295 U.N.T.S. , No. 21424. https://www.un.org/Depts/los/LEGISLATIONAN.DTREATIES/PDFFILES/TREATIES/URY-ARG1973MB.PDF. See Eduardo Jiménez de Aréchaga, "Argentina-Uruguay. Report Number 3-2," in Charney and Alexander, *International Maritime Boundaries*, 757–776. Also Lilian del Castillo, *The Río de la Plata and Its Maritime Front Legal Regime* (Leiden, The Netherlands: Brill 2008), 131–132.

[16] Eduardo Jiménez de Aréchaga, "Brazil-France (French Guiana). Report Number 3-3," in Charney and Alexander, *International Maritime Boundaries*, 777–783.

[17] Eduardo Jiménez de Aréchaga, "Brazil-Uruguay. Report Number 3-4," in Charney and Alexander, *International Maritime Boundaries*, 785–792.

[18] Rubén Carpio Castillo, *El Golfo de Venezuela y el Tratado Herrera Campins-Turbay Ayala*(Caracas, 1980), 104–110. The 1980 draft agreement was unsuccessful in setting up lines accommodating the respective positions. Also Tomas D. Anderson, "The Gulf of Venezuela Sea Boundary: A Problem Between Friends," *Yearbook (Conference of Latin Americanist Geographers* 15 (1989): 101–102.

In close connection with the development of new maritime spaces as part of the evolution of the Law of the Sea, it is also relevant to look at historical maritime agreements and awards in Latin America and the Caribbean region, considering not only their geographical scope and the criteria chosen to define the nature of the maritime spaces but also as their relationship with UNCLOS, as well as the applicable regime and the practice entertained by the parties concerned.[19] In that regard, the Gulf of Fonseca, as a semi-enclosed sea and a historical bay bordered by three states, El Salvador, Honduras, and Nicaragua, provides an example of this challenge. In 1917, the Central American Court of Justice declared that the Gulf of Fonseca was the property of the three countries surrounding it, except for an exclusive three-mile fringe along the littoral of each riparian State.[20] In 1992, the ICJ recalled the undivided status of the Gulf jointly inherited by the three states, remarking that it was "in a state of community, which entails a condominium or co-ownership of these waters."[21] The outward delimitation in the Pacific from the closing line of the Gulf is another relevant issue.

III. From History to Practice and from Practice to Theory

Historical circumstances have shaped the delimitation processes in Latin America, including those prevailing when adherence to new concepts in the Law of the Sea dramatically expanded in the region. Past dispute settlement experiences, existing treaties, and international awards applicable to territorial questions with maritime consequences have all influenced states in their appraisal of theoretical elements of delimitation under international law, such as the role and meaning of equitable principles, equitable results, relevant circumstances, and equidistance or median line. It is also noticeable that the resolve to advance in a judicial or arbitral type of settlement applicable to delimitation has shown the prevalence of special sensitivities about where to invoke customary law to address maritime entitlements. Overall, delimitation seems less connected to a regional trend than to approaches that respond to circumstances.

From a global perspective, it is well-known that consensus and the package-deal methodology imbued negotiations of UNCLOS with a particular character from 1973 onward. Whereas there was arduous discussion about methodologies

[19] A pedagogical overview of the evolution of international law of maritime delimitation in Stephen Fietta and Robin Cleverly, *A Practitioner's Guide to Maritime Boundary Delimitation* (Oxford: Oxford University Press 2016), 3–29.

[20] *The Republic of El Salvador v. The Republic of Nicaragua*, Central Am. Ct. of Justice, Opinion and Decision of the Court, March 9, 1917, *American Journal of International Law* 11 (July 1974): 674–696.

[21] *Land, Island and Maritime Frontier Dispute* (*El Salvador v. Honduras*: Nicaragua intervening), Judgment, 1992 I.C.J. 599–600, ¶ 401.

and preferred approaches to delimitation, views on regionalism and universalism at the time of negotiation and adoption of UNCLOS seem to have been less present in bilateral discussions or subregional settings.[22] Altogether, the regional practice on delimitation includes negotiation and submissions to international courts and tribunals, encompassing procedural and substantive international legal matters. Also, as in other regions, geographical configurations have been part of the challenge, as illustrated by the presence of islands, including cays, which are salient features in the Caribbean.[23]

Moreover, the shifting status of maritime spaces, including the addition of extended maritime spaces, has acted upon this scenario, leading to processes of boundary determination. Regarding the action of courts and tribunals, the allegiance to this method of settling controversies enjoys distinct levels of adherence, with a marked preference by some states, as the practice of Nicaragua and Costa Rica indicates. On the other hand, alleged international legal uncertainties or questionings enriched by domestic political debates have also been part of the prevailing scenario, as was the case between Chile and Argentina after the Beagle Channel arbitral award in 1977 on the maritime projection of their coasts.[24]

History recalls that the creation of a maritime zone of two hundred nautical miles comprising the subsoil, the sea floor, the water column, and natural resourceswas early conceived together with the method of "the parallel at the point at which the land frontier of the States concerned reaches the sea." This is evident in the language of the Declaration on the Maritime Zone of 1952 adopted by Chile, Perú and Ecuador, which refers to "an island or group of islands belonging to one of the countries making the declaration is situated less than 200 nautical miles from the general maritime zone belonging to another of those countries."[25] A parallel line method was confirmed by the Agreement relating to a Special Maritime Frontier Zone (1954),[26] which set up a special zone "at a distance of 12 nautical miles from the coast, extending to a breadth of 10 nautical miles on either side of the parallel which constitutes a maritime boundary between the two countries."

[22] Société française pour le droit international, *Régionalisme et Universalisme dans le Droit international contemporain* (Paris: Pedone, 1977).

[23] *Territorial and Maritime Dispute between Nicaragua and Honduras in the Caribbean Sea (Nicaragua v. Honduras)*, Judgment, 2007 I.C.J., 672, ¶¶ 28–29; *Territorial and Maritime Dispute (Nicaragua v. Colombia)*, Judgment, 2012 I.C.J. 640–641, ¶ 24.

[24] Eduardo Jiménez de Aréchaga, "Argentina-Chile, Report Number 3-1," in Charney and , *International Maritime Boundaries*, 791–755.

[25] Declaration on the Maritime Zone, 1952, ¶ 3, IV. https://www.un.org/Depts/los/LEGISLATIONANDTREATIES/PDFFILES/TREATIES/CHL-ECU-PER1952MZ.PDF.

[26] Agreement by exchange of notes of identical content between the Republic of Peru and the Republic of Ecuador, May 2, 2011, 2756 U.N.T.S. I-48631. https://treaties.un.org/doc/Publication/UNTS/Volume%202274/v2274.pdf

In 2014, the ICJ, deciding on a case concerning Peru and Chile, dictated that "the Court has before it an Agreement which makes clear that the maritime boundary along a parallel already existed between the Parties. The 1954 Agreement is decisive in this respect. That Agreement cements the tacit agreement."[27] The Court further said that the 1954 Agreement did not indicate the nature and extent of this boundary, although there was a signal that it extended beyond twelve nautical miles from the coast. An all-purpose maritime boundary was reasserted in this case.

By exchange of notes, Peru and Ecuador—parties to the same tripartite treaties—agreed in 2011 that their single maritime boundary extended along the geographic parallel of latitude from the convergence point of their respective baselines, up to two hundred nautical miles.[28] The agreement seems to admit the interpretation that it enshrines a thorough delimitation that confirms a long-standing line in the subregion while underscoring the common desire to recognize the Gulf of Guayaquil as a historic bay. In 2010, Ecuador published Nautical Chart IOA42, referring to the 1952 and 1954 tripartite agreements and plotting the geographic parallel maritime boundary with Peru.[29] In turn, Colombia and Ecuador, along the lines of the Southeast Pacific tripartite instruments, adopted in 1975 an Agreement on a maritime boundary following the geographic parallel intersecting the point at which the land frontier between the two countries reached the sea.[30] In 2012, by a Joint Declaration, Colombia and Ecuador identified the coordinates of the land boundary terminus.[31] In addition, a parallel line composes one of the sections of the all-purpose maritime boundary between Honduras and the Cayman Islands (United Kingdom), according to the 2001 Treaty,[32] as well as of Honduras and Cuba.[33]

When states choose to undertake a procedure to delimit, it may be inferred that consistency and predictability are crucial values, and that those elements

[27] *Maritime Dispute* (*Peru v. Chile*), Judgment, 2014 I.C.J., 39, ¶ 91.

[28] See Agreement by exchange of notes of identical content between the Republic of Peru and the Republic of Ecuador.

[29] Foreign Minister Ricardo Patiño Aroca, Letter to U.N. Secretary General Ban Ki-Moon, March 9, 2011, Note No. 4998CGJ/GM/2011, United Nations, New York, accessed August 12, 2024, https://www.un.org/depts/los/LEGISLATIONANDTREATIES/PDFFILES/ecu_2010_decree_english.pdf.

[30] Agreement Concerning Delimitation of Marine and Submarine Areas and Maritime Cooperation between the Republics of Colombia and Ecuador (August 23, 1975). https://www.un.org/Depts/los/LEGISLATIONANDTREATIES/PDFFILES/TREATIES/COL-ECU1975MC.PDF.

[31] Ecuadorian Ministry of Foreign Affairs, Trade, and Integration, http://www.mmrree.gob.ec/2012/ecu_ col_0612.pdf.

[32] Carlos López Contreras and Michael C. Wood, "Honduras-United Kingdom (Cayman Islands), Report Number 2-23," in *International Maritime Boundaries*, ed. David A. Colson and Robert W. Smith, (Washington, DC: The American Society of International Law, 2005), 3564–3574.

[33] Carlos López Contreras, "Cuba-Honduras. Report Number 2-33," in Lathrop, *International Maritime Boundaries*, 4735–4743.

are part of the outcome expected from courts and tribunals. The Latin American context does not seem to show variation from this general contention. In the region, arguments raised before international tribunals, such as the certainty of an agreement on delimitation challenged by another state, or the way a preliminary line of delimitation should be adjusted in judicial proceedings, and the role of the proportionality test, are indicative of the broad spectrum of elements that states invoke to influence the result. As in any other region, delimitation by agreement in Latin America and the Caribbean shows a range of methods.[34]

Another feature of the maritime delimitation processes in Latin America has been the combination of factors spanning from territorial entitlements to geographical and geostrategic elements. The issue of the point at which the land boundary reaches the sea or the extension of the seashore and its bearing on the determination of the previously mentioned point has also been subject to deliberation before international tribunals.

These elements have interacted—as in any delimitation process—with legal concepts and geopolitical definitions both in negotiations, and in the presentation of relevant positions by parties in adjudicative proceedings. Among the most notorious cases, the *Nicaragua v. Colombia* proceedings before the ICJ (2001–2012) was critical, as the dispute encompassed title to territory and maritime delimitation.[35] In a supervening controversy titled Alleged Violations of Sovereign Rights and Maritime Spaces in the Caribbean Sea, between these states, before the ICJ, Law Of The Sea issues were well present, such as the content of the contiguous zone and protected areas declared by Colombia, as well as the baselines of Nicaragua, all of which were closely related to the area delimited in 2012, in the Caribbean.[36]

Moreover, the maritime and territorial ingredients have been well entrenched in the case of the Gulf of Fonseca,[37] with three coastal states enjoying their respective historical entitlements over a common maritime space, the Gulf. Another example of this complexity can be found in the definitions structuring the settlement in the 1984 Treaty of Peace and Amity between Chile and Argentina and the ensuing delimitation in the Mar de la Zona Austral (Southern Zone Sea).[38] This Treaty, concluded under the mediation of the Holy See, shows how complex

[34] Matthias Forteau and Jean-Marc Thouvenin (eds.), *Traité de Droit International de la Mer* (Paris: Editions A. Pedone, 2017), 576–584.

[35] *Territorial and Maritime Dispute* (*Nicaragua v. Colombia*), Judgment, 2012 I.C.J. 624.

[36] *Alleged Violations of Sovereign Rights and Maritime Spaces in the Caribbean Sea* (*Nicaragua v. Colombia*), 2022 I.C.J. Judgment (April 21), https://www.icj-cij.org/public/files/case-related/155/155-20220421-JUD-01-00-EN.pdf.

[37] *Land, Islands and Maritime Frontier Dispute* (El Salvador/Honduras: Nicaragua intervening), Judgment, 1992 I.C.J. (September 11), https://www.icj-cij.org/public/files/case-related/75/075-19920911-JUD-01-00-BI.pdf

[38] Treaty of peace and friendship (with annexes and maps), 1984, https://treaties.un.org/doc/Publication/UNTS/Volume%201399/volume-1399-I-23392-English.pdf.

the search for a settlement can be whenever the parties invoke elements other than maritime projections.

These cases are only a part of the arrangements and solutions shaping the Latin American and Caribbean legal and political maritime delimitation landscape. There is also an emerging problem of broader concern: fluctuating boundaries and their bearing on the provisional nature of a boundary, an issue that is present in the Caribbean setting.

As a background to this subject, the impact of a fluctuating boundary or a segment of it has been discussed before the ICJ. The Court has confirmed that a mobile line was acceptable for a short extension. These situations do not call for generalizations, as they have applied to limited distances from a coast. The *Nicaragua v. Honduras*[39] and *Costa Rica v. Nicaragua*[40] show that the ICJ has been able to deal with this matter while defining that it was up to the parties involved to agree on a course of the delimitation line between the endpoint of the land boundary and the starting point of the single maritime boundary. Fluctuating boundaries, while present to a limited extent between Honduras and Nicaragua and Costa Rica and Nicaragua in cases before the ICJ, have also been used to identify the starting point of the maritime boundary. Further, the existence of high instability and narrowness of the sandspit near the mouth of the San Juan River was invoked to explain the difficulties arising from the choice of a basepoint or to connect a point on the sandspit to the fixed point at sea for the first part of the delimitation line. Views differ regarding the grounds on which this method should be applied in maritime boundaries whose course could change whenever coastlines change, thereby changing points from which measurements are taken.[41]

IV. The Search for an *opinion juris* and UNCLOS as a Reference Framework in Maritime Delimitation

Entitlement to maritime spaces and how their definitions may have a bearing on delimitation is part of the global discussion. The natural prolongation factor in the continental shelf definition, together with preferences for a distance-based

[39] *Territorial and Maritime Dispute between Nicaragua and Honduras in the Caribbean Sea* (*Nicaragua v. Honduras*), Judgment, 2007 I.C.J. 659, ¶ 321, (4).

[40] *Maritime Delimitation in the Caribbean Sea and the Pacific Ocean* (*Costa Rica v. Nicaragua*) and Land Boundary in the Northern Part of Isla Portillos (*Costa Rica v. Nicaragua*), Judgment, 2018 I.C.J. Rep. 139, ¶ 104.

[41] Massimo Lando, "Stability of Maritime Boundaries and the Challenge of Geographical Change: A Reply to Snjólaug Árnadóttir," *Leiden Journal of International Law* 35 (2022): 379–395; Sniólaug Árnadótttir, "Provisional boundaries and alternative solutions to maritime delimitation," *Leiden Journal of International Law* 35 (2022): 397–406.

method to measure the continental shelf regardless of geomorphology,[42] became crucial over the years, and was recognized by UNCLOS. In this context, the question may arise as to the relationship between the continental shelf and the EEZ and its impact on the prevalence of one single line or two different delimitation lines, depending on the maritime zone.

In a region where the concept of a patrimonial sea was born as an antecedent of the EEZ that included the column of water, the soil, and subsoil natural resources, with few exceptions that favored an extended territorial sea, this situation has been reflected in maritime delimitation agreements. The practice shows an inclination toward an integrative approach, as shown by the 2012 agreement between Cuba and Honduras[43] and the treaties concluded between Colombia and Costa Rica in 1977 and 1984.[44] While in the first case the EEZ and the continental shelf are mentioned by their names, in the second example, the terms used are "marine and submarine areas." The maritime delimitation treaty signed by Colombia and Honduras in 1986 also refers to a maritime frontier encompassing the continental shelf resources (hydrocarbons and natural gas deposits).[45] Delimitation governed by a single regime line seems to reflect a general trend.

The Treaty of Peace and Friendship of 1984[46] between Argentina and Chile raises questions about the correspondence between the two maritime spaces. Article 7 settles the maritime boundary whose final section runs from a point at sea south from the most southerly point of Isla Hornos at coordinates 56°22.8'South latitude and 67°16.0' West longitude (point E). According to the Treaty, the line of longitude shall continue South to a point whose coordinates are 58°21.1'South latitude and 67°16.0' West longitude (point F). The Treaty states that "the exclusive economic zones of the Argentina Republic and the Republic of Chile shall extend respectively to the east and west of the

[42] Chile and the West African states. See also Doc A/CONF.62/C.2/L.17 (July 23, 1974), Official Records of the Third United Nations Conference on the Law of the Sea, vol. III, 195 (Nicaragua); Doc A/CONF.62/C.2/L.31/Rev.1 (August 16, 1974), Official Records of the Third United Nations Conference on the Law of the Sea, vol. III, 211 (Japan); Doc A/CONF.62/86 (August 22, 1979), Official Records of the Third United Nations Conference on the Law of the Sea, vol. XII, 69 (Group of Islamic States).

[43] Cuba-Honduras, Report No. 2-33, in *International Maritime Boundaries*, 4735–4743,

[44] Treaty on Delimitation of Marine and Submarine Areas and Maritime Cooperation between the Republic of Colombia and the Republic of Costa Rica (March 17, 1977) United Nations, New York, accessed August 12, 20 24,https://www.un.org/depts/los/LEGISLATIONANDTREATIES/PDFFILES/TREATIES/COL-CRI1977MC.PDF; Treaty on the Delimitation of Marine and Submarine Areas and Maritime Cooperation between the Republic of Colombia and the Republic of Costa Rica, additional to the Treaty signed at San José on March 17, 1977, April 6, 1984, United Nations, New York, accessed August 12, 2024, https://www.un.org/depts/los/LEGISLATIONANDTREATIES/PDFFILES/TREATIES/COL-CRI1984MC.PDF.

[45] Maritime Delimitation Treaty between Colombia and Honduras, August 2, 1986, United Nations, New York, accessed August 12, 2024, https://www.un.org/depts/los/LEGISLATIONANDTREATIES/PDFFILES/TREATIES/COL-HND1986MD.PDF.

[46] 1399 U.N.T.S. No. 23392.

boundary thus described." And then it sets out that "To the south of the end of the boundary (point F), the exclusive economic zone of the Republic of Chile shall extend, up to the distance permitted by international law, to the west of the meridian 67°16,0' West longitude, ending on the east at the high sea." A 2021 Chilean initiative[47] to illustrate a two-hundred-nautical-miles continental shelf extending from Diego Ramírez islands to the West of the above-mentioned longitude, South of Point F, below the high sea, as well as the delineation of an extended continental shelf by Argentina to the East of such longitude and South of Point F, as depicted in Law 27,557 of 2020, shows a difference in the interpretation of the effect of the 1984 Treaty over the concept of high sea and EEZ as limited by the longitudinal line South of Point F.[48]

As an antecedent to assess the place and role of UNCLOS, the 1958 Geneva Conventions on the Territorial Sea and the Continental Shelf, respectively, although limited in participation, provided for delimitation clauses that were deeply scrutinized when negotiating the 1982 Convention, in terms of both their customary value and their methodological content. As is known, the relevant provisions of the aforesaid 1982 UNCLOS clauses regarding delimitation of the territorial seas, EEZs, and continental shelves, were the subject of a tough debate during the Conference, where Latin American countries were not absent.

On the other hand, some Latin American countries are still not parties to UNCLOS,[49] and this fact may also be analyzed in terms of their approach to maritime delimitations. So far, in the Territorial and Maritime Dispute between *Nicaragua v. Colombia*, the ICJ noted that "since Colombia is not party to UNCLOS, the Parties agree that the applicable law is customary international law."[50] The same has been said regarding Articles 15, 74, and 83 of UNCLOS in terms that acknowledge their declaratory nature as customary international law.[51]

In cases involving the exclusive economic zone and the continental shelf, the above-mentioned provisions aim to provide a framework rather than impose a technical course of action. The phrase in Articles 74 and 83, according to which the delimitation "shall be affected by agreement on the basis of international law, as referred to in Article 38 of the Statute of the International Court of Justice, in order to achieve and equitable solution," contained in paragraph 1 of both

47 Decree No. 95 of the Ministry of Foreign Affairs of Chile, which determines the maritime jurisdictional areas from Punta Puga to Diego Ramírez Islands, of August 23, 2021, https://www.bcn.cl/leychile/navegar?i=1164205.

48 "Diplomatic row between Argentina and Chile erupts over maritime borders," https://www.batimes.com.ar/news/latin-america/diplomatic-row-between-argentina-and-chile-erupts-over-maritime-borders.phtml.

49 Colombia, El Salvador, Perú, and Venezuela.

50 *Territorial and Maritime Dispute* (*Nicaragua v. Colombia*), Judgment, 2012 I.C.J. 673, ¶ 137.

51 Ibid., ¶¶ 137–138.

Articles, does not add much to the selection of methods by the parties. As has been noted, courts and tribunals are showing a preference for the construction of a provisional line followed by a second stage of adjustment and proportionality testing. After establishing the entitlement and the relevant area, the delimitation process accommodates to a two- or a three-stage approach.[52]

Regarding the influence of UNCLOS, in addition to the technical considerations, this study is also aware of Lathrop's argument that maritime delimitation under UNCLOS is results-oriented to the extent that it aims at achieving an equitable result.[53] It follows from this argument that the successive tests applied to draw a boundary line shed light on the fact that the selection of elements by a court or tribunal depends on its own understanding of how to apply international law in every case, according to its merits.

The analysis of the regional practice, in conjunction with the global tendencies, indicates the presence of more alignment than discrepancies between them. The above reflections are not indifferent to the relationship between the maritime delimitation process with customary law, which may appear as definitive in certain conjunctures. On the other hand, although customary law may look like a starting point, it is difficult to assess its weight in the negotiation of maritime boundaries in terms of mandating the use of a preferred methodology.[54] A different situation stems from delimitations resulting from adjudication processes, which are useful for understanding how judges' arguments play a significant role in framing established practice in legal terms. This is the scenario whenever the terms of an equitable solution emerge in decisions issued by courts and tribunals.

In this sense, the affirmation that customary law has contributed to establishing a law of delimitation is correct, although it does not determine the selection of a consistent set of elements that shape the application of said customary source. On this matter, the major input flows from the didactic exercise of judicial formulation with authoritative value through the case law of the ICJ, arbitral tribunals, and the International Tribunal for the Law of the Sea (ITLOS).[55]

Deference toward the role of customary law is noticeable in the case law after the adoption of UNCLOS. Thus, it is worth noting that in the 2006 arbitration

[52] Malcolm D. Evans, "Maritime Boundary Delimitation," in *The Oxford Handbook of the Law of the Sea*, ed. Donald R. Rothwell(Oxford: Oxford University Press, 2015), 259–261.

[53] Coalter Lathrop, "The Provisional Equidistance Line," in *Maritime Boundary Delimitation: The Case Law*, ed. Alex G(Cambridge: Cambridge University Press, 2018), 221.

[54] A fair description of methods used in delimitation by negotiations in *Handbook on the Delimitation of Maritime Boundaries, Division for Ocean Affairs and the Law of the Sea* (Office of Legal Affairs, United Nations, 2000), 47–62.

[55] See reflections of former ICJ President Gilbert Guillaume to the Sixth Committee of the General Assembly of the United Nations, October 31, 2001, https://www.icj-cij.org/public/files/press-releases/5/2995.pdf

between *Trinidad and Tobago v. Barbados*, both parties to UNCLOS, the arbitral court invoked customary law as a source that helped "to shape the considerations that apply to any process of delimitation."[56] In fact, since the 1990s the ICJ and arbitral tribunals have in general followed the practice of first establishing a provisional equidistance line and then adjusting it, if necessary, to achieve an equitable result, as part of a process founded in customary law. The decisions embedded in the arbitral awards under Annex VII of UNCLOS in *Barbados/ Trinidad and Tobago* (2006)[57] and *Guyana/Surinam* (2007)[58] follow this methodology.

In cases between Latin American countries, the ICJ has also asserted that the aim of certainty is part of the process of delimitation. This has been enunciated in *Nicaragua v. Honduras* and *Nicaragua v. Colombia*, which appealed to the role of the equidistance line "unless in either case there are compelling reasons as a result of which the establishment of such a line is not feasible."[59] Also, the Court has stressed that for the territorial sea, equidistance is still the general rule as articulated in Article 15 of UNCLOS, unless due regard has to be paid to the presence of special circumstances. The Court has admitted that the general practice for single maritime boundaries is to begin with a provisional equidistance line, even if the equidistance method does not automatically have priority over other methods, and that in certain circumstances, there may be factors which make the application of the equidistance method inappropriate.[60]

That seems to have been the situation in the controversy between Nicaragua and Honduras, after the Court concluded that there was no traditional boundary along a parallel of latitude. Here, the Court chose a single line running along a bisector and acknowledged the right to a twelve-mile territorial sea of the islands (cays) belonging to Honduras and Nicaragua. This decision is one of the maritime boundary delimitations where the Court would determine an all-purpose maritime boundary, considering the claims of both parties to a territorial sea of twelve nautical miles for the islands. The Honduran islands ended up with a territorial sea of twelve miles in a semi-enclaved position in the Nicaraguan EEZ, and were not used as basepoints to establish an equidistance line for the entire boundary.

When deciding to use the bisector line in the *Nicaragua v. Honduras* case (2007), without praising the virtues of a provisional equidistance line, the Court

[56] Arbitration between Barbados and Trinidad and Tobago (2006), ¶ 223, https://legal.un.org/riaa/cases/vol_XXVII/147-251.pdf.

[57] Ibid., https://legal.un.org/riaa/cases/vol_XXVII/147-251.pdf.

[58] Arbitration between Guyana and Suriname (2007), https://legal.un.org/riaa/cases/vol_XXX/1-144.pdf.

[59] *Territorial and Maritime Dispute* (*Nicaragua v. Colombia*), Judgment, 2012 I.C.J. 965, ¶ 191.

[60] *Territorial and Maritime* Dispute between Nicaragua and Honduras in the Caribbean Sea (*Nicaragua v. Honduras*), Judgment, 2007 I.C.J. 741, ¶ 272.

would emphasize that it was doing so given the extreme instability of the relevant coasts that made it impossible to identify stable basepoints and to construct an equidistance line. Furthermore, the Court underlined the resemblance of the bisector line with the equidistant line, both lines being geometrical ones.

A different situation was assessed by the judgment of the ICJ on *The Question of Delimitation of the Continental Shelf between Nicaragua and Colombia beyond 200 Nautical Miles from the Nicaraguan Coast*.[61] Considering the answers of each party to the questions raised by the Court in this respect,[62] and after analyzing the practice of states that had submitted studies of extended continental shelves to the Commission on the Limits of the Continental Shelf (CLCS, UNCLOS body), and the underlying compromises in the EEZ and the continental shelf as embodied in UNCLOS, the Court concluded that, "under customary international law, a State's entitlement to a continental shelf beyond 200 nautical miles from the baselines from which the breadth of its territorial sea is measured may not extend within 200 nautical miles from the baselines of another State."[63] This assertion contains a distinction between the entitlement to an extended continental shelf and its extension within the two hundred-mile continental shelf of another state. One salient point in this judgment is the value given to the practice of states in the CLCS framework as an expression of *opinio juris*.

V. Unity and Diversity: A False Choice

From an overall perspective, the ICJ has worked out a reasoning aimed to provide certainty to the law of maritime delimitation of the EEZ and the continental shelf, through a development that former President Guillaume associated with the 1985 Libya/Malta case,[64] where the equidistance line was installed as a provisional line to delimit the continental shelves between the two countries. Then, the line could be corrected to achieve an equitable result, according to the Court's view.

[61] *Question on the Delimitation of the Continental Shelf between Nicaragua and Colombia beyond 200 Nautical Miles from the Nicaraguan Coast* (*Nicaragua v. Colombia*), Judgment, 2023 I.C.J. (July 13, 2023).

[62] *(1) Under customary international law, may a State's entitlement to a continental shelf beyond 200 nautical miles from the baselines from which the breadth of its territorial sea is measured extend within 200 nautical miles from the baselines of another State?. Question of the Delimitation of the Continental Shelf between Nicaragua and Colombia beyond 200 Nautical Miles from the Nicaraguan Coast* (*Nicaragua v. Colombia*), Order of October 4, 2022, 2022 I.C.J. 563.

[63] *Question on the Delimitation of the Continental Shelf between Nicaragua and Colombia beyond 200 Nautical Miles from the Nicaraguan Coast* (*Nicaragua v. Colombia*), Judgment, 2023 I.C.J. 29, ¶ 78 (July 13).

[64] *Continental Shelf* (*Libyan Arab Jamahiriya/Malta*), Judgment of June 3, 1985, 1985 I.C.J. 13 (1985).

In conclusion, consistency and predictability in applying the rule of law emerge as core criteria of the rule of law in maritime delimitation.[65] The resulting inference of this methodology is retaken in paragraph 179 of *Peru v. Chile*, where the ICJ said that it would proceed "on the basis of the provisions of Articles 74, paragraph 1, and 83, paragraph 1, of UNCLOS which, as the Court has recognized, reflect customary international law."[66] The ICJ referred to previous controversies where that conceptual analysis had prevailed, including a case between Nicaragua and Colombia.[67]

The identical texts of the UNCLOS provisions applicable to the delimitation of the EEZ and the continental shelf, as set out in Articles 74 and 83, respectively, were highlighted by the Court. The differences between Peru and Chile were not about the applicability of these provisions as distinguished from the existing agreements between the parties but mostly about the role of the agreements (even tripartite ones) passed together with the proclamations of the extended maritime zones before the adoption of UNCLOS, and their prevalence at the time Peru submitted the case to the ICJ. As noted above, in 2014, the ICJ admitted the existence of a tacit agreement based on the geographic parallel of latitude extending up to eighty miles from the coast.[68]

As Weil pointed out more than three decades ago, the law on maritime delimitation has changed as it aims to be more predictable and where the judge plays a role in asserting its content and application.[69] Thus, one of the main issues discussed in current delimitation bibliography is the combination of proportionality and consistency in adjudicative processes, from the perspective of Articles 74 and 83 of UNCLOS. Altogether, and in whatever way the normativity of these provisions was defined, their wording seems impressionistic. According to one author, the articles are characterized by their vagueness.[70] In that respect, ad hoc judge Orrego Vicuña would make the point of the need for consistency when considering Article 74, paragraph 1, of the 1982 UNCLOS as reflecting an understanding "considering equitable results of maritime delimitation, not in isolation from, but in conjunction with agreements between the parties, all of it effected on the maritime dispute basis of international law.[71] The accent put on

[65] Ibid., 39, ¶ 45.

[66] *Maritime Dispute* (*Peru v. Chile*), Judgment, 2014 I.C.J. 65, ¶ 179.

[67] *Maritime Delimitation and Territorial Questions between Qatar and Bahrain* (*Qatar v. Bahrain*), Merits, Judgment, 2001 I.C.J. 91, 167; *Territorial and Maritime Dispute* (*Nicaragua v. Colombia*), Judgment, 2012 I.C.J. (II), 674, ¶139.

[68] *Maritime Dispute* (*Peru v. Chile*), Judgment, 2014 I.C.J. 47, ¶ 117.

[69] Prosper Weil, *The Law of Maritime Delimitation-Reflections* (Cambridge: Cambridge University Press, 1989), 277–288.

[70] Massimo Lando, *Maritime Delimitation as a Judicial Process* (Cambridge: Cambridge University Press, 2019), 294.

[71] Separate opinion, partly concurring and partly dissenting, of Judge ad hoc Orrego Vicuña, ¶ 36. Maritime Dispute (*Peru v. Chile*), Judgment, 2014 I.C.J. 3.

existing agreements on delimitation challenges the assumption that those articles are empty of content. In turn, Judge Wolfrum added another element when valuing the case law as an *acquis judiciaire* remarking that it is "a source of international law to be read into articles 74 and 83 of the Convention."[72]

Another factor that is not alien to the above reasoning in the delimitation process is the recourse to a disproportionality test as a stage in the delimitation process. Its application shows variation when the delimitation is the product of negotiations (as in the case of the agreement between the Netherlands and Venezuela),[73] or if it is part of a judicial or arbitral decision. Tanaka[74] highlights that the test has been clearly present in the jurisprudence since the 2009 Black Sea case, where the ICJ—referring to a possible disparity in coastal lengths—underscored that "This remains in each case a matter for the Court's appreciation, which it will exercise by reference to the overall geography of the area."[75]

Along the above views, there have been questions whether the disproportionality test developed through the jurisprudence is adequately objective and scientific in international law, and if it aims to correct the line considering a strict correlation of the lengths of the coast and the relevant areas. The case law in Latin American disputes shows that it has been invoked in one way or the other, in cases such as *Nicaragua v. Colombia* and *Costa Rica v. Nicaragua*. In *Peru v. Chile*, the ICJ stated that "the existence of an agreed line running for 80 nautical miles along the parallel of latitude presents it with an unusual situation,"[76] and "the calculation does not purport to be precise and is approximate."[77]

On the other hand, the treatment of equidistance and basepoints seems not to vary dramatically between the Latin American case law and the general trend. Strict equidistance to determine a provisional delimitation of the EEZ and the continental shelf has been applied in two arbitrations in the region (*Guyana v. Suriname* and *Barbados v. Trinidad and Tobago*). Lathrop's comment on the selection of basepoints by courts and tribunals and its subjective nature is pertinent in this regard, as he argues that such a preference could influence the course of a provisional median line disproportionally to their size and importance.[78] Furthermore, in both arbitrations, the awards show coincidences in

[72] *Declaration of Judge Wolfrum, Delimitation of the maritime boundary in the Bay of Bengal (Bangladesh/Myanmar)*, Judgment, ITLOS, 137 (2012).

[73] Kaldone G. Nweihed, "The Netherlands (Antilles)-Venezuela Report Number 2-12," in Charney and Alexander, 615–637 *International Maritime Boundaries* (Amsterdam: Martinus Nijhoff,1993).

[74] Yoshifumi Tanaka, *Predictability and Flexibility in the Law of Maritime Delimitation* (2nd ed., London: Hart, 2019), 232–233.

[75] *Maritime Delimitation in the Black Sea* (*Romania v. Ukraine*), Judgment, 2009 I.C.J. 129, ¶ 213.

[76] *Maritime Dispute* (*Peru v. Chile*), Judgment, 2014 I.C.J. 69, ¶ 193.

[77] Ibid.

[78] Coalter Lathrop, "The Provisional Equidistance Line," in *Maritime Boundary Delimitation: the Case Law*, ed. Alex G. Oude Elferink, Tore Henriksen, and S. Veierud Busch, 218–219 (Cambridge: Cambridge University Press, 2018).

terms of applying a provisional equidistance line as a first step, and as a "hypothesis and a practical starting point,"[79] and of applying Articles 74(1) and 83(1) of UNCLOS in a way that admits a corrective-equity approach in light of relevant circumstances. In the *Guyana v. Suriname* case, the Tribunal discarded the application of a bisector method for the EEZ and the continental shelf and highlighted the primacy of the median line in the territorial sea, according to Article 15 of UNCLOS.

The selection of basepoints was also part of the delimitation in the 2012 *Nicaragua v. Colombia* case, where the Court considered whether basepoints on certain islands would have a "marked effect upon the course of the provisional median line which would be out of all proportion to its size and importance."[80] The treatment of base points and the construction of a provisional equidistance line in the Court's 2014 judgment in *Peru v. Chile*, starting at a point (Point A) on the geographic parallel at eighty nautical miles from the coast, is another example of latitude in the construction of a maritime boundary.[81] It is to be noted that soon after the decision, the parties in this case jointly implemented the measurement of points of the maritime boundary as decided by the ICJ as a sign of allegiance to its validity.[82]

Finally, there are two hypotheses regarding whether the role of equity or the adapted version of the equitable principles or equitable result predominate in Latin America. On the one hand, negotiations reflect what the parties believe is appropriate for them and in that sense, the outcome reflects an equitable result. This idea stems from agreements such as those adopted by Argentina and Uruguay, Ecuador and Colombia, Colombia and Panama, and Chile and Argentina. On the other hand, delimitations decided by courts or tribunals in cases to which Latin American states have been parties, in terms of the reasonings contained in the awards and judgments, that do not substantively differentiate from the general practice, follow the foundations advanced by courts and tribunals regarding the applicability of the relevant legal sources in the law of the sea. The discussion about the strength of regionalism, so present in the history of the Law of the Sea and the Latin American participation in shaping UNCLOS, does not show a precise correlation in terms of the sources of delimitation.

It is worth recalling that the ICJ judgment in 1969 enunciated that delimitation is to be effected by agreement in accordance with equitable principles, and

[79] RIAA 214-215, ¶ 242.

[80] *Territorial and Maritime Dispute* (*Nicaragua v. Colombia*), Judgment, 2012 I.C.J. 699, ¶ 202.

[81] Natalie Klein, "Chile-Peru. Report Number 3-5 (2)," in Lathrop, *International Maritime Boundaries*, 4749–4758.

[82] Minutes of the Joint Field and Office Work Related to the Measurement of Points of the Maritime Boundary between Peru and Chile Pursuant to the Judgment of the International Court of Justice. In "Chile-Peru, Report Number 3-5 (2)," in Lathrop, *International Maritime Boundaries*, 4762–4764.

taking account of all the relevant circumstances in such a way as to leave as much as possible to each party all those parts of the continental shelf that constitute a natural prolongation of its land territory into and under the sea, without encroachment on the natural prolongation of the land territory of the other.[83] This assertion enshrined a definition of principles and criteria that have had a lasting significance.[84]

In this landscape of delimitation by adjudication, colonial and postcolonial effectivities and *uti possidetis juris* have also been invoked. The doctrine relates to the Latin American assumption that there was no *terra nullius* in the continent at the end of the colonial era.[85] From this, the right to succeed to the motherland in all its rights and territorial claims would be implied. Determining boundaries between states should be a consequence of the doctrine and not the origin itself. Therefore, the transposition of the *uti possidetis juris* to the Latin American maritime scenario and its bearing on the establishment of zones and maritime delimitations could not be overlooked. The real impact of the doctrine would relate to the alleged succession of states to already settled boundaries or the interplay between boundaries and possessions, whether terrestrial or maritime ones. Inspiring cases have been the 1922 Frontier Case between Colombia and Venezuela[86] and the Frontier Dispute between Burkina Faso and the Republic of Mali before the ICJ,[87] where the Court admitted that the said principle was applicable by deliberate choice of the parties.

The validation by the case law of this doctrine as a primary principle in maritime delimitation has not been evident in disputes between Latin American countries, but that does not imply that the *uti possidetis juris* will not be argued in the future. Tribunals have based their decisions either on the nonexistence of an established maritime delimitation line before the independence of the concerned states or on the different legal nature of the maritime spaces to delimit as compared with those governed by the existing maritime delimitations agreed by a predecessor state. In an ICJ case, there have been views valuing the evidence

[83] 1969 I.C.J. 53–54.

[84] Hugo Caminos and Vicente Marotta-Rangel, "Sources of the Law of the Sea," in René-Jean Dupuy and Daniel Vignes, *Handbook on the New Law of the Sea* (Amsterdam: Martinus Nijhoff, 1991), 130.

[85] Giuseppe Nesi, "Uti possidetis Doctrine," *Max Planck Encyclopedia of Public International Law*, https://opil.ouplaw.com/view/10.1093/law:epil/9780199231690/law-9780199231690-e1125?rskey=oBWbno&result=1&prd=MPIL.

[86] Affaire des frontières Colombo-vénézuéliennes (Colombie contre Vénézuéla), Reports of International Arbitral Awards, Vol. I, 228, https://legal.un.org/riaa/cases/vol_I/223-298.pdf

[87] The ICJ stated that "there is no doubt that the obligation to respect pre-existing international frontiers in the event of a State succession derives from a general rule of international law, whether or not the rule is expressed in the formula uti possidetis." *Frontier Dispute*, Judgment, 1986 I.C.J., 566–567, ¶¶ 24, 26 (1986). The respect of borders existing on the achievement of independence had also been discussed in the *Frontier Dispute* (*Benin/Niger*), Judgment, 2005 I.C.J. 148, ¶ 140; and in *Frontier Dispute* (*Burkina Faso/Niger*), Judgment, 2013 I.C.J. 74, ¶ 63.

of pre-independence exploitation of seabed areas as a sign of an acquiesced de facto delimitation or a divide that could have traditionally served as a maritime boundary.[88]

In the *Territorial and Maritime Dispute between Nicaragua and Honduras* (1999–2007),[89] Honduras maintained that the *uti possidetis juris* principle referred to in the Gámez-Bonilla Treaty and the 1906 Award of the King of Spain applied to the maritime area off its coasts and those of Nicaragua. Thus, Honduras asserted that the 15th parallel of latitude constituted the traditional line of maritime delimitation and that both countries had succeeded to a maritime area extending up to six miles. The Court decided that the principle did not apply to the maritime delimitation in this case, recalling that the 1906 Arbitral Award "which indeed was based on the *uti possidetis juris* principle," did not deal with the maritime delimitation. The Court said that the Award fixed "the extreme boundary points on the coast of the Atlantic," which among other things, determined the point of commencement of the territorial boundary westward. In addition, the Court found no indication in the Award that the 15th parallel was agreed as the boundary line.[90] In summary, the Court did not uphold either the contention that the *uti possidetis juris* principle provided grounds for an alleged "traditional" maritime boundary along that parallel[91] or that a de facto boundary existed based on a tacit agreement, related to postcolonial *effectivités*. According to the Court, a distinction should be drawn between "a provisional line found convenient for a period of time" and an international boundary.[92] The phrase that "evidence of a tacit legal agreement must be compelling"[93] was then enunciated by the ICJ.

On delimitation, the 2007 *Nicaragua v. Honduras* judgment assumes the application of a single line to delimit maritime spaces. Its study also serves as another reference to the appraisal of the equitable principles/relevant circumstances method as a suitable one for achieving an equitable result. In another case of the same subregion, the 2012 *Nicaragua v. Colombia* case, the *uti possidetis juris* would be invoked by each party regarding certain maritime features, but the ICJ did not rule based on the said principle.[94] On a different note, but also related to historical elements, in the Guyana/Suriname case, the Arbitral Tribunal considered historical arrangements "of an unusual nature," including

[88] *Continental Shelf (Tunisia/Libyan Arab Jamahiriya)*, Judgment, 1982 I.C.J., sep. op. Judge Jiménez de Aréchaga, 132, ¶ 102. Also, *Continental Shelf (Tunisia/Libyan Arab Jamahiriya)*, Judgment, 1982 I.C.J., sep. op. Judge Ago, 97–98, ¶ 5.

[89] *Territorial and Maritime Dispute between Nicaragua and Honduras in the Caribbean Sea (Nicaragua v. Honduras)*, Judgment, 2007 I.C.J. 659.

[90] Ibid., 729, ¶¶ 235–236.

[91] Ibid., 727, ¶ 229.

[92] Ibid., 735, ¶ 253.

[93] Ibid., 735, ¶ 253.

[94] *Territorial and Maritime Dispute (Nicaragua v. Colombia)*, Judgment, 2012 I.C.J. 651, ¶ 65.

navigational interests, to determine a territorial sea boundary along a line from three nautical miles to the twelve-nautical-mile limit.[95]

Latin America also assumes other formulas in delimitation processes: cooperative arrangements. One example is the Caribbean Sea, where equidistance lines are present with innovations in terms of cooperative arrangements (joint development agreement [JDA], or joint regime or joint scientific research and fishing zone). These unique formulas are typified in agreements adopted between Colombia and the Dominican Republic, by means of a Joint Scientific Research and Common Fishing Exploitation Zone (1978),[96] and Colombia and Jamaica, setting up a joint regime area (1993).[97] By a 2007 Framework Treaty relating to the unitization of hydrocarbon reservoirs that extend across the delimitation line, Venezuela and Trinidad and Tobago agreed on a legal and operational framework to deal with those resources. It was followed by a unitization agreement for the exploitation and development of hydrocarbon reservoirs of the Loran-Manatee Field.[98] Also, between Barbados and Guyana, a JDA was introduced in a 2003 delimitation agreement titled Exclusive Economic Zone Co-operation Treaty that reiterates Articles 74(3) of UNCLOS.[99] This JDA aims—among other goals—to exercise of joint jurisdiction, control, and management development within an area over which a bilateral overlap occurs between the EEZs of the parties and beyond the limits of the EEZ of other states. The delimitation of maritime spaces joined by clauses about collaboration over the resources is present in cases in which their transboundary management becomes part of the final arrangement.

Cases are not abundant, but a 2000 agreement between Mexico and the United States is an interesting sample of interconnecting resources and the delimitation of the extended continental shelves. Here, the Treaty refers to the exploration of the shelf and the exploitation of its natural resources, particularly oil and gas. In the presentation of the treaty to the Senate, the US government referred to UNCLOS as an instrument that "reflects customary international law in this respect" and that it provides "a more scientifically-based definition of the continental shelf."[100] In respect to Jamaica and Colombia, a 1993 Treaty assumes

[95] *Arbitration between Guyana and Suriname* (2007), XXX RIAA, ¶¶ 323–325.

[96] Kaldone G. Nweihed, "Colombia-Dominican Republic Report Number 2-2," in Charney and Alexander, *International Maritime Boundaries*, 477–490.

[97] Kaldone G. Nweihed, "Colombia-Jamaica Report No. 2-18," in *International Maritime Boundaries*, ed. Jonathan I (Amsterdam: The American Society of International Law, Martinus Nijhoff, 1998), 2179–2204.

[98] Derek Smith, "Trinidad Tobago–Venezuela Report 2-13 (4)," in Lathrop, *International Maritime Boundaries*, 4649–4681.

[99] U.N.T.S. Vol. 2277, No. 40555.

[100] *Treaty between the Government of the United States of America and the Government of the United Mexican States on the Delimitation of the Continental Shelf in the Western Gulf of Mexico beyond 200 nautical miles.* 2000. P.VI, https://www.state.gov/wp-content/uploads/2020/02/US_2000_withExtension.pdf

that a boundary may exist in an area beyond two hundred nautical miles.[101] Additionally, delimitations between Barbados and France (Guadeloupe and Martinique)[102] and Suriname and France (French Guiana) cover continental shelf areas beyond two hundred miles.[103] Another case may be the delimitation of the Uruguay-Argentina extended continental shelves. In these examples, parties have submitted their respective studies concerning the continental shelf to the CLCS.[104]

VI. General Review: Cases, Comparisons, and Differences

From a macro-geographical perspective, considerations based on the assumption that the region is a single unit for the sake of delimitation methodologies may lead us to overemphasize the common features and overlook the singularities of the resulting maritime delimitations. At a point in time, it was worth considering that the delimitation landscape in the South American coast over the Pacific Ocean followed a system based on the parallel of latitude drawn from the point where the land boundary reaches the sea.[105] At the same time, maritime delimitations over the Atlantic coast of South America have been depicted as following in general an equidistance line. The first assertion would deserve more attention given the judgment of the ICJ in *Peru v. Chile*, issued in 2014.[106]

Aware of these matters, some elements can be underscored from the above study:

- In the case of delimitation agreements, whether directly agreed upon by the parties or set up through diplomatic procedures with the assistance of third parties, an agreement may reflect choices and preferences regarding geographical settings and the role attributed to coastal configurations, islands, and other features' presence, but also other interests and preferences.

[101] Nweihed, "Colombia-Jamaica Report No. 2-18," 2198.

[102] Carl W. Dundas, "Barbados-France (Guadeloupe and Martinique) Report Number 2-30," in *International Maritime Boundaries*, ed. David A. Colson and Robert W. Smith, 4223–4231 (Amsterdam: Brill Nijhoff, 2014).

[103] Agreement on maritime delimitation between the Government of the French Republic and the Government of the Republic of Suriname (with map), 2017,. https://www.un.org/Depts/los/LEGISLATIONANDTREATIES/PDFFILES/TREATIES/France-Suriname%20treaty.pdf

[104] Leonardo Bernard and Clive Schofield, "Disputes Concerning the Delimitation of the Continental Shelf beyond 200 Nautical Miles," in *New Knowledge and Changing Circumstances in the Law of the Sea*, ed. Thomas Heidar, 178–179 (Leiden, The Netherlands: Brill Nijhoff, 2020).

[105] Eduardo Jiménez de Aréchaga, "South American Boundaries," in Charney and Alexander, *International Maritime Boundaries*, 287–286; Weil, "Geographic Considerations in Maritime Delimitation," in Charney and Alexander, *International Maritime Boundaries*, 126.

[106] *Maritime Dispute* (*Peru v. Chile*), Judgment, 2014 I.C.J. 3

- Although these factors are relevant in delimitation processes conducted either by direct negotiations or in arbitral/judicially decided cases, the method of a specific process of delimitation by agreement may assign a different weight to certain factors where accommodation is considered. For example, different weight could be given to factors such as marine resources and their weight in the national or local economies, persistent maritime uses and interests (navigation, access to semi-enclosed zones, overflight), and environmental concerns. These elements may be part of the comprehensive assessment of each state when choosing the elements that will support a future agreement.
- Although it is difficult to appraise the role of the concept of *effectivités* in the cases analyzed in this study, it is noticeable that in some examples, it has been present either as an element of an alleged historic understanding or as an argument elicited to strengthen a position regarding the persistent presence of a coastal state or its population, as well as through the exercise of jurisdiction or control in a particular maritime sector.
- On the methods used in the delimitation processes by agreement, as reflected in the resulting formulas, such as the recourse to equidistance and the relevant circumstances as a basis to achieve an equitable result, it is difficult to deconstruct the wording employed by the parties. Nevertheless, the final presentation of the resulting line may serve to capture the essence of what the parties esteemed as acceptable.
- On the other hand, the study prepared by Jiménez de Aréchaga in the early 1990s,[107] which examines the practice as it stood at the time and his own assessment of the existing delimitation agreements, suggests that the set of valid methods and arrangements present on the Pacific and the Atlantic coasts of South America are indicative of the amplitude with which international law looks at the process of maritime delimitation.

While states may be aware of the existing practice as well as of the legal theory on maritime delimitation, and the possible prevalence of geometrical lines and the role of physical elements, such as basepoints and islands, agreements do not always allow us to infer which element was definitive in the final outcome. It is also worth noticing that in certain cases, the method employed can be explicit in the text of an agreement that explains whether the line chosen is an all-purpose maritime boundary or if it applies only to a specific maritime space. Besides, the selection of criteria underlying the consent of the parties in concluding delimitation agreements can be analyzed separately from the work of international courts and tribunals in charge of a delimitation case. The analysis of Tanaka is

[107] Jiménez de Aréchaga, "South American Maritime Boundaries," 285–286.

instructive in this respect.[108] Thus, selecting a preferred method may be a sign of adherence to the theory of delimitation based on predictable lines, which is one of the reasons for involving international courts and tribunals in the delimitation process. This is without prejudice to the fact that the predictable nature of the application of existing rules, or even alleged existing delimitation agreements, appears to be susceptible to challenges in the case law.

As has been suggested, the fact that some cases have been subject to decisions by courts or tribunals is also worth considering.[109] This study assumes the validity of the assertion that the modes of delimitation agreed upon by negotiations and those influencing judicial or arbitral decisions show a "world of difference," as Jiménez de Aréchaga highlighted in a case decided by the ICJ.[110] These examples show that whenever the delimitation is the object of a dispute and is brought before a court or tribunal, even when historical factors and doctrinal traditions are involved, the approach followed by an adjudicative body is mostly based on its own understanding of the applicable international law, particularly when it finds that there is no agreement between the parties concerned, or the agreement is a limited one. Concepts such as relevant coasts, relevant circumstances, the choice of base points, and the application of a (dis)proportionality test are present in the case law in Latin America and the Caribbean.

Based on the characteristics of the cases dealt with in this study, delimitations have been set up following a single all-purpose boundary line applicable to the EEZs and the continental shelves. This extended line may show variations from the line drawn to delimit territorial seas. It is always pertinent to dig into the weight given to the baselines and basepoints, either in direct agreements or in judgments and awards. In the latter case, scholars note the role of judicial discretion.[111]

In some cases, the delimitation line postulated by the parties had been part of a unique process of affirmation of the common adherence to an all-encompassing maritime zone of two hundred nautical miles. This was a salient characteristic of the *Peru v. Chile* proceedings, where the ICJ took note of the different approaches by each state regarding the two-hundred-mile maritime zone. While Chile had become party to the 1982 Convention and employed its terms, Peru sustained a single maritime domain extending up to two hundred nautical miles. In paragraph 178 of the 2014 judgment, the Court states, "Both Parties claim 200-nautical-mile maritime entitlements. Neither Party claims an

[108] Tanaka, *Predictability and Flexibility in the Law of Maritime Delimitation*, 187–194.

[109] *Arbitration Barbados v. Trinidad & Tobago* (2006); *arbitration Guyana v. Surinam* (2007); 2014 I.C.J., *Perú v. Chile*; 2012 I.C.J. *Nicaragua v. Colombia* (2012); 2018 I.C.J., *Costa Rica v. Nicaragua*; 1992 I.C.J. El Salvador/Honduras, Nicaragua intervening; 2007 I.C.J., *Nicaragua v. Honduras* (2007).

[110] Sep. op., *Continental Shelf (Tunisia/Libyan Arab Jamahiriya)*, Judgment, 1982 I.C.J. 117, ¶ 91.

[111] Davor Vidas, "The Delimitation of the Territorial Sea, the Continental Shelf, and the EEZ," in Oude Elferink et al., *Maritime Boundary Delimitation*, 55–56.

extended continental shelf in the area with which this case is concerned. Chile's claim consists of a 12-nautical-mile territorial sea and an exclusive economic zone and continental shelf extending to 200 nautical miles from the coast. Peru claims a 200-nautical mile "maritime domain." The Court also noted that Peru's Agent formally declared on behalf of his government that "[t]he term 'maritime domain' used in [Peru's] Constitution is applied in a manner consistent with the maritime zones set out in the 1982 Convention." The Court then affirmed that this was a formal undertaking by Peru.[112]

Another feature present in the Latin American and Caribbean situations is the close relationship between territorial and maritime disputes, as shown in ongoing cases before the ICJ. These cases may not explicitly refer to delimitations, but the issue of the maritime entitlement over areas allegedly appurtenant to the states concerned is worth noticing. At present, two cases of this characteristic are pending before the ICJ.[113] In these cases, the colonial and postcolonial titles are part of the legal discussions.

Apart from changing the bilateral legal and political landscape, a judgment or award may also have connections with the boundaries of a party to the case with third parties, despite that the judgment or award is not binding on third parties. The potential for encroachment is eventually possible.

Throughout this study, the influence of nongeographical factors in the delineation of maritime boundaries, as well as the weight accorded to them in the construction of an agreement between the concerned states, and the overall subregional context, subtlety surrounds the understanding of the legal geography of the maritime delimitations.

[112] *Maritime Dispute* (*Peru v. Chile*), Judgment, 2014 I.C.J. 65, ¶ 178.

[113] *Guatemala's Territorial, Insular and Maritime Claim* (*Guatemala/Belize*) initiated in 2019, and *Arbitral Award of October 3, 1899* (*Guyana v. Venezuela*), initiated in 2018.

25

Latin America and the Codification of the Law of State Responsibility

A Tale of Juridical Equality and Nonintervention

Fernando Lusa Bordin and Federica Paddeu

I. Introduction

In a lecture given at the Hague Academy of International Law, the late Judge Antônio Augusto Cançado Trindade emphasized how "Latin American legal doctrine has remained consistently attentive to general principles of international law, has duly acknowledged their importance, and has sustained their ineluctable incidence in distinct domains of international law."[1] Those principles include respect for the juridical equality of states and nonintervention in the internal or external affairs of states. Not only were juridical equality and nonintervention articulated in a pioneering fashion in the regional codification efforts that resulted in the 1933 Montevideo Convention on the Rights and Duties of States,[2] they have also informed the participation of Latin American states in global efforts to codify and progressively develop international law, especially the law of state responsibility.

In an opinion prepared in 1962, the Inter-American Juridical Committee articulated a list of postulates of "an American doctrine of the responsibility of the State," reflecting a "continental juridical concept" that started with the following: "Intervention in the internal or external affairs of a State is not admissible to enforce the responsibility of said State." On the contrary, intervention establishes the responsibility of the intervening state.[3] In the Committee's view, this first postulate was based on the "incontrovertible legal ground [of] the

[1] Cançado Trindade, "The Contribution of Latin American Legal Doctrine to the Progressive Development of International Law," *Recueil des cours* 376, no. 9 (2014): 91.

[2] Montevideo Convention on the Rights and Duties of States, Arts. 4 and 8 (proclaiming that States are "juridically equal" and "enjoy the same rights' based on 'the simple fact of [their] existence [persons] under international law," and that "[n]o state has the right to intervene in the internal or external affairs of another").

[3] Inter-American Juridical Committee, Contribution of the American Continent to the Principles of International Law that Govern the Responsibility of the State, Opinion prepared in accordance

Fernando Lusa Bordin and Federica Paddeu, *Latin America and the Codification of the Law of State Responsibility* In: *Latin American International Law in the Twenty-First Century*. Edited by: Alejandro Chehtman, Alexandra Huneeus, and Sergio Puig, Oxford University Press.
DOI: 10.1093/9780197754016.003.0025

fundamental right of the states to juridical equality."[4] It followed that intervention could not "be used to enforce the responsibility of a State."[5] This was a rule that, in the Committee's view, "revolutionized the question of the responsibility of the State."[6]

To reflect on the mark that Latin America has left on the codification of the law of state responsibility, this chapter reflects on how Latin American states have pushed, and continue to push, for ideals of juridical equality and non-intervention in two instances: their contributions to the International Law Commission's articulation of rules on countermeasures (section II) and their support for the adoption of a convention on state responsibility (section III).[7]

II. The Codification of Countermeasures: Learning from a History of Interventionism

Reprisals and Intervention in Latin America

To understand the Latin American stance on the law of countermeasures, it is necessary to have in mind the continent's historical experience with intervention. Throughout the nineteenth century and early twentieth centuries, Latin American states were often targeted with reprisals by (primarily) European powers seeking to obtain the payment of debts owed to their nationals and, on occasion, also to "avenge [their] outraged honour."[8] Such claims were usually

with Resolution CIV of the Tenth Inter-American Conference, Resolution VI of the Third Meeting and Resolution XII of the Fourth Meeting of the Inter-American Council of Jurists (OAS, 1962), 6.

[4] Ibid., 9, quoting its "Instrument Relating to Violations of the Principle of Nonintervention,, approved on October 23, 1959.

[5] Ibid., 9.

[6] Ibid., 9.

[7] In this chapter, our focus will be on Latin American states, on the assumption that they serve as proxies, however imperfectly, for the continent's professional legal communities and the legal culture in which those communities operate. We recognize, nonetheless, that a fuller account would require considering the contributions of key individuals, from Latin American ILC members to legal advisers and law academics. For a discussion of the contributions of Latin American jurists to the work of the ILC, especially at its inception, see Maria Cristina Rodríguez and Gloria Rosenberg, "El Pensamiento de Juristas Latinoamericanos en los Estudios de la Comisión de Derecho Internacional: Principios y Doctrinas Americanas," in *Cuaderno de Derecho Internacional* V (2010): 85.

[8] See *Journal de débats* in connection with the so-called Pastry war, quoted by William S. Robertson, "French Intervention in Mexico in 1838," *Hispanic American Historical Review* 24 (1944): 222, 231. Those were so-called public reprisals, as opposed to the earlier practice of "private" reprisals. See Federica Paddeu, *Justification and Excuse in International Law: Concept and Theory of General Defences* (Cambridge: Cambridge University Press, 2018), 228–229 (and references cited therein).

based on little evidence and often used as a pretense to coerce these States into changing their behavior more widely.

A few notable examples suffice to illustrate the point.[9] In 1838, France blockaded Mexican ports in response to Mexico's alleged failure to, among other things, pay debts to French nationals and its refusal of France's demand that it extend most-favored-nation treatment to its nationals. The blockade eventually led to the so-called Pastry War.[10] In 1861, the United Kingdom blockaded Brazilian ports in connection with the murder of the British passengers and the plunder of the cargo of the foundered *Prince of Wales*, and the arrest and interrogation of British officials from the frigate *Forte* on Brazilian soil. The United Kingdom demanded, and enforced through reprisals, investigations regarding both incidents, compensation for the victims, and an apology for the offense suffered by Britain.[11] Brazil agreed to pay damages relating to the *Prince of Wales* and to submit the matter of the *Forte* to arbitration—in which, eventually, it was held that no offense had been caused to Britain.[12] Perhaps most notably, in 1902, Britain, Italy, and Germany blockaded Venezuelan ports to coerce the government to settle certain debts owed to their citizens.[13] A letter from British officials to their German counterparts neatly (and candidly) encapsulates the attitude of European powers toward measures of coercion in Latin America (and likely beyond). These measures, UK officials stated:

> [F]orm[ed] a convenient *mitior usus* which is suitable to the case of a recalcitrant petty State in controversy with Great Powers of overwhelming strength, who, while desiring to obtain proper redress, are unwilling to dismember or destroy a puny antagonist.[14]

Latin American lawyers reacted against this practice by elaborating an extensive and robust doctrine of nonintervention. The earliest statement of the doctrine came from Venezuelan jurist Andrés Bello in his *Principios de Derecho de*

[9] The Inter-American Juridical Committee listed fourteen instances of reprisals against Latin American States: Inter-American Juridical Committee, *Contribution*, 3–5.

[10] See *Journal de débats* in connection with the so-called Pastry war, quoted by: Robertson, "French Intervention in Mexico in 1838, 231.

[11] Paddeu, *Justification and Excuse*, 232.

[12] See Albert G. de Lapradelle and Nicolas Politis, *Recueil des arbitrages internationaux* (Paris: Pedone, 1905) vol. 2, 236ff (Award at 241–242).

[13] For an overview of the claims by the blockading nations, see A. S. Hershey, "The Venezuelan Affair in the Light of International Law," *University of Pennsylvania Law Review* 51 (1903): 249, 249–251.

[14] Memorandum for Communication to Count Metternich, November 29, 1902, cited in Christophe Wampach, *Armed Reprisals from Medieval Times to 1945* (Baden-Baden, Germany: Nomos, 2020), 200.

jentes, first published in 1832.[15] While Bello did not address questions of international responsibility,[16] his work influenced the development of certain Latin American doctrines aimed at limiting the scope of reprisals for the repayment of debts, including the Calvo and Drago doctrines.[17] In his *Droit international théorique et pratique*, Argentine jurist Carlos Calvo directly addressed nonintervention in the context of responsibility and repayment of debts. He denounced the European practice of reprisals against Latin American states as unequal, and as a manifestation of, among others, "outdated traditions of the colonial system" and European states' failure to see, and therefore respect, them as equal independent nations.[18] Shortly after, so-called Calvo Clauses, limiting or excluding the exercise of diplomatic protection by a foreigner's home state, began to be incorporated in the constitutions of Latin American states and in contracts with foreigners.[19] Subsequently, in the early twentieth century, and in response to the blockade of Venezuelan ports, Luis María Drago, then Foreign Affairs Minister in Argentina, wrote to US President Theodore Roosevelt arguing that the forcible collection of public debt was incompatible with state sovereignty and the principles of equality and nonintervention.[20] The United States later raised a modified version of the doctrine during the Hague Peace Conference of 1907,[21] leading to the adoption of the 1907 Drago-Porter Convention, which limited recourse to force for the collection of public debts.[22] But the Convention had not gone as far as Latin American states had hoped, and many entered reservations

[15] Andrés Bello, *Principios de Derecho Internacional* (3rd rd., Paris: Garnier Hermanos, 1873), 29–30, 52–53. The text was originally published as *Principios de Derecho de Jentes* in 1832. It was renamed for subsequent revised editions, published 1844 and 1864.

[16] Responsibility was not treated as a discrete field of international law until later in the nineteenth century, on which, see James Crawford, Thomas Grant, and Francesco Messineo, "Towards an International Law of Responsibility: Early Doctrine," in *International Law and the Quest for Its Implementation: Liber Amicorum Vera Gowlland-Debbas*, ed. Laurence Boisson De Chazournes and Marcelo Kohen (eds), 377 (Amsterdam: Martinus Nijhoff, 2010).

[17] Juan Pablo Scarfi, "In the Name of the Americas: The Pan-American Redefinition of the Monroe Doctrine and the Emerging Language of American International Law in the Western Hemisphere, 1898-1933," *Diplomatic History* 40 (2016): 189, 199.

[18] Carlos Calvo, *Le droit international théorique et pratique* (4th ed., Paris: Pedone-Lauriel, 1887) vol. 1, 349 (§ 204).

[19] These clauses also asserted the equality between nationals and foreigners, and thus the primacy of domestic remedies for the resolution of contractual disputes with foreigners. On these clauses, see M. R. García-Mora, "The Calvo Clause in Latin American Constitutions and International Law," *Marquette Law Review* 30 (1950): 1; Chittharanjan Amerasinghe, *Diplomatic Protection* (Oxford: Oxford University Press, 2008), ch. 12.

[20] Letter by Drago, Minister of Foreign Relations of the Argentine Republic, to García Mérou, Minister of the Argentine Republic to the United States (December 29, 1902), *American Journal of International Law* 1 (1907): Suppl. 1. Drago subsequently developed his argument in: Luis María Drago, *Cobro coercitivo de deudas públicas* (Buenos Aires: Coni Hermanos, 1906).

[21] James Brown Scott, *The Proceedings of the Hague Peace Conferences, The Conference of 1907* (Oxford: Oxford University Press, 1920), vol. I, 55.

[22] Convention on the Limitation of Employment of Force for Recovery of Contract Debts (The Hague, adopted October 18, 1907, in force January 26, 1910), 205 CTS 250. On this development: John Williams, "Le droit international et les obligations financières internationales qui naissent d'un contrat," *Recueil* 1 (1923): 289, 326–336.

to the text.[23] Their disappointment was such that twenty years after its adoption, they had not become party to it.[24]

Latin America's Influence on the Shaping of the Law of Countermeasures

The historical experience of being at the receiving end of reprisals and intervention significantly shaped the approach of Latin American states to the International Law Commission's codification of countermeasures, in the context of the Articles on the Responsibility of States for Internationally Wrongful Acts (ARS), from the 1980s onward. By then, of course, the use of force and forcible countermeasures had been prohibited.[25] But non-forcible reprisals, involving non-performance of the target state's rights, such as by means of asset-freezing and other means of economic coercion, were still permissible. These remained a concern for Latin American states, especially as attempts to ban economic coercion had been repeatedly unsuccessful.[26] Guns and gunboats would no longer threaten their coasts, but the specter of coercion remained on the horizon.

Latin American states did not directly raise this historical experience in their comments on the International Law Commission (ILC) work, but the general tenor of their observations was evocative of it. The concern for juridical equality and non-intervention was central to their engagement in the debate on countermeasures. The words of the Uruguayan delegation at the Sixth Committee of the UN General Assembly neatly captured this mood: countermeasures, it said, "seemed to be antithetical to some fundamental principles, including the principle of sovereign equality of States, equality before the law, and the principle of peaceful settlement of disputes."[27] This mood meant that Latin American states approached the topic with a significant degree of circumspection.

Overall, thirteen Latin American states participated in these debates,[28] often speaking for larger regional groups.[29] These states were divided on the underlying

[23] The Convention had only limited, rather than outlawed, resort to force in a specific number of cases. For an assessment, see Wampach, *Armed Reprisals*, 220–225.

[24] K. Strupp, "L'intervention en matière financière," *Recueil* 8 (1925): 3, 104.

[25] Paddeu, *Justification and Excuse*, 239–242.

[26] Attempts to ban such coercive measures by broadening the concept of "force" to include economic coercion were made during the drafting of the UN Charter in the mid-1940s, and later during the negotiations on Article 52 of the VCLT in the 1960s, and on UNGA Resolutions 2625 and 3314, in the 1970s and 1980s

[27] A/C.6/47/SR.27 (1992), § 10.

[28] To the best of our knowledge, the following states commented on these provisions during the debates in the Sixth Committee of the UN General Assembly or submitted written observations to the ILC: Argentina, Brazil, Chile, Colombia, Costa Rica, Cuba, Ecuador, Guatemala, Haiti, Mexico, Trinidad and Tobago, Uruguay, and Venezuela.

[29] In this context, Venezuela spoke on behalf of the Andean Pact in 1979: A/C.6/34/SR.44; and Colombia on behalf of the Rio Group in 2000: A/C.6/55/SR.23. Overall, twenty of thirty-three Latin

question of the permissibility of countermeasures, and whether they should be included in the ARS. On the one hand, there were States—including Brazil,[30] Cuba,[31] Mexico,[32] and Uruguay[33]—that firmly opposed countermeasures and argued that they should be excluded from the project. Mexico and Brazil were the resolute staunchest opponents of this institution, frequently commenting on the ILC's proposals. As Brazil remarked, evoking the "first postulate," to recognize and codify "the legitimacy of countermeasures meant denying the equality of States and actually heightened their inequality."[34] On the other, there were states that were more sanguine about these measures. These states generally proceeded from the assumption that, in light of the decentralized character of international society, countermeasures remained a necessary tool of enforcement.[35] As explained by Argentina, for example, without countermeasures, it was "the injured State [which] could find itself unable to bring about the cessation of wrongful acts in a timely manner, and could turn out to be the main victim of a decentralized system of international sanctions."[36]

Regardless of their principled stance on countermeasures, all the Latin American states that took part in the discussions agreed that the institution must be restrained to avoid the risk of abuse. Several Latin American states endorsed the first reading proposal to "link" countermeasures to mandatory dispute settlement.[37] The first reading draft, completed in 1996, contained a complex dispute settlement mechanism that would have allowed a state subject to countermeasures to resort to arbitration.[38] But this "link" proved highly controversial.[39] As many states argued, these proposals unjustifiably privileged the

American and Caribbean States commented on these provisions, either individually or through regional groups.

[30] Brazil: A/C.6/34/SR.45 (1979), § 28; A/C.6/47/SR.25 (1992), §§ 39–40; A/C.6/49/SR.25 (1994), §§ 1–2; A/C.6/50/SR.17 (1995), §§ 18–21; A/C.6/51/SR.34, § 34.

[31] Cuba: A/C.6/47/SR.29 (1992), § 60. Its position remained unchanged during the second reading of the project: Cuba: A/C.6/54/SR.28 (1999), § 94.

[32] Mexico: A/C.6/49/SR.25 (1994), § 26; A/C.6/50/SR.21 (1995), § 61; A/C.6/53/SR.18 (1999), § 18; A/C.6/55/SR.20 (2000), § 37

[33] Uruguay: A/C.6/47/SR.27 (1992), § 20; A/C.6/49/SR.27 (1994), §§ 21–23; A/C.6/50/SR.21 (1995), § 22.

[34] A/C.6/47/SR.25 (1992), § 40.

[35] Costa Rica: A/C.6/55/SR.17 (2000), § 64; Ecuador: A/C.5/47/SR.30 (1992), § 49; Chile: A/C.6/55/SR.17 (2000), § 48.

[36] Argentina: A/C.6/51/SR.36 (1996), § 42.

[37] E.g., Brazil: A/C.6/49/SR.25 (1994), § 2, A/C.6/50/SR.17 (1995), § 15, A/C.6/51/SR.34 (1996), 65; Chile: A/C.6/54/SR.22 (1999), § 25; Guatemala: A/C.6/50/SR.18 (1995), § 23.

[38] See Draft Art. 48, Draft Articles on the Responsibility of States for Internationally Wrongful Acts adopted on first reading, Report of the ILC on the work of its forty-eighth session, ILC Yearbook 1996, vol. II(2).

[39] Comments by Governments on all the Draft Articles, U.N. Doc. A/CN.4/488 and Add.1-3, ILC Yearbook 1998, vol. II(1), 142–146; Topical summary of the discussion held in the Sixth Committee of the General Assembly during its fifty-fifth session prepared by the Secretariat, U.N. Doc. A/CN.4/513 (February 15, 2001), §§ 19–21.

state that had committed the wrongful act: a unilateral right to initiate arbitration was given to the responsible state, but not to the injured state.[40] Dispute settlement was eventually removed from the articles under Special Rapporteur James Crawford, on the understanding that such provisions could be introduced later—perhaps during negotiations toward a treaty on state responsibility.[41]

Aside from dispute settlement provisions and their ability to limit and oversee the taking of countermeasures, the Latin American states generally endorsed strict limits on the taking of countermeasures. Speaking on behalf of the eighteen members of the Rio Group, Colombia noted in 2000 that "[t]he Rio Group delegations had reservations concerning the provisions on countermeasures" and thought they needed to be "strictly regulated to prevent abuses."[42] Through the work of at least three Special Rapporteurs, and over many years, the Commission finally devised a regime presented to states in 2001. This regime significantly narrowed the function of countermeasures, now only permissible to enforce the obligations of cessation and reparation,[43] and placed some important limitations on these measures, both substantive and procedural. Substantively, countermeasures must be a response to a wrongful act and be temporary and proportionate.[44] They are prohibited with respect to a specific list of obligations.[45] Procedurally, states must call on the responsible state to comply, notify the state of their intention to take countermeasures, and offer to negotiate. Some of these requirements were recognized at customary law, but others—in particular, the requirements of prior notification and negotiation[46]—most likely involve elements of progressive development.[47]

States' views on this regime were mixed. It was strongly opposed by a handful of states, in particular the United Kingdom and the United States, on the grounds that it was unduly strict and not rooted in state practice.[48] However, the regime

[40] Crawford second report, § 387. There was also a risk that this would incentivize injured states to take countermeasures, to induce the responsible state to resort to arbitration.

[41] ILC Report 2001, § 73. For an overview of the reasons and discussions leading to this, seeJames Crawford, Jaqueline Peel, and Siman Olleson, "The ILC's Articles on Responsibility of States for Internationally Wrongful Acts: Completion of the Second Reading," *European Journal of International Law* 12 (2001): 963.

[42] A/C.6/55/SR.23, §4. As of 2000, the Rio Group comprised eighteen members: Argentina, Brazil, Colombia, Mexico, Panama, Peru, Uruguay, Venezuela, Bolivia, Ecuador, Chile, Paraguay, Costa Rica, El Salvador, Guatemala, Honduras, Nicaragua, and Dominican Republic, http://s017.sela.org/celac/quienes-somos/antecedentes/grupo-de-rio/estados-miembros/. See also, e.g., Argentina: A/C.6/51/SR.36 (1996), § 42; Brazil: A/C.6/55/SR.18 (2000), § 64; Chile: A/C.6/55/SR.17 (2000), § 48; Costa Rica: A/C.6/55/SR.17 (2000), § 64; Ecuador: A/C.5/47/SR.30 (1992), § 49; Venezuela: A/C.6/50/SR.20 (1995), § 2.

[43] ARS Art. 49.

[44] Ibid., art. 51.

[45] Ibid., art. 51. Ibid., art. 51. Ibid., art. 50.

[46] Ibid., art. 52(1)(b).

[47] The procedural requirements are included in ibid., Art. 52.

[48] United Kingdom: A/C.6/55/SR.14 (2000), §§§28, 33–36; United States: A/C.6/55/SR.18 (2000), §§ 68–70; A/C.6/56/SR.14 (2001), § 74.

was broadly satisfactory to most States. Among Latin American States, only six addressed the regime in their observations on the final draft of the articles.[49] Their views, too, were mixed. Some objected to the regime, but for reasons opposite to those of the United States and United Kingdom. For these states, the regime had not gone far enough in restricting the use of countermeasures. Colombia was the most negative of all:

> Even though the draft articles laid down stringent criteria for the use of countermeasures, States' margin of discretion in that respect was much too wide and upset the requisite balance of the articles. Countermeasures were not a logical, automatic consequence of State responsibility and therefore had no place in the law on the responsibility of States.[50]

Others were content with the balance struck by the ILC. Argentina "endorsed the rules proposed by the Commission, which were balanced and conducive to limiting any resort to countermeasures, as well as to preventing any abuse."[51] Venezuela expressed similar views.[52] Mexico observed that "like all products of compromise, the articles left some room for doubt and reservations."[53] However, the delegation "felt that the final result was balanced and reinforced the principles that countermeasures were limited in scope, were restricted to the purpose of securing compliance with the obligation breached and must be proportionate to the injury suffered."[54] In between were states like Brazil and Haiti. Brazil "attached great importance to the criteria for avoiding abuse" but regretted that some elements remained subjective.[55] Both states would have wished stronger provision for mandatory and peaceful dispute settlement.[56]

For all their differences in opinion, the interventions of Latin American states in the debate reveal a regional sensibility manifested in two main attitudes. First, one of skepticism against an institution that had been at the root of so many abuses against states in the region. Second, a commitment to upholding principles of equality and its corollary, nonintervention; a commitment, in other words, to endorse the "first postulate" articulated by the Inter-American Juridical Committee, as one of the main contributions made by Latin America to this area of international law. To be sure, Latin American states were not the only ones to approach countermeasures in this way. Many other states had expressed similar

[49] Six Latin American States commented on the final draft in 2001: Argentina, Brazil, Colombia, Haiti, Mexico, and Venezuela.
[50] A/C.6/56/SR.15 (2001), § 40.
[51] A/C.6/56/SR.15 (2001), § 53.
[52] A/C.6/56/SR.15 (2001), § 37.
[53] A/C.6/56/SR.14 (2001), § 10.
[54] A/C.6/56/SR.14 (2001), § 10.
[55] A/C.6/56/SR.15 (2001), § 2.
[56] Brazil: A/C.6/56/SR.15 (2001), § 2; Haiti: A/C.6/56/SR.23 (2001), § 37.

concerns, in particular with respect to abuses of the institution and the desire to restrict the application of countermeasures as much as possible.[57] Indeed, the three ILC Special Rapporteurs who addressed the regime of countermeasures (Riphagen, Arangio-Ruiz, and Crawford) also shared a restrictive approach to countermeasures. But they found difficult to find the right balance that would ensure the protection of the injured state's rights while limiting the risk of abuse. In Arangio-Ruiz's words, this difficult task involved a balance between two conflicting concerns: "[t]he first was to ensure that countermeasures were not abused by allegedly injured States. The second was to articulate a regime of countermeasures that was effective enough to guarantee cessation and reparation."[58] Mexico's observation that countermeasures were one of the most difficult aspects of the codification of the law of responsibility, and one that could delay completion of the project, was not overstated.[59] Successive proposals by the ILC on countermeasure restrictions had been opposed by states in the Sixth Committee. By throwing their weight behind the ILC's desire to constrain countermeasures, and regularly commenting on the Commission's proposals and pushing for restrictive regulation, Latin American states significantly contributed to shaping the compromise regime eventually adopted.

Even if the regulation of coercive methods for the enforcement of state responsibility did not go as far as many Latin American states wished, and even if the Articles leave open the possibility of coercive (if non-forcible) methods for the enforcement of international law, Latin American states seemed on the whole more satisfied with the compromises reached in 2001 in Geneva and New York than the compromises reached in 1907 in the Hague. Not long after the adoption of the Articles, Mexico, one of the staunchest opponents and critics of the proposals on countermeasures, relied on this doctrine to (unsuccessfully) justify domestic measures that affected US investors, contrary to North American Free Trade Agreement (NAFTA) protections.[60] Some skeptics remain, nevertheless. Twenty years after the adoption of the ARS, Brazil, commenting on the application of international law in cyberspace, noted that "[t]here are different views on the existence of widespread state practice and *opinio juris* capable of giving rise to customary international law on the legality and the requirements of countermeasures."[61]

[57] See, e.g., Iraq: A/C.6/38/SR.37 (1982), 16 ("the necessity for the establishment of law and order and the need of the injured State to take appropriate measures for self-preservation").

[58] Arangio-Ruiz, 2238th Meeting, ILC Yearbook 1991, vol. I, 209 (§ 22).

[59] A/C.6/49/SR.25 (1994), § 25.

[60] *Archer Daniels Midland Company and Tate & Lyle Ingredients Americas, Inc v. Mexico*, ICSID Case No. ARB/(AF)/04/5, Award, November 21, 2007; *Corn Products International, Inc v. Mexico*, ICSID AF Case No ARB/(AF)/04/1, Decision on Responsibility, January 15, 2008; *Cargill, Inc v. Mexico*, ICSID Case No. ARB/(AF)/05/2, Award, September 18, 2009.

[61] U.N. G.A., Official compendium of voluntary national contributions on the subject of how international law applies to the use of information and communications technologies by States submitted by participating governmental experts in the Group of Governmental Experts on Advancing

III. A Convention on State Responsibility: Multilateralism in the Service of Legal Certainty

Latin America's Pursuit of a Convention on State Responsibility

When the ILC completed the Articles on State Responsibility in 2001, it departed from its usual practice, at least up to that point, of proposing that states convene a diplomatic conference to adopt a convention based on the draft articles.[62] Instead, it recommended that the UN General Assembly take note of the Articles in the first instance, leaving the consideration of whether to pursue a convention for a later time.[63] This decision was made following a heated debate.[64] Some ILC members feared that a diplomatic conference would reopen debate on polemical issues; upset the balance of a text that the ILC had carefully crafted over four decades of work; and ultimately result in "reverse codification" if reluctance to ratify the convention called into question the status of customary rules restated by the Articles. Other members dismissed those concerns as exaggerated and pointed to the virtues of carrying out codification by treaty, which results in an instrument that is both more certain and reliable and also binding.

Accepting the ILC's recommendation, the General Assembly adopted Resolution 56/83 of December 12, 2001, where it "[took] note of the articles on responsibility of States for internationally wrongful acts, presented by the International Law Commission, and [commended] them to the attention of Governments without prejudice to the question of their future adoption or other appropriate action."[65] The resolution also reproduced the text of the ARS as an annex and included the topic of state responsibility in the provisional agenda of the fifty-ninth session of the General Assembly (held in 2004). A pattern then emerged of the Sixth Committee of the General Assembly revisiting the Articles once every three sessions, to discuss the pros and cons of three potential outcomes: (1) negotiating a convention based on the Articles; (2) issuing a declaration or resolution to adopt the Articles; or (3) leaving the Articles in their current form, at least for the time being.

As was the case within the Commission, the debates at the Sixth Committee reveal a continuing disagreement among delegations as to what form the

Responsible State Behaviour in Cyberspace in the Context of International Security established pursuant to General Assembly resolution 73/266, U.N. Doc. A/76/136 (July 13, 2021), 21/142.

[62] On which see Galvão Teles, "The Impact and Influence of the Articles on State Responsibility on the Work of the International Law Commission and beyond," *EJIL:Talk!* (August 3, 2021), https://www.ejiltalk.org/the-impact-and-influence-of-the-articles-on-state-responsibility-on-the-work-of-the-international-law-commission-and-beyond/.

[63] ILC Report 2001, §§72–73.

[64] Ibid., §§ 61–66.

[65] U.N. G.A. Res. 56/83 (2001).

codification of state responsibility should take.[66] There does not seem to be much of an appetite for a declaration or resolution, so the debate has been polarized between the option of adopting a convention and the option of maintaining the status quo of leaving it to state practice and international dispute settlement bodies to rely on the ARS as appropriate. While support for the status quo comes mostly from northern Europe, North America, and Oceania, the developing world has generally favored the convention option.

Latin American states have been playing a decisive role in advocating for a convention on state responsibility. For one, they have been unanimous in their support for codification by treaty, both in individual statements and in statements made on behalf of the Community of Latin American and Caribbean States (CELAC) group, which they formed with states from the Caribbean. One of the main reasons the group offers for its position is the desire to achieve "greater clarity and legal certainty by addressing existing gaps in international law, which would have a positive impact on the overall development of international law."[67] That partly reflects a regional preference for depending on treaty law rather than on the more elusive customary rules that the ARS are thought to reflect, to varying extents.[68] As El Salvador has stated in the Sixth Committee, "[t]he adoption of the articles in the form of a legally binding instrument would provide a more solid basis for the different means of implementation of the international responsibility of a State," as "they would become a source of law and have a greater constraining effect on national legal orders and a stronger impact on the practice of State organs."[69] Expressing a similar sentiment, Mexico has lamented the "imbalance that would be created where primary rules were more comprehensively codified than secondary rules," an imbalance which "could in the long term be detrimental to the coherence and effectiveness of international law."[70] A specific concern in this regard relates to how the ARS have been construed and applied thus far. Guatemala has suggested "a need for clear and uniform guidelines to assist those tribunals and help them avoid . . . political interpretations."[71] In a recent intervention, Cuba sharply criticized (unspecified)

[66] For a comprehensive discussion of the debates up to 2018, see Federica Paddeu, "To Convene or Not to Convene? The Future Status of the Articles on State Responsibility: Recent Developments," *Max Planck Yearbook of United Nations Law* 21 (2018): 83. More recently, see Arman Sarvarian, "The Ossified Debate on a UN Convention on State Responsibility," *International & Comparative Law Quarterly* 70 (2021): 769.

[67] A/C.6/71/SR.9 (2016), § 27.

[68] For a discussion of the relationship between the ARS and customary international law, see Fernando Lusa Bordin, "Reflections of Customary International Law: The Authority of Codification Conventions and ILC Draft Articles in International Law," *International & Comparative Law Quarterly* 63 (2014): 535.

[69] A/C.6/74/SR.13 (2020), § 33.

[70] A/65/96 (2010), at 3–4, § 4.

[71] A/C.6/68/SR.15 (2014), § ,10.

states that "force" ambiguous rulings on others by leaving the law in the hands of tribunals (presumably in the investment protection field) chaired by jurists educated in the Global North and ignorant of the realities of the developing world.[72]

While emphatic in their support for a convention, Latin American states have not been very vocal about what rules they would take the opportunity to clarify or what gaps they would like to fill if a diplomatic conference on state responsibility were convened. In the debates, delegations from other regions have referred to specific provisions they would like reassessed. Chief among them is perhaps the regime of countermeasures. Singapore, for example, has continued "to question the desirability of providing a legal regime for countermeasures within the framework of State responsibility because of their potentially negative implications."[73] Similarly, Iran expressed the hope that a future convention would "bring certainty and predictability to the application of the convention and prevent abuse in the form of excessive or unjustified invocation of countermeasures against other countries,"[74] and China has singled out countermeasures as a topic around which "differences in interpretation and major concerns" persisted.[75]

In contrast, Latin American delegations have been keeping their cards closer to their chest, offering comparatively vague statements. They have refrained, at least in plenary debates, from criticizing the Articles—in a rare instance, Mexico mentioned "the weaknesses in the articles, which have been extensively studied and identified in the literature and by State themselves" but did not elaborate on what those "weaknesses" were.[76] That might suggest a genuine commitment on their part to support the balance achieved by the ILC even in areas where they did not get the outcome they would have favored, in particular, in the field of countermeasures and dispute settlement. At the same time, one can sense in the debates that Latin American states remain guided by the values that have informed their contributions to the ILC debates, in particular, their suspicion of unilateral action and their commitment to that "first postulate" of "American international law": nonintervention. For example, Guatemala has expressed the view that "[c]odification of the articles would prompt States to seek greater unity in promoting the fundamental values of the Charter of the United Nations and to

[72] Intervención de la Delegación Cubana en el Tema 73 "Responsabilidad del Estado por Hechos Internacionalmente Ilícitos," October 13, 2022, https://www.un.org/en/ga/sixth/77/pdfs/statements/resp_of_states/14mtg_cuba.pdf.

[73] A/C.6/71/SR.9 (2016), § 46.

[74] Ibid., § 66.

[75] A/C.6/74/SR.13 (2020), § 17.

[76] A/71/79 (2016), at 5. For a recent contribution highlighting what may be some of the Articles' weaknesses in the light of recent state and judicial practice, see Maurizio Arcari, "The Future of the Articles on State Responsibility: A Matter of Form or of Substance?" *Questions of International Law, Zoom-in* 93 (2022): 3 (concluding that "[i[view of the controversial nature of some of the provisions included in the ARSIWA, and of their dubious conformity with international customary law, there seems [to be] little point in insisting on the solution, still stubbornly suggested by certain States, consisting of waiting for a further "sedimentation" of the Articles in international case-law").

strength multilateralism, protect human rights and consolidate the rule of law."[77] Cuba was even more explicit in noting that a convention would "curb the dangerous trend towards unilateral action by certain States . . . and help to protect States that were victims of wrongful acts."[78]

An exchange from the session of the ILC where the Articles were completed further captures that sensibility. French member Alain Pellet criticized Bernardo Sepúlveda Amor, who was later to become the Mexican judge at the ICJ, as holding "the classic nineteenth century notion that [only] treaties made the law."[79] Sepúlveda Amor replied that "Mr. Pellet"s reference to nineteenth century notions of the law [had] reminded him of the chapter in Mexican history when French intervention had prompted Mexico to devise a set of basic tenets of State responsibility" and added that it was "[t]o ensure that such experiences were not repeated" that it was "essential to produce a legal text to enshrine State responsibilities and guarantee that they were fulfilled."[80] A convention could help by, among other things, formalizing substantive and procedural requirements for the taking of countermeasures and by creating a dispute settlement mechanism.[81]

The UN General Assembly is yet to decide on how to proceed. But while disagreement as to the final status of the ARS persists, the character of the debate has changed since 2016, thanks in great part to the concerted efforts of Latin American states. Delegations favoring the convention route have turned their attention to procedural mechanisms that can move the debate forward. In that spirit, Mexico and Guatemala have joined forces with the Czech Republic, Portugal, and South Africa to organize side events "to raise awareness of the process and to prepare for deciding on future action to be taken,"[82] and a Working Group has been established to structure the discussion, with the support of Latin American states and having the Brazilian delegation as chair.[83]

Those procedural initiatives have proved a clever way to galvanize support for a convention, reacting to the inertia that the pattern of having pro forma discussions in plenary every three sessions had created. This is evidenced by the

[77] A/C.6/68/SR.15 (2014), § 10.

[78] Ibid., § 8.

[79] Pellet, 2671st Meeting, ILC Yearbook 2001, vol. I, at 32.

[80] Sepúlveda, ibid.

[81] Speaking explicitly in favor of including dispute settlement, Guatemala, A/C.6/68/SR.15 (2014), § 11: "A treaty would also entail a mechanism for the settlement of disputes, which would guarantee the protection of rights and obligations under the treaty and make binding decisions possible." As noted above, when the ILC decided to recommend that the General Assembly merely take note of the ARS, it omitted from the Articles any proposals for dispute settlement.

[82] A/C.6/68/SR.15 (2014), § 11.

[83] See the oral reports of the representatives of Brazil, Patrick Luna and Maitê de Souza Schmitz, on the discussions of the Working Group on responsibility of states for internationally wrongful acts in the 74th and 77th sessions of the U.N. G.A.: A/C.6/71/SR.31 (2016), §§ 1–9 and A/C.6/74/SR.34 (2019), §§ 13–21.

resolutions that the UN General Assembly adopted in 2001, which have changed over time. Until 2013, those resolutions limited themselves to inviting states to submit written comments and information on their own practice and to request the Secretary-General to prepare compilations of international decisions referencing the Articles.[84] The resolutions adopted in 2016 and 2019 took a step further by acknowledging "the possibility of requesting the Secretary-General to provide the General Assembly with information on all procedural options regarding possible action on the basis of the articles," referencing "the constructive dialogue in the context of the working group of the Sixth Committee" and encouraging states to "continue the substantive dialogue on an informal basis" in between sessions.[85] And the latest resolution on the topic, adopted in 2022, delivered on the promise of a previous couple of resolutions by asking the Secretary-General to prepare said report "based on precedents regarding action taken on other products of the International Law Commission," in advance of the eightieth session of the General Assembly to be held in 2025.[86] Whether those procedural initiatives will result in concrete action remains to be seen, but they show how Latin American States, in cooperation with like-minded delegations, have succeeded in pulling their weight to create momentum for the conclusion of a convention on state responsibility.

Latin America's Confidence in Codification by States

One of the main concerns about convening a diplomatic conference on state responsibility is that states may not yet share a vision of the substantive goal to be achieved by the convention, that is, of the balance between continuity and revision of the ARS that needs to be struck. Latin American states do not share that anxiety, however. As the Dominican Republic representative stated, speaking on behalf of CELAC, the group remains "convinced that a consensus agreement could be reached at a diplomatic conference and that the interests of the international community would prevail over the interests of individual states."[87] The regional sensibility is nicely captured by another eloquent intervention that Bernardo Sepúlveda Amor made at the ILC debates, which merits quoting at length:

> The ability of States to adapt to new circumstances and needs should not be underestimated. It had been asserted that Governments would not accept norms

[84] G.A. Res. 59/35 (2004); Res. 62/61 (2007); Res. 65/19 (2010); Res. 68/104 (2013).
[85] G.A. Res. 71/133 (2016) and 74/180 (2019).
[86] G.A. Res. 77/97 (2022).
[87] A/C.6/71/SR.9 (2016), § 29.

> that represented a progressive development of international law they regarded as too bold. Yet that interpretation was not borne out by the facts. In 1958, some had thought that the three-mile limit for the territorial sea was inviolable. In 1969, a regime for the seabed and ocean floor had been considered absurd. In the beginning, there had been little support for establishing an exclusive economic zone so that coastal States would benefit from the ocean resources within a 200-mile limit. In the early 1960s, jus cogens had been a very strange legal concept. Until recently, an international criminal court had seemed impossible. Many other examples could be cited.[88]

In short, Sepúlveda Amor suggested, "in principle States acted in a responsible manner."[89] That speaks to the historical experience of Latin American states in contributing to global and regional codification efforts. Arnulf Becker Lorca provides an illuminating account of how, in codification processes in the first half of the twentieth century, Latin American jurists and states seized the opportunity to articulate rules. Such rules "changed the structure of modern international law," including "a formal definition of statehood, non-recognition of territorial acquisitions obtained by force, equality between states, and declaratory, unconditional and irrevocable doctrine of recognition," all of which paved the way for the emergence of a doctrine of nonintervention that has found its way into the corpus of international law.[90] For Latin American states, engaging in codification was a way to assert their equality with (and vis-à-vis) the European powers and to remake international law on the foundations of a more robust and inclusive conception of equality.[91] That transpired in objections that Latin American states made at the 1907 Hague Peace Conference both against the Drago-Porter Convention, as noted earlier, and against a procedure for electing judges for a proposed permanent court that would have favored the European powers; the opposition of Latin American states to the idea of an international minimum standard in the failed attempts to codify the law of state responsibility (then focused on the treatment of foreigners and foreign property) in the League of Nations Codification Conference of 1930; and the turn of Latin American states to the regional codification processes that culminated in the adoption 1933 Montevideo Convention on the Rights and Duties of States, the instrument

[88] Sepúlveda, 2671st Meeting, ILC Yearbook 2001, vol. I, at 28.

[89] Ibid.

[90] Arnulf Becker Lorca, *Mestizo International Law* (Cambridge: Cambridge University Press, 2014), 351.

[91] As Cançado Trindade has observed, "[t]he convening of the Second Hague Peace Conference of 1907, with the presence of Latin American States, gave concrete expression to the principle of the juridical equality of States, grouping together the most powerful and the more fragile or vulnerable States of the world": "The Presence and Participation of Latin America at The Second Hague Peace Conference of 1907," in *Topicality of the 1907 Hague Conference, the Second Peace Conference* (Amsterdam: Nijhoff, 2008), 51, 61–62.

that articulated their view of juridical equality and nonintervention most emphatically and influentially.[92]

Tellingly, the history of Latin American participation in codification was not always one of prioritizing consensus with the world at large. Rather, it was also characterized by an attitude of principled opposition in defense of values that the region believed were deserving of universal acceptance.[93] While the tone of Latin American delegations in the current debates on state responsibility has been less antagonistic vis-à-vis states that favor keeping the Articles in their current form, it seems that they remain enthusiastic about the prospects of exercising the agency that the juridical equality for which they fought so hard allows. In light of their own historical experience, it is not surprising that they should share a certain confidence in the process and be willing to take risks. That good outcomes can come out of engagement even when the path is not linear is part of the regional ethos.

IV. Concluding Remarks

Parsing out the contribution and influence of a vast and diverse region of the world on the codification of a subfield of international law involves a degree of imagination and simplification. However, a close look at the approach that Latin American states have taken on two issues in which they have been most invested—the law of countermeasures and the question of the final status of the Articles on State Responsibility—takes us back to two key postulates of "American international law": juridical equality of states and nonintervention. Drawing on their historical experience, Latin American states have played an active role in advocating for an orderly and restrictive regime of countermeasures to curb unilateral action and interventionism. They have also remained committed to asserting their juridical equality and actively shaping international law through codification, and thus favor the adoption of a convention on state responsibility. Through this effort, they hope the international community will come together in an earnest multilateral endeavor to create greater legal certainty.

[92] See generally Becker Lorca, *Mestizo International Law*, ch. 9. On Latin America's defense of juridical equality, see further Cançado Trindade, "The Presence and Participation," 61–66.

[93] The opposition of Latin American States to the Drago-Porter Convention, previously discussed, on the grounds that it would only limit rather than outlaw resort to force to collect debts is also an example.

PART V
CONTEMPORARY CHALLENGES

26

Corruption and International Law in Latin America

From the Washington Consensus to Human Rights

Ezequiel Gonzalez-Ocantos and Wayne Sandholtz

I. Introduction

The 2015 United Nations Sustainable Development Goals are committed to "significantly reduce illicit financial and arms flows, strengthen the recovery and return of stolen assets and combat all forms of organized crime," and "substantially reduce corruption and bribery."[1] The view that corruption is a global problem and that it requires global commitments such as these to tackle it is relatively new. In fact, policymakers started to think of corruption in such terms during the "corruption eruption" of the 1990s.[2] Institutionally, this period witnessed the rise of what might be termed an international anticorruption regime, a multilayered juridical structure of treaties, conventions, and reform templates designed to cement domestic capacity and channels of transborder cooperation to combat graft.[3]

This chapter analyzes how Latin American countries grappled with the "corruption eruption," translating and creating internationally sanctioned anticorruption standards. In so doing, it traces an important shift in how the international community has framed the issue of corruption since the late 1980s. Initially, corruption gained salience during the region's transition to more open market economies. During this period, the phenomenon was linked to large and unaccountable public sectors and was seen as a major obstacle to nurturing an attractive investment climate conducive to economic development. This led

[1] Sustainable Development Goals, United Nations, https://www.un.org/sustainabledevelopment/peace-justice/ [Accessed 4 March 2021].

[2] Moises Naim, "The Corruption Eruption," *The Brown Journal of World Affairs* 2, no. 2 (1995): 245–261.

[3] Mette Eilstrup-Sangiovani and Jason C. Sharman, *Vigilantes Beyond Borders: NGOs as Enforcers of International Law* (Princeton, NJ: Princeton University Press, 2022).

Ezequiel Gonzalez-Ocantos and Wayne Sandholtz, *Corruption and International Law in Latin America*
In: *Latin American International Law in the Twenty-First Century*. Edited by: Alejandro Chehtman, Alexandra Huneeus, and Sergio Puig, Oxford University Press.
DOI: 10.1093/9780197754016.003.0026

to a series of international treaties and concomitant changes to domestic legal frameworks and key law enforcement institutions to bolster horizontal accountability. Today, though corruption continues to be regarded as a source of inefficiencies and higher transaction costs, it is increasingly seen as a human rights issue. This is true in terms of the consequences of corruption for ordinary citizens (as opposed to economies) and the negative side-effects of the tough anticorruption measures made possible by the institutional innovations implemented during the first period.

Section II of the chapter discusses how democratization and the spread of neoliberalism led to landmark treaties and favored the operationalization of the commitment to fight corruption espoused in those documents. This process resulted in sharper legal definitions of corrupt behavior in penal codes and nominally stronger law enforcement institutions, especially prosecution services. Section III of the chapter explores a shift in the conceptualization of corruption from an economic to a human rights issue. We look closely at incipient attempts by institutions of the Inter-American System of Human Rights, namely, the Commission and the Court, to clarify state responsibilities in the fight against corruption and to regulate the exercise of anticorruption prerogatives. The concluding section discusses factors that could explain the shift from an economic to a human rights framing of corruption.

II. Latin America and the Rise of the International Anticorruption Regime

The international anticorruption regime began to take shape well before the 1990s. As early as the 1970s, the United States played a leading role in creating such a regime. In response to high-profile corruption scandals, in 1977, the US Congress enacted the Foreign Corrupt Practices Act (FCPA), which made companies liable for corruption crimes perpetrated abroad. Initially, the United States was the only country where law enforcement agents had such prerogatives. This put American companies at a disadvantage vis-à-vis their counterparts in other countries, especially when economic globalization accelerated following the fall of the Berlin wall. In response, the Clinton administration led a concerted effort to export the FCPA model.[4] Specifically, the United States pressed other OECD (Organisation for Economic Co-operation and Development) countries to enact the 1997 Convention on Combating Bribery of Foreign Public Officials in International Business Transactions.

[4] Indira Carr and Opi Outwaite, "The OECD Anti-Bribery Convention 10 Years On," *Manchester Journal of International Law* 5, no. 1 (2008): 3–35.

Developing countries faced similar pressures. In line with the Washington Consensus, institutions such as the World Bank and the International Monetary Fund advised governments in Latin America and elsewhere to adopt measures conducive to financial and commercial liberalization. To be sure, Latin American economists were the primary architects of the (misnamed) Washington Consensus.[5] That framework likewise aimed to shrink the public sector. The mantra at the time was that states with a large economic footprint were inefficient and stifled growth, partly because they incentivized corruption and rent-seeking. With these objectives in mind, former World Bank officials created Transparency International in 1993, and the Bank made anticorruption a priority. The growing anticorruption movement led to the introduction in 1996 of new corruption prevention standards and the creation of the Global Corporate Governance Forum jointly with the OECD, an initiative that emphasized close attention to corporate practices in emerging markets.[6]

The 1996 Inter-American Convention against Corruption, sponsored by the United States, marked a major step forward in the construction of an international legal architecture to reduce corruption.[7] Signatories agreed on measures to enhance transparency in the public sector, strengthen oversight agencies, and improve protections for whistle-blowers. Notably, the Convention listed acts of corruption and encouraged states to criminalize the supply, demand, and acceptance of bribes. It also established the basis for international cooperation, including the relaxation of banking secrecy rules. In addition, the United Nations promoted the 2000 Convention against Organized Crime[8] and the 2003 Convention against Corruption.[9] The latter contained multiple advances, including committing parties to the criminalization of bribery and the embezzlement of public funds, and highlighted the importance of interstate cooperation for repatriating the proceeds of corruption.

Throughout this period, Latin America was primarily a standard-taker. Governments throughout the region had multiple incentives to partake in the emerging international anticorruption regime. First, enacting significant legislation or ratifying treaties such as the Inter-American Convention against Corruption allowed states to signal adherence to the fight against corruption when many were implementing ambitious economic reforms. Adherence

[5] Nancy Birdsall, Augusto de la Torre, and Felipe Valencia Caicedo, "The Washington Consensus: Assessing A 'Damaged Brand'," in *The Oxford Handbook of Latin American Economics*, ed. José Antonio Ocampo and Jaime Ros (Oxford: Oxford University Press, 2011).

[6] Jennifer McCoy and Heather Heckel, "The Emergence of a Global Anti-Corruption Norm," *International Politics* 38, no. 1 (2001): 65–90.

[7] Inter-American Convention against Corruption, March 29, 1996, Inter-American Treaties B-58. The treaty entered into force on March 6, 1997, and has been ratified or acceded to by thirty-four states.

[8] Convention against Transnational Organized Crime, November 15, 2000, 2225 U.N.T.S. 209.

[9] Convention against Corruption, October 31, 2003, 2349 U.N.T.S. 41.

to the anticorruption values at the heart of the Washington Consensus was seen as a necessary step to encourage aid and foreign investment at this delicate moment of economic policy change, even when gaps inevitably remained between the law on the books and the law in action. Brazil, for example, enacted significant legislation, including the Law on Administrative Impropriety in 1992, the Law on Criminal Organizations in 1995, and the Law on Money Laundering in 1998, partly with this goal in mind.[10] The money-laundering law inspired the creation of "a specialized financial crime unit in the Central Bank, and specialized courts for money laundering."[11] In the following decade, Brazil ratified the OECD (2000), Inter-American (2002), UN Organized Crime (2004), and UN Corruption (2005) conventions, as well as the Inter-American Convention on Mutual Assistance in Criminal Matters (2008). To comply with the OECD Convention, the Brazilian Congress also passed the Anti-Corruption Law. It reformed the Law on Criminal Organizations in 2013, allowing for "the possibility of collaboration agreements between criminal authorities and suspects, and of leniency agreements with civil effects."[12] In line with the FCPA, the law made companies liable for corruption perpetrated in Brazil and abroad.

Second, enhanced prosecutorial competence and power came to be seen as a critical component of the neoliberal project: retrenching the state could not be completed without simultaneously discouraging rent-seeking by politicians and bureaucrats. To this end, major donors such as the US government or the World Bank funded ambitious judicial reform initiatives.[13] A crucial part of the reforms was a shift from inquisitorial to adversarial criminal justice systems, removing investigative responsibilities from the courts and placing them under prosecutors. Judges would become full-time overseers of due process, thus helping to align criminal justice systems with the rule of law aspirations of the new democracies

[10] Luciano Da Ros and Matthew Taylor, *Brazilian Politics on Trial: Corruption and Reform Under Democracy* (Boulder, CO: Lynne Rienner, 2022).

[11] Sergio Praça and Matthew Taylor, "Inching Toward Accountability: The Evolution of Brazil's Anticorruption Institutions," *Latin American Politics and Society* 56, no. 2 (2014): 27–48, at 39.

[12] Michelle R. Sanchez-Badin and Arthur Sanchez-Badin, "Anticorruption in Brazil: From Transnational Legal Order to Disorder," *AJIL Unbound* 113 (2019): 326–330, at 327.

[13] Linn Hammergren, "Twenty Five Years of Latin American Judicial Reforms: Achievements, Disappointments, and Emerging Issues," *Whitehead Journal of Diplomacy and International Relations* 9, no. 1 (2008): 89–104. International actors, including donors, were only one of many driving forces behind these institutional changes. For example, changes to the status of the prosecution services in Brazil were also sponsored by groups of prosecutors from within. See Azul Aguiar-Aguilar, "Reforms of the Public Prosecutor's Office in Brazil, Chile and Mexico: The Role of Justice Sector Interest Groups," in *Beyond High Courts: The Justice Complex in Latin America*, ed. Matthew Ingram and Diana Kapiszewski (Notre Dame, IN: University of Notre Dame Press, 2019). Furthermore, the transition away from the accusatorial model was the pet project of a network of Latin American criminal lawyers, which, in 1988, published the Model Code of Criminal Procedure for Iberoamerica. See Alberto Binder, *Ideas y Materiales para la Reforma de la Justicia Penal* (Buenos Aires: Ad Hoc, 2000).

established across the region.[14] More central to our story is that thanks to these reforms, countries could also enhance the autonomy of the prosecution services and encourage the specialization of elite prosecutorial units in the types of criminal activity identified by the new institutions of the international anticorruption regime. In addition to macro-institutional changes, donors promoted American-style legislation, including plea bargain agreements, to enable prosecutorial selectivity and facilitate inroads into complex criminal organizations.[15] Along with adopting oral proceedings, these reforms were designed to promote capacity, speed, and zeal in the fight against corruption, giving extra teeth to international conventions and standards.[16]

Brazil is the paradigmatic example of prosecutorial empowerment during this period. Though the 1988 constitution did not adopt the accusatorial model, it did grant the Ministério Público Federal full autonomy from the executive and judicial branches. The new constitution also shifted the mandate of the prosecution services to focus on defending fundamental rights and monitoring officeholders. During the 1990s, some within the Ministério Público began to take this new mission very seriously, prioritizing the fight against white-collar crime. For instance, in some states, prosecutors deployed their newly expanded administrative autonomy to create units specialized in corruption.[17]

Similarly, the 1998 Ecuadorian Constitution established the autonomy of the public prosecution services, which had previously operated under the orbit of the Executive branch, and embraced the accusatorial model. Complementary institutional innovations adopted subsequently include the approval of a new criminal code that provides clear definitions for a variety of white-collar crimes such as graft (art. 278), illicit enrichment (art. 279), the acceptance and demand of bribes (art. 280 and 281, respectively), influence-peddling (art. 285), involvement in the use of figureheads (art. 289), and money-laundering (arts. 317–319).

[14] James Bischoff, "Reforming the Criminal Procedure System in Latin America," *Texas Hispanic Journal of Law & Policy* 9 (2003): 27–54; Veronica Michel, *Prosecutorial Accountability and Victims' Rights in Latin America* (New York: Cambridge University Press, 2018).

[15] Maximo Langer, "From Legal Transplants to Legal Translations: The Globalization of Plea Bargaining and the Americanization Thesis in Criminal Procedure," *Havard Internarional Law Journal* 45, no. 1 (2004): 1–64; Maximo Langer, "Revolution in Latin American Criminal Procedure," *American Journal of Comparative Law* 55 (2007): 617–676.

[16] Ezequiel Gonzalez-Ocantos et al., *Prosecutors, Voters and the Criminalisation of Corruption in Latin America: The Case of Lava Jato* (New York: Cambridge University Press, 2023).

[17] Maria Teresa Sadek and Rosangela Batista Cavalcanti, "The New Brazilian Public Prosecution: An Agent of Accountability," in *Democratic Accountability in Latin America*, ed. Scott Mainwaring and Christopher Welna (Oxford: Oxford University Press, 2003); Rogelio Arantes, "The Federal Police and the Ministério Publico," in *Corruption and Democracy in Brazil: The Struggle for Accountability*, ed. Timothy Power and Matthew Taylor (Notre Dame, IN: University of Notre Dame Press, 2011); Salo Coslovsky, "Relational Regulation in the Brazilian Ministério Publico: The Organizational Basis of Regulatory Responsiveness," *Regulation and Governance* 5, no. 1 (2011): 70–89.

The updated law also enabled the creation of elite prosecutorial units to investigate some of the crimes identified in the new legislation.

Peru is yet another case of prosecutorial empowerment. The transition to an accusatorial criminal justice system started in 2004 by adopting a new Code of Criminal Procedure. Although implementation was initially slow, it was brought forward by a few years for corruption cases. The new code affords prosecutors complete control over investigations and more time for the preliminary investigation of complex crimes. It also includes a series of abridged proceedings where defendants seek to cooperate with the authorities. Furthermore, beginning in 2007, the prosecution services appointed new prosecutors specialized in organized crime, corruption, money-laundering, crimes against the environment, human trafficking, tax fraud, and customs and intellectual property crimes, thus boosting overall capacity to comply with the obligations emerging from the international anticorruption regime.

Third, the adoption of anticorruption legislation has become a condition for access to free trade deals or membership in international organizations. The United States typically insists that governments aspiring to sign a trade agreement implement anticorruption reforms. For example, between 2009 and 2010, the Peruvian Congress passed laws that explicitly criminalize international bribery. Another typical request is for creating corporate liability regimes (such as the one put in place by Brazil in 2013), which mirror the American FCPA model in providing incentives for companies to cooperate with corruption investigations. Joining the OECD now requires similar action. Jorge explains that the "paradigm seeks to calibrate the enforcement response in a context of scarce investigative resources, the transnational nature of 'grand corruption,' and the difficulties of identifying individual wrongdoers within complex, usually multinational corporations."[18]

Fourth, in addition to rewarding states that establish more robust anticorruption tools and institutions, the international community has also, on occasion, directly pressured countries to confront corruption. Particularly noteworthy are instances in which foreign governments or international institutions encourage the creation of specialized anticorruption agencies with various prevention and enforcement prerogatives. The so-called commission model[19] can be traced back to the 1950s when Singapore created its Corrupt Practices Investigations Bureau. The global diffusion of the model, however, took place in the 1990s and accelerated after the signing of the UN Convention in 2003. In the early 2000s, for example, Guatemala came under international pressure

[18] Guillermo Jorge, "The Impact of Corporate Liability on Corruption in Latin America," *AJIL Unbound* 113 (2019): 320–325, at 321.

[19] Robert Rotberg, *The Corruption Cure: How Citizens and Leaders Can Combat Graft* (Princeton, NJ: Princeton University Press, 2017), 110.

to act against organized crime networks of politicians, businessmen, and security officers that had infiltrated the state following the end of the civil war. The United States removed Guatemala from the list of countries considered allies in the war on drugs. The problems of organized crime and corruption were also addressed during a series of loan negotiations with the International Monetary Fund (IMF). After arduous discussions, in 2006, the government agreed to create the UN-sponsored Commission against Impunity in Guatemala (CICIG). Until 2019, when it was dismantled, the CICIG helped fortify a weak judicial system, promoting reforms that improved investigative practices among select and specialized groups of judges and prosecutors (e.g., the so-called high-risk tribunals).[20] The commission also cooperated with local prosecutors to identify seventy criminal organizations and initiate prosecutions in over a hundred cases, including some against former presidents and vice presidents, cabinet ministers, and congressmen. The wave of corruption prosecutions produced more than four hundred convictions.[21]

In sum, the rise of a treaty infrastructure and a network of practitioners orbiting around it facilitated the diffusion of institutional reform templates. The spread of internationally sanctioned models for defining corruption in criminal codes, for instance, led law enforcement agents in many countries to start prioritizing corruption, outlined their responsibilities more clearly, and led to specialization and investments in capacity building. Together with other innovations—such as the transition from inquisitorial to accusatorial criminal justice systems—these changes boosted the capacity to combat graft. Furthermore, institutional diffusion facilitated the emergence of communities of enforcers with comparable prerogatives and responsibilities. These individuals often have similar professional dispositions and are willing to share best practices and deepen international penal cooperation during salient corruption investigations.

As we shall see in section III, these reforms were far from inconsequential in promoting greater capacity and zeal in the fight against grand corruption. In fact, those countries that aligned their laws and institutions with the imperatives of the international anticorruption regime saw spectacular anticorruption crusades.

[20] International Crisis Group, *Learning to Walk Without a Crutch: An Assessment of the International Commission Against Impunity in Guatemala* (New York: International Crisis Group, 2011); Roddy Brett, "Peace without Social Reconciliation? Understanding the Trial of Generals Rios Montt and Rodriguez Sanchez in the Wake of Guatemala's Genocide," *Journal of Genocide Research* 18, no. 2–3 (2011): 285–303.

[21] For the CICG's Final Report, accessed June 30, 2022, https://www.cicig.org/cicig/informes_cicig/informe-de-labores/informe-final-de-labores/.

III. Latin America Confronts the Dilemmas of Aggressive Anticorruption Efforts

Latin America's insertion in the international anticorruption regime gave law enforcement agents new tools, prerogatives, and organizational resources to go after white-collar criminals, including corrupt politicians. Over the past decade or so, some of these agents have taken their new mandate more seriously than ever before, leading to a few unprecedented anticorruption efforts.

Perhaps the most famous was Operation Lava Jato, an investigation that started in Brazil in March 2014 and lasted roughly until 2021, when it suffered significant setbacks at the Supremo Tribunal Federal.[22] Within months, federal prosecutors and police officers discovered a gigantic corruption scheme involving top executives of the state-owned oil company Petrobras, local business conglomerates, and politicians from twenty-eight different political parties. Between 2014 and 2022, law enforcement officials signed a flurry of leniency and plea bargain agreements, issued an impressive number of indictments, imposed millions of dollars in fines, and convicted over two hundred defendants. Among those implicated in the scandal was former President Luiz Inácio "Lula" Da Silva from the Workers' Party. Through this and other high-profile measures, Lava Jato exacerbated the country's acute political crisis, contributing to President Dilma Rousseff's downfall in 2016 and the rise of far-right populist Jair Bolsonaro in 2018.

Lava Jato reverberated throughout the region. US prosecutors revealed that the company at the heart of the bribery scheme in Brazil, construction giant Odebrecht, had used a similar modus operandi to bribe public officials in at least nine other Latin American countries in exchange for preferential treatment in the allocation of large infrastructure projects.[23] This prompted authorities outside Brazil to start their national chapters of Lava Jato, resulting in "the largest foreign bribery case in history."[24] While some countries saw little by way of effective criminalization (e.g., Argentina, Colombia, and Mexico), others experienced anticorruption crusades that ravaged politics. In Peru, for example, the investigation initially focused on bribes paid to secure three public works projects but quickly expanded. Five former presidents, as well as leading opposition figures,

[22] Paul Lagunes and Jan Svejnar (eds.), *Corruption and the Lava Jato Scandal in Latin America* (London: Routledge, 2020); Luciano Da Ros and Matthew Taylor, "Kickbacks, Crackdown, and Backlash: Legal Accountability in the Lava Jato Investigation," in *The Limits of Judicializacion: From Progress to Backlash in Latin America*, ed. Sandra Botero, Daniel Brinks, and Ezequiel Gonzalez-Ocantos (New York: Cambridge University Press, 2022).

[23] Ezequiel Gonzalez-Ocantos and Viviana Baraybar, "Lava Jato Beyond Borders: The Uneven Performance of Anti-Corruption Judicial Efforts in Latin America," *Taiwan Journal of Democracy* 15, no. 1 (2019): 63–89.

[24] Linda Pressly, "The Largest Foreign Bribery Case in History," *BBC* (April 20, 2018).

capital city mayors, and regional governors, were investigated and ordered to spend time in detention. Lava Jato also contributed to a presidential resignation in 2018, the shutdown of Congress in 2019, and the impeachment of another president in 2020.[25] In Ecuador, the investigation did not last as long as it did in Brazil or Peru and did not radically expand its original remit, but prosecutors were arguably more effective. They secured several high-profile convictions relatively quickly, including convictions against financial intermediaries, former government ministers, former president Rafael Correa, and former vice president Jorge Glas.

One distinctive characteristic of the countries where Lava Jato made more progress is that they had reformers who went further to increase the autonomy of prosecution services; to adopt the accusatorial model and/or American-style legislation on plea bargains and leniency agreements; to modify the organization of the prosecution services so that cohorts of prosecutors could become experts in white-collar crime; and to embrace the practice of assigning complex cases of macro-criminality to specialized task forces.[26] When such institutional and organizational factors were present, the standards and reform templates promoted by the international anticorruption regime trickled down, and prosecutors could act quickly and skillfully, for example, to extract confessions or sign international cooperation agreements with Brazil. The latter was critical to guarantee the flow of high-quality evidence and required the presence of shrewd legal minds capable of aligning the obligations outlined in various international conventions regarding penal cooperation with domestic criminal law (laws against double jeopardy, limits on the principle of prosecutorial selectivity, etc.).

Corruption probes like Lava Jato are characterized by extremely high levels of prosecutorial and judicial zeal, leading to a frenzy of investigative and punitive measures. These zealous judges and prosecutors present themselves as relentless envoys in a crusade against evil politicians, justifying unorthodoxy in the name of a higher-order mission to defeat corruption for the sake of the welfare of society. Crucially, they make creative use of the available legal framework to ease the procedural and evidentiary constraints that normally limit investigations into macro-criminal behavior, including the unorthodox use of criminal definitions, the redefinition of evidentiary standards, heavy reliance on

[25] At the time of writing, there were few convictions, but the most high-profile lines of inquiry were making their way to trial courts. See Viviana Baryabar and Ezequiel Gonzalez-Ocantos, "Prosecutorial Agency, Backlash and Resistance in the Peruvian Chapter of Lava Jato," in *The Limits of Judicialization: From Progress to Backlash in Latin America*, ed. Sandra Botero, Daniel Brinks, and Ezequiel Gonzalez-Ocantos (New York: Cambridge University Press, 2022).

[26] For a full account of how countries' variable insertion in the international anti-corruption regime led to differences in the progress of the Lava Jato investigion, see Gonzalez-Ocantos et al., *Prosecutors, Voters and the Criminalisation of Corruption*, chs. 2–4.

new tools such as plea bargains, and innovative interpretations of international law to facilitate transnational cooperation between prosecutorial agencies.

Many observers value these investigations for their deterrent qualities or simply because punishing wrongdoing is right. Others, however, caution that the aggressive criminalization of corruption may be a devil in disguise. By casting doubt on the integrity of politicians, sometimes entire political parties or party systems, law enforcement agents may destabilize democracy. Perhaps more importantly, from a rule of law perspective, critics argue that prosecutorial and judicial zeal usually come at the expense of strict respect for the due process and political rights of defendants, for example, when politicians are at the receiving end of long pretrial detention orders, when they are preventively banned from running for office, and when indictments (or even convictions) stand on limited evidence or third-party confessions.[27] Finally, while some of these critics are ready to concede that without the adoption of unorthodox and creative strategies it is hard to imagine how grand corruption networks could ever be exposed and dismantled, that is, how international anticorruption norms could ever come to bite, they also maintain that those high levels of zeal compromise the legitimacy and staying power of transparency efforts. In their view, prosecutorial and judicial aggression provide the perfect ammunition for corrupt actors to successfully cry foul, ultimately emerging from these episodes unscathed.

The legal controversies elicited by zealous investigators are not the only rule of law "stress test" triggered by corruption probes. Politicians don't just let prosecutors destroy their careers; they fight back. Unusual displays of prosecutorial and judicial aggression invite backlash because they impose high costs, even when investigations fall short of a conviction.[28] In Latin America, many of those prosecuted by Lava Jato belonged to left-wing parties and were eager to denounce the investigation as an attempt by the right to engage in "lawfare," weaponizing legal proceedings to undermine progressive causes.[29] In addition to defending themselves in court (and in the court of public opinion), defendants also resorted to myriad extralegal tactics to delegitimize, block, or

[27] Fabio De Sa e Silva, "From Car Wash to Bolsonaro: Law and Lawyers in Brazil's Illiberal Turn," *Journal of Law and Society* 47 (2020): 90–110; Mariana Mota-Prado and Marta Rodriguez Machado, "Turning Corruption Trials into Political Tools in the Name of Transparency," in *The Limits of Judicializacion: From Progress to Backlash in Latin America*, edited by Sandra Botero, Daniel Brinks and Ezequiel Gonzalez-Ocantos (New York: Cambridge University Press, 2022); João Guilherme Bastos dos Santos and Esther Solano Gallego, "Fighting Corruption, Dismantling Democracy: Antagonism, Communication, and the Political Use of Lava Jato in Brazil," in Botero et al., *The Limits of Judicialization.*

[28] Rachel Bowen, "Backlash against State Strengthening Reforms: The Rise and Fall of the CICIG in Guatemala," in Botero et al., *The Limits of Judicialization*; Da Ros and Taylor, Kickbacks, Crackdowns and Backlash; Baraybar and Gonzalez-Ocantos, *Prosecutorial Agency.*

[29] Catalina Smulovitz, "Del Descrubrimiento de la Ley al Lawfare, o Cómo las Uvas se Volvieron Amargas," *Revista SAAP* 16, no. 2 (2022): 231–259

dismantle investigations, including blunt intimidation tactics and court-packing initiatives, as well efforts to rein in judicial and prosecutorial power through counterreforms.[30]

As the law on the books started "to bite," what was hitherto deemed an incontrovertible international obligation and political aspiration, namely, eradicating corruption, began to clash with other values, including democratic stability and respect for due process. The "lawfare" narrative gained traction in many countries partly because of the political power and appeal of those crying foul and partly because judges and prosecutors sometimes crossed red lines. But the success of this narrative is also explained by the fact that debates over the merits of the various chapters of Lava Jato and other major anticorruption crusades (e.g., the one spearheaded by Guatemala's CICIG) unfolded at a time when the issue of corruption was being reframed. Whereas the "corruption eruption" of the 1990s and the origins of the international anticorruption regime were defined by the view that corruption is primarily an economic problem, key actors subsequently started to see corruption as a human rights issue.

Controversies over prosecutorial zeal during Lava Jato crystallized this paradigm shift. Those who championed the cause defended unorthodox approaches to criminalization, arguing it is necessary to adopt exceptional measures to combat a phenomenon that severely infringes fundamental rights. For example, according to one of the leading prosecutors in Brazil:

> International studies on corruption encourage us to abandon the perspective of the rotten apple and seek systemic changes in organizational structures to curb behaviour. Corruption of these proportions must be punished more firmly than homicide because it kills many people. It also steals schools, running water, medicine and the safety of millions of Brazilians.[31]

Furthermore, when prosecutors were under attack, they sometimes relied on human rights institutions to defend themselves. Peru is a case in point. The Instituto de Defensa Legal, a leading human rights and anticorruption nongovernmental organization (NGO), filed a complaint before the Inter-American Commission on Human Rights denouncing threats to the autonomy of the

[30] For instance, in response to corruption probes affecting members of Argentina's ruling coalition, the Peronist government inaugurated in 2019 proposed (but failed to pass) legislation aimed at curbing the autonomy of the prosecution services. Pro-government legislators also pushed for the early implementation of a select group of provisions of the new Code of Criminal Procedures to protect defendants convicted of corruption in lower courts from spending time in jail. Similarly, in February 2022, legislators on the Justice and Human Rights Committee of the Peruvian Congress gave the green light to a bill intended to weaken incentives for witnesses to enter plea bargains. At the time of writing, the bill had not yet reached the floor.

[31] Fausto Macedo and Ricardo Brandt, "'Maior Parte das Acusações Ainda Virá,' Diz Procurador," *O Estado de Sao Paulo* (March 16, 2015).

prosecutor in charge of investigating a high-profile politician as part of the local Lava Jato probe. Interestingly, those at the receiving end of these accusations similarly resorted to human rights institutions to question the merits of anticorruption. Most notably, Cristina Fernandez de Kirchner, who served as Argentina's president between 2007 and 2015, went to the Inter-American Commission claiming to be the victim of "political discrimination and persecution" and singled out "lawfare" as a major threat to democratic stability in Latin America.[32]

What is noteworthy about the shift from an economic to a human rights framing of the problem of corruption is that Latin America ceased to be a standard-taker, as it was in the early stages of the international anticorruption regime, to become a standard-maker through the institutions of the Inter-American System of Human Rights. Section IV explores how the Inter-American Court and Commission have transformed the international discourse and legal environment around corruption.

IV. The Turn to Human Rights

Global perceptions of the corruption problem have shifted. Corruption was initially seen as an obstacle to economic development, whereas more recently, the political consequences of corruption have attracted concern. Corruption is increasingly viewed as corroding political institutions and legitimacy[33] and imposing costs on society.[34] In line with this perception, influential actors and institutions are beginning to frame corruption as a human rights issue.[35]

The link between corruption and compliance with human rights obligations has been explicitly highlighted in international fora. A UN General Assembly report highlights "the convergence between core principles in the fight against corruption and human rights."[36] Furthermore, the UN High Commissioner for Human Rights has stated that corruption erodes the capacity of a state to achieve "progressively the full realization of the rights recognized in the International Covenant on Economic, Social and Cultural Rights."[37] Indeed, reducing

[32] "Cristina Kirchner Files 'Lawfare' Writ with the IACHR," *BA Times*, May 20, 2020.

[33] Joel Ngugi, "Making the Link Between Corruption and Human Rights: Promises and Perils," *Proceedings of the Annual Meeting–American Society of International Law* 1, no. 4 (2010): 247.

[34] Julio Bacio-Terracino, "Linking Corruption and Human Rights," *American Society of International Law Proceedings* 147 (2010): 243–246.

[35] James Thuo Gathii, "Defining the Relationship Between Human Rights and Corruption," *University of Pennsylvania Journal of International Law* 31, no. 1, (2009): 125–202, at 147.

[36] UN G.A., *Informe Sobre la Marcha de los Trabajos del Comité Asesor del Consejo de Derechos Humanos sobre las Consecuencias Negativas de la Corrupción en el Disfrute de los Derechos Humanos*, A/HRC/26/42, ¶ 21 (2014).

[37] Office of the High Commissioner for Human Rights and the Government of Poland, U.N. Conference on Anti-Corruption Measures, Good Governance and Human Rights, Background Note, ¶ 3, HR/POL/GG/SEM/2006/2 (November 8–9, 2006).

corruption and promoting human rights are mutually reinforcing, particularly regarding core civil and political rights. Whistleblower laws and other initiatives designed to increase transparency and reduce corruption support the right to freedom of expression, while political environments where civil and political rights are routinely protected enable the public to call attention to corrupt practices.[38] Similarly, strong protections of the rights to freedom of association and assembly enhance the ability of citizens publicly to oppose corrupt actors and systems.[39]

As Bacio-Terracino has pointed out, however, the link between anticorruption and human rights goes further. On the one hand, human rights norms can sometimes be seen as hindering anticorruption efforts, especially when they are invoked to rein in the zeal of committed investigators. On the other, anticorruption practices can occasionally impinge on human rights.[40] As Rotberg suggests, "the more legal provisions curtail (unfortunately) a potential defendant's civil liberties, the easier it is for the prosecutors. Indeed, in several nations that have successfully reduced corruption, prosecutors have possessed broad powers of search and seizure, have been permitted to enter hearsay evidence, and have been allowed [. . .] to infer guilt merely from suspicious actions."[41] Such tensions reinforce the centrality of human rights discourses in debates about corruption and anticorruption.

The institutions of the Inter-American System of Human Rights, especially the Court and the Commission, are active participants in this global conversation and have made interesting contributions to the framing of corruption as a human rights issue, as well as valiant attempts to try to ease the conflict between anticorruption practices and human rights norms. Here, we highlight three jurisprudential developments that are particularly relevant to understanding Latin American contributions to international anticorruption law.

1. *Linking corruption and human rights.* The inter-American system has participated in the global trend toward recognizing the links between corruption and human rights, putting forward tentative arguments that link (systemic) corruption with human rights violations, especially those stemming from structural inequality and institutional atrophy. Indeed, the Inter-American Commission on Human Rights (IACHR) has recognized corruption as a direct violation of human rights or an upstream cause of human rights violations. Since the early 2000s, the IACHR has recognized the inhibiting effect of corruption on a country's ability to comply with human rights obligations. For instance, the Commission's 2001 country report on Paraguay links corruption in

[38] Gathii, "Defining the Relationship," 150.
[39] Bacio-Terracino, "Linking Corruption," 244.
[40] Ibid.
[41] Rotberg, *The Corruption Cure*, 78–79.

public institutions to reduced societal enjoyment of human rights in general.[42] The report further explores the connection between corruption and human rights violations, on the one hand, and democratic stability on the other. This position is echoed in later statements, such as a 2015 IACHR country report on Guatemala, which portrays corruption as damaging the right to human development.[43]

This innovative conceptualization effort has yet to have legal or practical consequences, partly because establishing a causal connection between corruption and human rights violations is hard.[44] While "corruption will lead to human rights violations," it "will not itself violate a human right."[45] The jurisprudence is nevertheless promising because it links the obligations stemming from the anticorruption and human rights regimes, providing yet another rationale for fully implementing the former. Linking corruption to human rights violations could bring a new set of legal principles and processes to bear against corruption. What is at stake is not just reframing corruption but leveraging a set of established human rights legal norms and institutions to identify, condemn, and penalize corruption.

2. *Prevention*. Arguments linking human rights to corruption later led to more explicit discussions of states' anticorruption obligations, with a decidedly preventive focus. In a 2009 report, the Commission declared that when "high levels of corruption that impede the adequate administration of justice"[46] are present, states should "implement the necessary measures to prevent, investigate, and sanction whatever form of corruption affects the good functioning of the justice system."[47] Another report published in 2017 on the situation in Venezuela echoes earlier statements portraying corruption as an obstacle to the complete protection of human rights. The Commission further stated that this connection between corruption and rights implies an obligation for states to take preventive measures against corruption to avoid rights violations. The Commission

[42] IACHR, *Tercer Informe sobre la Situación de los Derechos Humanos en Paraguay*, OEA/Ser/L/VII.110. Doc. 52, p rr. 41 (March 9, 2001). In the same vein, see IACHR, *Informe Anual de la Comisi n Interamericana de Derechos Humanos 2005*, chap. 4, "Desarrollo de los Derechos Humanos en la Región–Ecuador," OEA/Ser/L/V/II.124. Doc. 7 (February 27, 2006), ¶¶ 130, 131.

[43] IACHR, "Situación de los Derechos Humanos en Guatemala: Diversidad, Desigualdad y Exclusión," OEA/Ser/L/V/II, Doc. 43/15 (December 31, 2015), ¶ 53.

[44] Claudio Nash, "Corrupción, Democracia, Estado de Derecho y Derechos Humanos: Sus Vínculos y Sus Consecuencias," in *Corrupción, Estado de Derecho y Derechos Humanos*, ed. Claudio Nash and Marie-Christine Fuchs (Bogota, Colombia: Kondrad Adenauer Stiftung, 2019).

[45] Bacio-Terracino, "Linking Corruption," 243.

[46] IACHR, "Informe Sobre Seguridad Ciudadana y Derechos Humanos," OEA/Ser/L/V/II. Doc. 57 (December 31, 2009), ¶¶ 33, 167 ("altos niveles de corrupción que impiden una adecuada administración de justiciar").

[47] IACHR, "Informe Sobre Seguridad Ciudadana," ¶¶ 33, 167 ("implementar los mecanismos necesarios para prevenir, investigar y sancionar cualquier forma de corrupción que afecte el buen funcionamiento del sistema de administración de justiciar").

declares that state fulfillment of that obligation will ensure that states "govern based on the principles of publicity, transparency, and effective public responsibility," which are essential for the functioning of a democratic society.[48] And in a 2017 resolution, the Commission reaffirmed "the importance of the fight against corruption in guaranteeing the effective enjoyment of human rights."[49]

In line with the goal of operationalizing state duties in this area, the Commission has extended the reach of long-standing jurisprudential standards on freedom of expression and the independence of judges to protect some of the actors that engineer anticorruption probes, including journalists and whistleblowers. Two cases concerning the assassination of reporters investigating corruption illustrate the evolution of the Commission's approach. In a 1999 case, the Commission inquired into the assassination of a Mexican reporter who was investigating a corruption case. Ultimately, the Commission recommended that the state "punish the perpetrators."[50] A 2016 report concerning a similar case in Brazil reveals a more assertive Commission. In this instance, the IACHR explicitly tied the reporter's murder to his work exposing the corruption. Rather than focusing merely on the failure to investigate, as in the 1999 case, the Commission concluded that the state was responsible "for violating the rights to life and to freedom of thought and expression enshrined in Articles 4 and 13 of the American Convention [. . .] and of the rights to humane treatment, fair trial and judicial protection."[51]

State obligations go beyond ensuring that journalists and whistleblowers can express themselves freely. The Commission has also issued precautionary measures in favor of judges and prosecutors facing personal and professional threats.[52] Perhaps more innovatively, commissioners have further proclaimed states' responsibility to contribute to international penal cooperation, defining what those efforts should look like in practice:

> The [Commission] highlights the importance of cooperation between justice systems, with a view to tackling a transnational phenomenon, such as the

[48] IACHR, "Institucionalidad Democrática, Estado de Derecho y Derechos Humanos en Venezuela," Informe de País, OEA/Ser/L/V/II. Doc. 209/17 (December 31, 2017), ¶¶ 146, 147 ("gobernar con base en los principios de publicidad, transparencia y responsabilidad pública efectiva").

[49] IACHR, Derechos Humanos y la Lucha Contra la Impunidad y la Corrupción, Resolution 1/17, September 12, 2017. See also Resolution 1/18, March 2, 2018.

[50] IACHR, Informe 50/99, Caso 11.739, *Héctor Félix Miranda (México)* (April 13, 1999), 52.

[51] IACHR, Informe 7/16, Caso 12.213, *Aristeu Guida da Silva y Familia (Brasil)* (April 13, 1999), ¶ 253.

[52] Measures in favor of prosecutors include: Resolución 11/2018, Medida Cautelar No. 917-17, *Douglas Arquímides Meléndez Ruiz.y familia respecto de El Salvador*, February 28, 2018; Resolución 55/2021, Medida cautelar No. 576-21, *José Domingo Pérez Gómez y su núcleo familiar respecto de Perú*, July 25, 2021. Measures in favor of judges include Resolución sobre Medida cautelar 431-17, *Gloria Patricia Porras y familia respecto de Guatemala*, August 29, 2017.

> exchange of information, the creation of multilateral investigation units that could facilitate [. . .] a coordinated policy of identification of asset flows destined for corruption.[53]

This type of cooperation is critical for the success of grand corruption probes, as they often involve multinational companies, intricate asset ownership structures, and the use of offshore accounts. Treaties such as the Inter-American and UN Conventions against corruption encouraged states to cooperate; the Commission's intervention reinforces the centrality of that obligation. Finally, the Commission has addressed the effects of corruption on judicial systems. In a 2013 report on Guarantees of Independence for Workers in the Justice System, the Commission addressed corruption and the absence of protection in the face of pressure from organized crime and other sectors as major obstacles for effective investigations.[54]

The IACtHR has similarly trained its eyes on state obligations vis-à-vis corruption investigations, paying special attention to prosecutorial independence. The Court's jurisprudence on judicial independence is well-established and highly influential.[55] States must protect judges from pressures coming from within and outside the judiciary. This jurisprudence, however, has an important blind spot as it does not deal with prosecutors and their distinct realities. This lacuna is potentially problematic. The reforms inspired by the international anticorruption regime empowered Latin American prosecutors and reduced the centrality of judges in criminal investigations. As a result, prosecutors have become key targets of those seeking to contain anticorruption initiatives. That prosecutors were not central to the criminal justice system (or in politically charged cases) does not fully explain why the IACtHR paid little attention to them. The issue of prosecutorial independence presents a series of complications, which may have led inter-American judges to sidestep the issue.[56] For one, the prosecution services are not strictly speaking a separate branch of government (even though they

[53] Resolución 1/18, *Corrupcion y Derechos Humanos*, March 2, 2018, 7.

[54] IACHR, Situación de los Derechos Humanos en Honduras, OEA/Ser/L/V/II. Doc. 42/15 (December 31, 2015), ¶¶ 9, 311–314; IACHR, Situación de los Derechos Humanos en Guatemala: Diversidad, Desigualdad y Exclusión, OEA/Ser/L/V/II. Doc. 43/15 (December 31, 2015), ¶¶ 57-61; IACHR, Hacia una Política Integral de Protección a Personas Defensoras de Derechos Humanos, OEA/Ser/L/V/II. Doc. 207/17 (December 29, 2017), recommendation no. 21.

[55] See *Castillo Petruzzi et al. v. Peru*, Merits, Reparations, and Costs, Inter-Am. Ct. H.R. (ser. C) No. 52 (May 30, 1999), ¶¶ 124, 125(a), (e), and (g), 134 (finding that military courts did not meet standards of judicial independence); *Reverón Trujillo v. Venezuela*, Preliminary Objections, Merits, Reparations and Costs, Inter-Am. Ct. H.R. (ser. C) No. 197 (June 30, 2009), ¶¶ 108, 114 (dismissal of a judge violated judicial independence); *López Lone et al. v. Honduras*, Preliminary Objections, Merits, Reparations and Costs, Inter-Am. Ct. H.R. (ser. C) No. 30 (October 25, 2015), ¶ 249 (lack of guarantee as to the impartiality of judges).

[56] The bias could also result from inter-American judges' inclination to privilege other judges in their jurisprudence.

may enjoy high levels of autonomy on paper). They also tend to be rather hierarchical organizations, meaning that internal independence may not be as robust at a structural level as it can be in the courts.

The IACtHR started to fill in this gap in jurisprudence in 2020 when, for the first time in its history, judges ruled that the arbitrary removal of prosecutors is illegal under the American Convention on Human Rights.[57] Crucially, the Court understands that prosecutors deserve the same protections as judges, regardless of the nature of institutional design. This could imply, for example, that untenured prosecutors, those formally under the orbit of the Executive branch, or those assigned to a case on an ad hoc basis (e.g., the anticorruption task forces in charge of Lava Jato in Brazil, Peru, or Ecuador) cannot be removed on a whim, even though politicians or senior prosecutors may have the formal prerogative to do so.

3. *The risks to human rights.* In addition to tackling corruption as a direct cause of human rights violations and clarifying state obligations around anticorruption, the inter-American system has addressed the potential risks to human rights that sweeping anticorruption efforts might pose. As previously noted, the investigation and prosecution of corruption can sometimes violate the due process rights of those being investigated and prosecuted.[58] With this in mind, the Court and the Commission have sought to strike a balance between international anticorruption obligations and the civil and political rights of defendants enshrined in the American Convention. In a broad, standard-setting report published in 2019, the Commission hinted at the tension between effectiveness and respect for due process at the heart of corruption prosecutions, emphasizing that both are necessary:

> States have a duty to be effective in the face of a complex phenomenon where traditional investigation techniques seem insufficient. The Inter-American Commission reaffirms the full validity of the human rights of the accused in matters of corruption. Likewise, it reiterates that it is the duty of the State to seriously investigate corruption cases, establish the truth, and punish those responsible. This means that the States have the obligation to respect the full enjoyment and exercise of all rights, particularly those that do not admit restrictions, such as the prohibition of torture.[59]

[57] *Martínez Esquivia v. Colombia*, Preliminary Objections, Merits and Reparations, IACtHR (ser. C) No. 412 (October 6, 2020), ¶¶ 84–86, 96 (guarantees of judicial independence apply also to prosecutors); *Casa Nina v. Peru*, Preliminary Objections, Merits, Reparations and Costs, IACtHR (ser. C) No. 419 (November 24, 2020), ¶ 69 (the safeguarding of the independence of judges applies also to prosecutors).

[58] Bacio-Terracino, "Linking Corruption," 160.

[59] "Corrupción y Derechos Humanos: Estándares Latinoamericanos," OEA/Ser.L/V/II. Doc. 236 (December 6, 2019), 142.

Furthermore, the Court has emphasized the limits of prosecutorial zeal, focusing on defendants' rights. This is hardly surprising given its long-standing jurisprudence on due process. The Court has ruled that the duration of corruption cases ought to be "reasonable." In this regard, investigators must never be tempted to prolong corruption investigations to prevent political opponents from participating in elections.[60] Moreover, the IACtHR insists that impartial courts must oversee the proceedings.[61] The Court has also held that prosecutors should pursue multiple lines of inquiry to avoid biased investigations against specific individuals or groups.[62] It has further made it clear that regardless of the challenges involved in obtaining incriminating evidence, investigators must not behave contrary to due process to secure valuable documentation or witness testimonies, and that decisions ought to be fully justified.[63] The Court has further ruled that even though punitive measures such as pretrial detentions are often necessary to preserve evidence or protect witnesses, they are only admissible when there is strong evidence that defendants perpetrated the crime and are in a position to obstruct justice effectively.[64] Finally, the court has intervened on the thorny issue of evidentiary standards. In one decision, the judges noted that the presumption of innocence must be respected, even when it is difficult to prove corruption crimes. The ruling claims that perpetrator confessions, critical to uncovering grand corruption schemes, cannot be the only evidence used to support a conviction.[65]

This fledging body of soft law seeks to both protect and regulate corruption probes. It draws attention to how different dimensions of the liberal international order, in this case those promoting human rights and good governance, can clash with and complement each other. If they ever become consolidated, inter-American standards on the responsibility of states to fight corruption and the legitimate means to do so could help enhance the effectiveness of pro-transparency efforts and lower the voltage of the political battles that accompany these legal dramas. While some national high courts have also intervened to check the legality of controversial prosecutorial and judicial moves in corruption cases (e.g., Brazil's Supremo Tribunal Federal (STF) decision to nullify all of Judge Moro's proceedings against Lula during the Lava Jato inquiry, or rulings

[60] *Andrade Salmón v. Bolivia*, Merits, Reparations and Costs, Judgment of December 1, 2016, IACtHR (ser. C) No. 330.

[61] *Zegarra Marín v. Peru*, Preliminary Objections, Merits, Reparations and Costs, Judgment of February 15, 2017, IACtHR (ser. C) No. 331.

[62] *Acosta et al. v. Nicaragua*, Preliminary Objections, Merits, Reparations and Costs, Judgment of March 25, 2017, IACtHR (ser. C) No. 334.

[63] *López Mendoza v. Venezuela*, Merits, Reparations, and Costs, Judgment of September 1, 2011, IACtHR (ser. C) No. 233; *Acosta et al. v. Nicaragua*; *Zegarra Marín v. Peru*.

[64] *Barreto Leiva v. Venezuela*, Merits, Reparations and Costs, Judgment of November 17, 2009, IACtHR (ser. C) No. 206.

[65] *Zegarra Marín v. Peru*.

by Peru's Constitutional Court limiting the use of pretrial detentions), the political neutrality of these interventions is usually called into question. By contrast, the Court and the Commission are far better positioned to assess contested legal fields. In fact, this is exactly what they did with similarly controversial issues such as the applicability of amnesty or statutes of limitations in cases of forced disappearances during dictatorships and armed conflicts.

Whether the inter-American system can promote substantive progress in prosecuting and thereby reducing corruption across Latin America remains an open question. It certainly lacks the capacity to bring corrupt actors under judicial scrutiny across the region or to effectively protect those willing to prosecute corruption in domestic courts. After all, the Inter-American Court cannot oversee the prosecution of corrupt officials; it can only determine whether corrupt official actions violate rights or whether corruption prosecutions infringe on defendants' rights. In principle, the Court could order states—as a remedy when it finds that corrupt acts have violated rights—to investigate, prosecute, and punish those responsible, as it has regularly done in cases involving gross physical integrity rights violations. But states rarely comply with the Court's orders to investigate and prosecute even the most grievous abuses. According to one analysis, states fully comply with only 10–14 percent of IACtHR orders to investigate, prosecute, and punish perpetrators.[66] Models developed by Pérez Liñan, Schenoni, and Morrison further show that orders to investigate, prosecute, and punish those responsible for rights violations have an "estimated time to full compliance" of eighty years (as compared to thirty-eight years for "rehabilitation" remedies).[67] The failure of recent efforts by the Court and the Commission to use precautiounary measures to safeguard anticorruption prosecutors in Guatemala is a case in point.[68] Still, though the inter-American system cannot by itself produce prosecutions for corruption, it could perhaps begin to shift perceptions of the legal tools available for prosecuting corruption under a framework of human rights law.

V. By Way of Conclusion: Explaining the Turn to Human Rights

In the 1980s and 1990s, the goal of economic development served as a key driver of anticorruption rhetoric and policy. The United States took the lead in enacting

[66] Lonardo Filippini et al., "La Efectividad del Sistema Interamericano de Protección de Derechos Humanos," *SUR: Revista Internacional de Direitos Humanos* 1, no. 1. (2002)

[67] Aníbal Pérez-Liñán, Luis Schenoni, and Kelly Morrison, "Compliance in Time: Lessons from the Inter-American Court of Human Rights," *International Studies Review* 25, no. 1 (2023).

[68] Jonathan Blitzer, "The Exile of Guatemala's Anti-Corruption Efforts," *New Yorker*, April 29, 2022.

laws against corruption and pushing other states to do the same. International organizations like the OECD, the World Bank, and the IMF likewise emphasized corruption as a drag on economic growth and anticorruption as a key to economic development. Anticorruption became part of the so-called Washington Consensus, a set of assumptions and related policy prescriptions that served as the basis of economic development policies worldwide. To be sure, the term "Washington Consensus" was a misnomer: its key prescriptions were "developed in Latin America, by Latin Americans,"[69] though US officials endorsed and diffused them. At the core of the Washington Consensus were the commitment to free-market economies and openness to international trade and investment. Corruption undermined and distorted markets and therefore skewed and inhibited trade and international investment. The imperative to reduce corruption became a component of the dominant economic development ideas of the era.

By the early years of the new century, the Washington Consensus had fallen apart.[70] Corruption, however, remained a challenge across Latin America. Though the multilateral anticorruption treaties remained in place, a new front opened in the struggle to reduce corruption: human rights. Linking human rights concerns to anticorruption initiatives is closely associated with the rise of the "good governance" movement.[71] Core tenets of good governance initiatives include transparency and accountability, which directly implicate the struggle against corruption.[72] Anticorruption in pursuit of economic growth and efficiency has thus partially given way to good governance for the sake of maintaining effective, democratic institutions that can fulfill rights obligations.

In addition to this global transition in dominant policymaking paradigms, there are more region-specific reasons for why the discourses of anticorruption and human rights have become increasingly intertwined in Latin America, leading to the emergence of an innovative corpus of jurisprudence and soft law. First, the inter-American system has asserted itself on an expanding set of sensitive social and political questions, including in vitro fertilization[73] and cross-border pollution.[74] When seen in light of this general willingness of the

[69] Daniel Yergin and Joseph Stanislaw, *The Commanding Heights: The Battle for the World Economy* (New York: Simon and Schuster, 2002), 237.

[70] Dani Rodrik, "Goodbye Washington Consensus, Hello Washington Confusion? A Review of the World Bank's Economic Growth in the 1990s: Learning from a Decade of Reform", *Journal of Economic Literature* 44 (2006): 973–987.

[71] Claudio Nash and Marie-Christine Fuchs (eds.), *Corrupción, Estado de Derecho y Derechos Humanos* (Bogota, Colombia: Kondrad Adenauer Stiftung, 2019).

[72] Ngugi, "Making the Link," 64.

[73] *Artavia Murillo et al. (In Vitro Fertilization) v. Costa Rica*, Preliminary Objections, Merits, Reparations and Costs, Inter-Am. Ct. H.R. (ser. C) No. 257 (November 28, 2012).

[74] The Environment and Human Rights (state obligations in relation to the environment in the context of the protection and guarantee of the rights to life and to personal integrity interpretation and scope of Articles 4(1) and 5(1) of the American Convention on Human Rights), Advisory Opinion OC-23/17 (ser. A) No. 23 (November 15, 2017).

Commission and the Court to step into new domains, it is not surprising that both institutions have targeted corrupt practices as causes of human rights violations. As Rojas and Fuchs observe, "There exists an obvious link between a complex understanding of the phenomenon of corruption and the erosion of the foundations of the democratic system and the rule of law."[75] Put differently, any attempt to understand the roots of poor rights enforcement in Latin America will sooner or later stumble upon the problem of systemic corruption. The Court and the Commission have begun to recognize these connections.

Second, the third wave of democratization stalled, and several countries experienced democratic erosion. The inter-American system started to receive cases that put into sharper focus the intimate relationship between human rights and corruption. For instance, the Commission's 2017 report on the situation in Venezuela explicitly draws a connection between outright autocratization, increasing institutional opaqueness, corruption, and human rights violations. Similarly, in 2019, the Court found that Venezuela had violated the right to freedom of expression by upholding a defamation conviction against a journalist who tried to expose corruption in the National Assembly.[76] Another set of cases brought attention to the weaponization of corruption accusations by (would be) autocrats. In fact, the leading case pertaining to the exercise of anticorruption prerogatives is arguably *Lopez-Mendoza v. Venezeula* (2011), in which the Court ruled against the use of administrative proceedings to ban an opposition politician accused of misuse of public funds from running for mayor of Caracas.

Finally, spectacular anticorruption crusades, including various national chapters of the Lava Jato investigation and the work of Guatemala's CICIG, led both accusers and accused to increasingly rely on human rights framings to justify their actions or defend themselves from attacks. The sheer zeal displayed by some judges and prosecutors in these cases magnified the tensions between anticorruption and human rights norms. And as embattled politicians lashed back, it also became clear that enforcing human rights was essential to preserve the integrity of sensitive investigations. All of this attracted the attention of the inter-American system. The Court and the Commission have had to perform a balancing act, treating corruption as a source of human rights violations and reviewing threats to judicial and prosecutorial independence, while also recognizing that overzealous corruption prosecutions can sometimes violate due process rights. In so doing, they have sought to reconcile the international anticorruption obligations of states and the civil and political rights of defendants enshrined in the American Convention. Because the inter-American system

[75] Nash and Fuchs, *Corrupción*, 23.

[76] *Álvarez Ramos v. Venezuela*, Preliminary Objection, Merits, Reparations and Costs, Judgment of August 30, 2019, Inter-Am. Ct. H.R. (ser. C) No. 380.

is designed not to prosecute wrongdoers but to stand up for victims' rights, its primary role in attacking corruption may be one of signaling inter-American law and standards to domestic prosecutors and judges. Given the gulf between the scale of human rights violations in the Americas and the small number of cases that are resolved in the inter-American system, that is a role to which the Commission and the Court must already be accustomed.

27

Strategic Uses of International Law in Peace Negotiations in Colombia

Helena Alviar García and Laura Betancur-Restrepo*

I. Peace in Colombia: Testing the Limits of the International in the Local

In his speech before the United Nations General Assembly in 2003, Álvaro Uribe defended what his government had called "alternative justice mechanisms" projected for the Justice and Peace Law draft. He argued that some forgiveness was necessary to face a conflict against more than thirty thousand terrorists. Uribe argued that, ultimately, peace was the best form of justice:

> "I understand the concern that arises from attenuating justice in the face of serious crimes, but it must also be understood that, in a context of 30,000 terrorists, definitive peace is the best justice for a Nation in which several generations have not known a day without acts of terror."[1]

Thirteen years later, Uribe's opinion had radically changed. In an interview with the Spanish newspaper ABC, the former Colombian president said forgiving certain crimes was not the best justice. On the contrary, forgiveness would necessarily generate new conflicts. He justified this attack in several ways, including the argument that this type of forgiveness was contrary to international treaties signed by Colombia:

> "The Government assures that the atrocious crimes will be tried and sentenced, but immediately afterwards it admits that those responsible will not go to jail and will enjoy full political participation. That goes against the American

* A shorter and earlier version of this argument was published in Spanish as: Helena Alviar García and Laura Betancur-Restrepo, "Usos estratégicos del Derecho Internacional en las Conversaciones de la Habana," in *Después del acuerdo: ¿Cómo va la paz en Colombia?*, vol. 1, ed. Laura Betancur-Restrepo and Angelika Rettberg (Bogotá, Colombia: Ediciones Uniandes, 2023).

[1] UN G.A., 58th Session of the United Nations General Assembly, *Statement by H.E. Mr. Alvaro Uribe Velez, President of Colombia* (September 30, 2003), https://www.un.org/webcast/ga/58/statements/coloeng030930.htm.

Helena Alviar García and Laura Betancur-Restrepo, *Strategic Uses of International Law in Peace Negotiations in Colombia* In: *Latin American International Law in the Twenty-First Century*. Edited by: Alejandro Chehtman, Alexandra Huneeus, and Sergio Puig, Oxford University Press.
 DOI: 10.1093/9780197754016.003.0027

> Convention on Human Rights, as well as the Statute of the International Criminal Court. And this is a bad example. The history of impunity is the history of the creation of new violence."[2]

Uribe's contradictory positions illustrate the central topic of this chapter: the strategic uses of international law. In the case of the speech before the UN, then-President Uribe argued that (in the tension between justice and peace) trying to achieve peace is a much more important objective than criminally processing thirty thousand terrorists (according to his numbers, some academics have said there were considerably fewer members). At the time, Uribe's interpretation of human rights and the consequences of human rights violations seemed more open, flexible, and detached from formalist readings. Thirteen years later, his reading is exactly the opposite. What he calls in 2003 "attenuating justice" becomes an act that goes against the American Convention on Human Rights and the Statute of the International Criminal Court (ICC).[3]

This chapter is framed within the contradictions of right-wing former president Uribe. It explores the clashes and contradictions between the aims of achieving peace and the demands imposed by international institutions and treaties. It discusses the negotiations and peace agreements between the Colombian government and the Revolutionary Armed Forces of Colombia (FARC) guerrillas. The case offers an interesting example of the tense, complex, and far-reaching interaction between international law and domestic goals of ending civil conflict. This example is deeply relevant as the negotiations were nourished by previous experiences in different parts of the world, and it is the first peace agreement achieved since the ICC entered into force. Several studies have analyzed international legal challenges during the Colombian peace talks;[4] however, none explore the different uses of

[2] Guillermo D. Olmo, "Álvaro Uribe: 'El acuerdo de Santos con las FARC no es de paz, es de impunidad,'" *ABC International*, March 31, 2016, https://www.abc.es/internacional/abci-alvaro-uribe-acuerdo-santos-farc-no-impunidad-201603300234_noticia.html?ref=https:%2F%2Fwww.google.com%2F

[3] In August 2021, Uribe again seemed to change his mind by proposing a "general amnesty as a way to move the country towards total peace." "Uribe propone amnistía general para lograr paz en Colombia," *DW Made for minds*, August 19, 2021, https://www.dw.com/es/expresidente-uribe-propone-amnist%C3%ADa-general-para-lograr-paz-en-colombia/a-58901845

[4] *AJIL Unbound* dedicated a symposium that collected contributions from various scholars. See Alexandra Huneeus and René Urueña, "Introduction to Symposium on the Colombian Peace Talks and International Law," *AJIL Unbound* 110 (2016): 161–164, https://doi.org/10.1017/S2398772300003007. See also Lina María Céspedes Báez and Enrique Prieto-Ríos (eds.), *Utopía u oportunidad fallida. Análisis crítico del Acuerdo de paz* (Bogotá, Colombia: Editorial Universidad del Rosario, 2017), https://doi.org/10.12804/tj9789587389289; Félix Vacas Fernández, *El conflicto de Colombia y los Acuerdos de Paz en perspectiva internacional* (Bogotá, Colombia: Ediciones Doctrina y Ley, 2017). From a legal perspective (not international), see Helena Alviar García and Isabel Cristina Jaramillo Sierra (eds.), *Perspectivas jurídicas para la paz* (Bogotá, Colombia: Ediciones Uniandes, 2016).

international law and the strategic way in which those discourses served certain agendas.[5]

Here, we present how some national and external actors (participating in the peace negotiations) presented international law as if it was univocal and universal and as if it were neutral in relation to local political discussions. Building upon this insight, we analyze how different actors made strategic use of international law according to their political preferences or economic goals. We divide the strategic uses of international law into three parts: a set of rules that impose strict limits on peace, a mechanism that offers new possibilities for dialogue, or a strong safeguard to protect what was agreed on.

To illustrate these divisions, the text analyzes some references to international law in the peace talks and the agreements that resulted after the Havana negotiations. The chapter also reviews certain public statements and interventions made before the Constitutional Court during the constitutionality reviews of the transitional legal framework aimed at evaluating the possibilities and implementation of what was agreed[6] upon and the Court's rulings in this area.[7] The main goal is to foreground the ideological content of these deployments of international law and what these uses conceal to understand who wins and who loses when a particular view prevails.

To present this analysis, we have organized the text as follows: Section II maps out the political divisions within the Colombian elite in general and how they define peace. These divisions help us understand the strategic uses discussed above and developed in section III. Section IV contains some conclusions.

[5] See, however, an interesting contribution to the discourses of human rights during the conflict, before the peace process: Juana Schlenker and Manuel A. Iturralde, "El uso del discurso de los derechos humanos por parte de los actores armados en Colombia: ¿Humanización del conflicto o estrategia de guerra?," *UN Análisis Político*, no. 56 (January–April 2006): 29–50, https://repositorio.unal.edu.co/handle/unal/50319.

[6] These statements examined the feasibility of adapting the internal Colombian legal system to allow negotiations and the transitional legal framework that accompanied them. See, in particular, the revision of the following norms: Congress of Colombia. Legislative Act 01 of 2012. By means of which legal instruments of transitional justice are established within the framework of article 22 of the Political Constitution and other provisions are issued. July 31, 2012. *Official Diary* No. 48.508; Congress of Colombia. Law 1806 of 2016. By means of which the plebiscite for the endorsement of the final agreement for the termination of the conflict and the construction of a stable and lasting peace is regulated. August 24, 2016. *Official Diary* No. 49.975; Congress of Colombia. Law 1820 of 2016. By means of which provisions on amnesty, pardon and special criminal treatment and other provisions are issued. December 30, 2016. *Official* Diary No. 50.102; Congress of Colombia. Legislative Act 02 of 2017. By means of which a transitory article is added to the Constitution with the purpose of providing stability and legal security to the final agreement for the termination of the conflict and the construction of a stable and lasting peace. May 11, 2017. *Official* Diary No. 50.230; Congress of Colombia. Law 1957 of 2019. Statutory Law of the Administration of Justice in the Special Jurisdiction for Peace. June 6, 2019. *Official* Diary No. 50.976.

[7] See the following judgments of the Constitutional Court of Colombia: C-579 of August 28, 2013; C-577 of August 6, 2014; C-332 of May 17, 2017; C-379 of July 18, 2016; C- 630 of October 11, 2017; C-674 of November 14, 2017; C-007 of March 1, 2018; C-017 of March 21, 2018; C-025 of April 11, 2018; C-070 of July 4, 2018; C-071 of July 4, 2018 and C-080 of August 15, 2018.

II. Mapping the Political Divisions within the Colombian Elite and Their Definition of Peace

Even though Colombia has more than thirteen political parties, the ideological landscape can be divided into three broad groups: liberals, conservatives, and social-democratic progressives. These groups call for the redistribution of power and resources. This section outlines their main characteristics, subdivisions, and ways of defining peace.

Colombian liberals follow classical principles: the individual is the center of society, the market is the best distributor of resources, and there is a clear separation between public and private spheres. They are divided into two groups mostly in relation to the degree of state intervention in the economy and society. Those in the center are deeply embedded in neoliberalism and embrace privatization, minimal state intervention, and means-tested social policies such as conditional cash transfers. Liberals on the left, also called interventionists, believe in the centrality of the individual, the market, and the separation between public and private, but they call for more state-led distribution and participation in the economy.

These competing views are translated into slightly different interpretations of what achieving peace entails. For neoliberals, such as former president Juan Manuel Santos, peace meant achieving individual transformation and a consensual agreement that would replace conflict with rules of civility which, in turn, would bring growth and prosperity. In 2014, he mentioned these ideas several times:

> "Peace implies changing our behavior, redrawing a line of civility that has been torn for decades, peace requires patience, care, conviction."[8]
>
> "With peace Colombia will be more attractive for tourists, for foreign investment and the more they visit us, the more companies go to Colombia, there will be more and better jobs."[9]

Liberal interventionists define peace similarly but emphasize correcting past harms through reparations. In Colombia, this view was crystallized in the Victim's law[10] and by granting privileged access to women, Indigenous

[8] Presidency of the Republic of Colombia, "Declaración del presidente Juan Manuel Santos al iniciar su visita a España," *YouTube*, January 21, 2014, https://www.youtube.com/watch?v=KHxCD4snkvo.

[9] News Radio Internacional Interview, Radio, TV. "Televisión Española: Juan Manuel Santos en Bruselas." *YouTube*, November 12, 2014, https://www.youtube.com/watch?v=HApEyzSfieE.

[10] "10 años de la Ley de Víctimas: Hablan sus Protagonistas," *El Espectador*, June 10, 2021, https://www.elespectador.com/colombia-20/paz-y-memoria/10-anos-de-la-ley-de-victimas-hablan-sus-protagonistas/.

populations, and Afro-descendants. They are interested in the state correcting the historical exclusion of those in the margins.[11]

The right—at the beginning slowly but in the last few years with such force and determination that those in the center or left of the center seemed to be surprised and completely unprepared—has opposed each of these projects with varying degrees of vigor. Conservatives are interested in protecting existing privileges (instead of allowing the market to distribute resources) of property owners, the landed elite, agribusiness, the financial sector, merchants, and industrialists. In addition, a strong discourse centers on moral values and nationalism.[12]

There are two different two strands within conservatives. One, "the family preservationist," is progressive in terms of distribution and extremely conservative in relation to the family, its role in society, and how it should be structured. This odd combination is a product of the Catholic Church's ideas about solidarity (in relation to the allocation of resources) aligned with its firm stance on heterosexual marriage and women's place in the household. The other strand, "the radical right," is economically and morally conservative. Their agenda is to prevent social and economic distribution at all costs and preserve Christian values in society and in the family.[13]

The most salient definition of peace was that embraced by the radical right in the words of former President Uribe Vélez (from *Centro Democrático* political party), peace meant, in the best-case scenario, winning the war against FARC and reaching an agreement that meant no peace without justice: "We were winning the war, in 2002 the FARC had thirty thousand members, in 2010 two thousand eight hundred. We all want peace, we were winning it, but peace with impunity is like ill made money."[14]

Finally, the left in Colombia is diverse and has changed over time. Until 2022, there had not been a left-wing government in the country. Their agenda follows the influence of dependency theory: a state-led development policy that protects national production and redistributes growth. In recent years, the left has also embraced environmental and gender equality concerns.[15] Consequently, their definition of peace is not simply the end of civil conflict; it necessarily entails

[11] For more on this position, see Helena Alviar García, "La Lucha por el Género en la Paz," in *Género en Transición*, ed. Isabel Cristina Jaramillo Sierra, 37–57 (New York: Peter Lang Verlag, 2020), https://doi.org/10.3726/b16140.

[12] The contemporary agenda of the right is synthesized in the program and goals of the political party founded by former president Álvaro Uribe Vélez, "¿Quiénes somos?" *Centro Democrático*, accessed December 19, 2023, https://www.centrodemocratico.com/quienes-somos.

[13] Emphasis on the family prevails in the Conservative Party's platform, accessed December 19, 2023, https://www.partidoconservador.com.

[14] Álvaro Uribe Vélez, "En Miami, Álvaro Uribe critica proceso de paz con las FARC," *YouTube*, November 7, 2015, https://www.youtube.com/watch?v=7WDe3TLRYdY.

[15] "Programa de Gobierno para una Era de Paz", *Voto por la igualdad*, accessed August 3, 2022, https://votoporlaigualdad.com/gustavo-petro/.

revisiting the neoliberal economic development model and the distribution of property and wealth.

During the peace negotiations, these political divisions among the elites were noteworthy in their approach to the peace agreement. As we will see in the following sections, international law was a strategic tool to advance their agendas.

All actors use the law for strategic purposes; this is a fact. Our argument here is to provide nuance to how international law was brought into the negotiations and the paths for peace. On the one hand, conservatives in Colombia opposed the agreement for economic, social, political, and legal reasons. The most salient were fears of a comprehensive resource and political power redistribution, the redesign of policies based on gender (understood as the result of social relations instead of a biologically determined fact), and the establishment of alternative forms of punishment that would lead to impunity.[16] To adequately boost the arguments for their resistance, conservatives used international law and argued that it imposed a strict limit to what could be negotiated. On the other hand, and as we will discuss in the next section, liberals and left-leaning progressives embraced a different interpretation of international law, presenting it less as a rigid frame and more as an enabler of peace and crucial discussions regarding resource and power redistribution.

III. Strategic Uses of International Law

International Law as a Set of Rules that Imposes Strict Limits to Peace

For the general public, one of the most controversial and striking interpretations of international law was the idea that it set a clear dividing line between things that could and couldn't be negotiated during the peace talks. From this perspective, international law is relevant because conversations took place within a global legal context that, according to the proponents of this interpretation, determines strict legal limits that must be respected by domestic legislation.

[16] For a detailed description of conservative opposition to the peace agreement in these topics, see Helena Alviar García and Karen Engle, "The Distributive Politics of Impunity and Anti-Impunity: Lessons from Four Decades of Colombian Peace Negotiations," in *Anti-Impunity and the Human Rights Agenda*, ed. Karen Engle, Zina Miller, and Dennis Davis, 216–254 (Cambridge: Cambridge University Press, 2016); Helena Alviar García, "Derechos de propiedad rural y desarrollo económico en tiempos de transición: Desempacando la lucha," in *Propiedad sobre la tierra en Colombia*, ed. Helena Alviar García and Tatiana Alfonso, 11–25 (Bogotá, Colombia: Ediciones Uniandes, 2021); and Alviar García, "La Lucha por el Género en la Paz," 37–57.

This instrumentalization of international law was particularly prevalent in discussions about international criminal law, international human rights law, and international humanitarian law, as well as issues of responsibility for international crimes and the benefits and sanctions that *could* and *could not* be included. For example, in the early stages of the negotiations, the FARC was emphatic in stating that Havana was not a process of submission or surrender in which their punishment or responsibility for their actions during the conflict would be.[17] Given this, part of the Colombian government's response was to point out that Colombia was bound by international treaties and was under the surveillance of international tribunals that demanded the prosecution of atrocious crimes.[18] In this sense, the roles of the Inter-American Court of Human Rights (IACtHR) and the ICC were presented as swords hanging over Colombia, threatening to fall on the agreement if its prohibitions were violated.

In addition, the ICC was perceived before the Havana negotiations as a clear limit to the peace negotiations and even as an obstacle to achieving a negotiated peace.[19] The content of the Rome Statute,[20] the constant pronouncements of the ICC[21] Prosecutor's Office (which opened a preliminary investigation of

[17] See, for example, the statement made by Jesús Santrich, one of the negotiators for the FARC guerrillas, after meeting with Kofi Annan, former secretary of the United Nations in the negotiations in Havana: "What remains for us is to reiterate our disagreement and repeat that those of us who exercise the right to rebellion against a regime of terror are not willing to pay a single day in jail. We did not come to Havana to attend a process of submission or surrender, but to seek solutions to the serious political, economic and social problems that Colombia has." "Kofi Annan se equivoca, no vamos a pagar ni un día de cárcel: FARC," *Semana*, March 2, 2015, https://www.semana.com/nacion/articulo/farc-dicen-que-no-pagaran-carcel-en-respuesta-declaraciones-de-kofi-annan/419700-3/.

[18] President Santos said at the time: "We do not want to sign an agreement that is later defeated in the courts." "¿Habrá cárcel en el posconflicto?" *Semana*, February 28, 2015, https://www.semana.com/nacion/articulo/habra-carcel-en-el-posconflicto/419342-3/

[19] Colombia signed and ratified the Rome Statute in 2002 but with a reservation that excluded war crimes from the Court's jurisdiction for seven years, until 2009. This was precisely to have more freedom in peace negotiations that the Government of Pastrana was carrying out with the FARC. After the failure of the Caguán negotiations and the entry into force for Colombia of the Rome Statute, several analysts wondered if the dialogue with the guerrillas had been closed since international law had set "effective limits to the type of negotiations that are valid" and because the margin of "impunity" that Colombia could negotiate was eliminated. "Con la entrada de la Corte Penal Internacional se cerraron puertas para diálogo con la guerrilla." *El Tiempo*, August 5, 2009, https://www.eltiempo.com/archivo/documento/CMS-5784290. See also Romero Rincón and Mary Luz, "Corte Penal Internacional: ¿Un obstáculo para la paz en Colombia?" *Revista Misión Jurídica* 8, no. 8 (January–June 2015): 133–148, https://doi.org/10.25058/1794600X.93.

[20] Article 17.1(b) of the Statute indicates that the Criminal Court will have jurisdiction to judge a case if the state decides not to initiate a criminal action for being unwilling to prosecute. Article 25.2 adds that whoever commits a crime within the jurisdiction of the Court "may be punished in accordance with the Statute." UN G.A., *Rome Statute of the International Criminal Court*, A/CONF. 183/9 (July 17, 1998), https://www.refworld.org/docid/3ae6b3a84.html.

[21] See, for example, the following reports from the Prosecutor's Office on Colombia. ICC Prosecutor's Office, "Situation in Colombia, Interim Report," *International Criminal Court*, (November 14, 2012), https://www.icc-cpi.int/NR/rdonlyres/3D3055BD-16E2-4C83-BA85-35BCFD2A7922/285102/OTPCOLOMBIAPublicInterimReportNovember2012.pdf; ICC Prosecutor's Office, "Report on Preliminary Examination Activities. Situations in Honduras and Colombia 2014,"

Colombia in 2004), and the long history of rejecting total amnesties for crimes against humanity and serious human rights violations in the Inter-American Human Rights System[22] influenced negotiating parties. In fact, these factors likely made FARC members change their initial position, rejecting all punishment and responsibility for their actions in the armed conflict and accepting an alternative justice proposal.

As can be deduced from the shift in the FARC's initial position (often used by critics of the agreement),[23] this strategic use had concrete consequences during the negotiations. This is why, in the final peace agreement[24] and Constitutional Court rulings,[25] there are direct references to compliance with international law (including international criminal law, international human rights law, and international humanitarian law) in the agreements. In the negotiations, it was clear that it was not possible to agree on a general amnesty law that would cover

International Criminal Court (December 2, 2014), https://www.icc-cpi.int/sites/default/files/iccdocs/otp/OTP-Hon-Col-2014.PDF; ICC Prosecutor's Office, "Report on Preliminary Examination Activities. Situations in Colombia and Honduras 2015," *International Criminal Court* (November 12, 2015), https://www.icc-cpi.int/iccdocs/otp/OTP-PE-rep-2015-Spa.pdf; and ICC Prosecutor's Office, "Report on preliminary examination activities. Situation in Colombia 2016," *International Criminal Court* (November 14, 2016), https://www.icc-cpi.int/sites/default/files/iccdocs/otp/161114-otp-rep-PE-Colombia.pdf.

[22] In particular, in several contentious cases, the Inter-American Court has considered that amnesty laws that include impunity for these types of crimes go against the inter-American *corpus iuris*. See, for example, *"White Van" (Paniagua-Morales et al.) v. Guatemala,* (merits), Inter-Am. Ct. H.R. (ser. C) No. 37 (March 8, 1998), https://www.corteidh.or.cr/docs/casos/articulos/seriec_37_ing.pdf; *Loayza-Tamayo v. Peru,* (reparations), Inter-Am. Ct. H.R., (ser. C) No. 32 (November 27, 1998); *Barrios Altos v. Peru,* Preliminary Objections, Merits, Reparations and Costs, Inter-Am. Ct. H.R., (ser. C) No. 75 (March 14, 2001), https://www.corteidh.or.cr/docs/casos/articulos/seriec_75_ing.pdf; and *Almonacid-Arellano et al v. Chile,* Preliminary Objections, Merits, Reparations and Costs), Inter-Am. Ct. H.R. (ser. C) No. 154 (September 26, 2006), https://www.corteidh.or.cr/docs/casos/articulos/seriec_154_ing.pdf.

[23] Other times, it was used in the discussion on political and related crimes that could be allowed or the debate on the eventual inclusion of the agreement as part of the constitutionality block.

[24] The preamble to the Final Agreement not only makes direct reference to international law but also refers to some areas and institutions including international criminal law and the decisions of the IACtHR: "Bearing in mind that the Final Agreement includes each and every one of the agreements reached on the Agenda of the General Agreement signed in Havana in August 2012; and that in order to achieve this, the National Government and the FARC-EP always and at all times adhere to the spirit and respect of the National Constitution, the principles of International Law, International Human Rights Law, and International Humanitarian Law (Agreements and Protocols), of what is mandated by the Rome Statute (International Criminal Law), of the rulings issued by the Inter-American Court of Human Rights regarding conflicts and their termination, and other rulings of universally recognized competences and pronouncements of authority relative to the subscribed topics." Government of Colombia and FARC-EP, *Acuerdo final para la terminación del conflicto y la construcción de una paz estable y duradera* (June 26, 2016), https://www.refworld.org.es/docid/5a8744d54.html.

[25] "The principle of selection is characterized by being framed exclusively within a transitional justice scenario; it does not constitute an example of self-amnesty incompatible with international human rights standards, it offers a balance between the rights of victims to truth, justice and reparation, the state duty to investigate and punish international crimes and the right to peace and national reconciliation." Constitutional Court of Colombia, C-577.

crimes against humanity or serious violations of human rights or international humanitarian law.

However, the scope of this limitation and what international law allowed or limited were the subject of further debate. The discussions covered the types of sanctions that should be imposed, the selection criteria for the cases that would be reviewed within the framework of the agreed transitional justice, and the benefits granted to those who had committed serious human rights violations.

Indeed, the compatibility of these criteria with international law was analyzed in some of the judicial reviews by the Constitutional Court of the legal framework of the peace agreements. In his intervention in ruling C-579/13,[26] the Office of the Procurator General[27] affirmed that the international legal framework for human rights:

> does not allow the legislator to issue laws that grant rights to truth, justice and reparation to only some victims (those who are victims of crimes against humanity, war crimes, systemic genocide and crimes committed by those in charge) and others exclude others (those who do not fall into the categories expressed in the law).[28]

Along the same lines, the former director for the Americas of Human Rights Watch (HRW), an international NGO that initially opposed some provisions of the Peace Agreement, said in his speech:

> Colombia has an international obligation to investigate and prosecute all those who share responsibility for violations of human rights and International Humanitarian Law, so the waiver of these powers regardless of whether it is carried out according to prioritization and selection criteria would be in breach of these obligations...
>
> [T] he obligation to investigate and prosecute those responsible for serious violations of human rights and International Humanitarian Law extends to everyone and not only to those most responsible for such conduct... [To] authorize those responsible for atrocious crimes to avoid Justice, endorsed by the Constitution, implies an irremediable setback for the rule of law, which is why

[26] This ruling considered the constitutionality of Legislative Act 1 of July 31, 2012. The reporting judge was Jorge Ignacio Pretelt, who was a judge of the Constitutional Court between 2009 and 2016 (the date on which he was suspended for a corruption case). Judge Pretelt was characterized by defending conservative positions.

[27] Between 2009 and 2016, the Office of the Procurator-General of Colombia was led by Alejandro Ordoñez, an exponent of the conservative family preservationist and a strong critic of the peace agreement.

[28] Procurator-General of Colombia, "Intervención de la Procuraduría ante la Corte Constitucional en la Sentencia C-579 de 2013," *Constitutional Court of Colombia 579/13* (August 28, 2013), https://www.corteconstitucional.gov.co/relatoria/2013/C-579-13.htm.

> Colombia would be exposed to the jurisdiction of specialized international courts such as the ICC.[29]

On the other hand, the then Attorney General of Colombia[30] defended the idea that what had been agreed satisfied international obligations as it was a transitional justice process:

> (i) prioritization satisfies the international obligation (that operates within a framework of protection from human rights violations) that the structures, their causes, the people who participated in these events in various ways, their beneficiaries and their consequences are unearthed. This way guaranteeing the rights of the victims and avoiding impunity (ii) the principle of selectivity which is framed exclusively within the terms of transitional justice and as such, it does not constitute an example of self-amnesty that is incompatible with international human rights standards, instead it offers a balance between the victims' rights to truth, justice and reparation, the duty of the state to investigate and punish international crimes and the right to peace and national reconciliation ... the prioritization and selection guarantee access to the administration of justice, in the light of national and international standards, as they are instruments that allow the State to comply with its duty to investigate serious human rights violations effectively, avoid impunity and guarantee the rights of the victims to clarify the facts.[31]

In yet another example of international law as a field open to interpretation, the ICC Prosecutor's Office gradually modified its position from rigid limits imposed by international criminal law to a more flexible position on transitional justice. Thus, after much criticism directed toward the first statement set forth by Prosecutor Bensouda (regarding the Colombian peace process), in 2015, the Deputy Prosecutor of the ICC, James Stewart, clarified that "the Prosecutor of the ICC hopes to play a positive and constructive role." In addition, Stewart stated that "[i]n sentencing, States have wide discretion [that] transitional justice measures offer broad scope" and that effective criminal punishment can take different forms (which don't necessarily require time in prison).[32] Finally, after signing the peace agreement in 2016, Prosecutor Bensouda issued a statement in

[29] Human Rights Watch, "Intervención de Human Rights Watch ante la Corte Constitucional en la Sentencia C-579/13," *Constitutional Court of Colombia C-579/13* (August 28, 2013), https://www.corteconstitucional.gov.co/relatoria/2013/C-579-13.htm.

[30] Eduardo Montealegre was Attorney General of Colombia between 2012 and 2016, and he defended a liberal interventionist agenda.

[31] Attorney General of Colombia, "Intervención de la Fiscalía General de la Nación ante la Corte Constitucional en la Sentencia C-579 de 2013," *Constitutional Court of Colombia C-579/13* (August 28, 2013), https://www.corteconstitucional.gov.co/relatoria/2013/C-579-13.htm.

[32] James Stewart, "Transitional Justice in Colombia and the Role of the International Criminal Court," *International Criminal Court* (May 13, 2015), 2–10, https://www.icc-cpi.int/iccdocs/otp/otp-stat-13-05-2015-ENG.pdf.

which she celebrated the agreement and agreed with the Special Jurisdiction for Peace, the limited amnesty it included, and the "focus on those directly responsible for the most serious crimes committed during the armed conflict."[33]

International Law as a Field that Offers New Possibilities for Dialogue and Inclusion

International law was also used as a tool to facilitate or offer new possibilities in a peace negotiation, allowing the active participation of some individuals and communities that would otherwise be excluded.

For example, both the negotiation process and the agreements were a platform for victims, communities that have special protection, minorities, rebels, and state agents to actively participate and seek access to political, social, economic, and legal resources. International human rights law was a legal framework that offered new possibilities and tools to vindicate the claims of various sectors of the population within the peacebuilding process.

In this sense, and for some academics and activists, victims' rights for truth and justice opened the door for different social sectors to formulate and implement transitional justice processes. Indeed, international law scholars have argued that the work of the Gender Subcommittee during the peace negotiations in Havana not only broadened the spectrum of participation for those who considered themselves victims (by including, for example, the suffering of the LGBTI population) but also included important considerations in relation to the role of women in conflict.[34]

Another example of this use of international law (which is also related to the use of international law as a limitation explained in section II) is the discussion regarding the type of punishment required in transitional justice processes and whether the agreement opened the door to impunity. Some commenters considered that international law, particularly international criminal law, instead of imposing an insurmountable barrier, offered a flexible legal framework with a broader scope of interpretation than, for example, the traditional interpretation of domestic criminal law. In this sense, the then Attorney General of Colombia defended the legal architecture of the agreement on several occasions, considering that international law, within a transitional justice process, allows a flexible

[33] ICC Prosecutor's Office, "Statement of ICC Prosecutor, Fatou Bensouda, on the conclusion of the peace negotiations between the Government of Colombia and the Revolutionary Armed Forces of Colombia–People's Army," *International Criminal Court* (September 1, 2016), https://www.icc-cpi.int/pages/item.aspx?name=160901-otp-stat-colombia.

[34] Huneeus and Urueña, "Introduction to Symposium on the Colombian Peace"; and Christine Bell, "Lex Pacificatoria Colombiana: Colombia's Peace Accord in Comparative Perspective," *AJIL Unbound* 110 (2016): 165–171, https://doi.org/10.1017/S2398772300003019.

interpretation regarding the types of penalties, political crimes, and amnesties, among others.[35]

International Law as a Strong Safeguard for Protection

A third use of international law was to present it as a mechanism to protect what was agreed upon. In this case, the discussion was about what can be considered international law and its relationship with domestic law. International law was presented as a legal tool to guarantee future compliance because if laws or regulations violated the agreements, there would be legal consequences at the global level.

This strategic use is evidenced by reviewing all the international instruments in which parties have faith. Although a peace agreement with a guerrilla group does not fit neatly into international law's traditional classifications of sources and subjects, the parties decided to settle the peace agreement in Switzerland; the Colombian government made a unilateral declaration to the Secretary General of the United Nations and requested the inclusion of the agreement in a Security Council Resolution.[36] Perhaps the most important resolution was that the negotiators in Havana decided that the peace treaty would constitute a special agreement in "terms of Article 3 common to all the Geneva Conventions of 1949." This strategy sparked discussion about the guerrillas' international legal status and the effects of such consideration.[37]

One of the first questions addressed by the International Committee for the Red Cross (ICRC), one of the foremost interpreters of the Geneva Conventions, was whether it is possible to consider a peace agreement as a special agreement under international law. Common Article 3[38] is unclear in determining

[35] Referring to the political participation of the ex-guerrillas, he stated that this intervention did not imply "a breach of the State's obligation to investigate and punish serious crimes against human rights and infractions of international humanitarian law as, by preventing the conflict from being prolonged, it is one of the instruments of transitional justice that allow the State to comply with the guarantee of non-repetition of serious human rights violations." Attorney General of Colombia, "Intervención de la Fiscalía ante la Corte Constitucional en la Sentencia C-577 de 2014," *Constitutional Court of Colombia C-577/14* (August 6, 2014), https://www.corteconstitucional.gov.co/relatoria/2014/C-577-14.htm.

[36] In this regard, former President Santos stated that "the legal agreement is legally protected, within the country and in front of the international community . . . I deposited the agreement with the United Nations Security Council. It is a declaration of the State that obliges compliance with it, which is non-derogable." Iván Darío Duva Ruiz, "Juan Manuel Santos cuestiona propuesta para derogar a la JEP," *RCN Radio* (November 10, 2020), https://www.rcnradio.com/politica/juan-manuel-santos-cuestiona-propuesta-para-derogar-la-jep.

[37] About this, see Laura Restrepo-Betancur, "The Legal Status of the Colombian Peace Agreement," *AJIL Unbound* 110 (2016): 188–192, https://doi.org/10.1017/S2398772300003056, and Bell, "Lex Pacificatoria Colombiana," 169–170.

[38] "The four Geneva Conventions of 1949 constitute a large part of the contemporary IHL [international humanitarian law] legal framework. Although the Geneva Conventions of 1949 refer

whether the content of special agreements is limited to exclusively developing international humanitarian law or whether it allows the inclusion of other content particular to a peace agreement. The ICRC stated in its last comment on Article 3 that a peace agreement could be considered a special one when it contains clauses that give rise to additional obligations derived from the Geneva Conventions and their Additional Protocols, other sources of humanitarian law, or other obligations derived from human rights law that help to implement humanitarian law (CICR 2016).[39]

However, while it is novel to consider a peace agreement as a special one according to common Article 3 of the Geneva Conventions of 1949, such consideration has been contested. In Colombia, the main controversy centered on its internal effects. An attempt was made to define whether that status would allow the peace agreement to be considered part of the constitutionality block. The constitutionality block is a jurisprudential doctrine (which has had developments in countries with legal regimes as different as the United States and France) whose objective is to establish that some principles or the contents of certain treaties are part of a country's constitution beyond the written text.[40] This expansion of what is strictly contained in the text expands the tools of interpretation used by judges. In Colombia, it has been used to establish that certain human rights treaties, as well as international humanitarian law conventions, have a constitutional status.

One of the first to mention this possibility was the then Attorney General of Colombia. In his intervention in Ruling C-379/2016 (which reviewed the demand for constitutionality of the draft statutory law that regulated the plebiscite)[41] he expressly stated that the status of a special agreement (in terms of common Article 3 of the Geneva Conventions) would make it part of the constitutionality block.[42] For its part, Dejusticia, a local NGO that mainly defends

mainly to international armed conflicts, Article 3 common to them includes obligations of the parties to a non-international armed conflict and in its third paragraph establishes: "the Parties to the conflict shall do everything possible to put in force, through special agreements, all or part of the other provisions of this Agreement."

[39] This is given that peace agreements allow the regulation of specific obligations of the parties to an armed conflict on the understanding that the consequences of war (and, therefore, the application of international humanitarian law or the law of war) do not end with the signing of the peace agreement. About this, see Betancur-Restrepo, "The Legal Status of the Colombian Peace Agreement," 191.

[40] For a complete analysis of the development of this concept in Colombia, see Rodrigo Uprimny, "El Bloque de Constitucionalidad en Colombia. Un Análisis Jurisprudencial y un ensayo de Sistematización Doctrinal," *Dejusticia* (2001), https://www.dejusticia.org/wp-content/uploads/2017/04/fi_name_recurso_46.pdf.

[41] In this ruling, the reporting judge was Luis Ernesto Vargas, a judge of the Constitutional Court between 2009 and 2017. In several of his interventions, Judge Vargas defended redistributive positions and the protection of economic, social and cultural rights, more akin to the left.

[42] "The peace agreements, in relation to the negotiation agenda, the end of the armed conflict, disarmament, demobilization, the reintegration of combatants and justice, can be constituted as

a liberal interventionist agenda, considered that an international custom was developing which gave peace agreements (with humanitarian clauses) the rank of special agreements. According to Dejusticia, this would not mean that they would automatically form part of the constitutionality block because agreements "go beyond the normative scope of the humanitarian concept."[43]

Congress accepted the argument of the former Attorney General, and thus Article 4 of Legislative Act 01 of 2016 established that the peace agreement "constitutes a Special Agreement under the terms of Article 3 common to the Geneva Conventions of 1949" and that "in order to offer guarantees of compliance with the Final Agreement, once it has been signed and entered into force, it will strictly enter the constitutionality block and must be taken into account during the period of its implementation as a parameter of interpretation and as a reference for the development and validity of the Norms and Laws of Implementation and Development of the Final Agreement."[44] The opponents, members of the radical right political party *Centro Democrático*, presented a constitutional challenge in court to the whole of the Legislative Act and particularly to this article. According to the lawsuit, the peace accords were mistakenly assimilated into international treaties and should be inadmissible for consideration as part of the constitutionality block.[45]

The Court, in Ruling C-332/2017,[46] declared itself unable to rule on the merits of this article due to the controversy unleashed by its eventual automatic entry into the constitutionality block and, particularly after the negative result of the plebiscite that sought to endorse the agreements. The discussion was settled with

special agreements in the terms of common article 3 of the Geneva Conventions. Due to this, they would become part of the constitutionality block, that is, they are binding for the different authorities given their legal nature; and not because of a popular pronouncement." Attorney General of Colombia, "Intervención de la Fiscalía ante la Corte Constitucional en la Sentencia C-379 de 2016," *Constitutional Court of Colombia C-379/16* (July 18, 2016), https://www.corteconstitucional.gov.co/relatoria/2016/c-379-16.htm.

[43] Dejusticia, "Intervención del Centro de Estudios Derecho, Justicia y Sociedad (Dejusticia) en el proceso de constitucionalidad PE0000045," *Dejusticia* (March 11, 2016): 10, https://www.dejusticia.org/wp-content/uploads/2017/04/fi_name_recurso_816.pdf.

[44] Congress of Colombia, Legislative Act 01 of 2016, Por medio del cual se establecen instrumentos jurídicos para facilitar y asegurar la implementación y el desarrollo normativo del acuerdo final para la terminación del conflicto y la construcción de una paz estable y duradera (July 7, 2016), *Official Diary* No. 49.927.

[45] "This agreement does not correspond to an international humanitarian human rights treaty, or to a labor convention, or to any other type of international standard that is admissible within said block." In the same way, they maintained that "the Legislative Act demanded seeks to assimilate the agreement for the termination of the conflict to a treaty of public international law, made with a counterpart of international law and that, however, the FARC does not have legal personality, nor are they a State, far from being a subject of international law." Centro Democrático, "Demanda ante la Corte Constitucional en la Sentencia C-332 de 2017," *Constitutional Court of Colombia C-332/17* (May 17, 2017), https://www.corteconstitucional.gov.co/relatoria/2017/C-332-17.htm.

[46] Antonio José Lizarazo, the reporting judge of this ruling (judge of the Constitutional Court since 2017) is characterized by defending neoliberal and liberal interventionist positions.

the issuance of Legislative Act 02 of 2017, which repealed article 4 of Legislative Act 1 of 2016 and established that only the provisions of the agreement referring to international humanitarian law norms or fundamental rights would be mandatory parameters of interpretation of the final agreement.[47]

What is relevant about this discussion for this chapter is that the negotiating parties saw international law as a useful and relevant tool to protect the agreement from possible undermining efforts of future governments. Indeed, the government of President Duque has not been able to "tear the peace agreement to shreds,"[48] as some of his co-supporters dreamed of, and right-wing president Duque has had to render reports to the UN Security Council and other international bodies.

IV. Conclusions

We are not arguing that there is a correct interpretation of international law. Some of its strategic uses are contradictory, while others could be complementary. Like all law, international law is a field in which interpretive battles are fought. In this struggle, different political actors have diverse ideological viewpoints and support their positions according to their beliefs. Their arguments present international law as a single, closed system with universal agreement.

We cannot deny that legal instruments such as international treaties and courts create discourses that have local influence and will consequently modify the context in which negotiations and agreements take place. However, their implementation and scope are largely subject to interpretation and adaptation processes instrumentalized by actors with different political motivations. Analyzing the strategic uses of international law reveals the political purposes hidden under the supposed neutrality of international law and, at the same time, provides a set of tools to understand who wins and who loses when a specific interpretation prevails.

[47] "In development of the right to peace, the contents of the Final Agreement for the termination of the conflict and the construction of a stable and lasting peace, signed on November 24, 2016, which correspond to norms of international humanitarian law or fundamental rights defined in The Political Constitution and those related to the previous ones, will be mandatory parameters of interpretation and reference of development and validity of the norms and laws of implementation and development of the Final Agreement, subject to the constitutional provisions." Congress of Colombia, Legislative Act 02 of 2017. About this, see Álvaro Francisco Amaya-Villarreal and Valeria Guzmán-Duarte, "La Naturaleza jurídico-internacional de los Acuerdos de Paz y sus consecuencias en la implementación," *International Law: Revista Colombiana De Derecho Internacional* 15, no. 30 (2017): 41–60, https://doi.org/10.11144/Javeriana.il15-30.njia.

[48] Colprensa, "¿Está completamente blindado el acuerdo de paz con las Farc?" *El País* (October 12, 2017), https://www.elpais.com.co/proceso-de-paz/esta-completamente-blindado-el-acuerdo-de-paz-con-las-farc.html.

We would also like to point out that, despite the differences these strategic uses of international law have had in the peace negotiations in Colombia, the three uses share the perception that the relationship between domestic and international law is unidirectional. as if only international law, whatever its use and meaning, could influence the domestic sphere.

This leaves aside the possibility of understanding a two-way relationship, one in which international law is not alien to domestic law but is constantly influenced and modified by it. It also obscures the possibility that interpreting, creating, and modifying international law come from different parts of the world, not only from specific knowledge centers (traditionally Europe or the United States) but also from states of the Global South that face particular legal and political challenges, and which respond with innovative, creative legal solutions (both international and national).

Indeed, legal instruments such as international treaties and tribunals create influencing discourses used strategically by internal actors in the peace process (including victims). But this is a two-way street. The Colombian case provides an opportunity to redefine and apply certain concepts, such as legal and illegal amnesties, impunity, and adequate punishment.

28

The Promise of Environmental Cooperation in Latin America

Enhancing Forest Conservation through Sustainable Supply Chains

Beatriz Garcia

I. Introduction

Forests now represent only 31 percent of the global land area.[1] The crucial role of primary forests in climate change mitigation is largely recognized in scientific and policy literature,[2] yet forests continue to be threatened by degradation and conversion to other land uses. To limit global warming and meet the goals of the Paris Agreement,[3] the world's remaining forests must be protected. This is true for all forests worldwide as well as forests in Latin America. The widespread forest fires of 2019 in the Amazon[4] and the outbreak of COVID-19—which badly hit populations, notably Indigenous peoples, in Latin American countries—revealed how cooperation is needed and how little prepared those countries are to take collective action and face the "new normal" of increased forest fires, both natural and human-caused. In response to the unprecedented fires, seven Amazon countries[5] gathered in Colombia at a Presidential Summit and signed

[1] *The State of the World's Forests* (Rome: Food and Agriculture Organization, 2024) 6.

[2] H. Keith et al., "Evaluating Nature-Based Solutions for Climate Mitigation and Conservation Requires Comprehensive Carbon Accounting," *Science of the Total Environment* 79 (2021): 144341; Brendan Mackey et al., "Understanding the Importance of Primary Tropical Forest Protection as a Mitigation Strategy," *Mitigation and Adaptation Strategies for Global Change* 25 (2020): 763; Charles Victor Barber et al., *The Nexus Report: Nature Based Solutions to the Biodiversity and Climate Crisis* (Hamburg, Germany: F20 Foundations, Campaign for Nature and SEE Foundation, 2020); Sassan S. Saatchi et al., "Benchmark Map of Forest Carbon Stocks in Tropical Regions across Three Continents," *Proceedings of the National Academy of Sciences of the United States of America* 108 (2011): 9899.

[3] Adopted December 12, 2015, entered into force November 4, 2016, 55 I.L.M. 740.

[4] Douglas Morton, head of the Biospheric Sciences Laboratory at NASA's Goddard Space Flight Center, notes that the timing and location of the fires were more consistent with land clearing than with regional drought. See "The Amazon Is on Fire—How Bad Is It?" *BBC News* (August 30, 2019); "Bolivian Wildfires Destroy Two Million Hectares of Forest," *BBC News* (September 10, 2019). See also Instituto Nacional de Pesquisas Espaciais, "Programas Instituto Nacional de Pesquisas Espaciais," accessed December 6, 2024, https://terrabrasilis.dpi.inpe.br.

[5] Bolivia, Brazil, Colombia, Ecuador, Guyana, Peru, and Suriname.

Beatriz Garcia, *The Promise of Environmental Cooperation in Latin America* In: *Latin American International Law in the Twenty-First Century*. Edited by: Alejandro Chehtman, Alexandra Huneeus, and Sergio Puig, Oxford University Press. © Oxford University Press 2025. DOI: 10.1093/9780197754016.003.0028

the Leticia Pact in 2019.[6] The Pact is a declaration of intent aimed at improving disaster response coordination. Still, it is yet to define future targets, resources, measurable actions, and milestones to tackle deforestation and mitigate fires.[7]

Beyond their common history, languages, and culture, Latin American countries share rivers, transboundary species, and ecosystems. These countries also share similar environmental problems—such as deforestation and forest degradation, biodiversity loss, wildlife trafficking, and water pollution—many of which require cooperation to be effectively addressed. Nevertheless, environmental cooperation has not been a significant feature in Latin America, particularly regarding forest conservation. There are several areas where regional cooperation is increasingly required but not sufficiently used—regarding, for instance, the protection and restoration of forests, including building resilience against forest fires;[8] the control of illegal activities, such as logging, agricultural conversion, gold mining, and wildlife trade; and the management of migratory species and shared ecosystems, such as transboundary protected areas and international watercourses. Can these problems be handled through regional cooperation based upon international law norms and principles, or is this primarily the role of individual states under domestic law?

There is extensive literature on the promise and hurdles of collective action in natural resource management, notably based on game theory.[9] From a legal standpoint, there has been significant academic debate on the limits of international law in ensuring the equitable use of transboundary natural resources and enabling international cooperation.[10] For instance, scholars have looked at how the implementation of and compliance with international treaties, including environmental agreements, can be strengthened,[11] which international

[6] Pacto de Leticia por la Amazonía, adopted September 6, 2019.

[7] Maria Antonia Tigre, "COVID-19 and Amazonia: Rights-Based Approaches for the Pandemic Response," *RECIEL* 162 (2021): 166.

[8] Edward A Morgan, Timothy Cadman, and Brendan Mackey, "Integrating Forest Management across the Landscape: A Three Pillar Framework," *Journal of Environmental Planning and Management* 64 (2021): 1735.

[9] As noted by Eyal Benvenisti, *Sharing Transboundary Resources: International Law and Optimal Resource Use* (Cambridge: Cambridge University Press, 2002), 33; Herbert Arthur Smith, *The Economic Uses of International Rivers* (1st ed., London: PS King 1931), 224.

[10] Daniel Bodansky, "Implementation of International Environmental Law," *Japanese Yearbook of International Law* 54 (2011): 62. For an earlier example, see L. F. E. Goldie, "Equity and the International Management of Transboundary Resources," *Natural Resources Journal* 25 (1985): 665.

[11] Edith Brown Weiss and Harold K Jacobson (eds.), *Engaging Countries, Strengthening Compliance with Environmental Accords* (Cambridge, MA: MIT Press, 1998), 515. This is the case of the Montreal Protocol on Substances that Deplete the Ozone Layer, adopted September 16, 1987, entered into force January 1, 1989, 1522 U.N.T.S. 3; and the Convention on the Prevention of Marine Pollution by Dumping of Wastes and Other Matter, adopted November 13, 1972, entered into force August 30, 1975, 1046 U.N.T.S. 138, when compared to other treaties—that is, the Convention Concerning the Protection of the World Cultural and Natural Heritage, adopted November 16, 1972, entered into force December 17, 1975, 1037 U.N.T.S. 151; the Convention on International Trade in Endangered Species of Wild Fauna and Flora, adopted March 3, 1973, entered into force July 1, 1975,

mechanisms to protect shared natural resources are effective,[12] and whether international law can create incentives for states to cooperate.[13] Transboundary natural resources are those to which only a few states have access, such as rivers and lakes, fisheries, hydrocarbon and mineral deposits, forests, and migratory species.[14] Historically, the principle of permanent and full sovereignty over natural resources has hindered the ideal that transboundary natural resources should be treated as shared and regulated by norms beyond each state's unilateral interests and national law.[15] It should be noted, however, that these resources are not all equal. While international rivers and lakes, fisheries, and air unequivocally transcend borders, other natural resources, such as forests, are confined within well-defined national borders. This is one of the reasons countries in Latin America and elsewhere have usually opposed global rules on forests and see forests primarily as a matter of national concern. These claims have been grounded on the principle of national sovereignty over natural resources.

Beyond the discussion of where regional cooperation may be most needed in Latin America, it is worth investigating *how* regional cooperation should take place. Is it time to move from the general provisions and nonprescriptive language that characterize most Latin American environmental agreements to more specific legal obligations? Would more prescriptive legal obligations lead to more targeted actions and real outcomes?[16] Against this background, this chapter investigates current forms of environmental cooperation in Latin America and examines whether new pathways could be open, especially regarding forest conservation, given new regulatory trends focused on global supply chains targeting commodities associated with deforestation and forest degradation. This discussion is relevant for Latin American countries because agricultural and forestry products represent a large share of their domestic markets, while commodity exports, particularly to China and the United States, are likely to grow.[17] This

993 U.N.T.S. 243; and the International Tropical Timber Agreement, adopted November 18, 1983, entered into force April 1, 1985, 1393 U.N.T.S. 671.

[12] Julio Barberis, "International Effects of Noncompliance with Environmental Standards," *Pace Environmental Law Review* 13 (1996): 607; Justry Patrick Lumumba Nyaberi, "Historical Analysis: Does International Environmental Law Provide Effective Environmental Protection?" *Journal of Environmental Policy and Law* 46 (2016): 408; Victoria Jenkins, "Sustainable Management of Natural Resources: Lessons from Wales," *Journal of Environmental Law* 30 (2018): 399. For a regionally specific example, see Justine Bendel and Tim Stephens, "Turning to International Litigation to Protect the Amazon?" *RECIEL* 30 (2021): 173.

[13] Benvenisti, *Sharing Transboundary Resources*, 161.

[14] Ibid., 3.

[15] Ibid., 18.

[16] Harold K. Jacobson and Edith Brown Weiss, "Assessing the Record and Designing Strategies to Engage Countries," in *Engaging Countries: Strengthening Compliance with Environmental Accords*, ed. Edith Brown Weiss and Harold K. Jacobson, 525 (Cambridge, MA: MIT Press, 1998).

[17] See Beatriz Garcia and Laurent Pauwels, "La Lucha contra la Deforestación a Través de las Cadenas de Suministro Globales: Una Oportunidad de Reenfocar la Cooperación Ambiental en América Latina," *AJIL Unbound* 116 (2022): 352.

leads to whether international norms targeting global supply chains could be instrumental in reshaping Latin American forest conservation efforts. The argument is that these regulations might provide an opportunity to refocus Latin American cooperation on more tangible actions toward forest and biodiversity conservation.

II. Trends in Forest Conservation Focusing on Global Supply Chains

Economic incentives targeting governments, businesses, and individuals for forest conservation are a popular approach to combatting tropical deforestation.[18] This is what the recent Regulation (EU) 2023/1115 of the European Parliament and of the Council *on the making available on the Union market and the export from the Union of certain commodities and products associated with deforestation* (EUDR) aims to achieve.[19] The Regulation covers commodities representing the largest share of EU-driven deforestation,[20] and its cornerstone is the prohibition of trading deforestation-linked products on the EU market.[21] Producer countries are motivated to produce sustainably if they wish to access the EU market rather than have their commodities rejected for not complying with EU standards. This practice is not new. For example, in the agricultural sector, countries set national and international standards for the trade of certain commodities, such as sanitary and phytosanitary measures, to reduce the risks of animal or plant diseases being introduced in their markets.[22] Other examples include legislation that prohibits the placing of illegal timber and timber products on internal markets, adopted by the EU, the United States, and

[18] See ibid. See also Kelly W. Jones et al., *Forest Conservation Incentives and Deforestation in the Ecuadorian Amazon* (Cambridge: Cambridge University Press, 2016).

[19] Regulation (EU) 2023/1115 of the European Parliament and of the Council of 31 May 2023, Official Journal of the European Union L 150/206 (EUDR). See also Proposal for a Regulation of the European Parliament and of the Council on making available on the EU market as well as exporting from the EU certain commodities and products associated with deforestation and forest degradation and repealing Regulation (EU) No 995/2010, COM(2021) 706 final (2021) (EU 2021 Proposal).

[20] EUDR preamble, recital 38.

[21] EUDR, art. 3.

[22] Examples include Council Regulation (EC) 882/2004 of April 29, 2004, on official controls performed to ensure the verification of compliance with feed and food law, animal health and animal welfare rules [2004] OJ L165/1; Commission Regulation (EC) 669/2009 of July 24, 2009, implementing Regulation (EC) No. 882/2004 of the European Parliament and of the Council as regards the increased level of official controls on imports of certain feed and food of non-animal origin and amending Decision 2006/504/EC, [2004] OJL 194/11; Council Directive (EC) 2000/29/EC of May 8, 2000, on protective measures against the introduction into the Community of organisms harmful to plants or plant products and against their spread within the Community [2000] OJL 169/1.

Australia,[23] as well as international guidelines, such as the Conflict-Free Gold Standard implemented by the World Gold Council member companies and other entities involved in the extraction of gold.[24] The novelty of the EUDR is in proposing *deforestation-free supply chains* for agricultural commodities linked to deforestation to protect forests, particularly primary forests.[25]

As noted earlier, the EUDR could help transform existing, albeit weak, Latin American environmental cooperation into something tangible—for example, targeting agricultural expansion, a major driver of deforestation in Latin American countries, by building deforestation-free supply chains. Despite the global relevance of the region's forests and biodiversity, regional cooperation in Latin America has remained limited in terms of forest conservation and restoration, as previously mentioned.[26] Collective efforts to address the main drivers of deforestation could, then, be a step forward in meeting the goals of the Paris Agreement and the emission reduction targets proposed by Latin American countries under their nationally determined contributions.

Looking forward, regional cooperation might be required to tackle the trade of forest-risk commodities—such as soy, cattle, timber, and gold—in domestic and international markets. Commodities associated with deforestation are consumed largely in national markets, but this is not uniform across commodities. For example, while nearly 64 percent of Brazil's soy production is exported, only 33 percent of its cattle production is directly exported.[27] Currently, domestic consumption of resources and manufactured products from commodities in Latin America dominates exports; however, with increased consumption from the growing population and from the industrialization of Latin American countries, as well as large economies such as China and India, the demand for Latin American commodities will continue to grow.[28] Ultimately, international norms such as the EUDR may trickle down supply and broadly change trade practices. Other developed countries will likely follow the European Union in setting standards for deforestation-free supply chains. Therefore, Latin American countries may need to change their production and commercial practices to meet higher forest conservation standards and access export markets. Regional efforts

[23] See Beatriz Garcia and Jonathan Verschuuren, "Complying with Australia's Illegal Logging Laws: Tough Reality after a Soft Start? Lessons from the United States and the European Union," *Asia Pacific Journal of Environmental Law* 22 (2019): 7.

[24] World Gold Council, Conflict-Free Gold Standard, October 2012.

[25] EUDR, art. 2 (13); See also Beatriz Garcia and Laurent Pauwels, "La Lucha contra la Deforestación a Través de las Cadenas de Suministro Globales: Una Oportunidad de Reenfocar la Cooperación Ambiental en América Latina," *AJIL Unbound* 116 (2022): 354.

[26] Michelle-Ann Williams, "Regional Environmental Agreements and Initiatives in the Americas," *Yearbook of International Environmental Law* 18 (2007): 74.

[27] Data from 2021/2022 harvest: Ministério da Agricultura, Pecuária e Abastecimento, *Projeções do Agronegócio: Brasil 2020/21 a 2030/31* (2021).

[28] Garcia and Pauwels, "La Lucha contra la Deforestación."

made so far toward forest and biodiversity conservation are discussed in section III.

III. Latin American Environmental Cooperation

Latin American countries began to adopt bilateral and regional cooperation treaties following their independence from the European colonial powers. They created their own regional organizations, most of which currently possess an environmental agenda.[29] Regional cooperation in Latin America has evolved in response to the shared geography, ecology, cultures, and economies in the region,[30] predominantly regarding transboundary natural resources such as international rivers, marine conservation, and fisheries. Almost all American countries are also parties to the major multilateral environmental agreements.[31]

Early examples of regional cooperation treaties in the Americas include the 1940 Convention on Nature Protection and Wildlife Preservation in the Western Hemisphere,[32] aimed at protecting native flora and fauna, scenery, and geologic formations.[33] During the 1970s, various bilateral treaties were adopted in Latin America to increase environmental awareness, which led to the 1972 United Nations Conference on the Human Environment held in Stockholm.[34] These included treaties on forests, wildlife protection, public health and sanitation, and cultural and scientific exchange.[35] Regional treaties were also adopted to conserve certain sites, shared ecosystems, and native species. Examples include the 1976 Convention on the Protection of the Archaeological, Historical, and Artistic Heritage of the American Nations, signed under the Organization of American States;[36] the 1978 Amazon Cooperation Treaty;[37] and the 1979 Convention for the Conservation and Management of the Vicuna.[38] Later on, states signed environmental cooperation agreements regarding natural resources in border

[29] See Beatriz Garcia, *The Amazon from an International Law Perspective* (Cambridge: Cambridge University Press, 2011).

[30] Williams, "Regional Environmental Agreements and Initiatives in the Americas," 65.

[31] Ibid., 68.

[32] Adopted October 12, 1940, entered into force May 1, 1942, 161 U.N.T.S. 193. See Simon Lyster, *International Wildlife Law: An Analysis of International Treaties Concerned with the Conservation of Wildlife* (Cambridge: Cambridge University Press, 1993).

[33] Article 1.

[34] Heraldo Muñoz, *Environment and Diplomacy in the Americas* (Boulder, CO: Lynne Rienner, 1992), 1.

[35] See Garcia, *The Amazon from an International Law Perspective*, chap. 6.

[36] Adopted June 16, 1976, entered into force September 27, 1978, 15 I.L.M. 1350. Parties include Costa Rica, Ecuador, El Salvador, Guatemala, Nicaragua, Panama, and Peru.

[37] Adopted July 3, 1978, entered into force August 12, 1980, 1202 U.N.T.S. 51. Parties include Bolivia, Brazil, Colombia, Guyana, Ecuador, Peru, Suriname, and Venezuela.

[38] Adopted December 20, 1979, entered into force March 19, 1982, IELMT 979: 94. Parties include Argentina, Bolivia, Chile, Ecuador, and Peru.

areas, such as the 1987 Agreement on the Protection and Improvement of the Environment in the Border Area between Mexico and Guatemala[39] and the 1990 Treaty between Brazil and Bolivia on the Preservation, Conservation and Monitoring of Natural Resources in Border Areas,[40] which controls the illegal trade of fauna and flora species.[41]

Regional cooperation in Latin America has also extended to international watercourses. Examples of treaties regulating the management of shared rivers and aquifers adopted by two or more states include the 1969 La Plata River Basin Treaty,[42] the 1973 Itaipu Treaty,[43] and the 2010 Guarani Aquifer Agreement.[44] Similar efforts have been made to protect the marine environment and migratory fishing stocks—for example, under the 1983 Convention for the Protection and Development of the Marine Environment in the Wider Caribbean Region (Cartagena Convention)[45] and the 1996 Inter-American Convention for the Protection and Conservation of Sea Turtles,[46] as well as through the establishment of the Inter-American Tropical Tuna Commission.[47] Given the links between trade and the environment, regional trade agreements have also incorporated environmental provisions,[48] such as the 1993 North American Agreement on Environmental Cooperation[49] under the former North American Free Trade Agreement[50] and the MERCOSUR 2001 Framework Agreement on the Environment.[51]

[39] Adopted April 10, 1987, entered into force March 22, 1988, 1509 U.N.T.S. 184. Parties include Mexico and Guatemala.

[40] *Brazilian Official Gazette*, April 14, 1999, 1.

[41] Article 5.

[42] La Plata River Basin Treaty, signed between Argentina, Bolivia, Brazil, Paraguay, and Uruguay on April 23, 1969, entered into force August 14, 1970, 875 U.N.T.S. 3.

[43] Itaipu Treaty signed by Brazil and Paraguay, Law 5,899/1973, adopted April 26, 1976, 923 U.N.T.S. 92.

[44] Adopted August 2, 2010, entered into force November 26, 2020. Parties include Argentina, Brazil, Paraguay, and Uruguay.

[45] Adopted March 24, 1983, entered into force October 11, 1986, 22 I.L.M. 1983. Parties include several American countries. See United Nations Environment Programme, "Cartagena Convention" (August 2021), accessed December 6, 2024, www.unep.org/cep/who-we-are/cartagena-convention.

[46] Adopted December 1, 1996, entered into force May 2, 2001, 2164 U.N.T.S. 29. Parties include several American countries. See ECOLEX, "Inter-American Convention for the Protection and Conservation of Sea Turtles," accessed December 6, 2024, www.ecolex.org/details/treaty/inter-american-convention-for-the-protection-and-conservation-of-sea-turtles-tre-001250/.

[47] Convention for the Establishment of an Inter-American Tropical Tuna Commission, adopted May 29, 1949, entered into force March 3, 1950, 80 U.N.T.S. 3. Parties include several American countries.

[48] Williams, "Regional Environmental Agreements and Initiatives in the Americas," 66.

[49] Adopted September 14, 1993, entered into force January 1, 1994, 32 I.L.M. 1480.

[50] Signed December 17, 1992, entered into force January 1, 1994, 32 I.L.M. 670 (NAFTA). The current agreement is the 2018 United States–Mexico–Canada Agreement, also known as the USMCA or "New NAFTA," adopted November 30, 2018, entered into force July 1, 2020.

[51] Adopted July 22, 2001, entered into force June 23, 2004, MERCOSUR/CMC/DEC No 2/01 436. Parties include Argentina, Brazil, Paraguay, and Uruguay.

In contrast to the more robust legal frameworks regarding freshwater and marine conservation, only a few treaties deal with forests in Latin America.[52] The only "forest agreement"[53] is the 1978 Amazon Cooperation Treaty, which involves eight South American countries sharing the Amazon region. The parties agreed to promote the development of the Amazon while ensuring the rational use of its natural resources through joint actions and efforts.[54] The treaty is based on the commitment to cooperate in different areas—for example, to rationally use water resources,[55] improve the navigation of Amazonian rivers,[56] and preserve native species of fauna and flora.[57] The Amazon Cooperation Treaty Organization was created in 2002 with a permanent secretariat based in Brasilia.[58] It currently supports regional projects on forest monitoring,[59] biodiversity conservation,[60] and wildlife species threatened by trade.[61]

Overall, the legal instruments adopted by Latin American countries contain a general duty to cooperate regarding international watercourses, marine resources, wildlife, health, and sanitation, as noted above.[62] These treaties, however, often lack specific legal obligations—setting targets and timetables, requiring parties to act in a certain way, and creating mechanisms to monitor and evaluate treaty implementation. The procedural obligations in these treaties often involve the duty to exchange information, conduct regular meetings, and designate national focal points to oversee national implementation.[63] For example, the Sea Turtle Convention and the Amazon Cooperation Treaty provide for the establishment of meetings of the parties with different functions, such as exchanging information, negotiating and adopting common policies

[52] Williams, "Regional Environmental Agreements and Initiatives in the Americas," 74.

[53] Ibid.

[54] Article 1.

[55] Article 5.

[56] Article 6.

[57] Article 7.

[58] Under the Protocol of Amendment to the Amazon Cooperation Treaty, adopted December 14, 1998, entered into force August 2, 2002, 2199 U.N.T.S. 163.

[59] Project "Monitoring of Deforestation, Forest Use and Changes in Land Use in the Pan Amazonian Forest," accessed December 6, 2024, http://otca.org/en/ctp_otca_projetos/monitoring-project-of-forest-cover-in-the-amazon-region-monitoring-of-deforestation-forest-use-and-changes-in-land-use-in-the-pan-amazon-forest/.

[60] Project "Institutional Strengthening of the Member Countries of ACTO in Forest Management Environmentally Responsible and Conservation of Biodiversity in Managed Forests of the Amazon," accessed December 6, 2024, http://otca.org/en/ctp_otca_projetos/project-institutional-strengthening-of-acto-member-countries-in-ecologically-responsible-forest-management-and-conservation-of-biodiversity-in-the-managed-forests-of-the-amazon-itto-cbd-acto/.

[61] "Bioamazon Project–Conservation of Species Threatened by Unsustainable Trade," accessed December 6, 2024, http://otca.org/en/ctp_otca_projetos/regional-project-for-the-management-monitoring-and-control-of-species-of-wild-fauna-and-flora-threatened-by-trade-bioamazon-project-conservation-of-species-threatened-by-unsustainable-trade/.

[62] See Garcia, *The Amazon from an International Law Perspective*, chap. 6.

[63] Ibid.

and additional rules, and monitoring compliance with the law.[64] Nevertheless, under the Amazon Cooperation Treaty, these meetings have not occurred regularly or created new and more precise legal obligations via treaty amendments and protocols. Consequently, the general duty to cooperate enunciated in the Amazon Cooperation Treaty has not been translated into legal obligations requiring the parties to take specific actions or to achieve results.[65] Moreover, treaty bodies usually lack the financial resources and technical expertise to address environmental concerns and ensure collective action.[66] Therefore, bilateral and regional environmental treaties have often had little practical impact due to a combination of factors that include the lack of legal obligations of an imperative or obligatory nature, weak compliance and enforcement mechanisms, and insufficient financial and human resources.

Despite their promise as cooperation tools, many treaties have failed to yield practical measures or foster enduring cooperation. The examples of broad regional cooperation discussed here indicate the ability of Latin American countries to garner political will around common environmental concerns, but what is needed is to transform the expressed political commitments into more substantial institutional and normative commitments.[67]

IV. National Environmental Law in Latin America

The natural resources of Latin American countries are generally recognized as part of the national patrimony or heritage of the state, which is sovereign in their utilization.[68] The sovereign right to use natural resources is often enunciated with the associated duty of the state to protect the diversity and integrity of the environment and to conserve areas of particular ecological importance.[69] Various Latin American constitutions explicitly recognize the right to a healthy environment[70] and the obligation of the state to defend and preserve that right.[71] States must effectively plan the use of natural resources to guarantee their sustainable

[64] Sea ECOLEX, "Inter-American Convention for the Protection and Conservation of Sea Turtles," art. 5; Amazon Cooperation Treaty, art. 20.

[65] See Rüdiger Wolfrum, "Obligation of Result versus Obligation of Conduct: Some Thoughts about the Implementation of International Obligations," in *Looking to the Future: Essays on International Law in Honor of W. Michael Reisman*, ed. Mahnoush H Arsanjani et al. (Leiden, The Netherlands: Brill, 2011).

[66] Williams, "Regional Environmental Agreements and Initiatives in the Americas," 93.

[67] Ibid., 95.

[68] 1993 Constitution of Peru, art. 66.

[69] 1991 Constitution of Colombia, art. 79; 1993 Constitution of Peru, art. 66.

[70] 1991 Constitution of Colombia, art 79; 2008 Constitution of Ecuador, arts. 1, 14; 1949 Constitution of Costa Rica, art. 50.

[71] 1949 Constitution of Costa Rica, art. 50.

development, conservation, restoration, or replacement.[72] National laws and environmental policies determine the conditions for using natural resources.[73] Some national constitutions impose a specific obligation on the state to protect the Amazon using appropriate legislation,[74] given its importance to the planet's environmental balance.[75] Some states also recognize the duty to cooperate with other nations to protect ecosystems in border areas.[76]

Because of their status as national patrimony or heritage, forests have been mainly regulated by national law in Latin America—for instance, through forest codes, national policies to prevent and control deforestation, and biodiversity and protected areas legislation.[77] For example, Brazil's 2012 Forest Code[78] sets norms for the management of native vegetation and creates different forms of protection depending on the types of forest areas. Despite these national laws, the recent widespread forest fires in the Brazilian Amazon and the high rates of deforestation during the Bolsonaro years have brought the question of Amazon conservation to the forefront of international debate.[79] The implementation of national and international environmental laws and their effectiveness in protecting the environment has also been the subject of extensive academic debate.[80]

There are significant examples of forest conservation efforts at the national level, based on domestic laws and policies and in the form of market-based instruments, such as forest certification, payments for ecosystem services (PES), and carbon mitigation schemes.[81] Many of these national schemes use

[72] 1991 Constitution of Colombia, art. 80.

[73] 1993 Constitution of Peru, art. 66; 2008 Constitution of Ecuador, arts. 391, 397(4), 400.

[74] 1993 Constitution of Peru, art. 69.

[75] 2008 Constitution of Ecuador, art. 250.

[76] 1991 Constitution of Colombia, arts. 80, 289.

[77] Garcia and Pauwels, "La Lucha contra la Deforestación."

[78] Law 12.651, May 25, 2012.

[79] See data from Brazil's National Institute for Space Research: National Institute for Space Research, accessed December 6, 2024. "PRODES-Amazônia," www.obt.inpe.br/OBT/assuntos/programas/amazonia/prodes. See Ricardo Pereira and Beatriz Garcia, "The Legal Protection of the Amazon Rainforest," *RECIEL* 30 (2021): 157.

[80] Neil Hawke, *Environmental Policy: Implementation and Enforcement* (London: Routledge, 2018); S. Maljean-Dubois and L. Rajamani, *Implementation of International Environmental Law* (Leiden, The Netherlands Brill, 2011); Paul Martin, Ben Boer, and Lydia Slobodian (eds.), *Framework for Assessing and Improving Law for Sustainability* (Geneva, Switzerland: International Union for Conservation of Nature, 2016); Paul Martin and Amanda Kennedy (eds.), *Implementing Environmental Law* (Cheltenham, UK: Edward Elgar, 2017); Brian Tomasovic, "Tradeoffs in Environmental Law," *Journal of Land Use and Environmental Law* 34 (2019): 93; Shirley Scott, "Does the UNFCCC Fulfil the Functions Required of a Framework Convention? Why Abandoning the United Nations Framework Convention on Climate Change Might Constitute a Long Overdue Step Forward," *Journal of Environmental Law* 27 (2015): 69. For an earlier example of this ongoing discourse, see Mary Ellen O'Connell, "Enforcement and the Success of International Environmental Law," *Indiana Journal of Global Legal Studies* 3 (1995): 47.

[81] See Edward A. Morgan et al., "Capturing Multiple Forest Ecosystem Services for Just Benefit Sharing: The Basket of Benefits Approach," *Ecosystem Services* 55 (2022): 101421.

forest conservation incentives—such as payments, loans, or tax incentives—directed to landholders and/or communities for their efforts to protect forests and biodiversity. For example, Ecuador's Socio Bosque program, created in 2008 and administered by the Ministry of the Environment, involves twenty-year contracts with landowners who commit to protect forest areas in exchange for payments granted by the government.[82] A condition for enrollment in the program is to possess a clear and uncontested land title.[83] Likewise, a well-studied PES scheme in Costa Rica makes direct payments from the National Forestry Fund (FONAFIFO) to private landowners based on five-year contracts involving activities related to forest protection, reforestation, sustainable forest management, or agroforestry.[84] The landowners transfer the "rights" for ecosystem services to FONAFIFO, which then sells credits to different buyers. PES schemes usually operate on a payment-by-results basis, with payments dependent on audited and verified outcomes.[85] Latin American countries have also engaged in carbon offset markets, by which project proponents—either communities or individual landowners—develop forest carbon projects such as REDD+ (Reducing Emissions from Deforestation and Forest Degradation) that generate tradable carbon credits, with the sales paid back to the project proponents.[86]

Other national initiatives target certain agricultural commodities associated with deforestation. These include Brazil's soy moratorium,[87] by which companies agreed not to purchase soy produced on forest land cleared after July 2006. Led by the soy industry, this voluntary and non-legally binding agreement was established in 2006 following demands from non-governmental organizations and civil society concerning deforestation in the Brazilian Amazon. Despite some

[82] Ina T. Porras and Nigel Asquith, *Ecosystems, Poverty Alleviation and Conditional Transfers* (London: International Institute for Environment and Development, 2018); Melissa Bollman and Scott D Hardy, "Institutional Rules in Action: A Multi-Level Analysis of Costa Rica's Payments for Environmental Services Programme," *Carbon & Climate Law Review* 5 (2011): 357; FONAFIFO, CONAFOR, and Ministry of Environment, *Lessons Learned for REDD+ from PES and Conservation Incentive Programs: Examples from Costa Rica, Mexico, and Ecuador* (Washington, DC: World Bank 2012), https://doi.org/10.1596/27164; Stefano Pagiola, "Payments for Environmental Services in Costa Rica," *Ecological Economics* 65 (2008): 712 <https://doi.org/10.1016/j.ecolecon.2007.07.033>; Brian C. Steed, "Government Payments for Ecosystem Services–Lessons from Costa Rica," *Journal of Land Use and Environmental Law* 23 (2007): 177; James Salzman et al., "Payments for Ecosystem Services: Past, Present and Future," *Texas A&M Law Review* 6 (2018): 199.

[83] Jones et al., *Forest Conservation Incentives and Deforestation in the Ecuadorian Amazon.*

[84] Morgan et al., "Capturing Multiple Forest Ecosystem Services for Just Benefit Sharing," 101421.

[85] Ibid.

[86] See Beatriz Garcia et al., "REDD+ and Forest Protection on Indigenous Lands in the Amazon," *RECIEL* 30 (2021): 207.

[87] Garcia and Pauwels, "La Lucha contra la Deforestación." See also Maria-Augusta Paim, "Zero Deforestation in the Amazon: The Soy Moratorium and Global Forest Governance," *RECIEL* 20 (2021): 220.

loopholes, the moratorium has helped reduce the direct conversion of land for soy production in the Amazon.[88]

Beyond those normative and voluntary initiatives, recent lawsuits in Latin America—some of which are based on the "rights of nature" doctrine[89]—may also introduce new forms of environmental protection and give effect to environmental law. The rights of nature doctrine recognizes that an ecosystem has the right to exist, flourish, regenerate its vital cycles, and naturally evolve without human-caused disruption. As such, an ecosystem can be declared a "subject of rights" and have the right to legal representation by a guardian—much like a charitable trust designates a trustee.[90] In 2018, in Colombia's *Future Generations v Ministry of the Environment* case,[91] a group of young plaintiffs filed a special constitutional claim (known as *tutela*), alleging that their fundamental rights to a healthy environment, life, health, food, and water were threatened by climate change and the government's failure to reduce deforestation in the Amazon. In this case, the Supreme Court recognized the Colombian Amazon as a "subject of rights"[92] like the Constitutional Court recognized the Atrato River in Choco, Colombia. Accordingly, the court declared that the Colombian Amazon was entitled to "protection, conservation, maintenance and restoration."[93] Likewise, in the Argentinean case *Asociación Civil por la Justicia Ambiental v Province of Entre Ríos et al.*,[94] the plaintiffs requested that the court declare the Paraná Delta a subject of rights and designate a "guardian" of its rights, who should be responsible for the conservation and sustainable use of its wetlands. In *Alvarez et al.*

[88] Paim, "Zero Deforestation in the Amazon," 224, citing Associação Brasileira das Indústrias e Óleos Vegetais, "Moratória Da Soja (Safra 2018/19): Monitoramento Por Imagens de Satélites Dos Plantios de Soja Em Desconformidade Com a Moratória Da Soja" 32 (2020).

[89] Oliver A. Houck, "Noah's Second Voyage: The Rights of Nature as Law," *Tulane Environmental Law Journal* 31 (2017): 1; Allison McKenzie, "Rights of Nature: The Evolution of Personhood Rights," *Joule: Duquesne Energy and Environmental Law Journal* 9 (2021): 27.

[90] See Tiffany Challe-Campiz, "The Rights of Nature–Can an Ecosystem Bear Legal Rights?" *Climate Law* (April 22, 2021), accessed December 6, 2024, https://blogs.law.columbia.edu/climatechange/2021/04/22/the-rights-of-nature-can-an-ecosystem-bear-legal-rights/; David R. Boyd, *The Rights of Nature: A Legal Revolution That Could Save the World* (Toronto: ECW Press, 2017); Christopher Stone, *Should Trees Have Standing? Law, Morality and the Environment* (Oxford: Oxford University Press, 2010); Cormac Cullinan, *Wild Law: A Manifesto for Earth Justice* (Newark, NJ: Green Books, 2011).

[91] Supreme Court of Justice of Columbia, STC4360-2018, No 11001-22-03-000-2018-00319-01 (2018). See further Brian J. Preston, "The Evolving Role of Environmental Rights in Climate Change Litigation," *Chinese Journal of Environmental Law* 2 (2018): 131, 156.

[92] *Future Generations*, 45 [14] (Reporting Judge Luis Armando Tolosa Villabona), accessed December 6, 2024, https://climatecasechart.com/non-us-case/future-generation-v-ministry-environment-others/

[93] Ibid.

[94] Supreme Court of Justice of the Argentine Nation, complaint filed February 7, 2020, decision pending. Transcript of the original filing, accessed December 6, 2024, https://climatecasechart.com/non-us-case/asociacion-civil-por-la-justicia-ambiental-v-province-of-entre-rios-et-al/.

v. Peru,[95] a group of Peruvian youths demanded the development of an action plan to reduce deforestation in the Peruvian Amazon to zero by 2025. It sought the recognition of the Peruvian Amazon as an entity subject to the rights of protection, conservation, maintenance, and restoration, referencing other nature rights cases in Ecuador, Colombia, and New Zealand. These and other lawsuits using a climate litigation approach provide avenues for demanding compliance by governments and businesses with environmental law.[96]

V. Regulatory Measures Tackling Deforestation and Forest Degradation in Tropical Countries

Without a global treaty on forests, the United Nations Framework Convention on Climate Change[97] has been a crucial forum in the international debate on forest conservation—including market mechanisms such as REDD+.[98] More recently, the Paris Agreement has urged states to conserve and enhance carbon sinks[99] as part of global climate mitigation efforts. Forest conservation has also inspired many declarations of intent, including the non-legally binding 1992 Forest Principles,[100] the 2014 New York Declaration on Forests,[101] and the more recent Glasgow Leaders' Declaration on Forests and Land Use, signed by several Latin American countries at COP-26 in 2021.[102] The last of these asserts

[95] Original filing, Constitutional Court of the Superior Court of Justice, Lima, December 10, 2019, decision pending. Transcript of the original filing, accessed December 6, 2024, https://climatecasechart.com/non-us-case/alvarez-et-al-v-peru/.

[96] Jacqueline Peel and Jolene Lin, "Transnational Climate Litigation: The Contribution of the Global South," *American Journal of International Law* 113 (2019): 679. See also Joana Setzer and Delton Carvalho, "Climate Litigation to Protect the Brazilian Amazon: Establishing a Constitutional Right to a Stable Climate," *RECIEL* 30 (2021): 197; Joana Setzer and Lisa Benjamin, "Climate Change Litigation in the Global South: Filling in the Gaps," *AJIL Unbound* 114 (2020): 56; Jacqueline Peel and Michael Power, "Climate Change Law: Lessons from the Californian Experience," *Environmental and Planning Law Journal* 27 (2010): 169; Cesar Rodriguez-Garavito, "Human Rights: The Global South's Route to Climate Litigation," *AJIL Unbound* 114 (2020): 40; Daniel G. Hare, "Blue Jeans, Chewing Gum and Climate Change Litigation: American Exports to Europe," *Merkourios-Utrecht Journal of International and European Law* 29 (2013): 65. For an earlier oversight of climate litigation in North America, see Julia Schatz, "Climate Change Litigation in Canada and the USA," *RECIEL* 18 (2013): 129.

[97] Adopted May 29, 1992, entered into force March 21, 1994, 1771 U.N.T.S. 107.

[98] Papua New Guinea and Costa Rica, "Reducing Emissions from Deforestation in Developing Countries: Approaches to Stimulate Action," UN Doc. FCCC/CP/2005/MISC.1 (November 11, 2005).

[99] New York Declaration on Forests Declaration and Action Agenda, Climate Summit 2014, September 23, 2012.

[100] Non-legally binding authoritative statement of principles for a global consensus on the management, conservation, and sustainable development of all types of forests, UN Doc. A/CONF.151/6 (April 21, 1992).

[101] New York Declaration on Forests Declaration and Action Agenda.

[102] Adopted November 12, 2021, accessed December 6, 2024, https://ukcop26.org/glasgow-leaders-declaration-on-forests-and-land-use/.

that trade and development policies are required to avoid commodity consumption and production continuing to drive deforestation and land degradation.[103] Some regulatory measures tackling deforestation, which are discussed here, aim to achieve that goal. These include the EUDR and timber regulations adopted by the EU and other markets.

The EUDR provides a template for forest conservation that targets global supply chains.[104] It applies to seven commodities and related products with the highest EU-embodied deforestation: cattle, cocoa, coffee, oil palm, rubber, soya and wood, called "relevant commodities."[105] The related products—listed in Annex I of the Regulation—contain, have been fed with, or have been made using the relevant commodities.[106] Being deforestation-free means that the relevant commodities and products were produced on land that has not been subject to deforestation after December 31, 2020.[107]

The rationale of the EUDR is to incentivize producers to implement sustainable production and ensure transparent supply chains. Compared to producers causing deforestation, those producers should gain in their share in the EU market and increase their competitiveness.[108]

The EUDR sets a demand-driven standard rather than imposing legal obligations on developing countries that have historically opposed global rules that are likely to limit their sovereign right to use their natural resources. However, there is ongoing discussion regarding the extraterritorial effects of the EUDR.[109] Under the Regulation, EU countries choose not to consume deforestation-linked products. In contrast, producing countries may choose to abide by the standard—although they have a financial incentive to produce sustainably to access the EU market. Other examples of demand-driven measures for tropical forest conservation include certification schemes and consumer campaigns.[110]

The EUDR targets operators who place relevant commodities and products on the EU market or export them from that market,[111] as well as traders who, during a commercial activity, make relevant commodities and products available

[103] Ibid., ¶ 2.

[104] Garcia and Pauwels, "La Lucha contra la Deforestación."

[105] Article 2(1).

[106] Article 2(2).

[107] Article 2(13).

[108] EU 2021 Proposal 9.

[109] Aline Beltrame de Moura, Carla Lerin, and Betina Machado Santos, 'Impactos extraterritoriais do Regulamento (UE) 2023/1115: a proibição da comercialização de matérias primas e produtos associados ao desmatamento e à degradação florestal' (2023) 8(2) *Revista de Ciências do Estado* 1.

[110] Martin Persson, Sabine Henders, and Thomas Kastner, "Trading Forests: Quantifying the Contribution of Global Commodity Markets to Emissions from Tropical Deforestation," Centre for Global Development, Working Paper 384 (October 2014).

[111] Art. 2(15).

on the EU market.[112] Its primary regulatory technique is a three-step due diligence process involving data collection, risk assessment, and risk mitigation.[113] The first step is to gather information regarding the relevant commodities and products; the second is to assess whether there is a risk that commodities and products entering the EU market are not compliant with the Regulation; and the third is to mitigate any risks to a negligible level.[114] Before placing commodities and products on the EU market or exporting them, due diligence should be performed. If there is no available information about the relevant commodities or products, or if associated risks cannot be mitigated, they should not be placed on the EU market.

Prior to the EUDR, other policies and regulations used similar techniques to target certain commodities, such as timber.[115] These include the EU Forest Law Enforcement Governance and Trade (FLEGT) Action Plan[116] and the EU Timber Regulation (EUTR),[117] which prohibited imports of illegally harvested timber into the European Union.[118] While these instruments tackle illegal logging and associated trade, they do not address deforestation and forest degradation more broadly.[119] The EUTR also introduces a due diligence process to ensure that companies collect, assess, and mitigate the risks of importing illegally harvested timber.[120] Other consumer countries worldwide have adopted similar legislative approaches. These include Australia, South Korea, Japan, and China; the last of these amended its Forest Law in 2019 to include a ban on buying, processing, and transporting illegal timber.[121] In the broader context of deforestation, this shows that the EU can impact and lead the way globally even with a decreasing market share.[122] Similar to what happened to the EUTR and subsequent timber regulations, other consumer countries are likely to introduce

[112] Article 2(17).

[113] Article 8.

[114] Article 11.

[115] Garcia and Pauwels, "La Lucha contra la Deforestación."

[116] Council Regulation (EC) 2173/2005/EC of December 20, 2005, on the establishment of a FLEGT licensing scheme for imports of timber into the European Community [2005] OJ L347/1, art. 4.1.

[117] Regulation (EU) 995/2010 of the European Parliament and of the Council laying down the obligations of operators who place timber and timber products on the market [2010] OJ L295/23.

[118] On timber regulations, see Garcia and Verschuuren, "Complying with Australia's Illegal Logging Laws: Tough Reality after a Soft Start?"

[119] Ibid., 2.

[120] Council Regulation (EU) 995/2010, art. 4.

[121] Commission Staff Working Document Fitness Check on Regulation (EU) No. 995/2010 of the European Parliament and of the Council of October 20, 2010, laying down the obligations of operators who place timber and timber products on the market (the EU Timber Regulation) and on Regulation (EC) No. 2173/2005 of December 20, 2005, on the establishment of a FLEGT licensing scheme for imports of timber into the European Community (FLEGT Regulation) Brussels, 17.11.2021 SWD (2021) 328 final 14 (Fitness Check).

[122] EU 2021 Proposal 6.

regulations targeting agricultural commodities that pose risks to forests or other ecosystems.

VI. What Role for Latin American Cooperation in Building Deforestation-Free Supply Chains?

Forests cover approximately 47 percent of Latin America's land area[123] and countries in the region face similar environmental problems, such as deforestation and biodiversity loss. Despite this, Latin American cooperation has not been strong in forest and biodiversity conservation. As proposed here, the EUDR and other similar norms could open a pathway for Latin American cooperation in reducing deforestation and forest degradation. Certainly, there are several challenges and issues associated with the EUDR, such as uncertainty about the robustness of its due diligence mechanism, its compatibility with World Trade Organization (WTO) rules,[124] and its potential extraterritorial reach, among others. Nevertheless, the EUDR could act as a trigger for mobilizing Latin American countries to address, both individually and collectively, agricultural-driven deforestation and forest degradation. What follows are some examples of how this could be done.

One of the challenges in implementing the EUDR—and other regulations concerning global commodity markets—is ensuring the availability and reliability of information on the relevant commodities and products. As noted earlier, EU operators must conduct a due diligence process to collect information and mitigate risks, if possible. It has proved challenging, however, for EU businesses to collect reliable product-specific information and assess associated risks conclusively.

In preparation for the EUDR, timber regulations and policies—notably the EUTR and FLEGT—were evaluated (called a "fitness check").[125] It revealed that one of the most critical issues for operators under the EUTR is the ability to verify the robustness of information on timber and timber products and to assess risks effectively, which are also steps required under the EUTR's due diligence process.[126] Weak governance and endemic corruption in the forest sector of many timber-producing countries often hinder requirements for improved transparency and information to fulfill due diligence obligations.

[123] Williams, "Regional Environmental Agreements and Initiatives in the Americas."

[124] Gracia Marín Durán, Joanne Scott, 'Regulating Trade in Forest-Risk Commodities: Two Cheers for the European Union' (2022) 34(2) *Journal of Environmental Law* 245.

[125] Garcia and Pauwels, "La Lucha contra la Deforestación."

[126] Fitness Check, 22.

The success of regulatory measures tackling tropical deforestation risks depends on cooperation with producing countries in Latin America and other tropical countries. In the context of the EUDR, the European Commission recognizes the need to engage with producer countries to support their transition to sustainable and transparent agricultural practices.[127] The challenges related to the operation of the due diligence obligation, identified in the EU fitness check document, will remain a central issue in the implementation of the EUDR. Partnerships and cooperation mechanisms to address this and other issues should involve, according to the European Union, structured dialogues, support programs, and actions aimed at ensuring the sustainable use of forests.[128] The Commission understands that it must work with and support producer countries in addressing the root causes of deforestation.[129] In this context, the following are some examples of where regional cooperation might be beneficial and contribute to global forest conservation efforts.

Regional cooperation could primarily be used to set regional standards for the sustainable production of forest-risk commodities. Other organizations, such as the ASEAN Tourism Standards, have set regional standards for specific industries.[130] The EUDR and other regulations tackling global supply chains use due diligence processes to ensure that businesses meet the traceability and information requirements imposed by law. This is where regional cooperation can play a role: it could be used to set regional standards for Latin American countries and businesses to ensure transparency in their commercial operations, notably in terms of the availability and quality of product-specific and other information required under due diligence processes or other requirements imposed by international regulations. Regional standards could guide relevant businesses about sustainable agricultural practices and commercial operations, which include generating and handling transparent and reliable information about relevant commodities and products. By doing so, Latin American producers may be better equipped to engage in the due diligence processes required under the EUDR and other similar regulations and ultimately access export markets. Common regional standards could also help minimize the risks of leakage, where companies may continue providing commodities and products from deforested land to domestic economies not subject to sustainability standards.[131]

Latin American countries already have regional cooperation frameworks—including, for example, the inter-American system—where states can discuss

[127] Article 28.

[128] Ibid.

[129] EUDR preamble, recital 27.

[130] ASEAN Secretariat, *ASEAN Tourism Standards* (2012), accessed December 6, 2024, https://asean.org/wp-content/uploads/images/2012/Economic/MATM/document/ASEAN%20Tourism%20Standards%20Book.pdf.

[131] Garcia and Pauwels, "La Lucha contra la Deforestación."

and adopt targeted actions aimed at forest and biodiversity conservation. This system comprises the Organization of American States, the Inter-American Development Bank, and other subregional organizations, such as the Andean Community, as well as trade blocs including the MERCOSUR, the Caribbean Community, and the Common Market. These organizations can provide a forum for debating and implementing joint actions regarding global supply chains and forest conservation.[132]

Looking forward, Latin American countries might develop their own national legal frameworks imposing further sustainability requirements on forest-risk commodities or introducing voluntary measures, like Brazil's soy moratorium. Consequently, if Latin American organizations, such as the Organization of American States, are already active in this space, they could provide useful guidance for individual states interested in developing national laws and policies to restrict the trade of forest-risk commodities and products. This might be needed because various commodities are consumed largely in national markets.[133] Regional cooperation could then be directed to assisting Latin American countries in developing domestic law, voluntary approaches, and mechanisms such as traceability tools for commodities associated with deforestation and forest degradation.

The EUDR imposes obligations on European operators and traders who place the relevant commodities on that market or export them from it.[134] However, the EU regulators have limited visibility into the supply chains, as they are downstream. This type of regulation would benefit from standards and/or regulations upstream of the supply chain—that is, in the (multiple) countries producing the goods subjected to the regulation.

VII. Conclusions

Environmental cooperation in Latin America is long-standing and has taken different forms—via cooperative measures foreseen under international treaties, decisions, and initiatives from regional organizations. While more significant regional cooperation efforts exist regarding certain transboundary resources, including watercourses and marine resources, forest conservation has been less explored for bilateral and regional cooperation. Some areas where regional cooperation is increasingly needed in terms of the protection and restoration of forests include building capacity against forest fires, controlling illegal activities,

[132] Williams, "Regional Environmental Agreements and Initiatives in the Americas," 94.
[133] Garcia and Pauwels, "La Lucha contra la Deforestación."
[134] Natural or legal persons must be established in the Union, see EUDR art. 2(21).

and managing migratory species and shared ecosystems. All these areas are probably better handled through collective action. This chapter has focused on one area where regional cooperation should be strengthened: agricultural expansion driven by global supply chains that pose risks to forests and other ecosystems.

Recent international regulations focused on global commodities associated with deforestation, such as the EUDR, could offer an avenue for Latin America to refocus and reshape cooperative efforts more actively toward forest and biodiversity protection. Despite the potential challenges related to its implementation, as mentioned earlier, the EUDR, and other similar regulations, could stimulate cooperative action among Latin American countries in developing deforestation-free supply chains, both in their domestic markets and as a regional practice.

Regional organizations, such as the Organization of American States, could play a role—for example, in setting regional standards for Latin American businesses to improve their agricultural and trade practices to reduce the environmental footprint of certain global commodities. Regional organizations could also provide useful guidance and support for individual Latin American countries in developing national laws and mechanisms targeting commodities and products linked to deforestation and forest degradation. Mobilizing national and regional cooperation efforts in this direction is particularly relevant, given that agricultural and forestry products represent a significant share of the domestic consumption and exports of Latin American states. Going forward, other consumer countries will likely join the European Union in setting higher environmental standards for global value chains. Therefore, Latin American countries can only benefit and become more competitive by preparing for export markets where the production and commercialization of forest-risk commodities may no longer be acceptable.

29

Can the Inter-American Court Tip Us toward Climate Justice?

Alexandra Huneeus

I. Introduction

In January 2023, Chile and Colombia requested that the Interamerican Court of Human Rights (IACtHR) render an advisory opinion on "the scope of State obligations . . . to respond to the climate emergency."[1] The petition was followed by an advisory opinion request before the International Court of Justice (ICJ) on the obligations of states to protect "the climate system and other parts of the environment from anthropogenic emissions of greenhouse gases [GHG]," and was preceded by a similar request before the International Tribunal for the Law of the Sea (ITLOS).[2] Meanwhile, the European Court of Human Rights (ECHR) held in April 2024 that states must take "measures for the substantial and progressive reduction of their respective GHG emission levels, with a view to reaching net neutrality within, in principle, the next three decades,"[3] and a cluster of climate justice cases are making their way through the Inter-American Commission on Human Rights (IACHR) which acts as the gateway to the Inter-American Court.[4]

The emerging climate docket of the international courts provides a site through which to examine Latin America's human rights system from a comparative perspective.[5] As this volume makes clear, if it wasn't already obvious, the

[1] Request for an Advisory Opinion on the Climate Emergency and Human Rights submitted to the Inter-American Court of Human Rights by the Republic of Colombia and the Republic of Chile, January 9, 2023, https://www.corteidh.or.cr/observaciones_oc_new.cfm?nId_oc=2634.

[2] Request for an Advisory Opinion of the International Court of Justice on the Obligations of States in Respect of Climate Change, U.N. G.A., March 1, 2023, A/77/L.58; Commission of Small Island States on Climate Change and International Law, Request for an Advisory Opinion, December 12, 2022, https://www.itlos.org/en/main/cases/list-of-cases/request-for-an-advisory-opinion-submitted-by-the-commission-of-small-island-states-on-climate-change-and-international-law-request-for-advisory-opinion-submitted-to-the-tribunal.

[3] *KlimaSeniorinnen v. Switzerland*, App. No. 53600/20, Eur. Ct. H.R., ¶ 548 (2024), https://hudoc.echr.coe.int/eng?i=002-13212.

[4] For contentious cases, litigants in the inter-American system must first file cases before the Inter-American Commission. If the Commission cannot resolve the case, it refers it to the Inter-American Court.

[5] this chapter focuses on international courts, as they play a unique role in the international system and are just now embarking on climate litigation. However, several international organizations

Alexandra Huneeus, *Can the Inter-American Court Tip Us toward Climate Justice?* In: *Latin American International Law in the Twenty-First Century*. Edited by: Alejandro Chehtman, Alexandra Huneeus, and Sergio Puig, Oxford University Press.
DOI: 10.1093/9780197754016.003.0029

Inter-American Human Rights System (IAHRS) is one of the unique and most influential features of Latin American international law in the twenty-first century. Now, the Inter-American Court, alongside its fellow international courts, is being called to weigh in on the most intractable issue of our time. What will it be able to offer?

Admittedly, it would be delusional to put much stock in what an international court can do in the face of the climate emergency, let alone a court on a shoestring budget in Central America (the IACtHR sits in Costa Rica). The turn to international courts is an act of despair for those who are most vulnerable to climate change, particularly small island developing states (SIDS).[6] The Intergovernmental Panel on Climate Change reports that under the current trajectory, states will not meet the Paris Agreement goal of keeping global temperature "well below 2C above pre-industrial levels."[7] It is precisely disillusionment with the United Nations Framework Convention on Climate Change regime, to which the Paris Agreement belongs, that is leading activists and SIDS into the arms of the international courts at this critical juncture. This will give those courts an opportunity to act, perhaps even to shine. But international courts are also state-created international organizations based on treaty law and could just as easily fail to spur state action. They will harm their own legitimacy if they issue judgments that contradict each other, offer vague generalities that merely parrot the Paris Agreement language, choose not to answer under the doctrine of *non liquet*, or otherwise fail to alter the politics around climate inaction.

That is why the courts must be tactical. This chapter argues that the inter-American system's legacy of confronting structural injustice will allow the Court to play a unique but limited role in the emerging international climate docket.[8]

have already issued resolutions and reports, particularly at the United Nations. *See* esp. Sumudu Atapattu, *UN Human Rights Institutions and the Environment: Synergies, Challenges, Trajectories* (London: Routledge, 2023). As of writing, there was no climate litigation before the African Court of Human and Peoples Rights. *See* Yusra Suedi and Marie Fall, "Climate Change Litigation Before the African Human Rights System: Prospects and Pitfalls: Practice Note: GNHRE Climate Litigation in Global South Project," *Journal of Human Rights Practice* (July 2023): 1–14, https://doi.org/10.1093/jhuman/huad024.

[6] Spurred by youth activists, SIDS were the ones to push for the Advisory Opinion requests before the ICJ and ITLOS. In the inter-American setting, Chile and Colombia submitted the request.

[7] IPCC, *Climate Change 2023 Synthesis Report: Summary for Policymakers* (2023), at A.4, or 10, https://www.ipcc.ch/report/ar6/syr/downloads/report/IPCC_AR6_SYR_SPM.pdf. ("well below" is the language of the Paris Agreement.)

[8] There is much hope being pinned on the Inter-American Court. See, for example, Maria Antonia Tigre, Castellanos Natalia Urzola, and Juan Sebastián, "A Request for an Advisory Opinion at the Inter-American Court of Human Rights: Initial Reactions," Climate Law Blog, February 17, 2023, https://blogs.law.columbia.edu/climatechange/2023/02/17/a-request- for-an-advisory-opinion-at-the-inter-american-court-of-human-rights-initial-reactions/; Lena Riemer and Luca Scheid, "Leading the Way: The IACtHR's Advisory Opinion on Human Rights and Climate Change," Verfassungsblog, January 18, 2024, https://verfassungsblog.de/leading-the-way/.

The chapter argues that the Inter-American Court could have the most impact through its climate docket if it were to adjudicate with an eye to its comparative advantages. Specifically, the Court should utilize the strengths of its jurisprudence on structural injustice to articulate state obligations regarding adaptation and the protection of the most vulnerable groups. It would thereby provide social movements with discursive tools to advance their causes at the national and international levels as the climate becomes more unstable. Simultaneously, the Court should reinforce what will be the other international courts' (likely) emphasis on mitigation of greenhouse gas (GHG) emissions by drawing on its groundbreaking jurisprudence on state obligations to *prevent* human rights violations. In this way, it may be able to push states toward greater compliance and more ambitious mitigation goals. The Court will be on weaker ground, substantively and politically, if it turns to questions of climate justice between states. These questions have been at the heart of international climate law and continue to hamper progress on states' commitments to mitigation. There will be pressure for the Inter-American Court to step in, but it should show restraint.

The prescription offered here looks to the future of human rights in Latin America with a dose of pragmatism. Drawing on law and society scholarship, it adopts a institutional and political lens, even as it is doctrinal.[9] For over a decade, scholars have been developing the field of climate change and human rights.[10] Much of this writing focuses on substantive doctrinal arguments and leaves aside the political and institutional context in which these arguments are deployed. However, an interesting line of study on climate litigation in national courts approaches the topic with a sociolegal lens, attending to the political and institutional contexts that constrain litigation and explain the shape it takes.[11] The analysis extends this sociolegal approach to the international courts' climate docket. It looks beyond the IACtHR's doctrine to consider the inter-American system in its entirety, including not only the states in the Organization of American States (OAS), the IACHR, and the civil society actors who litigate before the court, but also legal opportunity structures at the national level,

[9] Gregory C. Shaffer, "The New Legal Realist Approach to International Law," *Leiden Journal of International Law* 28, no. 2 (2015): 189–210, https://doi.org/10.1017/S0922156515000035. Jeffrey Omari, Pablo Rueda-Saize, and Richard Wilson, "New Legal Realism at 20: Rethinking Law in an Era of Populism and Social Movements," *Connecticut Law Review* 57 (2023): 1–51.

[10] *See*, for example, Sumudu Atapattu, *Human Rights Approaches to Climate Change* (New York: Routledge, 2016); Sébastien Duyck, Sébastien Jodoin, and Alyssa Johl (eds.), *Handbook on Human Rights and Climate Governance* (New York: Routledge, 2018); Stephen Humphreys (ed.), *Human Rights and Climate Change* (Cambridge: Cambridge University Press, 2009), to name just a few.

[11] See Lisa Vanhala, "The Social and Political Life of Climate Litigation: Mobilizing the Law to Address the Climate Crisis," in *Litigating the Climate Emergency: How Human Rights, Courts, and Legal Mobilization Can Bolster Climate Action*, ed. César Rodríguez-Garavito (Cambridge: Cambridge University Press, 2022), 84–94.

including national judiciaries, governments, nongovernmental organizations (NGOs), and constitutional law. This larger context is the unit of comparison that matters when looking at the relative strengths and weaknesses of the four international courts.[12] In thus broadening the lens, the analysis reflects the recent path Latin American international law (LAIL) scholarship has taken as it begins to incorporate interdisciplinary theory and methods.[13]

Section II begins by explaining the legal opportunity structure of the IACtHR in comparison to the three other international courts being called to issue judgments on the climate emergency. The next section highlights the features of the jurisprudence of the Inter-American Court that will be relevant to the climate docket. Section IV advances a prescription for the Court as it approaches its climate docket over the coming years. The chapter concludes with reflections on the unique historical role of Latin American human rights law in addressing structural injustice and economic and social rights, and how this can shape its future in the new climactic regime.[14]

II. The Legal Opportunity Structure

An axiom of thee sociology of law is that social movements turn to courts when other, more political avenues of achieving change are blocked. Another of axiom is that courts acting alone are unable to create sweeping social change.[15] Read together, the axioms suggest that little will be achieved by turning to international courts in the face of inadequate state action on climate change. Perhaps international court judgments will be just as ineffective as the Paris Agreement and associated treaties in forcing states to meet the "well under 2C" target. But scholars have also shown that international courts do, under certain conditions, alter international and domestic politics. "Through 'alliances' with cause-lawyers and domestic interlocutors, ICs [international courts] can be agents of national and international change."[16] Even when international courts cannot

[12] Lisa Vanhala, "Legal Opportunity Structures and the Paradox of Legal Mobilization by the Environmental Movement in the UK," *Law & Society Review* 46, no. 3 (2012): 523–556, https://www.jstor.org/stable/23252253.

[13] *See* Puig, chapter 7, in this volume; *see also* Alexandra Huneeus, "Human Rights Between Jurisprudence and Social Science," *Leiden Journal of International Law* 28, no. 2 (2015): 255–266, https://doi.org/10.1017/S0922156515000060.

[14] Bruno Latour uses the term "new climactic regime" to emphasize that climate change is not a crisis that will pass, but here to stay. Bruno Latour, *Facing Gaia: Eight Lectures on the New Climactic Regime*, trans. Catherine Porter (Cambridge: Polity Press, 2017), 3.

[15] Gerald Rosenberg, *The Hollow Hope: Can Courts Bring About Social Change?* (1991).

[16] Karen Alter, "Tipping the Balance: International Courts and the Construction of International and Domestic Politics," *Cambridge Yearbook of European Legal Studies* 13, no. 1 (October 2011): 1–21, at 2, https://doi.org/10.5235/152888712801752979. See also Karen Alter, *The New Terrain of International Law: Courts, Politics, Rights* (Princeton, NJ: Princeton University Press, 2014).

create direct change in the behavior of the state, they provide discursive tools for social movements, fortifying them and, at times, opening paths to further litigation at the domestic level or helping them reshape the way people think about a particular issue. In considering the position of the IACtHR relative to that of other international courts, it therefore makes sense to pay attention not only to State Parties to the Convention but also civil society and domestic judiciaries.

States and GHG Emissions

The world's first international human rights climate petition was filed before the IACHR in 2005. In that case the Inuit people, through the Circumpolar Conference, filed a petition asking the Commission to declare that the United States and Canada had violated their rights through harmful GHG emissions that were affecting their rights to life, health, and culture, among other violations.[17] The Commission declined the petition but nonetheless held a hearing, which is often described as the birth of the climate change and human rights nexus.

The Inuit petition pitted an Indigenous people against the world's largest GHG emitter at the time: the United States. But the challenge currently facing the IACtHR is that—in contrast to the Commission—neither the United States nor Canada falls under its purview. Of the twenty states under the Court's jurisdiction, none has been a major GHG emitter historically, and only one (Brazil) sits among the top twenty emitting states in recent years. By contrast, the ECHR has jurisdiction over most Western European states, ITLOS has jurisdiction over all the top ten emitters minus the United States, and the ICJ's judgments will address the responsibility of all of the world's major emitters.

This poses a challenge for the Inter-American Court. There is clearly something incongruous in laying responsibility for the climate crisis at the feet of developing states that did not play a role in creating the problem. Nor would it be acceptable for Latin American states to take shelter under the doctrine of Common but Differentiated Responsibility to argue that it only states such as the United States, Western European states, and China that must invest in mitigation, adaptation, and loss and damage from climate change, putting the problem outside the grasp of the Inter-American Court. Relative to the ECtHR, ICJ, and ITLOS, the IACtHR's position as having jurisdiction only over developing

[17] Sheila Watt-Cloutier, Petition to the Inter American Commission on Human Rights Seeking Relief from Violations Resulting from Global Warming Caused by Acts and Omissions of the United States (2005), https://earthjustice.org/document/petition-inter-american-commission-human-rights-behalf-inuit-circumpola.

and middle-income states from the global south is an opportunity but also a liability.[18]

Civil Society and Litigation

Karen Alter distinguishes two types of international courts.[19] Old-style international courts, of which the ICJ and ITLOS are examples, have contentious jurisdiction over disputes between states and do not have mandatory jurisdiction. New-style international courts, such as the human rights courts, see cases brought by non-state actors, including individuals, and have compulsory jurisdiction over states. This distinction is significant for the international climate docket. ICJ and ITLOS contentious litigation is brought exclusively by states against states. As a result, litigation before these tribunals is less frequent and is shaped by state interest. Further, states can decline to be sued and still participate in the regime. By contrast, litigation before human rights courts is initiated by individuals and civil society as well as states, and the only way to avoid jurisdiction is through withdrawal from the underlying treaty. The human rights courts, therefore, have more active dockets and civil society plays a more direct role in shaping the docket of the courts (which means states play less of a role in defining the docket). For these reasons, the ECHR and IACtHR will likely become more frequent sites for climate litigation than the old-style international courts.

For civil society, human rights litigation also has the advantage of giving a human face to the harm of climate change. These differences are attenuated when the IACtHR works through its advisory jurisdiction, as there is no specific victim-plaintiff. But even as the IACtHR issues its advisory opinion on climate change, it should consider that it is creating discursive tools for future litigation on its own contentious docket. In contrast to the ICJ and ITLOS, the IACtHR judgment will be of direct use for litigation driven by the same NGOs that submitted amicus briefs and appeared before the Court in its advisory opinion hearings. Domestic climate litigation in the region is becoming more frequent.[20]

[18] The African Court of Human and People's Rights will also be in this position as its climate docket develops. See Suedi and Fall, "Climate Change Litigation before the African Human Rights System."

[19] Alter, *The New Terrain of International Law*, 5.

[20] Maria Antonia Tigre, Natalia Urzola, and Alexandra Goodman, "Climate Litigation in Latin America: Is the Region Quietly Leading a Revolution?" *Journal of Human Rights and the Environment* 14, no. 1 (2023): 67–93; Juan Auz, "Human Rights-Based Climate Litigation: A Latin American Cartography," *Journal of Human Rights and the Environment* 13, no. 1 (2022): 114–136, accessed May 26, 2024, https://doi.org/10.4337/jhre.2022.01.05.

The Domestic Legal Complex

The inter-American system is deeply embedded in national jurisdictions.[21] Many Latin American states receive the American Convention on Human Rights (ACHR) as part of their constitutional law and as directly justiciable. Indeed, in some states, IACtHR judgments themselves have a direct effect. That means that individuals can sue for violations of the ACHR in national court, and that national judiciaries play an important role in developing the meaning of the ACHR alongside the IACtHR. The resulting judicial dialogue between national courts and the Inter-American Court has been a focal point of LAIL scholarship.[22] Scholars have argued that the Inter-American Court should treat national courts as partners in developing the ACHR.[23] By contrast, the ICJ and ITLOS have a more distant connection to national courts and domestic litigation, which does not typically involve state-to-state contests. In issuing judgments on state responsibilities around the climate crisis, the IACtHR will create discursive tools for domestic social movements to use in *local* litigation, and it should consider what domestic judiciaries have already resolved on these matters.[24]

Two conclusions follow from this analysis of the Inter-American Court's relative political and institutional context. In contrast to the other international courts, the IACtHR's jurisdiction does not include major GHG-emitting states. This will pose a challenge, particularly where it considers state responsibility for

[21] *See* Laurence R. Helfer, "Redesigning the European Court of Human Rights: Embeddedness as a Deep Structural Principle of the European Human Rights Regime," *European Journal of International Law* 19, no. 1, (February 2008): 125–159, https://doi.org/10.1093/ejil/chn004.

[22] *See*, in this volume, Landau, chapter 18; Cespedes et al., chapter 23; and Contesse, chapter 19.

[23] Alexandra Huneeus, "Courts Resisting Courts: Lessons from the Inter-American Court's Struggle to Enforce Human Rights," *Cornell International Law Journal* 44, no. 3 (2011): 493–533, https://scholarship.law.cornell.edu/cilj/vol44/iss3/2.

[24] See Jorge Contesse, "The Final Word? Constitutional Dialogue and the Inter-American Court of Human Rights," *International Journal of Constitutional Law* 15, no. 2 (April 2017): 414–435, https://doi.org/10.1093/icon/mox034 (arguing that the Inter-American Court should also heed domestic courts). See also Eduardo Ferrer MacGregor, "El control de convencionalidad como un vehículo para el diálogo judicial entre la Corte Interamericana de Derechos Humanos y los tribunales de América," in *Anuario de Derecho Constitucional Latinoamericano*, ed. Marie Christine Fuchs and Christian Steiner (Berlin: Konrad Adenauer Stiftung, 2016); Humberto Noguero Alcala, "Diálogo interjurisdiccional y control de convencionalidad entre los tribunales nacionales y la Corte Interamericanade Derechos Humanos en Chile," *Anuario De Derecho Constitucional Latinoamericano Ano* 19 (2013): 9; Antonio Moreira Maués et al., "Judicial Dialogue between National Courts and the Inter-American Court of Human Rights: A Comparative Study of Argentina, Brazil, Colombia and Mexico," *Human Rights Law Review* 21, no. 1 (March 2021): 108–131, https://doi.org/10.1093/hrlr/ngaa047; Ezequiel Gonzalez-Ocantos and Wayne Sandholtz, "Constructing a Regional Human Rights Legal Order: The Inter-American Court, National Courts, and Judicial Dialogue, 1988–2014," *International Journal of Constitutional Law*19, no. 5 (December 2021): 1559–1596, https://doi.org/10.1093/icon/moab094. For a general review of constitutional law and international law in the region, see Alejandro Chehtman, "Constitutions and International Law," in *The Oxford Handbook of Constitutional Law in Latin America*, ed. Conrado Hübner Mendes, Roberto Gargarella, and Sebastián Guidi (Oxford: Oxford University Press, 2022).

GHG mitigation. However, the IACtHR has relative strengths as well. In contrast to the ICJ and ITLOS, it has the opportunity to create discursive tools and standards that will be used directly in national litigation as well as litigation in its own docket, and it can draw from existing rights jurisprudence from national courts. The next section turns from institutional and political context to law and jurisprudence.

III. The Inter-American System's *Corpus Iuris*

The preamble to the Paris Climate Agreement notes that "Parties should, when taking action to address climate change, respect, promote, and consider their respective obligations on human rights."[25] It then points to the right to health, and "the rights of indigenous peoples, local communities, migrants, children, persons with disabilities and people in vulnerable situations and the right to development, as well as gender equality, empowerment of women and intergenerational equity."[26] With this brief preambular clause, the treaty built a bridge between two distinct branches of international law.[27] Scholars and activists have been working to bring the two into further conversation ever since. Climate activists have filed rights-based cases before courts around the globe, and national courts have begun to render their interpretations of the climate/rights nexus. Indeed, since 2015, human rights-based climate cases have "proliferated at a steady pace . . . even as (and sometimes as a reaction to) progress stalled with regard to the implementation of the 2105 Paris Agreement."[28]

This section considers what the IACtHR has to offer *as a matter of doctrine* to the emerging international climate docket. All four international courts considered here have subject matter jurisdiction over human rights,[29] and the ECHR and IACtHR, in particular, have developed a nuanced and rich understanding of human rights obligations over hundreds of cases. But the IACtHR has a distinct political and institutional history that has led it to emphasize the development of rights doctrines focused on structural injustice. This began with its early jurisprudence on mass, state-sponsored atrocity. More recently,

[25] Paris Agreement to the United Nations Framework Convention on Climate Change (2015), Preamble.

[26] Ibid.

[27] John H. Knox, "The Paris Agreement as a Human Rights Treaty," in *Human Rights and 21st Century Challenges: Poverty, Conflict, and the Environment*, ed. Dapo Akande et al. (Oxford: Oxford University Press, 2020); Online ed. Oxford Academic, April 23, 2020).

[28] César Rodríguez-Garavito, "Litigating the Climate Emergency: The Global Rise of Human Rights-Based Litigation for Climate Action," in Rodríguez-Garavito, *Litigating the Climate Emergency*, ed. 10.

[29] But see Chris Whomersley, "UNCLOS at 40: What about Human Rights?" *Marine Policy* 148 (2023): 105424 (arguing that UNCLOS has limited human rights jurisdiction).

it has developed environmental justice doctrines, particularly in the context of Indigenous peoples, that also focus on structural harm.

The IAHRS and Structural Injustice

It is often noted that while the ECHR came of age in a region of well-functioning relatively prosperous democracies, the IACtHR came of age in a region of high inequality where democracy was constantly in question. This rosy account of ECHR history has been debunked, given that several core states of the early ECHR strategically excluded their colonial territories from its purview.[30] But it is true that the two courts developed different jurisprudential strengths, with the IACtHR advancing a more progressive *corpus iuris*. Through decades of litigation, the Court has developed a rich legacy of victim-centered, reparatory practices in the face of structural harms. Rather than view a human rights violation as a single event that can be repaired by monetary reparation, the IACtHR views violations as symptomatic of failed state policies and demands reform to avoid future violations.[31] This structural approach is reflected in the doctrinal development of the duty to prevent human rights violations, the duty of integral reparation that includes structural remedial orders, the idea of a "differential lens" where certain groups suffer harm in distinctive ways, and the development of socioeconomic rights. Each of these doctrines has spread beyond the inter-American system—one of the Court's and Commission's many contributions to global human rights doctrine—but plays a particularly prominent role in the inter-American setting.

From its first case, the IACtHR held that the American Convention Article 1.1 duty to respect human rights includes a duty to prevent human rights violations.[32] Not only do states have an obligation to refrain from actions that violate human rights, but they also have the forward-looking obligation to exert due diligence in preventing them.[33] This doctrine, developed over hundreds of

[30] Alexandra Huneeus and Mikael Rask Madsen, "Between Universalism and Regional Law and Politics: A Comparative History of the American, European and African Human Rights Systems," *International Journal of Constitutional Law* 16, no. 1 (2018): 136–160.

[31] Víctor Abramovich, "From Massive Violations to Structural Patterns," *SUR* 11 (2009), accessed May 26, 2024, https://sur.conectas.org/en/massive-violations-structural-patterns/.

[32] *Velásquez Rodríguez v. Honduras*, Inter-Am. Ct. H.R. (ser. C) No. 4 (1988).

[33] For discussion of due diligence in the inter-American system, see Y. C. Álvarez López, N. Ferrer Araújo, and Y. Garrido Ochoa, "Estándar interamericano de la debida diligencia: aplicación por las altas cortes colombianas en los casos de delitos de violencia sexual contra mujeres en el conflicto armado," *Revista Jurídica Mario Alario D'Filippo* (2014): 37–49; Y. Abreu, and J. C. Abreu, "La debida diligencia en la investigación de graves violaciones de derechos humanos [En términos de la jurisprudencia de la Corte Interamericana de Derechos Humanos]," Instituto Nacional de Ciencias Penales (2019); J. S. Lozano Parra and M. F. Jaimes Melgarejo, "Principio De Debida Diligencia En Los Procesos Judiciales Colombianos: Hacia Un Estándar Interamericano De Obligación Y Deber Estatal En Derechos Humanos," *Revistas ICDP* 1 (2014).

cases, has a twofold significance for the climate change setting. GHG emission is not itself an act that violates human rights. However, GHG emissions at a certain level will create human rights violations in the future, in which case it can be argued that states have a duty to prevent that outcome under Article 1.1 of the American Convention. Second, that duty could extend to preventing non-state actors, such as corporations, from emitting GHG at levels that would impact human rights in the future.[34] In this way, human rights law includes mitigation obligations that are consonant with the international climate treaties' mitigation obligations but can be enforced via individual rights litigation.

The IACtHR's emphasis on structural causes of human rights violations also led it to develop a unique reparatory regime.[35] In contrast to the ECtHR, the IACtHR was not content to order monetary damages alone but began to order structural reparatory orders from early on, arguing that the state had a duty to guarantee nonrepetition of the underlying human rights violation. In the *Cottonfields Case*, for example, it was not enough to say that the state must provide monetary compensation to families of the women and girls who had been killed or disappeared in Ciudad Juarez. Nor was the problem limited to a few bad actors who had to be prosecuted and punished. Rather, in addition to ordering the state to compensate and prosecute, the Court ordered Mexico to adapt its practices for investigating forced disappearance, sexual abuse, and femicide in accordance with particular international instruments.[36] The Court used its judgment not only to declare a violation and demand reparation for the victims but as an instrument to spur cultural and institutional reform. Further, the Court began to monitor state compliance to its reparatory orders through open and closed hearings and meetings with government actors directly involved in specific areas of governance. These reparatory practices could play a meaningful role in litigation on both mitigation and adaptation in climate law.

Equally significant for the climate docket are the Inter-American Court's doctrines on socioeconomic rights and differential harm, which extend beyond the work of the ECtHR in these areas. Although the American Convention on Human Rights, like the European Convention on Human Rights, focuses predominantly on civil and political rights, the American Convention includes an article on socioeconomic rights (Article 26). In *Lagos del Campo v. Peru* (2017),

[34] Some scholars argue that corporations have direct human rights obligation. See Daniel Iglesias Márquez and Lucas Sebastián de Erice Aranda, "La Diligencia Debida Empresarial Como Mecanismo Para Reforzar El Respeto De Los Derechos Humanos Laborales En América Latina," *Homa Publica-Revista Internacional De Derechos Humanos Y Empresas* 6, no. 1 (2022). https://periodicos.ufjf.br/index.php/HOMA/article/view/37339; Daniel Uribe Terán, Pablo Alarcón Peña, and Pamela Aguirre Castro, "La debida diligencia corporativa y los derechos humanos: un análisis desde el derecho comparado," *Actualidad Jurídica* no. 47 (2023): 355–374.

[35] See Claudio Grossman, chapter 20, in this volume.

[36] *González et al. ("Cotton Field") v. Mexico*, Inter-Am. Ct. H.R. (ser. C), No. 205, 148 (2009), https://www.corteidh.or.cr/docs/casos/articulos/seriec_205_ing.pdf.

the Court allowed direct justiciability of economic, social, and cultural rights (ESCR) under article 26.[37] Additionally, a subgroup of states has ratified the American Convention on Human Rights in the realm of ESCR, known as the Protocol of San Salvador (which includes a right to environment, as discussed below). In this work, the Court draws on a rich regional tradition of domestic ESCR. Starting with Mexico's 1917 constitution, which was the world's first to include socioeconomic rights, Latin American constitutions have been leaders in the recognition of socioeconomic rights. In some countries, notably Colombia, Brazil, and Costa Rica, these rights have been extensively litigated.[38] Insofar as climate change impacts socioeconomic rights, the Inter-American Court will be well positioned, as a matter of doctrine, relative to the other international courts.[39]

Finally, the Inter-American Court's reparatory practice acknowledges that structural discrimination creates distinct vulnerabilities. The Court has held that equal protection and nondiscrimination require states to refrain from arbitrary differential treatment, but they also imply "an affirmative concept related to the obligation of States Party to create real equal conditions toward groups who have been historically excluded or who are exposed to a greater risk of being discriminated."[40] In the *Cottonfields Case* discussed above, for example, the Court broke new ground when it found that the murders of women and girls in Ciudad Juarez were "gender-based murders of women, also known as femicide,"[41] and demanded that the state conduct its investigations using a "gender perspective."[42] Given that climate change will disproportionately affect

[37] *But see* Liliana Ronconi and María Barraco, "La Consolidación de los DESCA en la Corte Interamericana de Derechos Humanos: Reflexiones a Propósito del Caso Lhaka Honhat vs. Argentina," *Revista de la Facultad de Derecho* [online] 50, e105 (2021): 1–27, https://doi.org/10.22187/rfd2020n50a5 (arguing that *Poblete Vilches v. Chile* is the first such case).

[38] Daniel Brinks and Varun Guari, "A New Policy Landscape: Legalizing Social and Economic Rights in the Developing World," in *Courting Social Justice: Judicial Enforcement of Social and Economic Rights in the Developing World*, ed. Daniel Brinks and Varun Guari (Cambridge: Cambridge University Press, 2008), 303–352.

[39] The scholarship on ESCR in the Americas is vast. See, for example, *El Derecho Constitucional Común Latinoamericano de los Derechos Económicos, Sociales, Culturales y Ambientales: La Contribución de las Clínicas Jurídicas*, ed. Armin von Bogdandy et al. (Bogotá, Colombia: Ediciones Uniandes–Max Planck Institute, 2023); *Interamericanización del derecho a la salud. Perspectivas a la luz del caso Poblete de la Corte IDH*, ed. Mariela Morales Antionazzi and Laura Clérico (Mexico City: Instituto de Estudios Constitucionales del Estado de Querétaro, 2019); G. S. Galán Melo, "La Justiciabilidad De Los Derechos Económicos, Sociales Y Culturales: Evolución de su aplicación en la Corte Interamericana De Derechos Humanos," *Iuris Tantum* 33, no. 30 (2019: 115–142; Viviana Krsticevic, "The Inter-American System, *Research Handbook on Economic, Social and Cultural Rights as Human Rights*, ed. Jackie Dugard et al. (Cheltenham, UK: Edward Elgar, 2020); Eduardo Ferrer Mac-Gregor, "Social rights in the jurisprudence of the Inter-American Court of Human Rights," in *Research Handbook on International Law and Social Rights*, ed. by Christina Binder et al., (Cheltenham, UK: Edward Elgar, 2020), 173–186.

[40] *Furlan and family v. Argentina,* Inter-Am. Ct. H.R. (ser. C) No. 246, ¶ 267(2012), https://www.corteidh.or.cr/docs/casos/articulos/resumen_246_ing.pdf.

[41] *González et al. ("Cotton Field") v. Mexico*, ¶ 143.

[42] Ibid., ¶ 147.

vulnerable groups, the Court's doctrines on differential impact could become a bulwark of the climate docket.[43]

The IAHRS and the Environment

Like most human rights instruments of its era, the American Convention of Human Rights makes no mention of nature, the environment, or the climate system. But the Inter-American Court has issued several groundbreaking judgments with significant implications for environmental protection and climate change.

The first of these focused on Indigenous and Tribal rights. Starting in the 1990s, indigenous and Afro-descendent peoples cases began invoking the American Convention to protect their territories from extractive industry projects such as mining. Through these cases, and in dialogue with national courts and ILO 169, the Inter-American Court developed doctrines affirming that the "special relation" that Indigenous and Tribal peoples hold with their territories requires a distinct type of protection. Its first case, *Awas Tingi v. Nicaragua*, held:

> [T]he close ties of indigenous people with the land must be recognized and understood as the fundamental basis of their cultures, their spiritual life, their integrity, and their economic survival. For indigenous communities, relations to the land are not merely a matter of possession and production but a material and spiritual element which they must fully enjoy, even to preserve their cultural legacy and transmit it to future generations.[44]

The Court has since extended the concept of the special relationship to include Afro-descendent communities or Tribal communities.[45] Thus, it has established a doctrine of heightened, differential protection for communities on the front lines of climate change.[46]

[43] It is quite possible, for example, that the Inter-American Court would use a gender lens to analyze a case such as *KlimaSiniorinnen v. Switzerland*, in which elderly women claimed the government was violating their ECHR rights by setting inadequately ambitious GHG mitigation goals. Their claim was that as women, they were particularly vulnerable, but the ECtHR did not take up this argument.

[44] *Mayagna (Sumo) Awas Tingni Community v. Nicaragua*, Inter-Am. Ct. H.R. (ser. C) No. 79, ¶ 149 (2001), https://www.corteidh.or.cr/docs/casos/articulos/seriec_79_ing.pdf.

[45] See, for example, *Moiwana Community v. Suriname*, Inter-Am. Ct. H.R. (ser. C) No. 124, ¶¶ 132–133 (2005), https://www.corteidh.or.cr/docs/casos/articulos/seriec_124_ing.pdf.

[46] See also *Indigenous Communities of the Lhaka Honhat (Our Land) Association v. Argentina*, Inter-Am. Ct. H.R. (ser. C) No. 400 (2020), https://www.corteidh.or.cr/docs/casos/articulos/seriec_400_ing.pdf.

In 2017, the Court issued an advisory opinion on human rights and the environment, its first judgment on environmental matters beyond the Indigenous and Tribal context.[47] It broke ground on several doctrines. The opinion held that there is a right to a healthy environment in the inter-American system and that states have an obligation to prevent environmental harm that could affect human rights. Drawing on principles of environmental law, the opinion found that states had responsibility for transboundary harm. It also noted that the obligation to prevent environmental harm was not just a doctrine of human rights but also of the environment as an end in itself (more on this later).

Recently, the IACtHR has begun to adjudicate contentious environmental cases beyond the Indigenous context. In November 2023, it issued a judgment on its first toxic pollution case, declaring that "environmental degradation can cause irreparable damage to human beings, which is why a healthy environment is a fundamental right for the existence of humanity."[48] It found violations of the rights to "the rights to a healthy environment, health, life, physical and mental integrity, dignity, and the rights of the child." This was a case in which a private company had created the pollution. The Court concluded that "States are obliged to use all means at their disposal in order to prevent activities carried out under their jurisdiction from causing significant damage to the environment. This obligation must be fulfilled under a standard of due diligence, which must be appropriate and proportional to the degree of risk of environmental damage" (¶ 126). Further, the Court showed the ambitious scope of reparatory orders that it is prepared to bring to the environmental context. It found that the state is obliged to (1) establish laws, regulations, and policies that ensure air quality standards do not constitute health risks; (2) monitor air quality and inform the population of possible health risks; and (3) carry out action plans to control air quality, which include the identification of the primary sources of air pollution, and implement measures to enforce air quality standards.[49]

Taken together, the Inter-American Court's emphasis on structural injustice and its development of the nexus between environmental protection and human rights leave it poised to make a distinct contribution to the international climate docket. The next section considers how it could leverage these doctrines to have the most impact in light of the legal opportunity structure outlined in section II.

[47] *The Environment and Human Rights*, Advisory Opinion OC-23/17, Inter-Am. Ct. H.R. (ser. A) No. 23 (2017), https://www.corteidh.or.cr/docs/opiniones/seriea_23_ing.pdf.

[48] *Inhabitants of La Oroya v. Perú*, Inter-Am. Ct. H.R. (ser. C) No. 511 (2023), ¶ 177, https://www.corteidh.or.cr/docs/casos/articulos/seriec_511_esp.pdf.

[49] *La Oroya v. Perú*, ¶120.

IV. Strategies for Impact

The term "climate justice" typically refers to justice between one of three sets of subjects. First, it can refer to justice between nation-states, in which the nation-state is the entity with rights and duties. A focal point of United Nations Framework Convention on Climate Change (UNFCCC) politics, the concern here is that the states most harmed by climate change are those least able to respond and, at the same time, the ones that have least contributed to the problem. Second, climate justice can refer to justice between present and future generations. By failing to take appropriate measures in the present, current generations condemn future generations to lives in which their most basic human rights may be impossible for states to guarantee. Third, climate justice can refer to justice among currently living individuals and groups, with concern for the most marginalized individuals and groups in society today. As with the least developed states, marginalized groups are the most harmed by climate change even as they contribute least to the problem.

All three sets are key areas of concern in the litigation appearing before international courts. The advisory opinion request and accompanying amicus briefs submitted to the Inter-American Court ask for clarification of state obligations in all three domains of climate justice. However, given the Court's comparative institutional, political, and legal context, it should prioritize the third. The key contribution of the Inter-American Court will be to address state duties in light of the most vulnerable individuals and groups as a matter of structural justice. The Court will have less to say on future generations, and the least to say on interstate obligations. Finally, there is a fourth set of subjects to which the term "climate justice" can refer: justice between humans and the nonhuman world, including animals, ecosystems, and "nature" or "mother earth" (*Pachamama*) and natural entities more generally. This is an emerging framing in the context of climate justice, and it has been put before the Inter-America Court in the climate change advisory opinion request. It is a question the Court should grapple with and contribute to, if with caution, in dialogue with high courts in the region.

Climate Justice for Front-Line Communities: A Pathbreaking Role

Front-line communities are those "who are the most vulnerable to and will be the most adversely affected by climate change and inequitable actions because of systemic and historical socioeconomic disparities, environmental injustice, or other forms of injustice."[50]

[50] National Oceanic and Atmospheric Administration, Climate Program Office, "Climate Adaptation Partnerships Program in the Justice40 Initiative," accessed May 4, 2024, https://cpo.noaa.gov/divisions-programs/climate-and-societal-interactions/cap-risa/justice40-initiative.

Of the four courts, the Inter-American Court is best poised to articulate state duties to protect these communities. Because the human rights systems allow direct petition, vulnerable communities working with civil society organizations will be able to bring their claims of climate-induced harm directly to the human rights courts. In fact, the European Court itself has a direct petition, whereas, in the inter-American system, litigants begin with the Commission. However, between the two human right courts, the IACtHR has the more sophisticated doctrines addressing structural obstacles and differential harm.

First, the Court can demand that climate mitigation strategies take into consideration their differential impact on vulnerable communities. In the context of Indigenous and tribal communities, mitigation strategies must be submitted to free, prior, informed consent processes. Second, the court's structural lens will be particularly important to developing doctrines on state obligations in the face of *adaptation* to climate change. Rights litigation at the national level thus far has focused on mitigation, not adaptation. The Court could prioritize the situation of front-line communities, ensuring that states use a differential lens in policymaking and implementation. The Court will be able to direct states to hold meaningful consultation with these communities on measures that affect them; to acknowledge the differential harm that they will suffer due to the unique relationship they have with their territories; and to afford them measures for adaptation and other reparatory measures (loss and damage) that are culturally appropriate.

In articulating these duties, the Court would contribute to the development of doctrines of adaptation and loss and damage, two areas that have remained less developed in the litigation unfolding in domestic courts.[51] It would hand a new set of discursive tools to a preexisting ecosystem of transnational civil society organizations and organized communities. These compliance constituencies would then be able to pursue enforcement through litigation in national court and the inter-American system.

Justice for Future Generations: An Echoing Role

From its first case, the Inter-American Court interpreted ACHR Article 1.1 to hold states responsible for respecting human rights by not violating them and by exercising due diligence in preventing foreseeable violations. The state has a forward-looking duty to prevent human rights violations in the future, without regard to a specific victim, but under a more generalized sense of who could be harmed. The duty to mitigate in climate law is also grounded in a duty to preserve

[51] Rodríguez-Garavito, "Litigating the Climate Emergency."

the climate for future generations (which is not the same as saying that future generations are rights-holders). By subsuming climate law mitigation duties into regional human rights law, the Court could open the door to domestic and international litigation around mitigation, which is not directly justiciable otherwise. In this way it can echo and amplify what the international courts such as ICJ and ITLOS can establish in terms of obligations under international law more generally. It can also echo developments in the Council of Europe system, where the ECtHR found that Switzerland had a duty to establish a regulatory framework for mitigation and to meet its stated emissions targets.[52] However, the IACtHR's overall contribution will be limited in the realm of mitigation, given that its membership is limited to developing and middle-income states that are not major GHG contributors, with the exception of Brazil.

Climate Justice among States: A Muted Role

Discussion of national mitigation goals immediately invokes the question of justice among states. What do developed states owe to SIDS and other vulnerable developing states as a matter of international law? Each advisory opinion request foregrounds this dimension of justice, a question that has been at the core of UNFCCC Conference of Party (COP) negotiations. It is also a question that lurks behind individual petitions that seek to hold states accountable for mitigation.

It might seem that the Inter-American Court should not weigh into this debate. In contrast to the other three courts, the IACtHR does not have developed states under its jurisdiction, as noted above. Further, the Inter-American Court is a human rights court, and states do not have human rights. In its Advisory Opinion OC-23, the Court held that states have transboundary obligations in the environmental context. But that obligation is to those whose human rights are violated rather than to the other state's rights insofar as the ACHR is concerned.

Yet the IACtHR has a unique if muted role to play here. While there are some states under its jurisdiction that are very poor, the Court is also home to OEDC states, such as Chile, Costa Rica, and Mexico, and home to Brazil, which is currently the world's sixth largest emitter of GHG emissions, and the seat of the Amazon Basin. The IACtHR will be able to speak to the responsibility of these more powerful states. Even if these states are not the main drivers of the problem, they cannot sidestep responsibility by merely pointing to developed states' responsibility. In this sense, the Court will have to be creative. Juan Auz argues that courts such as the IACtHR should formulate remedies that incorporate a duty to

[52] *KlimaSeniorinnen v. Switzerland*, App. No. 53600/20.

cooperate across borders: "The defendant state could be mandated to perform its best when it comes to finding international assistance and cooperation, particularly with those states that pollute the most or with financial institutions that might provide appropriate funding."[53]

Climate Justice for Nature: A Visibilizing Role

Latin American judges, activists, Indigenous social movements, and legislatures have been at the forefront of the movement for rights of nature, or doctrines that recognize the rights of nonhuman entities, such as rivers, mountains, and Indigenous territories.[54] This is not a uniquely Latin American trend: there are examples as far east as India and New Zealand and as far north as the United States and Canada. But Latin American courts have been leading the development of these doctrines through rights litigation. Indeed, the Inter-American Court is the first international court to acknowledge this development in its 2017 Advisory Opinion on the environment, declaring that the right to a healthy environment "protects nature and the environment, not only because of the benefits they provide to humanity . . . but because of their importance to the other living organisms with which we share the planet that also merit protection in their own right."[55]

Perhaps taking note of this development, the request for an advisory opinion on climate change asks the Court to clarify state obligations in responding "to the climate emergency within the framework of international human rights law, paying special attention to the differentiated impacts of this emergency on individuals from diverse regions and population groups, *as well as on nature*" (my emphasis).[56] Several amicus briefs push the court in this direction in the advisory opinion on climate change. The Inter-American Court does not have jurisprudence on nature rights. However, the Court, in its ongoing dialogue with national courts, will have the opportunity to shine a light on this doctrine. For example, it could reiterate its observations on the scope of the

[53] Juan Auz, "Two Reputed Allies: Reconciling Climate Justice and Litigation in the Global South," in Rodríguez-Garavito, *Litigating the Climate Emergency*, 152.

[54] Ecuador and Colombia are the countries where doctrines of nonhuman rights have seen the most development. See Rommel Lara Ponce, Jenny García Ruales, and Alex Valle Franco, *Derechos de la Naturaleza y Territorio en Ecuador. Diálogos desde los saberes, quehaceres jurídicos y antropológicos* (Quito: Abya Yala, UPS, 2024); Eduardo Gudynas, *Derechos de la naturaleza: ética biocéntrica y políticas ambientales* (Buenos Aires: Tinta Limon, 2014); Camila Bustos and Whitney Richardson, "Implementando los derechos de la naturaleza en Colombia: las experiencias del Atrato y el Amazonas," *Revista Derecho del Estado* 54 (2023): 227–275; Javier Alfredo Molina Roa, *Derechos de la Naturaleza: histórica y Tendencia Actual* (Bogotá: Universidad Externado de Colombia, 2014).

[55] *The Environment and Human Rights*, Advisory Opinion OC-23/17.

[56] Request for an Advisory Opinion of the International Court of Justice.

right to a healthy environment, and it could delve further into the analysis of the jurisprudence of the Ecuadorian and Colombian constitutional courts on these rights. In Colombian jurisprudence, grants of personhood to natural entities typically stem from the demands of Indigenous and Black Colombian communities that live in close connection to that entity. Thus, the grant of personality is also an act of intercultural dialogue, and part of Colombia's constitutional commitment to legal pluralism. Further, these judgments emphasize a relational understanding: the claim that the Atrato River has rights is not a claim that the river holds rights as *against* humans but rather an acknowledgment that the two—humans and their environment—live so closely in relation that erosion of the rights of one harms the other. It is also an acknowledgment that some peoples view their nonhuman environment as imbued with a meaning that is not captured in the term "property," but should be acknowledged in some fundamental legal form. The Court can make these developments more visible by acknowledging and further analyzing them, even if it does not find similar rights within the inter-American instruments.

In summary, the Court should be able to weigh into these four realms of climate justice as its climate docket grows. But its strongest and most distinctive contribution will be in the area of structural injustice and differential harm.

V. Conclusion: Are We Dreaming?

Of the international courts, the Inter-American Court is the one that has shown the greatest concern for the most vulnerable groups in society. That should continue to be the focal point as it considers states' legal responsibilities in the face of climate change. Until now, even rights-based climate litigation at the national level has focused on developing mitigation rather than adaptation, and it has not focused on the effects of climate change on the most vulnerable but on future generations and society at large. Focusing on adaptation from the perspective of the most vulnerable is an auspicious path for the IACtHR climate docket. The outcome will not be a changed world. But the Court could play a role in helping those who help the most vulnerable face climate harm.

30

Health Law and Pandemics in Latin America

Pedro A. Villarreal

I. Introduction

In many ways, the unfolding of pandemics in Latin America is another shard in the mirror of rampant economic inequality and social exclusion prevailing in the region.[1] The protection against communicable diseases does not escape this context, and some of its main normative concerns stem from colonial times. Against such a backdrop, the chapter discusses overarching regional challenges in the field of international health law, with an emphasis on communicable disease pandemics. While COVID-19 represents the most acute disease-related problem in an entire century, the chapter shows how the regional dimension not only plays a role but may actually be a determinant factor in the pandemic's short- and longer-term impact.

First, the scene is set through an overview of the Latin American background in the spread of communicable diseases.[2] Historical insights on how health law in the region emerged as a response to pandemic threats shed light upon distinctive regional features. Second, the chapter puts forward a mapping of regional human rights law, particularly the right to health. The role of the Inter-American Human Rights System (IAHRS) in this regard represents a unique regional institutional constellation, due to both substantive and procedural innovations in the protection of the right to health and its justiciability. Third, this chapter looks at broader trends in the region's health profile to identify the structural ailments that ask for a normative agenda. Lastly, the chapter concludes by underscoring how the legal challenges posed by the COVID-19 pandemic in the region should be understood in light of the aforementioned rampant economic inequality and the resulting social exclusion of marginalized groups.

[1] United Nations Economic Commission for Latin America and the Caribbean (CEPAL), *Panorama Social de América Latina* (Santiago, Chile: United Nations, 2019), 13.

[2] The Latin American region referred to in the current analysis encompasses all Pan-American Health Organization (PAHO) members, and not only those that are or have been members of the broader Inter-American System of Human Rights at one point (including Venezuela, Trinidad and Tobago, and Nicaragua).

Pedro A. Villarreal, *Health Law and Pandemics in Latin America* In: *Latin American International Law in the Twenty-First Century*. Edited by: Alejandro Chehtman, Alexandra Huneeus, and Sergio Puig,
Oxford University Press. © Oxford University Press 2025. DOI: 10.1093/9780197754016.003.0030

II. Health Law in Latin America: Between Atavisms and US Hegemony

A Historical Note

One of the distinctive features of the Latin American region is the evolution of legal mechanisms for redress for Indigenous peoples. In this chapter, Indigenous peoples are strictly understood as persons who inhabited the continent before the arrival of European conquistadors, leading to a common background of discrimination and oppression.[3] Such a definition is, by nature, vague and has blurry contours. Despite this, at the moment of writing, the United Nations estimates the number of Indigenous peoples in Latin America at around 50 million.[4]

Historical accounts have shown how the introduction of then-novel European diseases in the Americas was the main cause of the decimation of Indigenous peoples.[5] Coupled with patterns of slavery and exploitation, the particularly vulnerable situation of Indigenous communities is present throughout the region. Indigenous peoples' distinctive plights are compounded by other cross-cutting global challenges, such as growing inequality and social exclusion.[6] Such a background is by no means limited to Latin America, encompassing the current territories of the United States and Canada, as well as other groups like Americans of African descent.[7]

In the late nineteenth century, after several waves of independence wars fought against European colonial powers, the Americas were almost on par with Europe in the emergence of international health law. On both continents, a series of Sanitary Conferences took place in the second half of such century. Countries' delegates gathered to discuss the best means to legally harmonize criteria on measures adopted for facing communicable diseases. These posed

[3] The category is taken from James Anaya, *Indigenous Peoples in International Law* (2nd ed., Oxford: Oxford University Press, 2004), 3–5; Sergio Puig, *At the Margins of Globalization: Indigenous Peoples and International Economic Law* (Cambridge: Cambridge University Press, 2021), 40–43.

[4] See also Martín de Dios, "The Situation of Latin America's Indigenous Population and the Impact of COVID-19," *United Nations Development Programme Blog* (May 14, 2020), https://www.undp.org/latin-america/blog/situation-latin-america's-indigenous-population-and-impact-covid-19.

[5] Certain accounts point to communicable diseases as responsible for up to 90 percent of all premature deaths of Indigenous peoples during the Conquest and the colonial period (i.e. ,from the sixteenth until the early nineteenth centuries. Angélica Mandujano, Luis Camarillo, and Mario Mandujano, "Historia de las epidemias en el México antiguo. Algunos aspectos biológicos y sociales," *Revista Casa del Tiempo* 9 (April 2003): 12–13.

[6] Armin von Bogdandy and René Urueña, "International Transformative Constitutionalism in Latin America," *American Journal of International Law* 114 (2020): 403.

[7] "Americans" is understood continent-wide. Matiangai Sirleaf, "Racial Valuation of Diseases," *U.C.L.A. Law Review* 67 (2021): 1823–1824; Luciano Bottini Filho, "Covid-19 Through Brazilian Courts: The Deserving and the Undeserving Vulnerable," *German Law Journal* 22 (2021): 1111.

the biggest medical threat, as multiple pandemics of cholera and plague were ravaging the world.[8] The need to protect the population from the cross-border spread of those diseases was balanced against governments' sovereign right to regulate public health matters, including which measures would be adopted and when. Quarantine was a source of major contempt, as the significant variation in its imposition from country to country hampered international trade. Economic interests lay at the core of the aim toward regulatory harmonization in international health.[9]

While the corresponding conferences of each region were held in parallel, one of them, the International Sanitary Conference of 1888, took place in Washington, DC and gathered representatives from both Europe and the Americas. It was the only such Conference to be held, and no definitive agreement was reached on a common legally binding instrument.[10] Instead, the first binding International Sanitary Convention entered into force only for European countries in 1893, whereas the Pan-American Convention on Health was signed in 1902. In sum, until that point, international health law was fully fragmented across regions and almost exclusively dealt with the adoption of measures such as quarantines. This was possible because medical technologies on pharmaceutical goods were in a much earlier stage. Nonpharmaceutical interventions such as quarantine were the most effective means to stop diseases from spreading,[11] and the need to regulate them stood at the core of international lawmaking.

Against that backdrop, the emergence of a regional health law in the Americas was not a predominantly Latin American development. Beyond the entry into force of treaties, the region's history has played a notable role in regard to the early international law instruments in the field. These initiatives were driven by the United States , leading to the foundation of the International Sanitary Bureau (ISB)—the first intergovernmental body with a mandate in the field of health[12]—in 1902 with its seat in Washington, DC. The organization was founded under the aegis of the International Union of American States, the predecessor of the Organization of American States (OAS). As argued elsewhere, the foundation of the ISB was based on the US goals of consolidating its interests in the region.[13]

[8] Niels Høiby, "Pandemics: Past, Present, Future. That Is Like Choosing between Cholera and Plague," *Acta Pathologica, Microbiologica, et Immunologica Scandinavica*, 129 (2021): 352–371.

[9] On this reason for the emergence of regional health law in the Americas, Myron Wegman, "A Salute to the Pan American Health Organization," *American Journal of Public Health* 67 (1977): 1198; on the European context, see Hélène De Pooter, *Le droit international face aux pandémies: vers un système de sécurité sanitaire collective?* (Paris: Editions A Pédone, 2015), 31.

[10] Norman Howard-Jones, *The Scientific Background of the International Sanitary Conferences 1851-1938* (Geneva: WHO, 1975).

[11] Ibid., 10.

[12] Elizabeth Fee and Theodore Brown, "100 Years of the Pan American Health Organization," *American Journal of Public Health* 92, no. 12 (2002): 1888.

[13] Ibid.

Following the trend established in the nineteenth century, the harmonization of measures to protect the international spread of disease became a key concern and was still one of the core objectives of the Pan-American Sanitary Code, approved in 1924.[14] A telling sign of the regional prevalence of medical and public health expertise from the United States is that until 1958, all the leaders of the ISB and the first leader of its successor organization, the Pan-American Health Organization (PAHO), were physicians from the United States.[15]

Prevailing US Regional Health Hegemony

The history of regional US health hegemony in the Americas prevails to this day, though to a different degree than in the past. Although PAHO director-generals are geographically more diverse than their predecessor,[16] the largest contributions to the PAHO's budget come from the US government.[17] This, in turn, makes the organization highly dependent on US domestic-level politics, particularly as its senate must approve these contributions.

The regional health hegemony played by the United States plays out not only at the financial and political level. The country has the largest volume worldwide of medical, particularly pharmaceutical, innovation.[18] National agencies with a regulatory role in the health field hold direct legal sway across the region. For instance, a 2021 study found that thirteen of twenty regulatory health agencies across Latin American and the Caribbean, encompassing thirty-four countries,[19] rely upon the US Food and Drug Administration (alongside the European Medicines Agency and Health Canada) for either direct recognition of

[14] Pan American Sanitary Code, art. 1(e) (1924).

[15] The position of ISB Chair was always held by the US Surgeon General in office. Myron Wegman, "A Salute to the Pan American Health Organization," *American Journal of Public Health* 67 (1977): 1198–1200.

[16] The director-general, at the moment of writing, is Dr. Jarbas Barbosa da Silva Jr., a Brazilian national. He succeeded Dr. Carissa Etienne, from Dominica, in February 2023, for a five-year term. Urdani Samarasekera, "Jarbas Barbosa da Silva Jr: New Director of PAHO," *The Lancet* 401 (2023): 426.

[17] For the 2022–2023 Biennium, 36.1 percent of PAHO's budget was based on contributions by the United States, with the World Health Organization being the second largest contributor with 24.8 percent. See PAHO, *Contributors*, accessed May 16, 2023), https://open.paho.org/2022-23/contributors.

[18] G. Alleyne, "The Pan American Health Organization's First 100 Years: Reflections of the Director," *American Journal of Public Health* 92 (2002): 1890–1894; Fee and Brown, "100 Years of the Pan American Health Organization."

[19] The Caribbean Regulatory System encompasses fifteen member states of the Caribbean Community (CARICOM), and its authorizations are valid across all of them. Lawrence Liberti et al., "An Evaluation of the Caribbean Regulatory System Centralized Assessment Process for Medicines Submitted 2017-2018 Using the OpERA Methodology," *Journal of Pharmaceutical Policy and Practice*, 13 (2020): 56.

those same products or an abbreviated process.[20] Conversely, no Latin American or Caribbean counterpart enjoys the same degree of deference.[21]

In terms of the financing of healthcare systems, the sway over the region of the Washington Consensus favoring fiscal discipline, financial deregulation, and trade liberalization[22] has been documented and discussed elsewhere.[23] A key component of the Consensus was privatizing several areas previously belonging to the public sector. Similarly, the World Bank played an impactful role in health through its influential but controversial report, *Investing in Health*,[24] which advocated the increase of competition between health service providers, allowing for the growth of the private sector.[25] Moreover, as part of its structural adjustment programs, the World Bank made lending conditional upon reforms that limited public spending while increasing privatization of services formerly provided by the state.[26] The underlying premise was that these reforms were necessary to ensure longer-term sustainability. Nevertheless, the impact of increased privatization of the healthcare sector in the subsequent years was noticeable.[27] The outcomes of this process reflect a worsening equity in access to healthcare services, affecting vulnerable groups in particular.[28]

Beyond its hegemonic role, US technical capacities in the field of health present a potential for effective collaboration. During the H1N1 Influenza pandemic of 2009–2010, the governments of Mexico, the United States, and Canada resorted to a partnership for pandemic preparedness and response.[29] This collaboration for information and pathogen sharing allowed for the rapid identification of the new strain of the influenza virus, circulating mostly across Mexico

[20] Carlos E. Durán et al., "Regulatory Reliance to Approve New Medicinal Products in Latin America and Caribbean Countries," *Revista Panamericana de Salud Pública* 45 (2021): e10.

[21] Ibid., fig. 1.

[22] John Williamson, "The Washington Consensus and Beyond," *Economic and Political Weekly* 38 (2003): 1476.

[23] César Rodríguez Garavito, "Towards a Sociology of the Rule of Law Field: Neoliberalism, Neoconstitutionalism and the Contest over Judicial Reform in Latin America," in *Lawyers and the Rule of Law in an Era of Globalization*, ed. Yves Dezalay and Bryan Garth (London: Routledge, 2012), 155–181.

[24] World Bank, *World Development Report 1993: Investing in Health* (New York: Oxford University Press, 1993), esp. 157–164.

[25] Kamran Abbasi, "The World Bank and World Health. Under Fire," *British Medical Journal* 318 (1999): 1004–1006.

[26] Sarah Babb and Bruce Carruthers, "Conditionality: Forms, Function and History," *Annual Review of Law and Social Science* 4 (2008): 13–29.

[27] Ronald Labonté and Arne Ruckert, *Health Equity in a Globalizing Era: Past Challenges, Future Prospects* (Oxford: Oxford University Press, 2019), 53–55; Leila Bernarda Donato Göttems and Maria de Lourdes Rollemberg Mollo, "Neoliberalism in Latin America: Effects on Health System Reforms," *Revista de Saúde Pública* 54 (2020): 4–6.

[28] Santosh Mehortra and Enrique Delamonica, "The Private Sector and Privatization in Social Services. Is the Washington Consensus 'Dead'?" *Global Social Policy* 5 (2005): 154–155.

[29] *North American Plan for Avian & Pandemic Influenza*, August 2007, https://2001-2009.state.gov/documents/organization/91311.pdf.

and the United States by April 2009.[30] Experience gained in the wake of this pandemic shows the positive synergies involved in a multicountry collaboration.

In sum, the United States has played a hegemonic role on both regional health law and the ensuing regulation of healthcare at the national level. An empirical analysis documenting the evolution of healthcare systems in the region is beyond the scope of this chapter. When it comes to regional technical capacities and policymaking in the field of health, the Latin American region cannot be addressed in isolation from the United States. The consequences of such hegemony, as argued elsewhere,[31] ought to be inherently suspect.

III. Health Law with a Latin American Twist

Whereas both the World Bank[32] and several Latin American countries have steered away from the Washington Consensus era of underestimated social policies,[33] it would be far-fetched to speak of a regional consensus on how actually to ensure an effective rights-based approach to health. Yet Latin America arguably does have its own self-standing perspective toward the social determinants of health. On this front, the US and Latin America have historically parted ways. Legal adjudication and policymaking in the US have rejected the implications of such an approach by, for instance, refusing to enshrine guarantees of universal healthcare access in case law.[34] By contrast, Latin American social justice has a long-standing tradition, dating back to the nineteenth century, of protecting socioeconomic rights. In fact, Latin America directly contributed to the emergence of international human rights with a socioeconomic dimension.[35]

[30] WHO, *Strengthening Response to Pandemics and Other Public Health Emergencies. Report of the Review Committee on the Functioning of the International Health Regulations (2005) and on Pandemic Influenza (H1N1) 2009* (2011), 29.

[31] Marcelo Kohen, "The Use of Force by The United States After the End of the Cold War, and Its Impact of International Law", in *United States Hegemony and the Foundations of International Law*, eds. Michael Byers and Georg Nolte, 197–231 (Cambridge: Cambridge University Press 2003).

[32] Kamran Abbasi, "The World Bank and World Health. Changing Sides," *British Medical Journal* 318 (1999): 869.

[33] This steer away from the Washington Consensus has been gradual and has yet to become a long-lasting feature of social policies. On the increase of public expenditure in education and health in Mexico, Brazil, and Chile since the 1980s, see Ilan Goldfajn, Lorenza Martínez, and Rodrigo Valdés, "Washington Consensus in Latin America: From Raw Model to Straw Man," *Journal of Economic Perspectives* 35 (2021): 112.

[34] David Orentlicher, "Rights to Healthcare in the United States: Inherently Unstable," *American Journal of Law & Medicine* 38 (2012): 326–327; Jennifer Prah Ruger, "The Elusive Right to Health Care under U.S. Law," *The New England Journal of Medicine* 372 (2015): 2558–2563.

[35] Mary Ann Glendon, "The Forgotten Crucible: The Latin American Influence on the Universal Human Rights Idea," *Harvard Human Rights Journal* 16 (2003): 35.

The widespread acceptance of socioeconomic rights in the region stands at the basis of the prevalent rights-based perspectives toward healthcare.[36] Indeed, all countries in Latin America are parties to international treaties enshrining the right to health, such as the Constitution of the World Health Organization, the International Covenant on Economic, Social and Cultural Rights (ICESCR), and the United Nations Convention of the Child.[37] Economic, social, and cultural (ESC) rights, in particular, are imprinted from a Latin American perspective. Some countries from the region actively contributed to the drafting of the Universal Declaration of Human Rights with regard to social values inspired by a catholic tradition.[38] Similarly, all Latin American countries are bound by Article 12 ICESCR, which legally obliges states to protect the right to health. These obligations have been further expanded by the United Nations Committee on Economic, Social, and Cultural Rights, which holds the mandate to formulate an authoritative interpretation of states' obligations. Notable among them are the elements of availability, accessibility, affordability, and quality (AAAQ).[39] These elements inform obligations for states to ensure that the provision of healthcare products and services conforms with recognized human rights standards.

The rights-based approach to healthcare in Latin American countries has led to a rise in litigation in national courts. A growing body of literature has scrutinized the trend toward increased health litigation and judicialization as a means of redressing shortcomings in access to healthcare products and services.[40] Broadly speaking, litigation has yielded mixed results in terms of

[36] On the distinctive features of a rights-based approach to healthcare can make, see Aeyal Gross and Colleen Flood, "Conclusion: Contexts for the Promise and Peril of the Right to Health," in *The Right to Health at the Public/Private Divide: A Global Comparative Study*, ed. Colleen Flood and Aeyal Gross, 451 (Oxford: Oxford University Press 2014); on the Latin American region in particular, see Alicia Ely Yamín, "The Right to Health in Latin America: The Challenges of Constructing Fair Limits," *University of Pennsylvania Journal of International Law* 49 (2019): 732–734.

[37] Pedro A. Villarreal, "El derecho a la salud en lo individual y en lo colectivo: la calidad en los servicios de salud a partir de *Poblete Vilches vs. Chile*," in *Interamericanización del derecho a la salud. Perspectivas a la luz del caso Poblete de la Corte IDH*, ed. Mariela Morales Antoniazzi and Laura Clérico (Mexico City: Instituto de Estudios Constitucionales del Estado de Querétaro, 2019), 285–286.

[38] Glendon, "The Forgotten Crucible."

[39] Committee on Economic, Social and Cultural Rights, General Comment 14—Article 12: The Right to the Highest Attainable Standard of Health (August 11, 2000), E/C.12/2000/4, ¶ 12.b; see also Brigit Toebes, "International Health Law: An Emerging Field of Public International Law," *Indian Journal of International Law* 55 (2016): 310–312.

[40] By now discussed extensively in the literature. See Paola Bergallo, "Courts and Social Change: Lessons from the Struggle to Universalize Access to HIV/AIDS Treatment in Argentina," *Texas Law Review* 89 (2011): 1611; Octavio Luiz Motta Ferraz, "Harming the Poor through Social Rights Litigation: Lessons from Brazil," *Texas Law Review* 89 (2011): p. 1643; Roberto Gargarella et al., "Courts, Rights and Social Transformation: Concluding Reflections," in *Courts and Social Transformation in New Democracies*, ed. Roberto Gargarella, Pilar Domingo, and Theunis Roux (London: Routledge, 2016), 255; Malcolm Langford, "Domestic Adjudication and Economic, Social and Cultural Rights: A Socio-Legal Review," *SUR-International Journal on Human Rights* 11 (2009): 91; Cesar Rodriguez-Garavito, "Beyond the Courtroom: The Impact of Judicial Activism on Socioeconomic Rights in Latin America," *Texas Law Review* 89 (2011): 1669; Alicia Ely Yamín and

enhancing persons' access to healthcare products and services.[41] The benefits thereof have not been equally distributed, and there have been documented instances of how only some sections of the population—usually those from a middle-income background—receive most of the benefits.[42] This awareness helps explain why resorting to courts for corrective justice is not always the best way to ensure access to health products and services. Instead, legislation and policymaking are still needed to tackle structural factors undermining such access.

The IAHRS has granted the international right to health an additional regional pedigree. Though not all of the broader Latin American countries are under its jurisdiction,[43] the impact of judicial and quasi-judicial decisions has been documented and appraised across the literature.[44] Standards developed within the IAHRS have strived to overcome the division between ESC rights, on the one hand, and civil and political rights, on the other hand. Under the Charter of the OAS and the American Convention on Human Rights (ACHR), Latin American states are bound to protect both. From a procedural perspective, the vague wording of Article 26 of the ACHR led in the past to a persistent reluctance by the IACtHR to issue rulings in contentious cases establishing a direct violation of ESC rights.[45] Consequently, cases dealing with human rights violations in healthcare settings resorted to civil and political rights, namely, the right to life as enshrined in Article 2 ACHR.[46] This was deemed the "indirect approach" in the justiciability of the right to health.[47]

Siri Gloppen (eds), *Litigating Health Rights: Can Courts Bring More Justice to Health?* (Cambridge, MA: Harvard University Press, 2011); Audrey Chapman, *Global Health, Human Rights and the Challenge of Neoliberal Policies* (Cambridge: Cambridge University Press, 2016), 14.

[41] Octavio Ferraz, *Health as a Human Right: The Politics and Judicialisation of Health in Brazil* (Cambridge: Cambridge University Press, 2020), 225–274.

[42] Yamín, "The Right to Health in Latin America," 732–733.

[43] Both Venezuela and Nicaragua have denounced the American Convention on Human Rights—with the latter withdrawing from the OAS altogether. See Mariela Morales, "Advisory Opinion OC-26/20, Denunciation of the American Convention on Human Rights and the Charter of the Organization of American States and the Consequences for State Human Rights Obligations," *American Journal of International Law* 116, no. 2 (2022): 410.

[44] See the overarching study by Armin von Bogdandy et al. (eds), *The Impact of the Inter-American Human Rights System: Transformations on the Ground* (Oxford: Oxford University Press, 2024).

[45] Underscored in Tara Melish, "The Inter-American Court of Human Rights. Beyond Progressivity," in *Social Rights Jurisprudence. Emerging Trends in International and Comparative Law*, ed. Malcolm Langford (Cambridge: Cambridge University Press, 2008) 375–376.

[46] See, e.g., *Albán Cornejo et al. v. Ecuador*, Judgment of November 22, 2007, Merits, Reparations, and Costs, Inter-Am. Ct. H.R. (ser. C) No. 171, ¶¶ 117–122.

[47] Óscar Parra Vera, "La protección del derecho a la salud a través de casos contenciosos ante el Sistema Interamericano de Derechos Humanos," in *Tratado de derecho a la salud*, ed. Laura Clérico, Martín Aldao, and Liliana Ronconi (Buenos Aires: Abeledo Perrot, 2013), 762.

Already under the "indirect approach," IASHR case law offered criteria for addressing the consequences of increased participation of the private sector in healthcare. In *Ximenes Lópes v. Brazil*, by recognizing the protection of health as a matter of "public interest," the IACtHR affirmed states' human rights duties related to acts committed by private healthcare institutions, including those of medical negligence.[48] While states are certainly not responsible due to the negative outcomes of healthcare practices per se, they must fulfill a supervisory role, on the one hand, and ensure that affected individuals have access to effective remedies, on the other hand.[49]

An interpretive turning point on the direct justiciability of the right to health in Latin America came with the IACtHR case *Poblete Vilches v. Chile* in 2017.[50] Here, the previously espoused "indirect" approach to the justiciability of the right to health ceded to a "direct" one. The case concerned the death of Mr. Vinicio Antonio Poblete Vilches, an elderly man, in 2001. In its reasoning, the IACtHR referred to the distinction between obligations of *progressive* and *immediate* fulfillment in the right to health. The Court emphasized that obligations of *immediate* fulfillment, in particular, entailed adopting effective measures that "guarantee access, without discrimination, to the benefits recognized for each right,"[51] which in the case at hand was the right to health.[52] Arguably, this case did not entail new substantive components that reshaped the right to health; instead, procedural innovations now allow applicants to claim a direct violation of the right as a basis for their complaints. In the wake of this case, the IACtHR constitutes, so far, the only regional human rights court establishing the direct justiciability of the right to health.[53] This raises multiple questions about whether and to what extent this offers a toolkit that includes protection against other health problems, such as pandemics.

Notably, in *Poblete Vilches v. Chile*, the IACtHR asserted an inter-American consensus on the right to health being enshrined in domestic constitutional law.[54] Having such a constitutional legal basis enables courts to conduct judicial review on whether national authorities have fulfilled their obligations according to a AAAQ perspective. Nevertheless, as is now a long-established trope,

[48] *Ximenes Lopes v. Brazil*, Judgment of July 4, 2006, Merits, Reparations and Costs, Inter-Am. Ct. H.R. (ser. C) No. 149, ¶¶ 85–90.

[49] Ibid., ¶ 89.

[50] *Poblete Vilches v. Chile*, Judgment of March 8, 2018 (Merits, Reparations and Costs), Inter-Am. Ct. H.R. (ser. C) No. 349.

[51] Ibid., ¶ 104.

[52] Ibid., ¶ 124.

[53] International Law Association, *Committee on Global Health Law*, 2020 Report, ¶ 104, https://www.ila-hq.org/index.php/committees

[54] The Court examined the constitutions and laws of twenty Latin American and Caribbean countries. *Poblete Vilches v Chile*, Inter-Am. Ct. H.R., ¶ 113.

the distance between "law in books" and "law in action"[55] is comparatively large in the region.

There are several limitations to judicializing the right to health in the IASHR. To mention a few, there is, first, a two-stage "funnel" in terms of which cases may eventually reach the judgment phase. Individuals may not directly submit a case to the IACtHR, but rather rely upon the Commission to do so,[56] which has led to a decades-long substantial backlog. Directly related to it, in terms of the average time span of individual cases, *Poblete Vilches v. Chile* took twenty years from Mr. Vilches's death for the case to reach a judgment at the IACtHR. In the face of more acute challenges, such as the COVID-19 pandemic, and drawing from the principle of subsidiarity,[57] the inter-American jurisdiction does not offer immediate remedies for individuals. Moreover, the Commission's and Court's precautionary and provisional measures, aimed at addressing "urgent" situations, do not encompass issues regarding health services and products and require the fulfillment of more stringent requirements than their national equivalents.[58] Arguably, belated and restricted access to justice is by design unfit to be a first-responding mechanism against the risk posed by acute communicable disease threats.[59] Nevertheless, as argued elsewhere, the IACHR and the Court partially compensate for these shortcomings by issuing structural remedies beyond individual cases and sometimes benefiting entire communities.[60]

[55] On this theme, Rachel Sieder, Karina Ansolabehere, and Tatiana Alfonso, "Law and Society in Latin America: An Introduction," in *Routledge Handbook of Law and Society in Latin America*, ed. Rachel Sieder, Karina Ansolabehere, and Tatiana Alfonso (New York: Routledge, 2019), 3.

[56] Alexandra Huneeus, "Courts Resisting Courts: Lessons from the Inter-American Court's Struggle to Enforce Human Rights," *Cornell International Law Journal* 44, no. 3 (2011): 499–500; Sabrina Ragone, "The Inter-American System of Human Rights: Essential Features," in *Transformative Constitutionalism in Latin America: The Emergence of a New Ius Commune*, ed. Armin von Bogdandy (Oxford: Oxford University Press, 2017), 290.

[57] Paolo Carozza, "Subsidiarity as a Structural Principle of International Human Rights Law," *American Journal of International Law* 97 (2003): 78–79; Pablo González Domínguez, "Reconfiguración de la relación entre el derecho internacional de los derechos humanos y el derecho nacional sobre la base del principio de subsidiariedad," *Anuario Mexicano de Derecho Internacional* 17 (2017): 742–743.

[58] Felipe González, "Urgent Measures in the Inter-American Human Rights System," *Sur* 7 (2010): 66.

[59] Pedro Villarreal, "The role of interstate adjudication in public health emergencies: Incompatible at the core", *QIL* 85 (2021): 43–45.

[60] Leidy Cornejo, "New Remedial Responses in the Practice of Regional Human Rights Courts: Purposes beyond Compensation," *International Journal of Constitutional Law* 15, no. 2 (2017): 386–390.

IV. Communicable Diseases and Health Law in Latin America: Overcoming Atavisms

In the twentieth century, the theory of epidemiological transition developed by Abdel Omran showed how communicable diseases were gradually receding as the cause of death in the global realm of disease.[61] Life expectancy increased globally, and until COVID-19, noncommunicable diseases represented the main causes of death and disability.[62] However, this transition certainly did not take place homogenously. On the contrary, multiple countries experience what is known as the "double burden of disease"[63] because, on the one hand, communicable diseases that are receding globally are still present in countries with weak health infrastructure; on the other hand, the population of these countries also faces the blight of noncommunicable diseases that increasingly affect low-, middle- and high-income countries. In the case of Latin America and before the COVID-19 pandemic, the burden posed by communicable diseases also followed a decades-long receding trend.[64] But, following the region's historical background explained in section II, vulnerable groups in the population have remained marginalized and do not enjoy, in general, the same degree of access to healthcare services.[65]

In past public health emergencies caused by disease outbreaks, like the H1N1 influenza pandemic and the Zika epidemic, Latin American countries have, for the most part, mostly left each other to their own devices. Absent a deeper institutional integration in the region, including in the OAS,[66] interstate health cooperation in the region has been ad hoc and without a unified front.

Regional legal standards on communicable diseases remain thin but are not nonexistent. The IAHRS has addressed the impact of communicable diseases on Indigenous peoples, in light of their vulnerability. While the obligations of the right to health apply to all inhabitants, and not just Indigenous communities, the need for a concrete approach in their case results from atavisms that persist

[61] Abdel Omran, "The Epidemiologic Transition: A Theory of the Epidemiology of Population Change," *Milbank Quarterly* 83 (2005): 731–757.

[62] GBD 2019 Diseases and Injuries Collaborators, "Global Burden of 369 Diseases and Injuries in 204 Countries and Territories, 1990–2019: A Systematic Analysis for the Global Burden of Disease Study 2019," *The Lancet* 369 (2020): 1218.

[63] Abdesslam Boutayeb, "The Double Burden of Communicable and Non-Communicable Diseases in Developing Countries," *Transactions of the Royal Society of Tropical Medicine and Hygiene* 100 (2005): 191–199.

[64] GBD 2019 Diseases and Injuries Collaborators, "Global Burden of 369 Diseases and Injuries," 1210–1212, fig. 2A.

[65] Organisation for Economic Cooperation and Development (OECD), *Primary Health Care for Resilient Health Systems in Latin America* (Paris: OECD Publishing, 2022), 21–23.

[66] Juan Herrera, *Las cláusulas durmientes de integración latinoamericana. Orígenes, funciones y opciones para despertarla* (México City: UNAM/Max Planck Institute for Comparative Public Law and International Law, 2019), 34–37.

to date.[67] Thus, in 1985, the IACHR relied upon the OAS Charter to address applications against both the Paraguayan[68] and Brazilian[69] governments, among other things, due to a lack of access to adequate medical goods and services to protect against communicable diseases.[70]

Disease outbreaks in the region have exposed the need for human rights obligations to offer more than just protection against their spread. The spread of Zika throughout the Americas peaked between 2015 and 2017.[71] Among its primary concerns was the correlation between exposure to the Zika virus, on the one hand, and the risk of microcephaly in newborns, on the other hand.[72] This risk was one of the main reasons why the World Health Organization (WHO) declared the spread of Zika through the Americas a public health emergency of international concern in February 2016,[73] with Brazil being the most affected country.[74]

The Zika outbreak underscored the region's prevailing limitations in access to sexual and reproductive services. Women from several Latin American countries could simply not opt for abortion in its wake.[75] More recently, the case *Beatriz v. El Salvador* regarding the full prohibition on abortion in El Salvador—the country in the Americas with the harshest restriction—is pending judgment at the IACtHR.[76] The facts of the case concern a mother, "Beatriz," who was denied the possibility to abort even though the fetus suffered from a severe malformation (anencephaly) and, additionally, her life was at risk because of the

[67] Puig, *At the Margins of Globalization.*

[68] The IACHR considered that the Paraguayan State's failure to guarantee access to medical goods and services to the Aché Tribe during epidemic events was a violation of Art. XI of the OAS Charter. IACHR, *Tribu Aché (Paraguay)* Resolution of 27 May 1977, OEA/Ser. L/V/II.43 doc. 21 corr. 1, 34–35.

[69] The Commission highlighted the devastating effect of epidemics of influenza, tuberculosis, measles, malaria, and venereal diseases in the Yanomami community, leading to a "considerable number of deaths." IACHR, Res. No. 12/85, Case No. 7615 (Brazil) (March 5, 1985), ¶ 10(f).

[70] Verą, "La protección del derecho a la salud a través de casos contenciosos ante el Sistema Interamericano de Derechos Humanos," 764.

[71] Neil Ferguson et al., "Countering the Zika Epidemic in Latin America," *Science* 353 (2016): 353. By 2017, the epidemic had receded. Rebecca Borchering et al., "Impacts of Zika Emergence in Latin America on Endemic Dengue Transmission," *Nature Communications* 10 (2019): 1.

[72] WHO, *WHO Statement on the First Meeting of the International Health Regulations (2005) (IHR 2005) Emergency Committee on Zika virus and observed increase in neurological disorders and neonatal transformations* (February 1, 2016), https://www.who.int/news/item/01-02-2016-who-statement-on-the-first-meeting-of-the-international-health-regulations-(2005)-(ihr-2005)-emergency-committee-on-zika-virus-and-observed-increase-in-neurological-disorders-and-neonatal-malformations.

[73] Ibid.

[74] Laith Yakob, "Zika Virus after the Public Health Emergency of International Concern Period, Brazil," *Emerging Infectious Diseases* 28 (2022): 837–840.

[75] Mabel Carabali et al., "The Zika Epidemic and Abortion in Latin America: A Scoping Review," *Global Health Research and Policy* 3 (2018): 1.

[76] Julia Zulver, "'Historic Moment' as El Salvador Abortion Case Fuels Hopes for Expanded Access across Latin America," *The Guardian*, March 24, 2023, https://www.theguardian.com/global-development/2023/mar/24/historic-moment-as-el-salvador-abortion-case-fuels-hopes-for-expanded-access-across-latin-america.

pregnancy. While this is a slightly different scenario than the one that mothers experienced due to Zika-related microcephaly in babies, both scenarios underscore prevailing limitations in the field of sexual and reproductive rights. These rights are further hampered by the activism of morally conservative lobby groups throughout the Americas, which deploy electoral and other political strategies to hamper their exercise.[77] The interface between the protection against communicable diseases and the exercise of sexual and reproductive rights is one where the latter remains without sufficiently widespread recognition and enshrinement

V. The Regional Future of Law and Pandemics after COVID-19

From the perspective of healthcare systems, the COVID-19 pandemic struck the Latin American region in the middle of a transition process. Most countries there had, even before the pandemic, reached the status of middle-income economies.[78] Nevertheless, despite the expansion of some type of insurance coverage overall, the provision of healthcare services is still heavily determined by levels of personal income.[79] The region's high degree of income inequality[80] leads to a dissonance in fulfilling basic healthcare needs. The most recent data on healthcare system expenditures shows that the proportion of private "out-of-pocket" expenses is comparatively high.[81] Thus, the accessibility of healthcare services continues to be stunted. Such a precarious setting may have worsened the impact of the COVID-19 pandemic. By March 2022, the region had reported 28 percent of all worldwide deaths despite having 8 percent of the global population.[82]

Latin America's distinctive rights-based approach must be part and parcel of any pandemic prevention, preparedness, and response strategy. Indeed, during responses to the COVID-19 pandemic, public health measures adopted for mitigating the spread of the disease should have been epidemiologically sound and context-sensitive.[83] Consequently, a regional approach toward pandemics

[77] Deisy Ventura et al., "A Rights-Based Approach to Public Health Emergencies: The Case of the 'More Rights, Less Zika' Campaign in Brazil," *Global Public Health. An International Journal for Research, Policy and Practice* 16 (2021): 1576–1589.

[78] Until 2021, of the forty-one countries and territories listed by the World Bank as being part of Latin America and the Caribbean, fourteen were listed as high income (with Chile, Uruguay, and several islands in the Caribbean), nineteen as upper middle income, and the remaining six as lower middle income. There were no low-income per capita countries by that point. World Bank, "The World by Income and Region," https://datatopics.worldbank.org/world-development-indicators/the-world-by-income-and-region.html.

[79] OECD, "Global Burden of 369 Diseases and Injuries," 11–12.

[80] CEPAL, *Panorama Social de América Latina.*

[81] Ibid.

[82] Alvaro Schwalb et al., "COVID-19 in Latin America and the Caribbean: Two Years of the Pandemic," *Journal of Internal Medicine* 292 (2022): 409.

[83] WHO, *Considerations for Implementing and Adjusting Public Health and Social Measures in the Context of COVID-19*, Interim guidance (March 30, 2023), 1.

could offer a clearer perspective of features that must be considered when tailoring those measures. Yet, in comparison to regional counterparts, such as the European or African Centers for Disease Prevention and Control and even the Caribbean Public Health Agency, which is a supranational agency, the PAHO lacks the same depth in its legal mandate—though granted, this is not an exclusively Latin American feature. Still, the PAHO may and does issue technical guidance, which can assist national authorities when deciding upon which pandemic strategies to follow.[84]

Incorporating a human rights perspective toward public health measures against pandemics is not only normatively desirable but has also been identified as a component of an overall effective response. The PAHO recommends incorporating context-sensitive human rights approaches to public policies against COVID-19 by incorporating individual and collective rights to improve Indigenous peoples' health and foster development.[85] As stated above, the judicial design of the IASHR does not allow for reviewing the human rights conformity of states' actions and omissions during acute disease outbreaks. Nevertheless, in the wake of the COVID-19 pandemic, the Inter-American Commission did issue several resolutions underscoring states' obligations to respect and fulfill human rights, focusing on both COVID-19 patients and the general population.[86]

Thus far, the PAHO has played a technical and supporting role in managing disease outbreaks and pandemics. However, it does have initiatives with the potential for a deeper role in terms of regional health cooperation. The PAHO hosts a so-called Revolving Fund to purchase medical goods, including vaccines.[87] The Fund has been deployed to procure vaccines during the H1N1 Influenza and the COVID-19 pandemics. As shown elsewhere, the amount of vaccines procured through the Revolving Fund during the H1N1 Influenza Pandemic only amounted to a fraction of the total volume procured by Latin American countries, with the vast majority being purchased directly from manufacturers through bilateral contracts.[88]

[84] Offering a summary of measures against COVID-19 in the European context and its relevance for the Americas, see PAHO, *Considerations on the Adjustments of Social Distancing and Travel-Related Measures in the Context of the Response to COVID-19 Pandemic* (April 24, 2020), 3–4.

[85] The PAHO, in particular, emphasizes how individual and collective rights can, by recognizing ancestral practices, help protect older Indigenous persons and promote biodiversity protection and sustainable economies. PAHO, *The Sociodemographic Situation of Indigenous Peoples in Latin America and the Caribbean. Analysis in the Context of Aging and COVID-19* (2023), 30–31.

[86] IACHR, *Pandemic and Human Rights in the Americas*, Res. 1/2020 (April 10, 2020); IACHR, *Human Rights of Persons with COVID-19*, Res. 4/2020 (July 27, 2020).

[87] Created in 1977. See Fariza Nasreen Seraj Ahmad et al., "Southeast Asia Needs a Revolving Fund for Vaccines," *The Lancet Global Health* 10 (2022): E1557–E1558.

[88] On the volumes of vaccine doses purchased during the H1N1 influenza pandemic, see Alba María Ropero Álvarez et al., "Pandemic Influenza Vaccination: Lessons Learned from Latin America and the Caribbean," *Vaccines* 30 (2012): 917.

The argument can be made that PAHO has sufficient tools to play a larger role in fostering a rights-based approach toward pandemic prevention, preparedness, and response. In its capacity as a regional WHO office, PAHO has historically enjoyed a high degree of autonomy with regard to the headquarters in Geneva.[89] Discussions on the future role of PAHO have focused on whether it is fit for its purpose, especially regarding a precarious financial situation.[90] Furthermore, the historically hegemonic undertone of the role of the United States in the region has not disappeared. For various reasons, unlike supranational health agencies of the European and African Unions and the Caribbean, no Latin America-wide institution plays such a role. While having a visible presence, neither the PAHO nor any of the regional or subregional bodies for integration[91] have explored the potential of a Latin American health law capable of capitalizing on its distinctive rights-based approach toward health.

VI. Conclusion: The Need for a Latin American Perspective in Health Law and Pandemics

By now, it is a truism to affirm that the spread of communicable diseases recognizes no national borders or, for that matter, regional distinctions. The COVID-19 pandemic exposed the preexisting vulnerability of healthcare systems. The unfulfilled health equity goals in Latin America and its relation to the pandemic response are not exclusive regional phenomena. However, how the disease affected Latin American countries merits closer inquiry. Understanding the social determinants of health must involve addressing specificities in every context. The Latin American region and how its colonial past[92] was fraught with the social exclusion of vulnerable groups, including Indigenous peoples, warrants in-depth studies focusing on how these features lead to consequences of public health measures and the lack thereof.[93]

The story of international law and pandemics in Latin America is mired in episodes where the broader themes have played out: a hegemonic role played

[89] For an in-depth study, see Tine Hanrieder, *International Organization in Time: Fragmentation and Reform* (Oxford: Oxford University Press 2015), 47–70.

[90] Arlene King, Jon Kim Andrus, and J. Peter Figueroa, "Financial Crisis at PAHO in the Time of COVID-19: A Call for Action," *The Lancet* 396 (2020): 96.

[91] Besides CARICOM, there are currently at least thirteen groupings of Latin American states with the goal of fostering integration. Herrera, *Las cláusulas durmientes de integración latinoamericana*, 35.

[92] On how the colonial past of countries can have a direct link to communicable disease outbreaks, with the particular example of the West African Ebola crisis of 2014, see Matiangai Sirleaf, "Responsibility for Epidemics," *Texas Law Review* 97 (2018): 309.

[93] For a similar plea, see Tamara Giles-Vernick et al., "Louis Pasteur, COVID-19, and the Social Challenges of Epidemic," *The Lancet* 400 (2022): 2166–2168.

by the United States; rampant inequality and exclusion inherited from colonial times; a trend of judicializing the right to health, with its ensuing prospects and pitfalls; and a trend of unfulfilled prospects posed by an economic transition.

Although this chapter does not argue for a Latin American public health exceptionalism, strategies to face pandemics would benefit from a contextualized, rights-based regional approach. So far, the fulfillment of the multiple layers of the right to health in the region continues to be bogged down by obstacles in access to quality healthcare products and services. The region's preceding health profile helps us understand how a pandemic such as COVID-19 struck in circumstances that were already adverse. Thus, the devastation brought upon by COVID-19 only reinforced the plight of healthcare in Latin America, saddled by unequal access to health products and services. These challenges continue to undermine the realization of the elements of the right to health's AAAQ formulation.

As the strengthening of healthcare systems in Latin America advances, new avenues are sketched along the different components of the right to health. Available data on access to healthcare shows an upward trend of persons legally entitled to basic medical care services in almost all countries from the region.[94] Aside from those experiencing severe financial crises before COVID-19, most Latin American countries had expanded the number of persons affiliated with the healthcare system. But, despite progress in this formal dimension of access, new questions have emerged about the next step in the health transition. According to recent studies, not all Latin American countries actually incorporate substantive components of the concept of health equity.[95] Notably, access to health products and services for vulnerable and marginalized groups continues to be especially restricted. This reflects a particularly tone-deaf neglect of historical processes. Despite instances in which access is enshrined in law, there is still an open question about the quality of such services.[96] Public health research shows how death rates of patients due to insufficient quality of services, including medical malpractice, remain quite high.[97] These and other burgeoning health challenges continue to underscore the need to take the regional dimension of the legal determinants of health more seriously.

[94] OECD, "Global Burden of 369 Diseases and Injuries."

[95] Matthew Kavanagh et al., "Planning for Health Equity in the Americas: An Analysis of National Health Plans," *Revista Panamericana de Salud Pública* 45 (2021): e35–e37.

[96] OECD, "Global Burden of 369 Diseases and Injuries."

[97] Data was taken from before the COVID-19 pandemic. See Committee on Improving the Quality of Health Care Globally, *Crossing the Global Quality Chasm: Improving Health Care Worldwide* (Washington, DC: National Academies Press, 2018), 2.

31

Latin America and the Regulation of Internet and Digital Trade

Rodrigo Polanco[*]

I. Introduction

The internet is supposed to be global, but its rules are primarily created in the North, and contributions from the South commonly go unacknowledged. We can appreciate this from the very origin of the proto-internet. For instance, it is well-known that the Advanced Research Projects Agency Network (ARPANET)—a US Department of Defense project developed in the late 1960s and implemented in the early 1970s—is one of the technical foundations of the internet. The first public demonstration of this new network technology took place in October 1972 at the International Computer Communication Conference (ICCC).[1]

However, it is largely unknown that around the same time, the Chilean project Cybersyn became a case of the so-called groupware and early "internet" communication or even what can be considered an initial form of the "cloud." Cybersyn was created as a distributed decision support system to manage the socialist economy under the Allende government from 1971 to 1973. Unfortunately, it was destroyed after the coup d'état that same year.[2]

This is just an example of how the involvement of Latin America—and the Global South—is often overlooked when it comes to internet development. In this chapter, we aim to present the participation of countries of the region in regulating the web, with particular emphasis on one of its more essential uses—digital trade. We do not claim that these countries have been crucial in

* I am grateful to Derek Bambauer, Carlos Espósito, Sergio Puig, Alejandro Chehtman, Alexandra Huneeus, and all other Latin American International Law workshop participants for their useful comments and suggestions. All errors and omissions are mine.

[1] Barry M. Leiner et al., *Brief History of the Internet* (Reston, VA: Internet Society, 1997), 3–4, accessed November 12, 2024, https://www.internetsociety.org/wp-content/uploads/2017/09/ISOC-History-of-the-Internet_1997.pdf.

[2] The project was largely developed by British Stafford Beer and the Chilean engineer Fernando Flores, with a team of Chilean and British engineers who developed a plan for a new technological system that would improve the government's ability to coordinate the state-run economy. See Eden Medina, *Cybernetic Revolutionaries: Technology and Politics in Allende's Chile* (Cambridge, MA: MIT Press, 2011); Katharina Loeber, "Big Data, Algorithmic Regulation, and the History of the Cybersyn Project in Chile, 1971–1973," *Social Sciences* 7 (2008): 65.

Rodrigo Polanco, *Latin America and the Regulation of Internet and Digital Trade* In: *Latin American International Law in the Twenty-First Century*. Edited by: Alejandro Chehtman, Alexandra Huneeus, and Sergio Puig, Oxford University Press. © Oxford University Press 2025.
DOI: 10.1093/9780197754016.003.0031

the technological development of the internet. Instead, Latin American countries have made a distinct contribution, advancing principles like open access and net neutrality. In addition, they have pioneered the inclusion of e-commerce and data flow provisions in preferential trade agreements (PTAs).

The chapter is organized as follows. After this introduction, we examine Latin America's participation in advancing the internet principles of open access and net neutrality. Section III provides a detailed description of e-commerce and data rules in PTAs that Latin American countries concluded. To finalize, section IV highlights potential conflicts between these countries' domestic regulations and international commitments concerning the internet and digital trade.

II. The Development of Internet Principles

The internet has been made possible through a mix of both technical and policy principles. There is essentially an agreement on the central tenets that allow the interconnection of computer networks to communicate with other networks and devices, like the Transmission Control Protocol (TCP), the Internet Protocol (IP), domain names system (DNS), and the Uniform Resource Locator (URL), among others. However, many would claim that there is no general internet policy architecture, only a set of unwritten traditions.

For some, international internet law includes five core principles: internet freedom, privacy, territorial jurisdiction adapted to cyberspace, interstate cooperation, and multistakeholder cooperation.[3] Members of the Organisation for Economic Co-operation and Development (OECD) have endorsed fourteen principles for internet policymaking. These include promoting and protecting the global free flow of information; promoting the open, distributed, and interconnected nature of the internet; promoting and enabling the cross-border delivery of services; and limiting internet intermediary liability.[4]

In this section, we draw attention to two internet principles Latin American countries have pushed forward: open access and net neutrality.

Open Access

Open access (OA) means free and unrestricted online access to scientific and scholarly information. In 2002, the Budapest Open Access Initiative (BOAI)

[3] Robert Uerpmann-Wittzack, "Principles of International Internet Law," *German Law Journal* 11 (2010): 1245.

[4] OECD, *Recommendation of the Council on Principles for Internet Policy-Making* (2014), accessed November 12, 2024, https://legalinstruments.oecd.org/public/doc/328/body-text.en.html.

defined it as "free availability on the public internet, permitting any users to read, download, copy, distribute, print, search, or link to the full texts of these articles, crawl them for indexing, pass them as data to software, or use them for any other lawful purpose, without financial, legal, or technical barriers other than those inseparable from gaining access to the internet itself. The only constraint on reproduction and distribution, and the only role for copyright in this domain, should be to give authors control over the integrity of their work and the right to be properly acknowledged and cited."[5]

Two complementary strategies are traditionally recommended to achieve OA goals: self-archiving of accepted manuscripts in open-access repositories ("green" road) and publishing in open-access journals ("gold" road).[6]

Although the OA movement began in the Global North, in 1991, with Paul Ginsparg's online repository of electronic preprints, later renamed to "ArXiv.org,"[7] academic publications in those countries still significantly rely on a mix of intellectual property rights (IPR) and open science. This framework is understood as a set of practices that increases the transparency and accessibility of scientific research, which includes open access.[8] For example, for the European Commission, there is no incompatibility between IPR and open science, and it actively promotes this model.[9] Leading academic publishers are mainly in the North. Although, over the years, they have included different OA mechanisms, like shortened embargo periods and paying for gold open access, a significant number of academic publications are still subject to IPR and partly rely on a traditional business model that considers subscription to journals. This explains the emergence (and success) of sites like Sci-Hub.[10]

Countries socially and historically excluded from the center of science can benefit from OA. For example, researchers from institutions unable to afford commercial journals and database subscriptions can access relevant literature. In addition, OA initiatives are expected to increase the visibility of those countries' research output.[11]

[5] BOAI, "Budapest Open Access Initiative" (February 14, 2002), accessed November 12, 2024, https://www.budapestopenaccessinitiative.org/read.

[6] Charles W. Bailey Jr., "What Is Open Access?" (February 7, 2007), accessed November 12, 2024, https://digital-scholarship.org/cwb/what-is-open-access.pdf.

[7] Open Access Network, History of the Open Access Movement, accessed November 12, 2024, https://open-access.network/en/information/open-access-primers/history-of-the-open-access-movement.

[8] Tim van der Zee and Justin Reich, "Open Education Science," *AERA Open* 4 (2018): 2332858418787466.

[9] Directorate-General for Research and Innovation (European Commission), *Open Science and Intellectual Property Rights: How Can They Better Interact? : State of the Art and Reflections. Report of Study* (Luxembourg: Publications Office of the European Union, 2022).

[10] Juan C. Correa et al., "The Sci-Hub Effect on Papers' Citations," *Scientometrics* 127 (2022): 99.

[11] Michelli Pereira da Costa and Fernando César Lima Leite, "Open Access in the World and Latin America: A Review since the Budapest Open Access Initiative," *Transinformação* 28 (2016): 33.

According to the United Nations Educational, Scientific and Cultural Organization (UNESCO), Latin America has a long tradition of providing OA to its research results in regional subject repositories. This process started in the 1980s with bibliographic records, and it was extended at the end of the 1990s to full texts, digital repositories, and multidisciplinary regional peer-reviewed journal portals.[12]

Furthermore, the region has contributed to the implementation of OA by strengthening the necessary infrastructure and adopting regional instruments like the "Declaration of Salvador" (2005), promoting "broad and equitable access to national and international sources of information and knowledge."[13] Since 2016, the Open Forum of Sciences of Latin America and the Caribbean (CILAC) has become a biannual regional space for debate and exchange Its purpose is to discuss how to strengthen and implement effective science, technology, and innovation policies in line with the Sustainable Development Goals of Agenda 2030, including open science as one of the tools to achieve those goals.[14]

Over the past decade, the region has been working to create policies and initiatives to encourage open science practices and promote access to publicly funded research. In this context, Argentina, Brazil, Chile, Colombia, Costa Rica, Mexico, and Peru have developed data policies and initiatives, including OA.[15]

Some countries have been great enablers of open access through domestic legislation mandating that state-funded research results be available in OA digital repositories. For example, Argentina[16] and Peru[17] approved such legislation in 2013, and Mexico did it in 2014.[18] These countries also created national repositories for their national research output.[19]

[12] UNESCO, "Latin America and the Caribbean," *Global Open Access Portal*, September 29, 2021, accessed November 12, 2024, https://goap.info/oa/access-by-region/latin-america-and-the-caribbean/.

[13] Ninth World Congress on Health Information and Libraries and Seventh Regional Congress of Information in Health Sciences, "Declaration of Salvador—Commitment to Equity" (September 23, 2005), accessed November 12, 2024, http://www.icml9.org/channel.php?lang=en&channel=91&content=438.

[14] CILAC, "About CILAC" (2022), accessed November 12, 2024, https://forocilac.org/en/about-foro-cilac/.

[15] Dominique Saugy de Babini and Laura Rovelli, *Tendencias recientes en las políticas científicas de ciencia abierta y acceso abierto en Iberoamérica* (Buenos Aires : CLACSO; Fundación Carolina, 2020), accessed November 12, 2024, https://www.jstor.org/stable/10.2307/j.ctv1gm02tq.

[16] Argentina, Ley 26.899, Repositorios digitales institucionales de acceso abierto, accessed November 12, 2024, http://servicios.infoleg.gob.ar/infolegInternet/anexos/220000-224999/223459/norma.htm.

[17] Peru, Ley que regula el repositorio nacional digital de ciencia, tecnología e innovación de acceso abierto, accessed November 12, 2024, https://portal.concytec.gob.pe/images/stories/images2013/portal/areas-institucion/dsic/ley-30035.pdf.

[18] Mexico, Decreto por el que se reforman y adicionan diversas disposiciones de la Ley de Ciencia y Tecnología, de la Ley General de Educación y de la Ley Orgánica del Consejo Nacional de Ciencia y Tecnología (Diario Oficial, May 20, 2014), accessed November 12, 2024, https://www.dof.gob.mx/nota_detalle.php?codigo=5345503&fecha=20/05/2014&print=true.

[19] These are "CONICET Digital" in Argentina, accessed November 10, 2023, https://ri.conicet.gov.ar/; "ALICIA" (Acceso Libre a la Información Científica) in Peru, accessed November 12, 2024,

In other countries, despite the absence of mandatory laws for OA in national research, government agencies are contributing to data sharing and reuse or managing national systems of digital repositories.[20] For instance, Brazil unsuccessfully introduced bills on OA in 2007 and 2011. However, since 2019, FAPESP (the Sao Paulo State funding agency) has required that all journal articles it has funded be publicly available in institutional OA repositories if this does not violate copyright rules.[21] In Chile, the National Agency for Research and Development (ANID) policy since 2022 is that any project financed in whole or in part through its instruments must consider the necessary mechanisms to manage open access to documents, publications, or research data.[22] In Colombia, the then Administrative Department of Science, Technology and Innovation (COLCIENCIAS)—now Ministry of Technology, Science and Information (MINCIENCIAS)—made public in December 2018 its "Guidelines for an Open Science In Colombia," which includes open access to the results of research financed with public resources.[23] In Costa Rica, in 2016, the National Council of Rectors (CONARE) created the National Repository "Kímuk," an OA tool whose objective is to enhance the online visibility of academic and scientific production as a crucial input for the scientific and technological development of the country.[24]

Historically, the leading publishers in the North have shown limited interest in publishing academic books and journals in Latin America. Few academic publishers exist in the region, and printed versions of books and journals have suffered from irregular publication and restricted circulation. Thus, scholarly legal writing from the region, either in Spanish or Portuguese, has generally been absent from international indexes, producing low visibility of the region's scientific research output.[25]

Furthermore, the regional editorial tradition does not consider a fee for authors or readers; publishing is traditionally scholarly led, owned, and

https://alicia.concytec.gob.pe/; and the National Repository in Mexico, accessed November 12, 2024, https://www.siicyt.gob.mx/index.php/repositorio-nacional.

[20] Leandro Torres and Ricardo Hartley, "Repositories for Academic Products/Outputs: Latin American and Chilean Visions," *F1000Research* 8 (2019): 1517.

[21] FAPESP, Portaria CTA no. 01/2019, Institui a "Política para Acesso Aberto às Publicações Resultantes de Auxílios e Bolsas FAPESP," accessed November 12, 2024, https://fapesp.br/12632/portaria-cta-no-012019.

[22] ANID, Política de acceso abierto a la información científica y a datos de investigación financiados con fondos públicos de la ANID, accessed November 12, 2024, https://s3.amazonaws.com/documentos.anid.cl/estudios/Politica_acceso_a_informacion_cientifica_2022.pdf.

[23] COLCIENCIAS, Lineamientos para una Política de Ciencia Abierta en Colombia, accessed November 12, 2024, https://minciencias.gov.co/sites/default/files/lineamientos_ciencia_abierta_17_dic_2018_version_aprobda_comite_de_direccion_udep.pdf.

[24] CONARE, Kimuk, accessed November 12, 2024, https://kimuk.conare.ac.cr/Content/aabierto.

[25] UNESCO, "Latin America and the Caribbean."

financed.[26] For these reasons, the free print distribution of scientific and academic publications has become the norm in the region.[27] The first platforms that started working were Latindex[28] and the Scientific Electronic Library Online (SciELO) in 1997.[29] They were followed by the Network of Scientific Journals of Latin America, the Caribbean, Spain, and Portugal (RedALyC) in 2003[30] and LA Referencia in 2012.[31] In addition, since 1998, the Latin American Council of Social Sciences (CLACSO), including research institutions in twenty-three countries across the region, developed a network of virtual libraries providing international visibility and free access to over 100,000 texts (including books, working documents, theses, and conference papers), and an 850 peer-reviewed journal collection.[32] A most recent initiative, AmeliCA (launched in November 2018), was developed to promote a nonprofit publishing model to preserve the scholarly and open nature of scientific communication.[33]

As of November 2024, of the 21,117 open access journals registered in the Directory of Open Access Journals (DOAJ), 3,416 journals are from Latin America (around 17 percent of the total journals).[34] Previously, it has been reported that by 2011, 74 percent of all Latin American journals were OA in the Scopus database, compared with a global total of 9 percent. Similarly, in Ulrich's Periodicals database, by 2005, 51 percent of all online journals were OA, compared with their global total of 7 percent. Some have suggested that 95 percent of all online journals published within the region are entirely OA.[35]

There are also institutional repositories to manage, giving visibility and access to the research output of each institution. By November 2024, OpenDOAR registered 816 digital repositories from Latin America and the Caribbean (from a global total of 5,949, representing around 14 percent of the total). Peru tops the list with 200, followed by Brazil (177), Colombia (126), Argentina (82), and

[26] Arianna Becerril-García and Eduardo Aguado-López, "The End of a Centralized Open Access Project and the Beginning of a Community-Based Sustainable Infrastructure for Latin America: Redalyc.Org after Fifteen Years," *22nd International Conference on Electronic Publishing* (Marseilles, France: OpenEdition Press, 2018), accessed November 12, 2024, https://hal.archives-ouvertes.fr/hal-01816693v1.

[27] Jorge Delgado, "Role of Open Access in the Emergence and Consolidation of Refereed Journals in Latin America and the Caribbean," *Educación Superior y Sociedad* 16 (2012).

[28] Latindex, accessed November 12, 2024, https://www.latindex.org/latindex/inicio.

[29] SciELO, accessed November 12, 2024, https://www.scielo.org/es/.

[30] RedALyC, accessed November 12, 2024, https://www.redalyc.org/.

[31] LA Referencia, accessed November 12, 2024, https://www.lareferencia.info/en.

[32] CLACSO, accessed November 12, 2024, https://www.clacso.org/.

[33] AmeliCA, accessed November 12, 2024, http://amelica.org/index.php/en/home/.

[34] DOAJ, accessed November 12, 2024, https://www.doaj.org/.

[35] Juan Pablo Alperin et al. (eds.), *Open Access Indicators and Scholarly Communications in Latin America* (Buenos Aires: CLACSO, 2014), 17, accessed November 12, 2024, http://biblioteca.clacso.edu.ar/clacso/se/20140917054406/OpenAccess.pdf.

Mexico (56). All these countries are also in the top thirty list of repositories by country worldwide.[36]

Net Neutrality

Net neutrality is understood as a principle that prevents specific contents or applications on the internet from being discriminated against in favor of others by the internet service provider (ISP) regarding the Internet end-user.[37]

However, this principle does not mean an entirely neutral net.[38] Some exceptions are commonly accepted, such as reasonable network management (practices necessary to maintain the integrity and security of a network, like blocking malicious traffic or limiting bandwidth for heavy users) and specialized services (e.g., telemedicine or self-driving car networks may have different technical requirements that justify other treatment).[39] Under European Union (EU) law, exceptions to network neutrality are limited to traffic management, compliance with a legal order, ensuring network integrity and security, and managing exceptional or temporary network congestion.[40]

But the source of internet content discrimination can also come from regulatory restrictions (e.g., child pornography) or "jawboning" (enforcement through governmental pressure or informal channels).[41] According to a 2014 survey on the importance of internet freedom, citizens' opposition to government restrictions is widespread in several Latin American countries, including Argentina, Bolivia, Brazil, Chile, Mexico, and Venezuela.[42] Overall, Latin America has not taken the path of "cybernationalism" or digital sovereignty, understood as the right of a state to govern its network according to national

[36] OpenDOAR, accessed November 12, 2024, https://v2.sherpa.ac.uk/opendoar/.

[37] Christoph B. Graber, "Bottom-up Constitutionalism: The Case of Net Neutrality," *Transnational Legal Theory* 7 (2016): 524.

[38] Christopher T. Marsden, *Net Neutrality: Towards a Co-Regulatory Solution* (London: Bloomsbury Academic, 2010), 105, accessed November 12, 2024, https://library.oapen.org/handle/20.500.12657/58677.

[39] Angele A. Gilroy, "Access to Broadband Networks: Net Neutrality," *Congressional Research Service: In Focus* (April 3, 2019), accessed November 12, 2024, https://crsreports.congress.gov/product/pdf/IF/IF10955/6.

[40] Regulation (EU) 2015/2120 of the European Parliament and of the Council of 25 November 2015 laying down measures concerning open internet access and retail charges for regulated intra-EU communications and amending Directive 2002/22/EC and Regulation (EU) No. 531/2012 2018.

[41] Derek E. Bambauer, "Against Jawboning," *Minnesota Law Review* 182 (2015): 52.

[42] Pew Research Center, "Emerging and Developing Nations Want Freedom on the Internet," *Pew Research Center's Global Attitudes Project* (March 19, 2014), accessed November 12, 2024, https://www.pewresearch.org/global/2014/03/19/emerging-and-developing-nations-want-freedom-on-the-internet/.

interests concerning matters such as commerce, security, and privacy, identified for example with China, Iran, Russia, and the EU.[43]

Latin American countries have been prominent supporters of net neutrality and have recognized it in domestic law and international agreements.[44] Chile was the first to pass a net neutrality law for the consumers and users of the internet in 2010,[45] a year before the Netherlands became the second country to take that step.[46] Colombia followed in June 2011 with Law 1450, which establishes that internet service providers may not block, interfere, discriminate, or restrict the right of any internet user to use, send, receive, or offer any lawful content or service over the internet.[47] The EU only regulated this principle in 2015.[48]

In 2014, Brazil's Marco Civil da Internet (MCI) guaranteed net neutrality, ensuring that ISPs and the government cannot restrict users' access to content, websites, or internet-based services, nor can they interfere with how consumers use the internet. In addition, the law establishes that telecom companies are not permitted to sell packages that distinguish prices based on the content accessed by users. However, the president, the Brazilian Internet Steering Committee, and the National Telecommunications Agency have the power to make exceptions in the case of emergencies, such as cases of public security or health.[49]

In July 2022, the countries of the Andean Community (Bolivia, Colombia, Ecuador, and Peru) approved Decision No. 897, which updates various guidelines for the protection of users' rights in telecommunications and includes, among others, net neutrality, understood as the principle whereby internet service operators and the governments that regulate them must provide equal treatment to all data traffic passing through the network without any arbitrary

[43] Martin Becerra and Silvio R. Waisbord, "The Curious Absence of Cybernationalism in Latin America: Lessons for the Study of Digital Sovereignty and Governance," *Communication and the Public* 6 (2021): 67.

[44] Patricia Adriana Vargas-Leon, "Net Neutrality: An Overview of Enacted Laws in South America," in *Net Neutrality Compendium: Human Rights, Free Competition and the Future of the Internet*, ed. Luca Belli and Primavera De Filippi (Cham, Switzerland: Springer International, 2016), https://doi.org/10.1007/978-3-319-26425-7_10.

[45] Ley 20.453, Consagra el principio de neutralidad en la red para los consumidores y usuarios de internet, accessed November 12, 2024, https://www.bcn.cl/leychile/navegar?idNorma=1016570.

[46] Carin Zissis and Rachel Glickhouse, "Net Neutrality Lessons from Latin America," *AS/COA* (May 9, 2014), accessed November 12, 2024, https://www.as-coa.org/articles/net-neutrality-lessons-latin-america.

[47] Roberto Triviño, Antonio Franco, and Rafael Leonardo Ochoa, "Net Neutrality and Enacted Laws in South America: A Literature Review," *Latin American Journal of Computing* 6 (2019): 17.

[48] Regulation (EU) 2015/2120 of the European Parliament and of the Council of 25 November 2015 laying down measures concerning open internet access and retail charges for regulated intra-EU communications and amending Directive 2002/22/EC and Regulation (EU) No. 531/2012 201.

[49] Lei 12.965 de 23 de abril de 2014, Estabelece princípios, garantias, direitos e deveres para o uso da Internet no Brasil, accessed November 12, 2024, http://www.planalto.gov.br/ccivil_03/_ato2011-2014/2014/lei/l12965.htm.

discrimination, in accordance with the internal regulations of each member country.[50]

Worldwide, only five PTAs explicitly recognize the principle of net neutrality, and most have been concluded between Latin American countries. These are the Additional Protocol to the Framework Agreement of the Pacific Alliance (PAAP), to which Chile, Colombia, Mexico, and Peru are parties (2014), the Argentina-Chile FTA (2017), the Brazil-Chile FTA (2018), the Chile-Ecuador Economic Complementation Agreement (ECA) (2020), and the Pacific Alliance-Singapore FTA (2022).[51]

The PAAP stipulates that each party shall adopt or maintain measures to ensure compliance with net neutrality, which shall be construed in accordance with the laws of each party.[52] Similarly, the Argentina-Chile FTA added a provision stating that net neutrality compliance shall be without discrimination or blocking of services.[53] In less binding terms, the Brazil-Chile FTA declares that to guarantee a free and competitive market for internet content, the parties undertake to study mechanisms to give effect to the principle of net neutrality in their domestic legislation, to prevent certain content or applications from being discriminated against in favor of others.[54]

According to the Chile-Ecuador ECA, parties shall, under their domestic law, adopt or maintain measures to ensure that public telecommunications services do not arbitrarily discriminate by blocking, interfering with, obstructing, or restricting the right of any internet user to use, send, receive or offer any lawful content, applications, or services over the internet. Likewise, parties cannot limit a user's right to use any device to connect to the network, as long as it is legal and does not harm the network or the quality of service. However, public telecommunications service providers may take such measures necessary to ensure their networks' operation, provided that they are not undertaken in a manner that constitutes arbitrary discrimination or anticompetitive conduct.[55]

Regardless of the regulations, it is important to note that implementing the net neutrality principle is not easy. One problem is technical: traffic is not always exchanged from a content provider to an end user, but it can also be between end users. Another issue is the dependency on the power of the local telecommunication regulator and the technical problems in monitoring compliance with such a principle.[56]

[50] Comunidad Andina, Decision No. 897, July 14, 2022, accessed November 12, 2024, decision897.pdf.

[51] Net neutrality is also implicitly endorsed in the TPP/CPTPP, art. 14.10.

[52] PAAP, art. 14.6 quáter.

[53] Argentina-Chile FTA, art. 10.10.

[54] Brazil-Chile FTA, art. 11.11.

[55] Chile-Ecuador ECA, art. 11.11.

[56] See, e.g., Joshua S. Gans, "Net Neutrality: A Simple Goal with Some Difficult Implementation Ahead," *CEPR* (June 11, 2014), accessed November 12, 2024, https://cepr.org/voxeu/columns/

III. The Regulation of Digital Trade

In the past decades, the development of the internet has allowed the growth of digital trade.[57] Traditional trade rules, like the law of the multilateral forum of the World Trade Organization (WTO), established in 1994, could be used as a starting point but are still tailored to regulate trade in tangible goods and brick-and-mortar businesses.

Efforts to deal with these issues at a multilateral level started in 1998. That year, after the WTO established a work program on electronic commerce, the members at the Ministerial Conference agreed on a temporary duty-free moratorium on all electronic transactions. This practice has been renewed at each WTO Ministerial Conference (MC).[58] In December 2017, forty-four WTO members made a joint declaration to initiate exploratory work toward future negotiations on trade-related aspects of electronic commerce.[59] As of November 2024, ninety-one WTO members participated in this joint statement initiative (JSI), which does not have a precise end date.[60] Any agreement would be, at its best, plurilateral. Burri pointed out that despite living in the "Fourth Industrial Revolution," we still had trade rules that were grounded at 1.0.[61]

However, the lack of consensus at the multilateral level does not mean that rules for digital trade are not created elsewhere. In fact, since the beginning of the twenty-first century, some countries have included provisions and chapters on digital trade and data flows in PTAs, free trade agreements (FTAs), the most common type of agreement having such provisions.

net-neutrality-simple-goal-some-difficult-implementation-ahead; Richard A Epstein, "The Problem With Net Neutrality," *Hoover Institution* (January 20, 2014), accessed November 12, 2024, https://www.hoover.org/research/problem-net-neutrality.

[57] Some literature has drawn distinctions between e-commerce and digital trade. E-commerce would refer to trade in goods bought by digital platforms (e.g., purchasing a book online) whereas digital trade focuses on digital contents or services, emphasizing data flows and largely ignoring trade in goods (e.g., providing an online streaming service). Henry Gao, "Digital or Trade? The Contrasting Approaches of China and US to Digital Trade," *Journal of International Economic Law* 21 (2018): 297. However, this chapter will use e-commerce and digital trade are interchangeably.

[58] WTO Work Programme on Electronic Commerce, "Ministerial Decision," *WTO* (June 17, 2022), accessed November 12, 2024, https://docs.wto.org/dol2fe/Pages/SS/directdoc.aspx?filename=q:/WT/MIN22/32.pdf&Open=True.

[59] WTO, "Joint Ministerial Statement on Electronic Commerce WT/MIN(17)/65. WT/L/1032," *WTO* (December 13, 2017), accessed November 12, 2024, https://www.wto.org/english/thewto_e/minist_e/mc11_e/documents_e.htm.

[60] WTO, Joint Initiative on E-commerce, accessed November 12, 2024, https://www.wto.org/english/tratop_e/ecom_e/joint_statement_e.htm.

[61] Mira Burri, "Introduction," in *Big Data and Global Trade Law*, ed. Mira Burri, 3 (Cambridge: Cambridge University Press 2021), accessed November 12, 2024, https://www.cambridge.org/core/books/big-data-and-global-trade-law/introduction/06137D47B15738D4813F5003FD75BCA1.

The advent of agreements including provisions on electronic commerce started with the new century after the well-known kick-off given by the EU and the US initiatives in this regard, such as the EU's 2000 Directive on e-commerce[62] and the US Digital Agenda (with the Bipartisan Trade Promotion Authority Act of 2002).[63] The relevant role other actors had in the development of these rules is not so well known. This section focuses on one group of Latin American countries (Chile, Colombia, Mexico, Peru, and Panama), which have been important vectors of including e-commerce and data rules in PTAs.

Digital Trade Provisions in Latin American PTAs

PTAs explicitly referring to digital trade are not a recent phenomenon, although they have evolved significantly in the past two decades. According to the TAPED dataset, of 432 PTAs concluded between 2000 and 2024, 235 include digital trade provisions, and 137 have dedicated chapters on this topic.[64] These agreements are highly heterogeneous and address issues such as customs duties, nondiscriminatory treatment of digital products, electronic signatures, paperless trading, unsolicited electronic messages (spam), consumer protection, data protection, data flows, and data localization.

Latin American countries have concluded around 31 percent of PTAs with digital trade provisions (sixty-eight agreements, forty-nine chapters). These agreements are concluded with thirty developed and thirty-eight developing economies, mainly from Latin America,[65] including regional agreements like the Pacific Alliance (2015) and MERCOSUR (2021). The earliest of these agreements is the Canada-Costa Rica FTA (2001), which included a Joint Statement on Global Electronic Commerce. The Chile-EU Association Agreement (2002)

[62] Directive 2000/31/EC of the European Parliament and of the Council of 8 June 2000 on certain legal aspects of information society services, particularly electronic commerce, in the Internal Market, OJ L 178 (2000).

[63] Bipartisan Trade Promotion Authority Act of 2002, Ch. 24, 19 U.S.C. §§ 3801–3813 (2002), accessed November 12, 2024, https://uscode.house.gov/view.xhtml?path=/prelim@title19/chapter24&edition=prelim.

[64] Data cited in this chapter comes from the "Trade Agreements Provisions on Electronic-Commerce and Data" (TAPED) dataset, accessed November 20, 2024, https://www.unilu.ch/en/faculties/faculty-of-law/professorships/burri-mira/research/taped/. Mira Burri and Rodrigo Polanco, "Digital Trade Provisions in Preferential Trade Agreements: Introducing a New Dataset," *Journal of International Economic Law* 23 (2020): 187; and Mira Burri, María Vásquez Callo-Müller, and Kholofelo Kugler, The Evolution of Digital Trade Law: Insights from TAPED," *World Trade Review* 23(2)(2024):190-207, doi:10.1017/S1474745623000472.

[65] Country classification is according to United Nations, Department of Economic and Social Affairs, *World Economic Situation and Prospects 2024* (2024), accessed November 12, 2024, https://www.un.org/development/desa/dpad/publication/world-economic-situation-and-prospects-2024/.

properly included e-commerce provisions in the text of the treaty. The first of these PTAs with a dedicated e-commerce chapter is the Chile-US FTA (2002).

PTAs with digital trade provisions are mainly intercontinental. Yet, according to TAPED, around one-third have at least one Latin American country as a contracting party. Digital trade provisions are in PTAs' dedicated sections or intellectual property chapters. They can also be found in other documents like annexes, joint statements, and side letters. Their level of detail has also significantly increased over the years.[66] It is worth noting that a Latin American country (Chile) is party to the Digital Economy Partnership Agreement (DEPA) with Singapore and New Zealand, the first agreement exclusively on digital trade issues not directly connected to a PTA.

A group of Latin American countries has pioneered e-commerce and data-flow provisions in preferential trade agreements. The countries leading this treaty-making practice in the region are Chile (twenty-three PTAs), Peru (fifteen PTAs), Colombia (fourteen PTAs), Panama (eight PTAs), and Costa Rica (seven PTAs). The number of Latin American PTAs with such provisions has increased over the years, simultaneously with the growing discussions on the digital economy in the policy agenda.

In the following sections, we will examine digital trade provisions of Latin American PTAs, distinguishing between "soft," "mixed," and "hard," or "binding" commitments.[67]

For that purpose, we will consider "Latin American PTAs" those trade agreements in which at least one or more parties are a country from the Latin American and Caribbean regions.

Some of these provisions are particularly important for international trade in general. For example, they reduce or eliminate barriers (e.g., nondiscrimination, customs duties exemption) or enhance confidence in e-commerce (e.g., consumer protection, recognition of electronic authentication). Others are critical for specific sectors like telecommunication, financial services, and digital products or services, which require rules allowing data sharing (e.g., personal data, data flows, and data localization).

Objectives and Principles

Latin American PTAs largely converge on several objectives relevant to international trade, like avoiding unnecessary barriers to e-commerce (thirty-nine

[66] For further details, see Rodrigo Polanco, "Regulatory Convergence of Data Rules in Latin America," in Burri, *Big Data and Global Trade Law*, 268–300.

[67] TAPED considers as "soft" those commitments that are not enforceable by the parties, like "best efforts" and cooperation commitments. "Hard" commitments oblige a party to comply with a rule or a principle and are enforceable by another party. Agreements with "mixed" commitments have both soft and hard commitments or references to other agreements partially applicable. Burri and Polanco, "Digital Trade Provisions in Preferential Trade Agreements," 5.

PTAs), addressing the needs of small and medium enterprises (forty PTAs), and promoting and facilitating its use (thirty-eight PTAs). These objectives and principles are also commonly found in PTAs concluded by countries outside the region.

These agreements have also recognized other principles that are less prevalent, like considering private participation in developing a regulatory framework for e-commerce (thirty PTAs), the principle of technological neutrality (sixteen PTAs),[68] and the principle of net neutrality explained above.

Applicability of WTO Rules

All Latin American countries that have concluded PTAs with digital trade provisions are WTO members. But that does not necessarily mean they consider WTO law to apply to digital trade. For example, with some differences across agreements, less than one-third of Latin American PTAs include provisions on the applicability of WTO rules to e-commerce (twenty-one PTAs).

Some treaties explicitly recognize the WTO rules' applicability to e-commerce without specifying which provisions.[69] For example, certain agreements aim to apply them "to the extent they affect electronic commerce"[70] or measures "affecting electronic commerce."[71] Other softer variations merely reaffirm their respective commitments under WTO Agreements.[72]

National Treatment and Most-Favored Nation

The number of Latin American PTAs, including provisions with explicit nondiscrimination commitments in digital trade, is relatively small. For example, only twenty-one agreements consider giving a treatment no less favorable than they accord domestically on digital trade (national treatment, or NT). In turn, eighteen Latin American PTAs include commitments to provide treatment no less favorable on digital trade than they accord to nonparties to the PTA (most favored nation, or MFN). Yet, most of these MFN and NT provisions are binding.[73]

[68] Technological neutrality is understood here as a nondiscrimination principle between products delivered electronically and other modes of supply (e.g., physical delivery). R. V. Anuradha, "Technological Neutrality: Implications for Services Commitments and the Discussions on E-Commerce," CWS/WP/200/51 Working Paper. Centre for WTO Studies, Indian Institute of Foreign Trade (2018), 83.

[69] E.g., DEPA, art. 1.2; Central America–Korea FTA, art. 14.1.1; Colombia-Panama FTA, art. 19.2.1; Canada-Panama FTA, art. 15.03.1.

[70] Canada-Honduras FTA, art. 16.2.

[71] E.g., Colombia-Costa Rica FTA, art. 16.2.1; Central America-Mexico, art. 15.2.1; Korea-Peru FTA, art. 14.1.1.

[72] Colombia-EC-EU-Peru FTA, art. 107.1.

[73] Brazil-Chile FTA, art. 10.4 recognizes this discussion without a specific commitment.

The majority of Latin American PTAs include separate provisions for NT[74] and MFN.[75] However, following the PAAP, some agreements consider NT and MFN together as part of a general commitment to the nondiscriminatory treatment of digital products.[76]

Customs Duties Exemption

One of the most common provisions in PTAs is the commitment not to impose customs duties on digital products, and Latin American agreements are no exception.

Despite being commonplace, these provisions have different wordings with two distinctive trends: autonomous and connected to the WTO practice. Most Latin American PTAs (forty-four agreements) provide a permanent moratorium on the duty-free treatment of digital or electronic products.[77] Yet, a group of these PTAs explicitly mentions that this rule does not extend to internal taxes or other charges.[78] Moreover, in certain agreements, electronic transmissions are only considered to provide services.[79]

Some Latin American PTAs merely reaffirm the WTO member's practice of not imposing customs duties on electronic transmissions.[80] Such commitment seems conditional to such practice, which has been heavily contested recently. In 2019, some countries like India and South Africa argued that the e-commerce moratorium in the WTO led to a loss of revenue as it gave such transmissions immunity from taxation and initially opposed its renewal. During the MC12 (June 2022) and the MC13 (February-March 2024), both countries again argued against the scope and application of the moratorium. So, the continuation of such practice is not guaranteed.[81]

[74] E.g., Panama-Singapore FTA, art. 13.3.2; Nicaragua-Taiwan FTA, art. 14.03.3; Chile-Colombia FTA, art. 12.4.1.

[75] E.g., Chile-US FTA, art. 15.4.2; Panama-Singapore FTA, art. 13.3.3; Nicaragua-Taiwan FTA, art. 14.03.4.

[76] PAAP, art. 13.4 bis; TPP/CPTPP, art. 14.4; Australia-Peru FTA, art. 13.4.1; USMCA, art. 19.4.1.

[77] Chile-US FTA, art. 15.3; Australia-Chile FTA, art. 16.4; Mexico-Panama FTA, art. 14.4; Central America-EU FTA, art. 201.3; Chile-Paraguay FTA, art. 7.3.1.

[78] E.g., Canada-Panama FTA, art. 15.04; Colombia-Panama FTA, art. 19.3; Peru-Singapore FTA, art. 13.1; Canada-Colombia FTA, art. 1503; PAAP, art. 13.4; TPP/CPTPP, art. 14.3; Chile-Uruguay FTA, art. 8.3; Brazil-Chile FTA, art. 10.3.

[79] Colombia-EC-Peru FTA, art. 162.3; Colombia-Israel FTA, Annex B, art. 1.3.

[80] MERCOSUR, Electronic Commerce Agreement, art. 3; Central America-EFTA, Annex II, art. 2.

[81] Peter Ungphakorn, "Getting to yes: What's behind the e-commerce standoff at the WTO?," *Trade β Blog*, September 5, 2024, accessed November 12, 2024, https://tradebetablog.wordpress.com/2024/09/05/getting-to-yes-whats-behind-the-e-commerce-standoff-at-the-wto/.

Electronic Authentication

Fifty-one Latin American PTAs have provisions on electronic authentication, representing around 42 percent of the agreements that include such clauses. Typically, they allow authentication technologies and mutual recognition of digital certificates and signatures. While earlier treaties included only best-efforts commitments in this field, recent agreements include more binding and mandatory clauses.

Canada-Costa Rica FTA (2001) merely acknowledged the necessity of policies to facilitate the use of technologies for authentication and secure e-commerce.[82] Other treaties included cooperation commitments on electronic authentication; activities to share information and experiences on laws, regulations, and programs on electronic signatures[83] or secure electronic authentication;[84] and "maintaining a dialogue" on facilitating cross-border certification services[85] or digital accreditation.[86]

Binding commitments on authentication and digital certificates establish restrictions on legislation, using both negative and positive obligations. Usually, under the negative obligation model, countries may not adopt or maintain laws that prevent or prohibit parties to an electronic transaction (1) from mutually determining appropriate authentication methods[87] or (2) from having the opportunity to prove in court that their electronic transaction complies with any legal requirements concerning authentication.[88]

Under the positive obligation model, countries should apply domestic legislation for electronic authentication, allowing parties to electronic transactions to (1) determine the appropriate authentication technologies and implementation models, without limiting their recognition, and (2) prove in court that their electronic transactions comply with any legal requirements.[89]

Further commitments on authentication establish that neither party may deny the legal validity of a signature solely because the signature is in electronic form.[90] Certain treaties allow some exceptions to this rule under the circumstances provided for in its domestic law, like performance standards for

[82] Canada-Costa Rica FTA, Joint Statement on Global Electronic Commerce.

[83] E.g., Central America-Mexico FTA, art. 15.5(b); Australia-Chile FTA, art. 16.10.1; Colombia-Northern Triangle FTA, art. 14.8(b).

[84] E.g., USMCA, art. 19.14(a)(iii); Australia-Peru FTA, art. 13.14(b)(v); Argentina-Chile FTA, art. 11.9(b).

[85] E.g., Colombia-Israel FTA, Annex B, art. 2.1(a); Central America-EU FTA, art. 202(a); CARIFORUM-EC EPA, art. 120.1(a).

[86] Colombia-EU-Peru FTA, art. 109(g).

[87] E.g., Chile-Colombia FTA, art. 12.7; Colombia-US TPA, art. 15.6; Peru-US TPA, art. 15.6.

[88] Mexico-Panama FTA, art. 14.9.1; PAAP, art. 13.10.1; Colombia-Northern Triangle FTA, art. 14.7.

[89] Chile-Thailand FTA, art. 11.7(e); Australia-Chile FTA, art. 16.6.3.

[90] See e.g., Brazil-Chile FTA, art. 10.6.2; USMCA, art. 19.6.2; Australia-Peru FTA, art. 13.6.2; Argentina-Chile FTA, art. 11.3.2; Chile-Uruguay FTA, art. 8.5.2; TPP/CPTPP, art. 14.6.2.

sensitive communications that require a higher degree of reliability and security, like electronic financial transactions.[91]

Some PTAs consider exceptions to these commitments, including the fact that a party may require certification of electronic signatures by an authority or a private accredited supplier.[92] Often, such requirements are objective, transparent, and nondiscriminatory and relate only to the category of transactions concerned.[93]

Consumer Protection

Fifty-one Latin American PTAs have provisions on consumer protection for digital trade, representing almost half of the universe of PTAs that include them. Most are nonbinding; like the first agreement with that feature, the Canada-Costa Rica FTA (2001) states that e-commerce consumers should be afforded no less transparent and effective protection than other commerce forms.[94]

Later agreements focused on international cooperation for the protection of consumers. Such activities include sharing information and experiences on regulations, laws, and programs on consumer protection[95] or consumer redress.[96] Others consider exchanging best practices to enhance confidence in e-commerce,[97] online security from fraudulent and misleading practices,[98] and online access to products and services.[99] Certain treaties also include cooperation between national consumer protection agencies on cross-border electronic commerce.[100] In the PAAP, countries agreed on further cooperation commitments. These include sharing information about suppliers punished for infringement of consumer rights, prevention measures, consumer information, and training initiatives.[101]

Some Latin American PTAs also consider adopting domestic standards concerning consumer protection, but mainly in a nonbinding fashion. Certain

[91] E.g., Pacific Alliance–Singapore FTA, art. 13.13; Brazil-Chile FTA, art. 10.6.1; USMCA, art. 19.6.1; Australia-Peru FTA, art. 13.6.1.

[92] E.g., Argentina-Chile FTA, art. 11.3.3; Chile-Uruguay FTA, art. 8.5.3; TPP/CPTPP, art. 14.6.3.

[93] EU-Mexico Modernised Global Agreement, Digital Trade Chapter, art. 6.3.

[94] Canada-Costa Rica FTA, Joint Statement on Global Electronic Commerce.

[95] E.g., Brazil-Chile FTA, art. 10.15(b), art. 10.7.4; Argentina-Chile FTA, art. 11.9(b); Chile-Uruguay FTA, art. 8.13(b).

[96] Australia-Peru FTA, art. 13.14(b)(ii); TPP/CPTPP, art. 14.15(b)(ii); Chile-Thailand FTA, art. 11.7.1(b).

[97] E.g., Mexico-Panama FTA, art. 14.3.2(f); Canada-Honduras FTA, art. 16.5(b); Central America-Mexico FTA, art. 15.5(b).

[98] E.g., DEPA, art. 6.3.7; Australia-Chile FTA, art. 16.10.1. Central America-Korea FTA, art. 14.7.1(d).

[99] E.g., Brazil-Chile FTA, art. 10.15(c); Argentina-Chile FTA, art. 11.9(c); Chile-Uruguay FTA, art. 8.13(c).

[100] E.g., Australia-Peru FTA, art. 13.7.3; Argentina-Chile FTA, art. 11.4.4; Chile-Uruguay FTA, art. 8.6.4.

[101] PAAP, art. 13.6.4.

treaties "recognize the importance" of transparent and effective measures to protect e-commerce consumers from fraudulent and deceptive commercial practices,[102] or encourage e-commerce suppliers to comply with consumer protection regulations in the territory where the consumer is located.[103] In only a handful of agreements, parties commit to adopting or maintaining consumer protection laws to prescribe these practices when they harm or potentially harm consumers.[104] Fewer treaties consider using alternative dispute resolution mechanisms[105] or even online dispute settlement.[106]

Latin American countries have rarely used more binding options to tackle consumer protection. Some agreements establish a criterion of "equivalence" that each party shall provide, where possible and appropriate, protection for e-commerce consumers that is at least equivalent to that offered to consumers under their respective domestic laws, regulations, and policies.[107] The Australia-Chile FTA (2008) further considers specific businesses' obligations to protect e-commerce consumers, including following fair business, advertising, and marketing practices. They include providing accurate, clear, and easily accessible information about goods or services offered; easy-to-use, secure payment mechanisms; and information on the security level such tools afford, avoiding ambiguity on intended purchases.[108]

Personal Data Protection

Fifty-four Latin American PTAs include provisions on privacy, usually under the concept of "data protection" (representing one-third of the 159 agreements with those clauses). But how such data is protected varies considerably, a mixed bag of binding and nonbinding provisions.

The Canada-Costa Rica FTA (2001) was the first to deal with privacy issues in a nonbinding declaration that was largely programmatic.[109] Later PTAs included international cooperation activities to enhance the security of personal data. These activities include sharing information and experience on domestic laws and regulations,[110] exchanging experts, establishing joint programs and

[102] E.g., Pacific Alliance–Singapore FTA, art. 13.8; DEPA, art. 6.3.1; Brazil-Chile FTA, art. 10.7.1; USMCA, art. 19.7.1.

[103] PAAP, art. 13.6.5.

[104] E.g., Australia-Peru FTA, art. 13.7.2; Argentina-Chile FTA, art. 11.4.2; Chile-Uruguay FTA, art. 8.6.2.

[105] E.g., DEPA, art. 6.3.8; Mexico-Panama FTA, art. 14.6.2; PAAP, art. 13.6.3; Colombia-Costa Rica FTA, art. 16.4.3.

[106] Brazil-Chile FTA, art. 10.7.4.

[107] Chile-Thailand FTA, art. 11.7(k); Chile-China FTA (2018), art. 54; Australia-Chile FTA, art. 16.7.1-2(a).

[108] Australia-Chile FTA, arts. 16.7.2(b), 16.7.3.

[109] Canada-Costa Rica FTA, Joint Statement on Global Electronic Commerce.

[110] E.g., Brazil-Chile FTA, arts. 10.8.5, 10.15(b); Central America-Korea FTA, art. 14.5.2; Argentina-Chile FTA, arts. 11.5.5, 11.9(b).

projects,[111] dialogues or consultations,[112] or other general cooperation activities.[113] On the other hand, some Latin American PTAs merely recognize the importance or benefits of protecting personal information online.[114]

In several treaties, countries specifically commit to adopting or maintaining legislation or regulations that protect personal data or the privacy of e-commerce users[115] concerning data processing and dissemination,[116] which may also include administrative measures.[117] Often, parties commit to publishing personal data protection information,[118] including how individuals can pursue remedies and how businesses can comply with any legal requirements.[119] In addition, some encourage encryption or security mechanisms for users' personal information and anonymization when said data is provided to third parties.[120]

Specific PTAs mandate considering international standards,[121] criteria, or guidelines of relevant international organizations or bodies when developing online personal data protection rules.[122] For example, the United States–Mexico–Canada Agreement (USMCA) explicitly recognizes the APEC Privacy Framework and the OECD Recommendation of the Council concerning Guidelines Governing the Protection of Privacy and Transborder Flows of Personal Data (2013) and the APEC Cross-Border Privacy Rules System.[123]

Few agreements consider qualifications for these rules, like the differences in existing systems for personal data protection.[124] A couple of PTAs encourage the development of mechanisms to promote compatibility between different regimes, recognizing that parties may take other legal approaches to protect personal information. These may include recognizing regulatory outcomes, whether accorded autonomously, by mutual arrangement, or in broader international frameworks and exchanging information.[125] The Colombia-EU-Peru FTA (2012)—which since 2017 has also included Ecuador—left the development of

[111] Chile-EC AA, art. 30.

[112] Colombia-EU-Peru FTA, art. 163.1(e); Australia-Chile FTA, art. 16.10.1.

[113] E.g., Central America-Korea FTA, art. 14.7.1(a); Colombia-Israel FTA, Annex-B, art. 2(e); Colombia-Panama FTA, art. 19.7.1(b).

[114] Central America-Korea FTA, art. 14.5.1; Canada-Honduras FTA, art. 16.2.2(e).

[115] E.g., Brazil-Chile FTA, art. 10.8.2; USMCA, art. 19.8.1-2; Australia-Peru FTA, art. 13.8.1-2.

[116] Central America-EFTA, Annex II, art. 1(c)(i); EFTA-Colombia FTA, Annex I, art. 1(c)(i); EFTA-Peru FTA, Annex I, art. 1(c)(i).

[117] E.g., Colombia-Costa Rica FTA, art. 16.6.1; Korea-Peru FTA, art. 14.7; Australia-Chile FTA, art. 16.8.

[118] Brazil-Chile FTA, art. 10.8.4.

[119] E.g., USMCA, art. 19.8.5; Australia-Peru FTA, art. 13.8.4; Chile-Uruguay FTA, art. 8.7.3.

[120] Brazil-Chile FTA, art. 10.8.6; Argentina-Chile FTA, art. 11.5.6; Chile-Uruguay FTA, art. 8.7.5.

[121] E.g., Argentina-Chile FTA, art. 11.5.1-2; Chile-Uruguay FTA, art. 8.7.2; Colombia-EU-Peru FTA, art. 162.2.

[122] E.g., TPP/CPTPP, art. 14.8.2; Mexico-Panama FTA, art. 14.8; Chile-Thailand FTA, art. 11.7(j).

[123] USMCA, arts. 19.8.2, 19.8.6.

[124] Chile-Thailand FTA, art. 11.7.1(j).

[125] DEPA, art. 4.2.6-7; Australia-Peru FTA, art. 13.8.5; TPP/CPTPP, art. 14.8.5.

guidelines and strategies on homologation processes of data protection systems to a working group as part of a cooperation agenda.[126]

But Latin American PTAs have also used more binding options to protect personal information online. One option recognizes principles for collecting, processing, and storing personal data without developing its content in detail. These include collection limitations, data quality, purpose specification, use limitations, security safeguards, transparency, individual participation, and accountability.[127] Some PTAs acknowledge the importance of compliance, ensuring that any restrictions on cross-border personal information flows are necessary and proportionate to the risks presented.[128] Certain PTAs recognize data protection "trustmarks" as a valid mechanism to facilitate cross-border information transfers while protecting personal information.[129]

A second option considers protecting individuals' privacy concerning the processing and dissemination of personal data and the confidentiality of individual records and accounts as exceptions in specific chapters of the agreement. These provisions are usually included in telecommunications chapters (to protect the privacy of non-public personal data of subscribers to public telecommunications services)[130] and financial services (adopting adequate safeguards to protect privacy and fundamental rights while permitting data transfer and processing).[131] Some PTAs add that where financial information or processing involves personal data, the treatment shall be under the domestic law regulating such data protection.[132]

A third option allows countries to adopt "appropriate measures" to ensure privacy protection while allowing the free movement of data. For example, the Argentina-Chile FTA (2017) established a criterion of "equivalence," meaning that personal data exchange is possible only where the party that receives it protects such data in at least an equivalent, similar, or adequate way compared to the party that supplies it. The parties shall negotiate reciprocal, general, or specific agreements in a broader international framework, admitting the private sector's implementation of contracts or self-regulation.[133]

[126] Colombia-EU-Peru FTA, art. 109(b).

[127] Argentina-Chile FTA, art. 11.2.5(f) n. 1; Chile-Uruguay FTA, art. 8.2.5(f), n. 3; DEPA, art. 4.2; Chile-Paraguay FTA, art. 7.8.

[128] USMCA, art. 19.8.3.

[129] DEPA, art. 4.2.9-10; Chile-Uruguay FTA, art. 8.2.5(b); Argentina-Chile FTA, art. 11.2.5(b).

[130] E.g., USMCA, art. 18.3.4; Australia-Peru FTA, art. 12.4.4; Argentina-Chile FTA, art. 10.3.4.

[131] E.g., USMCA, Annex 17-A; Australia-Peru FTA, art. 10.21; TPP/CPTPP, Annex 11-B.

[132] E.g., Australia-Peru FTA, Annex 10-A; TPP/CPTPP, Annex 11-A; Korea-Peru FTA, Annex 12-B.

[133] Argentina-Chile FTA, art. 11.5.7.

Cross-Border Data Flows

Several Latin American PTAs include general provisions on cross-border data flow, either in digital trade chapters or sectoral chapters where data flows have a central role, like telecommunications and financial services. Around half of all FTAs, including such provisions, have been concluded by Latin American countries.[134]

We find two types of data-related provisions on these PTAs: those referring to the cross-border flow of data and those banning or limiting data localization requirements. The former is more common but with different levels of commitment across agreements.

Data Flows

Latin American PTAs represent almost a third of the agreements that include data flow clauses (twenty-two of sixty-one). There are two types of these provisions: binding, which directly guarantees the free flow of data, and nonbinding, which considers cross-border information flows part of cooperation activities. In addition, few agreements consider some "intermediate" clauses, including best endeavor provisions and commitments to future negotiations on data flows.

Nonbinding provisions on data flows appeared earlier. In the first agreement with such provision, the Taiwan-Nicaragua FTA (2006), the parties affirmed the importance of working "to maintain cross-border flows of information as an essential element to promote a dynamic environment for electronic commerce" as part of the cooperation activities.[135] Later agreements concluded by Peru, Mexico, Colombia, Costa Rica, and other Central American countries use similar wording.[136]

In an intermediate type, the parties agree to consider commitments related to the cross-border flow of information in future negotiations. For example, this type of clause is found in the PAAP[137] and the EU-Mexico Global Agreement's modernization, which is currently agreed upon "in principle."[138]

Mexico-Panama FTA (2014) was the first PTA with a binding provision on cross-border information flows. According to this treaty, each party "shall allow its persons and the persons of the other Party to transmit electronic information, from and to its territory, when required by said person, under the

[134] For further details, see Polanco, "Regulatory Convergence of Data Rules in Latin America."

[135] Nicaragua-Taiwan FTA, art. 14.05(c).

[136] Canada-Peru FTA, art. 1508(c); Korea-Peru FTA, art. 14.9(c); Central America-Mexico FTA, art. 15.5(d); Colombia-Costa Rica FTA, art. 16.7(c); Canada-Honduras FTA, art. 16.5(c).

[137] PAAP (2014), art. 13.11.

[138] EU-Mexico Modernised Global Agreement, Digital Trade Chapter, art. XX.

applicable legislation on the protection of personal data and taking into consideration international practices."[139] A more detailed clause is found in the 2015 amended version of the PAAP. According to that provision, countries shall allow the cross-border transfer of data by electronic means, including personal information, when this activity is for a covered personal business, recognizing that each country may have its regulatory requirements concerning information transfer by electronic means. Furthermore, this transfer shall not prevent a party from adopting or maintaining measures to "achieve a legitimate public policy objective," provided that the measure is not applied in a manner that would constitute a means of arbitrary or unjustifiable discrimination or a disguised restriction on trade. It shall also not impose restrictions on transfers of information greater than are required to achieve the objective.[140] The same provision was included in the TPP/CPTPP, DEPA, and the Pacific Alliance-Singapore FTA and has influenced subsequent agreements concluded by Chile, Argentina, Peru, Mexico, and Brazil.[141]

Under USMCA, no party shall prohibit or restrict the cross-border transfer of information, including personal information, by electronic means if this activity is for the conduct of the business of a covered person. Again, this does not prevent a party from adopting or maintaining a measure that is necessary to achieve a "legitimate public policy objective," provided that the measure is not applied in a manner that would constitute a means of arbitrary or unjustifiable discrimination or a disguised restriction on trade, and does not impose restrictions on transfers of information greater than are necessary to achieve the objective. It is presumed that a measure does not achieve a legitimate public policy objective if "it accords different treatment of data transfers solely on the basis that they are cross-border in a manner that modifies the conditions of competition to the detriment of the service suppliers of the other Party."[142] According to the Argentina-Chile FTA, both countries shall apply to the data received from the other party a level of protection that is at least similar to that applicable to the party from which the data originates through mutual, general, or specific agreements.[143]

Data Localization

Some PTAs have also started to include data localization provisions, banning or limiting requirements on the location or use of data. An essential difference between data flow provisions analyzed in the previous section is that most data

[139] Mexico-Panama FTA, art. 14.10.

[140] PAAP (2015), art. 13.11.

[141] E.g., Pacific Alliance-Singapore FTA, art. 13.14; DEPA, art. 4.3; TPP/CPTPP, art. 14.11. Chile-Uruguay FTA, art. 8.10; Australia-Peru FTA, art. 13.11; Brazil-Chile FTA, art. 10.12; Chile-Paraguay FTA, art. 7.11.

[142] USMCA, art. 19.11, n. 5.

[143] Argentina-Chile FTA, art. 11.5.7.

localization provisions are binding. Again, Latin American PTAs represent over one-third of these provisions (fourteen of thirty-eight).

According to the amended version of the PAAP, no party may require a covered person to use or locate computing facilities in that party's territory as a condition for exercising its business activity. An exception in this regard considers that nothing shall prevent a party from adopting or maintaining measures to achieve a legitimate public policy objective, provided that such measures are not applied in a manner that constitutes a means of arbitrary or unjustifiable discrimination or a disguised restriction to trade.[144] Brazil-Chile FTA (2018) and the Pacific Alliance–Singapore FTA (2022) include a similar provision.[145]

TPP/CPTPP and the Chile-Uruguay FTA (2016) mainly considered the same clause, requiring that such measures not impose restrictions on the use or location of computing facilities greater than are necessary to achieve the objective.[146] DEPA also has similar wording to the PAAP, adding that the parties recognize that each party may have its own regulatory requirements regarding the use of computing facilities, including provisions that seek to ensure the security and confidentiality of communications.[147]

USMCA includes the same type of provision without considering any exception, merely stipulating that no party shall require a covered person to use or locate computing facilities in that party's territory as a condition for conducting business there.[148]

Argentina-Chile FTA includes one of the few provisions on data localization that are not directly binding. Instead, parties merely "recognize the importance" of not requiring the use or location of computing facilities in a country's territory as a condition for conducting business in that territory. Instead, parties undertake to exchange good practices, experiences, and regulatory frameworks regarding the location of servers.[149] Chile-Paraguay FTA adds that nothing shall prevent a party from adopting or maintaining measures to pursue a legitimate public policy objective, provided that the measure is not applied in a manner that would constitute a means of arbitrary or unjustifiable discrimination or a disguised restriction on trade.[150]

The EU-Chile Interim Trade Agreement, signed in December 2023, also includes a provision on data localization. It prohibits a party from restricting cross-border data flows by: a) requiring the use of computing facilities or

[144] PAAP (2015), art. 13.11.bis.

[145] Pacific Alliance-Singapore FTA, art. 13.15; Singapore-Sri Lanka FTA, art. 9.10; Australia-Peru FTA art. 13.12; Brazil-Chile FTA, art. 10.13.

[146] TPP/CPTPP art. 14.13; Chile-Uruguay FTA, art. 8.11.

[147] DEPA, art. 4.4.

[148] USMCA, art. 19.12.

[149] Argentina-Chile FTA, art. 11.7.

[150] Chile-Paraguay FTA, art. 7.12.

network elements in the territory of that party for processing; b) requiring the localization of data in the territory of that party for storage or processing; c) prohibiting storage or processing in the territory of the other party; and d) making the cross-border transfer of data contingent upon the use of computing facilities, network elements, or localization requirements in the territory of that party.[151]

IV. Conclusion

Latin America's contributions to internet and digital commerce regulation are typically overlooked. However, a group of countries from that region has fostered the internet principles of open access and net neutrality and pioneered the inclusion of digital trade and data flow provisions in PTAs. Such developments are not necessarily aligned with the Northern dichotomy of an EU or US model.

Latin America has largely embraced open-access principles for their research, like promoting access to publicly funded research, fostering self-archiving in domestic and regional repositories, and developing open-access journals. However, it has primarily done it at the level of domestic laws and policies, with few international commitments in this regard, mostly soft law instruments like the Declaration of Salvador" (2005) and CILAC (2016). The discussion about OA as a general rule is now gaining traction in Europe[152] and the United States—but largely without considering the Latin American experience.

At the same time, only Latin American PTAs have explicitly recognized the principle of net neutrality in their domestic laws and international agreements.

That does not mean all is going smoothly. For example, some have criticized Brazil's MCI for containing a provision requiring websites to maintain data on consumers' access for six months, which raises privacy concerns.[153] In addition, though regulations concerning net neutrality exist in the region, they do not appear to be an obstacle to preventing ISPs from circumventing them, and organizations responsible for ensuring compliance do not have the necessary competencies or resources for carrying out this function.[154]

[151] EU-Chile Interim Trade Agreement, art. 19.5, accessed November 12, 2024, https://policy.trade.ec.europa.eu/eu-trade-relationships-country-and-region/countries-and-regions/chile/eu-chile-agreement/text-agreement_en.

[152] See, e.g., European Commission, Directorate-General for Research and Innovation (2021), Horizon Europe, open science–Early knowledge and data sharing, and open collaboration (Luxembourg: Publications Office of the European Union), accessed November 12, 2024, https://data.europa.eu/doi/10.2777/18252.

[153] Zissis and Glickhouse, "Net Neutrality Lessons from Latin America."

[154] Derechos Digitales Latin America, *Latin America in a Glimpse* (Santiago, Chile: 2015), accessed November 12, 2024, https://www.derechosdigitales.org/wp-content/uploads/glympse_ingl__s1.pdf.

Digital trade provisions in Latin American PTAs converge on objectives, principles, and specific commitments such as nondiscrimination, the moratorium on customs duties, consumer protection, electronic authentication, personal data, data flows, and data localization. Such principles and obligations were primarily elaborated in PTAs with developed partners.

Latin American countries also have advanced new principles on digital trade. Around half of all PTAs, including data flow provisions on telecommunications or financial services, have been concluded by Latin American countries. Mexico-Panama FTA (2014) was the first to have a general binding clause on cross-border information flows. Moreover, Latin American PTAs are the largest group that includes provisions banning or limiting data localization requirements. Further testimony of Latin American countries' creative role on these topics is the conclusion of DEPA, which covers a range of emerging digital trade issues, like electronic invoicing, digital identity, artificial intelligence, and open government data.[155]

However, consistency is not necessarily good. A few PTAs explicitly exclude the protection of personal data—the information held, collected, or processed by or on behalf of a party. These provisions put states in an asymmetrical position vis-à-vis international traders, service providers, and investors. They exclude governmental data collection and processing from the disciplines dealing with personal data treatment. Around half of all PTAs with these provisions have been concluded by Latin American countries.[156]

Likewise, not all these Latin American countries have had the same consistency at the domestic level. As a result, national regulations on specific topics in PTAs lag what has been committed to in those agreements, particularly domestic barriers to digital trade and data protection.

For example, except for Costa Rica, all other Latin American countries leading the conclusion of PTAs with digital trade provisions have moderate to significant digital trade restrictions at a domestic level.[157] Simultaneously, these countries have moderate (Chile, Colombia, Costa Rica, Peru) or limited (Panama) data protection.[158] While data protection provisions in PTAs concluded by these countries are primarily soft or mixed, general provisions on data flows and specific sectors (financial services and telecommunications) are mostly binding.

[155] DEPA, art. 2.5, 7.1, art. 8.2, art. 9.5.

[156] Brazil-Chile FTA, art. 10.2.2(c); USMCA, art. 19.2.1(b); Australia-Peru FTA, art. 13.2.3(b); Argentina-Chile FTA, art. 11.2.2(c); Chile-Uruguay FTA, art. 8.2.2(b); TPP/CPTPP, art. 14.2.3(b); PAAP, art. 13.2.2(a).

[157] Janos Ferencz, "The OECD Digital Services Trade Restrictiveness Index," accessed November 12, 2024, https://www.oecd-ilibrary.org/trade/the-oecd-digital-services-trade-restrictiveness-index_16ed2d78-en.

[158] DLA Piper, "Global Data Protection Laws of the World" (June 26, 2019), accessed November 12, 2024, https://www.dlapiperdataprotection.com/.

The different levels of commitment and approaches concerning these issues between international and domestic regulation and its implementation (or lack thereof) potentially create future conflicts if some countries want to change the domestic data protection regime. If both regimes are not well-coordinated, Latin American countries could be limited in their policy space to enact rules contradicting international commitments. It is not clear why Latin American countries have such different levels of commitment concerning digital trade restrictions and data protection, and future research is needed in this regard. One hypothesis would be that this is merely an issue of lack of coordination or awareness between different state agencies.[159]

Only Colombia, Panama, and Peru have established a criterion of equivalence for the international transfer of personal data from the countries mentioned above. Those countries agree that personal data may be exchanged when the party receiving it undertakes to protect it in at least an "adequate" way (which can mean having equivalent or similar regulations). In all the PTAs examined in this chapter, we only find such a rule in the 2017 Argentina-Chile FTA.

In several countries, discussions are taking place to reform data protection laws according to a model closer to the European Union's General Data Protection Regulation (GDPR). However, the EU has determined that only two Latin American countries have "adequate" data protection under the GDPR: Argentina and Uruguay.[160] What will happen if other Latin American countries make a policy change to be GDPR adequate and implement their adequacy policies? Could that violate PTA commitments to allow the cross-border transfer of information electronically that do not include such exceptions?[161] Something similar would happen if Latin American countries abandoned principles like the duty-free moratorium of digital products and the prohibition of data localization, which developing economies have increasingly contested.[162]

This scenario also begs the question of what Latin American countries should do regarding digital trade integration. Should they sign more PTAs with e-commerce or digital trade provisions to pressure domestic reform or reduce the gap between PTA's commitments and domestic law? Whichever path these countries choose, the issue of implementation is crucial.

[159] For further details, see Rodrigo Polanco, "Regulatory Convergence of Data Rules in Latin America," in Burri, *Big Data and Global Trade Law*, 268–300.

[160] European Commission, "Adequacy Decisions" (June 2024), accessed November 12, 2024, https://ec.europa.eu/info/law/law-topic/data-protection/international-dimension-data-protection/adequacy-decisions_en.

[161] Only Peru considers that international treaties with provisions on cross-border flow of personal data in which Peru is a party may be an exception to the domestic "adequacy" rule.

[162] Neha Mishra, "Data Localization Laws in a Digital World: Data Protection or Data Protectionism?" *The Public Sphere: Journal of Public Policy* 4 (2016): 135.

Latin American countries could prioritize topics like nondiscrimination, electronic authentication, and online payments (the latter, largely absent in PTAs) to raise awareness in the region's companies about the benefits of using e-commerce. The Inter-American Development Bank (IADB) has suggested that Latin American countries ensure that small and medium enterprises (SMEs) have a level playing field in digital trade, with clear rules on taxes and fees applicable to online purchases, and that postal packages are fully trackable.[163]

Further research could explore why these Latin American countries have pioneered the development and diffusion of internet principles of open access and net neutrality, as well as electronic commerce and data flow provisions in PTAs. Is this out of necessity? Is it "path dependency" or the influence of developed countries? Or a reaction to economic interests? Is it a route to push or lock in domestic reforms through international commitments, or the will to be rule-makers and not only rule-takers?

Finally, it is important to note that the level of consistency that Latin American countries have achieved concerning open access, net neutrality, and digital trade regulation is not necessarily replicable in other regions. For example, in recent years, some Asian countries have embraced an OA policy (like Indonesia and India),[164] while African countries are largely missing out on this opportunity.[165] African and Asian economies seem to have different "ecosystems" in this regard, probably affected by their cultural, normative, and economic realities. As explained in the introduction of this book, there are several reasons Latin America is a class of its own. The pace and reach of technological developments—including the internet and digital trade—transform human experiences and capabilities, creating new disruptions in the region. To address these concerns, Latin American countries have reacted not always in alignment with the United States, Europe, or other traditional "rule-makers," looking for solutions that are at times innovative and contradictory.

[163] Reena B. Gordon and Kati Suominen, *Going Global: Promoting the Internationalization of Small and Mid-Size Enterprises in Latin America and the Caribbean* (Washington, DC: Inter-American Development Bank, 2014), accessed November 12, 2024, https://publications.iadb.org/en/going-global-promoting-internationalization-small-and-mid-size-enterprises-latin-america-and.

[164] 164 In fact, Indonesia is today the country with the most open-access journals in the world. Accessed November 12, 2024, https://openaccessasia.org/.

[165] Maina Waruru, "Africa Is Missing Out on Open-Access Publishing Opportunities," *University World News, Africa Edition*, August 29, 2023, https://www.universityworldnews.com/post.php?story=20230827201809889.

Epilogue

The Birth of a New Canon in Latin American International Law

Alejandro Chehtman, Alexandra Huneeus, and Sergio Puig

I. Introduction

We close our volume with a brief, bold claim born of reflection on the essays in this volume: there is a new canon of Latin American international law (LAIL) in our time. It is characterized by broader participation of different actors within society than in the past; by greater pluralism in theory and scholarly methodology; by an emphasis on international human rights as an important language of domestic as well as regional law and politics; and, most crucially, by a turn away from the United States and Europe as the main sources of cultural and economic influence. We begin by revisiting the two main regionalist projects of the past, juxtaposing them to the current era. We close by considering the limits and fragility of the current LAIL project and calling for further study of the shifting LAIL landscape.

II. The Traditional LAIL Canon and Countercanons

Over the last two centuries, the leading legal and political project among Latin American international lawyers was Alejandro Álvarez's pan-Americanism.[1] At the center of Álvarez's interest was developing a hemispheric project built

[1] Notably, pan-Americanism has extended well beyond international law, influencing a large number of fields, including the sciences, economics, architecture, art, fashion and culture more broadly. See, e.g., J. Senillosa, *Panamericanismo cultural* (Valmadonna, Italy: Pedemonte, 1924), R. Cándida Smith, *Improvised Continent: Pan-Americanism and Cultural Exchange* (College Park: University of Pennsylvania Press, 2017), and even A. Alvarez, *El derecho internacional del porvenir* (Madrid: América, 1916), 14.

around the United States and its Monroe Doctrine, albeit construed in a purely anti-interventionist spirit—with European countries on the offending side. Insofar as "failure of payment of financial obligations [was] not a characteristic of [American] states,"[2] Álvarez deemed that the Monroe Doctrine was more favorable than the Drago and Calvo Doctrines to the interests of American states, for it was more effective in preventing European powers from regaining possession and exercising military pressure on American soil. This approach assumed some form of "hemispheric exceptionalism," and many of its proponents viewed the "friendly face of US hegemony over Latin America" as justified, and even beneficial.[3]

Three further features of pan-Americanism are worth mentioning. First, pan-Americanism is a project of the Western Hemisphere's elites. It has been described as "an alliance forged between diplomats and politicians in the United States and in Latin America."[4] Simón Bolívar first posited a regional project of integration in the United States of *Hispanoamérica* in his message to the Congress of Angostura (1910). Similarly, in 1844 a prominent Argentine jurist, Juan Bautista Alberdi, called for the reorganization of Spanish American republics into a broader federation.[5] He further advocated the creation of a permanent "international peace court" to sort out disputes within the continent. But this regional project never gained traction and, instead, a different one materialized, with the United States at its center.[6] Pan-Americanism was partly forged by the competition among Latin American elites for foreign resources. As suggested by Petersen, the persistent popularity and influence of pan-Americanism cannot be conceived outside its potential to advance the personal, professional, national, and international goals of the Latin American elites who shaped approaches to international law.[7]

[2] Álvarez, *El derecho internacional del porvenir,* 334. See, further, D. Sheinin, "Rethinking Pan Americanism: An Introduction," in *Beyond the ideal: Pan-Americanism in inter-American Affairs,* ed. D. Sheinin (New York: Praeger, 2000).

[3] See Stephen C. Neff, *Justice Among Nations: A History of International Law* (Cambridge, MA: Harvard University Press, 2014), 292.

[4] R. Salvatore, "Epilogue. Pan-Americanism and the Changing Nature of US Hegemony," in *The New Pan-Americanism and the Structuring of Inter-American Relation*, ed. Juan Pablo Scarfi and David M. K. Sheinin(London: Routledge, 2022), 164.

[5] J. B. Alberdi, "Report on the Suitability and Aims of a General American Congress," in *Documents on Inter-American Cooperation*, ed. R. N. Burr and R. D. Hussey, (College Park: University of Pennsylvania Press, 1955), 89. Domingo F. Sarmiento more modestly advocated for a Federation around the Río de la Plata between Argentina, Uruguay and Paraguay (see his *Argirópolis* (1850)).

[6] For a contemporary analysis of why this ambitious regional project has little chances of succeeding, even today, see. A. Malamud and P. Castro, "Are Regional Blocs Leading from Nation States to Global Governance? A Skeptical View from Latin America," *Iberoamericana. Nordic Journal of Latin American and Caribbean Studies* 37, no. 1 (2007): 115–134.

[7] M. J. Petersen, "Architects, Exchange, and the consolidation of Pan-American Cooperation, 1914-40," in Scarfi and Sheinin, *The New Pan-Americanism*, 37.

Second, pan-Americanism was shaped by US policies toward Latin America. The US reaction to the Drago Doctrine had been the 1904 Roosevelt Corollary to the Monroe Doctrine, clarifying that if any country within its sphere of influence were to threaten the property rights of US citizens, the United States would be entitled to intervene in the internal affairs of the recalcitrant country.[8] Argentine diplomat Vicente Quesada had denounced US "imperialism" in the Caribbean in the late 1880s. Accordingly, pan-Americanism was used to soften US hegemonic aspirations over the continent. Aída Rodriguez recounts that the term "inter-American" was introduced to replace "Pan-American" in light of the increasingly imperialistic tone ascribed to the latter.[9] Furthermore, in the 1960s and 1970s, pan-Americanism was directly linked to the fight against communism.[10] Nonintervention and these precursors were used to fight Soviet-inspired guerrillas and political movements as foreign interventions on the sovereign rights of Latin American republics.[11]

Finally, pan-Americanism was animated by a deep confidence in free markets and a commitment to peace, commerce, and "civilization," typically construed in racist terms. Then Argentina's future president Roque Sáenz Peña closed his speech at the First Pan-American Conference in Washington, DC (1890), with the now famous "*¡Que sea América para la humanidad!*"[12] This sensibility was generally accompanied by a mission in which international law, and Pan-American approaches to international law in particular, could have a distinct "civilizing" mission or role in the world. Jorge Reyes (Argentine *chargé d'affairs* in Havanna) went as far as justifying military intervention by the United States in Cuba as a reasonable response against political insurrection, using deeply racist terms.[13]

The influence of pan-Americanism has been profound. It lies at the core of institutions such as the Organisation of American States (OAS), the Pan-American Health Organization (PAHO), and the Inter-American System of

[8] Notably, Roosevelt's "Good Neighbor Policy" and the US's softening of its hegemonic expectations and military interventions in Latin America came when the United States needed to counter German and Italian propaganda in the mid-1930s. Already in the 1950s, it was clear for commentators that Latin America was vital to the security interests of the United States at the time of Monroe, during World War II and the Cold War against the Soviet Union. See E. O. Guerrant, *Roosevelt's Good Neighbor Policy* (New York: Literary Licensing, 1950), 213.

[9] A. Rodríguez, "Imperial Pan-Americanism," in Scarfi and Sheinin, *The New Pan-Americanism*, 12.

[10] A. McCarthy-Jones and A. Greig, "Somos hijos de Sandino y Bolívar: Radical Pan-American Traditions in Historical and Cultural Context," *Journal of Iberian and Latin American Research* 17, no. 2 (2011): 237.

[11] David M. K. Sheinin, "The Colombo-Lanusse Doctrine: Cold War Anti-interventionism and the End of Pan-Americanism," in Scarfi and Sheinin, *The New Pan-Americanism*, 122–123.

[12] Roque Sáenz Peña and Miguel Cané, *Derecho público americano: Escritos y discursos* (Gale, Making of Modern Law, 1905).

[13] Ibid., 118.

Human Rights (IASHR), which in many senses stems from the American Institute of International Law.[14] It encapsulates a worldview that has been enormously influential among Latin American elites, reflecting how they understand their status, values, and place and role in world affairs. While some believed pan-Americanism was "destined to disappear,"[15] it has had a long and influential life, especially in Latin America.[16]

III. The Pan-Hispanic Countercanon

Although dominant, pan-Americanism was not the only relevant regional framework that took root among Latin American international lawyers. From the early twentieth century there were movements that were anti-imperialist (and anti-American in particular) and (relatively) more inclusive (Pan-Hispanic).[17] In general, this political sensibility grew as a reaction to the projects of "order and progress" of the local criollo elites, led by political figures such as Roca in Argentina, Núñez in Colombia, Da Fonseca in Brazil, Porfirio Díaz in México, Rufino Barrios in Guatemala, Latorre in Uruguay, and Guzmán Blanco in Venezuela.[18] It was also a reaction to growing US influence in the region. At the end of World War I, the United States became "the most important investor and trading partner of most Latin American countries."[19]

This current of thought was articulated by a number of public intellectuals, including José Carlos Mariátegui in Peru, Juan B. Justo in Argentina, Luis Emilio Recabarren in Chile, José Martí in Cuba and Ricardo Flores Magón in México. Notably it also construed itself as an embodiment of the intellectual tradition inaugurated by Andrés Bello and followed by Calvo and Drago. Mexican jurist and diplomat Isidro Fabela was a leading forerunner. These thinkers flatly rejected the Monroe Doctrine, particularly under the Roosevelt Corollary

[14] See M. Petersen and C-A. Schulz, "Setting the Regional Agenda: A Critique of Posthegemonic Regionalism," *Latin American Politics and Society* 60, no. 10 (2018): 115–116.

[15] Lorenzo Anadón, "Informe confidencial, presentado al Excmo Señor Ministro de Relaciones Exteriores, Dr. Luis M Drago, con ocasión del Congreso de México sobre cuestiones de política americana" (1903), cited in M. J. Petersen, "Architects, Exchange, and the Consolidation of Pan-American Cooperation, 1914-40," in Scarfi and Sheinin, *The New Pan-Americanism*, 22.

[16] A. P. Whitaker, *The Western Hemisphere Idea: Its Rise and Decline* (Ithaca, NY: Cornell University Press, 1954), 154 and footnotes. After World War II, the United States largely relinquished its hemispheric project in favor of a more global agenda.

[17] J. A. Britton, "Redefining Intervention: Mexico's Contribution to anti-Americanism," in *Anti-Americanism in Latin America and the Caribbean*, ed. A. McPherson (London: Berghahn Books, 2006).

[18] Roberto Gargarella, *Latin American Constitutionalism 1810-2010* (Oxford: Oxford University Press, 2013), 84.

[19] Friederich Katz, *The Secret War in Mexico: Europe, the United States, and the Mexican Revolution* (Chicago: University of Chicago Press, 1981), 527.

(1904). The US intervention in Veracruz in 1914 clarified to the Mexican revolutionaries that their political cause was at stake. Accordingly, Fabela forcefully stated that "the Monroe Doctrine constitutes an arbitrary protectorate, imposed over countries that have neither requested it, and nor do they need it."[20] He further complained that, as the umpire of the world, the powerful influence of the United States has made the Monroe Doctrine widely accepted in the region (i.e., by his leading, pan-Americanist colleagues).[21] His approach opposed the more broadly internationalist, liberal Wilsonian project and favored both a more egalitarian and nationalist approach. Accordingly, the Estrada Doctrine, named after Mexican Secretary of Foreign Affairs Genaro Estrada, posited that Mexico would not issue any declaration recognizing or failing to recognize foreign governments (and was clearly influenced by the nonrecognition of Mexican President Álvaro Obregón by the United States).

Fabela further resented the Pan-American stance adopted in 1915 by Argentina, Brazil, and Chile and complained that, by offering to mediate in the conflict with the United States after the Veracruz operation, they were intervening in Mexico's internal affairs. He was arguably responsible for the Carranza Doctrine, which advocated a stronger (absolute) version of the principle of nonintervention. As articulated by Serrano Migallón, the Carranza Doctrine not only advocated the (sovereign) equality before the law between states but also rejected the Monroe Doctrine as a hegemonic principle imposed by the United States on Latin America.[22] By this token, international law and diplomacy should neither protect particular interests against universal fraternity nor serve big powers to exercise pressure and intervene against the governments of weaker nations. Fabela thereby complained that the emerging League of Nations had failed to incorporate a strong anti-interventionist principle, that could counteract, *inter alia*, the Monroe Doctrine.[23] In the words of Russian exile Leon Trotsky, "fighting for its national independence, political and economic . . . is the basic meaning of the Mexican revolution at this stage."[24]

Some of the key ideas in this counteraction have often been ascribed to the 1917 Mexican Constitution. This constitutional process was characterized by what has been subsequently called the "politics of presence," that is, the participation of representatives of marginalized groups in the Constitutional Assembly.[25]

[20] Isidro Fabela, *Intervención* (Mexico City: UNAM, 1959), 138. His book, *Los Estados Unidos contra la Libertad* (1920) examines in detail the US (ab)use of the Monroe Doctrine to intervene in Latin America, and it even opens with a reference to the intervention in Veracruz in 1914 against the Carranza regime.

[21] Ibid., 311.

[22] Fernando Serrano Migallón, "La Doctrina Carranza," in *Isidro Fabela y la diplomacia mexicana* (Buenos Aires: Porrua, 1981), 161, 192–193.

[23] F. S. Northedge, *The League of Nations: its Life and Times, 1920-1946* (Teaneck, NJ: Holmes & Meier, 1988), 324.

[24] L. Trotsky, "Mexico and British Imperialism," *Socialist Appeal* (June 25, 1938).

[25] See Anne Phillips, *The Politics of Presence* (Oxford: Oxford University Press, 1995).

Constitutionalist Luis Cabrera eloquently claimed that the Constitution had to "be in agreement with the blood, the races and the necessities of the aborigines" rather than a document "copied from the French or the U.S. Constitution."[26] Article 27 of the Mexican Constitution famously established that expropriation was lawful under Mexican Law, subject to being in the interest of public utility and compensation, and, perhaps most significantly, that all subsoil mineral resources were the property of the state. By 1917, 90 percent of Mexico's oil reserves were owned by foreign companies.[27]

This political sensibility was passed through generations in part through populist movements from the left in the 1940s–1950s, the endorsement of the nonaligned movement, the Cuban Revolution, and the left-wing political movements in the 1970s in Chile and Nicaragua, leading to the ambitious (if ultimately unsuccessful) institutional projects of ALBA-TCP (in opposition to the US-led Free Trade Area for the Americas), and Unasur, led by Hugo Chavez and some of the governments of the so-called "pink tide." At points, it has been characterized by extreme conceptions of (absolute) nonintervention, nationalist discourse, and a marked rejection of imperialist projects, particularly of the influence of the United States in Latin American internal politics.[28] Figures in this tradition include, *inter alia*, Jorge Castañeda (Mexico), Alfonso García Robles (Mexico) and Lucio M. Moreno Quintana (Argentina).[29]

IV. A Twenty-First-Century LAIL Canon Emerges

A defining theme of LAIL, then, has been the relationship Latin American states forge with the United States. But Latin American international law has entered a new phase. The volume's chapters read together suggest that LAIL is distancing itself from the US/anti-US dialectic that shaped the region's international law practice and theory in the nineteenth and twentieth centuries. As in the past, LAIL harbors many different strands. But the strands, taken together, exhibit four features that distinguish it from the past.

The most striking feature is that, whereas the regional projects of the past sought to insert Latin America into the Europe/US-led community of nations

[26] Cited in Gargarella, *Latin American Constitutionalism*, 103.

[27] W. Dirk Raat and Michael M. Brescia, *Mexico and the United States: Ambivalent Vistas* (Athens: University of Georgia Press, 2010), 126.

[28] *See*, e.g., Ezequiel Ramírez Novoa, *La Farsa del Panamericanismo y la Unidad Indoamericana* (Bogotá, Colombia: Indoamericana, 1955); and Carlos Pereyra, *El Mito Monroe* (Charleston, SC: Nabu Press, 1959).

[29] See, e.g., Francisco-José Quintana, "Small Powers, International Organizations, and the Role of Law: Jorge Castañeda's Views from Mexico," *European Journal of International Law* 34, no. 2 (2023): 319–344.

on more equal terms, the new regional project is not only about projecting Latin America into the international sphere. Certainly, the OAS human rights project grew in part from the US impetus to shield the Western hemisphere from communism during the Cold War: that is part of its history (though not the entirety as Sikkink and Jensen argue). However, human rights has become a regional practice and doctrine focused on Latin America itself and its people. It is not only about the relationship between regions but also about relations between government and individuals, and government and peoples, as well as relations among the states within the region. It is largely mediated by lawyers, civil society organizations, domestic courts, diplomats, publicists, and international courts and tribunals. It is a more plural, more inward-looking regional project of international law. This is evidenced as well by the way Latin American states use the ICJ to mediate regional disputes, the way Latin American domestic courts draw so much of their international law practice from each other (as opposed to, for example, the United States), and the way that a growing number of scholars are studying the history of international law in the region for its own sake, and not only to show its relation to European international law or U.S. foreign relations. All this is not to say that the negotiation of Latin America's position in the world is no longer part of the story. Relations with China and the United States are constructed in important part through treaties, and it is through international relations with the EU, Beatriz Garcia argues, that Latin America's forestry practices could change. But we believe that the greater focus on LAIL as a tool of domestic and regional governance instead of international relations, alongside the other characteristics outlined below, demarcate a new LAIL era.

A second feature is that LAIL has come to include a broader set of actors. Increasingly international law is constructed not only by diplomats and international law publicists, but also by judges, civil society organizations, Indigenous peoples, and others who were previously absent from or overlooked by the general debates about the role of international law. Sergio Puig points to how new sociolegal approaches expand the range of actors studied in the making of LAIL, an observation borne out in many of the chapters. David Landau highlights the important role played by judges in constructing human rights law, while Céspedes-Báez points to the role of communities of practice, which includes actors such as nongovernmental organizations (NGOs) and activists, in the same project. Barragán shows how the region's Afro-descendent peoples have shaped international law and used international law, in turn, to reshape domestic law governing their peoples. Lack of access to law remains a serious challenge across the region, and it is still the case that law is an elite-driven project. Compared to the past, however, there are more points of access for non-state actors, and scholars have begun to look beyond the evolution of doctrine and the role of judges in their study of international law.

Third, the volume points to the law of human rights, constructed through the inter-American system in dialogue with domestic courts and other actors and institutions, as the area of greatest cohesion, development, and originality of LAIL. Human rights doctrine has expanded such that it now touches on many areas of governance. In fact, in designing this volume, we asked for chapters on health law and pandemics, feminism, corruption, the laws of war, peace-making, transitional justice, and climate. Each of these chapters wound up discussing regional human rights law and how international law was used to pursue domestic agendas. The new LAIL canon, then, not only subsumes the *uti posseditis*/nonintervention doctrines of the past but includes a new set of doctrines and institutions linked to a human rights system that is key to the identity of LAIL in the present. This insight echoes the arguments made by *ius commune* scholars such as Mariela Morales, Armin von Bodansky, and René Urueña.[30] However, it integrates this development into the longer LAIL tradition.[31]

Fourth is a change in the scholarship of LAIL. Contemporary scholarship continues to revisit the old doctrines, debates, and writers of the past. However, it does so with a different sensibility. As noted in the introduction, scholarship now includes historians, political theorists, and lawyers. Thus, they engage with different theoretical debates that come from their disciplines and employ new methods. In this way, Fawcett, a scholar of international relations, analyzes doctrines such as *uti posseditis* and non-intervention not as legal rules but as a part of Latin America's effort to pronounce and define itself through international relations. These new takes also include more players. Fawcett brings to her study the overlooked contributions of women thinkers of the 19th century. Becker Lorca and Alvez discuss the same classical set of doctrines—such as *uti possidetis*—but with a critical twist. They argue that these doctrines were crafted by a particular class of Latin Americans, *criollos*, as a way of excluding Indigenous peoples from foreign relations, self-determination, and sovereignty. Additionally, several chapters critically investigate how international law serves as a tool for particular group interests at the expense of other groups.[32] This is

[30] Armin von Bogdandy et al. (eds.), *Transformative Constitutionalism in Latin America: The Emergence of a New Ius Commune*, (Oxford: Oxford University Press, 2017); Armin von Bogdandy and R. Urueña, "International Transformative Constitutionalism in Latin America," *American Journal of International Law* 114, no. 3. (2020): 403–442, https://doi.org/10.1017/ajil.2020.27.

[31] See also Alejandro Rodiles, "The Great Promise of Comparative Public Law for Latin America: Toward *Ius Commune Americanum*?' in *Comparative International Law*, ed. Anthea Roberts et al.(New York: Oxford University Press, 2018), 501–526.

[32] As we went to press, a collection of essays on international law in the Americas from a critical, Third World approaches to international law perspective was also in being published. *See* Liliana Obregón Tarazona, et al. (eds.), *The Oxford Handbook of International Law and the Americas* (Oxford: Oxford Academic, online ed., February 23, 2023), accessed August 15, 2024, https://doi.org/10.1093/oxfordhb/9780197661062.001.0001.

not new, but for international law to be more effective as a tool for governance, scholarship must try to provide an account of the different ways in which legal doctrine can be deployed to support particular sets of interests. Contemporary scholarship thus breaks through the unitary analysis of the state (and the region) to reveal the fractious use of law between and within Latin American states.

Our claim of a twenty-first-century LAIL that is more plural and autonomous than the LAIL of the past may sound complacent or teleological in a 1990s way. Yet we publish this volume at a moment in which political polarization and authoritarianism are growing in the region, just as they are in so many parts of the world. This poses a risk for democracy and human rights, just as growing nationalism poses a risk for regionalism. Witness, for example, the flourishing of autocratic legalism—a rhetorical use of the language of international law and its institutions to pursue goals distant from its most basic normative commitments.[33] In other words, it could be that we publish this volume and our claims about a new phase of LAIL just as it is on the cusp of change again. Even so, the observation that the current era stands as distinct from the past is important, not least because it shows how Latin American international law is moving beyond the US-led geopolitical era, and may help us discern its future course.

V. Conclusion

We began with the goal of conveying the diversity of scholarly approaches emerging from the flourishing study of international law in contemporary Latin America. We end on a humbler note by noting the limits of the volume, which reflect the challenges present in further advancing the field. The diversity of LAIL practice is greater than what we were able to capture through this exercise, and many voices are not represented in this volume. Although the volume includes scholars from across Latin America, it is short on Central American and Caribbean scholars. These are two key subregions that need further study, yet they appear here fleetingly. Further, even if LAIL is more plural and inclusive than it was in the past, our list of authors suggests that it is still dominated by what we might term *criollos*, and the authors hail mostly from the countries that have stronger international scholarly networks in place. International law practice and scholarship are still practices of exclusion. And of course, inevitably, the volume is an incomplete catalog of LAIL, missing discussion of important institutions and doctrines such as Mercosur, the Court of Justice of the Andean

[33] Kim Lane Scheppele, "Autocratic Legalism," *University of Chicago Law Review* 85, no. 2 (2018): 545–584. See also David Landau, "Abusive Constitutionalism," *UC Davis Law Review* 47 (2013): 189–262.

Community, the Central American Court of Justice, and the classical LAIL doctrine of political asylum, which is shifting even as we write this epilogue. No volume can capture everything, but we also believe these absences point to areas that need further development in the existing scholarship.

We close, therefore, with a call for greater investment in regional academic associations, networks, and publications that focus on LAIL. We believe that a stronger intellectual field around LAIL can promote research of genuine ambition and further engage the new generations of international lawyers who are already doing groundbreaking work. But we must do so while ensuring greater sustained inclusion of topics that affect marginalized peoples in the region, from their perspective, as a core part of Latin American international law. In this way, the study of LAIL will be more able to identify problems and fashion responses to the challenges ahead.

Index

For the benefit of digital users, indexed terms that span two pages (e.g., 52–53) may, on occasion, appear on only one of those pages.